World Literature in Spanish

World Literature in Spanish

AN ENCYCLOPEDIA

Volume 1: A–F

Maureen Ihrie and Salvador A. Oropesa, Editors

 ABC-CLIO

Santa Barbara, California • Denver, Colorado • Oxford, England

Copyright 2011 by Maureen Ihrie and Salvador A. Oropesa

Library of Congress Cataloging-in-Publication Data

World literature in Spanish : an encyclopedia / edited by Maureen Ihrie and Salvador A. Oropesa.
   v. cm.
   Includes bibliographical references and index.
   ISBN 978–0–313–33770–3 (set : acid-free paper) — ISBN 978–0–313–08083–8 (ebook) 1. Spanish literature—Encyclopedias. 2. Spanish American literature—Encyclopedias. 3. Hispanic American literature—Encyclopedias. 4. African literature (Spanish)—Encyclopedias. I. Ihrie, Maureen. II. Oropesa, Salvador A., 1961–
PQ6006.W68   2011
860.9—dc22   2011007599

ISBN: 978–0–313–33770–3
EISBN: 978–0–313–08083–8

15 14 13 12 11   1 2 3 4 5

This book is also available on the World Wide Web as an eBook.
Visit www.abc-clio.com for details.

ABC-CLIO, LLC
130 Cremona Drive, P.O. Box 1911
Santa Barbara, California 93116-1911

This book is printed on acid-free paper ∞

Manufactured in the United States of America

Contents

VOLUME I

Acknowledgments   *vii*

Introduction   *ix*

List of Entries   *xv*

Guide to Related Topics   *xxxi*

Entries A–F   1

VOLUME 2

List of Entries   *vii*

Guide to Related Topics   *xxiii*

Entries G–Q   405

VOLUME 3

List of Entries   *vii*

Guide to Related Topics   *xxiii*

Entries R–Z   827

Appendix A: Chronological Listing of Entries by Century   1055

Appendix B: Listing of Entries Related to Specific Geographic Areas   1079

Glossary of Literary and Cultural Terms   1103

Select Bibliography of Recent Print Resources in English   1121

Selected List of Publicly Available, Free Electronic Sources Related to Hispanic Literature and Culture   1135

About the Editors and Contributors   1143

Index   1151

Acknowledgments

Almost 200 scholars from Australia, Canada, Europe, Spanish America, Africa, Asia, and the United States have contributed to this encyclopedia. We sincerely appreciate the time and knowledge they contributed and have included their names in the list of contributors. Recognition is also due to the support of consulting editors David William Foster, Regents' Professor of Spanish and Women and Gender Studies at Arizona State University; Janet Pérez, Horn Professor and Qualia Chair of Spanish at Texas Tech University; and ABC-CLIO editor John Wagner and PreMedia Global project manager Magendravarman Nithyanandam. We both appreciate the valuable assistance of interlibrary loan services at our respective institutions. Salvador Oropesa gratefully acknowledges Kansas State University for granting him a one-semester sabbatical leave. Maureen Ihrie expresses sincere gratitude to Elon University for a one-semester sabbatical leave and several course releases. Without such support, this encyclopedia would not have seen print.

On a more personal note, this project has been charged with an infinite scope but has possessed finite resources. At times, it has proved overwhelming to us and to our families. Our deepest gratitude is due to our families, and especially to our spouses, Leonides Oropesa and Bob Ihrie.

Maureen Ihrie and Salvador Oropesa

Introduction

This encyclopedia takes as its subject literatures throughout the world that are written in Spanish. Entries are arranged alphabetically and composed by expert contributors. *World Literature in Spanish* provides a well-contextualized introduction to the globally extended, vibrantly complex tradition of literature composed in Spanish and demonstrates the distinguished and numerous contributions of Spanish literature to world civilization. This linguistically based (rather than nationally defined) understanding of Spanish literature transcends genres, time periods, and political boundaries and recognizes that the growing diversity within national borders and the increasing interdependence between nations require new ways of understanding "national" literature.

The intended audience of this work is nonspecialist high school, undergraduate college, and adult readers and anyone interested in the diversity, resilience, and creativity of Hispanic cultures and literature. Within the United States, the increasing visibility of Latinos has generated much public interest in Hispanic culture, which constitutes more and more of the U.S. national profile. To address these readers, entries avoid jargon and highly specialized terminology without diluting content unnecessarily. Information is strongly contextualized to provide clear connections between the historical events and social and cultural changes that inform the corpus of Spanish-language writing.

The project devotes solid attention to the political and cultural dimensions of Spanish-language texts over centuries, but particularly from the 20th century until today. Almost one-third of the 848 entries found in the encyclopedia's three volumes employ a cultural or thematic rather than biographical approach. Some entries view literature as a chronicle of historical events, a response to social changes, or a supplemental version of events that departs from the "official story." Other entries discern shared aspects and/or unique elements of literary texts and traditions; still others reference their subject with an eye to understanding contemporary social and political concerns.

Such a focus necessarily omits literatures in Spanish-speaking countries that are not written in Spanish (e.g., the literature of Spain, written in Galician, Catalan, or Euskara); texts written in Mayan (from Mexico and Central America), Quechua (from Bolivia, Peru, Chile), Tagalog (from the Philippine Islands), or English (by U.S. Latino writers with no Spanish-language publications) are not covered. Our comprehensive approach to Spanish-language texts does, however, include information on neglected Spanish-language literature from Africa and Asia and the diversity of black literature in Spanish.

With the exception of Morocco, whose modern Spanish-language literary production is a recent phenomenon, each country possessing a literary tradition in Spanish receives one entry titled by the country name. The purpose of these entries is to provide readers with quick access to an overview of the history, culture, and literature of a specific geographic location, not to suggest or create differences that may not exist. To that end, almost one-third of the entries are delimited by a time period, genre or specific work, theme, cultural phenomenon, geographic region, or sociopolitical aspect. Some entries present broader angles of analysis, including that of the Hispanic world. Many thematic entries are especially original because they deal with neglected topics like soccer in literature. In entries devoted to individuals, we have tried to respond to the question of what makes each author literarily relevant rather than compiling biographical data and enumerating lists of works that are easily accessible elsewhere. Because of the encyclopedia's emphasis on a more contextualized, thematic consideration of Spanish literature, writings of some important authors are covered in one or more topical entries, and their names do not appear as titles to individual entries. Thus, to fully access the rich variety of information within the encyclopedia's topical focus, readers will need to consult the Guide to Related Topics, the chronological and geographical appendices, and the general subject index.

The subject of literature in Spanish is vast, and this encyclopedia does not in any way pretend to be exhaustive. *World Literature in Spanish* provides a solid general review of literature before 1900, and concentrates somewhat more on works produced since then. Entry length does not necessarily correlate with a subject's importance; well-studied canonical subjects are included, but readers desiring more exhaustive consideration of particular items should consult the general bibliography of reference works in print and the annotated bibliography of publicly available online resources. For reasons of length, the two-part bibliography found at the end of most entries is extremely limited and intended only to point readers toward a few primary and secondary sources. English-language translations of primary sources and recent English-language criticism available in print are cited where possible.

General Format of Entries

Entry titles may be biographical names, literary titles or characters, cultural institutions, cultural phenomena, country names, literary or cultural movements, significant time periods, relevant terms, and other clearly defined topics. Specific dates (biographical, publication, composition, duration, title translations) or other information is included in many titles to further orient readers. Punctuation is consistent with the following examples: "Equatorial Guinea's *Generación del Silencio* (The Generation of Silence)";

"Puerto Rico: *Generación del treinta* (1930s Generation)"; and "Universities in Spain and the New World: Beginnings to 1900." Canonized saints are listed under their first names, thus Santa Teresa de Jesús appears as "Teresa de Jesús, Santa (1515–1582)" in the entry title. Noncanonized religious figures and all other biographical figures are catalogued under their surnames, unless the individual is much more recognized by a stage name, as in the case of "Selena," or a pen name, such as "Azorín."

Within the main text of entries, Spanish language quotes and other terms in Spanish are usually translated or paraphrased to English. Book-length publications are italicized, while published individual short stories and poems appear in quotes. The first time a published Spanish-language title is mentioned it is followed by a published or literal translation to English (unless the title is the name of a place, person, or character) in parentheses. These English-language translations are preceded by the original publication date of the Spanish title, unless the date is mentioned in the text. If the work has a published English-language translation, that published title is given, followed by a recent publication or printing date. As much as possible, only readily available English-language translations are provided. Journal, newspaper, and similar titles are usually not translated, unless they are relevant. The citation for a novel or other book-length work with a published English-language translation reads as follows: *La virgen de los sicarios* (1994; *Our Lady of the Assassins*, 2001). A similar text with no published English-language translation is listed as follows: *Las memorias de la mamá blanca* (1932; The Memories of the White Mama). Short fiction and individual poems that have been published appear according to the following example: "El matadero" (written 1839, pub. 1871; "The Slaughter House," 1959). As in the prior example, when composition (or performance) and publishing dates differ strikingly, both are usually provided.

Most entries finish with a brief two-part bibliography. Part one selects one or more relevant works or translations of a key primary work; part two provides a short list of recent criticism with at least one English-language item, when available. In a handful of entries devoted to a little-known subject, a somewhat more extensive bibliography is included. Criteria for selecting among recent bibliographic items were in large part left to the discretion of contributors. This information is provided solely as a starting point for interested readers.

English alphabetical order has been followed; *ch*, *ll*, and *ñ* are interfiled and not treated as separate letters. As is customary, when alphabetizing English-language titles, *a*, *an*, and *the* are ignored; similarly, when alphabetizing Spanish-language titles, *el*, *la*, *los*, *las*, *un*, *una*, *unos*, and *unas* have been ignored. Entry titles usually begin after any definite or indefinite article, so that, for example, *La carreta* is listed as *Carreta, La* (1952; *The Oxcart*, 1969).

Asterisks (*) have been used to provide cross-referencing of topics, titles, biographical figures, movements, or other aspects that appear as main entries elsewhere in the encyclopedia. The first mention of such items is identified with an asterisk placed immediately before the part of the name or title under which it appears. Country names, however, are not asterisked. All other appropriate references to related topics are listed at the very end of the main text of entries. In some cases, plural forms or possessive forms of an entry have been asterisked even though the entry appears in its singular, nonpossessive form. All entries conclude with the author's name, following the bibliography.

Access Tools

The general subject index lists all names, topics, titles, and other items found in the encyclopedia. Because *World Literature in Spanish* presents a linguistically based understanding of Spanish literature and aims to present information through a contextualized topical and thematic approach, a variety of other resources have also been prepared to allow nonspecialist readers to access, understand, and research subjects effectively.

Guide to Related Topics and Appendices

The Guide to Related Topics and two appendices allow readers full access to information regarding broad topic areas and specific subjects of interest. The Guide to Related Topics lists entries related to literary styles, subject areas, relevant social and political themes, cultural movements, cultural institutions, genres and subgenres, major works, and similar items.

Appendix A: The Chronological Listing of Entries by Century groups entries by century, following birthdates, publication dates, or dates of onset for movements and other items. Nations are listed according to the date when a Spanish presence arrived.

Appendix B: The Listing of Entries Related to Specific Geographic Areas provides alphabetical listings of relevant entries for each Spanish-speaking nation (Argentina, Bolivia, Chile, Colombia, Costa Rica, Cuba, Dominican Republic, Ecuador, El Salvador, Equatorial Guinea, Guatemala, Honduras, Mexico, Nicaragua, Panama, Paraguay, Peru, Philippine Islands, Spain, Venezuela, and Uruguay), Morocco, the geographic areas of Puerto Rico, and Latinos located in the mainland United States. In the case of biographically based titles, when individuals are born in one country but then relocate early on, their names appear under both nations.

Glossary of Literary and Cultural Terms

Language used in this reference work is intended to be jargon-free. Necessary specific concepts and terms that may be unfamiliar to general readers have been explained in entries as much as possible. Nonetheless, every discipline uses a specific vocabulary for discussion of its topic, and some terms, concepts, or ideas may still be sufficiently specialized to be foreign to certain readers. The Glossary of Literary and Cultural Terms is designed to provide or refresh reader understanding of basic vocabulary used in literary study and explain some basic cultural features of Hispanic society.

Selected Bibliographic Resources

The encyclopedia offers two bibliographies. The Select Bibliography of Recent Print Resources in English lists major reference works and other specialized sources for further study. The Selected List of Publicly Available, Free Electronic Sources Related to Hispanic Literature and Culture offers an annotated description of major academic Web sites, well-established electronic journals, and similar sites.

List of Entries

Abad, Antonio (1894–1970)

Abreu Gómez, Ermilo (1894–1971)

Acto

Ada, Alma Flor (1938–)

Adán, Martín (1908–1985)

Adoum, Jorge Enrique (1926–2009)

Afro-Hispanic Literature in Spanish America

Afro-Hispanic Writers of Costa Rica

Agosín, Marjorie (1955–)

Aguilar, Rosario (1938–)

Aguilar, Camín, Héctor (1946–)

Agustini, Delmira (1886–1914)

Aira, César (1949–)

Alarcón, Pedro Antonio de (1833–1891)

Alberdi, Juan Bautista (1810–1884)

Alberti, Rafael (1902–1999)

Aldecoa, Ignacio (1925–1969)

Aldecoa, Josefina (1926–2011)

Alegría, Ciro (1909–1967)

Alegría, Claribel (1924–)

Aleixandre, Vicente (1898–1984)

Alfaro, Óscar (1921–1963)

Alfonso X, "el Sabio" (1221–1284)

Algarín, Miguel (1941–)

Allende, Isabel (1942–)

Almodóvar, Pedro (1949–)

Alonso, Dámaso (1898–1990)

Altamirano, Ignacio Manuel (1834–1893)

Altolaguirre, Manuel (1905–1959)

Alva Ixtlilxóchitl, Fernando de (1568–1648)

Álvarez Gardeazábal, Gustavo (1945–)

Álvarez Quintero, Serafín (1871–1938) and Álvarez Quintero, Joaquín (1873–1944)

Amazon Theme in Spanish American Literature

Andreu, Blanca (1959–)

Ángel, Albalucía (1939–)

Anzaldúa, Gloria (1942–2004)

Aponte Alsina, Marta (1945–)

Apóstol, Cecilio (1877–1938)

Arce, Manuel José (1935–1985)

Arciniegas, Germán (1900–1999)

Arenas, Reinaldo (1943–1990)

Aréstegui, Narciso (1823–1869)

Arévalo Martínez, Rafael (1884–1975)

Argentina: History, Culture, and Literature

Argentine Novel after the Recovery of Democracy: 1983–2006

Argentine Theater by Women: 1900 to Present

Arguedas, Alcides (1879–1946)

Arguedas, José María (1911–1969)

Argueta, Manlio (1935–)

Arias, Arturo (1950–)

Arlt, Roberto (1900–1942)

Arms and Letters

Arniches, Carlos (1866–1943)

Arreola, Juan José (1918–2001)

Arroyo, Justo (l936–)

Ascensio Segura, Manuel (1805–1871)

Asturias, Miguel Ángel (1899–1974)

Atencia, María Victoria (1931–)

Atxaga, Bernardo (1951–)

Aub, Max (1903–1972)

Autobiography in Spain: Beginnings to 1700

Autobiography in Spain: 1700 to Present

Autobiography in Spanish America

Avant-Garde Poetry in Spanish America

Avant-Garde Prose in Spanish America

Aventuras de Don Chipote, o cuando los pericos mamen, Las (1928; The Adventures of Don Chipote, or When Parrots Breast-Feed, 2000)

Ávila Laurel, Juan Tomás (1966–)

Ayala, Francisco (1906–2009)

Azaña, Manuel (1880–1940)

Azorín (pseudonym of José Martínez Ruiz) (1873–1967)

Aztlán

Azuela, Mariano (1873–1952)

Ballagas, Emilio (1908–1954)

Balmori, Jesús (1886–1948)

Balsero ("Rafter")

Barcelona in Literature

Barea Ogazón, Arturo (1897–1957)

Barnet, Miguel (1940–)

Baroja y Nessi, Pío (1872–1956)

Barrio, El

Barrios, Eduardo (1884–1963)

Barros, Pía (1956–)

Bécquer, Gustavo Adolfo (pseudonym of Gustavo Adolfo Domínguez Bastida) (1836–1870)

Bellatin, Mario (1960–)

Belli, Gioconda (1948–)

Bello, Andrés (1781–1865)

Belpré, Pura (c. 1899–1982)

Benavente, Jacinto (1866–1954)

Benedetti, Mario (1920–2009)

Benet, Juan (1927–1993)

Benítez Rojo, Antonio (1931–2005)

Berceo, Gonzalo de (c. 1190s–c. 1260s)

Berman Goldberg, Sabina (1956–)

Bernabé, Manuel (1890–1960)

Biblioteca de Autores Españoles (BAE)

Biography in Spain: Beginnings to 1700

Biography in Spain: 1700 to Present

Biography in Spanish America

Black Legend

Blasco Ibáñez, Vicente (1867–1928)

Blest Gana, Alberto (1830–1920)

Bogotazo, el

Bolaño, Roberto (1953–2003)

Bolívar, Simón, in Contemporary
Literature and Culture

Bolivia: History, Culture, and Literature

Bombal, María Luisa (1910–1980)

Bonasso, Miguel (1940–)

Borge, Tomás (1930–)

Borges, Jorge Luis (1899–1986)

Borrero, Juana (1878–1896)

Boullosa, Carmen (1954–)

Bousoño, Carlos (1923–)

Bretón de los Herreros, Manuel
(1796–1873)

Brunet, Marta (1897–1967)

Bryce Echenique, Alfredo (1939–)

Buenos Aires in Literature

Buero Vallejo, Antonio (1916–2000)

Buitrago, Fanny (1943–)

Bullrich, Silvina (1915–1990)

Burgos, Carmen de (1867–1932)

de Burgos, Julia (1914–1953)

Caballero Calderón, Eduardo
(1910–1993)

Cabezas, Ómar (1950–)

Cabrera, Lydia (1900–1991)

Cabrera Infante, Guillermo (1929–2005)

CADA (1979–1985)

Cadalso, José (1741–1782)

Calderón de la Barca, Pedro (1600–1681)

Cambaceres, Eugenio (1843–1889)

Campo, Estanislao del (1834–1880)

Campo Alange, Condesa de (1902–1986)

Campobello, Nellie (1900–1986)

Campos, Julieta (1932–2007)

Canary Islands Writers

Cancionero Poetry in Spain

Cané, Miguel (1851–1905)

Canetti Duque, Yanitzia (1967–)

Cantar de Mío Cid

Capetillo, Luisa (1879–1922)

Caro y Cuervo Institute

Carpentier, Alejo (1904–1980)

Carranza, María Mercedes (1945–2003)

Carrasquilla, Tomás de (1858–1940)

Carrera Andrade, Jorge (1902–1978)

Carreras, Roberto de las (1875–1963)

Carreta, La (1952; *The Oxcart*, 1969)

Carrión Mora, Benjamín (1897–1979)

Casal, Julián del (1863–1893)

Casona, Alejandro (pseudonym of
Alejandro Rodríguez Álvarez)
(1903–1965)

Castellanos, Rosario (1925–1974)

Castillo, Amelia del (1923–)

Castro, Rosalía de (1837–1885)

Castro Quesada, Américo (1885–1972)

causa por la raza, la (The Cause for the
Mexican Race)

Cela, Camilo José (1916–2002)

Celaya, Gabriel (1911–1975)

Celestina, La in Spain and the New World

Censorship and Literature in Spain

Cepeda Samudio, Álvaro (1926–1972)

Cerda, Martha (1945–)

Cernuda, Luis (1902–1963)

Cervantes, Miguel de (1547–1616)

Cervantes, de Salazar, Francisco (1514/1518?–1575)

Chacel, Rosa (1898–1994)

Champourcin, Ernestina de (1905–1999)

Changó, el gran putas (1983; *Changó, the Biggest Badass*, 2010)

Chaviano, Daína (1957–)

Chicano

Chicano Movement: Literature and Publishing

Chicano Writers

Children's Literature in Spain: 1900 to Present

Children's Literature in Spanish in the United States

Chile: History, Culture, and Literature

Chilean Theater: 1900 to Present

Chilean Women Writers: The *Ergo Sum* Project

Chile's Generation of 1950

Chile's Generation of 1980: The New Scene

Chivalry Literature in Spain and the New World

Cien años de soledad (1967; *One Hundred Years of Solitude,* 1970)

Cisneros, Luis Benjamín (1837–1904)

Civil War Literature in Spain

Clarín (pseudonym of Leopoldo Alas) (1852–1901)

Clavel, Ana (1961–)

Codorniz, La Literary Magazine (1941–1978; The Quail)

Collazos, Óscar (1942–)

Colombia: History, Culture, and Literature

Colombian Exile Writers

Colombian Modernist Writing: 1885–1915

Colombian Women Writers: 1950 to Present

Colón, Jesús (1901–1974)

Colonial Baroque Writing in Spanish America

Colonialism and Anticolonialism in Spanish American Literature

Colonial Religious Chronicles in Spanish America

Colonial Theater in Spanish America

CONAIE (Confederación de Nacionalidades Indígenas del Ecuador)

Conde Abellán, Carmen (1907–1996)

Contemporáneos Group

Contemporary Guatemalan Indigenous Authors

Contemporary Moroccan Literature Written in Spanish

Contemporary Puerto Rican Short Story Writers: 1980 to Present

Conti, Haroldo (1925–1976)

Convent Writing in Spain and the New World

Converso Literature in Spain

Coronado, Carolina (1823–1911)

Coronel Urtecho, José (1906–1994)

Corpi, Lucha (1946–)

Correa, Miguel (1956–)

Cortázar, Julio (1914–1984)

Cossa, Roberto (1934–)

Costa Rica: History, Culture, and Literature

Costumbrismo in Spanish America

Cota Cárdenas, Margarita (1941–)

Cotto-Thorner, Guillermo (1916–1983)

Criollista Novel in Spanish America

Cruz, Ramón de la (1731–1794)

Cruz, Sor Juana Inés de la (1648–1695)

Cruz Varela, María Elena (1953–)

Cuadra, Pablo Antonio (1912–2002)

Cuba: History, Culture, and Literature

Cuban American Writers

Cuban Exile Writing outside the United States

Cuban *Special Period* Fiction

Cueto, Alonso (1954–)

Cultural Icons of Chicanos

Cultural Icons of Cuban Americans

Cultural Icons of Spain

Cultural Icons of Spanish America

Cultural Institutions for Hispanism in the United States

Curanderismo and *Brujería*

Dalton, Roque (1935–1975)

Darío, Rubén (1867–1916)

Dávila Andrade, César (1918–1967)

Décima

Delibes, Miguel (1920–2010)

Denevi, Marco (1922–1998)

Detective and Mystery Fiction in Spain

Detective and Mystery Fiction in Spanish America

Díaz, Jesús (1941–2005)

Díaz Arrieta, Hernán (pseudonym Alone) (1891–1984)

Díaz Castro, Eugenio (1803–1865)

Díaz del Castillo, Bernal (1492–1584)

Díaz-Mas, Paloma (1954–)

Diego, Gerardo (1896–1987)

Diosdado, Ana (1938–)

Discépolo, Armando (1887–1971)

Discovery and Conquest Writings: Describing the Americas

Documentary Narrative in Spanish American Literature

Dominican Republic: Contemporary Literature by Women Writers

Dominican Republic: History, Culture, and Literature

Don Juan Archetype in the Hispanic World

Donoso, Joés (1924–1996)

Donoso Pareja, Miguel (1931–)

Don Quijote de la Mancha in Spanish American Literature and Culture

Dorfman, Ariel (1942–)

Dragún, Osvaldo (1929–1999)

Droguett, Carlos (1912–1996)

Echegaray, José (1832–1916)

Echeverría, Esteban (1805–1851)

Ecuador: History, Culture, and Literature

Edwards, Jorge (1931–)

Égüez, Iván (1944–)

Eguren, José María (1874–1942)

Elizondo, Salvador (1932–2006)

El Salvador: History, Culture, and Literature

El Salvador's *Generación Comprometida* (1956–1972)

Eltit, Diamela (1949–)

Encina, Juan del (1468–1529)

Enlightenment in Spain: 1700–1800

Enlightenment in Spanish America

Epic Poetry in the Hispanic World

Equatorial Guinea: History, Culture, and Literature

Equatorial Guinea: Poets

Equatorial Guinea: Writers in Exile

Equatorial Guinea: Writers Living in the United States

Equatorial Guinea´s *Generación del Silencio* (The Generation of Silence)

Erauso, Catalina de (1592–1650)

Eroticism in Contemporary Spanish Women Writers: 1975 to Present

Escobar Galindo, David (1943–)

Escoto, Julio (1944–)

Espronceda, José de (1808–1842)

Esquivel, Laura (1950–)

Estévez, Abilio (1954–)

Estrada, Santiago (1841–1891)

Estupiñán Bass, Nelson (1912–2002)

Etxebarria, Lucía (1966–)

Exile Literature by Spanish Civil War Émigrés

Exile Writing in the Hispanic World

Fagundo, Ana María (1938–2010)

Falcón, Lidia (1935–)

Falcones, Ildefonso (1958–)

Fallas, Carlos Luis (1909–1966)

Felipe, León (1884–1968)

Feminism in Spain: Precursors to 1700

Feminism in Spain: 1700 to Present

Feminism in Spanish America

Fernández, Macedonio (1874–1952)

Fernández Cubas, Cristina (1945–)

Fernández de Lizardi, José Joaquín (1776–1827)

Fernández de Moratín, Leandro (1760–1828)

Fernández Retamar, Roberto (1930–)

Fernández Santos, Jesús (1926–1988)

Fernán-Gómez, Fernando (1921–2007)

Ferré, Rosario (1938–)

Figuera Aymerich, Ángela (1902–1984)

Flores, Marco Antonio (1937–)

Flor y canto

Formica, Mercedes (1918–2002)

Forner, Juan Pablo (1756–1797)

Fortún, Elena (pseudonym of Encarna Aragoneses) (1886–1952)

Francoism, Fascism, and Literature in Spain

Fuenmayor, José Félix (1885–1966)

Fuentes, Carlos (1928–)

Fuero Juzgo

Fuertes, Gloria (1917–1998)

Gala, Antonio (1936–)

Galeano, Eduardo (1940–)

Gallegos, Rómulo (1884–1969)

Galván, Manuel Jesús de (1834–1910)

Gálvez, Manuel (1882–1962)

Gálvez, de Cabrera, María Rosa (1768–1806)

Gambaro, Griselda (1928–)

Gamboa, Federico (1864–1939)

Gana, Federico (1867–1926)

Ganivet García, Ángel (1865–1898)

García Canclini, Néstor (1939–)

García Gutiérrez, Antonio (1812–1884)

García Lorca, Federico (1898–1936)

García Márquez, Gabriel (1927–)

García Montero, Luis (1958–)

García Morales, Adelaida (1945–)

García Pavón, Francisco (1919–1989)

Garcilaso de la Vega (1501–1536)

Garcilaso de la Vega, El Inca (1539–1616)

Garro, Elena (1920–1998)

Gauche Divine Cultural Movement

Gaucho Literature

Gelman, Juan (1930–)

Gender in Spanish American Literature

Gender in Spanish Literature

Generation "Crack" or "Crack Group"

Generation of 1898 in Spain

Generation of 1914 in Spain

Generation of 1927 in Spain

Generation of the 1950s in Spain

Generation X in Spain

Género chico criollo and the Río de la Plata *Saineteros* (*Sainete* Composers)

Giardinelli, Mempo (1947–)

Girondo, Oliverio (1891–1967)

Glantz, Margo (1930–)

Gómez Carrillo, Enrique (1873–1927)

Gómez de Avellaneda, Gertrudis (1814–1873)

Gómez de la Serna, Ramón (1888–1963)

Gómez Ojea, Carmen (1945–)

Góngora y Argote, Luis (1561–1627)

Gonzales-Berry, Erlinda (1942–)

González, Ángel (1925–2008)

González Echevarría, Roberto (1943–)

González Prada, Manuel (1844–1918)

González Suárez, Federico (1844–1917)

Gorostiza, José (1901–1973)

Gorriti, Juana Manuela (1818–1892)

Goytisolo, Juan (1931–)

Goytisolo, Luis (1935–)

Gracián y Morales, Baltasar (1601–1658)

Grandes, Almudena (1960–)

de Greiff, León (1895–1976)

Gringo

Grupo Barranquilla

Grupo de Guayaquil

Guatemala: History, Culture, and Literature

Guerra, Rosa (d. 1864)

Guerra Cunningham, Lucía (1943–)

Guerrero, Fernando María (1873–1929)

Guerrero Zacarías, Evangelina (1904–1949)

Guerrilla Poetry

Guevara, Che (1928–1967)

Guido, Beatriz (1924–1988)

Guillén, Jorge (1893–1984)

Güiraldes, Ricardo (1886–1927)

Gutiérrez, Juan María (1809–1878)

Gutiérrez Nájera, Manuel (1859–1895)

Guzmán, Martín Luis (1887–1976)

Guzmán de Alfarache

Haiti as Theme in Dominican Republic Writing

Hartzenbusch, Juan Eugenio (1806–1880)

Havana in Literature

Henríquez Ureña Family and Their Relation with the United States

Heredia, José María (1803–1839)

Hernández, Felisberto (1902–1964)

Hernández, Miguel (1910–1942)

Herrera, Fernando de (1534–1597)

Herrera y Reissig, Julio (1875–1910)

Hidalgo, Alberto (1897–1968)

Hierro, José (1922–2002)

Hijuelos, Oscar (1951–)

Hinojosa-Smith, Rolando (1929–)

Hispanic Heritage Month

Hispanism: Past and Present

Hispano-Arabic and Hispano-Judaic Literature and Culture in Spain

Honduras: History, Culture, and Literature

Huasipungo (1934; *The Villagers*, 1964)

Huidobro, Vicente (1893–1948)

Humanism in Spain

Ibárruri, Dolores (1895–1989)

Icaza, Carmen de (1899–1979)

Ignacio de Loyola, San (1491–1556)

Imperialism as Theme in Colonial Spanish America

Indigenismo in Spanish American Literature

Ingenieros, José (1877–1925)

Inquisition and Literature in the Hispanic World

Inquisition and the Hispanic World

Insularismo

Iparraguirre, Sylvia (1947–)

Iriarte, Tomás de (1750–1791)

Isaacs, Jorge (1837–1895)

Islamic Presence in Spain

Isleño

Jaimes Freyre, Ricardo (1868–1933)

Janés, Clara (1940–)

Jara, Víctor (1932–1973)

Jara Idrovo, Efraín (1926–)

Jardiel Poncela, Enrique (1901–1952)

Jarnés, Benjamín (1888–1949)

Jíbaro

Jiménez, Blas R. (1949–2009)

Jiménez, Juan Ramón (1881–1958)

Journals in Spanish America

Jovellanos, Gaspar Melchor de (1744–1811)

Juan de la Cruz, San (1542–1591)

Juan Manuel, Don (1282–1348)

Juaristi, Jon (1951–)

Judeo-Spanish Writing in Spanish America

Kahlo, Frida (1907–1954)

Krausism in Spain

Laforet, Carmen (1921–2004)

Laguerre, Enrique (1906–2005)

Lange, Norah (1906–1972)

Lara, Jesús (1898–1980)

Larra, Mariano José de (1809–1837)

Latinos and Latinas in the United States: History, Culture, and Literature

Latino Theater in the United States: Social Cohesion and Activism

Latorre Court, Mariano (1886–1955)

Laviera, Tato (1951–)

Lazarillo de Tormes: (*La vida de Lazarillo de Tormes y de sus fortunas y adversidades* [The Life of Lazarillo de Tormes and His Fortunes and Adversities])

Lazo, Agustín (1896–1971)

Lejárraga, María de la O (aka María Martínez Sierra) (1874–1974)

León, Fray Luis de (1527–1591)

Lezama Lima, José (1910–1976)

Liberation Theology in the Hispanic World

Libro de buen amor (1330?; *Book of Good Love*, 2005)

Literary Prizes in Spain and Spanish America

Literature and Film in Spain

Literature and Memory in the Hispanic World

Loaeza, Guadalupe (1946–)

Lobo, Tatiana (1939–)

López, Vicente Fidel (1815–1903)

López Velarde, Ramón (1888–1921)

Loynaz, Dulce María (1902–1997)

Lucas Guevara (1914; Eng. trans., 2003)

Lucía Jerez (1885)

Lugones, Leopoldo (1874–1938)

Lyceum Club Femenino

Lynch, Benito (1885–1951)

Lynch, Marta (1925–1985)

Machado y Ruiz, Antonio (1875–1939)

Machado y Ruiz, Manuel (1874–1947)

Madrid in Literature

Maeztu Whitney, Ramiro de (1875–1936)

Magical Realism

Mallea, Eduardo (1903–1982)

Malvinas/Falklands War Literature

Mañach, Jorge (1898–1961)

Mañas, José Ángel (1971–)

Manrique, Jorge (1440?–1479)

Mansilla, Lucio V. (1831–1913)

Mansilla de García, Eduarda (1834–1892)

Manzano, Juan Francisco (1797–1854)

Maravall Casesnoves, José Antonio (1911–1986)

Marechal, Leopoldo (1900–1970)

Marianism in Spanish America

Marías, Javier (1951–)

Mariel Writers Generation

Mármol, José (1817–1871)

Marqués, René (1919–1979)

Marsé, Juan (1933–)

Martí, José (1853–1895)

Martínez, Antonio José (1793–1867)

Martínez, Gregorio (1942–)

Martínez, Tomás Eloy (1934–2010)

Martínez de Pisón, Ignacio (1960–)

Martínez Estrada, Ezequiel (1895–1964)

Martínez Sierra, Gregorio (1881–1947)

Martín Fierro

Martín Gaite, Carmen (1925–2000)

Martín-Santos, Luis (1924–1964)

Mastretta, Ángeles (1949–)

Matto de Turner, Clorinda (1852–1909)

Matute, Ana María (1926–)

Mayan Literature

Mayoral, Marina (1942–)

McOndo

Mejía Vallejo, Manuel (1923–1998)

Memorias de Bernardo Vega (1930; *Memories of Bernardo Vega*, 1984)

Mena, Juan de (1411–1456)

Menchú, Rigoberta (1959–)

Mendoza, Eduardo (1943–)

Mera, Juan León (1832–1894)

Mesonero Romanos, Ramón (1803–1882)

Mexico City in Literature

Mexico: History, Culture, and Literature

Mexico: Twentieth-Century Organizers of Culture

Mihura Santos, Miguel (1905–1977)

Millán Astray, Pilar (1879–1949)

Millás, Juan José (1946–)

Miró, Gabriel (1879–1930)

Misogyny in Spanish Literature: Beginnings to 1700

Mistral, Gabriela (1889–1957)

Mitre, Bartolomé (1821–1906)

Modernismo in Hispanic Literature

Moix, Ana María (1947–)

Moix, Terenci (1942–2003)

Molina, Tirso de (pseudonym of Gabriel Téllez) (1580?–1648)

Monsiváis, Carlos (1938–2010)

Monteforte Toledo, Mario (1911–2003)

Montero, Mayra (1952–)

Montero, Rosa (1951–)

Monterroso, Augusto (1921–2003)

Montseny Mañé, Federica (1905–1993)

Mora, Pat (1942–)

Morejón, Nancy (1944–)

Moreno, Marvel (1939–1995)

Morisco

Morosoli, Juan José (1899–1957)

Movida, La (1978–1983)

Mozárabe

Mudéjar

Mújica, Elisa (1916–2003)

Mujica Láinez, Manuel (1910–1984)

Muñoz Molina, Antonio (1956–)

Muñoz Seca, Pedro (1879–1936)

Mutis, Álvaro (1923–)

Mysticism and Asceticism in Spain

Mythology in Spanish Golden Age Writing

Naranjo Cato, Carmen (1928–)

National Association of Latino Arts and Culture (NALAC)

National Catholicism

Nelken y Mausberger, Margarita (1896–1968)

Neohistoricism in the Contemporary Spanish Novel

Neruda, Pablo (1904–1973)

Nervo, Amado (1870–1919)

New Narrative in the Dominican Republic: 1978 to Present

Nicaragua: History, Culture, and Literature

Nissán, Rosa (1939–)

Nobel Prize Literature in Spanish

Nóvas Calvo, Lino (1905–1983)

Novel in Spain: Beginnings to 1700

Novel in Spain: 1700–1900

Novel in Spain: 1900 to Present

Novel in Spanish America: 1800–1900

Novel in Spanish America: *Boom*
Literature: 1950–1975

Novel of the Cuban Revolution

Novel of the Mexican Revolution

Novo, Salvador (1904–1974)

Nuestra América (Our America)

Núñez, Enrique Bernardo (1895–1964)

Nuyorican

Nuyorican Poets Café

Obaldía, María Olimpia de (1891–1984)

Ocampo, Silvina (1903–1994)

Ocampo, Victoria (1890–1979)

Oliver, María Rosa (1898–1977)

Olmedo, José Joaquín (1780–1847)

Olmo, Lauro (1922–1994)

Onetti, Juan Carlos (1909–1994)

Operation *Pedro Pan*

Oreamuno, Yolanda (1916–1956)

Orphée, Elvira (1930–)

Orrego Luco, Luis (1866–1948)

Ors y Rovira, Eugenio d' (1882–1954)

Ortega y Gasset, José (1883–1955)

Ortiz, Adalberto (1914–2003)

Ortiz, Fernando (1881–1969)

Ospina, William (1954–)

Otero Muñoz, Blas de (1916–1979)

Pacheco, Cristina (1941–)

Pacheco, José Emilio (1939–)

Pachuco

Padilla, Heberto (1932–2000)

Padrón, Justo Jorge (1943–)

Palacio Valdés, Armando (1853–1938)

Palma, Clemente (1872–1946)

Palma, Ricardo (1833–1919)

Panama Canal as Theme in Literature

Panama: Contemporary Women Writers

Panama: History, Culture, and Literature

Panero Family (20th Century)

Paraguay: History, Culture, and Literature

Pardo Bazán, Emilia (1851–1921)

Pardo y Aliaga, Felipe (1806–1868)

Parra, Marco Antonio de la (1952–)

Parra, Nicanor (1914–)

Parra, Teresa de la (pseudonym of Ana
Teresa Sanojo) (1898–1936)

Paso, Alfonso (1926–1978)

Pastorela

Pavlovsky, Eduardo (1933–)

Payador

Paz, Octavio (1914–1998)

Pellicer, Carlos (1897–1977)

PEN Club in the Hispanic World

Pereda, José María de (1833–1906)

Perera, Hilda (1926–)

Pérez de Ayala, Ramón (1889–1962)

Pérez de Zambrana, Luisa (1835–1922)

Pérez Firmat, Gustavo (1949–)

Pérez Galdós, Benito (1843–1920)

Pérez Reverte, Arturo (1951–)

Peri Rossi, Cristina (1941–)

Peru: History, Culture, and Literature

Philippine Islands: History, Culture, and
Literature

Philippine Literature in Spanish

Philosophy and Literature in Spain

Picaresque Literature in the Hispanic World

Piglia, Ricardo (1941–)

Piñera, Virgilio (1912–1979)

Pitol, Sergio (1933–)

Pla, Josefina (1903–1999)

Poetry in Spain: Beginnings to 1700

Poetry in Spain: 1700–1900

Poetry in Spain: 1900 to Present

Poetry in Spanish America: 1922–1975

Poetry in Spanish America: 1945 to Present

Poetry in the Dominican Republic: 1900 to Present

Poniatowska, Elena (1932/1933–)

Ponte, Antonio José (1964–)

Preciado Bedoya, Antonio (1941–)

Primo de Rivera y Sáenz de Heredia, José Antonio (1902–1936)

Project "Año 0"

Puértolas, Soledad (1948–)

Puerto Rican Poetry and Poetry Journals: 1960–2000

Puerto Rican Writers in Mainland United States

Puerto Rico: *Generación del treinta* (1930s Generation)

Puerto Rico: History, Culture, and Literature

Puig, Manuel (1932–1990)

Queer Literature in Contemporary Spain

Queer Literature in Spanish America

Quesada, José Luis (1948–)

Quesada, Roberto (1962–)

Quevedo, Francisco de (1580–1645)

Quintero Rivera, Ángel (1947–)

Quiroga, Elena (1921–1995)

Quiroga, Horacio (1879–1937)

Rabasa, Emilio (1856–1930)

Rama, Ángel (1926–1983)

Ramírez, Sergio (1942–)

Ramón y Cajal, Santiago (1852–1934)

Ramos Otero, Manuel (1948–1990)

Raza cósmica, La (1925; *The Cosmic Race*, 1997)

Real Academia Española de la Lengua (Royal Spanish Academy of Language)

Realism and Historical Fiction in the Dominican Republic

Realism and Naturalism in Spain

Recovering the U.S. Hispanic Literary Heritage Project

Recto, Claro (1890–1960)

Renaissance in Spain

Repertorio Español (Spanish Repertory)

Residencia de Estudiantes (Students' Residence)

Residencia de Señoritas (Young Women's Residence)

Restrepo, Laura (1950–)

Revueltas, José (1914–1976)

Reyes, Alfonso (1889–1959)

Ribeyro, Julio Ramón (1929–1994)

Ridruejo, Dionisio (1912–1974)

Riesco, Laura (1940–2008)

Río, Marcela del (pseudonym of Mara Reyes) (1932–)

Río, Nela (1938–)

Rivera Martínez, Edgardo (1933–)

Rivero, Eliana (1940–)

Rizal, José (1861–1896)

Roa Bastos, Augusto (1917–2005)

Robles, Mireya (1934–)

Rodas, Ana María (1937–2009)

Rodó, José Enrique (1871–1917)

Rojas, Ricardo (1882–1957)

Rojas Pizarro, Gonzalo (1917–2011)

Rojas Zorrilla, Francisco de (1607–1648)

Romance (Ballad) Tradition in the Hispanic World

Romantic Novel in Spain

Romanticism in Spain

Romero Esteo, Miguel (1930–)

Romero Olmedo, Felipe (1929–1998)

Rosales, Guillermo (1946–1993)

Rosales, Luis (1910–1992)

Rosencof, Mauricio (1933–)

Rossetti, Ana (1950–)

Rossi, Anacristina (1952–)

Ruiz de Alarcón, Juan (1581?–1639)

Ruiz Iriarte, Víctor (1912–1982)

Ruiz Zafón, Carlos (1964–)

Rulfo, Juan (1917–1986)

Sábato, Ernesto (1911–2011)

Saer, Juan José (1937–2005)

Sahagún, Bernardino de (1499–1590)

Salarrué (pseudonym of Efraín Salazar Arrué) (1899–1975)

Salinas, Pedro (1891–1951)

Salisachs, Mercedes (1916–)

Sampedro, José Luis (1917–)

Sánchez, Florencio (1875–1910)

Sánchez, Luis Rafael (1936–)

Sánchez Ferlosio, Rafael (1927–)

Sanín Cano, Baldomero (1861–1957)

Santería

Santiago de Compostela Myth

Santillana, Iñigo López de Mendoza, Marqués de (1398–1458)

Santos Chocano, José (1875–1942)

Sarduy, Severo (1936–1993)

Sarlo, Beatriz (1942–)

Sarmiento, Domingo Faustino (1811–1888)

Sastre, Alfonso (1926–)

Science Fiction in Spanish America

Scorza, Manuel (1928–1983)

Selena (stage name of Selena Quintanilla-Pérez) (1971–1995)

Selva, Salomón de la (1893–1959)

Semprún, Jorge (1923–2011)

Sender, Ramón José (1902–1982)

Senequism

Sephardic Literature in Spain

Serrano, Marcela (1951–)

Serrat, Joan Manuel (1943–)

Short Fiction in Spain: 1700–1900

Short Fiction in Spain: 1900 to Present

Short Fiction in Spanish America

Siale Djangany, José Fernando (1961–)

Silva, José Asunción (1865–1896)

Silva, Lorenzo (1966–)

Sinán, Rogelio (pseudonym of Bernardo Domínguez Alba) (1904–1994)

Skármeta, Antonio (1940–)

Slavery and Antislavery Literature in the Caribbean

Sleepy Lagoon Trial

Soccer (*Fútbol*) and Hispanic Literature

Solares, Ignacio (1945–)

Soriano, Osvaldo (1943–1997)

Soto, Pedro Juan (1928–2002)

Southern Cone Writing: Literature of Transition from Argentina and Chile

Spain and Self-Identity in the Nation

Spain: History, Culture, and Literature

Spanglish

Spanish American Poetry by Women

Spanish Civil War and the Dictatorship of General Franco (1936–1975)

Spanish Harlem (*El Barrio latino*)

Spanish-Language Writers from Catalonia, Spain

Stavans, Ilan (1961–)

Storni, Alfonsina (1892–1938)

Suárez y Romero, Anselmo (1818–1878)

Subercaseaux, Elizabeth (1945–)

Tablada, José Juan (1871–1945)

Teatro abierto (Open Theater, 1981–1985)

Teatro campesino (Farm Workers' Theater)

Teitelboim, Volodia (1916–2008)

Tejeira, Isis (l936–)

TENAZ (Teatro Nacional de Aztlán)

Teresa de Jesús, Santa (1515–1582)

Testimonial Writing in Central America

Theater in Spain: Beginnings to 1700

Theater in Spain: 1700–1900

Theater in Spain: 1900–1975

Theater in Spain: 1975 to Present

Theater in Spanish America: 1900 to Present

Tierno Galván, Enrique (1918–1986)

Tomás, Consuelo (1957–)

Tomeo, Javier (1932–)

Torre, Guillermo de (1900–1971)

Torrente Ballester, Gonzalo (1910–1999)

Torture in Modern Spanish American Literature

Toruño, Juan Felipe (1898–1980)

Toscana, David (1961–)

Traba, Marta (1930–1983)

Transculturation in the Hispanic World

Treaty of Guadalupe Hidalgo (1848)

Triana, José (1931–)

Trujillo as Theme in Dominican Republic and Hispanic Writing

Turcios, Froylán (1874–1943)

Tusquets, Esther (1936–)

Ulibarrí, Sabine (1919–2003)

Umbral, Francisco (1932–2007)

Umpierre, Luz María (Luzma) (1947–)

Unamuno y Jugo, Miguel de (1864–1936)

Universities in Spain and the New World: Beginnings to 1900

Urbina, Nicasio (1958–)

Uruguay: History, Culture, and Literature

Usigli, Rodolfo (1905–1979)

Valdés, Gabriel de la Concepción (1809–1844)

Valdés, José Manuel (1767–1843)

Valdés, Zoé (1959–)

Valencia, Guillermo (1873–1943)

Valente, José Ángel (1929–2000)

Valenzuela, Luisa (1938–)

Valera, Juan (1824–1905)

Valero, Roberto (1955–1994)

Valle-Inclán, Ramón María del (1866–1936)

Vallejo, César (1892–1938)

Vallejo, Fernando (1942–)

Vargas Llosa, Mario (1936–)

Vasconcelos, José (1882–1959)

Vaz Ferreira, María Eugenia (1875–1924)

Vázquez Montalbán, Manuel (1939–2003)

Vega, Ana Lydia (1946–)

Vega y Carpio, Lope de (1562–1635)

Velasco Mackenzie, Jorge (1949–)

Vélez de Guevara, Luis (1579–1644)

Veloz Maggiolo, Marcio (1936–)

Venezuela: Contemporary Women Poets

Venezuela: History, Culture, and Literature

Venezuelan Artistic Groups

Venezuelan Contemporary Narrative: 1980–2000

Venezuelan Writer-Statesmen

Vicent, Manuel (1936–)

Vilalta, Maruxa (1932–)

Villaurrutia, Xavier (1903–1950)

Villaverde, Cirilo (1812–1894)

Viñas, David (1929–2011)

Violencia, la: 1946–1953

Vitier, Cintio (1921–2009)

Vives, Juan Luis (1492–1540)

Vodanovic, Sergio (1926–2001)

Watanabe, José (1946–2007)

Wolff, Egon (1926–)

Women Writers in Cuba: 1900–1959

Women Writers in Cuba: 1959 to Present

Women Writers in Spain: Beginnings to 1700

Women Writers in Spain: 1700–1900

Women Writers in Spain: 1900 to Present

Yáñez, Agustín (1904–1980)

Yánez Cossío, Alicia (1928–)

...Y no se lo tragó la tierra (1971; *And the Earth Did Not Part,* 1971)

Zaldumbide, Gonzalo (1885–1965)

Zamora, Daisy (1950–)

Zamudio, Adela (1854–1928)

Zapata Olivella, Juan (1927–2008)

Zapata Olivella, Manuel (1920–2004)

Zarzuela

Zavala, Iris (1936–)

Zayas y Sotomayor, María de (1590–c.1660)

Zea, Leopoldo (1912–2004)

Zeno Gandía, Manuel (1855–1930)

Zoot Suit

Zorrilla y Moral, José (1817–1893)

Zunzunegui, Juan Antonio de (1901–1982)

Zurita, Raúl (1951–)

Guide to Related Topics

Absurdism

Argentine Theater by Women: 1900 to Present

Arreola, Juan José

Chilean Theater: 1900 to Present

Codorniz, La Literary Magazine

Contemporary Puerto Rican Short Story Writers: 1980 to Present

Dragún, Osvaldo

Eroticism in Contemporary Spanish Women Writers: 1975 to Present

Gambaro, Griselda

Jardiel Poncela, Enrique

Marqués, René

Mihura Santos, Miguel

New Narrative in the Dominican Republic: 1978 to Present

Onetti, Juan Carlos

Theater in Spain: 1900–1975

Theater in Spanish America: 1900 to Present

Tomeo, Javier

Vilalta, Maruxa

Vodanovic, Sergio

Afro-Hispanic Literature and Culture

Afro-Hispanic Literature in Spanish America

Afro-Hispanic Writers of Costa Rica

Avant-Garde Poetry in Spanish America

Ballagas, Emilio

Barnet, Miguel

Cabrera, Lydia

Carpentier, Alejo

Changó, el gran putas

Colón, Jesús

Contemporary Moroccan Literature Written in Spanish

Costa Rica: History, Culture, and Literature

Cuba: History, Culture, and Literature

Ecuador: History, Culture, and Literature

El Salvador: History, Culture, and Literature

Equatorial Guinea: History, Culture, and Literature

Equatorial Guinea: Poets

Equatorial Guinea: Writers in Exile

Equatorial Guinea: Writers Living in the United States

Equatorial Guinea's *Generación del Silencio* (The Generation of Silence)

Estupiñán Bass, Nelson

Grupo de Guayaquil

Gómez de Avellaneda, Gertrudis

Hispanism: Past and Present

Jiménez, Blas R.

Journals in Spanish America

Laviera, Tato

Lobo, Tatiana

Manzano, Juan Francisco

Martínez, Gregorio

Montero, Mayra

Morejón, Nancy

Ortiz, Adalberto

Ortiz, Fernando

Panama Canal as Theme in Literature

Panama: History, Culture and Literature

Preciado Bedoya, Antonio

Puerto Rico: *Generación del treinta* (1930s Generation)

Puerto Rico: History, Culture and Literature

Robles, Mireya

Rossi, Anacristina

Santería

Short Fiction in Spanish America

Slavery and Antislavery Literature in the Caribbean

Suárez y Romero, Anselmo

Transculturation in the Hispanic World

Valdés, Gabriel de la Concepción

Valdés, José Manuel

Velasco Mackenzie, Jorge

Women Writers in Cuba: 1900–1959

Women Writers in Cuba: 1959 to Present

Zapata Olivella, Juan

Zapata Olivella, Manuel

Archetypes and Icons in Literature and Culture

Almodóvar, Pedro

Bolívar, Simón, in Contemporary Literature and Culture

Cantar de Mío Cid

causa por la raza, la (The Cause for the Mexican Race)

Celestina, La in Spain and the New World

Cultural Icons of Chicanos

Cultural Icons of Cuban Americans

Cultural Icons of Spain

Cultural Icons of Spanish America

Don Juan Archetype in the Hispanic World

Don Quijote de la Mancha in Spanish American Literature and Culture

Gaucho Literature

Guevara, Che

Kahlo, Frida

Marianism in Spanish America

Martí, José

Martín Fierro

Pachuco

Picaresque Literature in the Hispanic World

Santiago de Compostela Myth

Selena

Serrat, Joan Manuel

Soccer (*Fútbol*) and Hispanic
  Literature

Zoot Suit

Avant-Garde Literature (Early 20th Century–1940s)

Adán, Martín

Adoum, Jorge Enrique

Alberti, Rafael

Altolaguirre, Manuel

Aub, Max

Avant-Garde Poetry in Spanish America

Avant-Garde Prose in Spanish America

Ayala, Francisco

Ballagas, Emilio

Bombal, María Luisa

Borges, Jorge Luis

Carrera Andrade, Jorge

Cernuda, Luis

Chacel, Rosa

Codorniz, La Literary Magazine

Contemporáneos Group

Coronel Urtecho, José

Cuadra, Pablo Antonio

Diego, Gerardo

Flores, Marco Antonio

García Lorca, Federico

Generation of 1927 in Spain

Girondo, Oliverio

Gómez de la Serna, Ramón

Gorostiza, José

Guatemala: History, Culture, and
  Literature

Huidobro, Vicente

Journals in Spanish America

Lazo, Agustín

López Velarde, Ramón

Marechal, Leopoldo

Mexico: History, Culture, and Literature

Mihura Santos, Miguel

Naranjo Cato, Carmen

Neruda, Pablo

Novo, Salvador

Ocampo, Silvina

Panama: History, Culture, and Literature

Panero Family (20th century)

Pellicer, Carlos

Pla, Josefina

Poetry in Spanish America: 1922–1975

Rojas Pizarro, Gonzalo

Selva, Salomón de la

Sinán, Rogelio (pseudonym of Bernardo
  Domínguez Alba)

Torre, Guillermo de

Vallejo, César

Villaurrutia, Xavier

Baroque and Neobaroque Literature

Cabrera Infante, Guillermo

Calderón de la Barca, Pedro

Canary Islands Writers

Carpentier, Alejo

Celestina, La in Spain and the New World

Colonial Baroque Writing in Spanish America

Colonial Theater in Spanish America

Contemporáneos Group

Gender in Spanish American Literature

Góngora y Argote, Luis

González Echevarría, Roberto

Gracián y Morales, Baltasar

Lezama Lima, José

Mexico: History, Culture and Literature

New Narrative in the Dominican Republic: 1978 to Present

Poetry in Spain: Beginnings to 1700

Poetry in Spanish America: 1922–1975

Poetry in Spanish America: 1945 to Present

Quevedo, Francisco de

Sarduy, Severo

Censorship and Literature

Arce, Manuel José

Arenas, Reinaldo

Argentina: History, Culture, and Literature

Argentine Novel after the Recovery of Democracy: 1983–2006

Ávila Laurel, Juan Tomás

Barcelona in Literature

Barros, Pía

Buero Vallejo, Antonio

CADA (1979–1985)

Cela, Camilo José

Censorship and Literature in Spain

Children's Literature in Spain: 1900 to Present

Chilean Women Writers: The *Ergo Sum* Project

Chile's Generation of 1980: The New Scene

Civil War Literature in Spain

Codorniz, La Literary Magazine (1941–1978; The Quail)

Cuban Exile Writing outside the United States

Documentary Narrative in Spanish American Literature

Dominican Republic: History, Culture, and Literature

Eltit, Diamela

Equatorial Guinea: Writers Living in the United States

Equatorial Guinea: Writers in Exile

Equatorial Guinea's *Generación del Silencio* (The Generation of Silence)

Exile Literature by Spanish Civil War Émigrés

Figuera Aymerich, Ángela

Francoism, Fascism, and Literature in Spain

Gambaro, Griselda

Gender in Spanish Literature

Generation of the 1950s in Spain

Gracián y Morales, Baltasar

Inquisition and Literature in the Hispanic World

Lazarillo de Tormes: (*La vida de Lazarillo de Tormes y de sus fortunas y adversidades*)

Mariel Writers Generation

Martín-Santos, Luis

Mujica Láinez, Manuel

Neohistoricism in the Contemporary Spanish Novel

Novel in Spain: 1900 to Present

Novel of the Cuban Revolution

Olmo, Lauro

Paraguay: History, Culture and Literature

Parra, Marco Antonio de la

PEN Club in the Hispanic World

Piglia, Ricardo

Piñera, Virgilio

Poetry in Spain: 1900 to Present

Poetry in Spanish America: 1945 to Present

Ponte, Antonio José

Queer Literature in Contemporary Spain

Rizal, José

Sánchez Ferlosio, Rafael

Sastre, Alfonso

Southern Cone Writing: Literature of Transition from Argentina and Chile

Spain and Self-Identity in the Nation

Teatro abierto

Testimonial Writing in Central America

Theater in Spain: 1900–1975

Theater in Spanish America: 1900 to Present

Torrente Ballester, Gonzalo

Torture in Modern Spanish American Literature

Trujillo as Theme in Dominican Republic and Hispanic Writing

Valle-Inclán, Ramón María del

Villaverde, Cirilo

Women Writers in Cuba: 1959 to Present

Chicanos and Chicano Literature

Acto

Anzaldúa, Gloria

Aventuras de Don Chipote, o cuando los pericos mamen, Las

Aztlán

causa por la raza, la

Chicano

Chicano Movement Literature and Publishing

Chicano Writers

Corpi, Lucha

Cota Cárdenas, Margarita

Cultural Icons of Chicanos

Feminism in Spanish America

Gonzales-Berry, Erlinda

Hinojosa-Smith, Rolando

Latinos and Latinas in the United States: History, Culture, and Literature

Latino Theater in the United States: Social Cohesion and Activism

Martínez, Antonio José

Mora, Pat

Pachuco

Sleepy Lagoon Trial

Teatro campesino

TENAZ

Ulibarrí, Sabine

... y no se lo tragó la tierra

Zoot Suit

Children's and Young Adults' Literature

Ada, Alma Flor

Afro-Hispanic Writers of Costa Rica

Alfaro, Óscar

Allende, Isabel

Anzaldúa, Gloria

Argentine Theater by Women: 1900 to Present

Atxaga, Bernardo

Belpré, Pura

Berman Goldberg, Sabina

Buitrago, Fanny

Caballero Calderón, Eduardo

Canetti Duque, Yanitzia

Casona, Alejandro (pseudonym of Alejandro Rodríguez Álvarez)

Celaya, Gabriel

Children's Literature in Spain: 1900 to Present

Children's Literature in Spanish in the United States

Colombian Exile Writers

Conde Abellán, Carmen

Corpi, Lucha

Escobar Galindo, David

Figuera Aymerich, Ángela

Fortún, Elena

Fuertes, Gloria (pseudonym of Encarna Aragoneses)

Giardinelli, Mempo

Gómez Ojea, Carmen

Martín Gaite, Carmen

Mistral, Gabriela

Montero, Rosa

Mora, Pat

Mújica, Elisa

Naranjo Cato, Carmen

Novel in Spain: 1900 to Present

Perera, Hilda

Poniatowska, Elena

Puértolas, Soledad

Rossetti, Ana

Ruiz Zafón, Carlos

Salarrué (pseudonym of Efraín Salazar Arrué)

Women Writers in Cuba: 1959 to Present

Yánez Cossío, Alicia

Zamudio, Adela

Cities in Literature

Aguilar Camín, Héctor

Arenas, Reinaldo

Barcelona in Literature

Benedetti, Mario

Bogotazo, el

Bolaño, Roberto

Buenos Aires in Literature

Cabrera-Infante, Guillermo

Carpenter, Alejo

Casal, Julián del

Cela, Camilo José

Chaviano, Daína

Contemporáneos Group

Cotto-Thorner, Guillermo

Detective and Mystery Fiction
  in Spain

Detective and Mystery Fiction in Spanish
  America

Dominican Republic: Contemporary
  Literature by Women Writers

Esquivel, Laura

Estévez, Abilio

Falcones, Ildefonso

Fernández de Lizardi, José Joaquín

Fuentes, Carlos

Gamboa, Federico

Género Chico Criollo and the
  Río de la Plata *Saineteros*
  (*Sainete* Composers)

Girondo, Oliverio

Guerra Cunningham, Lucía

Guzmán, Martín Luis

Havana in Literature

Larra, Mariano José de

Lezama Lima, José

López Velarde, Ramón

Lucas Guevara

Machado y Ruiz, Antonio

Madrid in Literature

Mañas, José Ángel

Marsé, Juan

Martín Santos, Luis

McOndo

Memorias de Bernardo Vega

Mendoza, Eduardo

Mesonero Romanos, Ramón

Mexico City in Literature

Mujica Láinez, Manuel

Muñoz Molina, Antonio

Novo, Salvador

Nuyorican Poets Cafe

Onetti, Juan Carlos

Pacheco, Cristina

Pérez Galdós, Benito

Pérez Reverte, Arturo

Poniatowska, Elena

Ponte, Antonio José

Project "Año 0"

Puerto Rican Writers in Mainland
  United States

Quesada, Roberto

Quiroga, Elena

Romero Olmedo, Felipe

Ruiz Zafón, Carlos

Valdés, Zoé

Valle-Inclán, Ramón María del

Vega y Carpio, Lope de

Velasco Mackenzie, Jorge

Villaverde, Cirilio

Colonialism and Colonial Writing (1492–1800)

Black Legend

Colonial Baroque Writing in Spanish America

Colonial Religious Chronicles in Spanish America

Colonial Theater in Spanish America

Cruz, Sor Juana Inés de la

Díaz del Castillo, Bernal

Discovery and Conquest Writings: Describing the Americas

Garcilaso de la Vega, el Inca

Imperialism as Theme in Colonial Spanish America

Mexico: History, Culture, and Literature

Nicaragua: History, Culture, and Literature

Paraguay: History, Culture, and Literature

Rama, Ángel

Ruiz de Alarcón, Juan

Sahagún, Bernardino de

Colonialism to Postcolonialism (1800 to Present)

(*See also* Imperialism and Anti-Imperialism)

Abad, Antonio

Adoum, Jorge Enrique

Afro-Hispanic Literature in Spanish America

Afro-Hispanic Writers of Costa Rica

Arciniegas, Germán

Arguedas, Alcides

Ávila Laurel, Juan Tomás

Cabrera, Lydia

Contemporáneos Group

Contemporary Moroccan Literature Written in Spanish

Criollista Novel in Spanish America

Dorfman, Ariel

Equatorial Guinea: History, Culture, and Literature

Equatorial Guinea: Poets

Equatorial Guinea: Writers in Exile

Equatorial Guinea: Writers Living in the United States

Equatorial Guinea's *Generación del silencio* (The Generation of Silence)

Exile Writing in the Hispanic World

Fernández Retamar, Roberto

García Canclini, Néstor

García Márquez, Gabriel

González Prada, Manuel

González Suárez, Federico

Guerra Cunningham, Lucía

Guerrero, Fernando María

Indigenismo in Spanish American Literature

Laguerre, Enrique

Lobo, Tatiana

López Velarde, Ramón

Mexico: Twentieth-Century Organizers of Culture

Monsiváis, Carlos

Naranjo Cato, Carmen

Novel in Spanish America: 1800–1900

Nuestra América (Our America)

Ortiz, Fernando

Philippine Literature in Spanish

Puerto Rico: Generación del treinta (1930s Generation)

Puerto Rico: History, Culture, and Literature

Rama, Ángel

Raza cósmica, La

Restrepo, Laura

Rizal, José

Rossi, Anacristina

Saer, Juan José

Sialy Djangany, José Fernando

Slavery and Antislavery Literature in the Caribbean

Soto, Pedro Juan

Transculturation in the Hispanic World

Vasconcelos, José

Valdés, Gabriel de la Concepción

Villaverde, Cirilio

Criollismo in Spanish America

Amazon Theme in Spanish American Literature

Brunet, Marta

Chile: History, Culture, and Literature

Colonialism and Anticolonialism in Spanish American Literature

Criollista Novel in Spanish America

Gallegos, Rómulo

Gana, Federico

Gaucho Literature

Género chico criollo and the Río de la Plata *Saineteros* (*Sainete* Composers)

Guatemala: History, Culture, and Literature

Güiraldes, Ricardo

Huasipungo

Indigenismo in Spanish American Literature

Laguerre, Enrique

Latorre Court, Mariano

Novel in Spanish America: *Boom* Literature: 1950–1975

Costumbrismo

Alfaro, Óscar

Aréstegui, Narciso

Ascensio Segura, Manuel

Chilean Theater: 1900 to Present

Cisneros, Luis Benjamín

Costumbrismo in Spanish America

Díaz Castro, Eugenio

García Pavón, Francisco

Isaacs, Jorge

Larra, Mariano José de

Mansilla de García, Eduarda

Martí, José

Morosoli, Juan José

Novel in Spanish America: 1800–1900

Palacio Valdés, Armando

Palma, Ricardo

Pardo y Aliaga, Felipe

Pereda, José María de

Pérez Galdós, Benito

Peru: History, Culture, and Literature

Philosophy and Literature in Spain

Romanticism in Spain

Short Fiction in Spain: 1700–1900

Vicent, Manuel

Cuban Americans and Cuban American Literature

Ada, Alma Flor

Arenas, Reinaldo

Balsero

Castillo, Amelia del

Cuban American Writers

Cultural Icons of Cuban Americans

Cultural Icons of Spanish America

Cultural Institutions for Hispanism in the United States

González Echevarría, Roberto

Hijuelos, Oscar

Latino Theater in the United States: Social Cohesion and Activism

Latinos and Latinas in the United States: History, Culture, and Literature

Mariel Writers Generation

National Association of Latino Arts and Culture (NALAC)

Novás Calvo, Lino

Operation *Pedro Pan*

Padilla, Heberto

PEN Club in the Hispanic World

Pérez Firmat, Gustavo

Rivero, Eliana

Cultural Institutions, and Initiatives in the Twentieth Century

Biblioteca de Autores Españoles (BAE)

Caro y Cuervo Institute

CONAIE (Confederación de Nacionalidades Indígenas del Ecuador)

Cultural Institutions for Hispanism in the United States

Hispanic Heritage Month

Hispanism: Past and Present

Literary Prizes in Spain and Spanish America

National Association of Latino Arts and Culture (NALAC)

Nuyorican Poets Café

PEN Club in the Hispanic World

Año 0

Real Academia Española de la Lengua (Royal Spanish Academy of Language)

Recovering the U.S. Hispanic Literary Heritage Project

Repertorio Español (Spanish Repertory)

Residencia de Estudiantes (Students' Residence)

Residencia de Señoritas (Young Women's Residence)

TENAZ (Teatro Nacional de Aztlán)

Cultural Movements and Literature in the 20th Century

(*See Also* Literary Generations and Groups)

Avant-Garde Poetry in Spanish America

Avant-Garde Prose in Spanish America

CADA (1978–1985)

Carrión Mora, Benjamín

Chicano Movement Literature and Publishing

Chilean Women Writers: The *Ergo Sum* Project

Cuban *Special Period* Fiction

Francoism, Fascism, and Literature in Spain

Gauche Divine Cultural Movement

Generation "Crack" or "Crack Group"

Grupo Barranquilla

Grupo de Guayaquil

Guevara, Che

Hispanism: Past and Present

Jara, Víctor

Latino Theater in the United States: Social Cohesion and Activism

Magical Realism

McOndo

Movida, La

Modernismo in Hispanic Literature

Nicaragua: History, Culture, and Literature

Novel of the Cuban Revolution

Novel of the Mexican Revolution

Nuyorican

Pachuco

Panama Canal as Theme in Literature

Serrat, Joan Manuel

Soccer (*Fútbol*) and Hispanic Literature

Spanish Civil War and the Dictatorship of General Franco (1935–1975)

Teatro abierto

Teatro campesino

Testimonial Writing in Central America

Valero, Roberto

Vasconcelos, José

Venezuelan Artistic Groups

Viñas, David

Detective Fiction

Benet, Juan

Bolaño, Roberto

Borges, Jorge Luis

Colombian Women Writers: 1950 to Present

Contemporary Puerto Rican Short Story Writers: 1980 to Present

Corpi, Lucha

Cuban *Special Period* Fiction

Cueto, Alonso

Denevi, Marco

Detective and Mystery Fiction in Spain

Detective and Mystery Fiction in Spanish America

Fernández, Macedonio

García Morales, Adelaida

García Pavón, Francisco

Mendoza, Eduardo

Novel in Spain: 1900 to Present

Novel of the Cuban Revolution

Paraguay: History, Culture, and Literature

Piglia, Ricardo

Pitol, Sergio

Queer Literature in Spanish America

Silva, Lorenzo

Southern Cone Writing: Literature of Transition from Argentina and Chile

Subercaseaux, Elizabeth

Vázquez Montalbán, Manuel

Venezuelan Contemporary Narrative: 1980–2000

Women Writers in Spain: 1900 to Present

Dictatorship and Literature

(*See Also* Political Protest and Literature)

Alberdi, Juan Bautista

Alberti, Rafael

Aldecoa, Ignacio

Alegría, Claribel

Alonso, Dámaso

Arciniegas, Germán

Arenas, Reinaldo

Arévalo Martínez, Rafael

Asturias, Miguel Ángel

Ayala, Francisco

Buero Vallejo, Antonio

Cela, Camilo José

Chilean Women Writers: The *Ergo Sum* Project

Contemporary Guatemalan Indigenous Authors

Dominican Republic: Contemporary Literature by Women Writers

Cuban-American Writers

Cuban Exile Writing outside the United States

Dominican Republic: History, Culture, and Literature

Dorfman, Ariel

Echeverría, Esteban

Equatorial Guinea: History, Culture, and Literature

Equatorial Guinea: Poets

Equatorial Guinea: Writers in Exile

Equatorial Guinea: Writers Living in the United States

Equatorial Guinea's *Generación del Silencio* (The Generation of Silence)

Exile Literature by Spanish Civil War Émigrés

Exile Writing in the Hispanic World

Francoism, Fascism, and Literature in Spain

Gambaro, Griselda

García Márquez, Gabriel

Guatemala: History, Culture, and Literature

Guerrilla Poetry

Liberation Theology in the Hispanic World

Machado y Ruiz, Manuel

Malvinas/Falklands War Literature

Mármol, José

Martínez Estrada, Ezequiel

Nicaragua: History, Culture, and Literature

Paraguay: History, Culture, and Literature

Poetry in the Dominican Republic: 1900 to Present

Roa Bastos, Augusto

Romero Esteo, Miguel

Sábato, Ernesto

Sarmiento, Domingo Faustino

Sastre, Alfonso

Semprún, Jorge

Soriano, Osvaldo

Southern Cone Writing: Literature of Transition from Argentina and Chile

Spain and Self-Identity in the Nation

Spanish Civil War and the Dictatorship of General Franco (1936–1975)

Teatro abierto

Testimonial Writing in Central America

Theater in Spain: 1900–1975

Torture in Modern Spanish American Literature

Trujillo as Theme in Dominican Republic and Hispanic Writing

Umbral, Francisco

Valenzuela, Luisa

Valle-Inclán, Ramón María del

Vargas Llosa, Mario

Veloz Maggiolo, Marcio

Viñas, David

Women Writers in Spain: 1900 to Present

Zurita, Raül

Discovery and Conquest in Literature

Adoum, Jorge Enrique

Autobiography in Spanish America

Biography in Spanish America

Black Legend

Cervantes de Salazar, Francisco

Colonial Religious Chronicles in Spanish America

Colonialism and Anticolonialism in Spanish American Literature

Díaz del Castillo, Bernal

Discovery and Conquest Writings: Describing the Americas

Epic Poetry in the Hispanic World

Garcilaso de la Vega, el Inca

Imperialism as Theme in Colonial Spanish America

Judeo-Spanish Writing in Spanish America

Mayan Literature

Mexico: History, Culture, and Literature

Peru: History, Culture, and Literature

Saer, Juan José

Sahagún, Bernardino de

Torture in Modern Spanish American Literature

Enlightenment (Neoclassicism)

Alberdi, Juan Bautista

Bello, Andrés

Enlightenment in Spain

Enlightenment in Spanish America

Feminism in Spain: 1700 to Present

Fernández de Moratín, Leandro

Forner, Juan Pablo

Gálvez de Cabrera, María Rosa

Gender in Spanish American Literature

Gender in Spanish Literature

Gómez de Avellaneda, Gertrudis

Iriarte, Tomás de

Jovellanos, Gaspar Melchor de

Madrid in Literature

Mexico: History, Culture, and Literature

Novel in Spain: 1700–1900

Philosophy and Literature in Spain

Poetry in Spain: 1700–1900

Short Fiction in Spain: 1700–1900

Spain: History, Culture, and Literature

Theater in Spain: 1700–1900

Valdés, José Manuel

Women Writers in Spain: 1700–1900

Erotic Literature and Eroticism

Aleixandre, Vicente

Contemporary Puerto Rican Short Story Writers: 1980 to Present

Darío, Rubén

Eroticism in Contemporary Spanish Women Writers: 1975 to Present

Gender in Spanish American Literature

Grandes, Almudena

Janés, Clara

Jarnés, Benjamín

Mayoral, Marina

Miró, Gabriel

Modernismo in Hispanic Literature

Montero, Mayra

Mujica Lainez, Manuel

Novel in Spain: 1700–1900

Novel in Spain: 1900 to Present

Padrón, Justo Jorge

Queer Literature in Contemporary Spain

Queer Literature in Spanish America

Río, Nela

Rodas, Ana María

Rossetti, Ana

Silva, José Asunción

Sinán, Rogelio (pseudonym of Bernardo Domínguez Alba)

Spanish American Poetry by Women

Turcios, Froylán

Tusquets, Esther

Umpierre, Luz María (Luzma)

Valdés, Zoé

Women Writers in Spain: 1900 to Present

Essay

Arciniegas, Germán

Arguedas, Alcides

Ávila Laurel, Juan Tomás

Azaña, Mañuel

Bolívar, Simón, in Contemporary Literature and Culture

Borges, Jorge Luis

Capetillo, Luisa

Carpentier, Alejo

Castellanos, Rosario

Castro Quesada, Américo

Colonialism and Anticolonialism in
  Spanish American Literature

Contemporary Moroccan Literature
  Written in Spanish

Dorfman, Ariel

Edwards, Jorge

Enlightenment in Spain: 1700–1800

Falcón, Lidia

Feminism in Spain: 1700 to Present

Fernández Retamar, Roberto

Forner, Juan Pablo

Galeano, Eduardo

Ganivet García, Ángel

García Canclini, Néstor

Generation of 1914 in Spain

González Echevarría, Roberto

González Prada, Manuel

Guerra, Rosa

Henríquez Ureña Family and
  Their Relation with the
  United States

Journals in Spanish America

Jovellanos, Gaspar Melchor de

Juaristi, Jon

Lezama Lima, José

Loaeza, Guadalupe

Mañach, Jorge

Maravall Casesnoves, José Antonio

Martí, José

Martínez Estrada, Ezequiel

Mexico: Twentieth-Century Organizers
  of Culture

Monsiváis, Carlos

Montero, Rosa

Montseny Mañé, Federica

Nelken y Mausberger, Margarita

Novo, Salvador

Nuestra América (Our America)

Ortega y Gasset, José

Ors y Rovira, Eugenio d'

Ospina, William

Pardo Bazán, Emilia

Paz, Octavio

Pérez de Ayala, Ramón

Peri Rossi, Cristina

Philippine Literature in Spanish

Philosophy and Literature in Spain

Puerto Rico: *Generación del treinta*
  (1930s Generation)

Raza cósmica, La

Reyes, Alfonso

Río, Marcela del (pseudonym of Mara Reyes)

Rodó, José Enrique

Sanín Cano, Baldomero

Sarlo, Beatriz

Short Fiction in Spain: 1700–1900

Tierno Galván, Enrique

Umbral, Francisco

Unamuno y Jugo, Miguel de

Venezuelan Writer-Statesmen

Vicent, Manuel

Exile Literature and Writers

Alberdi, Juan Bautista

Alberti, Rafael

Alegría, Ciro

Allende, Isabel

Altolaguirre, Manuel

Arce, Manuel José

Arenas, Reinaldo

Argentine Theater by Women: 1900 to Present

Argueta, Manlio

Aub, Max

Ayala, Francisco

Barea Ogazón, Arturo

Belli, Gioconda

Bello, Andrés

Benedetti, Mario

Bonasso, Miguel

Cabrera Infante, Guillermo

Cané, Miguel

Casona, Alejandro (pseudonym of Alejandro Rodríguez Álvarez)

Castillo, Amelia del

Castro Quesada, Américo

Cernuda, Luis

Champourcin, Ernestina de

Civil War Literature in Spain

Colombian Exile Writers

Correa, Miguel

Cruz Varela, María Elena

Cuban American Writers

Cuban Exile Writing outside the United States

Díaz, Jesús

Donoso, José

Donoso Pareja, Miguel

Dorfman, Ariel

Echeverría, Esteban

Equatorial Guinea: Poets

Equatorial Guinea: Writers in Exile

Equatorial Guinea: Writers Living in the United States

Equatorial Guinea's *Generación del Silencio* (The Generation of Silence)

Estévez, Abilio

Exile Literature by Spanish Civil War Émigrés

Exile Writing in the Hispanic World

Felipe, León

Fernández de Moratín, Leandro

Flores, Marco Antonio

Fortún, Elena (pseudonym of Encarna Aragoneses)

Gambaro, Griselda

Gelman, Juan

Giardinelli, Mempo

Goytisolo, Juan

Guillén Jorge

Gutiérrez, Juan María

Guzmán, Martín Luis

Heredia, José María

Ibárruri, Dolores

Jarnés, Benjamín

Latino Theater in the United States: Social Cohesion and Activism

Mañach, Jorge

Mariel Writers Generation

Martí, José

Martínez, Tomás Eloy

Menchú, Rigoberta

Mitre, Bartolomé

Monteforte Toledo, Mario

Neruda, Pablo

Novás Calvo, Lino

Padilla, Heberto

Pavlovsky, Eduardo

Perera, Hilda

Pérez de Ayala, Ramón

Pérez Firmat, Gustavo

Philippine Literature in Spanish

Rivero, Eliana

Rizal, José

Roa Bastos, Augusto

Rosales, Guillermo

Salinas, Pedro

Sanín Cano, Baldomero

Sarmiento, Domingo Faustino

Scorza, Manuel

Semprún, Jorge

Sender, Ramón José

Soriano, Osvaldo

Spain and Self-Identity in the Nation

Spanish American Poetry by Women

Triana, José

Usigli, Rodolfo

Valdés, Zoé

Vasconcelos, José

Villaverde, Cirilo

Feminism and Feminist Writers

Aguilar, Rosario

Alegría, Claribel

Allende, Isabel

Ángel, Albalucía

Anzaldúa, Gloria

Aponte Alsina, Marta

Argentina: History, Culture, and Literature

Argentine Theater by Women: 1900 to Present

Barros, Pía

Belli, Gioconda

Berman Goldberg, Sabina

Bombal, María Luisa

Boullosa, Carmen

Bullrich, Silvina

Burgos, Carmen de

de Burgos, Julia

Campo Alange, Condesa de

Capetillo, Luisa

Castellanos, Rosario

Castro, Rosalía de

Chacel, Rosa

Chicano Writers

Chilean Women Writers: The *Ergo Sum* Project

Chile's Generation of 1950

Colombian Women Writers: 1950 to Present

Colonial Baroque Writing in Spanish America

Contemporary Puerto Rican Short Story Writers: 1980 to Present

Coronado, Carolina

Cota Cárdenas, Margarita

Cruz, Sor Juana Inés de la

Detective and Mystery Fiction in Spain

Dominican Republic: Contemporary Literature by Women Writers

Ecuador: History, Culture, and Literature

Eroticism in Contemporary Spanish Women Writers: 1975 to Present

Falcón, Lidia

Feminism in Spain: 1700 to Present

Feminism in Spain: Precursors to 1700

Feminism in Spanish America

Ferré, Rosario

Formica, Mercedes

Fuertes, Gloria

Gálvez de Cabrera, María Rosa

García Morales, Adelaida

Garro, Elena

Gender in Spanish American Literature

Gender in Spanish Literature

Gómez Ojea, Carmen

Gonzales-Berry, Erlinda

Gorriti, Juana Manuela

Guerra Cunningham, Lucía

Guerrero Zacarías, Evangelina

Guido, Beatriz

Henríquez Ureña Family and Their Relation with the United States

Icaza, Carmen de

Laforet, Carmen

Lange, Norah

Lejárraga, María de la O (aka María Martínez Sierra)

Liberation Theology in the Hispanic World

Lobo, Tatiana

Lyceum Club Femenino

Lynch, Marta

Mansilla de García, Eduarda

Marianism in Spanish America

Martín Gaite, Carmen

Mastretta, Ángeles

Matto de Turner, Clorinda

Moix, Ana María

Montero, Rosa

Montseny Mañé, Federica

Morejón, Nancy

Moreno, Marvel

Naranjo Cato, Carmen

Nelken y Mausberger, Margarita

Nicaragua: History, Culture and Literature

Novel in Spain: 1900 to Present

Oreamuno, Yolanda

Panama: Contemporary Women Writers

Pardo Bazán, Emilia

Parra, Teresa de la (pseudonym of Ana Teresa Sanojo)

Philippine Literature in Spanish

Pla, Josefina

Poetry in Spanish America: 1945 to Present

Poniatowska, Elena

Puerto Rican Poetry and Poetry Journals: 1960–2000

Puerto Rico: *Generación del treinta* (1930s Generation)

Puerto Rico: History, Culture, and Literature

Río, Marcela del (pseudonym of Mara Reyes)

Río, Nela

Rivero, Eliana

Rodas, Ana María

Romanticism in Spain

Rossi, Anacristina

Rossetti, Ana

Short Fiction in Spain: 1900 to Present

Short Fiction in Spanish America

Slavery and Antislavery Literature in the Caribbean

Spanish American Poetry by Women

Storni, Alfonsina

Teresa de Jesús, Santa

Testimonial Writing in Central America

Theater in Spain: 1700–1900

Traba, Marta

Tusquets, Esther

Valdés, Zoé

Valenzuela, Luisa

Vaz Ferreira, María Eugenia

Venezuela: Contemporary Women Poets

Women Writers in Cuba: 1900–1959

Women Writers in Cuba: 1959 to Present

Women Writers in Spain: 1900 to Present

Yánez Cossío, Alicia

Zamora, Daisy

Zamudio, Adela

Film, Television, and Visual Arts in Literature

(*See Also* Music, Radio, and Popular Culture in Literature)

Almodóvar, Pedro

Arias, Arturo

Arreola, Juan José

Bolívar, Simón, in Contemporary Literature and Culture

Cabrera Infane, Guillermo

Children's Literature in Spain: 1900 to Present

Clavel, Ana

Costumbrismo in Spanish America

Cultural Icons of Chicanos

Cultural Icons of Cuban Americans

Cultural Icons of Spain

Cultural Icons of Spanish America

Don Quijote de la Mancha in Spanish American Literature and Culture

Dorfman, Ariel

Eguren, José María

Esquivel, Laura

Fernán-Gómez, Fernando

Francoism, Fascism, and Literature in Spain

Fuertes, Gloria

Gauche Divine Cultural Movement

Generation of 1927 in Spain

Generation X in Spain

Kahlo, Frida

Literature and Film in Spain

Mexico: Twentieth-Century Organizers
of Culture

Mihura Santos, Miguel

Moix, Ana María

Moix, Terenci

Movida, La

Pacheco, Cristina

Paso, Alfonso

Puig, Manuel

Quesada, Roberto

Río, Marcela del (pseudonym of Mara
Reyes)

Ruiz Iriarte, Víctor

Salarrué (pseudonym of Efraín Salazar
Arrué)

Semprún, Jorge

Skármeta, Antonio

Villaverde, Cirilo

Vodanovic, Sergio

Zurita, Raúl

Gaucho Literature

Argentina: History, Culture,
and Literature

Borges, Jorge Luis

Campo, Estanislao del

Criollista Novel in Spanish America

Epic Poetry in the Hispanic World

Estrada, Santiago

Gaucho Literature

Güiraldes, Ricardo

Lugones, Leopoldo

Lynch, Benito

Mansilla de García, Eduarda

Martín Fierro

Sarmiento, Domingo Faustino

Uruguay: History, Culture,
and Literature

History

Aguilar Camín, Héctor

Alfonso X, "el Sabio"

Alva Ixtlilxóchitl, Fernando de

Arguedas, Alcides

Castro Quesada, Américo

Colonial Religious Chronicles in Spanish
America

Cervantes de Salazar, Francisco

Díaz del Castillo, Bernal

Discovery and Conquest Writings:
Describing the Americas

Falcones, Ildefonso

Forner, Juan Pablo

Garcilaso de la Vega, El Inca

González Suárez, Federico

Henríquez Ureña Family and Their
Relation with the United States

López, Vicente Fidel

Maravall Casenoves, José Antonio

Mitre, Bartolomé

Neohistoricism in the Contemporary
Spanish Novel

Ortiz, Fernando

Ospina, William

Pérez Galdós, Benito

Ramírez, Sergio

Sahagún, Bernardino de

Solares, Ignacio

Zea, Leopoldo

Historical Fiction, Documentary Fiction, and Testimonial Writing

Afro-Hispanic Literature in Spanish America

Agosín, Marjorie

Alegría, Claribel

Alva Ixtlilxóchitl, Fernando de

Ángel, Albalucía

Arias, Arturo

Autobiography in Spanish America

Azuela, Mariano

Barea Ogazón, Arturo

Barnet, Miguel

Belli, Gioconda

Bonasso, Miguel

Borge, Tomás

Cabezas, Ómar

Campobello, Nellie

Cané, Miguel

Carranza, María Mercedes

Cervantes de Salazar, Francisco

Changó, el gran putas

Colón, Jesús

Contemporary Guatemalan Indigenous Authors

Cruz Varela, María Elena

Dalton, Roque

Díaz del Castillo, Bernal

Documentary Narrative in Spanish American Literature

El Salvador: History, Culture, and Literature

Exile Writing in the Hispanic World

Falcones, Ildefonso

Grandes, Almudena

Guatemala: History, Culture, and Literature

Guerra Cunningham, Lucía

Latinos and Latinas in the United States: History, Culture, and Literature

Literature and Memory in the Hispanic World

Lobo, Tatiana

López, Vicente Fidel

Manzano, Juan Francisco

Mastretta, Ángeles

Neohistoricism in the Contemporary Spanish Novel

Nissán, Rosa

Novel of the Cuban Revolution

Novel of the Mexican Revolution

Núñez, Enrique Bernardo

Pacheco, Cristina

Panama Canal as Theme in Literature

Pérez Reverte, Arturo

Poniatowska, Elena

Realism and Historical Fiction in the Dominican Republic

Río, Marcela del

Río, Nela

Rivera Martínez, Edgardo

Romantic Novel in Spain

Romero Olmedo, Felipe

Rosencof, Mauricio

Rossi, Anacristina

Saer, Juan José

Sahagún, Bernardino de

Scorza, Manuel

Soccer (*Fútbol*) and Hispanic Literature

Solares, Ignacio

Soto, Pedro Juan

Southern Cone Writing: Literature of Transition from Argentina and Chile

Testimonial Writing in Central America

Torture in Modern Spanish American Literature

Trujillo as Theme in Dominican Republic and Hispanic Writing

Valdés, Zoé

Vargas Llosa, Mario

Velasco Mackenzie, Jorge

Women Writers in Cuba: 1959s to Present

Women Writers in Spain: 1900 to Present

Imperialism and Anti-Imperialism

(*See Also* Colonialism to Postcolonialism: 1800 to Present)

Abad, Antonio

Adoum, Jorge Enrique

Alberdi, Juan Bautista

Alegría, Claribel

Apóstol, Cecilio

Arciniegas, Germán

Belli, Gioconda

Borge, Tomás

Cabezas, Ómar

Colonial Religious Chronicles in Spanish America

Contemporary Moroccan Literature Written in Spanish

Criollista Novel in Spanish America

Cuadra, Pablo Antonio

Dorfman, Ariel

Dragún, Osvaldo

Escoto, Julio

Guerrilla Poetry

Imperialism as Theme in Colonial Spanish America

Insularismo

Liberation Theology in the Hispanic World

Maeztu Whitney, Ramiro de

Modernismo in Hispanic Literature

Neruda, Pablo

Nicaragua: History, Culture, and Literature

Panama: Contemporary Women Writers

Philippine Literature in Spanish

Poetry in Spanish America: 1945 to Present

Puerto Rican Poetry and Poetry Journals: 1960–2000

Recto, Claro

Soto, Pedro Juan

Spanish American Poetry by Women

Testimonial Writing in Central America

Transculturation in the Hispanic World

Zamora, Daisy

Indigenism and Indigenous Writing

Abreu Gómez, Ermilo

Adoum, Jorge Enrique

Afro-Hispanic Writers of Costa Rica

Alegría, Ciro

Altamirano, Ignacio Manuel

Alva Ixtlilxóchitl, Fernando de

Amazon Theme in Spanish American Literature

Aréstegui, Narciso

Argentina: History, Culture, and Literature

Arguedas, Alcides

Arguedas, José María

Asturias, Miguel Ángel

Bolivia: History, Culture, and Literature

Campos, Julieta

Chile: History, Culture, and Literature

Colombia: History, Culture, and Literature

Colonialism and Anticolonialism in Spanish American Literature

Contemporary Guatemalan Indigenous Authors

Costa Rica: History, Culture, and Literature

Criollista Novel in Spanish America

Discovery and Conquest Writings: Describing the Americas

Ecuador: History, Culture, and Literature

El Salvador: History, Culture, and Literature

Epic Poetry in the Hispanic World

Garcilaso de la Vega, El Inca

González Prada, Manuel

Gorriti, Juana Manuela

Guatemala: History, Culture, and Literature

Heredia, José María

Huasipungo

Indigenismo in Spanish American Literature

Journals in Spanish America

Laguerre, Enrique

Lara, Jesús

Mansilla, Lucio V.

Matto de Turner, Clorinda

Mayan Literature

Menchú, Rigoberta

Mera, Juan León

Monteforte Toledo, Mario

Novel in Spanish America: 1800–1900

Ospina, William

Panama Canal as Theme in Literature

Peru: History, Culture, and Literature

Pla, Josefina

Riesco, Laura

Rulfo, Juan

Sahagún, Bernardino de

Salarrué

Scorza, Manuel

Testimonial Writing in Central America

Transculturation in the Hispanic World

Valdés, Gabriel de la Concepción

Valdés, José Manuel

Individual and Collective Identity and Literature

(Limited to non-biographical entries. *See Also* Spanish America and Cultural Identity; and Country Entries in Appendix B)

Afro-Hispanic Literature in Spanish America

Afro-Hispanic Writers of Costa Rica

Amazon Theme in Spanish American Literature

Argentine Novel after the Recovery of Democracy: 1983–2006

Autobiography in Spain: 1700 to Present

Autobiography in Spanish America

Barcelona in Literature

Biography in Spain: Beginnings to 1700

Biography in Spain: 1700 to Present

Biography in Spanish America

Black Legend

Bryce Echenique, Alfredo

Buenos Aires in Literature

Canary Islands Writers

Changó, el gran putas

Chicano Movement Literature and Publishing

Chicano Writers

Chilean Theater: 1900 to Present

Colombian Women Writers: 1950 to Present

Contemporary Guatemalan Indigenous Authors

Contemporary Moroccan Literature Written in Spanish

Contemporary Puerto Rican Short Story Writers: 1980 to Present

Costumbrismo in Spanish America

Converso Literature in Spain

Criollista Novel in Spanish America

Cuban Exile Writing outside the United States

Cuban American Writers

Cultural Icons of Chicanos

Cultural Icons of Cuban Americans

Cultural Icons of Spain

Cultural Icons of Spanish America

Detective and Mystery Fiction in Spain

Detective and Mystery Fiction in Spanish America

Dominican Republic: Contemporary Literature by Women Writers

Enlightenment in Spain: 1700–1800

Enlightenment in Spanish America

Epic Poetry in the Hispanic World

Equatorial Guinea: Poets

Equatorial Guinea: Writers in Exile

Equatorial Guinea: Writers Living in the United States

Equatorial Guinea's *Generación del Silencio* (The Generation of Silence)

Exile Literature by Spanish Civil War Émigrés

Exile Literature in the Hispanic World

Feminism in Spain: 1700 to Present

Feminism in Spanish America

Francoism, Fascism, and Literature in Spain

Gaucho Literature

Gender in Spanish American Literature

Gender in Spanish Literature

Generation of 1898 in Spain

Generation X in Spain

Género Chico Criollo and the Rio de la Plata *Saineteros* (*Sainete* Composers)

Haiti as Theme in Dominican Republic Writing

Havana in Literature

Indigenismo in Spanish American Literature

Insularismo

Jíbaro

Journals in Spanish America

Judeo-Spanish Writing in Spanish America

Latinos and Latinas in the United States: History, Culture, and Literature

Latino Theater in the United States: Social Cohesion and Activism

Liberation Theology in the Hispanic World

Literature and Memory in the Hispanic World

Madrid in Literature

Malvinas/Falklands War Literature

Marianism in Spanish America

McOndo

Mexico City in Literature

Mexico: Twentieth-Century Organizers of Culture

Misogyny in Spanish Literature: Beginnings to 1700

Movida, La

National Catholicism

Novel in Spain: 1900 to Present

Novel in Spanish America: *Boom* Literature: 1950–1975

Novel of the Cuban Revolution

Nuyorican

Nuyorican Poets Café

Pachuco

Panama: Contemporary Women Writers

Philippine Literature in Spanish

Poetry in Spanish America: 1945 to Present

Puerto Rican Writers in Mainland United States

Puerto Rico: *Generación del treinta* (1930s Generation)

Puerto Rico: History, Culture, and Literature

Queer Literature in Contemporary Spain

Queer Literature in Spanish America

Romance (Ballad) Tradition in the Hispanic World

Santiago de Compostela Myth

Short Fiction in Spain: 1900 to Present

Soccer (*Fútbol*) and Hispanic Literature

Spain and Self-Identity in the Nation

Spanish Civil War and the Dictatorship of
General Franco (1936–1975)

Spanish-Language Writers from
Catalonia, Spain

Teatro campesino

Theater in Spain: 1975 to Present

Theater in Spanish America: 1900 to
Present

Venezuela: Contemporary Women Poets

Women Writers in Cuba: 1900–1959

Women Writers in Cuba: 1959 to Present

Women Writers in Spain: 1700–1900

Women Writers in Spain: 1900
to Present

. . . y no se lo tragó la tierra

Islamic Influences, Themes, and Literature

Alarcón, Pedro Antonio de

Alfonso X, "el Sabio"

Cantar de Mío Cid

Contemporary Moroccan Literature
Written in Spanish

Dragún, Osvaldo

Epic Poetry in the Hispanic World

Falcones, Ildefonso

Goytisolo, Juan

Hispano-Arabic and Hispano-Judaic
Literature and Culture in Spain

Inquisition and Literature in the Hispanic
World

Islamic Presence in Spain

Morisco

Mozárabe

Mudéjar

Mysticism and Asceticism in Spain

Mythology in Spanish Golden Age
Writing

Neohistoricism in the Contemporary
Spanish Novel

Novel in Spain: Beginnings to 1700

Pérez Galdós, Benito

Romero Olmedo, Felipe

Sephardic Literature in Spain

Spain: History, Culture, and Literature

Universities in Spain and the New World:
Beginnings to 1900

Judeo-Spanish Presence and Literature

Agosín, Marjorie

Alfonso X, "el Sabio"

Aub, Max

Berman Goldberg, Sabina

Black Legend

Borges, Jorge Luis

Celestina, La in Spain and the New World

Converso Literature in Spain

Cultural Icons of Spain

Díaz-Mas, Paloma

Francoism, Fascism, and Literature in Spain

Gelman, Juan

Glantz, Margo

Goytisolo, Juan

Guzmán de Alfarache

Hispano-Arabic and Hispano-Judaic Literature and Culture in Spain

Inquisition and Literature in the Hispanic World

Isaacs, Jorge

Judeo-Spanish Writing in Spanish America

Misogyny in Spanish Literature: Beginnings to 1700

Mysticism and Asceticism in Spain

Mythology in Spanish Golden Age Writing

Neohistoricism in the Contemporary Spanish Novel

Nissán, Rosa

Pavlovsky, Eduardo

Philosophy and Literature in Spain

Romero Olmedo, Felipe

Rosencof, Mauricio

Sephardic Literature in Spain

Spain: History, Culture, and Literature

Stavans, Ilan

Torture in Modern Spanish American Literature

Vives, Juan Luis

Literary Generations and Groups

(Limited to topical entries. *See Also* Cultural Movements and Literature in the Twentieth Century)

CADA (1978–1985)

Canary Island Writers

Chilean Women Writers: The *Ergo Sum* Project

Chile's Generation of 1950

Chile's Generation of 1980: The New Scene

Colombian Exile Writers

Contemporáneos Group

Contemporary Puerto Rican Short Story Writers: 1980 to Present

El Salvador's *Generación Comprometida* (1956–1972)

Equatorial Guinea: Writers Living in the United States

Equatorial Guinea: Writers in Exile

Equatorial Guinea's *Generación del Silencio* (The Generation of Silence)

Exile Literature by Spanish Civil War Émigrés

Exile Literature in the Hispanic World

Gauche Divine Cultural Movement

Generation "Crack" or "Crack Group"

Generation of 1898 in Spain

Generation of 1914 in Spain

Generation of 1927 in Spain

Generation of the 1950s in Spain

Generation X in Spain

Grupo Barranquilla

Grupo de Guayaquil

Magical Realism

Mariel Writers Generation

McOndo

New Narrative in the Dominican Republic: 1978 to Present

Novel in Spanish America: *Boom* Literature: 1950–1975

Nuyorican Poets Café

Puerto Rican Poetry and Poetry Journals: 1960–2000

Puerto Rican Writers in Mainland United States

Venezuela: Contemporary Women Poets

Puerto Rico: *Generacion del treinta* (1930s Generation)

Venezuelan Artistic Groups

Venezuelan Contemporary Narrative: 1980–2000

Literary Journals

Avant-Garde Poetry in Spanish America

Chicano Movement Literature and Publishing

Codorniz, La Literary Magazine

Contemporáneos Group

Generation of 1914 in Spain

Generation of 1927 in Spain

Journals in Spanish America

Mexico: Twentieth-Century Organizers of Culture

Puerto Rican Poetry and Poetry Journals: 1960–2000

Puerto Rico: *Generación del treinta* (1930s Generation)

Literary Prizes and Prizewinners (Nobel, Cervantes Prize, Casa de las Américas, National Prizes)

Ada, Alma Flor

Alberti, Rafael

Alegría, Claribel

Aleixandre, Vicente

Alonso, Dámaso

Andreu, Blanca

Arciniegas, Germán

Argueta, Manlio

Arias, Arturo

Asturias, Miguel Ángel

Azaña, Manuel

Ballagas, Emilio

Balmori, Jesús

Bellatin, Mario

Belpré, Pura

Benavente, Jacinto

Benítez Rojo, Antonio

Bernabé, Manuel

Cabrera Infante, Guillermo

Carpentier, Alejo

Cela, Camilo José

Conti, Haroldo

Cossa, Roberto

Cruz Varela, María Elena

Díaz, Jesús

Diego, Gerardo

Donoso Pareja, Miguel

Donoso, José

Droguett, Carlos

Echegaray, José

Edwards, Jorge

Etxebarria, Lucía

Flores, Marco Antonio

García Canclini, Néstor

García Márquez, Gabriel

Gelman, Juan

Giardinelli, Mempo

Gómez Ojea, Carmen

Gorostiza, José

Guerrero Zacarías, Evangelina

Guillén, Jorge

Hijuelos, Oscar

Hinojosa-Smith, Rolando

Jara Idrovo, Efraín

Jiménez, Juan Ramón

Laforet, Carmen

Lange, Norah

Literary Prizes in Spain and Spanish
    America

Loynaz, Dulce María

Marechal, Leopoldo

Martín Gaite, Carmen

Mastretta, Ángeles

Matute, Ana María

Menchú, Rigoberta

Mistral, Gabriela

Monsiváis, Carlos

Monteforte Toledo, Mario

Morejón, Nancy

Muñoz Molina, Antonio

Naranjo Cato, Carmen

Neruda, Pablo

Nobel Prize Literature in Spanish

Olmo, Lauro

Ortiz, Adalberto

Parra, Nicanor

Paz, Octavio

Philippine Literature in Spanish

Piglia, Ricardo

Piñera, Virgilio

Quiroga, Elena

Roa Bastos, Augusto

Rodas, Ana María

Rojas Pizarro, Gonzalo

Rosales, Luis

Ruiz Iriarte, Víctor

Rulfo, Juan

Sábato, Ernesto

Saer, Juan José

Salisachs, Mercedes

Sampedro, José Luis

Sánchez Ferlosio, Rafael

Skármeta, Antonio

Vargas Llosa, Mario

Velasco Mackenzie, Jorge

Veloz Maggiolo, Marcio

Zavala, Iris

Zunzunegui, Juan Antonio de

Zurita, Raúl

Modernismo

Agustini, Delmira

Apóstol, Cecilio

Borrero, Juana

Canary Islands Writers

Carreras, Roberto de las

Casal, Julián del

Champourcin, Ernestina de

Colombian Modernist Writing: 1885–1915

Darío, Rubén

Eguren, José María

Gana, Federico

Gender in Spanish American Literature

Generation of 1898 in Spain

Gómez Carrillo, Enrique

Guatemala: History, Culture, and Literature

Guerrero, Fernando María

Güiraldes, Ricardo

Gutiérrez Nájera, Manuel

Henríquez Ureña Family and Their Relation with the United States

Herrera y Reissig, Julio

Huidobro, Vicente

Jaimes Freyre, Ricardo

Jiménez, Juan Ramón

Journals in Spanish America

Lejárraga, María de la O (aka María Martínez Sierra)

Lugones, Leopoldo

Machado y Ruiz, Manuel

Martí, José

Martínez Estrada, Ezequiel

Mexico History, Culture, and Literature

Modernismo in Hispanic Literature

Nervo, Amado

Nicaragua: History, Culture, and Literature

Novel in Spanish America: 1800–1900

Palma, Clemente

Philippine Literature in Spanish

Pla, Josefina

Poetry in Spain: 1700–1900

Poetry in Spain: 1900 to Present

Poetry in the Dominican Republic: 1900 to Present

Rodó, José Enrique

Sanín Cano, Baldomero

Santos Chocano, José

Science Fiction in Spanish America

Short Fiction in Spain: 1900 to Present

Short Fiction in Spanish America

Silva, José Asunción

Spanish American Poetry by Women

Storni, Alfonsina

Toruño, Juan Felipe

Turcios, Froylán

Uruguay: History, Culture, and Literature

Valencia, Guillermo

Valle-Inclán, Ramón María del

Vaz Ferreira, María Eugenia

Venezuelan Artistic Groups

Yáñez, Agustín

Music, Radio, and Popular Culture in Literature

(*See Also* Film, Television, and Visual Arts in Literature)

Alfaro, Óscar

CADA

Campobello, Nellie

Carpentier, Alejo

Children's Literature in Spain: 1900 to Present

Chilean Women Writers: The *Ergo Sum Project*

Diego, Gerardo

Generation X in Spain

Género Chico Criollo and the Río de la Plata *Saineteros* (*Sainete* Composers)

González Prada, Manuel

Hernández, Felisberto

Jara, Víctor

Mexico: Twentieth-Century Organizers of Culture

Modernismo in Hispanic Literature

Monsiváis, Carlos

Mutis, Álvaro

Panama: History, Culture, and Literature

Paraguay: History, Culture, and Literature

Parra, Nicanor

Payador

Preciado Bedoya, Antonio

Puig, Manuel

Quintero Rivera, Ángel

Romance (Ballad) Tradition in the Hispanic World

Selena (stage name of Selena Quintanilla-Pérez)

Serrat, Joan Manuel

Teitelboim, Volodia

Tierno Galván, Enrique

Uruguay: History, Culture, and Literature

Vaz Ferreira, María Eugenia

Venezuela: History, Culture, and Literature

Zamora, Daisy

Zarzuela

Neorealism, Social Realism, and Dirty Realism

(*See Also* Realism in Spanish Literature)

Aldecoa, Ignacio

Barcelona in Literature

Bolaño, Roberto

Cela, Camilo José

Chile: History, Culture, and Literature

Cuban *Special Period* Fiction

Ecuador: History, Culture, and Literature

Fallas, Carlos Luis

Fernández Santos, Jesús

Generation "Crack" or "Crack Group"

Generation X in Spain

Grupo de Guayaquil

Havana in Literature

Laforet, Carmen

Mañas, José Ángel

McOndo

Mexico City in Literature

New Narrative in the Dominican Republic: 1978 to Present

Novel in Spain: 1900 to Present

Novel of the Cuban Revolution

Pacheco, Cristina

Restrepo, Laura

Sampedro, José Luis

Sánchez Ferlosio, Rafael

Sastre, Alfonso

Sender, Ramón

Teitelboim, Volodia

Theater in Spain: 1900–1975

Wolff, Egon

Women Writers in Cuba: 1959 to Present

Novel

(Limited to non-biographical items)

Afro-Hispanic Literature of Spanish America

Amazon Theme in Spanish American Literature

Argentine Novel after the Recovery of Democracy: 1983–2006

Avant-Garde Prose in Spanish America

aventuras de Don Chipote, o cuando los pericos mamen, Las

Celestina, La in Spain and the New World

Changó, el gran putas

Cien años de soledad

Criollista Novel in Spanish America

Detective and Mystery Fiction in Spain

Detective and Mystery Fiction in Spanish America

Documentary Narrative in Spanish American Literature

Don Quijote de la Mancha in Spanish American Literature and Culture

Exile Literature by Spanish Civil War Émigrés

Gaucho Literature

Guzmán de Alfarache

Huasipungo

Indigenismo in Spanish American Literature

Judeo-Spanish Writing in Spanish America

Lazarillo de Tormes: (*La vida de Lazarillo de Tormes y de sus fortunas y adversidades*

Literature and Film in Spain

Literature and Memory in the Hispanic World

Lucas Guevara

Lucía Jerez

Magical Realism

Memorias de Bernardo Vega

Neohistoricism in the Contemporary Spanish Novel

New Narrative in the Dominican Republic: 1978 to Present

Novel in Spain: 1700–1900

Novel in Spain: 1900 to Present

Novel in Spain: Beginnings to 1700

Novel in Spanish America: 1800–1900

Novel in Spanish America: *Boom Literature: 1950–1975*

Novel of the Cuban Revolution

Novel of the Mexican Revolution

Panama Canal as Theme in Literature

Picaresque Literature in the Hispanic World

Realism and Historical Fiction in the Dominican Republic

Realism and Naturalism in Spain

Romantic Novel in Spain

Science Fiction in Spanish America

Slavery and Antislavery Literature in the Caribbean

Southern Cone Writing: Literature of Transition from Argentina and Chile

Testimonial Writing in Caribbean Literature

Torture in Modern Spanish American Literature

Trujillo as Theme in Dominican Republic and Hispanic Writing

. . . Y no se lo tragó la tierra

Philosophy

Biblioteca de Autores Españoles (BAE)

Enlightenment in Spain

Enlightenment in Spanish America

Ganivet, Ángel

Gracián y Morales, Baltasar

Humanism in Spain

Krausism in Spain

Maravall Casesnoves, José Antonio

Ortega y Gasset, José

Philosophy and Literature in Spain

Senequism

Tierno Galván, Enrique

Unamuno y Jugo, Miguel de

Zavala, Iris

Zea, Leopoldo

Picaresque Literature

Autobiography in Spain: Beginnings to 1700

Autobiography in Spain: 1700 to Present

Autobiography in Spanish America

Aventuras de don Chipote, o cuando los pericos mamen, Las

Celestina in Spain and the New World

Cervantes, Miguel de

Collazos, Óscar

Costumbrismo in Spanish America

Don Quijote de la Mancha in Spanish American Literature and Culture

Fernández de Lizardi, José Joaquín

Guzmán de Alfarache

Lazarillo de Tormes: La vida de Lazarillo de Tormes y de sus fortunes y adversidades

Lobo, Tatiana

Mendoza, Eduardo

Mexico City in Literature

Novel in Spain: Beginnings to 1700

Novel in Spain: 1700–1900

Novel in Spanish America

Picaresque Literature in the Hispanic World

Queer Literature in Spanish America

Quevedo, Francisco de

Renaissance in Spain

Rossetti, Ana

Tierno Galván, Enrique

Vélez de Guevara, Luis

Poetry

(Limited to non-biographical entries)

Afro-Hispanic Literature in Spanish America

Afro-Hispanic Writers of Costa Rica

Avant-Garde Poetry in Spanish America

Cancionero Poetry in Spain

Cantar de Mío Cid

Colombian Modernist Writing: 1885–1915

Convent Writing in Spain and the New World

Don Quijote de la Mancha in Spanish American Literature and Culture

El Salvador's *Generación comprometida*

Epic Poetry in the Hispanic World

Equatorial Guinea: Poets

Exile Literature by Spanish Civil War Émigrés

Feminism in Spain: 1700 to Present

Feminism in Spain: Beginnings to 1700

Feminism in Spanish America

Flor y canto

Generation of 1927 in Spain

Generation of the 1950s in Spain

Guerrilla Poetry

Hispano-Arabic and Hispano-Judaic Literature and Culture in Spain

Manrique, Jorge

Martín Fierro

Modernismo in the Hispanic World

Mysticism and Asceticism in Spain

Poetry in Spain: 1700–1900

Poetry in Spain: 1900 to Present

Poetry in Spain: Beginnings to 1700

Poetry in Spanish America: 1922–1975

Poetry in Spanish America: 1945 to Present

Poetry in the Dominican Republic: 1900 to Present

Puerto Rican Poetry and Poetry Journals: 1960–2000

Romance (Ballad) Tradition in the Hispanic World

Silva, José Asunción

Spanish American Poetry by Women

Venezuela: Contemporary Women Poets

Political Protest and Literature

(*See Also* Dictatorship and Literature; Social Disorder, War, and Revolution in Literature)

Acto

Alegría, Claribel

Arce, Manuel José

Argentine Novel after the Recovery of Democracy: 1983–2006

Argentine Theater by Women: 1900 to Present

Asturias, Miguel Ángel

Blasco Ibáñez, Vicente

CADA

Capetillo, Luisa

Chicano Movement Literature and Publishing

Chilean Women Writers: The *Ergo Sum* Project

Civil War Literature in Spain

Colombia: History, Culture, and Literature

Colombian Women Writers: 1950 to Present

Contemporary Puerto Rican Short Story Writers: 1980 to Present

Detective and Mystery Fiction in Spain

Documentary Narrative in Spanish American Literature

Dominican Republic: Contemporary Literature by Women Writers

Eltit, Damiela

Equatorial Guinea: Poets

Equatorial Guinea: Writers in Exile

Equatorial Guinea: Writers Living in the United States

Equatorial Guinea's *Generación del Silencio* (The Generation of Silence)

Feminism in Spain: 1700 to Present

Feminism in Spanish America

Flores, Marco Antonio

Fuertes, Gloria

Galeano, Eduardo

Gambaro, Griselda

Generation of the 1950s in Spain

Guerrilla Poetry

Guillén, Jorge

Hernández, Miguel

Jara, Víctor

Lara, Jesús

Liberation Theology in the Hispanic World

Mariel Writers Generation

Martínez, Antonio José

Montseny Mañé, Federica

Neruda, Pablo

Novel in Spain: 1900 to Present

Novel in Spanish America: *Boom* Literature: 1950–1975

Philippine Literature in Spanish

Poetry in Spain: 1900 to Present

Project "Año 0"

Puerto Rican Poetry and Poetry Journals 1960–2000

Puerto Rican Writers in Mainland United States

Queer Literature in Contemporary Spain

Queer Literature in Spanish America

Revueltas, José

Romanticism in Spain

Rosencof, Mauricio

Sastre, Alfonso

Semprún, Jorge

Short Fiction in Spanish America

Spanish American Poetry by Women

Teatro abierto

Teatro campesino

Testimonial Writing in Central America

Theater in Spain: 1975 to Present

Theater in Spanish America: 1900 to Present

Torture in Modern Spanish American Literature

Trujillo as Theme in Dominican Republic and Hispanic Writing

Valdés, Zoé

Valenzuela, Luisa

Women Writers in Spain: 1900 to Present

Positivism

Arguedas, Alcides

Canary Islands Writers

González Prada, Manuel

Ingenieros, José

Mexico: Twentieth-Century Organizers of Culture

Modernismo in Hispanic Literature

Pérez Galdós, Benito

Sánchez, Florencio

Postmodernism

Almodóvar, Pedro

Andreu, Blanca

Arenas, Reinaldo

Arias, Arturo

Avant-Garde Prose in Spanish America

Benítez Rojo, Antonio

Bolaño, Roberto

Boullosa, Carmen

Cerda, Martha

Clavel, Ana

Cultural Icons of Spain

Chile's Generation of 1980: The New Scene

Chile: History, Culture, and Literature

Díaz-Mas, Paloma

Documentary Narrative in Spanish American Literature

Dorfman, Ariel

Eltit, Diamela

Eroticism in Contemporary Spanish Women Writers: 1975 to Present

Etxebarria, Lucía

Fuentes, Carlos

García Montero, Luis

Gauche Divine Cultural Movement

Generation "Crack" or "Crack Group"

Generation X in Spain

González, Ángel

Goytisolo, Juan

Grandes, Almudena

Hijuelos, Óscar

Loaeza, Guadalupe

Mariel Writers Generation

McOndo

Montero, Rosa

Movida, La

Neohistoricism in the Contemporary
 Spanish Novel

Neruda, Pablo

New Narrative in the Dominican
 Republic: 1978 to Present

Peri Rossi, Cristina

Philosophy and Literature in Spain

Piglia, Ricardo

Poetry in Spain: 1900 to Present

Poetry in Spanish America: 1922–1975

Poetry in Spanish America: 1945 to Present

Queer Literature in Contemporary Spain

Queer Literature in Spanish America

Restrepo, Laura

Riesco, Laura

Rossetti, Ana

Sarlo, Beatriz

Short Fiction in Spain: 1900
 to Present

Soccer (*Fútbol*) and Hispanic Literature

Southern Cone Writing: Literature of
 Transition from Argentina and Chile

Spain and Self-Identity in the Nation

Theater in Spain: 1975 to Present

Tusquets, Esther

Vargas Llosa, Mario

Vicent, Manuel

Watanabe, José

Women Writers in Spain: 1900
 to Present

Queer Themes and Literature

Anzaldúa, Gloria

Arenas, Reinaldo

Ballagas, Emilio

Berman Goldberg, Sabina

Borges, Jorge Luis

Cernuda, Luis

Contemporáneos Group

Cruz, Sor Juana Inés de la

Díaz Arrieta, Hernán (pseudonym Alone)

Donoso, José

Erauso, Catalina de

Eroticism in Contemporary Spanish
 Women Writers: 1975 to Present

Fuertes, Gloria

Gambaro, Griselda

García Lorca, Federico

Gender in Spanish American Literature

Gender in Spanish Literature

Goytisolo, Juan

Lezama Lima, José

Martín Fierro

Mexico City in Literature

Mistral, Gabriela

Moix, Ana María

Moix, Terenci

Mujica Láinez, Manuel

Novo, Salvador

Peri Rossi, Cristina

Piñera, Virgilio

Puig, Manuel

Queer Literature in Contemporary Spain

Queer Literature in Spanish
America

Ramos Otero, Manuel

Rossetti, Ana

Sánchez, Luis Rafael

Mariel Writers Generation

Tusquets, Esther

Umpierre, Luz María

Villaurrutia, Xavier

Realism

(*See Also* Neorealism, Dirty Realism and
Social Realism)

Alarcón, Pedro Antonio de

Asturias, Miguel Ángel

Azuela, Mariano

Bello, Andrés

Benavente, Jacinto

Blest Gana, Alberto

Caballero Calderón, Eduardo

Cambaceres, Eugenio

Cervantes, Miguel de

Chile: History, Culture, and Literature

Clarín

Delibes, Miguel

Flores, Marco Antonio

Gamboa, Federico

Honduras: History, Culture, and Literature

Isaacs, Jorge

*Lazarillo de Tormes: La vida de Lazarillo
de Tormes y de sus fortunes y
adversidades*

Mújica, Elisa

Novel in Spain: 1700–1900

Novel in Spanish America: *Boom*
Literature: 1950–1975

Novel of the Mexican Revolution

Olmo, Lauro

Palacio Valdés, Armando

Palma, Ricardo

Pardo Bazán, Emilia

Pereda, José María de

Perera, Hilda

Pérez Galdós, Benito

Rabasa, Emilio

Realism and Naturalism in Spain Ruiz
Zafón, Carlos

Salarrué (pseudonym of Efraín Salazar
Arrué)

Sánchez Ferlosio, Rafael

Sastre, Alfonso

Short Fiction in Spain: 1900 to Present

Spain: History, Culture, and Literature

Suárez y Romero, Anselmo

Teitelboim, Volodia

Theater in Spanish America: 1900 to the
Present

Toscana, David

Valera, Juan

Women Writers in Cuba: 1959
to Present

Religion and Literature

Alfonso X, "el Sabio"

Alonso, Dámaso

Autobiography in Spain: Beginnings to 1700

Berceo, Gonzalo de

Black Legend

Bousoño, Carlos

Clarín (pseudonym of Leopoldo Alas)

Colonial Baroque Writing in Spanish America

Colonial Religious Chronicles in Spanish America

Colonial Theater in Spanish America

Convent Writing in Spain and the New World

Converso Literature in Spain

Cruz, Sor Juana Inés de la

Cultural Icons of Chicanos

Cultural Icons of Cuban Americans

Cultural Icons of Spain

Cultural Icons of Spanish America

Curanderismo and *Brujería*

Delibes, Miguel

Discovery and Conquest Writings: Describing the Americas

Falcones, Ildefonso

Generation of 1898 in Spain

Gracián y Morales, Baltasar

Guerrilla Poetry

Hispano-Arabic and Hispano-Judaic Literature and Culture in Spain

Ignacio de Loyola, San

Islamic Presence in Spain

Juan de la Cruz, San

Krausism in Spain

Lazarillo de Tormes: La vida de Lazarillo de Tormes y de sus fortunes y adversidades

León, Fray Luis de

Lezama Lima, José

Liberation Theology in the Hispanic World

Maeztu Whitney, Ramiro de

Martínez, Antonio José

Marianism in Spanish America

Mara, Juan León

Miró, Gabriel

Modernismo in Hispanic Literature

Montseny Mañé, Federica

Morisco

Mudéjar

Mysticism and Asceticism in Spain

Mythology in Spanish Golden Age Writing

National Catholicism

Nervo, Amado

Nissán, Rosa

Novel in Spanish America: *Boom* Literature: 1950–1975

Ors y Rovira, Eugenio d'

Otero Muñoz, Blas de

Picaresque Literature in the Hispanic World

Poetry in Spain: Beginnings to 1700

Quevedo, Francisco de

Santería

Santiago de Compostela Myth

Senequism

Slavery and Antislavery Literature in the
  Caribbean

Teresa de Jesús, Santa

Testimonial Writing in Central America

Theater in Spain: Beginnings to 1700

Unamuno y Jugo, Miguel de

Universities in Spain and the New World

Vallejo, César

Vallejo, Fernando

Valdés, José Manuel

Women Writers in Spain: Beginnings
  to 1700

Romanticism

Alarcón, Pedro Antonio de

Bécquer, Gustavo Adolfo (pseudonym of
  Gustavo Adolfo Domínguez Bastida)

Cadalso, José

Echeverría, Esteban

Eguren, José María

Espronceda, José de

Gálvez de Cabrera, María Rosa

García Gutiérrez, Antonio

Gorriti, Juana Manuela

Heredia, José María

Isaacs, Jorge

Larra, Mariano José de

Mármol, José

Mesonero Romanos, Ramón

Nervo, Amado

Novel in Spain: 1700–1900

Novel in Spanish America:
  1800–1900

Olmedo, José Joaquín

Romanticism in Spain

Short Fiction in Spain: 1700–1900

Valdés, Gabriel de la Concepción

Valera, Juan

Zorrilla y Moral, José

Science Fiction

Carrera Andrade, Jorge

Chaviano, Daína

Dorfman, Ariel

Esquivel, Laura

Mendoza, Eduardo

Modernismo in Hispanic Literature

Queer Literature in Spanish America

Ramón y Cajal, Santiago

Science Fiction in Spanish America
  Literature

Women Writers in Cuba:
  1959 to Present

Short Fiction

Aldecoa, Ignacio

Aldecoa, Josefina

Arévalo Martínez, Rafael

Arreola, Juan José

Arroyo, Justo

Arlt, Roberto

Barros, Pía

Benedetti, Mario

Borges, Jorge Luis

Contemporary Puerto Rican Short Story Writers: 1980 to Present

Cortázar, Julio

Darío, Rubén

Detective and Mystery Fiction in Spain

Detective and Mystery Fiction in Spanish America

Droguett, Carlos

Fuentes, Carlos

Gana, Federico

McOndo

Moreno, Marvel

Morosoli, Juan José

New Narrative in the Dominican Republic: 1978 to Present

Pacheco, José Emilio

Palma, Ricardo

Pardo Bazán, Emilia

Pereda, José María de

Piglia, Ricardo

Quiroga, Horacio

Ribeyro, Julio Ramón

Río, Nela

Rodas, Ana María

Rulfo, Juan

Short Fiction in Spain: 1700–1900

Short Fiction in Spain: 1900 to Present

Short Fiction in Spanish America

Sinán, Rogelio (pseudonym of Bernardo Domínguez Alba)

Tejeira, Isis

Tomás, Consuelo

Urbina, Nicasio

Zunzunegui, Juan Antonio de

Social Disorder, War, and Revolution in Literature

(*See Also* Political Protest and Literature)

Aldecoa, Ignacio

Álvarez Gardeazábal, Gustavo

Ángel, Albalucía

Arce, Manuel José

Argueta, Manlio

Arms and Letters

Aub, Max

Azuela, Mariano

Barcelona in Literature

Buenos Aires in Literature

Barea Ogazón, Arturo

Bogotazo, el

Borge, Tomás

Campobello, Nellie

Cantar de Mío Cid

Carpentier, Alejo

Cela, Camilo José

Cervantes de Salazar, Francisco

Civil War Literature in Spain

Contemporary Moroccan Literature Written in Spanish

Dalton, Roque

Díaz del Castillo, Bernal

Documentary Narrative in Spanish American Literature

El Salvador's *Generación comprometida* (1956–1972)

Exile Literature by Spanish Civil War Émigrés

Exile Writing in the Hispanic World

García Márquez, Gabriel

Guerrilla Poetry

Guzmán, Martín Luis

Hernández, Miguel

Hierro, José

Laforet, Carmen

Literature and Memory in the Hispanic World

Malvinas/Falklands War Literature

Martín Gaite, Carmen

Mastretta, Ángeles

Matute, Ana María

Mejía Vallejo, Manuel

Menchú, Rigoberta

Mexico City in Literature

Moreno, Marvel

Neruda, Pablo

Novás Calvo, Lino

Novel of the Cuban Revolution

Novel of the Mexican Revolution

Poniatowska, Elena

Testimonial Writing in Central America

Theater in Spain: 1975 to Present

Vallejo, Fernando

Vargas Llosa, Mario

Viñas, David

Violencia, la

Spanish America and Cultural Identity

(*See Also* Indigenism and Indigenous Writing; Individual and Collective Identity and Literature; Judeo-Spanish Presence and Literature)

Afro-Hispanic Literature in Spanish America

Afro-Hispanic Writers of Costa Rica

Amazon Theme in Spanish American Literature

Aztlán

Borges, Jorge Luis

Buenos Aires in Literature

Caro y Cuervo Institute

Carpentier, Alejo

Chicano

Chicano Writing

Colonial Baroque Writing in Spanish America

Colonialism and Antocolonialism in Spanish America

Contemporary Guatemalan Indigenous Authors

Costumbrismo in Spanish America

Criollista Novel in Spanish America

Cultural icons of Chicanos

Cultural Institutions for Hispanism in the United States

Enlightenment in Spanish America

Cultural Icons in Spanish America

Fernández Retamar, Roberto

Galeano, Eduardo

Gallegos, Rómulo

Galván, Manuel Jesús de

García Canclini, Néstor

Gaucho in Literature

Gender in Spanish American Literature

Guevara, Che

Havana in Literature

Hispanic Heritage Month

Hispanism: Past and Present

Imperialism as Theme in Colonial
    Spanish America

Indigenismo in Spanish American Literature

Ingenieros, José

Inquisition and Literature in the
    Hispanic World

Insularismo

Isaacs, Jorge

Journals in Spanish America

Judeo-Spanish Writing in Spanish America

Latinos and Latinas in the United States:
    History, Culture, and Literature

Latino Theater in the United States:
    Social Cohesion and Activism

Liberation Theology in the Hispanic
    World

Loaeza, Guadalupe

Marianism in Spanish America

McOndo

Mexico City in Literature

Mexico: Twentieth-Century Organizers
    of Culture

Monsiváis, Carlos

Novel in Spanish America: *Boom*
    Literature: 1950–1975

Nuestra América (Our America)

Nuyorican

Ortiz, Adalberto

Ortiz, Fernando

Ospina, William

Pachuco

Panama Canal as Theme in Literature

Panama: Contemporary Women Writers

Panama: History, Culture, and Literature

Pérez Firmat, Gustavo

Ponte, Antonio José

Puerto Rico: *Generación del treinta*
    (1930s Generation)

Quintero Rivera, Ángel

Rama, Ángel

Raza cósmica, La

Recto, Claro

Rodó, José Enrique

Rojas, Ricardo

Sahagún, Bernardino de

Sanín Cano, Baldomero

Santería

Santos Chocano, José

Slavery and Antislavery Literature in the
    Caribbean

Soccer (*Fútbol*) and Hispanic Literature

Stavans, Ilan

Transculturation in the Hispanic World

Vasconcelos, José

Zea, Leopoldo

Surrealism

Afro-Hispanic Literature in Spanish America
Alberti, Rafael
Aleixandre, Vicente
Alfaro, Óscar
Andreu, Blanca
Asturias, Miguel Ángel
Bombal, María Luisa
Bousoño, Carlos
Canary Islands Writers
Casona, Alejandro (pseudonym of Alejandro Rodríguez Álvarez)
Cela, Camilo José
Celaya, Gabriel
Cernuda, Luis
Cortázar, Julio
Donoso, José
Fuertes, Gloria
García Lorca, Federico
Generation of 1927 in Spain

Guerrilla Poetry
Marechal, Leopoldo
Neruda, Pablo
Ortega y Gasset, José
Poetry in Spanish America: 1922–1975
Poetry in the Dominican Republic: 1900 to Present
Queer Literature in Contemporary Spain
Queer Literature in Spanish America
Rojas Pizarro, Gonzalo
Sender, Ramón José
Sinán, Rogelio (pseudonym of Bernardo Domínguez Alba)
Spanish American Poetry by Women
Theater in Spain: 1900–1975
Torre, Guillermo de
Valenzuela, Luisa
Valle-Inclán, Ramón María del
Vallejo, César
Venezuelan Artistic Groups

Theater

Abad, Antonio
Acto
Alberti, Rafael
Álvarez Quintero, Serafín and Álvarez Quintero, Joaquín
Argentine Theater by Women: 1900 to Present
Arniches, Carlos
Ascensio Segura, Manuel
Aub, Max
Ávila Laurel, Juan Tomás

Balmori, Jesús
Benavente, Jacinto
Berman Goldberg, Sabina
Bretón de los Herreros, Manuel
Buero Vallejo, Antonio
Calderón de la Barca, Pedro
Carreta, La
Chilean Theater: 1900 to Present
Colonial Theater in Spanish America
Cossa, Roberto
Costumbrismo in Spanish America

Cruz Ramón de la

Diosdado, Ana

Discépolo, Armando

Don Quijote de la Mancha in Spanish American Literature and Culture

Dorfman, Ariel

Dragún, Osvaldo

Echegaray, José

Fernán-Gómez, Fernando

Gala, Antonio

Gálvez de Cabrera, María Rosa

Gambaro, Griselda

García Gutiérrez, Antonio

García Lorca, Federico

Género chico criollo and the Río de la Plata *Saineteros* (*Sainete* Composers)

Hartzenbusch, Juan Eugenio

Iriarte, Tomás de

Jara, Víctor

Lazo, Agustín

Lejárraga, María de la O

Marqués, René

Martínez Sierra, Gregorio

Mihura Santos, Miguel

Millán Astray, Pilar

Molina, Tirso de (pseudonym of Gabriel Téllez)

Muñoz Seca, Pedro

Mythology in Spanish Golden Age Writing

Olmo, Lauro

Pardo y Aliaga, Felipe

Parra, Marco Antonio de la

Paso, Alfonso

Pavlovsky, Eduardo

Piñera, Virgilio

Repertorio Español (Spanish Repertory)

Ribeyro, Julio Ramón

Rojas Zorrilla, Francisco de

Romero Esteo, Miguel

Rosencof, Mauricio

Ruiz de Alarcón, Juan

Ruiz Iriarte, Víctor

Sánchez, Florencio

Sastre, Alfonso

Sender, Ramón José

Siale Djangany, José Fernando

Southern Cone Writing: Literature of Transition from Argentina and Chile

Teatro abierto

Teatro campesino

Theater in Spain: 1700–1900

Theater in Spain: 1900–1975

Theater in Spain: 1975 to Present

Theater in Spanish America: 1900 to Present

Triana, José

Unamuno y Jugo, Miguel de

Usigli, Rodolfo

Vega y Carpio, Lope de

Vélez de Guevara, Luis

Vilalta, Maruxa

Wolff, Egon

Zarzuela

Zayas y Sotomayor, María de

Zorrilla y Moral, José

Travel Writing

Aira, César

Ángel, Albalucía

Autobiography in Spain: 1700 to Present

Autobiography in Spain: Beginnings to 1700

Autobiography in Spanish America

Biography in Spanish America

Cané, Miguel

Carrera Andrade, Jorge

Cela, Camilo José

Delibes, Miguel

Discovery and Conquest Writings: Describing the Americas

Erauso, Catalina de

Estrada, Santiago

Girondo, Oliverio

Gómez Carrillo, Enrique

Gómez de Avellaneda, Gertrudis

Guevara, Che

Janés, Clara

Mansilla de García, Eduarda

Mansilla, Lucio V.

Mármol, José

Nissán, Rosa

Novo, Salvador

Project "Año 0"

Sahagún, Bernardino de

Short Fiction in Spain: 1700–1900

Silva, Lorenzo

Tablada, José Juan

Valera, Juan

Vicent, Manuel

Women Writers in Cuba: 1900–1959

A

Abad, Antonio (1894–1970)

Also a dramatist, journalist, and educator, he is considered the greatest Phil-Hispanic novelist after José *Rizal (1861–1896). Abad wrote four novels (three of which won Philippine literary prizes): *El ultimo romántico* (1927; The Last Romantic), *La oveja de Nathan* (1927; Nathan's Sheep), *El campeón* (1939; The Champion), and *La vida secreta de Daniel España* (1960; The Secret Life of Daniel España). Set during World War I, *La oveja de Nathan*, his best-known work, movingly expresses the nation's desire for independence from the United States.

Even more productive as a dramatist—he penned a total of nine plays—his award-winning three-act play *Dagohoy* (1939) features a native who waged an eight-decade revolt against Spanish colonial authorities in the 18th century. His other theatrical works include *Calvario de un alma* (1918; A Soul's Calvary), *La cicatriz* (1920; The Scar), *Las hijas de Juan* (1924; Juan's Daughters), *La redimida* (1925; The Redeemed), *Los desorientados* (1930; The Disoriented), *La Gloria* (1930; Glory), *Cuando los lobos se vuelven corderos* (1930; When Wolves Become Sheep) and *Sor Sagrario* (1937). Abad also worked as a journalist for such newspapers as *El Precursor, La Revolución, El Espectador, La Vanguar-*dia, *El Debate, La Defensa*, and *The Cebu Advertiser*. He eventually found himself at the helm of *La Opinión*.

After World War II (1939–1945), Abad devoted his energies to rebuilding the Department of Spanish of the University of the Philippines, during which time he authored several Spanish textbooks, including several Phil-Hispanic literary anthologies, and mentored a fresh crop of teachers of Spanish.

Wystan de la Peña

Work About:

81 Years of Premio Zóbel: A Legacy of Philippine Literature in Spanish. Makati: Georgina Padilla y Zóbel and Filipinas Heritage Library, 2006.

García Castellón, Manuel. "*La oveja de Nathán*, de Antonio M. Abad (1894–1970), novelador hispano-filipino del anhelo de independencia patria." *Revista Filipina:A Quarterly Journal of Hispano-Philippine Literature and Linguistics* 1.4 (Spring 1998): no pagination.

Abreu Gómez, Ermilo (1894–1971)

One of the Yucatan Peninsula's greatest writers, this literary critic, novelist, dramatist, short story author, and educator served as a director in the Pan-American Union's Department of Cultural Affairs and was a member of the Mexican Academy of Letters. Born in Mérida, his early dramatic writing contributed to the zenith of Yucatan theater between 1919 and 1926. Later, while living in Mexico City, his pioneering criticism assisted in the rediscovery of Sor Juana Inés de la *Cruz's work.

Abreu Gómez's most recognized and acclaimed work, *Canek* (1940; *Canek: History and Legend of a Maya Hero*, 1979), presents a poetic story of friendship between Jacinto Canek, a historical indigenous leader who led a rebellion against the Spanish in 1761, and a white boy, considered a simpleton by his aristocratic family. His novel *Naufragio de indios* (1951; Shipwreck of Indians) narrates the resistance to the French occupation of Mexico. Lastly, *La conjura de Xinum* (1958; The Conspiracy of Xinum) tells the story of Yucatan's Caste War (1847–1855). The lyricism of his writings, his treatment of indigenous themes, and his literary criticism make him a respected figure in Mexican literature.

Alicia Muñoz

See also Indigenismo in Spanish American Literature; Mexico: Twentieth-Century Organizers of Culture.

Work By:

Canek: History and Legend of a Maya Hero. Trans. Mario L. Dávila and Carter Wilson. Berkeley: University of California Press, 1979.

Work About:

Casanova, Jorge Pech. *La sabiduría de la emoción: vida y literatura de Ermilo Abreu Gómez*. Mexico: CONACULTA, 1998.

Whitsitt, Julia. "The Name of Canek Was Voice and Echo: Reading the Mosaic of Canek." *Confluencia: Revista Hispánica de Cultura y Literatura* 2.2 (Spring 1987): 100–107.

Acto

In 1965, aspiring Chicano playwright Luis Valdez joined the struggle of civil rights activist César Chávez to organize California's Mexican American farm workers into protest and nonviolent resistance of their unjust, even deplorable, work and living situations. To reach this powerless, largely illiterate group, Valdez created short, improvisational one-act skits featuring typical encounters between farm workers, their bosses, and similar stock characters. Devoid of scenery, using only masks and signs as props, these workers and students performed the *actos* for coworkers. The sketches used colloquial Spanish and English, rapid-fire dialogue, and humor to raise self-awareness, as well as to inspire solidarity of the workers and help mobilize them to improve their lot with nonviolent protest, strikes, and other forms of resistance.

This *teatro campesino* (farm workers' theater) soon left the farm fields and, over the next 20 years, broadened its focus to other issues (bilingual education for children, discrimination) faced by rural and urban working-class Chicanos and led to the establishment of Chicano and Latino theatrical groups across the country.

Maureen Ihrie

See also Cultural Icons of Chicanos; Latino Theater in the United States: Social Cohesion and Activism; Latinos and Latinas in the United States: History, Culture and Literature.

Work About:

Kanellos, Nicolás. "Hispanic Theatre in the United States: Post-War to the Present." *Latin American Theater Review* (Spring 1992): 197–209.

Ada, Alma Flor (1938–)

This prolific bilingual author, translator, and educator was born in Camagüey, Cuba, and moved permanently to the United States after studying in Madrid (undergraduate), Lima (MA, PhD in Spanish literature), and at Harvard as a Fulbright scholar. Ada's "transformative" approach to children's literacy values diverse cultural and linguistic heritages by integrating the participation of readers, families, educators, and writers.

Since the mid-1970s, Ada has authored scores of literary works for and about bilingual U.S. children, often collaborating with writer-translators F. Isabel Campoy and Rosalma Zubizarreta. Most of these titles—which include fiction, drama, poetry, folklore, biography, memoir, and reading textbooks—are available in both Spanish and English. A successful example is the alphabet picture book *Gathering the Sun* (1997). With illustrator Simón Silva, Ada honors the experiences of migrant farm workers with original poems featuring themes corresponding to the letters of the Spanish alphabet, each paired with Zubizarreta's English translation. Ada is also the Spanish translator of over 50 children's books, including such classics as Margery Williams's *The Velveteen Rabbit*.

In three decades as a professor of education at the University of San Francisco, Ada drew on the socially engaged pedagogy of Paulo Freire to promote bilingual literacy. Among her many honors is a 1998 Pura Belpré Award.

Laura Kanost

See also Children's Literature in Spanish in the United States.

Work By:

Gathering the Sun. New York: Lothrop, Lee and Shepard, 1997.

Work About:

Manna, Anthony L., Janet Hill, and Kathy Kellogg. "Alma Flor Ada and the Quest for Change." *Language Arts* 82.1 (2004): 76–79.

Adán, Martín (1908–1985)

One of Peru's greatest 20th-century poets, his birth name was Rafael de la Fuente Benavides, but he wrote under the pen name Martín Adán. Chronologically, he belongs to the avant-garde generation, thanks to his novel *La casa de cartón* (1929; *The Cardboard House*, 1990). In poetry collections like *La rosa de la espinela* (1939; The Rose and the Gem) and *Travesía de extramares* (1950; Beyond the Sea), however, he moves away from experimental writing to produce sonnets of rigorous formal perfection.

Adán defines poetry as a lonely journey into the unknown reality of the absolute. A case in point is *La mano desasida* (1964; The Unheld Hand) and its sequel *La piedra absoluta* (1966; The Absolute Stone), a monologue addressed to the ancient Inca ruins of Machu Picchu, in which the mystery of the human condition, seen as a multilayered experience, is symbolically explored. Adán's last two verse collections, *Mi diario* (1966; My Diary) and *Diario de poeta* (1966–1973; A Poet's Diary), continue to search for the absolute amidst intense feelings of futility and despair, for the only truth in his long journey is the acceptance of human mortality.

César Ferreira

See also Décima.

Work By:

The Cardboard House. Trans. Katherine Silver. St. Paul, MN: Graywolf, 1990.

Obra poética en prosa y verso. Ed. Ricardo Silva-Santisteban. Lima: Pontificia Universidad Católica del Perú, 2006.

Work About:

Kinsella, John. "The Theme of Poetry in Martín Adán's *Travesía de extramares*." *Bulletin of Hispanic Studies* 64.4 (October 1987): 349–58.

Moore, Melisa. "Fugitive Signs: Mapping Metaphors and Meaning in *La casa de cartón* by Martín Adán." *Bulletin of Hispanic Studies* 84.5 (2007): 625–43.

Adoum, Jorge Enrique (1926–2009)

Themes of social justice converge with a search for avant-garde aesthetic expression in writings by this significant Ecuadorian poet, novelist, and committed Marxist. From age 18 to 20, he worked as secretary for Chilean Nobel Prize–winner Pablo *Neruda, who later referred to Adoum as Latin America's finest poet. Later diplomatic and cultural positions, along with the 1970 military coup, led him to live abroad (France, China, Switzerland) for several decades. A widely traveled intellectual, Adoum contributed various newspaper and magazines, published at least 10 poetry volumes, three novels, and a theatrical piece, and translated to Spanish the poetry of such artists as Langston Hughes, Jacques Prévert, and Joseph Brodsky.

The year 1949 saw publication of his first poem collection, *Ecuador amargo* (Bitter Ecuador), which shows clear influences of Neruda. Over roughly the next decade, Adoum worked on four poetry volumes that made up *Los cuadernos de la tierra* (1963; Notebooks of the Earth). The individual volume titles and publication dates are *Los orígenes* (1952; Origins); *El enemigo y la mañana* (1952; The Enemy and Morning); *Dios trabaja la sombra* (1957; God Works the Shade);

Eldorado, and *Las ocupaciones nocturnas* (1961; [The Golden One] and [Nocturnal Occupations]). Together, they offer an epic narration of violent conquest and colonization of indigenous peoples by the Spanish, set against the powerful, prodigious terrain of Latin America.

Primarily due to political difficulties in Ecuador, Adoum and his family lived abroad (Paris, Beijing, Geneva) for most of the 25 years between 1963 and 1987, as he found work as an English teacher, a translator, with UNESCO, and in other positions. *Curriculum mortis* (1968) takes inspiration from these travels, but Ecuador still figures as a theme, and a concern for injustice remains in the foreground.

Adoum's first novel, *Entre Marx y una mujer desnuda* (1976; Between Marx and a Nude Woman), features a Marxist protagonist who falls deeply in love. It is a densely complex, experimental work that rejects traditional literary conventions of character, plot, and situation, all of which correlate with the author's rejection of the Pinochet dictatorship. The work was internationally acclaimed and adapted to film in 1996. Fragmentation of space and time are found in his second novel, *Ciudad sin ángel* (1995; City without an Angel).

In the final decade of the 20th century, Adoum published two verse collections: *...no son todos los que están: Poemas 1949–1979* (1979; Not All Those Who Are Here Are [Crazy]: Poems, 1949–1979) and *...ni están todos los que son...* (1999; ...Not All Those Who Are [Crazy] are Here...). Both contain telluric verse.

Martínez has characterized Adoum's poetry as field reports from a war correspondent of society, as they consistently document abuses of power, colonialism, imperialism, and neocolonial pressures on the continent.

Maureen Ihrie

See also Indigenismo in Spanish American Literature.

Work By:

Poesía hasta hoy, 1949–2008. Quito: Archipiélago, 2008.

The Sun Trampled beneath the Horses' Hooves. Trans. David Arthur McMurray, Robert Marquez. *Massachusetts Review* 15.1–2 (Spring 1974): 285–324.

Work About:

Martínez Arévalo, Pablo. *Jorge Enrique Adoum: Ideología, estética e historia (1944–1990).* Lexington: University of Kentucky, 1990.

Martínez, Pablo. "Strategies of Representation in the New Ecuadorian Novel: *Between Marx and a Naked Woman* and the Aesthetics of Violence." *New Novel Review* 3.1 (October 1995): 83–106.

O'Bryan-Knight, Jean. "Love, Death, and Other Complications in Jorge Enrique Adoum's *Ciudad sin Ángel.*" *Hispanic Journal* 20.2 (Fall 1999): 291–309.

Afro-Hispanic Literature in Spanish America

This category of writing privileges Afro-Hispanic characters in Spanish American literature, regardless of each author's race.

However, there is an Afrocentric discourse that underscores the author's ancestry; these writers provide insights into the lives of blacks, though not all choose to write exclusively about black themes. Spanish American politicians and intellectuals promote a nationalist Eurocentric discourse based on their own image of the nation and discourage other racial and ethnic identities. With few exceptions, Afro-Hispanic writers have been excluded from the canon; nonetheless, as a whole, Afro-Hispanic literature continues to thrive, challenging the established order with different interpretations of historical and cultural events. A substantial body of literature emerges in population centers with significant numbers of Afro-Hispanics.

The first blacks in Spanish American literature are found in Alonso de Ercilla y Zúñiga's *epic poem "La araucana" (1569–1594; *The Araucaniad*, 1945), specifically in Wolof, the black executioner of Mapuche Indian leader Caupolicán; and in Silvestre de Balboa's "Espejo de paciencia" (1608; Mirror of Patience), with Bishop Altamirano's Ethiopian savior, Salvador. As a literary movement, Afro-Hispanic literature can be traced to Cuban literary critic Domingo del Monte (1804–1853), who encouraged writers in his literary circle to compose a national literature that included the black slave. These early works include Anselmo *Suárez y Romero's *Francisco* (written 1839); Félix Tanco y Bosmeniel's *Escena de la vida privada en la Isla de Cuba* (written 1838; Scenes from Private Life on the Island of Cuba); José Morilla's "El ranchador" (written in 1838; The Slave Hunter); and Cirilo *Villaverde's *Cecilia Valdés* (1839, 1882), Cuba's national novel.

Formerly a slave, poet Juan Francisco *Manzano also belongs to this group. He wrote *Poesías líricas* (1821; Lyrical Poems) and *Flores pasajeras* (1830; Passing Flowers), published many poems in magazines of the day, and penned his *Autobiografía* (1835; *The Autobiography of a Slave*, 1996), Spanish America's only slave autobiography. Manzano taught himself to read and write at a time when slaves were prohibited from receiving a formal education; he narrates both good and bad moments under slavery, and justifies his escape from slavery. Like other antislavery works, this autobiography could not be published in Cuba at the time it was written. However, it reached a wider English audience in Richard Madden's *Poems by a Slave in the Island of Cuba*, published in London in 1840. A transcript of Manzano's autobiography was not available in Spanish until 1937, and a more accurate transcription only appeared in 2004. Manzano also wrote the play *Zafira* (1840). His works place him as the center pillar of Cuba's national literature.

Other Cuban authors wrote during this period. Plácido, the popular name of Gabriel de la Concepción *Valdés (1809–1844) made a living by composing poems to celebrities and officials. He also wrote poetry of resistance against authorities and in favor of Cuba's emergent national culture. These include "El bardo cautivo" (The Captive Poet), a denunciation of Spain's control over the island; "La flor de la caña" (The Cane Flower), a subversion of the racial and caste systems; and "El juramento" (The Contract), a defiant criticism of the colonial order. Although Plácido had many enemies, he was more popular than any of his contemporaries. Plácido was accused of leading the Ladder Conspiracy (1844), a black and mulatto uprising that Spanish authorities orchestrated to eliminate a growing and prosperous class of nonwhites. Before his execution, Plácido composed four poems, including the well-known "Plegaria a Dios" (Prayer to God).

Cuban-born Gertrudis *Gómez de Avellaneda (1814–1873) did not belong to the Del Monte group, but while living in Spain she authored *Sab* (1941), which follows a slave's willingness to sacrifice his life and future for his mistress. Though set in Cuba, the novel responds to liberal ideas associated with Spanish Regent María Cristina. In the second half of the 19th century, writers who provided a more aggressive response to slavery include Antonio Zambrana, who rewrote Suárez y Romero's earlier mentioned novel by adding the adjective "black" to the title of *El negro Francisco* (1873); Francisco Calcago, who authored *Aponte* (1901) and *Romualdo uno de tantos* (1881; Romualdo, One Among Many); and Afro-Cuban Martín Morúa Delgado, who rewrote Villaverde's novel as *Sofía* (1891) and published *La familia Unzúazu* (1901; The Unzúazu Family). Morúa is remembered as the president of Cuba's Senate in 1909 and author of the Morúa law, which forbade political parties based on racial color. The law was used to massacre members of the Partido Independiente de Color in 1912, two years after Morúa's death.

Other 19th-century Spanish American writers of African descent include Peruvian José Manuel *Valdés (1767–1843), who studied at the Convent of San Ildefonso and graduated from the University of San Marcos with a medical degree in 1807. He wrote such religious verse as *Poesías sagradas* (1819; Sacred Poems) and *Poesías espirituales, escritas a beneficio y para el uso de las personas sencillas y piadosas* (1833; Spiritual Poems, Written for the Benefit and Use of Simple and Pious People). In Colombia, the writings of Candelario Obeso (1849–884) should be noted. A poet, playwright, and novelist, his *Cantos populares de mi tierra* (1877; Popular Songs of My Land) captures the oral traditions of the Magdalena region, whose residents were mainly of African descent. Obeso rejected formal writing in favor of documenting an oral or spoken tradition. Panama's *modernismo* poet Gaspar Octavio Hernández also penned a collection of short stories and notes titled *Iconografías* (1915; Iconographies), the poem collection *Melodías del pasado* (1915; Past Melodies) and the posthumous *La Copa de Amatista* (1923; The Amethyst Challis).

The *negrismo* movement of the 1920s and 1930s celebrated black images, speech, and sounds. Spaniard Alfonso Carmín's "Elogio de la negra" (In Praise of the Black Woman), Cuban Emilio *Ballagas's "Bailadora de rumba" (Rumba Dancer), Cuban José Zacarías Tallet's "La rumba" (The Rumba) and Puerto Rican Luis Palés Matos' "Pueblo negro" (Black Town) gave birth to a poetic style that gained immediate recognition. White writers concentrated on the aesthetic representations of blacks, without negating some social concerns, as is the case with Ballagas's "María Belén Chacón," who dies of hard work. Palés Matos in particular has been criticized for sexualizing blacks in such poems as "Majestad negra" (Black Majesty), of *Tun tun de pasa y grifería* (1937; Drumbeats of Kink and Blackness).

Negrismo poets of African descent concentrated on the cultural and religious aspects of the poetry. Nicolás Guillén, arguably one of the few canonical writers of African heritage, composed Afro-Cuban poetry and distinguished himself with *Motivos de son* (1930; Son Motifs), *Sóngoro cosongo* (1931), and *West Indies Ltd.* (1934). Although his early poems underscored the musicality of the verse, as in "Canto negro" (Black Chant) and "Canción del bongó" (Song of the Bongo), Guillén also combined racial pride and social meaning. In "Sabá," the poetic voice tells Sabá to control his hunger and demand what is his; "Negro bembón" (Thick-Lipped Black) and "Mulata" refer to racial pride; and "Sensemayá" and "Balada del Güije" (Güije Ballad) pertain to Afro-Cuban religions. Guillén also poeticized social concerns that transcended the Afro-Cuban experience and encompassed other facets of Cuban life. *Cantos para soldados y sones para turistas* (1937; Songs for Soldiers and Sones for Tourists), *El son entero* 1947; The Whole Son), and *La paloma del vuelo popular* (1959; The Dove of Popular Flight), contain poems with social and political referents, as well as such other

works composed in the Cuban revolution as *Tengo* (1964; I Have), *El gran zoo* (1967; The Great Zoo), and *El diario que a diario* (1972; The Daily Diary). Among Afro-Cuban poets, Marcelino Arozarena's *Canción negra sin color* (1983; Black Song without Color) and Regino Pedroso's *Poesías* (1984) deserve mention. *Negrismo* developed late in the Dominican Republic with Manuel del Cabral and works like *Trópico negro* (1942; Black Tropic) and *Compadre Mon* (1948; Godfather Mon).

During and after *negrismo*, Cuban Alejo *Carpentier's early works stand out. He lived in Paris, was part of the surrealist movement, and incorporated aspects of this trend in his works. He entered the literary community with *Poèms des Antilles* (1930; Antillean Poems) and *Dos poemas afro-cubanos (deux poems afro-cubais)* (1930; Two Afro-Cuban Poems), with music by Alejandro García Caturla. His short story collection *Guerra del Tiempo* (1958; *War of Time*, 1970) contains the much-cited "Viaje a la semilla" (1944; Journey Back to the Source), about a black man who causes time to march backward. Carpentier also wrote longer works that referred to the black experience: "Histoire de lunes" (1933; Moon Tales) and *¡Écue Yamba-O!* (1933; Lord, Praised Be Thou) describe life among Afro-Cubans, and *El reino de este mundo* (1949; *The Kingdom of This World*, 1970) depicts the crucial period before and after the Republic of Haiti's founding. In the latter he expounds the ideas of marvelous realism, which led to what has been termed *magical realism. A reading of Carpentier's prologue and novel suggests the coming together of the magic of African religions and the realism of European culture, but the magic is a European perception of something Africans consider "normal." The history and legends about blacks are gathered in Lino *Novás Calvo's novelized life of the famed slave trader, *El negrero: vida novelada de Pedro Blanco Fernández de Trava* (1933; The Slave Trader), and Lydia *Cabrera's *Cuentos negros de Cuba* (1940; Black Stories from Cuba), respectively.

Guillén's poetry and travels throughout the Americas encouraged Afro-Hispanic writers to express their proud heritage. Similar poetic movements develop in countries like Uruguay, with a significant black population. Pilar Barrios, founder of the journal *Nuestra Raza* (1917; Our Race), authored *Piel negra* (1947; Black Skin), *Mis cantos* (1949; My Songs), and *Campo afuera* (1959; The Countryside); Virginia Brindis de Salas wrote *Pregón de Marimorena* (1946; Street Cries) and *Cien cárceles de amor* (1949; One Hundred Love Cells); and Juan Julio Arrascaeta composed such poems as "Samba bo." Of the three, Brindis de Salas was the most defiant and active within the community of Afro-Uruguayan intellectuals during the 1930s and 1940s. Scholar Ildefonso Pereda Valdés also contributed to the diffusion of the black voice in works like *Antología de la poesía negra americana* (1936; Anthology of American Black Poetry).

While Venezuelans hail Rómulo *Gallegos's *Doña Bárbara* (1929), his *Pobre negro* (1937; Poor Blackman), a tale of white exploitation of blacks after emancipation, was considered flawed. Afro-Venezuelan

Juan Pablo Sojo was more successful with *Nochebuena negra* (1943; Black Christmas Eve), which captures the social and political life of his country's Barlovento region and offers insight into the region's traditions and customs, often conveyed through the character Crisanto Marasma. Sojo coined the term Afro-Venezuelans in his essay collections *Temas y apuntes afrovenezolanos* (1943; Afro-Venezuelan Notes and Themes).

The noted Ecuadorian writer Adalberto *Ortiz wrote poetry volumes like *Tierra son y tambor* (1945; Earth, Sound and Drums), and such short story collections as *La entundada* (1971; The Bewitched). However, his reputation rests on *Juyungo* (1943), a novel about racial identity and social freedom against oppression in Esmeraldas province; the novel also explores the relationship between blacks and mestizos. Fellow compatriot Nelson *Estupiñán Bass composed *Canto negro por la luz* (1954; Black Songs through the Light), *Timarán y Cuabú* (1956), *and El desempate* (1980; The Playoff); also a fine novelist, he authored *Toque de queda* (1978; The Curfew), a profile of Ecuadorian dictator General Espinoza, *El último río* (1966; The Last River), about Esmeraldas governor José Antonio Pastrana, and *Cuando los guayacanes florecían* (1954; When the Guayacanes Were in Bloom) which discusses the Concha rebellion in Esmeraldas.

Afro-Peruvian authors have also contributed to this body of literature. Enrique López Albújar's *De la tierra brava. Poemas afroyungas* (1938; From the Untamed Land, Afro-Yunga Poems) contains poems about mestizos; Nicomedes Santa Cruz was celebrated for his *décimas*, as in *Décimas* (1959), *Cumanana* (1964), and *Canto a mi Peru* (1966; I Sing to My Peru). Santa Cruz wrote about the Afro-Peruvian experience but also gave voice to other groups of his region.

In Colombia, Jorge Artel authored *Tambores en la noche* (1940; Drums in the Night), *Poemas con botas y banderas* (1972; Poems with Boots and Banners), and *Sinú, riberas de asombro jubiloso* (1972; Sinú, Riverbanks of Joyous Wonder); a play, *De rigurosa etiqueta* (With Strict Etiquette); and the novel *No es la muerte . . . es el morir* (1979; It's Not the Death . . . It's the Dying). Such poems as "Velorio del boga adolescente" (Wake of the Adolescent Rower) and "Ahora hablo de gaítas" (Now I Speak of Bagpipes) in his first book reflect the happiness and sorrow of his people. Other noteworthy Afro-Hispanic writers include Panama's Carlos Guillermo Wilson (1941–), Costa Rica's Quince Duncan (1940–), Dominican Republic's Blas *Jiménez (1949–2009), and Colombia's Yvonne Truque (1955–2001).

Colombia's Manuel *Zapata Olivella occupies a singular place in Afro-Hispanic literature. A medical doctor turned ethnographer, he produced numerous works about the black experience in Colombia. They include *Chambacú, corral de negros* (1963; *Chambacu: Black Slum*, 1989) and *En Chimá nace un santo* (1964; *A Saint Is Born in Chima*, 1991). But his epic *Changó, el gran putas* (1983; *Changó, The Biggest Badass*, 2010), which has more in common with Spanish American *Boom* novels than those of the post-*Boom*

periods, merits placement alongside the best works of Spanish American literature. Based on African culture and oral traditions, the living, the dead, and the deities occupy the same time and space. *Changó* narrates 500 years of slavery and racial oppression in the New World. It begins with a long ritualistic poem invoking the Orishas (gods) and the Ancestors, explaining why Changó, the deity of fire and lighting, cursed his people into slavery, from which they must free themselves before making their way back home. The story is told by multiple narrators, some from this world, others from the next, and some of divine intervention. All tell a common narrative in different regions: the arduous transatlantic slave traffic; the New World arrival to Cartagena, where the reader uncovers the lives of Benko Biojo and his guardian Father Pedro Clavel; the Haitian rebellion with Mackandal, Bouckman, Toussaint Louverture, Jacque Dessaline, and other black and mulatto generals; the Brazilian sculptor Aleihandriho; and the Mexican priest José María Morelos. The novel concludes with a long chapter on slavery and racism in the United States during the 19th and 20th centuries. In the present, Elegua, god of the Crossroads, has chosen Agne Brown, and Marcus Garvey and Malcolm X are proclaimed prophets. *Changó* is an important yet dense and difficult novel; it requires readers to abandon a Western frame of mind and become black to truly understand the black experience.

While the Cuban revolution has been insistent on presenting a unified racial vision of the nation, the topic of Afro-Cubans cannot be avoided. Of immense significance is Miguel *Barnet's *Biografía de un cimarrón* (1966; *The Autobiography of a Runaway Slave*, 1968), a testimonial novel based on interviews with a 106-year-old slave, who describes his life in slavery, emancipation, and in the republic; despite historical changes, Montejo's life remains the same. There are indications that the interviews continued into the present time of the revolution, but these have been omitted from the text.

The Cuban revolution has produced a significant number of Afro-Cuban writers, even though political authorities have quelled any notion of Afro-Cuban identity in favor of a colorless nation, based on the ideas of the white ruling class. Nevertheless, Nancy *Morejón has written revolutionary poetry, as in *Cuaderno de Granada* (1984; *Grenada Notebook*, 1984), but has also composed other poems about her African ancestry, including *Richard trajo su flauta* (1967; Richard Brought His Flute). Morejón's much anthologized "Mujer negra" (Black Woman) has become a classic, as it offers an alternate vision of history from a black woman's perspective. Other women writers include Georgina Herrera, Exilia Saldaña, Marta Rojas, and poet Eloy Machao, "El Ambia."

Three areas of current research should be noted. First, scholars are uncovering the literature of Afro-Argentine writers. Though many Afro-Argentines died in wars against Spain, Brazil, and Argentina's indigenous people, and Europeans were invited to "civilize" the country, there is clear evidence of an African presence in Argentine culture that flourished

in the 19th century. Second, Equatorial Guinea is receiving increased publicity. Once a colony of Spain, it gained independence in 1968, only to fall into the hands of dictators Macías Nguema and Obiang Nguema, who assassinated his uncle to assume power. Equatorial Guinean writers at home and in exile are producing an important literature that will broaden Afro-Hispanic literature and influence postcolonial studies. In April 2009, Hofstra University sponsored a significant interdisciplinary conference that brought together for the first time writers, artists, and cultural promoters from within and outsider of the country. The *Afro-Hispanic Review* 28.2 (2009) published a monograph issue on Equatorial Guinea.

Finally, Afro-Latino literature, written in the United States in Spanish, English, and *Spanglish, is helping erase the linguistic and cultural boundaries between Hispanic and Anglo cultures. As the fourth-largest Spanish-speaking country in the world, an important Hispanic/Latino literature, with an Afro-Latino component, documents the culture of this population. It includes Afro-Puerto Rican writers like Arturo Alfonso Schomberg, Jesús *Colón, Piri Thomas, and Tato *Laviera. Other Latino writers like Cristina García rely on Afro-Cuban religions to narrate the lives of their protagonists.

The field of Afro-Hispanic literature continues to grow, as writers use race to challenge the traditional Eurocentric discourses that misrepresent the Afro-Hispanic experience. As expressed in the introduction to the English translation of *Changó*, blacks in the Americas represent a symbol against oppression and injustice and promote equality for all.

William Luis

See also Afro-Hispanic Writers of Costa Rica; Equatorial Guinea: Poets; Equatorial Guinea: Writers Living in the United States; Equatorial Guinea: Writers in Exile; Equatorial Guinea's *Generación del Silencio* (The Generation of Silence); Journals in Spanish America; Martínez, Gregorio; Slavery and Antislavery Literature in the Caribbean.

Work About:

DeCosta Willis, Miriam, ed. *Blacks in Hispanic Literature: Critical Essays.* Port Washington, NY: Kennikat, 1977.

Jackson, Richard. *The Black Image in Latin American Literature.* Albuquerque: University of New Mexico Press, 1976.

Jackson, Richard. *Black Writers in Latin America.* Albuquerque: University of New Mexico Press, 1979.

Luis, William. *Literary Bondage: Slavery in Cuban Narrative.* Austin: University of Texas Press, 1990.

Afro-Hispanic Writers of Costa Rica

Writings by Afro-Costa Ricans, who currently represent about 3 percent of the country's population, constitute a significant aspect of that nation's literature, notable through four prominent writers. Occasionally, such writers are erroneously classified as "West Indian," a term that fails to acknowledge their Spanish language production. African heritage is visible in Central American music, cuisine, colloquial vocabulary, stories and fables, and this population group has contributed to the agricultural expansion and infrastructure of such nations as Costa Rica and Panama.

Present as slaves from the beginning of the colonial era, Costa Rica's black population increased during the 17th century with the expansion of cacao production along the eastern seaboard, in Matina province. The colonial elite who owned plantations preferred to remain in San José, the capital city near the Pacific coast; thus the African-origin community lived separately in enclaves, where they continued their own language and ancient traditions. Occasionally, runaway slaves from Caribbean islands joined these communities.

During the late 18th century, slaves were freed in great numbers when the economic burden became too heavy for plantation owners. Social change came with independence; in 1822, Mexico and Central America abolished slavery, making it official by law in 1824. New governments and elite power disallowed black participation, pushing them into *barrios* and to work as servants in the capital. Costa Rica became a rather poor country after independence, but in 1871 construction of a railway system (to transport goods to ships) was launched, requiring an extensive workforce. While some were recruited locally, many black laborers were imported from Jamaica (mostly) and some from the British West Indies. Since African-origin peoples bear the last names of former slaveholders, English-language surnames (reflecting British rule in Jamaica) now appeared in ensuing generations of

Afro-Costa Ricans. Following the railroad enterprise, the banana industry arrived, and United Fruit Company—based in the Limón province along the eastern coast—tapped essentially the same workforce.

By the 1920s, due in part to an activist labor movement, Afro-Costa Ricans achieved some improvement in economic status; however, white Costa Ricans soon drove them out of jobs and businesses. Not until 1948, following a civil war, did Afro-Costa Ricans gain status as citizens. It is these experiences and histories that are revealed in the works of contemporary Afro-Costa Rican writers and poets.

Two early 20th-century figures are important. Texts by Eulalia Bernard (1935–) exhibit innovative structures and linguistic techniques, with language play and neologisms combining Spanish, English, indigenous, and African Creole vocabulary. Her poetry collections span 20 years, with some translations to English, and she has published a lengthy essay on political philosophy. Bernard identifies cultural connections between Africa and the Americas, revealing them in Costa Rican society; *Carnaval*, for example, serves as entertainment for white Costa Ricans and a release of personal experience for Afro-Costa Ricans. The highly prolific Quince Duncan (1940–) has penned six novels, historical criticism and essays, and children's stories (many works translated to English). He draws out contrasts between racialized populations in Costa Rican society, and stark social and class realities. His narrative captures linguistic heritage and political manipulations by various power systems and voices in Costa Rica.

Two more recent poets of prominence are Sally Campbell Barr (1965–) and Delia McDonald Woolery (1965–); their verse evokes striking images. McDonald Woolery's epic poem "...la lluvia es una piel..." (1999; ...rain is a skin...) demonstrates a sense of *otherness* acquired in the school system and the workplace—rain is equated with a person's skin or appearance. Her brevity encourages pondering on daily urban routines, experiences of personal heritage in grade school and at home, and racist societal reactions. (Born in San José, one of her parents was from Limón, the other from Panama.) Both poets reveal the historical experience of Afro-Costa Rican women, which now is as much urban as regional. Campbell's poetry evokes strong female consciousness caught between opposite poles, and similar to the poles between heritage and nation. Her poetry volume *Rotundamente negra* (1994; Profoundly Black) asserts female strength and Afro-Costa Rican national presence.

Like their predecessor Bernard, Campbell's and McDonald's poetry promoted a greater consciousness about Costa Rican society and history, particularly with regard to the impact and influence of African and indigenous cultural traditions on national heritage. In its vocabulary, with such social practices as voo-doo, and festivities like *Carnaval* (the pre-Lent festival), Costa Rica is a nation where an African ethos is ever-present and warrants conscious acknowledgement. In the verses of these poets, the schoolchildren, household maids, and workers at the factory and in agriculture all emerge from invisibility. In addition, these poems open readers' eyes to the plight of girls and women, an overlooked problem in all cultural groups.

Elizabeth Coonrod Martínez

Work By:

Bernard Little, Eulalia. *Ritmohéroe*. San José: Costa Rica, 1996.

Bernard Little, Eulalia. *Ciénega*. San José, Costa Rica: Asesores Gráficos, 2001.

Campbell Barr, Shirley. *Naciendo*. San José: Arado, 1988.

Campbell Barr, Shirley. *Rotundamente negra*. San José: Arado, 1994.

Duncan, Quince. *The Best Short Stories of Quince Duncan*. Trans. Dellita Martín-Ogunsola. San José: Costa Rica, 1995.

Duncan, Quince. *Voice of a Limonise*. Miami: Latin American and Caribbean Center, Florida International University, 1985.

Duncan, Quince. *Un mensaje de Rosa: una novela en relatos*. San José: Universidad Estatal a Distancia, 2007.

Woolery, Delia McDonald. . . . *La lluvia es una piel* . . . San José: Ministerio de Cultura, 1999.

Work About:

Harpelle, Ronald N. *The West Indians of Costa Rica: Race, Class, and the Integration of an Ethnic Minority*. Montreal: McGill-Queen's University Press, 2001.

Lobo Wiehoff, Tatiana, and Mauricio Meléndez Obando. *Negros y blancos: todo mezclado*. San José: Universidad de Costa Rica, 1997.

McKinney, Kitzie. "Costa Rica's Black Body: The Politics and Poetics of Difference in Eulalia Bernard's Poetry." *Afro-Hispanic Review* 15:2 (Fall 1996): 11–20.

Mosby, Dorothy E. *Place, Language, and Identity in Afro-Costa Rican Literature*. Columbia: University of Missouri Press, 2003.

Ramsay, Paulette. "Quince Duncan's Literary Representation of the Ethno-Racial Dynamics between Latinos and Afro-Costa Ricans of West Indian Descent." *Afro-Hispanic Review* 17.2 (Fall 1998): 52–60.

Sharman, Russell Leigh. "Poetic Power: The Gendering of Literary Style in Puerto Limón." *Afro-Hispanic Review* 19.2 (Fall 2000): 70–79.

Agosín, Marjorie (1955–)

A poet, literary critic, professor, and human rights activist, Agosín was raised in Chile but moved to the United States after Chile's 1973 coup d'état. She writes both in English and Spanish. Her poetry collection *Sagrada memoria: Reminicencias de una niña judía en Chile* (1994; *A Cross and a Star: Memoirs of a Jewish Girl in Chile*, 1995) reflects her Jewish roots and Hispanic heritage. Much of Agosín's poetry deals with her family. *Always from Somewhere Else: A Memoir of my Chilean Jewish Father* (1998) and *Poems for Josefina* (2004) respectively chronicle her father's and grandmother's lives.

Agosín's bilingual poem collection *Dear Anne Frank* (1994) offers tribute to the extraordinary courage of the iconic Jewish girl who died in a concentration camp during World War II. *Uncertain Travelers* (1999), tells stories of her European family's search for refuge in Chile and recounts interviews with European and Latin American Jewish women immigrants to the United States. The bilingual poem book *Absence of Shadows* (1998) commemorates the 50th anniversary of the United Nations' Declaration of Human Rights. It echoes two earlier works: *Zones of Pain* (1988) and *Circle of Madness: Mothers of the Plaza de Mayo* (1992)— each pay homage to "the spirits of the disappeared" in Chile and El Salvador and to the Holocaust of Jews "in the country of the dead." The theme of human rights figures in all her work: *Writing Toward Hope: The Literature of Human Rights in Latin America* (2006) anthologizes texts by prominent Latin American authors.

Silvia Nagy-Zekmi

See also Documentary Narrative in Spanish American Literature; Judeo-Spanish Writing in Spanish America; Torture in Modern Spanish American Literature.

Work By:

Dear Anne Frank. Trans. Richard Schaaf, Cola Franzen, and Monica Bruno. Hanover, NH: University Press of New England, 1998.

Work About:

Gil, Lydia M. "A Balancing Act: Latin American Jewish Literature in the United States (or Towards a Jewish-Latino Literature). *A Companion to* *U.S. Latino Literatures*. Ed., intro. Carlota Caulfield and Darién Davis. Rochester, NY: Tamesis, 2007, 177–90.

Aguilar, Rosario (1938–)

Although this very important Nicaraguan novelist does not consider herself a feminist writer, her protagonists are Nicaraguan women whose conversations, situations, and experiences display feminist concerns. The first woman admitted to Nicaragua's Academy of Language, Aguilar's best known novels include *Primavera sonámbula* (1964; Sleepwalking Spring), *Quince barrotes de izquierda a derecha* (1965; Fifteen Bars from Left to Right), *Rosa Sarmiento* (1968), *El guerrillero* (1976; The Guerrilla), *La niña blanca y los pájaros sin pies* (1992; *The Lost Chronicles of Terra Firma*, 1997), and *La promesante* (2001; The Promising Girl).

Rosa Sarmiento centers on the world of Rosa Sarmiento, mother of famed Nicaraguan Modernist poet Rubén *Darío. It begins with Rosa's thoughts as she awaits the birth of her son, intertwining her marital discontent with the fear of maternity. After the birth of her child, she feels herself as an object and rejects the submissive role that her husband and society have imposed on her. Aguilar's focus on Rosa Sarmiento is an original one, as the mother scarcely receives mention in other biographies about Darío.

Set during the conquest of the Americas, *La niña blanca y los pájaros sin pies* captures the lives of six women: three from Spain, two indigenous, and one mestiza. Narrated by a Nicaraguan newspaperwoman who writes about women of that period, the success of this historical novel rests on the presentation of the conquest through women's eyes. Although barely mentioned in official chronicles, they also played roles in settling the New World.

María José Luján

See also Feminism in Spanish America.

Work By:

The Lost Chronicles of Terra Firma. Trans. Edward Waters Hood. Fredonia, NY: White Pine, 1997.

Work About:

Barbas-Rhoden, Laura. "Personal Stories and Historical Events in the Fiction of Rosario Aguilar." *Writing Women in Central America. Gender and Fictionalization of History.* Columbus: Ohio University Press, 2003, 80–120.

González, Ann. "Las mujeres de mi país: An Introduction to the Feminist Fiction of Rosario Aguilar." *Revista Interamericana* 23.1–2 (1993): 63–72.

Aguilar Camín, Héctor (1946–)

A Mexican novelist, historian and journalist, his creative works borrow heavily from the political life of 20th-century Mexico. Born in Chetumal, Quintana Roo, he earned a doctorate in history from El Colegio de México.

In his first novel, *Morir en el golfo* (1985; Dying in the Gulf), the investigation into a series of murders provides a pretext for more general observations regarding political corruption and greed. However, his second novel, *La guerra de Galio* (1990; Galio's War), is generally considered Aguilar Camín's most accomplished work; it provides a close look at the fraught relationship between Mexican political power and journalism during the 1970s. The government's extralegal means for suppressing an emergent guerrilla movement raise questions regarding the importance of an independent press in a functioning democracy.

Aguilar Camín's comprehensive history of Mexico since 1910, *A la sombra de la revolución mexicana* (1989; *In the Shadow of the Mexican Revolution*, 1993) coauthored with Lorenzo Meyer, has been recognized as a key text for students of contemporary Mexican politics.

Paul L. Goldberg

See also Mexico City in Literature.

Work By:

La guerra de Galio. Madrid: Alfaguara, 1994.

Work About:

Cabrera, Enriqueta. "The Freedom of Political Fiction." Trans. Kathy A. Ogle. *Américas* 58 (2006): 20–25.

Moreiras, Alberto. "Ethics and Politics in Héctor Aguilar Camín's *Morir en el golfo* and *La guerra de Galio.*" *South Central Review* 21 (2004): 70–84.

Agustini, Delmira (1886–1914)

Born in Montevideo, Uruguay, to an upper middle-class family, she is one of the most original voices of the Latin American literary movement *modernismo*. At an early age, she started composing poems that soon became inflamed with eroticism. Agustini's first book of poems, *El libro blanco (Frágil)* (1907; The White Book [Fragile]) was very well received by intellectuals of her day. This collection was followed by *Cantos de la mañana* (1910; Morning Songs) and *Los cálices vacíos* (1913; Empty Chalices). She also planned a book to be called *Los astros del abismo* (Stars from the Abyss) that was never completed. Her ex-husband, Enrique Job Reyes, whom she had divorced six weeks after their marriage in 1914, murdered her in their last clandestine sexual encounter and then killed himself. Agustini's spectacularly tragic death has often diverted attention from the extraordinary quality of her unique verses.

Tina Escaja

See also *Modernismo* in Hispanic Literature; Spanish American Poetry by Women.

Work By:

Poesías completas. Ed., intro. Magdalena García Pinto. Madrid: Cátedra, 1993.
Selected Poetry of Delmira Agustini: Poetics of Eros. Trans., intro. Alejandro Cáceres. Foreword Willis Barnstone. Carbondale: Southern Illinois University Press, 2003.

Work About:

Escaja, Tina. *Salomé Decapitada: Mujer y representación finisecular en la poesía de Delmira Agustini*. Amsterdam: Rodopi, 2001.

Varas, Patricia. "Modernism or *Modernismo*? Delmira Agustini and the Gendering of Turn-of-the-Century Spanish-American Poetry." *Modernism, Gender and Culture. A Cultural Studies Approach*. Ed. Lisa Rado. New York and London: Garland, 1997, 149–60.

Aira, César (1949–)

Born in the Buenos Aires province of Argentina, this influential writer and translator is arguably the nation's most prolific literary author of recent times, having published over 50 novella-length texts since the early 1990s. Aira values process over product in his writing, and this apparent frenzy becomes itself a theme in his writing. His entire literary practice rests on such motifs as the "flight forward" (*huida hacia adelante*), which upholds virtuous improvisation as the rationale for storytelling. Aira's distinctive writing often addresses the gap between art and life, as he experiments both with a certain continuity between creation and experience (*el continuo*) and radical moments of rupture (*fogonazos*).

Aira's short stories, novels, and essays defy classification. He often draws from and subverts one or more literary genres at a time, such as autobiography, in the imaginative re-creation of a year in the life of a child in *Cómo me hice monja* (1993; *How I Became a Nun*, 2006), or travel literature and *gauchesca* (South American cowboy literature) in the account of a German painter's misadventures in the pampas in *Un episodio en la vida del pintor viajero* (2000; *An Episode in the Life of a Landscape Painter*, 2006). Overall, his works uniquely combine lighthearted, humoristic prose with philosophical speculation and reflections on the act of creation.

Héctor M. Hoyos

Work By:

How I Became a Nun. Trans. Chris Andrews. New York: New Directions, 2007.

Work About:

Reber, Dierdra. "Cure for the Capitalist Headache: Affect and Fantastic Consumption in César Aira's Argentine 'Baghdad'." *Modern Language Notes* 122.2 (2007): 371–99.

Alarcón, Pedro Antonio de (1833–1891)

Narratives by this Spanish author, whose writing spans the end of *romanticism and the beginning explosion of realism, possess romantic themes, style, and techniques but also hint at what realism will become in writings by such contemporaries as Benito *Pérez Galdós and Emilia *Pardo Bazán.

Perhaps his best known novel is *El sombrero de tres picos* (1874; *The Three-Cornered Hat*, 2004), which recounts the popular tale of the *comendador*, or governor, who pursues the miller's wife but is ultimately outwitted by her and her husband. In this short text, Alarcón describes and criticizes the early 19th-century Spain of the *ancién régime*, where the abuse of authority and an honor-based society stood at the center of Spanish life.

A positive reception was also accorded his chronicle *Diario de un testigo de la guerra de África* (1860; Diary of A Witness of the War in Africa). Additionally, Alarcón wrote short stories of horror and the fantastic, in the manner of Edgar Allen Poe (whom he read extensively). These texts and several other novels received little critical attention, prompting Alarcón to abandon literary creation.

Vicente Gomis-Izquierdo

See also Realism and Naturalism in Spain.

Work By:

The Three-Cornered Hat. Trans. Peter Bush. London: Hesperus, 2004.
"The Nail" and Other Stories. Trans. Robert Fedorchek. Intro. Cyrus C. DeCoster. Cranbury, NJ: Associated University Presses, 1997.

Work About:

DeCoster, Cyrus C. *Pedro Antonio de Alarcón*. Boston: Twayne, 1979.

Alberdi, Juan Bautista (1810–1884)

One of 19th-century Argentina's influential intellectuals, this writer formed part of the "Generation of '37," a group of elite liberals influenced by Enlightenment ideas, where reason was considered to be the principal source of and legitimacy for authority.

Alberdi opposed the tyrannical government of Juan Manuel de Rosas (1793–1877) and, from exile in Montevideo, Europe, and Chile, wrote extensively against the dictator. One of his political plays, *El gigante Amapolas y sus formidables enemigos* (1842; Giant Amapolas and his Formidable Enemies), depicts Rosas as Giant Amapolas, a gigantic cloth puppet that intimidates every sector of the population through fear and his silence.

One of his most significant writings, "Bases y puntos de partida para la organización política de la república Argentina" (1952; Bases and Starting Points for the Political Organization of the Argentine Republic), heavily influenced the writing process of the 1853 Argentine Constitution. Alberdi supported using foreign capital and European immigration to populate the country, coining the aphorism *gobernar es poblar* (to govern is to populate). For him, "to populate" also implied to educate, to improve, and to civilize effectively, following the U.S. model; however, he also emphasized that the civilization process could be better attained by "transplanting" people with highly developed skills and a clear comprehension of what liberty entails.

Alejandra K. Carballo

See also Enlightenment in Spanish America.

Work By:

El gigante Amapolas y sus formidables enemigos. Buenos Aires: Teatro Municipal General San Martín, 1984.

Work About:

Herrero, Alejandro. "La imagen de España en Juan Bautista Alberdi." *Cuadernos Hispanoamericanos: Revista Mensual de Cultura Hispánica* 500 (1992): 189–99.

Labinger, Andrea G. "Something Old, Something New: *El gigante Amapolas.*" *Latin American Theatre Review* 15.2 (1982): 3–11.

Alberti, Rafael (1902–1999)

This prolific Spanish author's first book of poetry, *Marinero en tierra* (1924; Sailor on Dry Land), won him (together with Gerardo *Diego) the prestigious 1925 Premio Nacional de Literatura Prize. During this first period of his artistic creation, after flirting with a career as a painter, Alberti formed part of the Spanish avant-garde and published two additional poetry collections: *La amante* (1926; The Mistress) and *El alba del alhelí* (1927; The Dawn of the Wallflower). His stay at Madrid's *Residencia de Estudiantes coincided with the death anniversary of Baroque poet Luis de *Góngora. Alberti, along with Federico *García Lorca, Luis Buñuel, Vicente *Aleixandre, Dámaso *Alonso, and others, participated in that celebration which gave rise to the *Generation of 1927 writers. His friendship with Lorca and Buñuel prompted him to participate briefly in the superrealist movement and publish two of his best volumes of poems, *Sobre los ángeles* (1929; Concerning the Angels, 1967) and *Cal y canto* (1929; Quicklime and Plainsong).

Before the 1931 advent of the Second Spanish Republic, Alberti acquired a political conscience, which led him to join Spain's Communist Party and marked the rest of his literary production. The first collection of poems reflecting this change, *Con los zapatos puestos tengo que morir* (1930; I Must Die with My Shoes On), is followed by *Consignas* (1933; Orders), *Un fantasma recorre Europa* (1933; A Spectre Is Haunting Europe), *13 bandas y 48 estrellas* (1936; 13 Bars and 48 Stars) and *El poeta en la calle* (1938; Poet in the Street). At the same time, Alberti began to write plays in a political and ideological vein, such as *El hombre deshabitado* (1930; The Empty Man), which sought renewal of the Spanish theater by recovering a dramatic genre that had virtually disappeared since the mid-18th century, the allegorical religious play or *auto sacramental*. During the Spanish Civil War (1936–1939), he published and staged *Fermín Galán* (1931), *De un momento a otro* (1938–1939; From One Moment to Another) and *Teatro de urgencia* (1938; Urgent Theater), a model of "agit-prop" literature that greatly influenced playwrights of the 1970s.

During his lengthy exile from Spain (1939–1977), Alberti worked in Argentina for Losada publishing house, publishing many of his works, such as *Entre el clavel y la espada* (1941; Between the Carnation and the Sword) and *A la pintura* (1945; *To Painting*, 1997), wherein he shows his predilection for painters and, especially, paintings in Madrid's Prado Museum. Themes of the sea and his native land appear in *Pleamar* (1944; High Tide) and in *Oda marítima* (1953; Maritime Ode). Alberti completed his dramatic production with a series of poetic dramas, *El trébol florido* (1940; Clover), and *La gallarda* (1940; The Brave), as well as two of his most important works, *El adefesio* (1944; The Dandy), influenced by Lorca (especially *La casa de Bernarda Alba*), and *Noche de guerra en el Museo del Prado* (1956; A Night of War in the Prado Museum). He also began to write the first part of his autobiography, *La arboleda perdida* (1942; *The Lost Grove*, 1981).

After a period in Rome, which inspired the poems of *Roma peligro para caminantes* (1968; Rome, Danger to the Traveler), he returned to Spain on April 27, 1977, spending the last years of his life in Puerto de Santa María, where one can now visit the Museo Fundación that bears his name. In 1983, Alberti was awarded the Premio Cervantes, the Spanish literary world's highest honor. He also captured the 1965 Lenin Peace Prize.

Fernando de Diego Pérez

See also Exile Literature by Spanish Civil War Émigrés; Poetry in Spain: 1900 to Present; Theater in Spain: 1900–1975.

Work By:

Concerning the Angels. Trans. Christopher Sawyer-Lauçanno. San Francisco: City Lights, 1995.

The Lost Grove. Trans. Gabriel Berns. Berkeley: University of California Press, 1981.

Selected Poems. Trans. Ben Belit. Berkeley and Los Angeles: University of California Press, 1966.

To Painting. Trans. Carolyn Tipton. Evanston, IL: Hydra, 1997.

Work About:

Gagen, Derek. "Thy Fading Mansion: The Image of the Empty House in Rafael Alberti's *Sobre los ángeles*." *Bulletin of Hispanic Studies* 64.3 (1987): 225–35.

Nantell, Judith. "Irreconcilable Differences: Rafael Alberti's *Sobre los ángeles*." *The Surrealist Adventure in Spain*. Ed. C. Brian Morris. Ottawa: Dovehouse, 1991, 145–65.

Popkins, Louise. *The Theater of Rafael Alberti*. London: Tamesis, 1977.

Urraca, Beatriz. "Autobiography Completes No Pictures: Fragmentation in Rafael Alberti's *La arboleda perdida*." *Hispanic Journal* 13.1 (1992): 51–58.

Web site of Fundación Rafael Alberti: http://www.rafaelalberti.es/.

Aldecoa, Ignacio (1925–1969)

One of the most remarkable writers of Spain's *Generation of the 1950s, his poetry used social realism to critique Franco's regime. Born to a bourgeois family in the Basque region, Aldecoa studied at the Universities of Salamanca and Madrid, meeting young dissident writers like Jesús *Fernández Santos, Rafael *Sánchez Ferlosio, Alfonso *Sastre, and his future wife, writer and pedagogue Josefina Rodríguez. Although Aldecoa published two poetry books first, he is better known for his short stories, which reveal influences of Italian neorealism, American authors like Ernest Hemingway and John Dos Passos and Spanish writers like Pío *Baroja. His texts evince sympathy for marginalized, deprived people who struggle to survive or be free; they include children, rural workers, beggars, and boxers. His knowledge of everyday language and customs add a unique realism to his writing. Aldecoa's short stories first appeared in literary journals and were later published in collections like *Vísperas de silencio* (1955; The Eve of Silence) and *El corazón y otros frutos amargos* (1959; The Heart and Other Bitter Fruits).

Aldecoa also published several novels: in *El fulgor y la sangre* (1954; Glare and Blood), realistic dialogues and the tension-filled wait of several Civil Guard wives dramatize the final discovery of which husband has been murdered in a shooting. *Con el viento solano* (1956; With the Desert Wind) retells the same story, this time from the perspective of the criminal, a Spanish gypsy trying to escape with his life. *Gran Sol* (1958; Great Sole) employs a highly technical nautical vocabulary and focuses on the harsh life of sailors at sea.

Alberto Villamandos

See also Aldecoa, Josefina (1926–2011); Civil War Literature in Spain.

Work By:

Cuentos. Ed. Josefina Rodríguez de Aldecoa. Madrid: Cátedra, 1991.

Work About:

Landeira, Ricardo, and Mellizo, Carlos, eds. *Ignacio Aldecoa: A Collection of Critical Essays*. Laramie: University of Wyoming, 1977.

Aldecoa, Josefina (1926–2011)

Born Josefina Rodríguez Álvarez in the province of León, this Spanish novelist and short story writer comes from a family of educators, holds a doctorate in education, and features teachers and students in many of her works. She has distinguished herself in literature and pedagogy, the dual facets of her life. Her mother and grandmother were associated with the famed Institución Libre de Enseñanza, a progressive educational project aimed at developing independent thinking, free of imposed dogma and state controls. In 1959, she founded the Colegio Estilo, a Madrid school influenced by the earlier model. She became part of a new generation of writers in the 1950s and married her colleague Ignacio *Aldecoa (1925–1969), acclaimed as a neorealist.

Beginning in the 1980s, Josefina Aldecoa began writing with renewed enthusiasm. Particularly notable, as well as commercially successful, is her novelistic trilogy *Historia de una maestra* (1990; Story of a Schoolteacher), *Mujeres de negro* (1994; Women in Black), and *La fuerza del destino* (1997; The Force of Destiny)—which cover the years prior to the Spanish Civil War (1936–1939) to the end of the 20th century. Education in Spain and Mexico provides the backdrop for the first two novels, and the third shows the now elderly protagonist suffering from a form of dementia. The portrait of devoted teachers in isolated villages of Spain and allusions to the lofty (and unrealized) pedagogical goals of the Second Republic give *Historia de una maestra* a special poignancy and depth of feeling.

Edward H. Friedman

See also Krausism in Spain.

Work By:

Historia de una maestra. Barcelona: Anagrama, 1990.
La fuerza del destino. Barcelona: Anagrama, 1997.
Mujeres de negro. Barcelona: Anagrama, 1994.

Work About:

Graham, Helen, and Jo Labanyi, eds. *Spanish Cultural Studies: An Introduction. The Struggle for Modernity.* Oxford: Oxford University Press, 1995.
Leggott, Sarah J. "History, Autobiography, Maternity: Josefina Aldecoa's *Historia de una maestra* and *Mujeres de negro*." *Letras Femeninas* 24.1–2 (1998): 111–27.

Alegría, Ciro (1909–1967)

Considered a leading writer of Latin America's indigenist movement, this journalist, politician and novelist was born in the Andean region of La Libertad, in northeastern Peru. There, he discovered firsthand the harsh living conditions of native Peruvians, the focus of his fiction. Imprisoned several times for political activism, Alegría was exiled to Chile and later lived in the United States. Critical praise greeted his novel *La serpiente de oro* (1935; *The Golden Serpent*, 1943), a love story between a city-dweller and a young indigenous woman living among the boatmen of the Marañón River; he became a writer of international stature with *El mundo es ancho y ajeno* (1941; *Broad and Alien Is the World*, 1984). This poetic story of the indigenous culture's virtues and intimate relationship with the environment traces their displacement and mistreatment at the hands of white landowners and the government. Alegría also authored the novel *Los perros hambrientos* (1938; The Hungry Dogs), works of short fiction, essays, and the memoir *Mucha suerte con harto palo* (1976; Lots of Luck and a Hard Beating).

César Ferreira

See also Amazon Theme in Spanish American Literature; *Indigenismo* in Spanish American Literature; Transculturation in the Hispanic World.

Work By:

Broad and Alien Is the World. Trans. Harriet de Onís. London: Merlin, 1984.
Novela de mis novelas. Ed. Ricardo Silva-Santisteban. Lima: Universidad Pontificia Católica del Perú, 2004.

Work About:

Escajadillo, Tomás G. *Para leer a Ciro Alegría.* Lima: Amaru, 2007.
Kokotovic, Misha. *The Colonial Divide in Peruvian Narrative: Social Conflict and Transculturation.* Sussex, United Kingdom: Sussex Academic Press, 2007, 32–64.

Alegría, Claribel (1924–)

Born in Nicaragua, her father's involvement in politics forced the family to move to El Salvador when Alegría was one year old. As a result, this poet, essayist, novelist, translator, and editor has always considered herself Salvadoran, although today she makes Nicaragua her home. She led a sheltered childhood until age seven, when she witnessed the army's 1932 mass executions of over 30,000 indigenous peasants from the window of her home. This traumatizing event provided what she calls the "seedbed" for her first novel, *Cenizas de Izalco* (1966; *Ashes of Izalco*, 1989), which recounts both a love story and the brutal killings in a diary left by the protagonist's recently deceased mother.

Alegría was schooled in the United States. Spanish modernist poet and later Nobel laureate Juan Ramón *Jiménez became her mentor and helped her publish her first poetry collection, *Anillo del silencio* (1948; Ring of Silence). She married U.S. diplomat Darwin "Bud" Flakoll, and together they established a literary partnership that endured until his death in 1995. In 1978, *Sobrevivo* (I Survive), won the prestigious Casa de las Américas Prize for poetry. At this point, her work took on a more pointed political bent; Alegría herself commented that the Nicaraguan revolution helped spur her decision to participate more fully in the region's tumults. Alegría told poet Carolyn Forché (the force behind her bilingual 1982 collection, *Flores del volcán/Flowers from the Volcano*), that she had no *fusil* (rifle), but still saw her poetry as a contribution to the struggle for human rights, democracy, and freedom. Thus, Alegría's weapons of words, in poetry, prose, history, and testimony, served as a voice for Central America's popular social movements.

A self-declared feminist long before it was fashionable, in many works, she creates a protagonist who questions her assigned gender role, and gradually comes to consciousness about women's rights as human rights. Such plot lines define the novellas *Album familiar* (1982; *Family Album*, 1989) and *Despierta, mi bien, despierta* (1986; Wake Up, My Dear, Wake Up), as well as the longer works *Cenizas de Izalco* and *Luisa en el país de la realidad* (1987; *Luisa in Realityland*, 1987). In *No me agarran viva* (1983; *They Won't Take Me Alive*, 1984), Alegría recounts the life of a Salvadoran guerrillera in the *testimonio* genre of personal witness to injustice.

Alegría and Flakoll also copublished books aimed to diffuse knowledge of political events, as in *Somoza: Expediente cerrado* (1993; *Death of Somoza*, 1996), *Nicaragua: La revolución sandinista; Una crónica política, 1855–1979* (1983; Nicaragua: The Sandinista Revolution), and *On the Front Line: Guerrilla Poetry of El Salvador* (1989). Remarkably, their *Fuga de Canto Grande* (1992; *Tunnel to Canto Grande*, 1996) recounts the dramatic escape of 48 political prisoners from a maximum-security facility in Peru. To document such a sensitive situation, the revolutionary movement invited Alegría and Flakoll to interview them for the story, based on their reputation from previous works.

In October 2006, Alegría was awarded the Neustadt International Prize for Literature, considered by some to be second only to the Nobel. Her most recent poetry collection, *Soltando amarras/Casting Off* (2003) speaks to her impending death and the life work of a poet.

Nancy Saporta Sternbach

See also Testimonial Writing in Central America.

Work By:

Saudade = Sorrow. Trans. Carolyn Forché. Willimantic, CT: Curbstone, 1999.

Soltando amarras = Casting Off. Trans. Margaret Sayers Peden. Willimantic, CT: Curbstone, 2003.

Thresholds = Umbrales. Trans. Darwin J. Flakoll. Willimantic, CT: Curbstone, 1996.

Work About:

"Claribel Alegría: 2006 Neustadt Prize Laureate." *World Literature Today* 81.3 (May–June 2007): 27–49. Special section devoted to Alegría.

McGowan, Marcia Phillips. "The Poetry of Claribel Alegría: A Testament of Hope." *Latin American Literary Review* 32.64 (July–Dec. 2004): 5–28.

Aleixandre, Vicente (1898–1984)

This Spanish Nobel Prize–winner is famous for his experimental, visual poetry associated with the *Generation of 1927 and for contributions to post–civil war poetic production in Spain. While contemporaries like Federico *García Lorca, Jorge *Guillén, and Luis *Cernuda were killed or fled Spain after the Spanish Civil War (1936–1939), Aleixandre stayed. His influence on postwar poets and his own diverse poetic production extended the impressive legacy of a talented group of exiled peers.

Aleixandre's first poetic collection, *Ámbito* (1928; Boundary), reflects the influence of the *poesía pura* movement with its natural imagery and unadorned forms. His style shifts, however, in works like *Espadas como labios* (1932; Swords Like Lips). Poems of this period employ free association and irrational imagery, as in the prose poetry of *Pasión de la tierra* (1935; Passion of the Earth). Aleixandre's most critically acclaimed surrealistic work, *La destrucción o el amor* (1935; *Destruction or Love*, 2000), employs his signature free-verse form. The text contemplates erotic love and links the irrational, subconscious forces of a unifying passion with the interconnectedness of the universe.

After the civil war, health problems forced Aleixandre to remain in Spain despite his rejection of the Nationalist dictatorship. His works were banned for several years, but when he could again publish, verses like those of *Sombra del paraíso* (1944; Shadow of Paradise) reestablished his poetic stature through innovative imagery and a rejection of the neoclassical forms crowding the postwar literary scene. Aleixandre's home became a gathering place for young poets, offering a space of freedom in the midst of the interior exile caused by the Franco dictatorship. With the publication of *Historia del corazón* (1954; History of the Heart) Aleixandre's work became more accessible, employing humanistic themes related to historical circumstances and a conception of poetry as communication. Texts like *En un vasto dominio* (1962; In a Vast Domain) contributed to the social poetry dominant during the Franco regime.

Near the end of the dictatorship, Aleixandre's poetic style shifted again, returning to more contemplative and difficult forms in collections like *Poemas de la consumación* (1968; Poems of Consummation) and *Diálogos del conocimiento* (1974; Dialogues of Knowledge). These final publications recall the antirational poetry of Aleixandre's youth, contemplating hermetic and contradictory images related to poetic philosophy, old age, and death. In 1977, Aleixandre received the Nobel Prize in Literature; in his acceptance speech he acknowledged the importance of his poetic inheritance, from the rich history of Spanish letters and from his Generation of 1927 contemporaries, who encouraged a culture of experimentation and whose legacies he continued in Spain after the war.

Debra Faszer-McMahon

See also Francoism, Fascism, and Literature in Spain; Nobel Prize Literature in Spanish; Poetry in Spain: 1900 to Present.

Work By:

A Longing for the Light: Selected Poems of Vicente Aleixandre. Trans. Lewis Hyde. Port Townsend, WA: Copper Canyon, 2007.

Work About:

Daydí-Tolson, Santiago. "Light in the Eyes: Visionary Poetry in Vicente Aleixandre." *Contemporary Spanish Poetry: The Word and the World.* Ed. Cecile West-Settle and Sylvia Sherno. Madison, NJ: Fairleigh Dickinson University Press, 2005, 25–38.

Murphy, Daniel. *Vicente Aleixandre's Stream of Lyric Consciousness.* Lewisburg PA: Bucknell University Press, 2001.

Alfaro, Óscar (1921–1963)

This teacher, journalist, poet, and short story writer is considered Bolivia's most important children's author. He belonged to the *Gesta Bárbara* cultural movement; originally founded in 1918, he and other left-leaning Bolivian intellectuals resurrected it in 1944. The group, known as *bárbaros* (barbarians), edited a literary magazine and organized counter cultural events in La Paz and other cities in an attempt to shock people and break with cultural traditions. They introduced surrealist elements to writing, and favored Marcel Proust's and James Joyce's stream-of-consciousness techniques and their literary distancing from morality. Being an eternal optimist and rather shy, despite his participation in this bohemian group, he avoided the more confrontational, sexual tone used by members like Gustavo Medinaceli.

Nicknamed "the children's poet," the body of works in *La Colección Alfaro* (The Alfaro Collection) contain children's poems and short story texts like *Cien poemas para niños* (1955; One Hundred Poems for Children), and *Alfabeto de estrellas* (1950; Alphabet of Stars). In both genres, he tends to incorporate dialogue and uses animals and nature as protagonists, giving his writing a fable-like quality and an ideological and didactic component. Two such examples are the poem "El pájaro revolucionario" (The Revolutionary Bird) and the short story "El circo de la araña" (The Spider's Circus). Alfaro is a *chapaco* (a local term for people born in the southern city of Tarija) and many collections, like *Cuentos chapacos* (1963; Chapaco Short Stories), reflect the *costumbrismo* (detailed depiction of regional customs and traditions) of his birthplace. Songs by Bolivian singer-songwriter Nilo Soruco have immortalized many of Alfaro's poems.

Fabiola Fernández Salek

Work By:

Cuentos chapacos. La Paz: Alfaro, 1963–1987.

Work About:

Bedregal, Yolanda. "Óscar Alfaro." *Antología de la poesía boliviana.* Cochabamba, Bolivia: Los Amigos del Libro, 1997, 378–81.

Alfonso X, "el Sabio" (1221–1284)

Born in Toledo in 1221 and crowned King of Galicia, Castile, and León in 1252, Alfonso X became one of the most significant rulers in Spanish history. His epithet "el Sabio" means both learned and wise, reflecting his support of a broad range of intellectual endeavors. Alfonso became the first Castilian monarch to make a serious, concerted effort to exert a presence in Europe. His principal ambition was to become Holy Roman Emperor; although elected *Rex Romanorum* in 1254, in 1275 he renounced his claim to the imperial crown.

Alfonso X fostered interaction among Christian, Jewish, and Islamic intellectuals as he promoted study in the arts and sciences and sponsored a major literary work. One product of this interest was the creation of the School of Translators of Toledo, where Arabs, Jews, and Christians translated important writings from Greek, Arabic, Hebrew, and Latin into Castilian, standardizing the syntax of this vernacular language and defining new words and concepts not previously understood. Many scientific texts in Greek or Arabic that contained knowledge that had been lost to Christian European realms were rediscovered through translations to Latin that were disseminated from Toledo. He was the first king to codify the Castilian language in written and spoken courtly records, thereby displacing Latin as the "official language" for government and intellectual pursuits.

Alfonso X's wide-ranging scholarly interests have led critics to deem him the first humanist before *Humanism. His main interests included historiography, astronomy, legal codifications, poetry and astrology. He cannot be simply catalogued as "cultural patron" because he involved himself directly and personally in the creation of all this work, always bearing in mind the objective of enriching the culture and knowledge of his time.

The legal writings produced under his supervision are indissolubly bound to the introduction of the Roman Legal Code in Castile and León. Under his reign, a large body of legal texts was organized, the most significant being the *Siete Partidas* (1251, 1256–1265; Seven Statutory Divisions). Composed in Castilian, the collection included commercial, canon, and civil laws that defined and regulated most aspects of the state. The historiographic activity of Alfonso X and his collaborators produced massive works like the *Estoria de España* (1260–1274; History of Spain) and the *General Estoria* (from the 1270s on; General History) a universal history which begins with the creation of the world. Both are written in Castilian.

Alfonso X's interest in human sciences prompted translations of important Greek and Arabic texts, including many texts related to astrology and astronomy, which at that time were overlapping disciplines. One such example is the *Libro del Saber de Astrología* (1276–1279; Book of the Knowledge of Astrology). In literature, his poem collections are written in Galician, the language reserved for poetry at that time. His most acclaimed poetic work is the *Cantigas de Santa Maria* (13th century; Canticles of Holy Mary), a collection of 420 poems that show formal complexity and clear narrative form. Some appear to be written by Alfonso himself. Although the *Cantigas* are not liturgical texts, they have a noticeable religious nature since they discuss the miracles of the Virgin Mary. They are accompanied by stunning illuminations (drawings of scenes depicted in verse), and musical scores. Alfonso X died in Seville.

Javier Domínguez García

Work By:

Las Siete Partidas. Ed. Robert I. Burns. Trans. Samuel Parsons Scott. Philadelphia: Pennsylvania University Press, 2001.

Work About:

Burns, Robert Ignatius. *Emperor of Culture: Alfonso X the Learned of Castile and His Thirteenth-Century Renaissance*. Philadelphia: University of Pennsylvania Press, 1990.

Parkinson, Stephen, ed. *Cobras e son: Papers on the Text, Music, and Manuscripts of the Cántigas de Santa María*. Oxford: Research Centre of the University of Oxford, 2000.

Rico, Francisco. *Alfonso el Sabio y la General estoria: tres lecciones*. Barcelona: Ariel, 1984.

Algarín, Miguel (1941–)

Poet, playwright, and professor emeritus at Rutgers University, Miguel Algarín is best known as cofounder of the *Nuyorican Poets Cafe (NPC). He is a founding father of the 1970s Nuyorican literary movement that reclaimed the once-derogatory term *Nuyorican (denoting second and third generation Puerto Ricans in New York). Algarín and NPC cofounder Miguel Piñero first captured the Nuyorican aesthetic in the groundbreaking collection they coedited, *Nuyorican Poetry: An Anthology of Puerto Rican Words and Feelings* (1975). Twenty years later, Algarín coedited (with Bob Holman) another volume of NPC poetry, *Aloud: Voices from the Nuyorican Poets Cafe*.

A translator of Pablo *Neruda, Algarín authored several collections of his own poetry. Like most Nuyoricans, his base language is often English. However, much of his poetry is bilingual, switching between Spanish and English within the same poem or presenting a poem in both languages. Such language use reflects Puerto Ricans' complex dual identity. Algarín's themes include love and desire and the sights, sounds, and characters of everyday life in Manhattan's Lower East Side.

Betsy A. Sandlin

See also Puerto Rican Writers in Mainland United States.

Work By:

Love Is Hard Work: Memorias de Loisaida. New York: Scribner, 1997.
Time's Now: Ya es tiempo. Houston: Arte Público, 1985.

Work About:

Campa, Ramón de la. "En la utopía redentora del lenguaje: Pedro Pietri y Miguel Algarín." *The Americas Review* 16.2 (1988): 49–67.

Hernández, Carmen Dolores. *Puerto Rican Voices in English: Interviews with Writers*. Westport, CT: Praeger, 1997.

Allende, Isabel (1942–)

One of the most popular Latin American female writers of the 20th century, Allende was born in Peru and raised in Chile. Her prolific writing career has yielded more than 15 novels, short story collections for adults and children, and several plays. Three of her novels have been adapted to film and her works have been translated into more than 27 languages. Although her narrative relies on *magical realism, she also focuses on women's issues, politics, social class, and Latin American history.

After the death of her cousin, Chilean president Salvador Allende, and the rise in power of Augusto Pinochet, Allende and her family moved to Venezuela to live in exile for 13 years. During that time she wrote her first novel, *La casa de los espíritus* 1982; *The House of the Spirits*, 1985), which narrates the Trueba family's story over four generations from a female perspective; structurally similar to Gabriel *García Márquez's *One Hundred Years of Solitude*, the novel's direct and honest style, its setting in Chile, and the predominance of female characters differentiate her novel from that of Garcia Márquez. Next, *De amor y de sombras* (1984; *Of Love and Shadows*, 1987) recounts a love affair set in an environment of political repression, social commitment, and human dignity. Three years later, Allende published *Eva Luna* (1987), the story of an orphan growing up in South America; this was followed by the short story collection, *Cuentos de Eva Luna* (1989; *The Stories of Eva Luna*, 1991).

In the late 1980s, Allende remarried and moved to the United States. Her ensuing novels include *Paula* (1994; Eng. trans., 1995), a letter to her daughter who fell into a coma and died in December 1992; *Inés del alma mía* (2005; *Ines of My Soul*, 2006), the story of a *conquistadora* (female conqueror) who played a key role in founding Santiago de Chile; *Zorro. Comienza la leyenda* (2005; Eng. trans., 2005), an account of the famous masked hero's life; and a trilogy for young adults set in the Amazon rainforest. More recently, *La suma de los días* (2007; *The Sum of Our Days*; 2008) delves into the author's inner life and her relationships after the death of her daughter Paula.

Allende has also established a foundation to protect women and children from violence and to provide education and health care. Her leadership in women's issues and literary success have influenced people all over the world.

Leonora Simonovis

Work By:

Daughter of Fortune. Trans. Margaret Sayers Peden. New York: Harper Perennial, 2006.
Inés of My Soul. Trans. Margaret Sayers Peden. New York: Harper Perennial, 2006.
The Sum of Our Days. Trans. Margaret Sayers Peden. New York: Harper Perennial, 2009.

Work About:

Jolley, Jason R. "Mother-Daughter Feminism and Personal Criticism in Isabel Allende's Paula." *Revista Canadiense de Estudios Hispánicos* 30.2 (Winter 2006): 331–52.

Meacham, Cherie. "Resisting Romance: Isabel Allende's Transformation of the Popular Romance Formula in *Hija de la fortuna*." *Latin American Literary Review* 35.69 (January 2007): 29–45.

Swanson, Philip. "Z/Z: Isabel Allende and the Mark of Zorro." *Romance Studies* 24.3 (November 2006): 265–77.

Almodóvar, Pedro (1949–)

A cultural icon and currently Spain's most acclaimed director, in 1968 he moved from his rural birthplace to Madrid, as an aspiring filmmaker. With no formal training, Almodóvar has nonetheless gone on to win numerous national and international awards. He started his cinematic career shooting Super 8 short films; lacking technical support and financial backing, Almodóvar himself learned to experiment and solve production problems. From the beginning, his work possessed a strong narrative component and a focus on popular culture, very unlike the reigning high-culture film adaptations of Spanish literary masterpieces. Almodóvar strongly identified with La *Movida*, a national pop culture movement that emerged after the death of dictator Francisco Franco in 1975.

His films exhibit a pastiche of diverse influences, including Andy Warhol, popular Hollywood movies, punk music, boleros, Spanish *tonadillas*, Spanish literary artistic tradition, melodramas, Latin American *Boom* literature, soap operas, comic books and scatological humor. This combination of high and low sources is bounded by a grotesque realism and a parodic approach to the most taboo issues of traditional Spanish culture.

Mercedes Guijarro-Crouch

See also Cultural Icons of Spain

Work About:

D'Lugo, Marvin. *Pedro Almodóvar*. Urbana and Chicago: University of Illinois Press, 2006.

Alonso, Dámaso (1898–1990)

This internationally recognized Spanish scholar and poet was born in Madrid. He directed the *Real Academia Española from 1968–1982 and in 1977 received the Cervantes Award (the Spanish literary world's highest honor). His linguistic and literary research combines erudition with acute sensitivity, covering a broad spectrum of authors from medieval to modern poets. An expert philologist, he introduced stylistic literary theory to Spain, which focuses textual analysis primarily on linguistic form and patterns. Alonso is particularly known for deciphering Luis de *Góngora's intricate language. Despite being a contemporary of Spain's *Generation of 1927 poets, his works belong to the first post–civil war poetic generation.

His first collection, *Poemas Puros* (1921; Pure Poems), features anguished meditations on human destiny, with direct language and rich imagery. His most famous book, *Hijos de la ira* (1944; Children of Wrath), represents the seminal work of "uprooted" or "existentialist" Spanish postwar poetry. The term "uprooted" describes the lack of foundations and direction in the chaotic world following the Spanish Civil War (1936–1939) and Word War II (1939–1945). Distraught by violence and injustice, the poet expresses a frantic quest for meaning. Written in long, blank verse lines and reminiscent of biblical Psalms, it also sharply denounces the cruelty of Franco's dictatorship.

Alonso's religious angst figures as another main theme of his verse. In *Hombre y Dios* (1955; Man and God) and *Antología de nuestro monstruoso mundo* (1985; Anthology of Our Monstrous World), he dialogues passionately with the Creator about the afflictions of human life. A remarkable critic and poet, Alonso voiced the anxiety of a world dominated by cruelty and fear, opening the door for Spanish existential poetry.

María-Cruz Rodríguez

See also Poetry in Spain: 1900 to Present; Spanish Civil War and the Dictatorship of General Franco (1936–1975).

Work By:

Children of Wrath. Trans. Elias L. Rivers. Baltimore: Johns Hopkins Press, 1971.

Work About:

Bradford, Carole A. "The Dramatic Function of Symbol in *Hijos de la ira.*" *Romance Quarterly* 28.3 (1981): 295–308.

Russell, Dominique. " 'Esta desgarrada incógnita': Monster Theory and *Hijos de la ira.*" *Atenea* 24.2 (Dec. 2004): 73–90.

Altamirano, Ignacio Manuel (1834–1893)

This Mexican soldier, lawyer, legislator, journalist, editor, novelist, and poet dreamed of forging a modern liberal nation, with social justice, public education, free enterprise, and democratic institutions—the total opposite of what Mexico then represented. Known as the "Indian from Guerrero," he viewed Mexico as a wild frontier in need of taming, and for him, the chosen tool was literature.

Altamirano's very humble origins (legend holds that even his surname was borrowed because his indigenous parents had no Spanish name) clearly informed his vision. He considered novels to be a means for educating people and giving them a sense of nationhood; consequently, in several novels he portrays a somewhat idealistic, nationalist vision of Mexico and Mexicans. Mexican scenery, the relevant role of Mestizo (Spanish and indigenous) and female characters as patriots and true Mexicans figure importantly in such novels as *Clemencia* (1869; Mercy), *Navidad en las montañas* (1871; Christmas in the Mountains) and *El Zarco* (1901, posthumously; *El Zarco. The Blue-eyed Bandit*, 2007). In another major accomplishment, he brought together writers of all political inclinations to contribute to the literary journal *Renacimiento*, which he founded.

Jorge Zamora

Work By:

El Zarco. The Blue-eyed Bandit. Trans. Ronald Christ. Santa Fe, NM: Lumen, 2007.

Work About:

Conway, Christopher. "Ignacio Altamirano and the Contradictions of Autobiographical Indianism." *Latin American Literary Review* 34.67 (January–June 2006): 34–49.

Altolaguirre, Manuel (1905–1959)

Associated with the *Generation of 1927, this Spanish poet from Málaga is known for his introspective verse and prolific activity as a publisher of such magazines as *Litoral*, which included the work of other members of the Generation of 1927. His work focused predominantly on the intimate nature of experience; central themes include the sea, solitude, loneliness, and love. Well-measured verses predominate in his work but fixed rhyme schemes are rarely used. His penchant for incorporating previously published poems in new collections has resulted in a complex poetic trajectory.

Altolaguirre's poetic production is usually divided into three parts. The first includes all poetry published before the outbreak of the Spanish Civil War (1936–1939). The second stage consists of his limited wartime production, and stage three involves postwar work produced in exile until his death.

His principal early collections include *Las islas invitadas y otros poemas* (1926; The Invited Islands and Other Poems) and *Ejemplo* (1927; Example). A common motif in such work is the closing of the self in the face of the outside world. Loneliness plays a significant role, as does a focus on the speaker's body. The link between personal experience, nature, and loneliness is explicitly tied to language and poetry through references to books and the page. These poems occasionally include avant-garde images and characteristics.

Like many other Spanish intellectuals of the time, Altolaguirre left Spain after the Civil War, living in Mexico until his death. Later works like *Fin de un amor* (1949; End of a Love) and *Poemas en América* (1955; Poems in America) deal with loneliness, nostalgia, and nature.

Paul Cahill

See also Exile Literature by Spanish Civil War Émigrés.

Work By:

Poesías completas. Ed. Margarita Smerdou and Milagros Arizmendi. Madrid: Cátedra, 1999.

Work About:

Cate-Arries, Francie. "Manuel Altolaguirre through the Looking Glass: The Art of Self-Reflection." *Anales de la literatura española contemporánea* 13.3 (1988): 209–24.

Crispin, John. *Quest for Wholeness: The Personality and Works of Manuel Altolaguirre*. Valencia/Chapel Hill: Albatros/Hispanófila, 1983.

Romojaro, Rosa. *La poesía de Manuel Altolaguirre (Contexto. Claves de su poética. Recepción)*. Madrid: Visor, 2008.

Alva Ixtlilxóchitl, Fernando de (1568–1648)

This Mestizo (Spanish and indigenous) historian and great-grandson of the last ruler of Texcoco (a city-state that formed part of the Aztec Triple Alliance in Mexico's Central Valley) studied at the Colegio de Santa Cruz in Tlatelolco and in later years worked as a court interpreter. His ancestor formed an alliance with Hernán Cortés that helped bring Moctezuma's reign to an end. Alva Ixtlilxóchitl's writings about these events emphasize the courage, moral values, and heroism of his people, placing them on an equal plane with their Spanish allies.

Considered his best, most important work, *Historia de la nación chichimeca* (17th c.; History of the Chichimeca Nation) spans from the creation of the world to the 1521 siege of Tenochtitlán by Cortés. In *Sumaria relación de la historia general de esta Nueva España* (17th c.; Brief Account of the General History of This New Spain), Alva Ixtlilxóchitl focuses on indigenous history before the Spanish presence. With the exception of *Historia de la nación chichimeca*, his works are repetitive and lack clear order. However, his extensive collection of primary material makes these writings an important contribution to early documentation of Mexican history.

Alicia Muñoz

See also Discovery and Conquest Writings: Describing the Americas.

Work By:

Ally of Cortés: Account 13, of the Coming of the Spaniards and the Beginning of the Evangelical Law. Trans. Douglass K. Ballentine. El Paso, TX: Western, 1969.

Álvarez Gardeazábal, Gustavo (1945–)

This novelist, essayist, journalist, and politician is considered one of Colombia's most irreverent writers. In early novels, set in Tuluá, a town just outside Cali, he offers social critiques. The best known, *Cóndores no entierran todos los días* (1971; They Don't Bury Condors Every Day), focuses on la *violencia and how these years (1946–1953) affected Tuluá and its residents. As one of the most important literary accounts of this bloody period in Colombian history, it was later adapted to film.

El bazar de los idiotas (1974; *Bazaar of the Idiots*, 1991), another important novel of his early period, belittles its main characters in a satire of Colombian society. In it, two mentally challenged boys are believed to have supernatural powers. During the early 1980s, *Bazar* inspired a television soap opera.

Álvarez Gardeazábal became very active in politics in the 1980s and 1990s, serving as mayor of Tuluá and then governor of the Valle del Cauca Department. As governor, he was investigated for illicit activities, judged guilty in 1999, and spent six years in prison. Since then, he has worked as journalist and broadcaster for an important Colombian radio station.

Jaime A. Orrego

Work By:

Bazaar of the Idiots. Trans. Susan F. Hill and Jonathan Tittler. Pittsburgh, PA:

Latin American Literary Review Press, 1991.

Work About:

Cano, Luis. "Metaforización de la violencia en la nueva narrativa colombiana." *Ciberletras* 14 (Dec. 2005): no pagination. http://www.lehman.cuny.edu/ciberletras/4/cano.htm.

Álvarez Quintero, Serafín (1871–1938) and Álvarez Quintero, Joaquín (1873–1944)

These Spanish playwrights, commonly known as *los Hermanos Quintero* (the Quintero Brothers), were born in Seville province; their collaborative writing career began early and endured until Serafín's death. As adults, both brothers followed their family to Madrid, where theaters gradually began to perform their works. Success followed. Serafín was invited to join Spain's *Real Academia Española in 1920, Joaquín in 1925. After Serafín died, Joaquín continued to write works under both brothers' names.

A prolific team, the two collaborated fully on all aspects of their writing—choosing the theme, outlining plot, and writing dialogue. They authored over 200 works, including one-act plays, full-fledged comedies, and lyrics for *zarzuelas, the musical theater of the period. Plots are generally simple, filled with humor and "real world" language, especially that of Andalusia. No single work stands out as a classic; instead, most plays pleased middle-class Spaniards because they reflected their own hopes, fears, prejudices, and joys. Emblematic of this mind-set was their attitude toward the Spanish Civil War (1936–1939); though both brothers sympathized with the (left-leaning) Republican cause, each chose to remain "neutral" in writings and public comments. After the war, many Quintero plays were adapted for film; about a dozen were produced in Franco's Spain, some more than once.

The brother wrote many popular *sainetes*, humorous one-act plays, usually with both sung and spoken dialogue. These brief pieces showcase the Quintero's facility for language and dialogue, verbal humor, and stage craft. Perhaps their best is *La buena sombra* (1898; Good Shade). Though the plot is conventional, the use of popular stock characters produces a pleasing spectacle. Another brief genre at which the brothers excelled was the *paso*, an even shorter, scene-length play, usually humorous, such as *Mañana de sol* (1905; A Sunny Morning). The plot is simple and direct: octogenarians Laura and Gonzalo meet one sunny morning and both realize that the other was their first great love, though neither lets on that they have recognized the other. They promise to meet the next day, and each leaves happily. Humor resides in the witty dialogue and the way they lie to each other about their past.

Though perhaps best known for their shorter works, the brothers also penned many lighthearted three-act plays. *El centenario* (1910; *A Hundred Years Old*, 1928) is typical. Protagonist Papá Juan plans a party to celebrate his hundredth birthday. All are invited: good, bad, young, and old.

At the party, anarchist Trino meets Papá Juan's great grandchild, Currita. Although the match initially seems doubtful, in the end, viewers sense that Papá Juan will have a great-grandchild, as Trino and Currita fall in love.

Though criticized by many intellectuals of the time for their one-sided portrayal of Spain and Spanish life, their contemporary *Azorín was more forgiving, observing that the brothers perfectly balanced individual and collective sentiment in their works.

Matthew A. Wyszynski

See also Theater in Spain: 1900–1975.

Work By:

Four plays: The Women Have Their Way, A Hundred Years Old, Fortunato, The Lady from Alfaqueque. Trans. Helen and Harley Granville-Barker. Boston: Little, Brown, 1928.

Amazon Theme in Spanish American Literature

For centuries, this massive geographical space has inspired and fascinated writers by its "otherness." Physically, the Amazon River basin is about 4,195 miles long, covering roughly 2,720,000 square miles in area. The basin is divided arbitrarily among the countries of Brazil, Bolivia, Colombia, Ecuador, and Venezuela. It is also an imaginary space linked to myth, starting with its name. According to legend, the conquistador Francisco de Orellana named it after the one-breasted female warriors of classical mythology.

Orellana was searching for El Dorado but instead got lost in a "green hell"; ever since, the Amazon has been associated with extreme danger and highly risky schemes to get rich quickly, usually through gold, rubber, or cocaine.

The Dominican friar Gaspar de Carvajal (1500–1584) first chronicled the expedition of Gonzalo Pizarro and Francisco de Orellana to the Amazon in *Relación del nuevo descubrimiento del famoso río Grande . . .* (1942; Story of the New Discovery of the Famous Grand River . . .). In addition to particulars regarding the expedition, it contains a rich trove of ethnological details regarding the indigenous peoples living along the river banks. Werner Herzog's 1972 movie *Aguirre* aptly illustrates the blinding greed of early explorers.

For Colombian José Eustacio Rivera, the Amazon's hell is the rubber-producing Colombian jungle of his novel *La vorágine* (1924; *The Vortex*, 2001). Venezuelan Rómulo *Gallegos sets his Amazon novel *Canaíma* (1935; Eng. trans., 1988) on the banks of the Orinoco River. In it, Canaíma, the god of evil, engages in a never-ending struggle with Cajuna, the spirit of good, which can be read as an allegory of Venezuela's different cultures and races.

Peruvian Nobel prizewinner Mario *Vargas Llosa continues to equate the rainforest with lawlessness, albeit with more humor. In three of his novels, the Amazon rainforest plays an important part. *La casa verde* (1966; *The Green House*, 2008) is a highly experimental novel about a group of smugglers and an indigenous woman who, after being educated by nuns, becomes both wife of a military sergeant and prostitute in a flourishing jungle brothel. *Pantaleón y las visitadoras* (1973; *Captain Pantoja and the Special Service*, 1978) continues with a similar theme: an army bureaucrat concerned about the urgent "special needs" of soldiers organizes in highly efficient fashion a "special service" of prostitutes, thus deeply embarrassing the Peruvian army. Much more serious is *El Hablador* (1987; *The Storyteller*, 2001), featuring a man who tries to write about the "storytellers" among the Machiguengas, an indigenous Amazonian group threatened with extinction.

The Amazon, however, is not only a green hell; it has also been regarded as an earthly paradise, a pristine wilderness that offers the possibility of redemption and renewal. In this sense, "going primitive," or going to the rainforest and leaving the modern world behind, implies a search for a true home and one's origins, a time before modern troubles arose. Writers like Anglo-Argentine William Henry Hudson, whose 1904 novel *Green Mansions* is set in Guyana (along the border it shares with Venezuela) and Juan León *Mera, author of *Cumandá* (1871; Eng. trans., 2007), continue the intellectual tradition of French intellectuals Jean-Jacques Rousseau and, particularly, François-René de Chateaubriand, who strongly espoused the natural goodness of humanity. The latter's novel *Atalá*, widely popular in Latin America, presented uncorrupted indigenous people living in close contact in a setting reminiscent of paradise, serving to illustrate all that is wrong with Western civilization. Needless to say, neither of these men had ever set foot in a tropical

jungle, but people in Latin America preferred being regarded as idealized natives rather than simple savages.

For Ángel Felicísimo Rojas, in his too-little-known novel *El éxodo de Yangana* (1949; The Exodus of Yangana), Ecuador's jungle offers angry villagers of Yangana an escape from a ruthless landowner and corrupt juridical system and hope for a better life and more just administration as they build a new community. In *Los pasos perdidos* (1953; *The Lost Steps*, 1971) by Cuba's Alejo *Carpentier, an ethnomusicologist travels to South America's jungle to escape his life in a decadent modern city; he first believes he finds inspiration and true love, but ultimately realizes that one cannot travel back in time. An interesting counterpart to the traditional quest for masculine identity is undertaken by the female protagonist in *La Selva* (2000; *The Rainforest*, 2006) by Argentine Alicia Steimberg; she finds spiritual renewal in a clinic in the Brazilian rainforest after having been mentally and physically abused by her drug-addicted son.

Most of the writers mentioned above, however, have little or no direct knowledge of the daily life, history, and economy in the Amazon. Peruvian Santiago Roncagliolo readily admits that when he wrote *El príncipe de los caimanes* (2006; The Prince of Crocodiles) he was living in Spain, had never visited the area, and derived his knowledge from other, perhaps equally fictitious, texts. Bolivian poet, philosopher, and academic Nicomedes Suárez-Araúz is actually from the area and as of 2009 is the director of Smith College's Center for Amazonian Literature and Culture. He learned to read and write at age 11, and maintains his late-blooming literacy taught him a different, more direct relationship with nature. He also is editor of the *Amazonian Literary Review*. In his work, Suárez-Araúz confronts stereotypes about the Amazon provinces and reiterates that the Amazon has large cities, as well as rivers and trees. More than just a symbol, he argues, the region possesses a rich cultural life and history which is often unknown or dismissed by outsiders.

May E. Bletz

Work About:

Sá, Lúcia. *Rain Forest Literatures: Amazonian Texts and Latin American Culture*. Minneapolis: University of Minnesota Press, 2004.

Smith, Anthony. *Explorers of the Amazon*. Chicago: University of Chicago Press, 1994.

Suárez-Araúz, Nicomedes, ed. *Literary Amazonia: Modern Writing by Amazonian Authors*. Gainesville: University Press of Florida, 2007.

Andreu, Blanca (1959–)

Born in the Galician city of A Coruña in northwest Spain, this extraordinary modern poet commands a startling, sophisticated use of language. Her first book, *De una niña de provincias que se vino a vivir a un Chagall* (1980; Of a Provincial Girl Who Came to Life at a Chagall), received the prestigious Adonais poetry award. The collection uses hallucinatory images and surprising twists of grammar to describe the quasi-mystical journey of a female protagonist who flees from a constraining reality to find liberty in an elaborate linguistic world. Influences of the *poéte maudits* (poets who live outside or against social norms), surrealism, and mysticism are evident. Her second text, *Báculo de Babel* (1982; Babel's Staff), attempts to unlock the mysteries of human existence by returning to an archaic poetic language linked to creation. In *Elphistone* (1988), an epic antihero launches himself on a quest for the source of knowledge and power. *La tierra transparente* (2002; The Transparent Land) transmutes the atheist mysticism of her first two collections into a very personal, divine mysticism in which the forest and deer of 16th-century Spanish mystic poet San *Juan de la Cruz become for Andreu the sea and the dolphin.

Despite her culturally influenced and surrealist references, Andreu stands out among the 1980s poetry generation for blending mysticism and a very particular use of language. Her verse combines a postmodern disillusion with the real world with an examination of the nature of language. On one hand, she believes that words can convey meaning to an ever-changing postmodern world; on the other, she fears that language, a self-contained reality, is another illusion within an illusory dream world.

María-Cruz Rodríguez

See also Mysticism and Asceticism in Spain.

Work By:

El sueño oscuro: recopilación 1980–1994. Madrid: Hiperión, 1994.

Work About:

Sherno, Sylvia. "Blanca Andreu: Recovering the Lost Language." *Hispania* 77.3 (1994): 384–92.

Ángel, Albalucía (1939–)

Born in Pereira, Colombia, she is one of the country's few women writers to be read and reviewed at the national and international level. Ángel started writing when Gabriel *García Márquez dominated the literary panorama; nonetheless, she took a totally independent path.

Her early years were indelibly impacted by the violence following *el *Bogotazo* (April 9, 1948). This violence that has plagued Colombia ever since appears as a nightmarish backdrop of her entire work. University studies in philosophy and political science at Bogotá's University of the Andes and extensive travels through progressive European cultures further inform Ángel's profound confrontation with, and critical analysis of, Colombia in her work. Her narrative searches for more equitable interactions between the sexes. *Estaba la pájara pinta sentada en el verde limón* (1975; The Spotted Bird Was Sitting in the Green Lemon Tree) is her best-known novel; it masterfully intertwines two decades of Colombian history with the characters' life experiences. The feminine subject interprets national history from her point of view, equating it to the search for her own identity. The difficulty of this search, according to the narrator, consists of finding "a space for feminine identity in a masculine history." Ángel's

personal and professional interest in feminism during the 1980s is also reflected in the novels *Misiá Señora* (1982; The Missus) and *Las andariegas* (1984; The Travelers).

Inca Molina Rumold

See also Feminism in Spanish America; *Violencia, la*: 1946–1953

Work By:

"The Guerrillero." *Other Fires. Short Fiction by Latin American Women*. Comp., trans. Alberto Manguel. New York: Potter, 1986, 118–21.

Work About:

Lindsay, Claire. "Wish You Weren't Here: The Politics of Travel in Albalucía Ángel's *¡Oh gloria inmarcesible!*" *Studies in Travel Writing* 7. 1 (March 2003): 83–98.

Anzaldúa, Gloria (1942–2004)

This Chicana poet and author was born in the Rio Grande Valley of South Texas, and received her BA from Pan American University and her MA from the University of Texas at Austin. Anzaldúa made contributions to various fields and disciplines. As a creative writer, she published poetry, short stories, autobiographical narratives, and children's books. Her work as a public school teacher led her to publish several bilingual children's books, among them *Prietita and the Ghost Woman/Prietita y la Llorona* (1996).

As a theorist, her works have deeply influenced the redefinition of contemporary *Chicano, female and lesbian, and queer identities. Anzaldúa's interest in cultural hybrids and the contradictory forces that determine identity for women of color in the United States led to the publication of *Borderlands/La Frontera: The New Mestiza* (1987). Included on the 100 Best Books of the Century List by the magazines *Hungry Mind* and *Utne Reader*, it presents, in a variety of styles, reflections on the conditions of existence for those living on the fringes of different cultures, languages, or races. Her use of the terms "mestiza" and "nepantlera" make reference to the existence of people who move in different and multiple worlds, linguistic systems, and social codes.

Begoña Vilouta-Vázquez

See also Chicano Writers; Children's Literature in Spanish in the United States; Transculturation in the Hispanic World.

Work By:

This Bridge Called My Back: Writings by Radical Women of Color. Watertown, MA: Persephone, 1981.

Borderlands/La Frontera: The New Mestiza. San Francisco: Spinsters/Aunt Lute, 1987.

Making Face, Making Soul/Haciendo Caras: Creative and Critical Perspectives by Feminists of Color. San Francisco: Aunt Lute Foundation Books, 1990.

Work About:

Davis-Undiano, Robert. "Mestizos Critique the New World: Vasconcelos, Anzaldúa, and Anaya." *Literature Interpretation Theory* 11.2 (2000): 117–42.

Hernández, Ellie. "Re-Thinking Margins and Borders: An Interview with Gloria Anzaldúa." *Discourse* 18.1–2 (1996): 7–15.

Aponte Alsina, Marta (1945–)

This Puerto Rican writer, translator, teacher, and editor can arguably be considered a neofeminist. Since she started publishing later in life, she does not belong to a particular literary generation. Although elements of Puerto Rican identity are fundamental to her subjects, her characters are also universal.

Aponte privileges marginality's point of view, often choosing society's outcasts as protagonists. Her four novels are *Angélica furiosa* (1994; Furious Angelica), *El Cuarto Rey Mago* (1996; The Fourth Wise Man), *Vampiresas* (2004; Female Vampires) and *Sexto Sueño* (2007; Sixth Dream). Dr. Violeta Cruz, narrator of the historically grounded *Sexto Sueño*, embalms bodies and composes musical boleros; while dissecting exiled Puerto Rican murderer Nathan Leopold, she tries to reconstruct his life and friendship with Sammy Davis Jr. In *Vampiresas*, protagonist Laura Damiani, who works as a messenger, befriends three older women who are vampires. Laura falls in love with the vampire lifestyle and with the vampire Gerardo, and decides to become one herself.

Aponte has also written critical essays and three short story collections: *La casa de la loca* (1999; The Crazy's House), *La casa de la loca y otros relatos* (2001; The Madwoman's House and Other Short Stories) and *Fúgate* (2005; Escape).

Fabiola Fernández Salek

See also Puerto Rico: History, Culture, and Literature.

Work By:

Sexto sueño. Madrid: Veintisiete Letras, 2007.

Work About:

De Maeseneer, Rita. "El cuento puertorriqueño a finales de los noventa." *Casa de las Américas* 224 (July–September 2001): 112–19.

Rivera-Villegas, Carmen. " 'La loca de la casa' de Marta Aponte Alsina: Reinvenciones románticas de un canon fundacional." *Confluencia* 23.1 (2007): 62–71.

Apóstol, Cecilio (1877–1938)

Together with Fernando María Guerrero and the Palma brothers (José and Rafael), this poet and journalist was involved in the Philippine–American War (1899–1902) as a staff member of the Emilio Aguinaldo government newspaper *La Independencia*. His anti-U.S. poems "¡Al Yankee!" (1899; To the Yankee) and "Al héroe nacional" (c. 1899; To the National Hero) are much anthologized. "¡Al Yankee!" expresses the anger of a writer who witnesses his country's destruction by the superior American military might. "Al héroe nacional" represents one of many poems celebrating Philippine national

hero José *Rizal in Apóstol's lone anthology. He is one of the literati who helped create the Rizal cult in Philippine literature in Spanish.

After the war, Apóstol continued to write poetry while engaging in politics, practicing law, and serving as a prosecutor in the colonial bureaucracy. Three years after his death, fellow writer Jaime de Veyra, who had collected his friend's poems, released them in a volume titled *Pentélicas* (1941; From Mt. Pentelicus). This publication showcases the classical education of Apóstol and his generation. There is abundant use of Greco-Roman motifs, a style which combined well with Nicaraguan Rubén *Darío's *modernismo* poetry style. The anthology contains many laudatory poems about different Philippine personalities, particularly Rizal. Some poems celebrate Spain as cultural mother of the Philippines, a representation differentiated from Spain as colonial master.

Wystan de la Peña

Work By:

Pentélicas. 2nd ed. Manila: Hispano-Filipina, 1950.

Arce, Manuel José (1935–1985)

Born in Guatemala, this remarkably versatile author of poetry, plays, and newspaper collaborations fought censorship for some 25 years before being forced into exile in 1979 under Guatemala's repressive military rule. Arce started his literary career as a poet but became deeply involved in popular theater as an actor, director, and drama professor. He believed theater provided a better way of communicating with large, uneducated audiences when promoting social change. Among his grotesque pieces, *Delito, condena y ejecución de una gallina* (1968; Crime, Punishment, and Execution of a Hen) remains a benchmark in Guatemalan drama, combining sarcasm, humor, and political insight. Arce also staged a successful adaptation of Miguel Ángel *Asturias's *Torotumbo*, using elements from Guatemalan indigenous and nonindigenous popular theater.

His poetry centers on love, showing his mastery of both traditional rhythms and nonconventional poetic devices; in 1978, Arce published a selection of his verse in *Palabras alusivas al acto y otros poemas con el tema del amor* (Words Allusive to the Event and Other Poems with the Theme of Love). However, in *Los episodios del vagón de carga* (1971; The Episodes on the Freight Train Wagon) he explores social issues, also the main concern of his plays. Arce's daily newspaper collaborations have been collected in *Diario de un escribiente* (1979; 1988) (Journal of a Scribe). He died in Paris.

Claudia S. García

Work By:

Anclado en esta tierra (antología). Guatemala: Editorial Cultura, 2007.

Diario de un escribiente. Guatemala: Piedra Santa, 2006.

Work About:

Obregón, Osvaldo. "Entrevista a Manuel José Arce." *Gestos* 3.5 (1988): 105–15.

Arciniegas, Germán (1900–1999)

This prolific, polemical Colombian intellectual was hailed in New York City by The Americas Foundation as "Man of the Americas" in 1986 by for his radical revisioning of Latin American history. A controversial historian, journalist, and essayist, his writing rejected European colonialist attitudes and credited the Americas—where settlers were freed from European notions of class, race, and social differences that stifled discovery and creativity—with reinvigorating European culture and ushering in the modern world.

Beginning in 1928, for seven decades he wrote editorials for *El Tiempo* newspaper, as well as journalistic pieces published in European and U.S. newspapers. Arciniegas undertook diplomatic missions in Europe and Venezuela and taught at Columbia University during the 10 years he lived in exile in New York City (1947–1957). In his first book, *El estudiante de la mesa redonda* (1932; Student at the Round Table), idealistic students filled with revolutionary passions are seated at a table in "the tavern of history" and visited by such figures as Erasmus, Simón *Bolívar, and other giants from history in a discussion about "the problem of America." Cobo Borda notes that this same topic and situation, enriched by a lifetime of study, informs Arciniegas's posthumously published novel *La taberna de la historia* (2000; The Tavern of History). Here, conversations about America's identity involve Queen Isabella, Christopher Columbus, Amerigo Vespucci, an indigenous American, Pope Alexander VI, and Vasco Núñez de Balboa.

Entre la libertad y el miedo (1952; Between Freedom and Fear) discusses the rise of dictators in Latin America, and what made it possible. Dictators reacted by banning his books, and Dominican Republic dictator Rafael Trujillo placed him on a hit list. Among a long list of significant texts, Ambrus observes that his masterpiece is probably *Biografía del Caribe* (1945; *Caribbean: Sea of the New World*, 1986). Stretching from the arrival of Columbus to the present, it depicts colorful pirates, conquerors, freedom fighters, and ordinary citizens through five tumultuous centuries of political, economic, and social development.

Maureen Ihrie

Work By:

Caribbean: Sea of the New World. Trans. Harriet de Onís. Miami: Ian Randle, 2004.
Why America? 500 Years of a Name. The Life and Times of Amerigo Vespucci. Trans. Jimmy Weiskopf. 2nd ed. Bogotá: Villegas, 2002.

Work About:

Ambrus, Steven. "Germán Arciniegas: Guardian of Our Distinct History." *Américas* (English ed.) 49.3 (May–June 1997): 40–45.
Cobo Borda, Juan Gustavo. "Carta de Colombia. Su libro póstumo o la resurrección de Arciniegas." *Cuadernos Hispanoamericanos* 608 (Feb. 2001): 87–90.

Arenas, Reinaldo (1943–1990)

Persecuted and imprisoned because of his homosexuality, Reinaldo Arenas left his native Cuba for the United States during the 1980 Mariel boatlift. Ten years later, incapacitated by AIDS, Arenas committed suicide shortly after completing his autobiography, *Antes que anochezca* (1992). A critical and commercial success, the English translation, *Before Night Falls* (1993), became a popular film in 2000. An uninhibited, homoerotic text, this and many of Arenas's works were published and acclaimed in French translation before the original Spanish versions appeared in print. *El mundo alucinante* (1969; *The Ill-Fated Peregrinations of Fray Servando*, 1987), won the 1969 prize for best foreign novel in France. Before his self-exile, Arenas defiantly subverted Cuban censorship by smuggling and publishing his works abroad. His literary production did not conform to a national literary aesthetic that advanced the Castro government's ideals.

As a social, political, and literary rebel, Arenas's fiction, poetry, and essays challenge systems of power that inhibit individual expression. Best known for his prose, Arenas wrote a series of five novels which he called a *pentagonía* to stress the agony which the characters suffer under oppressive authoritarian systems. Intratextuality (relationships between the different parts of a text) marks the *pentagonía*, where mutating characters reappear in different narratives that contain multiple authorial voices. Arenas's fiction also utilizes intertextuality, repeatedly alluding to well-known literary works or creating a parodic version of a classic.

Rebeca Rosell Olmedo

See also Mariel Writers Generation; Torture in Modern Spanish American Literature.

Work By:

Arenas, Reinaldo. *The Color of Summer*. Trans. Andrew Hurley. New York: Viking, 2000.

Work About:

Soto, Francisco. *Reinaldo Arenas*. New York: Twayne, 1998.

Aréstegui, Narciso (1823–1869)

This Peruvian novelist, lawyer, prefect, and university professor ardently defended the disenfranchised native Indian majority and national industry in Cuzco, his birthplace. He won national acclaim for his first novel, *El padre Horán. Escenas de la vida en el Cuzco* (1848; Priest Horan. Scenes of Life in Cuzco), published in installments in Lima's *El Comercio* shortly before *Peru embraced economic liberalism. Considered the earliest *indigenista* novel in Republican Peru for its liberal denunciation of head taxes and priestly abuse, and for its sympathetic depiction of urban indigenous poor, the novel also offers a significant model for an emerging non-aristocratic identity. Aréstegui used the opposing forces of enlightened civilization and sensationalist melodrama and adapted

representational strategies of sentimental *costumbrismo*, *romanticism, and realism to produce a civic citizen that would regenerate a region ravaged by civil wars, exploitative labor relations, and unrestrained free trade.

Hard work, selflessness, benevolent interethnic sympathy, enlightened Christianity, Hispanic culture, industrialism, and ambivalence toward the marketplace were key components in this civic vision. While paternalistic when seen in historical terms, Aréstegui's vision constituted an ethical regional response to economic liberalism and informed the ways in which writers like Juan Bustamante and Clorinda *Matto imagined Andean modernity throughout the 19th century.

Soledad Gálvez

See also Indigenismo in Spanish American Literature.

Work By:

El padre Horán. Escenas de la vida en el Cuzco. Lima: Universo, 1969.

Work About:

Kristal, Efraín. *The Andes Viewed from the City. Literary and Political Discourse on the Indian in Peru (1848–1930)*. New York: Peter Lang, 1987.

Arévalo Martínez, Rafael (1884–1975)

This distinguished Guatemalan short story writer, poet, novelist, and diplomat was an editor of and contributor to literary magazines since his teenage years and director of Guatemala's National Library from 1926 to 1946, when he became the nation's representative before the Pan American Union in Washington, D.C., for a year.

Arévalo Martínez is most recognized for his so-called "psychozoological short stories," in which characters appear to have complex and often contradictory personalities resembling certain animals. Among his most celebrated works are such short stories as "El hombre que parecía un caballo" (1914; "The Man Who Resembled a Horse," 1915), which portrayed Colombian poet Porfirio Barba Jacob, who was allegedly unpolished, self-centered and amoral, but also elegant and attractive. In "Las fieras del trópico" (1922; Tropical Beasts) the figure of the tiger described the then-dictator of Guatemala, Estrada Cabrera (1898–1920), who was clean and smooth, but also very dangerous. This last short story belongs to the popular genre of "dictatorship literature" in Latin America.

Ana Serra

Work By:

"El hombre que parecía un caballo." *The Oxford Book of Latin American Short Stories*. New York: Oxford University Press, 1997, 131–41.

Work About:

Rosser, Harry L. "Reflections in an Equine Eye: Arévalo Martínez's 'Psycho-Zoology.' " *Latin American Literary Review* 14 (1986): 21–30.

Salgado, María. *Rafael Arévalo Martínez.* Boston: Twayne, 1979.

Argentina: History, Culture, and Literature

Although viewed as the most European nation of Latin America, Argentina is a country where heterogeneity has been suppressed. Authoritarian practices have attempted to eliminate differences to fulfill the ideals of modernization and global capitalism. Now estimated at 40 million people, Argentina's demographics are the result of waves of European immigration, notably Italians and Spanish, between the mid-19th and 20th centuries, mixed with indigenous, African and Creole populations and, most recently, such other South American nationalities as Bolivians and Paraguayans. The long-held view that Argentina was an empty land was based upon the encounter with nomadic peoples (Pampas, Guaraníes, Mapuches, Yamanas, etc.) by 16th-century Spanish conquistadors arriving at the River Plate. Founding father Domingo Faustino *Sarmiento proclaimed the nation's need to populate the land, asserting in his classic *Facundo* (1845; Eng. trans., 2003), that Argentina's curse was its vast, empty land holdings.

Founded in 1536, Buenos Aires remained marginal to the Spanish Empire until the creation of the Viceroyalty of the Provinces of Río de la Plata in 1776. However, Napoleon's invasion of Spain soon weakened the Empire, precipitating the fall of colonial rule. Creole leaders voted for removal of the viceroy on May 25, 1810, after the citizens of Buenos Aires defeated two British invasions (1806 and 1807) without help from the Spanish military. By then, the city was a dynamic center of commercial and cultural activity. Connections with the motherland provided the elite class with access to European authors and revolutionary ideas.

Yet it would take José de San Martín, the Creole son of a Spanish officer, to end the colonial order. His liberation army, which was 40 percent Afro-Argentine, defeated the Spaniards in lands that would become Argentina, Chile, and Peru. Independence was declared in the northwestern city of Tucumán, on July 9, 1816. Nevertheless, a bloody struggle raged for four decades between the region of Buenos Aires, now able to participate in the world market, and the remnants of colonial enclaves still subsisting in the interior. In 1835, the *caudillo* (political leader) Juan Manuel de Rosas seized control of Buenos Aires in what would become Argentina's longest and most contentious dictatorship. The country remained divided between two distinct political factions, Federalist and Unitarist. While the former fought for provincial autonomy, the latter advocated for a centralized system led by Buenos Aires.

Rosas's Federalist rule exacerbated this antagonism: his party felt that the Unitarists allied themselves with foreign interests and scorned the lower classes, while Unitarists viewed Federalists as backwards, tyrannical, and strongly tied to the needs of *gauchos and Africans. Testimony to the Unitarists' contempt of Rosas and his followers is romantic intellectual Esteban *Echeverría's portrayal of the physical and metaphorical frontiers dividing the population of Buenos Aires, *El matadero* (written 1838–1840, published 1871; *The Slaughterhouse*, 1980). Echeverría's is a passionate account of the torture and murder of an educated young Unitarist by a gang of gaucho and black supporters of Rosas. A graphic portrayal of violence, the text reveals the frontier as a catalyst for social and racial conflicts that permeate future realities and literary representations of Argentina. The ferocity of these persistent conflicts gradually diminishes with the signing of the Constitution in 1853. Concurring with Sarmiento's earlier admonition, one important political thinker of the day, Juan Bautista *Alberdi, declared that "to govern is to populate."

Following the establishment of the republic, the remaining Amerindian population was virtually wiped out through military campaigns, notably after the last "Campaign to the Desert" (1876–1880) which displaced or killed the remaining indigenous peoples of the Pampas and eastern Patagonia. In allusion to the thousands of disappeared of the recent military dictatorship (1976–1983), contemporary writer David *Viñas called Amerindians the first "disappeared" inhabitants of Argentina. On the other hand, gauchos (Mestizos of European and indigenous ancestry) did manage to adapt to the needs of modernization. José *Hernández's poem *Martín Fierro* (1872, 1879; *The Gaucho Martín Fierro*, 1935) assumes the voice of a gaucho outlaw who rebels against the state system of oppression and trickery that forces him into the military draft. The second part of the poem testifies to the assimilation of this social group, as it shows how Fierro mends his behavior and complies with the rules of modern society.

By 1880, Argentina had consummated the process of national organization. Julio A. Roca, one of the "heroes" of the military campaign against the Amerindians and president between 1880 and 1886, led the country into order and progress and paved the way for a grandiose, oligarchic conclusion to the century. Sarmiento's dream of a European-like nation was becoming a reality for the ruling class by 1910, a century after independence.

Progress, however, was not even; except for specific pockets, the economic boom excluded most of the interior provinces. Millions of poor Europeans arrived at the port of Buenos Aires following promises of opportunity that were in fact scarce outside Buenos Aires province and a few urban centers. In the city, social mobility was the exception, as most immigrants either joined the incipient working class or were left out altogether. These latter groups inhabited the *conventillos* (tenements) and precarious housing of the city's outskirts, such as La Boca neighborhood, whose dockworkers were immortalized in the brush of avant-garde painter Benito Quinquela Martín (1890–1977). Ironically, this working class *barrio* is today a major attraction for international tourism, though at the time only poor health, prostitution, and delinquency reigned. Such was the environment that gave birth to Río de la Plata's world-famous tango music and dance in the 1880s. Spain's Andalusian flamenco, Cuban habanera, and milonga (an Afro-Argentine dance) influenced the early musical developments of tango, which would later become a complex dance and music accompanied by a national canon of *lunfardo* (slang) poetry.

The turn of the century gave birth to the myth of Argentina as a new, modern nation, with a capital regarded as the Paris of South America. The capital became a sanctuary for architects, builders, and artists who would soon turn the *gran aldea* (large village) into a sophisticated, cosmopolitan center. Lola Mora's monumental sculptures inspired in Italian neoclassicism, or the Barolo Palace (1923) by Italian architect Mario Palanti, who took inspiration from Dante's *Divine Comedy* to create the building, are illustrative of this period. The economic expansion and political participation of this era enabled social mobility and the formation of a large middle class. The mandatory, secret, and "universal" vote was established in 1912, although women's suffrage would wait until 1947, when Juan Domingo Perón's wife, Eva Duarte, granted women this right.

The first decades of the century were propitious for an incipient feminist writing, such as Alfonsina *Storni's, to flourish. It was also the time of avant-garde poetry and art. Such writers as Oliverio *Girondo, Jorge Luis *Borges and Leopoldo *Marechal published in the journal *Martín Fierro* (1924–1927), while Xul Solar, Emilio Pettoruti, and Antonio Berni absorbed European surrealism, futurism, cubism and dadaism and incorporated local realities and inventive esthetics to create unique Latin American art forms. Public schools enabled the children of immigrant families and the poor of the provinces to be educated under an increasingly homogenizing concept of citizenship.

In 1930, General José F. Uriburu ousted Unión Cívica Radical (UCR) president Hipólito Yrigoyen from office, inaugurating a series of military coups that crushed the dreams of democracy and growth for decades. A major turning point in Argentine history came with the arrival of Perón to the political arena in 1943. One of the most multifaceted phenomenon in the country's history, *peronismo* was based on the alliance between Perón and the unions, and on the empowerment of the working class. His wife, affectionately called Evita by workers but despised by the upper classes, played a major role in implementing welfare policies and building the symbolic forces that sustained the movement through time, changing Argentine politics forever. In his novel *Santa Evita* (1995; Eng. trans., 1996), Tomás Eloy *Martínez portrays the almost religious devotion that she drew from the lower classes. Often accused of being authoritarian and sympathetic to European fascism, the Peróns awakened a passionate hatred in two of Argentina's best-known writers, Julio *Cortázar and Borges.

This social and political schism continued after Perón was overthrown in 1955, and found new expressions in the ensuing national and global revolutionary environment of the 1960s and 1970s. Perón's 18-year exile and political proscription led to the formation of a Peronist resistance and creation of the left-wing Montoneros guerrilla group. Political turmoil was a breeding ground for artistic and cultural revivalism, and public universities included the radical thinking of Jean-Paul Sartre, Karl Marx, and Ernesto "Che" *Guevara in their curriculum. Founded in Buenos Aires in 1963, the Di Tella Institute hosted pop art, happenings, and cultural experimentation. In May 1969, in the so-called *Cordobazo*, students and union workers organized a series of militant demonstrations in the city of Córdoba to protest the repressive military government of Juan Carlos Onganía (1966–1970).

After Perón's death in 1974, an escalation of violence between right-wing death squads and left-wing guerrilla groups led to the military coup of 1976. The 1976–1983 military dictatorship was the most brutal period in Argentine history, with 30,000 people disappeared and thousands tortured, imprisoned, and exiled. In 1982, the military tried to gain support for their then-discredited regime by invading the contested British Falkland Islands (*Malvinas). The strategy backfired when British Prime Minister Margaret Thatcher sent her navy to defend the islands. Popular discontent after Argentina's defeat forced the military to call for elections in 1983.

Art and literature produced under the dictatorship speaks of violence and brutality. Some artists openly denounced state terrorism, while others used metaphors and allegories to convey horrifying realities. In broad daylight, the mothers and grandmothers of the *Plaza de Mayo* wore white shawls and raised banners with pictures of their missing children, and later became major agents in the transition toward democracy. Raúl Alfonsín, of the moderate Unión Cívica Radical party, was popularly elected in December 1983.

The desire for political consensus and the preservation of democratic institutions after decades of turmoil and brutality replaced the revolutionary dreams of the 1960s and 1970s. In an unprecedented move in the history of human rights violations, and with strong support from civic organizations, Alfonsín took the military to trial in 1985. But, under pressure from the armed forces, he soon approved laws to put an end to trials and forgive low-ranking officers. In 1989 and 1990, President Carlos Menem signed final amnesties to free all convicted officers, causing outrage and massive protests.

Since their initial gathering in 1977, the Mothers of the Plaza de Mayo have continued to march every Thursday around the Mayo Pyramid, in Buenos Aires's main square, to demand the "Apparition with Life" (*aparición con vida*) of their children. These mothers, along with the Grandmothers of the Plaza de Mayo, still search for grandchildren born in detention and extermination camps or kidnapped along with their parents. With help from other organizations and by pressuring the legislature to pass laws preserving the right to identity, they have managed to locate close to 90 disappeared children. Since the mid-1990s, the members of the organization HIJOS (Sons and Daughters for Identity and Justice and Against

Forgetfulness and Silence) have looked for missing siblings and vindicated the struggle of their disappeared parents. In strong opposition to the conciliatory policies of amnesties and pardons, they have organized *escraches* (public denunciations) against military and police officers who have remained free despite violating human rights.

Under Menem's two subsequent presidencies (1989–1999), Peronism experienced its most startling metamorphosis. Though the old populist slogans appealed to the same class of dispossessed, the neoliberal policies that he implemented followed a divergent path. His government continued the economic liberalization and privatization of public resources undertaken by the military juntas. This restored the country's financial credibility even as it dragged millions of people below the poverty line. This era saw the transformation of citizens into consumers. Investigative journalism grew in prominence, as corruption, scandals, and violence entered the daily discourse and new identity groups based on gender, sexual orientation, ethnicity, and class gained voice.

As the 2001 economic collapse drew people out onto the streets, new art forms involving the occupancy of public spaces emerged. After president Fernando de la Rúa was forced to resign by popular uprisings in December 2001, and following a series of short-term presidencies, Néstor Kirchner was elected in 2003. A renewed struggle for human rights has been ongoing since then, and more so since his wife, Cristina Fernández de Kirchner, took office in 2007. Literature, films, and TV have followed the revival by addressing events of the last military dictatorship in richer, original, and more mature ways.

Julieta Vitullo

See also Appendix B, for other entries related to Argentina.

Work About:

Foster, David William, Melissa Fitch, and Darrel B. Lockhart. *Culture and Customs of Argentina*. Westport, CT: Greenwood, 1998.

Nouseilles, Gabriela and Graciela Montaldo, eds. *The Argentina Reader. History, Culture, Politics*. Durham and London: Duke University Press, 2002.

Argentine Novel after the Recovery of Democracy: 1983–2006

Argentine fiction written after the last military dictatorship (1976–1983) can be classified into two major strands: one which started during the 1960s and continues to this day, and another that began in the mid-1990s and has strengthened in recent years.

The first strand is characterized by allusion and allegory, the two narrative strategies inherited from the roughly 1940s anti-Peronist fiction written in collaboration by Jorge Luis *Borges and Bioy Casares. These two strategies required an engaged reader capable of deciphering veiled connections to the historical moment. Similarly, Argentine literature during the 1976–1983 dictatorship could only allude to political

repression, torture, and assassination. Paradigmatic novels of that dictatorship, such as Ricardo *Piglia's *Respiración artificial* (1980; *Artificial Respiration*, 1994), encouraged emerging writers to pursue a more indirect rhetoric. By the 1990s, the allusive style began to wane, and writers started to reconnect literary discourse to social identity. New readings of such authors as Osvaldo Lamborghini, who in the 1970s used political jargon and psychoanalysis in their work, encouraged the new direction.

In the second strand (1990–present), narrative allusion makes space for a literary discourse more interested in engaging directly with history, politics, and reality. By stressing multiple narrative voices and the coexistence of different narrative times, fiction becomes more realistic. Memory becomes a central topic in a literary discourse that addresses the time before the last dictatorship as well as the impact of the past on the present, as in Rodolfo Fogwill's novels. Faced with the social unrest of late 2001, literature began to represent what had until then been unnamed realities. Such novels as Florencia Abbate's *El grito* (2004; The Scream) reference past traumas that resonate with present-day uncertainties; and such texts as Sergio Chejfec's *Boca de lobo* (2000; The Wolf's Mouth) reference Argentine history to question the notion of community.

Karina Vázquez

Work By:

Abbate, Florencia. *El grito*. Buenos Aires: Emecé, 2004.

Chejfec, Sergio. *El aire*. Buenos Aires: Aguilar-Alfaguara, 1992.

Fogwill, Rodolfo. *En otro orden de cosas.* Barcelona. Mondadori, 2001.

Fogwill, Rodolfo. *La experiencia sensible.* Barcelona: Mondadori, 2001.

Fogwill, Rodolfo. *Vivir afuera.* Buenos Aires: Sudamericana, 1998.

Gusmán, Luis. *Ni muerto has perdido tu nombre.* Buenos Aires: Sudamericana, 2003.

Gusmán, Luis. *Villa.* Buenos Aires: Alfaguara, 1995.

Lamborghini, Osvaldo. *Novelas y cuentos.* Buenos Aires: Sudamericana, 2003.

Martínez, Tomás Eloy. *The Perón Novel.* Trans. Helen Lane. New York: Vintage, 1998.

Saer, Juan José. *Nobody Nothing Never.* Trans. Helen Lane. London and New York: Serpent's Tail, 1993.

Shua, Ana María. *Patient.* Trans. David William Foster. Pittsburgh: Latin American Literary Review, 1997.

Work About:

Avellaneda, Andrés. "Recordando con ira: Estrategias ideológicas y ficcionales argentinas a fin de siglo." *Revista Iberoamericana* 202 (January–March 2003): 119–35.

Reatti, Fernando. *Nombrar lo innombrable. Violencia política y novela argentina. 1975–1985.* Buenos Aires: Legasa, 1992.

Argentine Theater by Women: 1900 to Present

Argentina boasts a significant theatrical tradition, but the majority of literary anthologies make scarce mention of female playwrights. In the first decades of the century, several female playwrights produced mainstream plays. Amelia Monti contributed *sainetes* (farces) like *El divorcio de Chichilo* (1924; Chichilo's Divorce), while Lola Pita Martínez wrote *alta comedia* plays like *Marcela* (1922), in which the heroine is abandoned by her bankrupt husband, and his actions ruin her life, forcing her to commit suicide. Other women dramatists like Salvadora Medina Onrubia and Alfonsina *Storni addressed more radical topics. Medina Onrubia's writing is recognized for its combination of feminist and anarchist views. Her first play, *Almafuerte* (1914; Strong Spirit), illustrates how the economic and social system victimizes women. Storni wrote numerous children's plays and several adult dramas. Her farce *Cimbelina en el 1900 y pico* (1931; Cymbeline in the Early 1900s) recreates the same stock characters as Shakespeare's text but presents them under the lens of new cultural and social conditions.

Even though such writers as Cristina Verrier, Maria Luisa Rubertino, and María Elena Walsh staged plays during the 1950s, it was not until the 1960s when, thanks to Griselda *Gambaro, women achieved widespread recognition as playwrights. Gambaro's play *El desatino* (1965; The Blunder), presents the passive compliance with which many Argentines accepted military repression. The work created strong controversy among followers of realism and those who support theater of the absurd, in which logical premises are stretched to patently nonsensical consequences. Similarly, *Viejo* *matrimonio* (1965; Old Married Couple) questions marital relationships. *Los siameses* (1967; The Siamese) reveals through odd brotherly relationships the human propensity to either be a victim or to victimize others; *El campo* (1968; *The Camp*, 2008) also formed part in the "realism versus absurd" discussions.

At the beginning of the 1970s, several authors mixed realism with political criticism in their plays. *Soldados y soldaditos* (1972; Soldiers and Little Soldiers) by Aida Bortnik offers a pacifist analysis of the military profession throughout history; in *El guardagente* (1970; The People Keeper), by Diana Raznovich, the main character rents a closet as living space to several tenants. Because of the political situation under the military dictatorship, these women writers eschewed themes related to women. Another good example of political theater is found in María Escudero's Córdoba-based theater collective *Libre teatro libre* (The Free Theater of Freedom), founded in 1969 with a strong left-wing political orientation. Many of its members were arrested or killed, and others, as well as Escudero, went into exile.

During 1981 and 1982, many of these female dramatists participated in the *Teatro abierto (Open Theater) movement that had been established to create a voice opposed to military repression. In Aida Bortnik's *Papa Querido* (1981; Dear Father), criticism of repressive power represents an example of the first cycle of this movement. Beatriz Mosquera participated in the movement's second cycle; her *Despedida en el lugar* (1982; Goodbye in the Place) creates a metaphoric drama in which a triumphant authoritarianism destroys both individuals and governmental institutions.

In the 1980s, particularly in Buenos Aires, *teatro joven*, or underground theater, appears. Playwrights like Andrea Garrote, Eva Halac, Gabriela Izcovich, Florencia Saraví Medina, and Susana Torres Molina are considered part of this group. They have enriched Argentine drama with their concern for "theatrical performance" and gender issues. They often present works in nonconventional locations like bars or clubs, and they use eclectic combinations of such performance elements as acrobatics, dance, mime, or Japanese theater. Cristina Escofet also belongs to this group because of her feminist themes and innovative use of dance and music in plays like *Las que aman hasta morir* (1985; Those Who Love until They Die), *Nunca usarás medias de seda* (1989; You Will Never Use Silk Stockings), and *Señoritas en concierto* (1993; Señoritas in Concert). Many of these authors continue to perform these older plays, as well as new ones.

With the democratic transition in 1983, a new theater emerged, one concerned with defining the social and cultural patterns created by gender differences. Many of these authors use their writings to transgress restrictions imposed by society. For example, Diana Raznovich's play *De atrás para adelante* (1993; Rear Entry), parodies a Jewish father with a transsexual son to reflect on the prejudices of a traditional family toward a child who is different.

In the 1990s, many new female playwrights were recognized, as well as others from previous decades, such as Adriana

Genta and Patricia Zangano, who began writing in the second half of the 1980s. Despite the recognition they have received, they still do not form part of the commercial or "official" theatrical arena. In response to this exclusion, these playwrights have created a didactic type of theater, and are very active in the Buenos Aires theatrical arena. They conduct workshops, participate in discussions about theater, and write and direct plays that depict the evolving relationship between women and society.

María R. Matz

See also Feminism in Spanish America.

Work By:

Defiant Acts: Four Plays by Diana Raznovich/Actos desafiantes: cuatro obras de Diana Raznovich. Ed. Diana Taylor and Victoria Martínez. Trans. Victoria Martínez, Lydia Ramírez, and Nora Glickman. Lewisburg, PA: Bucknell University Press. 2002.

Gambaro, Griselda. *Information for Foreigners: Three Plays by Griselda Gambaro*. Trans. Marguerite Feitlowitz. Evanston, IL: Northwestern University Press, 1992.

Seven Plays by Argentine Playwright Susana Torres Molina (Strange Toy, That's All That, Mystic Union, Sirens' Song, Paradises Lost, Zero, and She). Trans., intro. María Claudia André and Barbara Younoszai. Lewiston, NY: Mellen, 2006.

Work About:

Larson, Catherine, and Margarita Vargas, eds. *Latin American Women Dramatists.*

Theater, Texts, and Theories. Bloomington: Indiana University Press, 1998.

Arguedas, Alcides (1879–1946)

This Bolivian historian and writer participated actively in politics. A member of the Liberal Party, he served as senator, congressman, minister of agriculture, and diplomat in Europe and America. His five-volume *Historia General de Bolivia* (1922; General History of Bolivia) represents the first effort to systematize Bolivian history.

Arguedas's two major literary works are the essay *Pueblo enfermo* (1909; Ill People) and *Raza de bronce* (1919; Race of Bronze), one of Spanish America's first indigenist novels. The two texts present complementary searches for a national identity. *Raza de bronce* depicts the unjust *hacienda* system, but also ridicules *indio* (Indian) traditions and portrays the *indio*'s perceived immorality. The novel is divided into two parts: *El valle* (The Valley), which describes the life of Abigail and his future wife Wuata Wuara as they journey to a hacienda with other Aymaras to procure seeds; and *El Yermo* (The Wasteland) which describes the abuses inflicted on *indios* by Pantoja, the *hacienda* owner, and civil, clerical, and military authorities. When Pantoja and his friends rape and kill Wuata Wuara, the *indios*, led by Abigail, revolt and kill their oppressors. Also by Arguedas, the novel *Wuata Wuara* (1904) was for years considered a primitive draft for *Raza de bronce*, until 1988, when it was published as a work in its own right by Lorente Medina. Critics believe, and Arguedas himself has stated, that it is as if he had written the same novel twice. The plot and protagonists of the two texts are identical; important differences are that in *Wuata Wuara*, details are much more bloody, and the landowners are from European heritage, while in *Raza de bronce* they are *cholos* (persons of mixed European and Indian lineage).

Pueblo enfermo offers a visceral critique of the *cholo* as a contemptible individual with inherent negative traits like laziness, and of the *caudillos* (populist leaders). According to Arguedas's positivist psychology and Eurocentric vision (product of his studies in Paris and prolonged European stays) the *cholo* is the source of the country's degeneration.

After losing the Acre region to Brazil in 1903 and the seacoast to Chile (territories conceded in 1904), Bolivian identity was left in a fragile state as it searched for a new identity. Arguedas felt compelled to construct such an identity and to denounce what he considered the country's social illnesses. At the same time, he judged the nation to be doomed as a modern state, due to its harsh environment and the *cholo*'s dominance in the Bolivian population. He held a more sympathetic, although paternalistic, view of the *indio*; portraying him as "the other," defined by hostile surroundings, he denounced the *indio*'s oppression, claiming that the indigenous population was a needed element of future nation building. Arguedas's ambivalent influence is palpable in modern-day Bolivia, where his pessimistic definition of nation and prejudiced postcolonial notions persist.

Fabiola Fernández Salek

See also Indigenismo in Spanish American Literature.

Work By:

Raza de bronce. Pittsburgh: University of Pittsburgh, 1989.

Work About:

Paz-Soldán, Edmundo. "The Indigenous Writer as a (Mis)Translator of Cultures: The Case of Alcides Arguedas." *Voice-Overs: Translation and Latin American Literature*. Ed. Daniel Balderston and Marcy E. Schwartz. Albany: State University of New York Press, 2002, 170–81.

Arguedas, José María (1911–1969)

This Peruvian anthropologist and novelist is one of the most celebrated defenders of Peru's indigenous and mestizo cultures. His first novel, *Yawar Fiesta* (1941), represents the indigenous opposition that fueled peasant movements of the 1950s and the breakup of landowner rule. It was followed by *El Sexto* (1961; Sexto Prison), which takes inspiration from the author's 1937 participation in student protests and subsequent detention in Sexto prison. Arguedas's most powerful work, *Los ríos profundos* (1961; *Deep Rivers*, 1997), offers a poetic portrayal of unequal power relationships in a country struggling to overcome its mid-20th-century feudalistic conditions.

The same year Arguedas became director of Peru's National Museum of History, he published *Todas las sangres* (1964; All Bloods), which examines Peru's goal of becoming a capitalist society and its impact on indigenous populations. His last, unfinished novel, *El zorro de arriba y el zorro de abajo* (pub. 1971; *The Fox from Above and the Fox from Below*, 2000) mixes narration of events in Chimbote and that of a personal struggle against depression.

Until his suicide, Arguedas was the nation's most impassioned advocate of Quechua culture and language, challenging the powerful ideologies of "modernization" and "national integration" that predicated the erasure of Peru's indigenous past. His writing extended beyond the mere portrayal of indigenous traditions and included the challenges of migration and modernity. In a famous speech that he gave when accepting the prestigious Garcilaso de la Vega, El Inca Award, he proclaimed himself not as an *aculturado* but as someone seeking a cultural pluralism that eschews the limits of narrow traditionalism.

Silvia Nagy-Zekmi

See also *Indigenismo* in Spanish American Literature.

Work By:

Deep Rivers. Trans. Frances Horning Barraclough. Austin: University of Texas Press, 1997.

The Fox from Up Above and the Fox from Down Below. Trans. Frances Horning Barraclough. Pittsburgh: University of Pittsburgh Press, 2000.

Work About:

Lambright, Anne. *Creating the Hybrid Intellectual: Subject, Space, and the Feminine in the Narrative of José María Arguedas*. Lewisburg, PA: Bucknell University Press, 2007.

Argueta, Manlio (1935–)

Born in El Salvador, this poet and novelist formed part of the *Generación comprometida* (Committed Generation) and the *Círculo Literario Universitario* (University Literary Circle), organizations which supported social change. Argueta's poetry expresses genuine solidarity with citizens who experienced governmental oppression from the 1932 massacre, *la matanza*, to the civil war (1980–1992).

His experimental social novel *Caperucita en la zona roja* (1978; Little Red Riding Hood in the Red Light District), which received the Casa de las Américas Prize, strongly advocates Salvadoran political reform. Written in exile, the novel focuses on the lives of ordinary people during the violent, pre–civil war years. *Un día en la vida* (1980; *One Day of Life*, 1992) offers readers another glimpse of ordinary citizens' wartime experiences, as well as the military's exploitation and mistreatment of peasants. As of this writing, Argueta is also the director of El Salvador's National Library. He has two unpublished novels.

Rhina Toruño-Haensly

See also El Salvador's *Generación comprometida* (1956–1972).

Work By:

Manlio Argueta, Poesía Completa, 1956–2005. Ed., intro. Astvaldur Astvaldsson. College Park, MD: *Hispamérica*, 2006.

Once Upon a Time (Bomb). Trans. Linda Craft. Lanham, MD: University Press of America, 2007.

One Day of Life. Trans. Bill Brow. New York: Vintage, 1992.

Work About:

Anderson, Robert. "Manlio Argueta: 'Committed' Third World Author." *South Eastern Latin Americanist* 43.1–2 (Summer–Fall 1999): 38–49.

Arias, Arturo (1950–)

One of Guatemala's outstanding 20th-century novelists, Arias was born in his nation's capital city and grew up in an environment of military street patrols, political repression, and censorship. Through the Alliance for Progress, he came to the United States to attend Boston University. While completing degrees there and at the Sorbonne in Paris, he wrote his first novel: *Después de las bombas* (1979; *After the Bombs*, 1990), based partly on his experiences growing up.

During the 1980s, Arias lived mostly in Mexico City. His second novel, *Itzam na* (1981), a Maya-inspired fantasy, received Cuba's prestigious Casa de las Américas Prize. He next wrote the award-winning screenplay for the U.S.-produced film *El norte* (1984; The North), which opened the door to his employment at U.S. universities. To date, Arias has published three additional novels, four books of literary criticism, and an edited text on the Rigoberta *Menchú controversy.

His novels are complicated and post-modern with philosophical and historical subtexts. *Los caminos de Paxil* (1991; The Road to Paxil) involves a ruthless Texas oilman and his son, whose enterprise is located deep in the Guatemalan jungle; two female characters embody the principles of Mayan agricultural philosophy. *Cascabel* (1998; *Rattlesnake*, 2003) adopts a linear style and features a CIA man, a malicious Guatemalan colonel, and a wealthy Guatemalan woman who works for both the government and the rebels. The ending is harrowing and unforgettable. Arias's sixth novel, *Sopa de caracol* (2002; Snail Soup) takes place mostly in Brazil, with a perplexing ending. In each case, his narratives adopt innovative colloquial and linguistic strategies. One critic has compared him to the remarkable Chilean writer Roberto *Bolaño.

Elizabeth Coonrod Martínez

Work By:

The Rigoberta Menchú Controversy. Minneapolis: University of Minnesota Press, 2001.

Taking Their Word: Literature and the Signs of Central America. Minneapolis: University of Minnesota Press, 2007.

Work About:

Craft, Linda. *Novels of Testimony and Resistance from Central America.* Gainesville: University Press of Florida, 1997, 132–57.

Roberts, Cheryl. "An Interview with Arturo Arias." *Speaking of the Short Story: Interviews with Contemporary Writers*. Ed. Farhat Iftekharuddin, Mary Rohrberger, and Maurice Lee. Jackson: University of Mississippi, 1997, 23–34.

Arlt, Roberto (1900–1942)

Born in Buenos Aires, Argentina, Roberto Arlt's literary work and essays combine grotesque humor with cynicism and social criticism. A journalist, essayist, novelist, short story writer, and playwright, his whimsical characters attempt to escape from poverty and alienation and are often drawn to chimerical worlds. Typically, their inability to distinguish fantasy from reality leads them to death, madness, or suicide. Arlt's bizarre literary creations influenced such notable writers as Jorge Luis *Borges and Julio *Cortázar. In his final years, he became increasingly drawn to the theater, composing plays with the same tragic themes as his fiction.

Arlt's most significant works are his novels *El juguete rabioso* (1926*; The Rabid Toy*, 2002), *Los siete locos* (1929; *The Seven Madman*, 1998), and the play *Saverio el cruel* (1936; Saverio the Cruel). *El juguete rabioso* portrays a young man, trapped in poverty, who dreams of becoming a brilliant scientist, a magnificent poet, or a Robin Hood–type hero. These are the same dreams of the young Arlt. The second novel depicts a group of misfits who attempt to escape their frustrations by forming a mysterious society that aspires to take over the world. Finally, his brilliant play weaves between reality and fantasy as a poor, timid dairyman accepts a role in a farce and eventually assumes the role of cruel tyrant as reality.

James Troiano

Work By:

Mad Toy. Trans. Michele McKay Aynesworth. Durham, NC: Duke University Press, 2002.

The Seven Madmen. Trans. Nick Caistor. London: Unesco, 1998.

Work About:

Civantos, Christina. "Language, Literary Legitimacy, and Masculinity in the Writings of Roberto Arlt." *Latin American Literary Review* 33.65 (January–June 2005): 109–34.

Arms and Letters

The phrase *armas y letras* represents, by metonymy, the twin roles of the ideal courtier: the warrior and the scholar/poet. Though the phrase may have originated in relationship to the roles of soldier and lawyer (*letrado*) and their equal importance to defending the republic, by the 16th century, *letras* was understood to mean the subjects of the *studia humanitatis*, especially rhetoric, moral philosophy, poetry, and history. The importance of knowledge of war and intellectual prowess for a courtier was expressly highlighted in Baldesar Castiglione's *Il Cortegiano* (1528; *The Book of the Courtier*, 1976), published first in Italian, and then translated to Spanish by *Garcilaso de la Vega's friend Juan Boscán in 1534.

Though originally understood as complementary aspects of an ideal for a *Renaissance noble, men who were either soldiers or scholars each came to see their role as the more important one, and thus, arms versus letters became a frequent debate. To practice writing in a rhetorical style, some school books assigned students to compose imaginary debates on this very subject. Miguel de *Cervantes develops the theme ironically in chapter 38 of *El ingenioso hidalgo don Quijote de la Mancha* (1605) for comic effect, and it was commonplace in Spanish Golden Age literature of the 16th and 17th centuries.

Matthew A. Wyszynski

Work About:

Castiglione, Baldesar. *Book of the Courtier.* Trans. George Bull. New York: Penguin, 1976.

Elliot van Liere, Katherine. "Humanism and Scholasticism in Sixteenth-Century Academe: Five Student Orations from the University of Salamanca." *Renaissance Quarterly* 53 (2000): 57–107.

Arniches, Carlos (1866–1943)

Born in Alicante, political instability prompted this Spanish dramatist's family to move to Barcelona. He lived there from 1880 until 1885, combining all sort of jobs with early poetry and novel writing. Later in Madrid, Arniches contributed to such newspapers as *El Diario Universal.* Living in Madrid's humblest neighborhoods (Lavapiés, Antón Martín) served as a catalyst for the realistic depiction of working-class lives in his characters' dialogues and settings. Soon, he expertly depicted popular Madrid types and their peculiar way of talking in *sainetes* (brief, humorous pieces) and longer plays, deriving inspiration from 19th-century *zarzuela* (Spanish musical theater) and *género chico* (less serious theater) traditions.

Arniches coined a new comic genre, the so-called *grotesque tragedy*, which displayed a peculiar combination of humor and bittersweet moral criticism of social conditions. *La señorita de Trevélez* (1916; Trevelez Lady) shows the petty, idle lives of bored young men in a provincial clubhouse who decide to play a very cruel joke on the town spinster, Florita, and her bachelor brother, Gonzalo. This work later served as inspiration for José Juan Antonio Bardem's film masterpiece *Calle Mayor* (1956; Main Street).

Overall, Arniches is highly respected for his control of dramatic technique, his skill with comic action and different linguistic registers, and his ability to depict his protagonists' daily lives.

Judith García-Quismondo García

See also Theater in Spain: 1900–1975.

Work By:

La señorita de Trevélez. ¡Que viene mi marido! Ed. Andrés Amorós. Madrid: Castalia, 2003.

Work About:

McKay, Douglas R. *Carlos Arniches.* New York: Twayne, 1972.

Ramos, Vicente. *Vida y teatro de Carlos Arniches.* Alicante: Biblioteca Virtual Miguel de Cervantes, 2006.

Arreola, Juan José (1918–2001)

Known for inventive, experimental short stories that introduced Mexican readers to existentialist themes and the aesthetics of the absurd, this energetic, if somewhat eccentric, promoter of literary culture earned a reputation for his enormous creativity and prodigious imagination. In the mid-1940s, Arreola began publishing stories in *Eos* and the Guadalajara literary magazine *Pan*, a periodical he edited in collaboration with fellow Jalisco luminary, Juan *Rulfo. Early in his career, Arreola harbored the ambition of becoming an actor and traveled to Paris in 1945 to study theater with celebrated French actor and director, Louis Jouvet. The trip was cut short by one of Arreola's frequent illnesses and he returned to Mexico to begin work as an editor for Fondo de la Cultura Económica publishing house. He later commented that his work at Fondo, writing copy for book jackets, helped polish his talent for concision and brevity.

Arreola's first book-length short story collection, *Varia invención* (*Other Inventions*, 1993), was published in 1949. His second collection, *Confabulario* (1952; Eng. trans., 1993), sealed his fame as one of Mexico's most inventive young writers and placed him squarely in the center of Mexican literary production and politics. Eschewing regionalism and *costumbrismo* (depiction of local customs, dress and speech), Arreola's cosmopolitan short stories often present characters grappling with the absurdity of modernity, consumerism, and Kafkaesque bureaucracies.

La hora de todos (1954), Arreola's only drama, was published in Ediciones Los Presentes, a series he founded with mid-century doyen of Mexican letters Alfonso *Reyes, to provide a literary platform for younger writers. Under Arreola's direction, Ediciones Los Presentes helped launch the careers of important Mexican writers like Carlos *Fuentes, Elena *Poniatowska, and Emmanuel Carballo. His only novel, *La feria* (1963; *The Fair*, 1977), weaves together the disparate voices of the inhabitants of Zapotlán, Mexico, as they discuss the upcoming annual fair. Important later works include *Palindroma* (1971; Palindrome) and *Bestiario* (1972; Bestiary). Borrowing from the classical and medieval tradition of bestiary (or list of beasts), *Bestiario* brings together short fables that function as ironic allegories of the shortcomings inherent to human nature.

Later in his career, Arreola became a minor television personality appearing on "Sábados con Saldaña." His sometimes caustic remarks about fellow writers and unconventional dress reinforced his reputation as an eccentric literary celebrity.

V. Daniel Rogers

Work About:

Burt, John R. "This Is No Way to Run a Railroad: Arreola's Allegorical Railroad and a Possible Source." *Hispania* 71 (1988): 806–11.

Herz, Theda. "Artistic Iconoclasm in Mexico: Countertexts of Arreola, Agustín, Avilés and Hiriart." *Chasqui: Revista de Literatura Latinoamericana* 18.1 (1989): 17–25.

Metzidakis, Stamos. "From Poetic to Prosaic Animal Portraits: Arreola's 'El elefante'." *Romance Review* (1994): 473–82.

Arroyo, Justo (1936–)

Perhaps Panama's best-known short story writer, this winner of numerous literary prizes in Central America was born in the Atlantic coastal city of Colón. Constants in his writing include the basic theme of relationships between men and women; use of everyday, realistic characters; simple, concise language; and a creative use of time.

Arroyo's most famous works are his short story collections: *Capricornio en gris* (1972; Capricorn in Gray), *Rostros como manchas* (1991; Faces Like Stains), *Para terminar diciembre* (1995; To Finish in December), and *Héroes a medio tiempo* (1998; Part Time Heroes). These stories describe the daily life of lower-middle-class people usually living on modest means in contemporary Panama. Single mothers, aging schoolteachers, and poverty stricken retirees number among his characters. The short story "Abuso de confianza" (Exploitation of Familiarity) from *Para terminar diciembre* tells the story of Catalina who, on becoming a widow at age 50, is expected to become a servant to her daughter. *Vida que olvida* (2002; Life That Forgets), his only historical novel, is set in early-20th-century Panama. It describes the life of a Colombian couple caught in Panama precisely when the nation changes from being part of Colombia to an independent country.

Finally, *Sin principio ni fin* (2001; Without Beginning or End) tells the story of Indian leader Victoriano Lorenzo, who was unjustly assassinated in 1903.

Maida Watson

Work About:

Watson, Maida. "Mujer, patria y narración en los cuentos de tres autores panameños: Rosa María Britton, Justo Arroyo y Antonio Paredes." *Revista Cayey* 85 (April 2008): 47–53.

Ascensio Segura, Manuel (1805–1871)

A playwright, journalist, and editor of *La Bolsa* newspaper, Peruvian Ascensio Segura wrote *costumbrista* pieces that depict early Republican Lima society and the aspirations of its emerging middle class from a localist perspective. The son of a Spanish military officer, Segura fought alongside the royalist army in the battle of Ayacucho (1824) but later embraced the republic and served in president Gamarra's army until 1842. His *costumbrista* comedies use local popular expressions and offer social criticism lightheartedly. The celebrated *El Sargento Canuto* (1839; Sergeant Canuto) attacks militarism through portrayal of the boastful soldier while *Ña Catita* (1856; Miss Catita) derides the adoption of foreign fashions and feigned religious zeal.

Segura's polemic with his literary rival, conservative writer *Pardo y Aliaga, over the direction of Peruvian *costumbrismo* circulated in several periodicals and was followed with interest by contemporaries. In the poem "La peli-muertada," subtitled "Epopeya de última moda" (1851; Epic of the Latest Fashion) Segura satirizes the classical references and erudition advocated by writers like Pardo as incomprehensible to the majority of Peruvians. By affirming his desire to identify himself with a larger audience and produce literary pieces understandable to the general public, Segura's work projected the identity of an emerging middle class.

Soledad Gálvez

Work By:

Obras completas. Ed., intro. Alberto Varillas. Lima: Universidad de San Martín de Porres, 2005.

Work About:

Cornejo Polar, Jorge. *Sobre Segura.* Arequipa, Peru: Universidad Nacional de San Agustín, 1970.

Asturias, Miguel Ángel (1899–1974)

Born in Guatemala City, Asturias became the best-known Central American writer of his generation. Crucial to his development was the time he spent as a child on his grandfather's ranch, where he came into contact with Guatemala's indigenous culture. He often expressed great pride in his Mayan ancestry. As a law school student, he wrote his thesis on the societal problems faced by the Indians; after graduating, he never practiced law. During his youth, Guatemala was ruled by the Estrada Cabrera dictatorship (1898–1920). Asturias spent much of the 1920s in Europe. In London, he visited the British Museum and discovered Mayan art, little appreciated in his homeland. While studying anthropology in Paris with specialists in Mayan culture, Asturias worked from a French translation to prepare a Spanish version of the *Popol Vuh*, the Mayan sacred book, and other Mayan texts. His time in Europe also allowed him to meet influential vanguard writers, which led him to experiment with surrealism and other new art forms.

Asturias's works use mythic elements of Mayan culture, experimental literary techniques, political themes, and social protest, as in his stories *Leyendas de Guatemala* (1930; Legends of Guatemala) and his novels *Hombres de maíz* (1949; *Men of Maize*, 1993) and *El Señor Presidente* (1946; Eng. trans., 1975). *El Señor Presidente* helped usher in Spanish America's "dictator novel," with its politically engaged satire conveying the horrors of dictatorship and the chaotic reality and atmosphere of fear it engendered. Unlike works of pure propaganda, the novel combines interior monologues, word play, and cubist perspectives with surrealistic scenes exploring dreams, myths, and the subconscious. The novels of Asturias's "banana trilogy"—*Viento fuerte* (1950; *Strong Wind*, 1969), *El Papa verde* (1954; *The Green Pope*, 1971), and *Los ojos de los enterrados* (1960; *The Eyes of the Interred*, 1973)—contain a strong message of protest with less emphasis on aesthetic features. Asturias won the Nobel Prize for literature in 1967.

Melvin S. Arrington Jr.

See also Indeginismo in Spanish American Literature; Mayan Literature; Nobel Prize Literature in Spanish.

Work By:

El Señor Presidente. Trans. Frances Partridge. New York: Atheneum, 1975.

Men of Maize. Trans. Gerald Martin. Pittsburgh and London: University of Pittsburgh Press, 1993.

Work About:

Prieto, René. *Miguel Ángel Asturias's Archaeology of Return.* Cambridge and New York: Cambridge University Press, 1993.

Atencia, María Victoria (1931–)

An acclaimed poet born in Málaga, she has been called the Emiliy Dickinson of Spain for her intensity, formal perfection, and ability to depict the human condition in spare verses that elevate the reader to the universal. Atencia's first poetry books (*Tierra mojada* [1953; Moist Earth]; *Cañada de los ingleses* [1961; Canebrake of the British]; *Arte y parte* [1961; Art and Report]) exalt life using alexandrines and classic forms (sonnets), and combine images and sounds to turn ordinary objects into ones of beauty. She captures the intensity of life, and creates her own inner sense of time, in a meditative tone, from the description of daily scenes.

After a decade of silence, perhaps due to the death of loved friends, her idyllic poems turn more concise, and subtle, to reflect on the fragility and temporality of humans that can only be overcome by beauty and poetic creativity. The contemplation of natural or artistic beauty creates a sense of plenitude that stops time. The exploration of feminine identity is another recurrent theme. Through literary characters, the poet presents the conflictive reality of women while discovering her own feminine condition. The silence imposed on women by the patriarchal system can only be defined by the poetic word. Such poems are collected in *La señal: Poesía 1961–1989* (1990; The Sign).

Among the motives present in her poetry are her city and feminine references, such as enclosed spaces, a fascination with childhood, the sea, and also culturalist elements, in keeping with the poetry of the 1980s, such as artwork (paintings, sculptures) or places where she has traveled, that serve to reveal a deeper reality palpably. The use of silence and literary and cinematic references are predominant characteristics of her poetry.

Atencia's work goes beyond any poetic group and surpasses the limitations of geography and time. She achieves a difficult balance between opposite forces, such as death and life, past and future, creating a unique perception of time in her verse, and pointing to a sense of abundance in contemplative verses. She has received many literature prizes and is a member of several Royal Academies of Fine Arts.

María-Cruz Rodríguez

Work By:

Antología poética 1961–2005. Ed. María José Jiménez Tomé. Málaga: Las 4 Estaciones, 2007.

Work About:

Ugalde, Sharon Keefe. "Masks of Canvas and Stone in the Poetry of María Victoria Atencia." *Anales de Literatura Española Contemporánea* 24.1–2 (1999): 227–42.

Atxaga, Bernardo (1951–)

Born in Asteasu in the Basque region of Spain, Bernardo Atxaga is the pseudonym of Joseba Irazu Garmendia, the best-selling, most highly acclaimed contemporary Basque writer. Famed for his short stories, novels, and children's books, Atxaga writes in the Basque language and translates many of his own works into Spanish. His landmark, internationally praised work, *Obabakoak* (1988; Those from Obaba), is set in a fictional, isolated village and presents a collage of stories that combine Basque legends with European and Middle Eastern tales to examine the meaning of literature itself.

During the 1990s, Atxaga's novels adopt a realistic yet lyrical tone to explore human frailties in *Gizona bere bakardadean* (1993; *The Lone Man*, 1996) and *Zeru horiek* (1995; *The Lone Woman*, 1999), whose protagonists are associated with the terrorist group ETA. Atxaga's later writings examine Basque nationalism, communication breakdowns, and the

challenges of community, making his narrative simultaneously local and universal.

Jason E. Klodt

Work By:

Obabakoak. Trans. Margaret Jull Costa. New York: Vintage, 1994.

Aub, Max (1903–1972)

This talented Spanish playwright and novelist, relatively unknown until 1939, lived in exile most of his life. Born in Paris to a German father and a French mother of Jewish origin, the family moved to Valencia, Spain, in 1914 after the breakout of World War I. Here, Aub was introduced to the avant-garde movement of the 1920s and 1930s, emerging as a promising young writer. Writing became his career and, regardless of genre, he always wrote in Spanish, his adoptive tongue. During the Spanish Civil War (1936–1939), he collaborated with French director André Malraux in filming *Sierra de Teruel* (1937; *Hope*) and went into exile in France in 1939 as the civil war ended.

Aub reached Mexico in 1942 and resumed his dedication to literature, publishing the majority of his work there. He composed plays, novels, short stories, magazines, poetry, screenplays, journal excerpts, studies on the Spanish novel, and a collection of essays. In 1969, he traveled to Spain for a short visit only to discover that neither the country nor he was the same after three decades apart. Aub returned to Mexico and wrote until his death.

Spain's civil conflict permeates all his writing, and takes front stage in his artistically and thematically impressive series of novels and short stories, entitled *El laberinto mágico* (1943–1968; The Magic Labyrinth). *Campo cerrado* (1943; Closed Field), *Campo de sangre* (1945; Bloody Field), *Campo abierto* (1951; Open Field), *Campo del moro* (1963; Field of the Moor), *Campo francés* (1965; French Field), and *Campo de los almendros* (1968; Field of Almond Trees) introduce hundreds of characters and multiple interrelated stories, making Aub's work a true labyrinth for the reader. In the absence of a hero, the peoples of Spain, as a collective voice, become the main character suffering the consequences of war. Through more than 2,000 pages, Aub paints a mural portraying a tale of survival. Expatriation, separation, loss, abandonment, absence, and memory play integral parts in his texts.

Initially influenced by avant-garde tendencies, Aub's later work moved toward a realism tainted with a strong social and political content in his lifelong attempt to comprehend the human being and the world around him. To date, only one of his novels has been translated to English.

José A. Sainz

See also Exile Literature by Spanish Civil War Émigrés.

Work By:

Jusep Torres Campalans. Trans. Herbert Weinstock. Garden City, NY: Doubleday, 1962.

Work About:

Altisent, Martha Eulalia, and Cristina Martínez-Carazo. *Twentieth-Century Spanish Fiction Writers*. Farmington Hills, MI: Thomson Gale, 2006, 137–56.

Amell, Samuel. *The Contemporary Spanish Novel: An Annotated, Critical Bibliography, 1936–1994*. Westport, CT: Greenwood, 1996, 1–65.

Faber, Sebastiaan. *Exile and Cultural Hegemony: Spanish Intellectuals in Mexico, 1939–1975*. Nashville: Vanderbilt University Press, 2002, 218–65.

Larson, Susan. *Peripheral Modernities of the Spanish Novel*. Washington, DC: Heldref, 2005, 221–31.

Ugarte, Michael. *Shifting Ground: Spanish Civil War Exile Literature*. Durham, NC: Duke University Press, 1989, 113–51.

Autobiography in Spain: Beginnings to 1700

This genre is defined as a life story usually written and narrated by a first-person "I" who is also the story's subject. These life stories, which can be subject to the emendations of a final editor, particularly when the protagonist is dead, can be traced back to very early times; for example, Saint Augustine's fourth-century *Confessions* provides one such a model for later writing. Critics once suggested that Spain produced few autobiographies, especially before 1700, but recently, additional first-person life stories have been identified among early texts, and autobiographical characteristics have been observed in other documents. Goetz discusses the presence of a poetic "I" in several medieval Spanish works; nonetheless, most medieval readers knew only of saints' and kings' biographies.

One very early life story is that of Leonor López de Córdoba. Her brief *Memorias* (1412; Memoirs), supposedly written in tribute to the Virgen Mary's protection, describes both the revenge (incarcerations, many deaths) King Henry took on her family for having supported his overthrown brother and, following release from prison, her efforts to reestablish a life and the family honor. Gitlitz opines that as early as the 1480s, confessions to the Inquisition constitute a common autobiographical genre, as they share aspects of other life writings of the period. Although not literary works, these oral confessions were transcribed and collected in Inquisition dossiers.

As society's focus shifted from collective to individual experience in the early modern period (early 1500s), Goetz classifies two types of first-person writing: introspective religious confessionals and experiential narratives. Saint Ignatius of Loyola dictated his autobiography to a confessor during several meetings from 1553–1555. This early model of religious narrative presents the young saint's early religious inclination, education, and travels. Santa *Teresa de Jesús's *Libro de la vida* (written c. 1565; *The Life of Teresa of Jesus: The Autobiography of Teresa of Ávila*, 1960) is doubly addressed to a confessor, who judges the speaker's conduct, and to God. The text traces her life from childhood through adulthood, narrating

daily experiences, illnesses, her calling to become a nun, personal struggles, and how to pray. Teresa's works circulated widely even before their first publication in 1588, influencing the writings and actions of other nuns.

Experiential autobiographies created during 16th- and 17th-century Spain include explorers' accounts and the soldier's life. Not intended for publication, a soldier's life recounts military activities and the quality of one's service, which includes some personal detail. The *Autobiografía de Jerónimo de Pasamonte* (1605) relates Pasamonte's childhood, entrance into military service, years as a captive galley slave, return to the military, and religious beliefs. The *Vida de Alonso de Contreras* (1630–1641; *The Adventures of Captain Alonso de Contreras*, 1989) records the adventures of a runaway who works as a sailor, then joins the Spanish army, leaves to become a hermit, and later undertakes army missions.

Born in an environment rich in first-person inquisition, religious, and documentary texts, the *picaresque novel (for example, *Vida de *Lazarillo de Tormes* [1554; *Lazarillo de Tormes*, 1969] and *La vida del buscón* [1626; *The Swindler*, 1969]) by Francisco de *Quevedo constitute a kind of false story about an unexemplary life, in which a lower-class rogue occupies various menial jobs with different masters and survives by his sharp wits. Picaresque travels and behavior emerge in other life stories, as in Santa Teresa's *Libro de fundaciones* (1582; *The Book of the Foundations*, 1893) and Estebanillo González's autobiography *Vida y Hechos*

(1646; Life and Deeds), as well as in many fictional autobiographical narratives by marginalized protagonists in the centuries to come.

Gwen H. Stickney

See also Convent Writing in Spain and the New World; Ignacio de Loyola, San (1491–1556); Inquisition and the Hispanic World

Work About:

Arenal, Electa, and Stacey Schlau. *Untold Sisters: Hispanic Nuns in Their Own Works*. Albuquerque: University of New Mexico Press, 1989.

Gitlitz, David. "Inquisition Confessions and *Lazarillo de Tormes*." *Hispanic Review* 68.1 (2000): 53–75.

Goetz, Rainer H. *Spanish Golden Age Autobiography in Its Context*. New York: Peter Lang, 1994.

Spadaccini, Nicholas, and Jenaro Talens, eds. *Autobiography in Early Modern Spain*. Minneapolis: Prisma Institute, 1988.

Autobiography in Spain: 1700 to Present

These narratives that people write about their own lives make up a complex genre with many possible variations and different names. Such terms as confession, life narrative, life writing, journal, and memoir, to name a few, indicate differences between forms of autobiography. After the early modern period (1500–1700), autobiography waned in Spain for a time, but a more recent, growing interest in life writings has led literary critics to seek unknown or forgotten autobiographical works and to read more texts from an autobiographical perspective.

Fernández argues that frequent political turmoil in Spain, such as military conflicts or changes in government, did not encourage leisurely reflection on an individual's personal development; thus, political events caused many of Spain's life writings to be historical in nature rather than literary. From the 18th and 19th centuries, critics frequently mention the autobiographies of Diego Torres Villarroel (1693–1770), a professor at the University of Salamanca, and of Joseph Blanco White (1775–1841), a former Spanish Catholic priest living in exile, father of an illegitimate son, and convert to the Anglican faith, and later Unitarianism, in England. Written and published in short sections, the *Vida de Torres Villarroel, escrita por él mismo* (1742–1758; *The Remarkable Life of Don Diego*, 1958) recounts the events of each decade of Villarroel's life and later adds concluding materials. This work is often compared to the picaresque novel of 1500–1700 because of the protagonist's frequent adventures, job changes, and roguish attitude. In contrast, Blanco White's *The Life of the Reverend Joseph Blanco White, Written by Himself* (1845), written in English after he fled to England during the French invasion of Spain, recalls external and psychological happenings in his life, reflecting on the shortcomings of religious denominations he had participated in and on his desire to heed his internal voice from God. Blanco White's text includes autobiographical narrative, journal entries, letters, and a final biography. A third significant life writing from this period is that of Pedro Antonio de *Alarcón (1833–1891); his *Diario de un testigo de la guerra de África* (1860; *Diary of a Witness . . . to the War in Africa*, 1988) is a widely read war report composed of sixty letters.

Numerous 19th- and 20th-century authors have penned autobiographical texts. Miguel de *Unamuno (1864–1936) wrote several, including his only recently published *Diario íntimo* (1970; Intimate Diary), which reveals his internal conflict about faith. Benito *Pérez Galdós (1843–1920) authored *Memorias de un desmemoriado* (1920; Memories of an Absent-Minded Man), 16 articles that discuss such topics as his university days, travels in Spain and abroad, and literary writings. A most recent autobiographical work, *Memorias, entendimientos y voluntades* (1993; Memories, Understanding and Wishes), by Nobel Prize–winner Camilo José *Cela (1916–2002), presents his life in the period before and after the Spanish Civil War (1936–1939) through to his publication of *La familia de Pascual Duarte* (1942; *The Family of Pascual Duarte*, 1964).

Political events in the 20th century have also affected the production of autobiographical writing. Some texts were penned after the civil war, often by Spaniards exiled during Franco's regime, such as Rafael *Alberti (1932–2001), Arturo *Barea (1897–1957), Rosa *Chacel (1898–1994), María Teresa León (1903–1988) and Rafael Cansinos Assens (1882–1964). Alberti's three-volume *La arboleda per-*

dida (1942–1987; *The Lost Grove*, 1976) traces his family life, friendships with other writers and artists, writing, and exile. Also three volumes, Barea's *La forja de un rebelde* (1951; *The Forging of a Rebel*, 1941) follows his childhood, military experience in Morocco and life during wartime, and exile. *La novela de un literato* (1983–1985; *The Novel of a Writer*, 2007), by Cansino Assens, portrays literary figures of the late-19th and early-20th centuries, while Chacel's *Desde el amanecer: Autobiografía de mis primeros diez años* (1972; Since Dawn: Autobiography of My First Ten Years) details her search for identity. Finally, León's *Memoria de la melancolía* (1970; Memory of Melancholy) presents a series of memories from her childhood through adult years, including the war and her postwar exile.

After Franco's death in 1975, autobiographical publications increased noticeably, due to greater freedom of expression and interest from readers and publishers. Composed of five previous publications, the collected memoirs of Carlos Barral (1928–1989), titled *Memorias* (2001), discuss his family life, education, sexual awakening, editorial work, and professional challenges. César Armando Gómez's edited publication of *Casi unas memorias* (1976; Almost a Memoir) by Dionisio *Ridruejo (1912–1975) contextualizes Ridruejo's recollection of his childhood, travels, writing, and leadership with the Falange and later political positions with parts of other documents, photographs, and a time line. Spain's first explicit gay autobiographer, Terenci *Moix (1942–2003), published the memoir collection *El peso de la paja* (1990; The Weight of Wank), which explores his youth, family, sexual awakening, and interest in popular culture.

Following in the Spanish tradition of fictional autobiography, Jorge *Semprún (1923–), writing in French and Spanish, has authored some life stories in Spanish. Despite having *autobiografía* in the title, *Autobiografía de Federico Sánchez* (1977; *The Autobiography of Federico Sánchez*, 1979) mixes fiction with Semprún's experiences as a Communist Party member, and his expulsion. Although writer Luis *Goytisolo does not always agree with his brother's memory, Juan *Goytisolo (1931–) has written several autobiographical works, including *Coto Vedado* (1985; *Forbidden Territory: The Memoir of Juan Goytisolo*, 2003) and *En los reinos de taifa* (1986; *Realms of Strife: The Memoir of Juan Goytisolo*, 2003), which depict Juan's family history, writing, and separation from family and country in order to find his true self.

Women have created significant autobiographical texts during the 20th century. In the tradition of Spanish fictional life writing, the widely acclaimed *Nada* (1944; *Nada*, 2007), by Carmen *Laforet (1921–2004), and *El cuarto de atrás* (1978; *The Back Room*, 2000) by Carmen *Martín Gaite (1925–2000), share a first-person structure with some personal details from the authors' lives set amid the fictions. María Martínez Sierra, also known as María de la O *Lejárraga (1874–1974) and María Teresa León (mentioned earlier) each wrote complex autobiographical texts. Martínez Sierra's *Una mujer por caminos de España* (1952; A Woman on Spain's Roads) tells of her experience doing propaganda for the Spanish Socialist Party in 1930s Spain. *Una mexicana en la guerra de España* (1964; *Trapped in Spain*, 1978), the artfully written and sinister testimony of Carlota O'Neill (1905–2000), whose husband (a captain) was killed in 1936 while defending a base in Melilla, describes women's prison experience in Franco's Spain.

In contrast to earlier observations that few autobiographies have been written in Spain, the 20th and 21st centuries are characterized by a growing interest in the production and criticism of life writings that seems unlikely to end soon.

Gwen H. Stickney

See also Picaresque Literature in the Hispanic World.

Work About:

Ballesteros, Isolina. *Escritura femenina y discurso autobiográfico en la nueva novela española*. New York: Peter Lang, 1994.

Caballé, Ana. *Narcisos de tinta: ensayos sobre la literatura autobiográfica en lengua castellana, siglos XIX y XX*. Málaga: Megazul, 1995.

Fernández, James D. *Apology to Apostrophe: Autobiography and the Rhetoric of Self-Representation in Spain*. Durham and London: Duke University Press, 1992.

Loureiro, Ángel G. *The Ethics of Autobiography: Replacing the Subject in Modern Spain*. Nashville: Vanderbilt University Press, 2000.

Autobiography in Spanish America

The word "autobiography" comprises three Greek parts: *autos* (self), *bios* (life), and *graphe* (writing); therefore, an autobiography is a life story written by oneself. In the last decades of the 20th century, critics began to define autobiographical writing in broader terms and to read texts with other functions, such as legal or religious writings, as autobiographies, which led to increased interest in the varied first-person texts from Spanish America. Colonial Spanish American autobiography has been influenced by the Americas' ties with Spain, but, as Molloy argues, it has also developed in ways that express the region's reality and concerns about national identity.

During Spain's exploration and settlement of the Americas, many peninsular works were read by Spanish explorers and residents, so early autobiographical texts often followed these models. One important kind of writing from Spanish America is chronicles, or first-person narratives of exploration and conquest. These related the travels of Spanish explorers in the New World, documented their observations about plants, animals, and indigenous residents, and often presented the writers and their agendas in a positive light to the king, who supported the expedition and could continue financial assistance for successful ventures. Many of these texts include autobiographical content, such as Hernán Cortes's *Cartas de relación* (1519–1526; *Letters from Mexico*, 1971), which presents the conquest of New Spain and the fall of Tenochtitlán; Alvar Núñez Cabeza de Vaca's *Naufragios* (1542; *Castaways*, 1993), which relates the loss of Cabeza de Vaca's ships during a storm in port and the difficult journey of a small number of his remaining crew as they traveled in the New World for almost a decade, even into what is now the United States; and Bernal *Díaz del Castillo's *Historia verdadera de la conquista de la Nueva España* (1632; *The Discovery and Conquest of Mexico*, 1956), another first-hand description of Hernán Cortés's expedition. Díaz del Castillo recounts the many battles that culminated in Spain's defeat of the Aztec empire, and what happened years after the conquest, including Cortés's return to Spain and his death. The early chronicles created an image of Spanish America for Europeans and paved the way for later travel writings that introduce foreigners and Spanish Americans alike to unfamiliar parts of the continent. Much more recently, Cuban Alejo *Carpentier's novel, *Los pasos perdidos* (1953; *The Lost Steps*, 1956), imitates a trip up the Orinoco, and Argentine revolutionary Ernesto (Che) *Guevara authored many texts, including travel diaries that were published after his death. Guevara's diaries include *Pasajes de la guerra revolucionaria: Congo* (1967; *The African Dream: The Diaries of the Revolutionary War in the Congo*, 2000) which details his trip to promote a Communist revolution in the Congo; his last diary, *El diario del Che en Bolivia* (1968; *The Bolivian Diary*, 1968) which is writing found when he was captured by the Bolivian army and executed; and *Diarios de motocicleta: notas de un viaje por América Latina* (2003; The *Motorcycle Diaries: A Journey around South America*, 1995), related to the 2004 film of the same title, about an extended road trip he took as a young man during the early 1950s.

Other autobiographical genres brought from Spain to Spanish America include confessional writing, the soldier's life, and fictional picaresque life stories of rogues. Many Spanish and Spanish American religious figures practiced confessional writing, which provided examples for others to follow and a way for the Church to monitor these writers' behavior, as with the illustrious Mexican nun and writer Sor Juana Inés de la *Cruz. Her letter to a bishop, later published as *Respuesta de la poetisa a la muy ilustre Sor Filotea de la Cruz* (1700; *The Answer*, 1994), contains autobiographical details about her childhood and schooling, and her defense of education for women. Arenal and Schlau's study includes two chapters with examples of Spanish American nuns' confessional writings from Peru and New Spain (Mexico).

Another genre from Spain, the soldier's life recounts military activities and the quality of one's service. An unusual example of a soldier's life from Spanish America, with religious and picaresque elements is Catalina de *Erauso's 17th-century *Vida i sucesos de la Monja Alférez* (1829; *Lieutenant Nun: Memoir of a Basque Transvestite in the New World*, 1996). As a young woman, the lieutenant nun escapes from a convent in Spain before professing and assumes a male identity. After working in Spain, she travels to the Americas and lives there as a man and respected soldier for 19 years before confessing her identity and returning to Spain. Later, Erauso came back as a man to New Spain, where she probably spent the rest of her life.

The fictional Spanish picaresque, which narrates the un-exemplary life story of a male or female rogue, also influenced Spanish American writing. Another autobiographical hybrid, Úrsula Suárez's *Relación autobiográfica* (1984; Autobiographical Account), probably written in about 1700, tells the story of a nun from an illustrious family who lived during the 17th and 18th centuries in a convent in Santiago, Chile. Suárez, a confident nun with troublemaker tendencies, escapes conflict with her mother by entering the convent after the death of her grandmother, who had favored and protected the young girl. While cloistered, the mischievous Suárez maintains ambiguous relationships with several men and has conflicts with other nuns. A later example of picaresque influence, José Joaquín *Fernández de Lizardi's *El Periquillo Sarniento* (1816; *The Itching Parrot*, 1942), humorously presents the story of a young man who learns a variety of trades from different masters and cheats to survive, along with moral and social critique.

Since the time of colonial-age first-person texts (such as exploration or travel narratives, confessional accounts, and picaresque writings), autobiographical styles have flourished in Spanish America, setting the stage for later firsthand witnessing texts. In early Spanish American letters, a personal note characterized autobiographical narratives. Argentina's Domingo Faustino *Sarmiento wrote various autobiographical texts, including *Recuerdos de provincia* (*1850; Recollections of a Provincial Past*, 2005), which presents Sarmiento as a reader and self-made man, influenced by Benjamin Franklin, despite the frontier environment.

One 20th-century autobiographical mode that is especially associated with Spanish America is *testimonio*, a life story told by an often illiterate speaker to a professional author who writes down the story. *Testimonio* is known for its first-person presentation of social injustices and struggles for human rights in Spanish America. Miguel *Barnet's *Biografía de un cimarrón* (1966; *Autobiography of a Runaway Slave*, 1968), the story of Esteban Montejo, who escaped and hid from civilization until slavery was abolished in Cuba, is often considered the first example of *testimonio*. A very well-known example, *Me llamo Rigoberta Menchú y así me nació la conciencia* (1983; I, *Rigoberta Menchú: An Indian Woman in Guatemala*, 1984), presents the life of *Menchú, the winner of the 1992 Nobel Peace Prize, who, with her family, faced many hardships to fight for social justice in Guatemala. Anthropologist Oscar Lewis's English-language *The Children of Sanchez: Autobiography of a Mexican Family* (1961; *Los hijos de Sánchez*, 1964) narrates the life story of a poor but hardworking father alongside the autobiographies of his four children. This example of a work about the socially marginalized constitutes a precursor of *testimonio*.

Contemporary writers have produced autobiographical works, sometimes with fictional details. In *Confieso que he vivido: memorias* (1974; *Memoirs*, 1977), the posthumous memoirs of Pablo *Neruda (born Neftalí Ricardo Reyes Basoalto), the Nobel Prize–winner recounts his rich life with poetic images, including his travels, time as a Chilean consul abroad, friendships with artists and political figures, romantic relationships, political beliefs, and writings. In *La tía Julia y el escribidor* (1977; *Aunt Julia and the Scriptwriter*, 1982) Nobel Prize-winner Mario *Vargas Llosa (who married an older family member as a young man) humorously presents the story of Varguitas, an aspiring writer who falls in love with a divorced, older relative parallel with a scriptwriter's story for a radio station's serial soap operas. In *Vivir para contarla* (2002; *Living to Tell the Tale*, 2003), Gabriel *García Márquez, also a Nobel Prize-winner, records the details of his family, education, and early writing career, framed by the violence of Colombian history. Completed decades before publication, Mexican writer, poet, television presenter and intellectual Salvador *Novo's *La estatua de sal* (1998; The Statue of Salt), a title with Biblical references to curiosity and sin, discusses his childhood and his publicly known homosexuality.

A trend in Spanish American autobiography that is likely to continue in the 21st century is that some authors of Spanish American descent who have settled in the

United States are producing autobiographical works in Spanish and/or English, sometimes mixing fiction with elements of their lives to different degrees. Chilean-American Isabel *Allende's *Paula* (1994; Eng trans., 1995) recounts Allende's life and family as well as the treatment of her terminally-ill daughter, Paula, whom Allende cared for until the daughter's death from porphyria.

Spanish American immigrant autobiographers often examine the formation of their new identities in the United States. Mexican-American Richard Rodriguez's *Hunger of Memory: The Education of Richard Rodriguez* (1982), portrays his assimilation to American culture in Sacramento, California, including his experiences with learning English and the U.S. educational system, and Esmeralda Santiago's *When I Was Puerto Rican* (1993), which she later published in Spanish as *Cuando era puertorriqueña* (1994), narrates Santiago's early years through her audition to Performing Arts High School, including her family's move from a rural area of Puerto Rico to New York City, where she learns English and attends public school.

Gwen H. Stickney

See also Convent Writing in Spain and the New World; Discovery and Conquest Writings: Describing the Americas; Picaresque Literature in the Hispanic World; Testimonial Writing in Central America; Torture in Modern Spanish American Literature.

Work About:

Arenal, Electa, and Stacey Schlau. *Untold Sisters: Hispanic Nuns in Their Own Works*. Albuquerque: University of New Mexico Press, 1989, 293–410.

Hunsaker, Steven V. *Autobiography and National Identity in the Americas*. Charlottesville and London: University Press of Virginia, 1999.

Molloy, Sylvia. *At Face Value: Autobiographical Writing in Spanish America*. Cambridge: Cambridge University Press, 1991.

Avant-Garde Poetry in Spanish America

During the first decades of the 20th century, different avant-garde currents began to appear with vertiginous zeal in Spanish America. These expressions are essentially revolutionary movements that break with ideas and practices of the past. Since they fall within a period of cultural transformation—the period of modernization, this artistic production is richly varied and diverse.

The poetic avant-garde has two main components, international and local. Its initial impetus is European and represents part of the Continent's literary historical process; it is localized because avant-garde writing has close ties to its historical moment and immediate environment. Some principal characteristics include: 1) the worship of images; 2) the search for what is original and surprising; 3) antisentimentality; 4) an antianecdotal approach; 5) new themes (the machine, the city, the worker); 6) irrationalism; 7) notes of humor and play; and 8) altered syntax, accentuation, and verse norms.

The first manifestation of the avant-garde in Spanish American poetry is *creacionismo* (creationism), a movement led by Chilean Vicente *Huidobro (1893–1948). The key to his writing is linguistic experimentalism, privileging the image as center of poetic discourse, accompanied by programmatic manifestos like "Non Serviam" (1914), wherein he rejects the principle of mimesis (imitation of nature) and affirms art's autonomy.

In Buenos Aires, poets, like Francisco Luis Bernárdez (1900–1978), Leopoldo *Marechal (1900–1970) and Ricardo Molinari (1898–1996), wrote in an avant-garde mode, but the most influential practitioners were Jorge Luis *Borges (1899–1986) and Oliverio *Girondo (1891–1967). Initially Borges was committed to *ultraísmo*, a poetic movement opposed to modernism, which privileges the noun, avoids adjectives, linking words and ornamentation, and features dense metaphors. Borges published numerous manifestos, essays and books of poems—*Fervor de Buenos Aires* (1923; Fervor of Buenos Aires), *Luna de enfrente* (1925; Moon across the Way), and *Cuaderno San Martín* (1929; San Martín Notebook)—in which he documents a more personal, intimate style through use of metaphor and free verse. For his part, Girondo collects poems in prose and verse, with aggressive humor, to depict the modernity of urban life in *Veinte poemas para ser leídos en el tranvía* (1922; Twenty Poems to be Read on the Tram) and *Calcomanías* (1925; Transfers).

In Mexico, the first avant-garde movement is *estridentismo* (stridentism), as seen in Manuel Maples Arce (1898–1981), author of *Andamios interiores* (1922; Inner Scaffoldings), *Vrbe* (1924; City), and *Poemas interdictos* (1927; Forbidden Poems). The *estridentistas* exalt the dynamism of the modern world, the machine, and the city. Subsequently, two outstanding publications responsible for innovating poetic activity appear: *Ulises* (1927–1928; Ulysses) and *Contemporáneos* (1928–1931; Contemporaries). Members of this "group without a group" include Xavier *Villaurrutia (1903–1950), Jaime Torres Bodet (1902–1974), Carlos *Pellicer (1897–1977), Salvador *Novo (1904–1974), and José *Gorostiza (1901–1973). These poets do not practice the typical rejection of literary antecedents and prior masters.

In the Caribbean region, the avant-garde impulse was very intense, although it did not manifest itself with the same force as in the rest of Spanish America. There were varied attempts like *diepalismo*, *noísmo*, and *egopirismo*, but it was the *negrismo* (blackness) of Luis Palés Matos (1898–1959) that obtained original verbal experimentation, incorporated surprising images, and assigned new importance to rhythm in its celebration of primitive cultures. In Cuba, the main avant-garde movement occurs around the literary magazine *Revista de avance* (1927–1930), with the collaboration of Emilio *Ballagas (1908–1954) and Mariano Brull (1891–1977).

In 1916, four issues of *Colónida*, a literary journal directed by Abraham Valdelomar (1888–1919), are published in Lima. After several periodic publications, *Amauta*, founded and directed by José Carlos Mariátegui (1894–1930), appears (1926–1930). Poetic activity proper is published in *Trilce* (1922), by César *Vallejo (1892–1938), *Simplismo* (1925; Simplicity), by Alberto Hidalgo (1897–1967), *Ande* (1926; Andean), by Alejandro Peralta (1899–1973), and *5 metros de poemas* (1927; Five Meters of Poems) by Carlos Oquendo de Amat (1905–1936). In Ecuador, the avant-garde finds its voice in Pablo Palacio (1906–1947). Renewed critical interest in avant-garde writing began in the 1980s, when several definitive studies were completed by Hugo J. Verani, Nelson Osorio Tejeda, Gloria Videla de Rivera, and Jorge Schwartz.

Daniel Altamiranda

See also Journals in Spanish America.

Work By:

Antología de la poesía latinoamericana de vanguardia (1916–1935). Ed. Mihai Grünfeld. Madrid: Hiperión, 1995.

The Cambridge Companion to Modern Latin American Culture. Ed. John King. Cambridge and New York: Cambridge University Press, 2004.

Twentieth-century Latin American Poetry: A Bilingual Anthology. Ed. Stephen Tapscott. Austin: University of Texas Press, 1996.

Work About:

Unruh, Vicky. *Latin American Vanguards: The Art of Contentious Encounters*. Berkeley: University of California Press, 1994.

Videla de Rivero, Gloria. *Direcciones del vanguardismo hispanoamericano. Estudios sobre poesía de vanguardia en la década del veinte*. Pittsburg: Instituto Internacional de Literatura Iberoamericana, 1994.

Avant-Garde Prose in Spanish America

While the literary movement marking the early 20th century is realism, diverse currents of artistic innovation evolved within or from it, including the trend of the *vanguardia* (avant-garde), a French term for revolutionary action that takes place on the front lines. Artistic works produced during this period established a foundation for subsequent novels, opening the way to the social novel, "*magical realism," and the late century postmodern novel. *Vanguardia* is the equivalent of modernism in the Western world, and should not be confused with the late-19th-century Spanish American literary movement of *modernismo* (initiated with Rubén Darío's *Azul*). *Vanguardia* artists rebelled against their predecessors' excessive use of passionate, exotic symbols and allusions to pristine nature. These writings rose from the trenches, rather than lofty towers of aesthetic principles. Initially, in various Latin American cities, this artistic tendency was referred to by terms like *futurismo*, *ultraísmo*, and *estridentismo*. A period still being defined by critics, it extends from as early as the second decade of the 20th century to as late as the 1940s, with principal works dating from 1922 to 1930. In a few isolated cases, most notably Chilean poet Vicente *Huidobro (1893–1948), an avant-garde aesthetic is visible as early as mid-1910 to 1920.

In narrative fiction or prose, prominent *vanguardia* writers include Mexico's Manuel Maples Arce (1898–1981) and Arqueles Vela (1899–1972); Peruvian Martín *Adán (née Rafael de la Fuente Benavides, 1908–1984); Ecuador's Pablo Palacio (1906–1946); and Argentinians Roberto *Arlt (1900–1942) and Macedonio *Fernández (1874–1952). Urban hubs of Cuba, Nicaragua, and Brazil also sprouted *vanguardia* movements, often launched with manifestos and dramatic actions.

These artists defied order and precision. They rebelled against "traditional" form (with a precise beginning, middle, and end) by composing brief narratives with abruptly shifting, telegraphic thoughts and images, often creating an erratic effect. Critics lambasted them, calling them fragments, or incomplete novels. The *vanguardia* goal was to eliminate the previous era's ornamentation and embellishment; it was more important to conjure images suggesting force and movement, with frequent allusions to mechanical devices, technology, and science. Such artistic experimentation directly connected to the frenetic changes occurring in modern society.

Universally, such artists are called *modern* for their sharp awareness of belonging to the fast-paced 20th century. The half-century before World War I (1914–1918) had seen the most remarkable period of economic growth in history, a technological revolution that produced the internal combustion engine, diesel engine, and steam turbine; electricity, oil, and petroleum as new sources of power;

the automobile, tractor, and motor bus; the telephone, typewriter, and voice-recording machine (the foundation of modern office organization); and the production of synthetic materials. Accompanying the invention of ocean travel, travel by air, faster automobiles, and faster systems of communication, life was speeding up. Populations shifted in great number to urban centers, factories proliferated, and large offices were established.

Greater access to literary culture benefitted artists, who conceived their works amid the dramatic changes affecting all aspects of society. New philosophical orientations, such as futurism, influenced politics as well as art. Actively involved in their urban settings, avant-garde artists responded to a call for universal social and political awareness.

By 1910, Mexico City's population reached 471,000, and increased substantially once the Mexican Revolution ended. Vela's novel *El café de nadie* (1926; Nobody's Café) depicts a sense of frenzied activity in this city, with trolley cars, factories, police detective work, fast train travel—in effect, a dehumanized society. With no "traditional" form or plot, he called his work an "antinovel." Consisting of three sections presented in reverse order of creation (part 3 was completed in 1922, part 2 in 1924, and part 1 in 1926), and each with entirely different characters and settings, critics understood the book as a collection of three "stories," but Vela replied that it was a novel. He belonged to the *estridentista* movement, active in Mexico City between 1922 and 1927; its members published manifestos and performed readings at a specific café. The group's antics attracted artists like painter Diego Rivera and Italian photographer Tina Modotti. Vela's narrative is the first in Mexico to represent the strategies of avant-garde prose, including abstract form and social commentary (using irony and parody), tendencies later employed by Latin American *Boom* and postmodern novelists.

In Perú, Adán's *La casa de cartón* (1928; *The Cardboard House*, 1990) takes to the extreme a seemingly plotless account focused on modernization occurring in the cliffside community of Barranco, on the outskirts of Lima. In effect, urbanization impacts a formerly self-enclosed community. His sharp descriptions, narrated by an adolescent observer, reflect a unique, idiosyncratic style and sense of awareness, and rich poetic language. In Ecuador, Pablo Palacio (1906–1946), with his novel *Débora* (1927) offers an early example of metafiction; the narrator is obsessed with a minor character and no one named Débora ever appears.

While avant-garde prose came into being to serve artistic experimentation, its primary purpose was to critique society's propagation of social injustice and dehumanization. Unlike the earlier Latin American *modernistas*, *vanguardia* artists were actively involved in their communities. Once their initial experimentation had run its course, subsequent novels of the 1930s and 1940s demonstrate continued innovative strategies. Writers such as Chilean María Luisa *Bombal (1910–1981), Venezuelan Arturo Uslar Pietri (1906–2001), and Guatemalan Miguel Ángel *Asturias (1899–1974), are now categorized as late *vanguardia* novelists as well

as precursors to *Boom* and/or *magical realism. Even the novel of social protest credits its beginnings to the "surrealistic" practices of *vanguardia* artists. The essence of avant-garde prose—its effective protest against traditional Western literature and reflection of the impact of technological change—launched in opposition to the literary mainstream is evident throughout Latin American literature.

Elizabeth Coonrod Martínez

Work About:

Lindstrom, Naomi. "Avant-Garde, Imaginative, and Fantastic Modes, 1920–1950." *Twentieth-Century Spanish American Fiction*. Austin: University of Texas Press, 1994.

Martínez, Elizabeth Coonrod. *Before the Boom: Latin American Revolutionary Novels of the 1920s*. Lanham, MD: University Press of America, 2001.

Pérez-Firmat, Gustavo. *Idle Fictions: The Hispanic Vanguard Novel*. Durham, NC: Duke University Press, 1982.

Unruh, Vicky. *Latin American Vanguards: The Arts of Contentious Encounters*. Berkeley: University of California Press, 1994.

Aventuras de Don Chipote, o cuando los pericos mamen, Las (1928; The Adventures of Don Chipote, or When Parrots Breast-Feed, 2000)

Rediscovered by Nicolás Kanellos in 1984; this slender novel by Daniel Venegas (of whom little is known) details in exaggerated, humorously satiric fashion the journey of an impoverished, simpleton peasant who travels north from Mexico in search of the "streets of gold" of the United States that a neighbor has described to him. Once there, Chipote secures a job with the railroad, is injured, and then goes to Los Angeles, finding work as a dishwasher. Throughout his journey, he encounters mistreatment, deception, exploitation, and prejudice from employers, shysters, and others he meets. Narrated in first person, the text abounds with *costumbrista* scenes (colorful sketches depicting local traditions, attire, and speech), most notably the colloquial language peppered with Anglicisms and neologisms. The work represents an important precursor of the Chicano literature movement that first flowered in the late 1960s. Critics have also observed the work's relation to Cervantes's masterpiece, *Don Quijote de la Mancha*, as well as its affiliation with the *picaresque.

Maureen Ihrie

See also Chicano Movement Literature and Publishing; *Don Quijote de la Mancha* in Spanish American Literature and Culture.

Work:

Venegas, Daniel. *The Adventures of Don Chipote, or, When Parrots Breast-Feed*. Ed. Nicolás Kanellos. Trans. Ethriam Cash Brammer. Houston: Arte Público, 2000.

Work About:

Fallon, Paul. "Staging a Protest: Fiction, Experience and the Narrator's Shifting Position in *Las aventuras de don Chipote o cuando los pericos mamen*." *Confluencia* 23.1 (Fall 2007): 115–27.

Kanellos, Nicolás. "*Las aventuras de don Chipote*, obra precursora de la novela chicana." *Hispania* 67.3 (September 1984): 358–63.

Ávila Laurel, Juan Tomás (1966–)

A native of the Equatorial Guinean island of Annobón, this prolific writer of more than a dozen books, including novels, plays, essays, and film scripts, has achieved widespread international recognition. Currently living in Malabo (the country's capital), he has chosen not to go into exile, despite pressures associated with his independent position in relation to the regime. Ávila Laurel has represented Equatorial Guinea in many international conferences and cultural events, has been an invited speaker in South Korea and Switzerland, and has held appointments as writer-in-residence in universities in Spain and the United States.

His work voices incisive criticism of social and economic inequalities, and political repression and ethnic discrimination in his country; he has reflected extensively on the traumatic historical and cultural legacies of European colonialism and occupation in Africa. Among his published titles are *Poemas* (1994; Poems); the play *Los hombres domésticos* (1994; Domestic Men), engaging with institutional corruption, social repression, and censorship; a second book of poetry, *Historia íntima de la humanidad* (1999; Intimate History of Humanity); the novels *La carga* (1999; The Burden), set in the colonial period circa 1940, and *Awala cu sangui* (2000; Awala with Blood), which unfolds in Annobón during the Francisco Macías dictatorship (1968–1979); the political essay *El derecho de pernada, o de cómo se vive el feudalismo en el siglo XXI* (2000; First Night, or Twenty-First Century Feudalism); and the novels *El desmayo de Judas* (2001; Judas Faints); and *Nadie tiene buena fama en este país* (2002; Nobody Has a Good Name in This Country).

Ávila Laurel returned to playwriting with *El fracaso de las sombras* (2004; The Failure of the Shadows). Staged in the country's capital during the 1990s oil boom, it denounced corruption and the fragility of institutional structures, issues which reemerge in *Cuentos crudos* (2007; Crude Short Stories) and the two essays *Cómo convertir este país en un paraíso, con otras reflexiones sobre Guinea Ecuatorial* (2005; How to Turn This Country into a Paradise, with Other Reflections on Equatorial Guinea) and *Guinea Ecuatorial. Vísceras* (2006; Equatorial Guinea. Entrails).

His most recent publications are novels with some autobiographical content: *Avión de ricos, ladrón de cerdos* (2008; Plane for the Rich, Thief of Pigs) is set in the city of Bata during the 1970s, and *Arde el monte de noche* (2009; The Forest Burns at Night) takes place in the same decade in Annobón. Forthcoming titles include the essay "Africa ya dejó de mamar" (Africa Stopped Suckling), and the documentary screen play "Un día vi cien mil elefantes" (One Day I Saw a Hundred Thousand Elephants). Ávila also directs *Atanga*, the only literary and cultural journal presently published in Equatorial Guinea.

Benita Sampedro Vizcaya

Work By:

Arde el monte de noche. Madrid: Calambur, 2009.
Avión de ricos, ladrón de cerdos. Barcelona: El cobre, 2008.

Work About:

Ávila Laurel, Juan Tomás. Author's Web page. http://www.guineanos.org/.
Sampedro Vizcaya, Benita. "Estudio introductorio." *Guinea Equatorial. Vísceras*. Valencia: Fundación Alfons el Magnánim, 2006, 7–24.

Ayala, Francisco (1906–2009)

The primary importance of this Spanish prose author is extraliterary; his longevity allowed Spaniards to link contemporary democratic Spain after the death of Dictator Francisco Franco (1892–1975) with the democratic Spain prior to the Spanish Civil War (1936–1939). Ayala became a living symbol of the nation's cultural resilience and the values and freedom that the *Generation of 1927 embodied.

Ayala started as an avant-garde novelist with *El boxeador y un ángel* (1929; The Boxer and the Angel) and *Cazador en el alba* (1930; Hunter at Dawn), in which he explores aesthetic and urban modernity. In

1929, he published *Indagación del cinema* (Inquiry of Cinema), a key text for understanding the deep impact that new art forms had on literature and the relationship between surrealism and cinematography. *Los usurpadores* (1949; *Usurpers*, 1987) collects seven narrations about the greed for power. *La cabeza del cordero* (1949; Head of the Lamb) compiles stories about the Spanish Civil War, disappointing in the fact that human passions are more prominent than social conflicts. In *Muertes de perro* (1958; *Death as a Way of Life*, 1964) Ayala denounces life under a dictatorship. His memoirs, *Recuerdos y olvidos* (1982–2006; Memories and Oblivions), written in different volumes, are key to understanding the intellectual life of Spain and the experience of exile that many Spanish writers confronted during the 20th century. As is common with writers formed during the avant-garde period, his exquisite prose adhered to the formalism and decorum of pre-Civil War Spain.

Salvador A. Oropesa

Work About:

Johnson, Roberta. "Francisco Ayala: Boxer and Angel." *Hispania* 89.4 (2006): 741–50.

Orringer, Nelson R. "The Baroque Body in Francisco Ayala's *El rapto*." *Monographic Review/Revista* Monográfica 10 (1994): 46–59.

Azaña, Manuel (1880–1940)

Although he was viewed as an intellectual with passion for literature—he penned plays and novels, winning Spain's National Prize for Literature—Azaña is much more recognized for his role as republican politician and president of the Second Spanish Republic. After being named Minister of War in the Second Republic's provisional government in April 1931, he undertook the much needed reform of the Spanish Army. When he became prime minister of the Republican coalition government in October of the same year, he carried out two other major projects: agrarian reform and education reform. Azaña always thought Spain could be transformed into a modern, democratic, secular state, and on those grounds he defended elimination of special privileges for the army, the landed aristocracy, and especially the Church. His conflicts with these factions forced his resignation on September 1933.

One year later, he founded the Republican Left party, and in early 1936 was instrumental in creating the Spanish Popular Front, a major left-wing coalition that won the February 1936 elections. Unfortunately, the Popular Front's triumph triggered the military uprising against the Second Republic on July 17, 1936, which marked the beginning of the Spanish Civil War (1936–1939). Azaña, who had been elected president of the republic two months before the military revolt, unsuccessfully tried to overcome the conflicts among different political groups that undermined the stability and political cohesion of the republic. After the fall of Barcelona to Nationalist troops in January 1936, he fled to France, where he died in November 1940.

José Manuel Reyes

Work By:

Vigil in Benicarló. Trans. Josephine Stewart and Paul Stewart. Rutherford, NJ: Fairleigh Dickinson University Press, 1982.

Work About:

Rivas Cherif, Cipriano de. *Portrait of an Unknown Man: Manuel Azaña and Modern Spain*. Trans. Paul Stewart. Madison, NJ: Fairleigh Dickinson University Press, 1995.

Azorín (pseudonym of José Martínez Ruiz) (1873–1967)

A leading member of the *Generation of 1898 (writers and intellectuals of Spain who examined their national character and history), José Martínez Ruiz became famous for his journalism, literary criticism, and prose, adopting the pen name of his fictional character Azorín (variously debated as meaning "little goshawk" or "little abashed one") in 1905. He is generally conceded to be author of the label "Generation of '98" since his use of the term, in *Clásicos y modernos* (1913), popularized it.

Azorín's literary style employs short, simple sentences full of nostalgia; descriptions of the Spanish landscape, villages, and people prevail in his, for that time, revolutionary aesthetics, in which plot matters little and the central theme is the essence of what it means to be "Spanish." In his youth he was strongly socialist, but later he departed from those beliefs,

serving five terms as a conservative deputy to Parliament (1907–1919) and choosing to live in Spain under Franco.

Jeffrey Oxford

Work By:

Las confesiones de un pequeño filósofo. Barcelona: Thule, 2003.
Los pueblos: ensayos sobre la vida provinciana. Madrid: Biblioteca Nueva, 2002.

Work About:

Wood, David. "Reportage, *Estampa*, and Socio-Historical Realities in Azorín's Spanish Towns." *Philological Review* 33.1 (Spring 2007): 15–43.

Aztlán

The 16th-century Ramírez Codex lists Aztlán as the mythical homeland of the Aztecs. This text, formally titled *Relación del origen de los indios que habitan esta Nueva España según sus historias* (Account of the Origin of Indians Inhabiting New Spain According to Their Histories) was most probably written by a Christianized Nahuatl Indian, and then copied by Juan de Tovar. Aztlán is geographically identified with northern Mexico and the Southwestern United States; for Mexican Americans, it later came to represent a political statement to reclaim their indigenous and sociocultural traditions.

In the Aztec creation myth, Mexica Indians left the bowels of the earth and settled in Aztlán, thus acquiring the name

Aztec. From there, they undertook a southward migration in search of a sign as to where they should resettle. The 20th-century Chicano civil rights struggle used this reference to a spiritual homeland in the title of the Chicano movement's first manifesto: *El plan espiritual de Aztlán* (1969; The Spiritual Plan of Aztlán).

Mercedes Guijarro-Crouch

Work About:

"El plan espiritual de Aztlán." http://clubs.asua.arizona.edu/~mecha/pages/PDFs/ElPlanDeAtzlan.pdf.

Sánchez, David A. *From Patmos to the Barrio. Subverting Imperial Myths.* Minneapolis: Fortress, 2008, 83–113, 129–135.

Azuela, Mariano (1873–1952)

This Mexican physician and novelist produced the iconic first novel about the Mexican Revolution (1910–1920). As a doctor, he joined Pancho Villa's forces in the revolution and was eventually forced into exile when the Carranza faction won. Azuela's first novel, *María Luisa* (1907), employed a naturalist style (characters defined by their social and biological environments); it was followed by a series of realist novels.

Los de abajo (1915; *The Underdogs*, 2008) first appeared as a serial in a Texas newspaper. A firsthand account of the revolution, it bluntly presents the brutality and absurdity of the war. Primary character Luis Cervantes is, like the author, a physician; unlikeable in his hypocrisy and cowardice, he supplies protagonist Demetrio Macías with ideological justifications for the civil conflict. The novel's stark narrative, fast-paced action, and cold, detached narrative voice make it one of the most modern Latin American novels of its day.

After the revolution, Azuela worked as a doctor caring for the indigent, and used these experiences in *La malhora* (1923; Bad Time) and *La luciérnaga* (1932; The Firefly). No other work approached the merits of *Los de abajo*. Awarded Mexico's National Prize for Arts and Sciences in 1949, he died in Mexico City three years later.

César Valverde

See also Novel of the Mexican Revolution.

Work By:

The Underdogs. Ed., trans., intro. Sergio Waisman. Foreword Carlos Fuentes. New York: Penguin, 2008.

Work About:

Duffy, J. Patrick. "A War of Words: Orality and Literacy in Mariano Azuela's *Los de abajo.*" *Romance Notes* 38.2 (Winter 1998): 173–78.

Laraway, David. "Doctoring the Revolution: Medical Discourse and Interpretation in *Los de abajo* and *El águila y la serpiente.*" *Hispanófila* 127 (September 1999): 53–65.

B

Ballagas, Emilio (1908–1954)

A notable Cuban poet and literary critic, he was a professor in Cuba, and worked in New York City for a year instructing blind students. Ballagas received the Cuban National Poetry Award in 1951. During his short life he cultivated numerous styles. His first book of poems, *Júbilo y fuga* (1931; Joy and Flight), relates to the Spanish avant-garde and is said to develop the concept of *pure poetry*, with a focus on sound and poetic imagery rather than on social realities. *Cuaderno de poesía negra* (1934; Book of Black Poetry) is the first of several anthologies that attempt to capture rhythms and traditions of Afro-Cubans. *Sabor eterno* (1939; Eternal Flavor) has been characterized as neoromantic; it depicts his feelings of guilt and self-disgust but also intense eroticism caused by homosexual desire. Toward the end of his life he wrote poems on personal spiritual experiences; of note is *Nuestra señora del Mar* (1943; Our Lady of the Sea) which also collects traditions surrounding the cult of Nuestra Señora del Cobre in Cuba. Due to his versatility as a poet, Ballagas can be compared with such notable Cuban figures as Nicolás *Guillén, José *Lezama Lima, and Dulce María *Loynaz, though he is much less well known.

Ana Serra

See also Afro-Hispanic Literature in Spanish America; Avant-Garde Poetry in Spanish America; Queer Literature in Spanish America.

Work By:

Burnt sugar Caña quemada: Contemporary Cuban Poetry in English and Spanish. Ed., trans. Lorie Marie Carlson and Oscar Hijuelos. New York: Free Press, 2006, 88–89.
Obra poética. Havana: Letras Cubanas, 1984.

Work About:

Arnedo, Miguel. "Afrocubanista' Poetry and Afro-Cuban Performance." *The Modern Language Review* 96.4 (2001): 990–1005.
Piñero, Virgilio. "Ballagas en persona." *Poesía y crítica*. Ed. Anton Arrufat. México DF: Consejo Nacional para la Cultura y las Artes, 1994, 192–209.

Balmori, Jesús (1886–1948)

This talented Philippine poet, fiction writer, humorist, and journalist came into the Phil-Hispanic literary scene in his late teens with the publication of his first poetry anthology, *Rimas Malayas* (1904; Malay Verses). Balmori became involved in controversy in 1908 when his three submissions—"Specs," "Vae Victis" (Woe to the Vanquished), and "Himno a Rizal" (Hymn to Rizal)—to a poetry contest organized by nationalist newspaper *El Renacimiento* to commemorate José *Rizal's execution won all three prizes. In a sonnet published in *El Renacimiento*, poet Cecilio *Apóstol protested the results. Balmori answered Apóstol's claims with a sonnet of his own, also published in *El Renacimiento*. Three rounds of sonnet exchanges ensued until Fernando María *Guerrero, with a sonnet of his own, asked the two poets to stop.

In 1904, when the Spanish *zarzuela* (musical theater) was still fashionable, Balmori composed *Aves de rapiña* (Birds of Prey). Its unsuccessful run made him abandon theater for the next two decades. Eventually he wrote two more plays which were later staged: *La Flor de Carmelo* (no date; Carmelo's Flower) and *Filipinizad a los Filipinos* (no date; Philippinize Philippines). There are, unfortunately, no known surviving copies. The latter play was an apparent jab at the colonial government's "Americanization" agenda.

In 1910, Balmori dared to do what no one had attempted in two decades: publish a novel. *Bancarrota de almas* (Moral Bankruptcy) presented a critique of the morality among the Manila-based socioeconomic elite, who viewed themselves culturally and morally superior to the lower classes. The novel touched on sensitive social issues of the time like prostitution, the upper class male's sexual exploitation of women, teenage pregnancy, and premarital sex.

A second novel, *Se deshojó la flor* (1915; The Flower Has Lost Its Petals)

continued *Bancarrota's* moralist orientation, attacking in particular the issue of male philandering and female resignation to this problem. The manuscript for Balmori's third novel, *Pájaros de fuego* (Birds of Fire), came three decades later, at the end of World War II (1939–1945). The text narrated life in the Philippines during the Japanese occupation. Literary histories say that the Philippine government acquired the rights to the work, but for years no one could pinpoint the location of the manuscript until a Spanish researcher, in 2006 or 2007, reportedly found a microfilm copy at the Ateneo de Manila University library. A critical edition is currently being prepared for publication.

Balmori's journalistic and humoristic writings appeared in Manila's Spanish language newspapers like *El Renacimiento, La Vanguardia, El Debate, Voz de Manila*, and even in the Spanish section of the *Philippines Free Press*. Before the Second World War, he wrote a column of satirical verses, "Vidas Manileñas" (Life in Manila), in *La Vanguardia* using the pseudonym *Batikuling* (Intestines). Balmori published these collected columns in *El libro de mis vidas manileñas* (1928; The Book of My Life in Manila). After the war, he resumed these satirical writings in his daily "Versos y berzas" (Verses and Cabbages) column in *La Voz de Manila*.

On the three occasions that Balmori earned a literary award, the recognition was met with controversy. In 1926, 18 years after his *El Renacimiento* triumph, Balmori and fellow poet Manuel *Bernabé (1890–1960) captured the Premio Zóbel for their poetic jousts called *Balagtasan*, named after Francisco Balagtas, the leading 19th-century Tagalog-language poet. Their public rejoinders (which debated topics like man vs. woman, and memory vs. oblivion) were significant social events, and staged at the Manila Opera House. One losing contestant protested the Balmori–Bernabé victory, saying they should no longer be eligible for the Zóbel Prize, as they were already the leading poets of the time.

Fourteen years later, during the 1940 Philippine Commonwealth Literary Contests, Balmori's poetry collection, *Mi Casa de Nipa* (1941; My Nipa Hut), won first place in the Spanish-language category. Flavio Zaragoza Cano, awarded second prize, dramatized his protest over the decision during the award ceremonies by ripping up the diploma of recognition that he had been given in front of high-ranking government officials and President Manuel Quezon.

Twenty-eight years after *Rimas Malayas*, Balmori released his second poetry book, *Nippon* (1932), inspired by a trip to Japan, a country which had captured the imagination of Phil-Hispanic writers, especially after the Russo–Japanese War (1904–1905). Philippine fascination with Japan would end with the 1941 bombing of Pearl Harbor and the Imperial Japanese Army's subsequent invasion of the Philippines. Balmori died the same day he finished his last poem, "A Cristo" (1947; To Christ).

Wystan de la Peña

Work By:

Cuentos de Balmori. Trans. Pilar Mariño. Metro Manila: National Book Store, 1987.
Philippine Short Stories in Spanish, 1900–1941. Trans. Pilar Mariño. Quezon City: University of the Philippines Diliman Office of Research Coordination, 1989, 36–49, 56–59, 130–41, 148–55, 348–53, 406–12.
The Other Stories, 1900–1910: English Translation of Selected Short Stories in Spanish. Trans. Teresita Alcantara et al. Mandaluyong City, Philippines: Carl Printing Press, 2002, 48–53, 61–65.

Work About:

Coronel, Reynaldo D. Jr. "Jesús Balmori: Poeta Modernista." *Cuadernos del Centro Cultural de la Embajada de España* 16 (August 1986): 20–22.
De la Peña, Wystan. "A Portrait of a Literary Descendant of María Clara: Ángela Limo in Jesús Balmori's *Bancarrota de Almas*." *Linguae et Litterae* (University of the Philippines Diliman), II (1997): 56–67.
De la Peña, Wystan. "Battlefield and Booty: The Early American Period Filipina in Jesús Balmori's Novels *Bancarrota de Almas* and *Se Deshojó la Flor*." *Philippine Humanities Review* (University of the Philippines Diliman) IX (2007): 46–58.

Balsero ("Rafter")

This term, which may be used pejoratively, denotes the tens of thousands of Cubans who have migrated primarily to the United States by use of small watercraft—often homemade from wood, tires, Styrofoam, and similar materials. The migration began in 1959, and, until the

Mariel boatlift of 1980, Cubans routinely received the favorable status of refugee upon arrival. Subsequently, relations between the United States and Cuba deteriorated: the United States began restricting immigration and implemented a series of punitive economic, social and propaganda policies which, from the Cuban perspective, contributed to dire living conditions and increasing unrest on the island. In 1994, after a violent riot in Havana, Fidel Castro lifted the prohibition on emigration and by July of that year, 500 Cubans refugees were arriving daily to southern Florida. President Clinton responded by intercepting all immigrants and detaining them at the U.S. Naval Base in Guantánamo. The United States detained 32,385 Cubans at Guantánamo, admitting them only some 15 months later. The 2002 documentary *Balseros*, directed by Carlos Bosch and Josep María Domènech, provides a compelling look at the *balsero* experience.

Maureen Ihrie

Work About:

The Cuban Rafter Phenomenon: A Unique Sea Exodus. http://balseros.miami.edu.

Barcelona in Literature

Barcelona is a complex city of Catalonia, Spain. Its linguistic, cultural, social, and economic diversity has meant that no single author has been able to capture its essential qualities. Indeed, Manuel Vázquez Montalbán suggests in *Barcelonas* (1987; *Barcelonas* 1992) that there is no single Barcelona to represent; rather, the city is made up of a multiplicity of contrasting, conflictive, and at times harmonious voices that dilute the possibility of a unique, urban grand narrative.

Indeed, although Don Quixote praises Barcelona's virtues in Part II (1615) of Miguel de *Cervantes's masterpiece, the city did not establish itself as a setting for literature in Spanish or Catalan until the second half of the 19th century, following its capitalist transformation during the preceding century. The absence of Barcelona is even common to literature written in Catalan prior to the 1890s, as the exponents of the 19th-century Catalan Renaissance largely saw the city as a place where Catalan cultural identity, customs, and traditions were diluted by contact with Spanish-speaking workers.

From the 1890s until the present day, however, a rich tradition of Catalan urban literature has developed in the works of Narcís Oller, Josep-Maria Sagarra, Carles Soldevila, Mercé Rodoreda, Manuel Pedrolo, Víctor Mora, Ana María *Moix, Montserrat Roig, and Quim Monzó, among others. Nevertheless, despite this tradition, and despite being the capital of the Catalan-speaking area, the popular image of Barcelona remains that of a cosmopolitan Spanish-speaking metropolis. This image is due to several factors, including the dominance of Spanish-language representations of Barcelona in works by Catalans who write in Castilian; the international strength of the Barcelona-based iconic Spanish-language publishing houses Anagrama, Planeta, Seix Barral, and Tusquets; and, finally, the mythical image of Barcelona as the refuge of so-called Latin American *Boom* writers, such as Colombia's Gabriel *García Márquez and Peruvian Mario *Vargas Llosa, who lived there during the 1960s and 1970s.

Barcelona truly became a literary subject in the 1860s with publication of numerous books in which authors blend historical enquiry with fiction, as in Antonio Altadill's *Barcelona y sus misterios* (1860; Barcelona and Its Mysteries) and Víctor Balaguer's *Las calles de Barcelona* (1866; The Streets of Barcelona). These Spanish-language writings gave way to urban literature in Catalan between the end of the 19th century and the Spanish Civil War (1936–1939), such as Oller's tale of business speculation and urban development in *La febre d'Or* (1892; Gold Fever) and Sagarra's story of Barcelona's red light district in *Vida privada* (1932; Private Life).

With Catalan prohibited by the postwar Franco regime, Barcelona came to be represented almost entirely in Castilian. Between 1943 and 1972, Ignacio Agustí produced a series of novels set in Barcelona between the late 19th century and the civil war, of which the best known is *Mariona Rebull* (1943). These novels paint Barcelona as a city of exciting possibilities, peopled with ambitious young men, but also a place of danger—a "City of Bombs"—in which social unrest and class conflict ultimately justify the 1936 military uprising.

The dominant representation of Barcelona during the early years of Francoism is that of a gray, defeated city, as exemplified in Carmen Laforet's *Nada* (1944; *Nada* 2007), winner of the first Nadal literary prize. *Nada* tells the story of a self-destructing family in a city without a future from the point of view of Andrea, a young 18-year-old girl who arrives in Barcelona from the Canary Islands after the civil war. Alienation, routine, materialism, and an aimless life are also at the heart of *La Noria* (1952; The Ferris Wheel) by Luis Romero, winner of the 1951 Nadal Prize. Unfairly compared to Camilo José *Cela's classic novel of postwar Madrid, *La colmena* (1951; *The Hive*, 1953), Romero attempts to represent the urban collective through 37 main and many more secondary characters. A similar approach is taken by Julio Manegat in *La ciudad amarilla* (1958; The Yellow City) which narrates one day in the life of a taxi driver as he takes passengers across the diverse social locations of Barcelona.

The 1950s economic boom that brought hundreds of thousands of immigrants from other parts of Spain to Barcelona also opened up new spatial settings in literature. Typical of literature in the late 1950s and 1960s are Luis *Goytisolo's avant-garde novel *Las afueras* (1958; The Outskirts) and the social realist narratives, *Fiestas* (1958; Fiestas) and *Donde la ciudad cambia su nombre* (1967; Where the City Changes Its Name), of Juan *Goytisolo and Francisco Candel respectively. All three novels focus on inequality and the often inhuman conditions in which immigrants to Barcelona must live to make a living. Perhaps the most important postwar Spanish-language novelist of Barcelona, Juan *Marsé represents more ironically the cultural and class divide between Castilian-speaking immigrants and the Catalan-speaking middle class in several novels, most notably *Últimas tardes con Teresa* (1966; Last Days with Teresa), in which the *murciano* Pijoaparte tries to win over the Catalan Teresa Serrat. Marsé returns to this theme in *El amante bilingüe* (1988; The Bilingual Lover), which satirizes the linguistic policies of the autonomous Catalan government.

Luis *Goytisolo's long, rambling experimental novel *Recuento* (1974; Retelling) narrates the story of Raúl, a bored, increasingly disillusioned, middle-class Catalan youth, while also exploring aspects of Barcelona's cultural, social, and economic development (chapters seven and eight), paying particular attention to its increasing political, social, and cultural marginalization within Spain, post 1714.

Following a decade of literary and linguistic experimentation in Spanish fiction, Eduardo *Mendoza's *La verdad sobre el caso Savolta* (1975; The Truth about the Savolta Case*, 1992) heralds a return to narrative storytelling. Set during and immediately after World War I, the novel recounts the political and social turmoil of Barcelona during this period. In a similar vein, Mendoza published *La ciudad de los prodigios* (1986; *The City of Marvels*, 1988), a Dickensian novel that chronicles the history of Barcelona from its Roman inception while ostensibly narrating the life of Onofre Bouvila, a *picaresque figure who, through astute business sense and a fair amount of chutzpah and bribes, becomes an important figure in the life of the city. Manuel *Vázquez Montalbán

represents the loss of historical memory in *El pianista* (1986; *The Pianist*, 1989) in which a group of 30-year-old friends deliberately overlook the struggles of previous generations in their scramble for political positions and cushy jobs. Rosa Regàs sets her novel, *Luna lunera* (1999; Moon, Moon Lover), in 1940s Barcelona. With echoes of Laforet's *Nada*, Regàs depicts the stifling atmosphere of the post–civil war city through the lives of several young siblings who suffer at the hands of their ultraconservative grandfather.

Spain's transition to democracy produced a new literary genre associated primarily with Barcelona: hardboiled crime fiction. The most famous exponent of the *novela negra* was Vázquez Montalbán, who chronicles the social, sexual, economic, and physical changes to the Catalan capital throughout the 17 novels and six short story collections which make up his Carvalho Series—named after the eponymous antihero—of which the best known is the Planeta Prize–winning *Los mares del sur* (1979; *Southern Seas*, 1981). During the almost 30 years of the series, Pepe Carvalho, a modern *flâneur* (idle person), observes and records the rapid changes that Barcelona has experienced and, as the series progresses, he becomes increasingly disoriented in the postmodern, post-Olympic Barcelona in which collective memory is slowly erased through land speculation and gentrification. Through the efforts of Vázquez Montalbán and such authors as Mendoza, Andreu Martín, Francisco González Ledesma, José Luis Muñoz, and Alicia Giménez-Bartlett, Barcelona has become undoubtedly the literary crime capital of Spain.

For female characters in works by contemporary women writers, the public spaces of the city largely signify their alienation. Writers Moix in *Julia* (1971), Esther *Tusquets in *El mismo mar de todos los veranos* (1978; *The Same Sea as Every Summer*, 1990), Nuria Amat in *La intimidad* (1997; Intimacy) and Maruja Torres in *Un calor tan cercano* (1997; A Warmth So Close) have all produced fictions in which the characters' search for self-expression takes them beyond the repressive domestic sphere to explore and to make theirs the city in which they live.

The theme of globalization and the mass movement of migrants from North Africa and Latin America enter Barcelonan literature from the mid- to late 1980s. Again, in such novels as Vázquez Montalbán's *El delantero centro fue asesinado al atardecer* (1987; *Offside*, 1995) and Francisco Casavella's *El triunfo* (1990; The Triumph), migrants are perceived as a threat to traditional social relations. Recently, however, extranational migrants, such as Asha Miró in *La hija del Ganges* (2004; *Daughter of the Ganges*, 2006), have begun to produce narratives based on their experiences of cultural conflict and integration in Barcelona.

Two trends dominate Barcelonan urban literature at the turn of the millennium. First, Barcelona has consolidated itself as the preeminent literary city in Spain through two best sellers with a historical bent. In the international publishing phenomenon *La sombra del viento* (2001; *The Shadow of the Wind*, 2004), Carlos *Ruiz Zafón paints a frightening gothic portrait of postwar Barcelona as seen through the eyes of a young boy, while Ildefonso *Falcones's *La Catedral del Mar* (2006; *Cathedral of the Sea*, 2008) centers on the building of the Gothic church Santa Maria del Mar during the Middle Ages. Second, such authors as Quim Aranda, Carlos Paramo, and Javier Pérez Andújar have produced Marsé-influenced works of critical social realism set in Barcelona's outskirts.

Stewart King

See also Censorship and Literature in Spain; Detective and Mystery Fiction in Spain.

Work About:

Carreras, Carles. *La Barcelona literària*. Una introducció geogràfica. Barcelona: Proa, 2003.

Dravasa, Mayder. *The Boom in Barcelona: Literary Modernism in Spanish and Spanish-American Fiction (1950–1974)*. New York: Peter Lang, 2004.

Resina, Joan Ramón. *Barcelona's Vocation of Modernity: Rise and Decline of an Urban Image*. Stanford: Stanford University Press, 2008.

Vázquez Montalbán, Manuel. *Barcelonas*. Trans. Andy Robinson. London: Verso, 1992.

Wells, Caragh. "The Case of Barcelona in Manuel Vázquez Montalbán's Detective Fiction." *Romance Studies* 25.4 (2007): 277–86.

Wells, Caragh. "The City's Renovating Virtue: Urban Epiphanies in the Novels of Carmen Laforet, Carmen Martín Gaite, Montserrat Roig, and Rosa Montero." *Journal of Romance Studies* 7.1 (2007): 7–19.

Barea Ogazón, Arturo (1897–1957)

Novelist, literary critic, and broadcaster, this Spanish intellectual lived in exile in England for much of his life due to the outbreak of the Spanish Civil War in 1936. As a young adult, Barea belonged to the Socialist General Union of Workers (*Unión General de Trabajadores*), and later helped found a militia corps called The Pen (*La Pluma*). Among his chief literary works is an autobiography titled *The Forging of a Rebel* (1941–1946; *La forja de un rebelde*, 1951), translated by Barea's wife Ilsa and first published in English in three volumes. This trilogy, later published in Spanish in 1951, contains *The Forge* (*La forja*), which relates details of the author's childhood experiences in Madrid between 1905–1914; *The Track* (*La ruta*), which expounds upon the Rif War of 1920–1926, where Barea served in the military (this conflict between Moroccan tribes and Spanish forces eventually led to Spain's repossession of present-day Spanish Morocco); and *The Clash* (*La llama*), which centers on the civil war period and the author's subsequent exile. This lengthy text, considered Barea's masterpiece, constitutes a vivid witness to the tensions in Spain before and during the war. Barea's exile in England led him to obtain English citizenship and eventually to work as a Spanish-language correspondent for the BBC. His written work also includes a short volume on *Generation of 1898 writer Miguel de *Unamuno, and another dealing with poet and playwright Federico *García Lorca.

David F. Richter

See also Autobiography in Spain: 1700 to Present; Civil War Literature in Spain; Exile Literature by Spanish Civil War Émigrés.

Work By:

The Forging of a Rebel. Trans. Ilsa Barea. New York City: Reynal & Hitchcock, 1946.

Work About:

Lunsford, Kern L. "*La forja de un rebelde* de Arturo Barea: Relato autobiográfico de las causas ideológicas de la Guerra Civil española." *Cincinnati Romance Review* 7 (1988): 75–84.

Barnet, Miguel (1940–)

This Cuban poet, essayist, screenwriter, and novelist, who studied ethnology under Fernando *Ortiz at the University of Havana, is best known for his ethnological portraits of Cuban society. Barnet had already published several volumes of poetry when he took the field of Afro-Cuban studies by storm in 1966 with *Biografía de un cimarrón* (*The Autobiography of a Runaway Slave*, 1966). This novelistic narrative account of Esteban Montejo, presented as "the oldest living runaway slave in the Americas," blurs the line between anthropological subject and object because it is sometimes unclear to what extent Montejo's narrative has been transformed by Barnet's editorial filter. *Biografía de un cimarrón* can be placed in dual historical and critical contexts: Barnet simultaneously continues the pioneering studies that Ortiz conducted earlier on Cuban character and reflects the egalitarian interests of the then-new Cuban Revolution, which sought to uncover previously silenced or forgotten perspectives on island life. In often gripping ways, *Biografía de un cimarrón* reveals an Afro-Cuban's attempts to retain his freedom and dignity while preserving his African heritage, during and after slavery. For these reasons, this work has become a foundational text of Latin American testimonial narrative.

Rudyard J. Alcocer

See also Afro-Hispanic Literature in Spanish America; Autobiography in Spanish America; Documentary Narrative in Spanish American Literature; Testimonial Writing in Central America; Slavery and Anti-Slavery Literature in Caribbean.

Work By:

The Autobiography of a Runaway Slave. Trans. Jocasta Innes. London: Bodley Head, 1966.
Rachel's Song. Trans. W. Nick Hill. Willimantic, CT: Curbstone Press, 1991.

Work About:

Luis, William. "The Politics of Memory and Miguel Barnet's *The Autobiography of a Runaway Slave*." *Modern Language Notes*. 104.2 (1989): 475–91.

Baroja y Nessi, Pío (1872–1956)

A significant Spanish novelist and member of the*Generation of 1898, he first studied to be a doctor but soon abandoned his rural medical practice for the down-and-out life of a writer in Madrid. After producing an early collection of dour stories and two rural novels, he began to compose a series of episodic adventure novels that conformed to the model of serialized narratives popular in the previous century. He never gave up interspersing such novels, which often had an important historical dimension, with his more definitive social commentaries. There is critical debate about whether such writing sapped Baroja's talents or is to be counted among his best work, with Spaniards generally opting for the latter view.

In his thirties and early forties, he began to produce novels in a style that combined refined naturalism with an impressionist, lyrical use of description. These qualities became a constant. Baroja additionally hit upon an almost formless type of narrative that conformed to his orderless, cynical view of human beings. After several very successful novels of this type, in 1901 and 1905 he published two avant-garde narratives, *Aventuras, inventos y mixtificaciones de Silvestre Paradox* (Adventures, Inventions, and Tricks of Silvestre Paradox) and *Paradox, Rey* (Paradox the King). Both are characterized by fantasy, one-line jokes, and clever political satire. After these novels he returned to the serious, fragmented narrative that was his norm, eventually producing two of his three best novels: *El árbol de la ciencia* (1911; *The Tree of Knowledge*, 1928) and *El mundo es así* (1912; The Way the World Is). The first, which is about an intellectual who tries to avoid unhappiness by refusing involvement in the corrupt society in which he must live, is generally regarded as the most influential Spanish novel of the first 50 years of the 20th century.

Following these two unqualified achievements, Baroja hammered out generally uninspired novels for another three decades, nearly all of them exhibiting a nihilist philosophy and a similar story—an unsociable man seeking happiness in a decadent Europe. At times, as in *Noches del Buen Retiro* (1934; Nights in the Retiro Gardens), he managed to reconnect with his old magic, but these successes were the exception. Baroja is generally viewed as a philosophical novelist, and many of his characters debate the more negative ideas of Kant, Schopenhauer, Nietzsche, and Spengler. His indirect but depressing social exposés had an immense impact on dissident Spanish writing during the post-war Franco years, and, conversely, his attacks on feminists and homosexuals were imitated by right-wing authors like Camilo José *Cela. Hemingway praised him for his allegedly "masculine" style and suggested him for the Nobel Prize.

Thomas R. Franz

Work By:

Zalacaín the Adventurer. Trans. James P. Diendl. Fort Bragg, CA: Lost Coast, 1997.

Work About:

Johnson, Roberta. *Crossfire: Philosophy and the Novel in Spain*, 1900–1934. Lexington: University of Kentucky Press, 1993.

Barrio, El

In general, a *barrio* is a Latino neighborhood. *El Barrio* or la *colonia hispana* was the name given by Puerto Rican immigrants to East Harlem and South Central Harlem in New York City during the 1920s. By 1950, these areas were predominantly populated by people of Puerto Rican descent, also called *Nuyorican. Nuyorican* Piri Thomas's *Down These Mean Streets* (1967) documents his experiences growing up there. Although Hispanic commercial and professional establishments have proliferated in these zones, drugs, crime, and the lack of education continue to plague *El Barrio's* residents.

The neighborhood also houses El Museo del Barrio. Founded in 1969 and located at Fifth Avenue and 104th Street, the museum is a leading cultural institution of the city, dedicated to promoting artistic expressions of all Latino cultures in the United States.

Mercedes Guijarro-Crouch

Work About:

Ciani Forza, Daniela. "Within and Without El Barrio: Piri Thomas's *Down These Mean Streets.*" *Cuadernos de literatura inglesa y norteamericana* 9.1–2 (May–November 2006): 63–81.

Thomas, Piri. *Down These Mean Streets.* New York: Vintage, 1997. http://www.elmuseo.org/.

Barrios, Eduardo (1884–1963)

This outstanding Chilean novelist and journalist is well known for psychological and social prose narratives that reflect the tragic view of life through sensitive, confused, and unhappy characters. One of Latin America's first writers of new narrative—a style that rejected traditional notions of reality and focused on the interior world of characters, Barrios introduced a psychological analysis of human existence.

As a child, Barrios was bullied at school and this may well have influenced his pessimistic writings. His most popular novels include *El niño que enloqueció de amor* (1915; *The Little Boy Driven Mad by Love*, 1967), *El hermano asno* (1922; *The Brother Ass*, 1985), and *Gran Señor y rajadiablos* (1948; Big Boss and Hell Raiser). Written as diaries, their descriptive language focuses on the physical sensations that human beings experience.

In *El niño que enloqueció de amor*, a 10-year-old boy records his love story involving an adult woman. Narrator and readers alike identify with the child, his words, "truth" and feelings, and the crisis that ultimately leads to his death. Its simple, powerful language, coupled with the innocent purity of a child who suffers at such an early age, strongly impacts the emotions of most readers. *El hermano asno* features a friar, Rufino, who has spent six years in a Franciscan order, struggling with his spiritual and material desires. His inability to separate physical love and love toward God results in tragedy.

Anna Hamling

Work By:

The Brother Ass. Trans. E. Sara Rowbotham. Appleton, WI: Lawrence University, 1985.

The Little Boy Driven Mad by Love. Trans. Robert E. Donaldson. Chicago: Roosevelt University, 1967.

Work About:

Brown, James. "*El hermano asno*: When the Unreliable Narrator Meets the Unreliable Reader." *Hispania* 71.4 (Dec. 1988): 798–805.

Barros, Pía (1956–)

Born in Chile's Melipilla province, the youth of this feminist writer and social activist was marked by the horror of Augusto Pinochet's 1973 coup d'état. During his 16-year dictatorship, Barros challenged the government with her writings, despite the sharp scrutiny of censors, and became one of the most representative authors of *Chile's Generation of 1980. This generation confronted dictatorship, seeking to reestablish democracy in Chile.

Mainly a short story writer, Barros has published two novels, *El tono menor del deseo* (1991; The Minor Tone of Desire) and *Lo que ya nos encontró* (2001; What Found Us). Death, solitude, torture, desire, repression, and the dichotomy between femininity and masculinity are recurrent themes in her fiction. Barros's narratives subtly interweave sexuality and politics to expose how women have simultaneously been victims of patriarchal repression and the dictatorship. Her characters challenge the establishment by reinventing male and female roles. Barros is considered a pioneer of the *microcuento* (micro short story) or *libro objeto* (object book), a new literary form. These extremely short texts, with eye-catching yet inexpensive design, are comparable to oral poetry, jokes, and graffiti. *Microcuentos* create a direct, emotional impact that allows readers to reflect critically on a familiar reality. Barros started publishing such texts during the dictatorship to reach readers at all economic levels.

Barros has also worked as a publisher, operating the underground feminist press Ergo Sum, which encouraged women to write against the dictatorship. Since 1976, Barros has run writer's workshops to help women learn to use words to demand their rights and express their own opinions.

Mercedes Guijarro-Crouch

See also Chilean Women Writers: The *Ergo Sum* Project; Feminism in Spanish America.

Work By:

"Scents of Wood and Silence." *What Is Secret: Short Stories by Chilean Women.* Ed., intro. Marjorie Agosín. Fredonia, NY: White Pine, 1995, 165–70.

Work About:

García-Corales, Guillermo. "Pía Barros y los senderos del deseo: Una perspectiva feminista de la Nueva Narrativa Chilena." *Dieciséis entrevistas con autores chilenos contemporáneos: La emergencia de una nueva narrativa.* Lewiston, NY: Mellen, 2005.

Bécquer, Gustavo Adolfo (pseudonym of Gustavo Adolfo Domínguez Bastida) (1836–1870)

Variously labeled a late romantic or post-romantic Spanish poet, Bécquer was orphaned throughout most of his youth, and for much of his life both sickly and unhappy. He inherited an artistic bent from his father, a well-known painter; and throughout his youth, Bécquer was viewed as something of an eccentric, preferring to spend time drawing and reading rather than playing with peers.

In 1854, he moved from his native Seville to Madrid, where he pursued employment as a journalist, translator, censor, and creative writer. He wed Casta Esteban in 1861 and fathered their three children, but the unhappy couple separated in 1868. It is said that Casta was the focal point for only one of Bécquer's published poems; although other women fascinated him, the identities of some of those who inspired his verses are shrouded in mystery.

If Bécquer is indeed to be classified as a romantic poet, his production must necessarily be viewed quite in contrast to that of José de *Espronceda, Ángel de Saavedra, the Duque de Rivas, and José de *Zorrilla. Whereas these poets showed no hesitation in openly demonstrating their emotions, Bécquer's writing is far more intimate. Some critics have argued, however, that it is precisely his tendency toward introspection that establishes him as more of a true romantic than his fellow countrymen, in that his works most closely resemble those of his German and British romantic counterparts.

Bécquer's poems were printed independently during his lifetime; only after his death were they collected and published in *Rimas* (1871; Eng. trans., 1985), his masterpiece. The thematic range of these brief pieces is narrow. The most memorable concern the nature of poetic art, the ethos of love, and feelings of nostalgia and despair; however, all share an overarching aesthetic quality.

The other works for which he is best known are *Desde mi celda* (1864; From My Cell), a series of literary letters, and his prose *Leyendas* (1858–1864; *Legends*, 2004), a collection of mysterious or fantastic stories set in the Middle Ages. The latter are so strikingly lyrical that they are often viewed as poetry masquerading as prose.

Bécquer's literary reputation has changed immensely over time. Although his poetry was esteemed by some during his lifetime, only after his death did he receive the acclaim that had eluded him during his brief life. His impact upon poets of the later modernist movement is largely undisputed, and many modern critics view him as the greatest poet of 19th-century Spain.

Charles Maurice Cherry

See also Poetry in Spain: 1700–1900; Romanticism in Spain.

Work By:

Rhymes and Legends (Selection)/Rimas y leyendas (selección): A Dual-Language Book. Ed., trans. Stanley Appelbaum. Mineola, NY: Dover, 2006.

Work About:

Bynum, B. Brant. *The Romantic Imagination in the Works of Gustavo Adolfo Bécquer.* Chapel Hill: University of North Carolina Department of Romance Languages and Literatures, 1993.

Montesinos, Rafael. *Bécquer: Biografía e imagen.* Seville: Fundación José Manuel Lara, 2005.

Bellatin, Mario (1960–)

This Mexican writer and cultural agent, known for his experimental fiction, was raised in Lima, Peru. He published his first books there before returning to Mexico, where he received the prestigious Xavier Villaurrutia Award for *Flores* (2000; Flowers). Bellatin's work examines the limits between art and life and between different creative media.

Autobiographical in oblique ways, Bellatin's novella-length books, over 15 to date, propose complex, open-ended intellectual games. Through a gripping descriptive language that has more to do with the disposition of objects and bodies in space than with actions, Bellatin involves his readers in distinctive atmospheres, such as that of oppression, in the story of a despotic dog trainer (*Perros héroes* [2000; *Hero Dogs*, 2006]) or of impending death by AIDS (*Salón de belleza* [1999; Beauty Parlor]). As the author elaborates in unexpected ways on common themes from one book to another, his readership follows an overarching yet unresolved tension between estrangement and familiarity, exhibition and secrecy, detachedness and intimacy. As such, the body of his works appears to be in constant mutation. Bellatin is director of the Escuela Dinámica de Escritores, a self-described "antiliterary" workshop that emphasizes immersion in the arts, broadly considered, in lieu of formal training in writing.

Héctor M. Hoyos

Work By:

El arte de enseñar a escribir. México: Fondo de Cultura Económica, 2007.
Chinese Checkers. Trans. Cooper Renner. Edmonds, WA: Ravenna, 2006.
Obra reunida. México: Alfaguara, 2005.

Work About:

Palaversich, Diana. "Apuntes para una lectura de Mario Bellatin." *Chasqui* 32.1 (2003): 25–38.

Belli, Gioconda (1948–)

Perhaps Nicaragua's most famous writer, Belli originally received recognition for her poetry, but is now better known for her prose. An underground member of the Sandinista National Liberation Front (FSLN), she later lived in exile in Costa Rica and Mexico. Her writing combines physical and intellectual passion with politics.

Belli's first two poetry books, *Sobre la grama* (1974; On the Grass), and *Línea de fuego* (1978; Firing Line), intertwine political, revolutionary, and erotic themes. Her memoir of the Sandinista revolution, *El país bajo mi piel: Memorias de amor y guerra* (2000; *The Country Under My Skin*, 2002) portrays her clandestine political and extramarital involvement with key members of the FSLN. *La mujer habitada* (1988; *The Inhabited Woman*, 1994)

details a woman's role in a revolution designed to free a country without changing its deeply rooted sexism. Her most recent novel, *El infinito en la palma de la mano* (2008; *Infinity in the Palm of Her Hand*, 2009), presents an award-winning revision of Adam and Eve's expulsion from the Garden of Eden, depicting woman as both an erotic and independent being.

Linda Ledford-Miller

Work By:

From Eve's Rib. Trans. Steven F. White. Willimantic, CT: Curbstone, 1989.
The Inhabited Woman. Trans. Kathleen N. March. Willimantic, CT: Curbstone, 1994.
The Scroll of Seduction. Trans. Lisa Dillman. New York: Harper Collins, 2006.

Work About:

Barbas-Rhoden, Laura. *Writing Women in Central America. Gender and the Fictionalization of History.* Athens: Ohio University, 2003, 48–79.
Craft, Linda J. *Novels of Testimony and Resistance from Central America.* Gainesville: University Press of Florida, 1997, 158–84.
Krugh, Janis. *Afrodita en el trópico: Erotismo y construcción del sujeto femenino en obras de autoras centroamericanas.* Potomac, MD: Scripta Humanistica, 1999, 3–23, 25–46, 47–59, 61–73, 135–52, 245–59.

Bello, Andrés (1781–1865)

Born in Caracas, in the Viceroyalty of New Granada (present-day Venezuela), this key transitional intellectual who bridged neoclassicism (in which reason furthers social progress) and romanticism (dominated by heightened passions, patriotism, and the individual) spent most of his life outside his native land. In 1810, he traveled with Simón *Bolívar, his former pupil, to London as a representative of Caracas's revolutionary junta and remained there for nearly two decades. During this time he absorbed the European literary and cultural milieu and met exiled Spanish liberals who, upon returning to Spain, carried with them romanticism's ideals. During this London phase Bello wrote his best-known poetry: "Alocución a la poesía" (1823; "Allocution to Poetry," 1997) and "A la agricultura de la zona tórrida" (1826; "Ode to Tropical Agriculture," 1997). Patriotic, optimistic, and nostalgic, these compositions employ the *silva*, an arbitrary combination of 7- and 11-syllable lines. The latter poem celebrates the simple life of the countryside and offers an idyllic portrait of the natural environment. Bello's emphasis, however, is on practical and utilitarian endeavors— agriculture rather than nature—and labor as a necessity in forging a new nation. The poem contributed notably to the newly emerging sense of a Spanish American identity.

In 1829, Bello returned to the Americas, settling in Chile for the remainder of his life. There he won fame as an educator, becoming the first rector of the University of Chile. His *Gramática de la lengua castellana destinada al uso de los americanos* (1847; Grammar of the Spanish Language for Spanish Americans) was a milestone publication that conferred on American Spanish a status equal to that of the Castilian "mother tongue." A neoclassicist at heart, Bello took part with Domingo Faustino *Sarmiento in a spirited, at times vitriolic polemic involving questions of language, culture, and, ultimately, the conflicting tenets of neoclassicism and romanticism. Journalist, humanist, and intellectual, Bello's writing covered a vast range of topics.

Melvin S. Arrington Jr.

Work By:

Selected Writings of Andrés Bello. Trans. Frances M. López-Morillas. Ed. Iván Jaksić. New York and Oxford: Oxford University Press, 1997.

Work About:

"Biblioteca de autor: Andrés Bello." October 9, 2007. http://www.cervantes virtual.com/bib_autor/Andresbello/.

Jaksic, Iván. *Andrés Bello: Scholarship and Nation-Building in Nineteenth-Century Latin America*. Cambridge: Cambridge University Press, 2001.

Belpré, Pura (c. 1899–1982)

This founding mother of U.S. Spanish-language children's literature was born in Cidra, Puerto Rico, between 1899 and 1903. After moving to New York City in 1920, Belpré began a long and innovative career as a public librarian, author, and translator.

Drawing on her talent for storytelling and knowledge of Puerto Rican folklore,

Belpré cultivated new bilingual library programs featuring Hispanic cultures. Her homeland also figures prominently in her writing, beginning with her first and best-known publication, *Pérez and Martina: A Portorican Folktale* (1932). Vibrantly illustrated by Carlos Sánchez, Belpré's rendition of the ill-fated love between a gallant mouse and a beautiful cockroach incorporates Spanish words and songs. Both the original and the author's 1960 Spanish translation have enjoyed extraordinary longevity. Lisa Sánchez González considers this work as an allegorical critique of colonial social hierarchies, and decries critics' failure to engage Belpré's writing as literature.

Of Belpré's eight children's books, most were published in the 1960s and 1970s; she translated three to Spanish herself. A young adult novel emerged posthumously. Belpré's other contributions to U.S. children's literature in Spanish include an annotated bibliography for librarians (1971) and some 20 translations. Since 1996, the Pura Belpré Award has honored this multifaceted legacy by recognizing outstanding Latino/a children's authors and illustrators.

Laura Kanost

Work By:

Pérez y Martina: Un cuento folklórico puertorriqueño. New York: Viking, 1991.

Work About:

Sánchez González, Lisa. *Boricua Literature: A Literary History of the Puerto Rican Diaspora*. New York: New York University Press, 2001, 71–101.

Benavente, Jacinto (1866–1954)

Born in Madrid, this enormously successful and prolific playwright won the *Nobel Prize for Literature in 1922. Reacting against the declamatory style of José *Echegaray and other predecessors, and influenced by Henrik Ibsen, August Strindberg, and their European followers, he brought a type of realism to the stage. Known for the creation of eloquent, well-developed female characters, some of his plays now seem highly stylized, while others strive for psychological depth. The great majority reflect the mores of the upper-middle class, which Benavente gently satirized, recognizing at the same time that the members of this group represented the theater audience of that day. His play *Rosas de otoño* (1905; *Autumnal Roses*, 1919) captures the spirit of much of his work. Its female protagonist does not walk away from her errant husband, but resigns herself to wait until he is too worn out to pursue other women. Benavente eschews the daring route of Ibsen's *A Doll's House*, and instead creates a secondary plot in which a younger woman is both impatient and rebellious. Despite Benavente's skills in the subgenre of what may be called parlor drama, his best-known work, *Los intereses creados* (1907; *The Bonds of Interest*, 1967), presents a variation on the classic Italian *Commedia dell'Arte*, and two of his most celebrated plays, *Señora ama* (1908; Lady of the House) and *La malquerida* (1913; *The Passionflower*, 1953), take place in rural settings and attempt to recreate the discourse, as well as the emotional intensity, of provincial Spain. Benavente also cultivated the short dramatic form, the *género chico*, in scores of plays.

Edward H. Friedman

See also Theater in Spain: 1700–1900.

Work By:

Plays by Jacinto Benavente. Trans. John Garrett Underhill. 4 vols. New York: Charles Scribner's Sons, 1923–1924.

Work About:

Peñuelas, Marcelino. *Jacinto Benavente*. New York: Twayne, 1968.

Benedetti, Mario (1920–2009)

This Uruguayan poet, essayist, novelist, playwright, and journalist is widely read in Spanish-speaking countries. Perhaps best known for his short stories, Benedetti's themes include relationships, love, alienation, loneliness, political commitment, and exile. Many writings center on the daily existence of the urban middle class. Benedetti has a great talent for speaking with different voices and points of view (his characters are young, old, male, and female). His best-known novel, *La tregua* (1960; *The Truce*, 1969), recounts the story of Martín Santomé, a widower who falls in love with a much younger woman. Their relationship, truncated by her death, opens a brief window of hope in his otherwise gray life. Equally important, *Gracias por el fuego* (1965; Thanks for the Fire), features as protagonist the son of a corrupt politician who commits suicide after failing to kill his father. The 1959 short story collection *Montevideanos* (Stories from Montevideo) offers a colorful collage of Uruguay's capital and its people. He is also well known for his *microcuentos*, very short stories or vignettes in which the situation presented overrides character development.

Benedetti's writings were banned after Uruguay's 1973 military coup, and he was forced into exile until the fall of the dictatorship in 1985, when he returned to Uruguay. He continued to write, dividing his time between Montevideo and Madrid. His poems, which sing of love and friendship, the man in the street and his concerns, and the political systems which separate human beings, have been sung by Catalan Joan Manuel *Serrat and Cuban Silvio Rodríguez, and his narrative has inspired several movies.

Gianna M. Martella

Work By:

Blood Pact and Other Stories. Ed. Claribel Alegría and Darwin J. Flackoff. Willimantic, CT: Curbstone, 1997.
Little Stones at My Window. Trans., intro. Charles D. Hatfield. Willimantic, CT: Curbstone, 2003.

Work About:

Dawes, Greg, ed. *Mario Benedetti, Contemporary Uruguayan Author*. Lampeter, UK: Edwin Mellen, 2008.

Benet, Juan (1927–1993)

Widely acknowledged as one of 20th-century Spain's most important writers, he produced plays, short stories, and numerous essays, but his *Región* novel series best revealed his distinctive voice among contemporaries. The first, most famous novel of the trilogy *Volverás a Región* (1967; *Return to Región*, 1987) was soon followed by *Una meditación* (1969; *A Meditation*, 1982) and *Un viaje de invierno* (1972; *A Winter Journey*, 1998).

The three novels take place in Región, a mythical place that has often been compared to William Faulkner's Yoknapatawpha. Región is highly reminiscent of many locations in rural Spain after the devastation of the civil war (1936–1939), but the reader never knows where it is or exactly what is happening. Likewise, characters are few and there is little information to successfully craft their story, given the chronological hopscotch and vagueness of their rare exchanges, either within particular novels or across the trilogy. From the very first Región novel, Benet's style is spectacularly dense, baroque, labyrinthine, and semantically precise in its painstaking detail. His prose is also syntactically intricate to such levels as to frustrate even the most willing reader. Sentences can be pages long, extending through paragraphs trussed by clauses that contribute to the ambiguity that his novels embody. Questions of time, memory, and loss, among others, figure at their core. Benet always eschews narratives of cause and effect; instead, readers must plunge into an enigmatic environment that grows more complicated with successive readings.

After publishing *El aire de un crimen* (1980; The Air of a Crime), a deceptively accessible crime novel that also took place in Región, *Saúl ante Samuel* (1980; Saul before Samuel) becomes another example of Benetian verbal virtuosity. The text retells (or deciphers) a conflict between brothers during the Spanish Civil War. The same conflict takes center stage in the 12-novel series *Herrumbrosas Lanzas* (1983–1986; Rusty Lances). This monumental work even includes a topographic map, drawn by Benet, but, as usually happens in his novels, the reader can draw no conclusions. Again, only a complex ambiguous world emerges: those two attributes provide the only coordinates to delineate the devastation that Región has endured.

Anton Pujol

See also Civil War Literature in Spain.

Work By:

Return to Region. Trans. Gregory Rabassa. New York: Columbia University Press, 1987.

Work About:

Manteiga, Roberto C., David K. Herzberger, and Malcom A. Compitello, ed. *Critical Approaches to the Writings of Juan Benet.* Hanover, NH: University Press of New England, 1984.

Vernon, Kathleen M., ed. *Juan Benet.* Madrid: Taurus, 1986.

Benítez Rojo, Antonio (1931–2005)

Born in Havana, Cuba, this widely translated novelist, essayist, and short story writer earned degrees in accounting, finance, and economics from the University of Havana. Benítez Rojo's vocation as writer was apparent as a child, but he pursued this career only after being confined to bed by illness. His first published fiction, the short story collection *Tute de reyes* (1967; King's Flush) won the prestigious Casa de las Américas Prize.

Benítez Rojo also authored the award-winning screenplay for Tomás Gutiérrez Alea's film *The Survivors*. As literary theorist, he is widely known for *La isla que se repite: el Caribe y la perspectiva posmoderna* (1989; *The Repeating Island: The Caribbean and the Modern Perspective*), which was awarded the 1992 Modern Language Association Katherine Singer Kovacs Prize. This text offers a profound analysis of common elements that unite the disparate Caribbean nations and islands. The concepts of machine—used to define the plantation system—and polyrhythm—describing widespread improvised cultural practices—cogently reference the historic and cultural circumstances that help define Caribbean identity.

Begoña Vilouta-Vázquez

Work By:

The Repeating Island: The Caribbean and the Postmodern Perspective. Trans. James Maraniss. Durham, NC: Duke University Press, 1996.

Sea of Lentils. Trans. James Maraniss. Amherst: University of Massachusetts Press, 1990.

A View from the Mangrove. Trans. James Maraniss. Amherst: University of Massachusetts Press, 1998.

Work About:

Paquet, Sandra Pouchet. "Documents of West Indian History: Telling a West Indian Story." *Callaloo* 20.4 (1997): 764–76.

Stavans, Ilan. "Carnival of Hyphens: A Conversation with Cuban Writer Antonio Benítez-Rojo." *Bloomsbury Review* 14.5 (1994): 5, 24–25.

Berceo, Gonzalo de (c. 1190s–c. 1260s)

Born in Berceo, La Rioja, Spain, he is the first poet in Spanish literature to break with the medieval tradition of *anonymatus* (maintaining authorial anonymity), initiating new interest in the individual as creator. By scattering information about his life in his works, readers have been able to reconstruct Berceo's literary persona. Documents from San Millán de la Cogolla monastery, where Berceo was educated, further help to assemble his biographical profile. Contrary to old suppositions, grounded in Berceo's misleadingly modest self-depiction as a low-ranking, simple priest, his innovative writing and the knowledge disseminated in his poems promote the assumption of a scholarly background and a solid medieval education in the so-called seven liberal arts—grammar, logic, rhetoric, arithmetic, geometry, astronomy, and music—and, most likely, studies of the Bible, patristic writings, hagiographies, and Latin. Furthermore, his stylistic similarities with other "*mester de clerecía*" works (a didactic poetic style used by clergy for texts directed to commoners) and his pragmatic use of literature suggest that Berceo's erudition might be connected with the University of Palencia.

Berceo's poetry has been classified in three groups: hagiographies, Marialogies and religious poems on diverse topics, always pedagogical in tone. The first group dealt with saints' lives and recommended exemplary conduct using each saint's virtues as a model. Some of these poems may have had a propagandistic, materialistic intent to help with the monastery's financial needs. Marialogies were poems fostering devotion for Virgin Mary; in this tradition, Berceo wrote his most extensive, important work, *Los Milagros de Nuestra Señora* (13th c.; *Miracles of Our Lady*, 2007).

As a *mester de clerecía* poet, Berceo composed all his work in *cuaderna vía* stanzas—four-line stanza poems with 14-syllable lines and consonant rhyme. Berceo's pragmatic goal of religious edification addressed both the clergy and laymen who were almost certainly illiterate in religious and pious matters. His relevance and originality lie in his transformation of erudite, primarily Latin sources into Castilian (Spanish), the shared language of his audience. Through Berceo, Castilian reached literary and artistic status. He did not invent new stories, but innovated by inserting folk elements into his verse and adding liveliness to his direct, first-person discourse with personal opinions, jokes, and personal feelings about different matters. He constantly seemed to address the nearby "you" (presence) of listeners. Vivacity, accentuated by the introduction of popular sayings and customs, helped create a world easily recognized by his public and augment the novelty of his work.

Mercedes Guijarro-Crouch

See also Poetry in Spain: Beginnings to 1700.

Work By:

The Collected Works of Gonzalo de Berceo in the English Translation. Ed. Annette Grant Cash. Trans. Jeannie K. Bartha, Annette Grant Cash, and Richard Terry Mount. Tempe, AZ: Arizona Center for Medieval and Renaissance Studies, 2007.

Work About:

Kelley, Mary Jane. "Blindness and Physical and Moral Disorder in the Works of Gonzalo de Berceo." *Hispanic Review* 73.2 (2005): 131–55.

Biblioteca Gonzalo de Berceo. http://www.vallenajerilla.com/berceo/.

Berman Goldberg, Sabina (1956–)

Born in Mexico City, this director, producer, journalist, screenwriter, novelist, essayist, and poet has also written and performed plays for children. Considered one of the "new dramatists of Mexico," her plays focus on gender roles and the struggle for power. Her work speaks to the difficulty of belonging to a minority group (lesbian, Jew) in Mexico, and she uses her writing to combat discrimination.

In 1993, Berman staged and directed *Entre Villa y una mujer desnuda* (*Between Villa and a Naked Woman*, 1997), a drama about gender roles where the main character tries to make her relationship with her lover a more committed one. Its theatrical success led to a 1996 screen adaptation. In later plays—*Molière* (1998), *¡Feliz nuevo siglo, doctor Freud!* (2000; Happy New Year, Dr. Freud!), and *65 contratos para hacer el amor* (2000; 65 Contracts for Lovemaking)—Berman makes use of European literary and scientific history to again develop her primary themes of gender and power.

Most recently inspired by the unsolved brutal murders of young Mexican women, her desire to call attention to these ongoing atrocities produced the screenplay, *El traspatio* (2009; *Backyard)*, set outside of the Mexican border town of Juárez.

María R. Matz

Work By:

Between Villa and a Naked Woman. Trans. Shelley Tepperman. *Theatre Forum* 14 (1997): 91–108.

The Theatre of Sabina Berman: The Agony of Ecstasy and Other Plays. Trans. Adam Versényi. Carbondale: Southern Illinois University Press, 2003.

Work About:

A'Ness, Francine. "The Challenges of Translation, the Deception of Reception: The Case of *Between Pancho Villa and a Naked Woman* by Sabina Berman." *Symposium: A Quarterly Journal in Modern Literatures* 61 (Winter 2008): 291–305.

Bernabé, Manuel (1890–1960)

This Philippine poet, politician, journalist, and educator enjoys the distinction of being the first Phil-Hispanic poet to be proclaimed national poet, the title bestowed him by the Dominican-run University of Santo Tomás in 1950, months before it began celebrating its 440th anniversary. For Bernabé, the honor came more than two decades after winning the Premio Zóbel—the highest literary award given to a Phil-Hispanic writer—twice in three years.

Bernabé garnered his first Zóbel in 1924 for his Spanish translation of Omar Khayyam's *Rubaiyat*. Two years later, he shared the prize with Jesús *Balmori (1886–1948) for their poetic jousts, called *Balagtasan*, after leading 19th-century Tagalog-language poet, Francisco Balagtas.

Aside from his literary laurels, Bernabé holds the record for producing the thickest poetry anthology of his generation, the 330-page *Cantos del Trópico* (1929; Songs from the Tropics). His second anthology, *Perfil de Cresta* (1957; Profile of a Rooster's Crest), contains poems demonstrating his generation's change in perspective vis-à-vis the United States: from hated colonizer to beloved mother. This new attitude is exemplified by references in the collection to "Madre América," a label

Bernabé reserved for Spain (Madre España) before World War II (1939–1945), undoubtedly influenced by the Allied forces' victorious return to the Philippines in October 1944. His most anthologized poems, "¡Bataan! ¡Corregidor!" and "Romería de la Muerte" (Pilgrimage of Death), lament the sufferings of Philippine and American soldiers after their defeat in Bataan and Corregidor Island in 1942.

For several years, Bernabé wrote for *La Democracia* and *La Vanguardia* newspapers. After the war, he contributed to *El Excelsior* magazine and taught Spanish in several universities and other educational institutions.

Wystan de la Peña

Work About:

Bautista, Erwin Thaddeus L. "Reflections of Impressionism in the Poetry of Manuel Bernabé," *Linguae et Litterae* I (December 1992): 25–28.

Bautista, Erwin Thaddeus L. "Cosmopolitanism in the Poetry of Manuel Bernabé." *Philippine Humanities Review* 3.1 (1996–1999): 85–106.

Biblioteca de Autores Españoles (BAE)

The complete title for this massive collection of masterpieces of Spanish literature is *Biblioteca de autores españoles desde la formación del lenguaje hasta nuestros días* (Library of Spanish Authors since the Formation of the Language until Our Time). Created in 1846 by Manuel de Rivadeneyra (1805–1872), the collection represents part of the historical formation of national consciousness in Spain. Miguel de *Cervantes (1547–1616), Lope de *Vega (1562–1635), and Francisco de *Quevedo (1580–1645) are some examples of the Spanish writers included in these volumes. Publication of the collection continues; to date, more than 300 volumes have appeared. In 2007, the collection began to be digitalized and is now available online.

Enric Mallorquí-Ruscalleda

Work By:

Biblioteca de Autores Españoles. http://www.cervantesvirtual.com.

Work About:

Agenjo Bullón, Xavier. "Nueva época de la Biblioteca de Autores Españoles (1999)." *Boletín de la Biblioteca Menéndez Pelayo* 75 (1999): 567–71.

Biography in Spain: Beginnings to 1700

Biography offers an account of an individual's life as described by another person. Although the term was probably first used in the late 17th century, critics have identified biographical elements in texts as early as the second millennium before Christ. Greeks and Romans also authored brief biographies, such as Plutarch's first-century *The Lives of the Noble Grecians and Romans*, which paired lives of notable Greek and Roman men with shared strengths or weaknesses. Medieval and early modern Spanish texts also commemorated lives of important subjects.

During the Middle Ages and later, biographical lives of rulers were popular. Completed long before its publication date, Pero López de Ayala's *Corónica de Enrique III* (1779; Chronicle of Henry III) traces Henry III of Castile's rule from his father's death in 1390 until his own in 1406. López de Ayala also wrote biographies of Pedro I, Enrique II, and Juan I. Hernán Pérez del Pulgar wrote *Crónica de los Reyes Católicos* (1490; Chronicle of the Catholic Monarchs), which recounts Ferdinand's and Isabella's lives from before their marriage through to the final years of the Moorish conflict, as well as chronicles of Juan II and Enrique IV. Gonzalo Chacón narrates Don Álvaro de Luna's 45 years in the royal court in *Crónica de Don Álvaro de Luna, Condestable de Castilla, Maestre de Santiago* (1546; Chronicle of Don Álvaro de Luna, Constable of Castile, Master of Santiago). When King Philip II died, a series of biographies presented his death, as well as his life, as an example for Spaniards to learn from, including Antonio Cervera de la Torre's *Testimonio auténtico y verdadero de las cosas notables*...(1599; A True and Authentic Testimony of the Remarkable Events...), Juan Íñiguez de Lequerica's *Sermones funerales*...(1601; Funeral Sermons...), Cristóbal Pérez de Herrera's *Elogio a las esclarecidas virtudes*... (1604; Eulogy to the Illustrious Virtues ...), and Baltasar Porreño's *Dichos y Hechos del Rey Don Felipe II* (1628; The Maxims and Deeds of King Don Philip II).

Biographies of saints, or hagiographies, were also widely read starting in the Middle Ages; Heffernan counts more than 8,000 in the *Bibliotheca Hagiographica Latina et Mediae Aetatis* (1898–1901). Different life narratives of Santa María Egipciaca date to the 13th and 14th centuries. For centuries, many biographers have written about St. *Teresa de Jesús's life; manuscripts of Fray Luis de *León's *De la vida, muerte, virtudes y milagros de* ... (1883; Of the Life, Death, Virtues, and Miracles of ...), Fray Diego de Yepes's *Vida, virtudes, y milagros* ... (1599; Life, Virtues, and Miracles ...), Padre Francisco de Ribera's *La vida de la Madre Teresa de Jesús* (1590; The Life of Mother Teresa of Jesus), Father Jerónimo de Gracián's *Fuentes históricas* ... (1582–1596; Historical Sources ...), Julián de Ávila's *Vida de Santa Teresa de Jesús* ... (1881; Life of St. Teresa of Jesus ...), and Ana García de San Bartolomé's "Últimos años de la Madre Teresa de Jesús" (ca. 1584–1585; Last Years of Mother Teresa of Jesus) date to the 16th century.

Following the classical tradition of penning collections of related, superior lives, several group accounts of themed exemplary lives were published in Spain. Juan Gil de Zamora wrote about saints, kings, and emperors in the late 13th-century *Liber illustrium personarum* (Book of Illustrius Persons). Fernán Pérez de Gúzman authored *Generaciones y semblanzas* (1512; Generations and Biographical Sketches), more than 30 brief discussions of men (and one woman), including rulers, archbishops, and other officials. *Claros varones de Castilla* (1486; Illustrious

Men of Castile), by Fernando del Pulgar, includes over 20 biographies of pre-eminent nobles and church officials.

As society's focus shifted from collective to individual experience, throughout Europe Renaissance intellectual trends renewed interest in individual lives of common people who were not rulers or saints. Whittemore credits Italians Benvenuto Cellini and Giorgio Vasari, respectively, for drawing attention to the flesh, instead of only the spirit, and presenting lives of artists, as well as kings and saints. In Spain, this transition also occurred. Francisco Pacheco included biographies of such artists as Diego Velázquez in *Arte de la pintura* (1638; Art of Painting). Fernando Pizarro y Orellana recounted the lives of several explorers, including Christopher Columbus, Hernán Cortés, and Francisco Pizarro, in *Varones ilustres del Nuevo Mundo* . . . (1639; Illustrious Men of the New World . . .).

Fewer biographies of women's lives exist, but there were individually authored (by a woman's confessor) and collected biographies of religious women of moral excellence. The Church may have used these biographies to monitor the activities of mystic women. Arenal and Schlau describe more than five examples of women's biographical narratives in *Untold Sisters*. Despite many challenges with writing and publishing, some women also wrote biographies, such as Ana de Castro y Egas's *Eternidad del Rey don Felipe Tercero* . . . (1629; Eternity of King Philip III . . .). Early biographies of important people in Spain were influenced by previous models, but the subjects and presentation

became less formal over time, a trend that continued in later Spanish biographies.

Gwen H. Stickney

See also Biography in Spain: 1700 to Present; Convent Writing in Spain and the New World; Renaissance in Spain.

Work About:

Arenal, Electa and Stacey Schlau. *Untold Sisters: Hispanic Nuns in Their Own Works*. Albuquerque: University of New Mexico Press, 1989.

Cruz, Anne J. "Challenging Lives: Gender and Class as Categories in Early Modern Spanish Biographies." *Disciplines on the Line: Feminist Research on Spanish, Latin American, and U.S. Latina Women*. Ed. Anne J. Cruz, Rosilie Hernández-Pecoraro, and Joyce Tolliver. Newark, DE: Juan de la Cuesta, 2003, 103–23.

Eire, Carlos M. N. *From Madrid to Purgatory: The Art and Craft of Dying in Sixteenth-Century Spain*. Cambridge: Cambridge University Press, 1995, 300–21, 371–400.

Heffernan, Thomas J. *Sacred Biography: Saints and Their Biographers in the Middle Ages*. New York: Oxford University Press, 1988.

Whittemore, Reed. *Pure Lives*: *The Early Biographers*. Baltimore: The Johns Hopkins University Press, 1988.

Biography in Spain: 1700 to Present

The term "biography," or a life story written by another, was first used in the late 17th century to name a genre that was becoming more standardized. Throughout the centuries, biographers have continued the early practice of writing about notable leaders, and in the 19th century there was a noticeable increase in such writing by journalists and members of the upper class. For example, national poet Manuel José Quintana's three-volume collection, *Vidas de los españoles célebres* (1807–1833; *Lives of Celebrated Spaniards: ...*, 1833), included detailed life narratives, based on the work of earlier writers, of such figures as El Cid, Gúzman el Bueno, Roger de Lauria, Vasco Núñez de Balboa, Francisco Pizarro, Don Álvaro de Luna, and Fray Bartolomé de las Casas.

A significant number of biographies of renowned historical figures appeared in print in the early- and late-20th century as well. Starting in 1929, the publishing house Espasa-Calpe produced "Las vidas españolas del siglo XIX," a series of approximately 60 biographies. Various publishers, including La Nave, F. Beltrán, and Seix-Barral, quickly followed suit with new biographical series in the 1930s. Such periodicals as *Biografías*, *La Gaceta Literaria*, *El Sol*, and *Revista de Occidente* featured some biographies in the 1930s. Significant biographies include numerous texts about Spanish military leader and post–civil war dictator Francisco Franco, Gregorio Marañón's work on the Duke of Olivares (1936), Salvador de Madariaga's studies on Christopher Columbus (1940) and Hernán Cortés (1941), and Jesús Pabón's publication on Catalan politician Francesc Cambó (1952), but there was less interest in the genre until the last part of the century.

Evidenced by books published and literary supplements, interest in biographies of important Spaniards and international subjects grew in the 1990s, which Morales Moya attributes to society's current interest in the individual. Some recent Spanish examples include Santos Juliá's work on the writer and president, *Manuel Azaña: Una biografía política: Del Ateneo al Palacio Nacional* (1990; Manuel Azaña: A Political Biography: From the Ateneo to the National Palace); J. Álvarez Junco's biography of a prime minister, *El emperador del Paralelo: Alejandro Lerroux y la demagogia populista* (1990; The Emperor of the Parallel: Alejandro Lerroux and the Populist Demagogy); John Huxtable Elliott's study of 17th-century politician and favorite of Phillip IV, *El conde-duque de Olivares: El político en una época de decadencia* (1990; The Count-Duke of Olivares: The Politician in a Period of Decadence); and Henry Kamen's *Felipe de España* (1997; *Philip of Spain*, 1997), *Felipe V: el rey que reinó dos veces* (2000; *Philip of Spain: The King Who Reigned Twice*, 2001), and *El gran duque de Alba: soldado de la España Imperial* (2004; *The Duke of Alba*, 2004). Isabel Burdiel and Manuel Pérez Ledesma discuss biographical methodology and collect 11 biographies of unconventional men and women, including Mariana Pineda, Juan Álvarez y Mendizábal, and Vicente *Blasco Ibáñez, in *Liberales, agitadores y conspiradores: Biografías heterodoxas del siglo XIX* (2000; Liberals, Agitators, and Conspirators: Heterodox Biographies from the 19th Century).

Modern Spanish biographers have composed many studies of writers. Miguel de

*Cervantes Saavedra, for example, has been the subject of numerous biographies throughout the centuries, including notable ones by Gregorio Mayans y Siscar (1737), Vicente de los Ríos (1773), Juan Antonio Pellicer y Pilares (1800), Martín Fernández de Navarette (1819), Jerónimo Morán (1862–1863), León Ramón Máinez (1876), Luis Astrana y Marín (1949–1953), and Jean Canavaggio (1986). Nicolás Antonio's extensive two-volume review of Spanish writers, *Bibliotheca Hispana Vetus* and *Bibliotheca Hispana Nova* (written in the late 17th century), was republished in 1788. In the 19th century, several biographical collections appeared, such as Cayetano Alberto de la Barrera y Leirado's *Catálogo bibliográfico y biográfico del teatro antiguo español, desde sus orígenes hasta mediados del siglo XVIII* (1860; Bibliographical and Biographical Catalogue of Old Spanish Theater, from Its Origins to the Middle of the Eighteenth Century) and Manuel Serrano y Sanz's *Apuntes para una biblioteca de escritoras españolas desde el año 1401 al 1833* (1903; Notes for a Collection of Spanish Women Writers from the Year 1401 to 1833).

José Romera Castillo makes apparent the interest in biographies of recent writers in the late 20th century. For example, Francisco *Umbral has authored various biographical narratives about other writers, such as *Miguel Delibes* (1970); *Larra: Anatomía de un dandi* (1965; Larra: Anatomy of a Dandy), about Mariano José de *Larra; and *Lorca: Poeta maldito* (1968; Lorca: Accursed Poet), about Federico *García Lorca. Many literary specialists have produced biographical studies. Rosa Navarro and Ángel García Galiano penned *Retrato de Francisco Ayala* (1996; Portrait of Francisco *Ayala), and Ian Gibson authored the following studies, in English and Spanish: *Vida, paón y muerte de Federico García Lorca* (1989; *Federico García Lorca: A Life*, 1989), *La vida desaforada de Salvador Dalí* (2003; *The Shameful Life of Salvador Dalí*, 1997), *Cela, el hombre que quiso ganar* (2003; Cela, The Man Who Wanted to Win) and *Ligero de equipaje: La vida de Antonio Machado* (2006; Light of Luggage: The Life of Antonio *Machado). Rosa *Montero includes some writers and other women from Spain and abroad in her collection *Historias de mujeres* (1995; Women's Stories), containing 15 biographies and a bibliography.

Family members have also written about writers. Camilo José Cela Conde published *Cela, mi padre: La vida íntima y literaria de Camilo José Cela* (1989; Cela, My Father: The Intimate and Literary Life of Camilo José *Cela), and Gonzalo Torrente Malvido penned *Torrente Ballester, mi padre* (1990; *Torrente Ballester, My Father).

Current demands for accessible and universal biographical information are generating the creation of reference materials in both electronic and book forms, a need that is likely to continue in the future. These often brief life histories share commonalities with medieval collections of biographical sketches. Víctor Herrero Mediavilla's *Archivo Biográfico de España, Portugal e Iberoamerica* (2000; Biographical Archive of Spain, Portugal, and Iberoamerica) contains 200,000 articles about prominent figures from the mid-19th to mid-20th centuries. The Real Academia de la

Historia is currently preparing the *Diccionario biográfico hispano* (Hispanic Biographical Dictionary) with approximately 40,000 biographical entries from all fields and historical periods.

Gwen H. Stickney

See also Biography in Spain: Beginnings to 1700; Biography in Spanish America.

Work About:

Morales Moya, Antonio. "Biografía y narración en la historiografía actual." *Problemas actuales de la historia.* Ed. José María Sánchez Nistal. Salamanca, Spain: Universidad de Salamanca, 1993, 229–55.

Romera Castillo, José. "Biografías literarias en la España actual." Universidad Nacional de Educación a Distancia Centro de Investigación de Semiótica Literaria, Teatral y Nuevas Tecnologías. March 19, 2011. http://www.uned.es/centro-investigacion-SELITEN@T/pdf/autobio/I7.pdf.

Romera Castillo, José, and Francisco Gutiérrez Carbajo, eds. *Biografías literarias (1975–1997).* Madrid: Visor, 1998.

Soguero García, Francisco Miguel. "Los narradores de vanguardia como renovadores del género biográfico: aproximación a la biografía vanguardista." *Hacia la novela nueva: Essays on the Spanish Avant-Garde Novel.* Ed. Francis Lough. Bern: Peter Lang, 2000, 199–217.

Biography in Spanish America

Biography, formed from Greek *bios* (life) and *graphe* (writing), narrates the story of a life. Biographers have authored life narratives about Spanish America's residents since the colonial period. The kinds of early biographies read in Spain, including those of important religious and political figures, were used in the Spanish colonies as models for writers documenting their travels. Arenal and Schlau indicate that colonial-era convents in Spanish America, as in Spain, produced biographies of religious women, such as Josefa de la Providencia's history of the founding of San Joaquín of Nazarene Nuns Monastery in Lima, Peru, which includes the biography of Antonia Lucía del Espíritu Santo.

Rose observes that the early 15th-century Spanish biographer Fernán Pérez de Gúzman and the chronicles of kings' lives offered organizational models for biographical portraits in New World explorers' narratives; such models were followed in Francisco López de Gómara's *Historia de la conquista de México* (1552; *Cortés: The Life of the Conquerer by His Secretary, 1964*) and Bernal *Díaz del Castillo's *Historia verdadera de la conquista de la Nueva España* (1575; *The Conquest of New Spain*, 1963), which include brief physical descriptions of Aztec ruler Montezuma's height, build, skin color, hair, and beard in this traditional order and then a moral description of his virtues and vices. Notable biographers of colonial figures include Juan de Castellanos, whose *Elegías de varones ilustres de Indias* (1589: Elegies of Illustrious Men from the Indies) traces American exploration and commemorates the deaths of soldiers, commanders, and political leaders; and Fernando Pizarro y

Orellana, whose *Varones ilustres del Nuevo Mundo* (1639: Illustrious Men of the New World) includes six biographies of figures like Christopher Columbus, Diego de Almagro, and Hernando Pizarro, plus an argument supporting compensation for their service.

For centuries, biographical collections have included such explorers as Christopher Columbus and Hernán Cortés. Many individual biographies have been published in Spanish America, including Spaniard Salvador de Madariaga's *Vida del muy magnífico señor don Cristóbal Colón* (1940; *Christopher Columbus, Being the Life of . . .*, 1940), a 1991 Spanish translation of Samuel Eliot Morison's *Admiral of the Ocean Sea: A Life of Christopher Columbus* (1942), and Madariaga's *Hernán Cortés* (1941; *Hernán Cortés, Conqueror of Mexico*, 1941).

Biography collections, popular among early Romans and Greeks as well as in Spain, have also abounded in Spanish America over the centuries. Josefina del Toro catalogues almost 500 collections in *A Bibliography of the Collective Biography of Spanish America* (1938), giving evidence of the plentiful general collections of mostly male historical, political, and literary figures during the 19th and 20th centuries. The collections range from a few to more than 100 entries. Del Toro located collections of many distinguished Mexicans among these texts, but collections exist for more than 15 other countries. During the late 19th century, Mexican Francisco Sosa was especially prolific, with biographical collections about religious and historical figures,

writers, and scholars. In the early 20th century, U.S. author William Belmont Parker published seven volumes containing hundreds of biographical sketches of leaders from varied disciplines in Cuba, Peru, Bolivia, Paraguay, Argentina, Uruguay, and Chile. Sara de Mundo Lo compiled the four-volume *Index to Spanish American Collective Biography* (1981–1985), which contains thousands of entries that classify and describe biographical narratives as well as indexes of authors, titles, countries, and biography subjects.

Trends in individual biographies in the later 20th and 21st centuries reveal that, as in Spain, publishers in the United States are producing works about Spanish American notables but Spanish American publishers, and even others internationally, are also actively at work. Best-selling Mexican biographer Enrique Krauze published *México: A Biography of Power: A History of Modern Mexico, 1810–1996* in the United States in 1997, but, in addition to many other works, in Mexico he published biographies on the following men in 1987: Emiliano Zapata, Francisco Villa, Lázaro Cárdenas, Venustiano Carranza, Francisco I. Madero, Plutarco E. Calles, Porfirio Díaz, and Álvaro Obregón.

Simón *Bolívar, the subject of Isidoro Sebastián's early *Biografía de Simón Bolívar* (1894; Biography of Simón Bolívar) and hundreds of 20th-century biographies, appears in more than 20 Spanish American biographies in the past decade, including David Bushnell's *Simón Bolívar: hombre de Caracas, proyecto de América: una biografía* (2001; Simón

Bolívar: Man of Caracas, Plan of America: A Biography) and in his English studies, including *The Liberator Simón Bolívar; Man and Image* (1970) and, with Frederick H. Fornoff, *El Libertador: Writings of Simón Bolívar* (2003). Che *Guevara, another popular biographical subject of multiple works recently published in Spanish America, Spain, and the United States, is the topic of Jorge G. Castañeda's *La vida en rojo: una biografía del Che Guevara* (also titled *Compañero: Vida y muerte del Che Guevara* [1997; *Compañero: The Life and Death of Che Guevara*, 1997]).

Spanish American and American biographers are also targeting contemporary writers and artists: several recent volumes about Jorge Luis *Borges, such as housekeeper Epifanía Uveda de Robledo and noted biographer Alejandro Vaccaro's *El señor Borges* (2004; Mr. Borges), Edwin Williamson's *Borges: A Life* (2004) and Émir Rodríguez Monegal's *Jorge Luis Borges: A Literary Biography* (1978) have appeared, as well as texts about Pablo *Neruda, including Edmundo Olivares Briones's *Pablo Neruda: Los caminos del mundo* (2001; The Paths of the World), Hernán Loyola's *Neruda: La biografía literaria* (2006; Neruda: Literary Biography), and Volodia *Teitelboim's *Neruda* (1984; *Neruda: An Intimate Biography*, 1991), which was published in Spain, Argentina, Mexico, Chile, the United States, and beyond. Frida *Kahlo is the topic of numerous biographies published in Mexico, Spain, the United States, and beyond, including Martha Zamora's *Frida: El pincel de la angustia* (1987; *Frida Kahlo: The Brush of Anguish*,

1990) and Hayden Herrera's *Frida: una biografía de Frida Kahlo* (1984; *Frida: A Biography of Frida Kahlo*, 1983).

Like Spanish and Spanish American autobiographical writings with varying forms and content, some recent biographical writing in Spanish America mixes biography with other disciplines or fiction. Two examples are Octavio *Paz's historical, biographical, and critical study, *Sor Juana Inés de la Cruz, o, Las trampas de la fe* (1982; *Sor Juana, or, The Traps of Faith*, 1988) and Elena *Poniatowska's biographical novel *Tinísima: novela* (1992; *Tinisima*, 1995) about photographer and revolutionary Tina Modotti. Twenty-first-century life narratives published in the United States by university presses, including Iván Jaksić's *Andrés Bello: Scholarship and Nation-Building in Nineteenth-Century Latin America* (2001), Miguel León Portilla's *Bernardino de Sahagún: First Anthropologist* (2002), and John Lynch's *Simón Bolívar: A Life* (2006), suggest that academic as well as popular interest in Spanish American notables is likely to continue in Spanish America and abroad.

Gwen H. Stickney

See also Biography in Spain: Beginnings to 1700; Biography in Spain: 1700 to Present; Convent Writing in Spain and the New World.

Work About:

Arenal, Electa and Stacey Schlau. *Untold Sisters: Hispanic Nuns in Their Own Works*. Albuquerque: University of New Mexico Press, 1989.

Monteón, Michael. "Biography and Latin American History." *Latin American*

Research Review 440.2 (2005): 193–206.

Rose, Sonia V. " 'The Great Moctezuma': A Literary Portrait in Sixteenth-Century Spanish American Historiography." *Modelling the Individual: Biography and Portrait in the Renaissance with a Critical Edition of Petrarch's* Letter to Posterity. Ed. K. A. E. Enenkel, Betsy de Jong-Crane, and Peter Liebregts. Amsterdam: Rodopi, 1998, 109–30.

Black Legend

This expression, coined by Spanish historian Julián Juderías, refers to the anti-Spanish propaganda spread for centuries by Protestant and Anglo-Saxon intellectuals, motivated in turn by territorial, religious, and political rivalries. Spanish writers Emilia *Pardo Bazán and Vicente *Blasco Ibáñez similarly objected to this defamatory campaign in conferences in París (1899) and Buenos Aires (1909) respectively. Starting with exaggerated, distorted portrayals of Spanish Catholicism and the *Inquisition, the legend also presented an incorrect picture of Spain's colonization of America. Many scholars note the present-day dissemination of the Black Legend through distorted historical accounts of Spanish presence in the Americas found in U.S. school textbooks. Likewise, the stereotypical attributes of tyranny, brutality, repression, and persecution that are accorded to Spanish historical characters in literature and film perpetuate such a view. This partial, hostile treatment toward Spanish history primarily derives from contemporary ignorance regarding mind-sets and worldviews of past centuries and the aforementioned self-interest of different nations.

The Black Legend gained vitality in about the 16th century, a time of strong Protestant–Catholic rivalry between England and Spain, and of international conspiracies between England, the Netherlands, and France to wrest control of land that Spain had conquered in the Americas. The 13th-century domination of Naples and Sicily by the Spanish Crown of Aragon first awoke a foreign resentment in the Italian peninsula, and reached its peak with the villainous, legendary behavior of the Spanish Valencian pope, Alexander VI Borgia, who assumed the papacy in 1492. Later, international reaction toward Spanish supremacy in Europe would cling to Spain's alleged "over-Catholicism" to protest the Inquisition's horrors. The Inquisition was not unique to Spain—France had had its own Inquisition for fighting heresy since the end of the 12th century, and Portugal and present-day Italy established Inquisition tribunals in the 16th century. Protestantism's emergence allowed Spain's Hapsburg possessions in the Netherlands and Austria to claim their opposition to Spain's religious fervor and attain political independence. Philip Wayne Powell confirms the rise of Nordicism (a belief in Nordic–Germanic racial superiority) in Europe from the 17th century on as a way to counter the Spanish-dominated southern region of Europe.

English Protestant polemicist John Foxe provided exaggerated and gory details of the Spanish Inquisition in *Book of Martyrs* (1554), and Girolamo Benzoni's *Historia del mondo nuovo* (1565; *History of the New World*, 1857) published a selective, biased account of Spain's conquest of America. Considerable responsibility for consolidation of the Black Legend must also go to such Spaniards as Protestant convert Reginaldo González de Montes, author of *Exposición de algunas mañas de la Santa Inquisición Española* (1567; Exposition of Some Vices of the Spanish Inquisition); Bartolomé de las *Casas, whose *Brevísima relación de la destrucción de las Indias* (1552; *The Devastation of the Indies, a Brief Account, 1992*), condemning the abuses in the colonization of Hispaniola (present Dominican Republic and Haiti), was heavily cited and printed both in England and other European nations; Antonio Pérez, former secretary to King Philip II, who, after falling from power, fled to England to attack the Spanish monarchy with his book *Relaciones* (1591; Relations/Correspondence).

In *Historia de la Leyenda Negra hispanoamericana* (1944; History of the Hispanic American Black Legend), Rómulo D. Carbia recognizes important omissions in English-language historical texts that demonize Spanish colonization, but fails to include logical motivations and positive results for these actions. Omitted aspects include evangelization of native people; large sums of money for education and the construction of churches, schools, universities, and hospitals; a clause in Queen Isabella's will claiming respect and dignity for American natives; accounts of brutality against natives launched by Spaniards themselves—such as las Casas—brave enough to oppose, fight, and empathize with others; interracial marriages; mixed settlements and gradual recognition of indigenous rights, centuries earlier than what occurred in colonies of other European empires. The United States, which began as British and Dutch colonies, alternated a strategy of annihilating native Indians with one of gradually forcing these populations to exist in enclosed reservations, and maintained segregation laws until the 1960s; and South Africa, originally a British colony, was ridden with apartheid until the 1990s.

Additionally, the popularity of the Spanish *Tercios* (a Spanish infantry section widely admired for bravery and courage) and the Duke of Alba's military campaigns in what is now the Netherlands and in other Spanish Hapsburg territories contributed to the Spanish profile of ferocity and greed. Abuses committed in America and criticized by las Casas were used by the Dutch to present an analogy with the Spanish control of their territories. Las Casas's text was reprinted 33 times between 1578 and 1648, and the Dutch press established an anti-Spain campaign to warn citizens of imminent perils wrought by Spaniards, including a conspiracy of the Holy Office to starve the Dutch people. All these texts were also used by the English to justify their constant and royally regulated piracy. Francis Drake was named "Sir" for his pillages and attacks on Spanish colonies and fleets. Ultimately, both Protestant Holland and England emerged as rivals of Spain in international colonialism, confirming their interest in promoting a derogatory image of a common enemy.

After its dominance during the 16th century, the Black Legend has reappeared intermittently until this day. During the 18th and 19th centuries, Philip II was criticized in German Friedrich Schiller's play *Don Carlos* and then in Italian Giuseppe Verdi's opera of the same name for the cruel imprisonment and death of his son Don Carlos. In late 18th and 19th century romanticism, many foreign visitors and travelers envisioned Spain as an exotic country, deeply rooted in superstition and rigid Catholicism. Matthew Lewis's *The Monk* (1796) established a connection between Gothic horror and English anti-Catholic sentiment through its depiction of a corrupt Spanish monk and sordid Inquisition. Prosper Mérimée's *Carmen* (1845; Carmen), on which Georges Bizet's opera was based, offered a connection between Spain and *andalucism*, where matadors, smugglers, bandits, and vulnerable officers were charmed by a passionate woman. In the 20th century, the inherent brutality of Spaniards seemed proven anew by the Spanish Civil War (1936–1939), and in present-day Spain, the Black Legend, almost exclusively attributed to Castilians, is used by the Nationalists in non-Castilian regions as a political excuse to justify claims of independence.

As far as the Hispanic world is concerned, the Black Legend is much in use by English-speaking populations, which denigrate Latinos with condescending clichés and overt omissions (laziness, barbarism, secondary role in American formation as a nation).

Judith García-Quismondo García

Work About:

DeGuzmán, María. *Spain's Long Shadow: The Black Legend, Off-Whiteness, and Anglo-American Empire*. Minneapolis: University of Minnesota Press, 2005.

Greer, Margaret Rich, Walter Mignolo, and Maureen Quilligan, eds. *Rereading the Black Legend: The Discourses and Racial Differences in the Renaissance Empires*. Chicago: University of Chicago Press, 2007.

Powell, Philip Wayne. *Tree of Hate: Propaganda and Prejudices Affecting United States Relations with the Hispanic World*. New York: Basic Books, 1971.

Schmidt, Benjamin. *Innocence Abroad. The Dutch Imagination and the New World, 1570–1670*. Cambridge: Cambridge University Press, 2001.

Blasco Ibáñez, Vicente (1867–1928)

Born in Valencia, Spain, this novelist was committed to social justice, protesting—among other things—opulence in the Catholic church, slave-like conditions in which various industries held workers, the monarchical system of Spanish government, and unrestrained bestial instincts of lower class Valencian society. Blasco Ibáñez is most recognized for his Valencian series of novels (1894–1902) written in the naturalist style, wherein humans are influenced, beyond their control, by environment and heredity.

Acclaim soon followed the 1901 French translation of Blasco Ibáñez's *La barraca* (1898; *The Cabin*, 1917), but it was the 1921 film adaptation of *Los cuatro jinetes del Apocalipsis* (1916; *The Four Horsemen of the Apocalypse*, 1918) that brought him world-wide fame. Political differences with the Spanish government after World War I prompted him to reside in Menton, France, until his death.

Jeffrey Oxford

See also Novel in Spain: 1700–1900; Realism and Naturalism in Spain.

Work About:

George, David. "Cinematising the Crowd; V. Blasco Ibáñez's Silent *Sangre y arena* (1916)." *Studies in Hispanic Cinemas* 4.2 (2007): 91–106.

Oxford, Jeffrey. "Blasco Ibáñez and Animal Portrayals: An Attempt at Societal Reformation." *Hipertexto* 8 (Summer 2008): 99–104.

Blest Gana, Alberto (1830–1920)

This Chilean novelist who bypassed *modernism and mixed romantic conventions and realistic social observation has been called the first realist writer in Spanish. His writing transpired during two periods of his life, separated by his political career. The precareer novels are better known and qualitatively superior.

His successful debut work, *La aritmética en el amor* (1860; The Arithmetics of Love), follows a man trying to climb the social ladder through marriage. This popular text was one of the first to incorporate contemporary Chilean characters. *Martín Rivas* (1862),

considered a rewrite of French writer Stendhal's *The Red and the Black*, depicts the poor son of a ruined miner who moves to the capital and, through persistence and honesty, achieves his two goals of climbing the social ladder and marrying his mentor's daughter. Through Martín's experiences, the narrator portrays Chile's working and middle-class societies, set against the nation's mid-19th century politics.

Vicente Gomis-Izquierdo

Work By:

Martín Rivas: A Novel. Trans. Tess O'Dwyer. New York: Oxford University Press, 2000.

Work About:

Araya, Guillermo. "Historia y sociedad en la obra de Alberto Blest Gana." *Revista de Crítica Literaria Latinoamericana* 7.14 (1981): 29–64.

Gotschlich, Guillermo. "Alberto Blest Gana y su novela histórica." *Revista chilena de literatura* 38 (1991): 29–58.

Bogotazo, el

On April 9, 1948, Colombia's popular Liberal Party presidential candidate, Jorge Eliécer Gaitán, was assassinated, sparking riots, looting, and the destruction of over 130 buildings in downtown Bogotá, leading to the death of over 2,000 civilians in the following days. Although the outburst in Bogotá was quelled, violence in the countryside surged in subsequent years, part of a period later called *la *Violencia*.

Maureen Ihrie

Work About:

Buitrago, Fanny. *El hostigante verano de los dioses*. Barcelona: Plaza & Janés, 1977.

Bolaño, Roberto (1953–2003)

A recent addition to the Latin American canon, this Chilean poet and fiction writer received widespread international acclaim in the early 2000s for his novels, novellas, and short stories. He left Santiago after the 1973 coup against President Salvador Allende, settling in Mexico and later in Spain. These places, along with many others, serve as settings for loosely auto-biographical writing in which journey and adventure constitute central motifs. Bolaño's prose combines narrative twists with provocative reflections on the role of the literary establishment in historical and political processes throughout the Spanish-speaking world and beyond.

His better known novel, *Los detectives salvajes* (1999; *The Savage Detectives*, 2007), follows two young poets, Arturo Belano and Ulises Lima, who lead a gritty, street-smart literary movement named "visceral realism"—modeled on the real-life *infrarrealismo* in which Bolaño participated. A comical yet dangerous plot takes them through five continents in search of the missing poet Cesárea Tinajero, illustrating the idea that literature, far from being confined to an ivory tower, belongs to matters of life or death. Bolaño revisits this theme through unlikely entanglements of literature and power. In *Nocturno de Chile* (2000; *By Night in Chile*, 2000), Pinochet's military junta asks a priest, who is also a literary critic, to give them lessons of Marxism. Similarly, *Literatura Nazi en América* (1996, *Nazi Literature in the Americas*, 2008) reads as an encyclopedia of the lives and works of an imaginary group of writers with heterogeneous right-wing tendencies. An expanded version of one of its storylines, that of a torturer who is also a poet, serves as the plot of *Estrella distante* (1996; *Distant Star*, 2004). Bolaño's stand against the perceived cultural hegemony of *magical realism, as well as his rich imagery, lyric language, and playful cosmopolitanism, have made him a highly influential figure for younger generations.

Héctor M. Hoyos

See also Project "Año 0."

Work By:

Bolaño, Roberto. *The Savage Detectives*. Trans. Natasha Wimmer. New York: Farrar, Straus and Giroux, 2007.

Work About:

Goldman, Francisco. "The Great Bolaño." *New York Review of Books* 54. 12 (July 19, 2007): 34–37.

Paz Soldán, Edmundo, and Gustavo Faverón. *Bolaño salvaje*. Barcelona: Candaya, 2008.

Bolívar, Simón, in Contemporary Literature and Culture

Often described as "The "Liberator of Latin America," historical texts have exalted the active, catalyzing role Simón Bolívar played in leading independence movements of Spanish colonial territories that became present-day Venezuela, Peru, Bolivia, Ecuador, and Colombia. Born in 1783 in Caracas, Venezuela, to a very wealthy Creole family, Bolívar had the opportunity to study in Caracas and in Spain. Among his many writings, most relevant are "Carta de Jamaica" (1815; "The Letter of Jamaica," 1818?), "Congreso de Angostura (1819; "Congress of Angostura," 1919), and his guidelines "Congreso de Panamá (1826; The Congress of Panama). These essays in particular have inspired admiration for Bolívar's political ideology, particularly his ideas concerning promotion of public education to reinforce Latin American identity and economic progress, his desire to establish alliances among nations, and his dream of creating the "Great Colombia," a solid, federal alliance of five nations. After serving as president of the Republic of Colombia from 1821 to 1830, he died shortly thereafter in Santa Marta, Colombia.

The many portraits of Bolívar created during his life generally depict his glorious military moments. Remarkably, this image varies noticeably in these paintings, so much so that it is sometimes difficult to recognize him as the same man. Some artists emphasize his European ancestry, painting him as a white man, while others portray him with darker skin, most probably to highlight his Mestizo roots.

In some literary texts and other cultural representations (sculptures, paintings, films) this initial glorious image has become more complicated. Bolívar is presented in terms of unknown moments of his life, as if he were deteriorating physically and emotionally. Such depictions include two recent novels: *El general en su laberinto* (1989; *The General in His Labyrinth*, 2004) by Colombian Gabriel *García Márquez, and *Las dos muertes del General Bolívar* (2004; The Two Deaths of General Bolívar) by Argentine Mario Szichman; Colombian Álvaro *Mutis's short story "El ultimo rostro" (1973; The Last Face) and Venezuelan Francisco Herrera Luque's essay *Bolívar de carne y hueso* (1983; Flesh and Blood Bolívar); and the films *Bolívar, Soy Yo* (2002; Bolívar, I Am) directed by Colombian Jorge Alí Triana and "Manuela Sáenz. La Libertadora del Libertador" (2000; Manuela Sáenz . The Liberator's Liberator) directed by Venezuela's Diego Risquez. While humanizing Bolívar, these fictional representations show him as a fragile man who questions his own words and actions and is influenced by political circumstances of his day, by friends close to him, and by his partner Manuela Sáenz.

Other challenging images of Bolívar can be found in the sculpture "Bolívar Desnudo" (1956–1962; Bolívar Nude), by Rodrigo Arenas Betancourt, in Pereira, Colombia, and in Chilean Juan Dávila's 1994 painting known as "The Liberator Simón Bolívar." The former displays Bolívar as deprived from his heroic investiture. The latter presents a fragmented characterization of a Bolívar who perhaps unites races and gender and yet never joins the hegemony of Latin American nations.

Yudis Contreras

Work By:

El libertador. Writings of Simón Bolívar. Trans. Frederick H. Fornoff. Ed., intro., notes David Bushnell. New York: Oxford University Press, 2003.

Work About:

Lynch, John. *Simón Bolívar, A Life*. New Haven, CT: Yale University Press, 2006.

Bolivia: History, Culture, and Literature

Located in central South America, southwest of Brazil, this nation of almost 1,100,000 square miles shares its border with Brazil, Argentina, Peru, Paraguay, and Chile. With an estimated population of slightly over 10,000,000 inhabitants (July 2011), Bolivia's ethnic composition is roughly 30 percent Quechua, 30 percent Mestizo (mixed white and Amerindian ancestry), 25 percent Aymara and 15 percent white. Some 95 percent of the population is Roman Catholic, while 5 percent is Protestant (Evangelical Methodist). Because of these strong ethnic constituencies, the nation recognizes three official languages, and millions of Bolivians are bilingual. Spanish is the first language of 60.7 percent, Quechua is the primary tongue of 21.2 percent, and Aymara is the native language of 14.6 percent. The name Bolivia derives from the surname of Latin American liberator *Simón Bolívar.

History

Before the Spanish conquest and exploration, the Aymara culture first inhabited the land of present-day Bolivia. Llama herds constituted their primary economic and food source. In 1438, the Incan empire, a conglomerate of languages, cultures, and peoples with various cultural traditions, acquired the territory. Cuzco, the center of the empire, imposed taxes on conquered areas, but did not institute new cultural norms. Spaniards arrived in 1524 and placed the territory under the control of the viceroy of Lima. The significant amount of silver that was extracted from the Potosí region played a crucial role in the economic development of 16th-century Europe.

In 1776, administrative control of the colony was transferred to the viceroy of Río de la Plata. In 1825, Bolivia secured independence from Spain; nonetheless, wars against Peru, Chile, and Argentina continued until national boundaries were determined. During the War of the Pacific (1879–1883) against Chile, Bolivia lost its maritime access. The state of Acre seceded in 1903 and joined Brazil. Bolivia also lost the Chaco War (1932–1935) against Paraguay and with it, the Chaco region. These losses halved the nation's territory, leaving the country with its present dimensions. Between 1952 and 1964, the Revolutionary Nationalist Movement (MNR) ruled and implemented universal suffrage.

Today, Chile and Peru reject Bolivia's claim to restore the Atacama corridor, ceded to Chile in 1884; Chile offers instead unrestricted but not sovereign maritime access through Chile for Bolivian natural gas and other commodities. In 1958, a mutual accord placed the long-disputed Isla Suárez/Ilha de Guajara-Mirim, a fluvial island on the Mamoré River, under Bolivian administration, but sovereignty remains in dispute. The current president is Evo Morales (1959–), a coca workers' leader of Aymara Indian descent. First elected in 2006, Morales was reelected in December 2009 for a second term of office that will run from 2010 to 2015. He belongs to the Movement to Socialism Party (MAS) and pursues a socialist agenda with support for ethnic identity. As an ethnic representative, he vividly personifies a demand for dignity and an end to the structural discrimination suffered by Bolivians of indigenous descent, who make up about half of the population.

In his first term, Morales nationalized the gas, telecommunications, and mining industries. The MAS government has markedly increased the budgets for education and social security, which includes the national health and pension systems. Conservative opposition to Morales's agenda dominates in eastern Bolivia. The clash between white or Mestizo population and the indigenous communities, the road to socialism or to a mixed economy, and the international market for Bolivian commodities will determine the future of Morales's reforms.

Culture

The major archeological ruins of Tiwanaku predate the Inca Empire. Samaipata is a pre-Inca temple of the Chane culture; Incallajta is an important Inca site; and Iskanwalla, also a pre-Inca site, belongs to the Mollo culture.

The most important Bolivian artists of the first half of the 20th century are Cecilio Guzmán de Rojas (1899–1950), a forerunner of indigenism in Latin American painting, and Arturo Borda (1883–1953), who also mastered civil portraits. Both artists made indigenous peoples and their concerns a primary theme of their painting. Their work deals with indigenous subjects with dignity and possessed of agency, rather than exotic figures. Avelino Nogales (1870–1930) was noted for portraiture and landscape. Ricardo Pérez Alcalá (1939–), the most important watercolorist in Bolivia, created a school of followers. In abstract art, the most important figures include María Luisa Pacheco (1919–1982) and Oscar Pantoja (1925–). Contemporary Bolivian painting is currently experiencing a boom, with international stars like Orlando Arias Morales (1954–), who combines color and perspective in his mestizo art. Aymara painter Roberto Mamani Mamani (1959–) creates stylized, naïve paintings that are extremely colorful and very well structured. Bolivian sculptors of international stature are Marina Núñez de Prado (1912–1996) and, working in wood, Marcelo Callaú (1946–).

With regard to popular culture, Bolivian food is rich. *Salteñas*, eaten for breakfast, are turnovers filled with meat and potatoes. *Humitas* are Bolivia's tamales, with corn husks or banana leafs wrapped around the seasoned corn dough. *Fritanga* is a spicy pork stew, and *charque de llama* is llama-meat jerky served with corn and cheese. In terms of dance, some traditional Bolivian dances are shared by other countries in the region, like the Chilean *cueca* and *caporales* from the Department of

Paz. Also from Paz is the Afro-Bolivian *saya*. Bolivian music was *criolla* until 1952, when a neoindigenous revolution took place and indigenous music and instruments gained prominence. Finally, the group *Los Kjarkas* has achieved international fame.

Literature

Adela *Zamudio (1854–1928) became an important romantic poet and author of short stories and plays for children; other works expressed concern for the role of women in society and the defense of femininity. Ricardo Jaimes Freyre (1868–1933) is one of the continent's most important modernist poets; because of the extensive time he spent in Argentina, he is also studied as an Argentine writer. Óscar *Alfaro (1921–1963) primarily composed poems for children.

In 2009, a commission of academics, writers, and editors of literature journals chose the 10 most relevant novels of Bolivian literature and 5 more books of national interest. The government is currently preparing these novels for publication in annotated editions. The 10 most relevant books are *Juan de la Rosa* (1885; Eng. trans., 1998) by Nataniel Aguirre (1843–1888); *Felipe Delgado* (1979) by Jaime Sáenz (1921–1986); *Jonás y la ballena rosada* (1987; *Jonah and the Pink Whale*, 1991) by José Wolfango Montes (1951–); *Los deshabitados* (The Uninhabited, 1957) by Marcelo Quiroga Santa Cruz (1931–1980); *Tirinea* (1969) by Jesús Urzagasti (1941–); *La Chaskañawi* (1947) by Carlos Medinacelli (1899–1949); *Otro gallo* (1982; Another

Rooster) by Jorge Suárez (1932–1998); *Aluvión de fuego* (1935; Downpour of Fire) by Óscar Cerruto (1912–1981); *Matías el apóstol suplente* (1968) by Julio de la Vega (1924–2010); and *Raza de bronce* (1919; Race of Bronce) by Alcides *Arguedas (1879–1946).

The other books selected for their particular national relevance include *Íntimas* (1913; Intimate) by Adela Zamudio; *Selección de historia de la Villa Imperial de Potosí* (1872; Tales of Potosí, 1975) by Bartolomé Arzans de Orzúa y Vela (1676–1736); *Selección de El Loco* (The Madman) by painter Arturo Borda (1883–1953)—a work that, by 1925, had nine unpublished volumes; *La virgen de las siete calles* (1941; The Virgin of the Seven Streets) by Alfredo Flores (1887–1987); and *El run run de la calavera* (1983; The Humming of the Skull) by Ramón Rocha Monroy (1950–).

Salvador A. Oropesa

See also Appendix B, for other entries related to Bolivia.

Work About:

Klein, Herbert S. *A Concise History of Bolivia*. Cambridge: Cambridge University Press, 2003.
Powers, William. *Whispering in the Giant's Ear: A Frontline Chronicle from Bolivia's War on Globalization*. London: Bloomsbury, 2006.

Bombal, María Luisa (1910–1980)

A significant avant-garde fiction writer, she is one of the first Latin American authors to break with realism and a key contributor to feminist writing in her native Chile. Born to a wealthy family in Viña del Mar, as an adolescent she moved to Paris, studying literature at the Sorbonne and becoming involved with the nascent avant-garde movement. Upon returning to the Americas, she moved to Buenos Aires and befriended vanguard writers Pablo *Neruda, Jorge Luis *Borges, Norah *Lange, and Oliverio *Girondo, among others, and published in Victoria *Ocampo's magazine, *Sur*. Eventually she returned to Chile, where she shot and wounded her lover, an incident that forced her to relocate to the United States, where she wrote fiction, several unpublished plays, and became her own English-language translator.

Bombal's publications include two novellas—*La última niebla* (1934; *The Final Mist*, 1982) and *La amortajada* (1938; *The Shrouded Woman*, 1948)—and a handful of short stories. Her most celebrated work, *La última niebla*, is a surrealist tale of amorous longings; the nameless female protagonist attempts to escape a loveless marriage through an affair with an imagined lover. The novella incorporates several thematic and stylistic innovations for which Bombal is known: the depiction of women as psychologically complex; a critique of heterosexual relationships; an interest in oneiric states, fantasy realms, and fairy tales; the use of symbols, particularly from nature; and an incorporation of poetic language, nonlinear plot structures, counterpoint, montage, and leitmotifs, among other literary experimentations. Her second novelette, *La amortajada*, continues to depict the female consciousness experimentally. The protagonist is dead; as she lies in her coffin surrounded by loved ones, a multiperspective narration reveals her thoughts and memories in her journey through life toward death. "El árbol" (1939; "The Tree," 1982), Bombal's most anthologized short story, uses music and sound to discuss her recurrent theme of women's painful dissatisfaction in marriage.

Resha Cardone

See also Avant-Garde Prose in Spanish America; Feminism in Spanish America.

Work By:

New Islands and Other Stories. Pref. Jorge Luis Borges. Trans. Richard and Lucía Cunningham. Ithaca, NY: Cornell University Press, 1988. 51–66.

Work About:

Kostopulos-Cooperman, Celeste. *The Lyrical Vision of María Luisa Bombal*. London: Tamesis, 1988.

Llanos M., Bernardita. *Passionate Subjects/ Split Subjects in Twentieth-Century Literature in Chile: Brunet, Bombal, Eltit*. Lewisburg, PA: Bucknell University Press, 2009.

Bonasso, Miguel (1940–)

Argentinian journalist, novelist, and left-wing politician, he has worked as a journalist for such magazines as *Leoplán*, *Análisis*, *Extra*, and *Semana Gráfica*, and *La Opinión* newspaper. In 1973, he became press secretary of the Frente

Justicialista de Liberación and advisor to President Héctor Cámpora. He sought exile in Rome in 1977, where he became a member of the Consejo Superior de Montoneros (a left-wing, Peronist guerrilla organization), and several years later moved to Mexico to work as an editor and foreign correspondent for several Latin American newspapers.

Bonasso's award-winning novel *Recuerdo de la muerte* (1984; Memory of Death) offers a testimony of kidnappings, incarcerations, and torture of prisoners at the Escuela de Mecánica de la Armada, a concentration camp run by Argentina's ruling military junta. In 1997, he received the prestigious Planeta Prize for *El presidente que no fue* (1997; The President Who Never Was) a biography of President Cámpora, President Juan Perón's personal friend, who facilitated Perón's return from exile. *Diario de un clandestino* (2000; Diary of a Clandestine Man) is based on the secret diary and chronicles of a 1960s militant, while *El palacio y la calle: crónicas de insurgentes y conspiradores* (2002; Palace and Street: Chronicles of Insurgents and Conspirators) reconstructs, through various documents and testimonies, the incidents leading to Argentina's financial and political crisis in December 2001.

María Claudia André

See also Documentary Narrative in Spanish American Literature; Torture in Modern Spanish American Literature.

Work By:

Diario de un clandestino. Buenos Aires: Planeta, 2000.

El presidente que no fue: Los archivos ocultos del peronismo. Buenos Aires: Planeta, 1997.

Work About:

Coira, María. "Versalles del horror." *Celehis: Revista del Centro de Letras Hispanoamericanas* 4.4–5 (1995): 167–83.

Borge, Tomás (1930–)

Born in Matagalpa, Nicaragua, this cofounder of the Sandinista National Liberation Front (FSLN) and interior minister of Nicaragua during Daniel Ortega's first government was also named vice-secretary of the FSLN in 1991, and in 2009 became Nicaragua's ambassador to Peru. The author of over eight books (novels, poetry, and essays on politics), his novels depict the Nicaraguan revolution, which sought to overthrow the regime of Anastasio Somoza Debayle (president 1967–1979). *Carlos, el amanecer ya no es una tentación* (1980; *Carlos, the Dawn Is No Longer Beyond Our Reach*, 1984) takes as its subject the revolutionary Carlos Fonseca, also a cofounder of the FSLN, whose assassination by Nicaragua's National Guard made him a martyr of the revolution, and *La paciente impaciencia* (1989; *The Patient Impatience*, 1992).

His poetry expresses both his political experiences and feelings of love. Because of their political dimension, most of Borge's writings are better known abroad than in Nicaragua.

María José Luján

See also Testimonial Writing in Central America.

Work By:

Carlos, the Dawn Is No Longer Beyond Our Reach. Trans. Russell Bartley. Willimantic, CT: Curbstone, 1989.

The Patient Impatience. Trans. Russell Bartley. Willimantic, CT: Curbstone, 1992.

Work About:

Beverly, John, and Mark Zimmerman. *Testimonial Narrative: Literature and Politics in the Central American Revolutions*. Austin: The University of Texas Press, 1990. 172–207.

Borges, Jorge Luis (1899–1986)

Born in Buenos Aires, this giant of Argentine literature grew up under the tutelage of Fanny Haslam, his paternal grandmother. Due to his father's increasing blindness, the Borges family went to Europe, remaining there for four years. He learned Latin, French, and German and read the contemporary classics of European literature. When World War I ended, they left Geneva for Spain. There, Borges met several avant-garde writers and contributed to poetry publications. Back in Buenos Aires, he began participating in the city's intellectual life, publishing in the renowned literary review *Martín Fierro*. In 1923, Borges published his first book of poems, *Fervor de Buenos Aires* (Fervor of Buenos Aires). Two years later, the poetry volume *Luna de enfrente* (1925;

Moon across the Way), appeared, and in 1929, *Cuaderno San Martín* (San Martín Notebook) won him second prize in Buenos Aires's annual literary contest. These three collections established his reputation as a poet. During the 1920s, Borges also wrote several books of essays for which he never authorized re-publication.

In 1930, he completed the biography *Evaristo Carriego*, and in following years, published *Discusión* (1932; Discussion), *Historia universal de la infamia* (1935; A Universal History of Infamy), and *Historia de la eternidad* (1936; A History of Eternity*, 1972). After a failed attempt to commit suicide, Borges underwent a series of transformative experiences in 1938, and then produced his first fantastic short story, "Pierre Menard, autor del Quijote" ("Pierre Menard, Author of the Quixote," 1962). In 1944, his short story collection *Ficciones* (Fictions; trans. under same title, 1962) appeared. This decade was crowned with publication of Borges's most celebrated book of fiction: *El Aleph* (1949; *The Aleph*, 1970).

In the 1950s, he published a new book of essays, *Otras inquisiciones* (1952; *Other Inquisitions*, 1964), and *El hacedor* (1960; *Dreamtigers*, 1964), a compilation of brief pieces in prose and verse. After the fall of Perón's government in 1955, Borges became director of the National Library, was named member of the Argentine Academy of Letters, and was appointed professor of English literature at the University of Buenos Aires. Concurrently, he received an honorary doctorate from the University of Cuyo and the National Prize for Literature. In 1986, Borges married María

Kodama, his former secretary and assistant. They took up residence in Geneva, where Borges died of cancer in June of that year.

As an aesthetic form, Borges prefers the short story to the novel. Due to its length and its realistic tone, the novel necessarily evolves into the psychological realm and characters require a life—a development of details unnecessary to the plot itself. But the short story, either fantastic or detective, may deal with just one particular problem and its explanation. Borges's ideal story implies the display of a purely geometrical problem that does not ignore the fallibility of human beings. For instance, in "El Aleph" the narrator (named "Borges") goes through a succession of photographs taken at different times in Beatriz Viterbo's life, a series of visits to her house after her death, an epic poem of Dante Argentino Daneri, and so on, to finally convince us with a personal testimony: he discovers that a certain spot in a particular house in Buenos Aires is a sort of compressed labyrinth from which one can observe the entire universe. In that way, the aleph is not only a story but an interpretation of it. Even more, it is also meaningful to the reader as a symbol of all Borges's writing.

Daniel Altamiranda

See also Avant-Garde Poetry in Spanish America; Avant-Garde Prose in Spanish America; Buenos Aires in Literature; Detective and Mystery Fiction in Spanish America; Gaucho Literature; Journals in Spanish America; Short Fiction in Spanish America.

Work By:

Collected Fictions. Trans. Andrew Hurley. New York: Viking, 1998.

Obras completas. 4 vols. Buenos Aires: Emecé, 2005.
Selected Non-Fictions. Ed. Eliot Weinberger. Trans. Esther Allen, Suzanne Jill Levine, and Eliot Weinberger. New York: Viking, 1999.
Selected Poems. Ed. Alexander Coleman. New York: Viking, 1999.

Work About:

Balderston, Daniel. *Out of Context: Historical Reference and the Representation of Reality in Borges*. Durham, NC: Duke University Press, 1993.
Bloom, Harold, ed. *Jorge Luis Borges*. New York: Chelsea, 1986.

Borrero, Juana (1878–1896)

Born in Havana, Cuba, the poet Juana Borrero lived and wrote in a time of political turmoil and literary effervescence. While Cuba struggled for independence from Spain, in literature the landscape was dominated by turn-of-the-century decadence and the influential Latin American movement called *modernismo*. Borrero actively participated in both politics and literature. Daughter of renowned intellectual and revolutionary Esteban Borrero Echevarría, she met the influential José *Martí during his exile in New York and was also a close friend of Julián del *Casal, a leader of the *modernismo* movement. Borrero followed this double path in her poetry, writing anguished poems in the elaborate style of *modernismo* and also verses of inflamed patriotism that defended Cuban independence. When accused of revolutionary involvement in 1896, the Borrero family went into exile in Key West, Florida. Several months later, Borrero died from typhoid fever, at age eighteen.

Tina Escaja

See also *Modernismo* in Hispanic Literature.

Work By:

Espíritu de estrella: Nuevas cartas de amor de Juana de Borrero. Havana: Academia, 1997.

Poemas de Juana Borrero. Havana: Academia de Ciencias de Cuba/Instituto de Literatura y Lingüística, 1966.

Work About:

Hauser, Rex. "Juana Borrero: The Poetics of Despair." *Letras Femeninas* 13.1–2 (1990): 113–20.

Boullosa, Carmen (1954–)

Born in Mexico City, this novelist, poet, playwright, essayist, and literary critic is one of Latin America's most prolific contemporary novelists. Boullosa obtained a fellowship from El Centro Mexicano de Escritores and was mentored by Juan *Rulfo. Her extensive work has been translated and studied in several languages, and performed on stage. As of 2010, she was a distinguished lecturer at City University of New York in the Foreign Languages Department.

Half of her published novels encapsulate a specific historical situation. Moctezuma, Cleopatra, the Costa brothers, and, more recently, Miguel de *Cervantes, have served as thematic axes of her novels. Within this scope, Boullosa explores subjects that articulate the cultural heterogeneity and plurality of difference that defy reductive categorizations. These two main features are intertwined in *Duerme* (1994; Sleep). *Duerme's* protagonist is Claire, a French woman who, dressed as a man, arrives in 17th-century Mexico as a male pirate. She strongly resembles the historical Spanish nun Catalina de *Erauso, known as "la monja alférez" (the lieutenant nun) who, in similar fashion, came to the New World as a soldier in 1632. In *Duerme*, Claire assumes different cultural and gender identities: a Mexican nobleman, an indigenous woman, a Mexican woman, and a male cadaver, defying and defeating her environment in these various roles and faces. *Duerme* shares techniques and themes with Boullosa's theater and with her novels *Son vacas, somos puercos* (1991; *They're Cows, We're Pigs*, 1997) and *El médico de los piratas* (1992; The Pirate's Physician). The world of these novels undercuts the organizing principle of social "order," destabilizing or blurring it. Boullosa addresses this theme throughout her writing.

María Fernández-Babineaux

See also Feminism in Spanish America

Work By:

Cleopatra Dismounts. Trans. Geoff Hargreaves. New York: Grove, 2003.

Work About:

Kroll, Juli. "(Re) Opening the Veins of Historiographic Visionary: Clothing,

Mapping and Tonguing Subjectivities in Carmen Boullosa's *Duerme.*" *Hispanófila* 141 (2004): 105–27.

Kuhnheim, Jill. "Postmodern Feminist Nomadism in Carmen Boullosa's *Duerme.*" *Letras Femeninas* 27.2 (2001): 8–23.

Bousoño, Carlos (1923–)

This Spanish poet, professor, and critic has decisively marked Spanish literary history through his poetic theories and analyses of literary movements. Bousoño's PhD thesis, *La poesía de Vicente Aleixandre* (1956; The Poetry of Vicente Aleixandre), set the tone for his career by analyzing the aesthetic shifts of the *Generation of 1927 and emphasizing the detachment and surrealism of modern poetic language. He argues that irrational metaphors offer an alternative *visión* that can represent experiences inaccessible to rational logic. Bousoño's influential *Teoría de la expresión poética* (1952; Theory of Poetic Expression) extended these ideas by distinguishing poetry from other genres based on defamiliarization (making the familiar seem strange, thus new) and metaphor. It remains canonical reading for students of Spanish literature.

Bousoño's own poetry moved from religious faith and existential anguish in works like *Subida al amor* (1945; Rising toward Love) and *Noche del sentido* (1957; Night of the Senses), to radical existentialism in *Invasión de la realidad* (1962; Invasion of Reality), where meaning is utterly secular and focused within the material realm. Later works like *Oda en la ceniza* (1967; Ode in the Ash) and *Las monedas contra la losa* (1973; Coins against the Gravestone) are innovative, metapoetic texts that offer the play of paradoxical language as a medium fit to explore the mysteries of experience. Bousoño taught literature at universities in Spain and the United States, and his pedagogical interests are reflected in such works as *Épocas literarias y evolución* (1981; Literary Epochs and Evolution) in which he argues that literary history from the Middle Ages to the present can be understood as an interaction (along the lines of José *Ortega y Gasset's *razón vital*) between particular authors and the cultural, economic, and political contexts of their times.

Debra Faszer-McMahon

Work By:

Bousoño, Carlos. *Teoría de la expresión poética.* 7th ed. Madrid: Gredos, 1999.

Work About:

Pao, Maria T. "Ekphrasis in Bousoño: 'Duro jarro', jarro que dura." *Revista Canadiense de Estudios Hispánicos* 28.1 (Fall 2003): 241–62.

Bretón de los Herreros, Manuel (1796–1873)

Born in la Rioja, Spain, after serving 10 years in the military, he became a translator of French plays for Spanish audiences, a member of the *Real Academia

Española, librarian of the National Library, theater critic, and playwright.

Although Bretón's works contain romantic elements, they portray and satirize the social milieu in which he lived, continuing the tradition of Leandro Fernández de *Moratín and providing a basic model for the *alta comedia* (plays written for the middle class that reflected and reinforced such "traditional" values as God, country, and king), popular from the mid-19th century until 1880.

Bretón's first success for the stage, *Marcela, o ¿cuál de los tres?* (1831; Marcela, or Which One of the Three?), deals with a young widow who, faced with choosing a husband, finally decides to do without a man because she enjoys her freedom too much. One of his most popular works, the hilarious *El pelo de la dehesa* (1840; The Country Bumpkin), presents a rich country bumpkin who has promised to marry the daughter of a poor noble family. With a light touch, Bretón examines the topics of honor, money, class, and marriage, popular themes in many of his works.

Matthew A. Wyszynski

Work By:

El pelo de la dehesa. Ed. José Montero Padilla. Madrid: Cátedra, 1997.

Work About:

Flynn, Gerard C. *Manuel Bretón de los Herreros*. Boston: Twayne, 1978.

Miret, Pau. *Las ideas teatrales de M. Bretón de los Herreros*. Logroño, Spain: Gobierno de La Rioja; Instituto de Estudios Riojanos, 2004.

Brunet, Marta (1897–1967)

This novelist from southern Chile grew up facing typical gender and class restrictions for aspiring women writers of that time. Brunet's parents accepted her chosen vocation, provided she stay at home and not dishonor the family name. Educated by governesses and private tutors, she also traveled in Europe and visited many countries with her parents. Much later in life, she held diplomatic posts in different Latin American nations.

In her early twenties, Brunet published *Montaña adentro* (1923; Back Country), a first novel about peasant life and the ways oppression worked within interpersonal relations. It caused considerable commotion in her small town and in the male literary establishment. Her prose garnered praised for being virile, sharp, and lucid. With the favorable endorsement of influential Chilean critic Hernán *Díaz Arrieta, she entered the literary national scene as a *criollista*, because the novel, and many to follow, depicted rural life. No attention was paid to her reconfiguration of language and its signs. Her questioning of the picturesque and later epic *criollista* tradition was overlooked.

A second literary phase appears in *Humo hacia el Sur* (1946; Smoke on the Southern Horizon), which introduces a subjective perspective through the main character's inner world. This more existential, confessional turn achieves its best expression in *María Nadie* (1953; Maria Nobody). Here, a single female denounces the sexist gender restrictions placed upon modern working women, hindering their development and freedom. This distraught, problematic character debunks *criollismo*'s picturesque façade to reveal the patriarchal, Catholic morality that controls public and private life.

Bernardita Llanos

See also *Criollista* Novel in Spanish America; Feminism in Spanish America.

Work About:

Agosín, Marjorie. "Marta Brunet: A Literary Biography." *Revista Interamericana de Bibliografía* 36 (1986): 452–59.

Llanos M., Bernardita. *Passionate Subjects/Split Subjects in Twentieth Century Literature in Chile: Brunet, Bombal and Eltit*. Lewisburg, PA: Bucknell University Press, 2009, 40–80.

Bryce Echenique, Alfredo (1939–)

One of Peru's most renowned contemporary novelists, he was educated in exclusive North American and British schools typically attended by Peru's elite. After completing university studies, in 1964 Bryce left for Paris and did not return to live in Peru until 1999. His most acclaimed novel, the *bildungsroman* (coming-of-age story) *Un mundo para Julius* (1970; *A World for Julius*, 1992), tells the tale of a sensitive, curious boy of the Peruvian upper class. *No me esperen en abril* (1995; Don't Expect Me in April) and *El huerto de amada* (2002; The Garden of Beloved) also explore the privileged Peruvian elite. In *La vida exagerada de Martín Romaña* (1981; The

Exaggerated Life of Martín Romaña), *La amigdalitis de Tarzán* (1998; *Tarzan's Tonsilitis*, 2001), and *Las obras infames de Pancho Marambio* (2007; The Infamous Deeds of Pancho Marambio), Bryce humorously explores the dilemmas of love, exile, and cultural identity.

César Ferreira

Work By:

A World for Julius. Trans. Dick Gerdes. Austin: University of Texas Press, 1992.

Tarzan's Tonsilitis. Trans. Alfred MacAdam. New York: Pantheon, 2001.

Work About:

Ferreira, César. "Alfredo Bryce Echenique." *Latin American Writers-Supplement 1*. Ed. Carlos A. Solé and Klaus Muller-Bergh. New York: Scribners, 2002.

Wood, David. *The Fictions of Alfredo Bryce Echenique*. London: King's College, 2000.

Buenos Aires in Literature

Founded in 1580 by Juan de Garay, the city that in 1880 became Argentina's capital has been depicted as a remote, hybrid, and mutating place. The city's demographic and architectural growths have never been gradual, and its many vertiginous changes have produced an array of expectations, fears, and reactions that can be traced in its literature.

During the 17th and 18th centuries, this city at the shores of the Río de la Plata

(River Plate) estuary appeared as a remote, empty location in texts written from about 1550 to 1650 but published many decades later. This is the case with Ulrich Schmidel's German-language chronicle of his experiences (1567), Luis de Miranda's *Romance Elegíaco* (1546; Elegiac Ballad), Martín del Barco de Centenera's narrative poem *La Argentina* (1602), and Ruy Díaz de Guzmán's *Argentina manuscrita* (1612; Handwritten Argentina). Unlike earlier chronicles of exploration of New World territories, which regularly exalted the success and heroism of the enterprise, texts concerning the foundations of Buenos Aires exhibit a sense of failure, negativism, and frustration. Miranda's medieval-style poem uses the literary construction of a duplicitous woman to denounce the conflicts between the Spanish crown and the conquering explorers. Barco Centenera's long poem, which inspired the country's name, vividly narrates the violence, hunger, and disenchantment experienced by Ortíz de Zárate and his men, who expected to find "argentine metal" (silver) there. Díaz de Guzmán's *Argentina manuscrita* is the first chronicle written by a *mancebo de la tierra* (Creole, born in Buenos Aires) many years after the city's founding. Because the narrator did not witness the events described, mythical elements prevail in this writing much more than in previous texts about Buenos Aires.

The idea of Buenos Aires as an empty land in need of European civilization—and at risk of native barbarism—becomes an important theme in 19th-century Argentine literature. Esteban *Echeverría's *El matadero* (1839; The Slaughter House), Domingo *Sarmiento's *Facundo* (1845; Eng. trans., 1960) and José *Mármol's *Amalia* (1851; Eng. trans., 2001) represented Buenos Aires both as the ideal scenario for a new civilization based on French philosophical Enlightment doctrines and, alternately, as a chaotic, barbaric locale.

After 1880, due to the arrival of millions of immigrants, mainly from Europe, Buenos Aires came to be perceived as an unpredictable, dangerous city. Eugenio Cambaceres's *Sin rumbo* (1885; Without Direction), Lucio López's *La gran aldea* (1882; The Grand Village), Antonio Argerich's *¿Inocentes o culpables?* (1884; Innocent or Guilty?), Miguel *Cané's *Juvenilia* (1884), and Lucio *Mansilla's *Mis memorias* (1907; My Memories) left a literary testimony of concerns, nostalgia, and fears among conservative writers after the city's abrupt demographic growth.

During the first decades of the 20th century, writers viewed Buenos Aires as a condensed metaphor of all desirable modernity and the center of unexpected social conflicts derived from such modernity. Leopoldo *Lugones's *Odas seculares* (1910; Secular Odes) celebrated urban beauty and grandeur; Baldomero Fernández Moreno's *Ciudad* (1917; City) and Evaristo Carriego's *Canción del barrio* (1912; Song of the Neighborhood) exalted the simplicity of the city's outskirts; Manuel *Gálvez's *Nacha Regules* (1919) depicted Buenos Aires with realistic prose; Roberto *Arlt created an alienating city in *Aguafuertes porteñas* (1930; Etchings from the Port); and the renown Jorge Luis *Borges wrote his first poetry book, *Fervor de Buenos Aires* (1923; *Fervor of Buenos Aires*, 1969) on the metropolis. In these poems, Borges first depicts the city as a vast space, spreading to the horizon that is internalized mentally and becomes a metaphor of his own solitude and sadness.

Buenos Aires delineates many of Borges's writings. From early avant-garde poems and essays like *Cuaderno San Martín* (1929; *San Martín Notebook*, 1969), *Inquisiciones* (1925; Inquisitions), and *El tamaño de mi esperanza* (1926; The Size of My Hope), to his mature books, including *Ficciones* (1944; *Fictions*, 1962), *El Aleph* (1949; *The Aleph*, 1970), and *Elogio de la sombra* (1969; In Praise of the Shadow), he eloquently expressed great love for his birth city, portraying Buenos Aires as a labyrinth, a cosmopolitan space, and a place where he would re-encounter his inner soul.

From the 1930s on, many works paint Buenos Aires as a mutating entity. Leopoldo *Marechal's *Adán Buenos Aires* (1948) offers a satirical depiction, while Manuel *Mujica Lainez in *Canto a Buenos Aires* (1943; Song to Buenos Aires) and *Misteriosa Buenos Aires* (1950; Mysterious Buenos Aires), Ezequiel *Martínez Estrada in *La cabeza de Goliat* (1946; Goliath's Head), Eduardo *Mallea in *La bahía del silencio* (1950; Silence Bay), and Adolfo Bioy Casares in *El sueño de los héroes* (1954; *The Dream of Heroes*, 1988) all inquire into hidden secrets of the city. These urban secrets, sometimes allegorical references to the political context of *peronismo* (political movement founded by three-time President Juan Perón) or metaphors of the various experiences a citizen should acquire in order to enter adulthood—as in the *bildungsroman* *Adán Buenos Aires*—are key elements in the literary construction of Buenos Aires as a mysterious city.

In the last half of the 20th century, danger and anonymity become central themes in literature about the metropolis. In *Rayuela* (1963; *Hopscotch*, 1966), *62/Modelo para armar* (1968; *62: A Model Kit*, 1972), and in many stories, Julio *Cortázar describes Buenos Aires as an unpredictable, oneiric city. Ernesto *Sábato's *Sobre héroes y tumbas* (1961; *On Heroes and Tombs*, 1981), César Fernández Moreno's *Buenos Aires me vas a matar* (1977; Buenos Aires You Are Going to Kill Me), Enrique Medina's *Strip-tease* (1976), David *Viñas's *Cuerpo a cuerpo* (1979; Melee), and Manuel *Puig's *The Buenos Aires Affair* (1973), among others, capture a sense of violence, threat, and repugnancy experienced in the megalopolis. Almost all of these literary works—the novel *Strip-tease* perhaps being the most representative—exemplify a process of demythification of Argentine culture, either by describing hallmarks of Buenos Aires or by incorporating a linguistic register characteristic of low sociocultural strata.

During the last military dictatorship (1976–1983), Buenos Aires functioned as backdrop of multiple sufferings and mysteries, as in Cortázar's *Deshoras* (1982; *Unreasonable Hours*, 1984), Alicia Dujovne Ortiz's *Buenos Aires* (1984), and

Luisa *Valenzuela's "Abril en Buenos Aires" (1983; "April in Buenos Aires," 1983). Following the state-inflicted violence during these seven years—a period known as *la guerra sucia* (the dirty war)—mourning, deterioration, and diaspora have become recurrent topics in postdictatorship literature about Buenos Aires, as in Ricardo *Piglia's *La ciudad ausente* (1992; *The Absent City*, 2000), Tununa Mercado's *En estado de memoria* (1990; *In a State of Memory*, 2001), and Rodolfo Enrique Fogwill's *Vivir afuera* (2000; Living Abroad), among others. More recently, novels such as Daniel Link's *Monserrat* (2006), María Sonia Cristoff's *Desubicados* (2006; Unsettled), and Bruno Morales's *Bolivia Construcciones* (2007; Bolivia Constructions), fictionalize the everyday life of newly arrived inhabitants, most of them immigrants from other Latin American countries, and their processes of settlement in a particular neighborhood of Buenos Aires.

As with the city itself, literature about Buenos Aires continues to increase its multiculturalism and diversity of voices. Such themes as immigration, extreme political oscillations, stories of exclusions and arbitrariness, along with fascinating depictions of the city and its people, remain constant features of the Buenos Aires literary map.

Natalia Crespo

See also *Género chico criollo* and the Río de la Plata *Saineteros* (*Sainete* Composers)

Work About:

Bernardson, Wayne. *Buenos Aires*. London: Lonely Planet, 1996.

Foster, David William. *Buenos Aires. Perspectives on the City and Cultural Production*. Gainesville: University Press of Florida, 1998.

Wilson, Jason. *Buenos Aires: A Cultural and Literary Companion*. Oxford: Signal, 1999.

Buero Vallejo, Antonio (1916–2000)

Arguably Spain's most important post–civil war dramatist, at the war's outbreak (1936), Buero joined Republican forces and served as an ambulance driver. When the Nationalists won in 1939, he was condemned to death; his sentence was later commuted to six years' servitude.

Buero submitted the play *Historia de una escalera* (1949; *History of a Staircase*, 2003) for the Lope de Vega Prize and won. *En la ardiente oscuridad* (*In the Burning Darkness*, 1985), also a 1949 entry for the prize, was subsequently performed to similar critical success. Buero authored some 30 more works for the stage.

Many of his plays deal with the alienation of individuals and their existential struggle against an oppressive society. *Historia* shows the struggle of three generations of neighbors in an apartment building and their inability to escape from near poverty, either because of their economic situation or their lack of motivation. His plays often use some sort of physical defect in one or more characters to symbolize alienation. Blindness, both figurative and literal, is a recurring theme in *En la ardiente oscuridad*. Only through confronting their blindness, rather than pretending it doesn't exist, do characters move toward the truth.

Francoist censors sometimes prohibited performance of his works in Spain, notably *La doble historia del Doctor Valmy* (written 1964; *Two Sides to Dr. Valmy's Story*, 1995), which premiered in England in 1968 but was not performed in Spain until after Franco's death in 1975. This drama directly attacks the torture that a dictatorship uses to maintain power, and critiques the inaction of "good" citizens to prevent such outrages. The connection to the real world of Franco's Spain is patent. In spite of these obstacles, Buero enjoyed continued success and his plays still delight critics and audiences.

Matthew A. Wyszynski

Work By:

Burning the Curtain: Four Revolutionary Spanish Plays. Trans. Gwynne Edwards. New York: Marion Boyers, 1995.

The Story of a Stairway. Trans. Peter Gibbs. Rock Hill, SC: Spanish Literature Publications, 2003.

Work About:

O'Leary, Catherine. *The Theater of Antonio Buero Vallejo: Ideology, Politics and Censorship*. London: Tamesis, 2005.

Buitrago, Fanny (1943–)

Born in Barranquilla, Colombia, Buitrago's extensive literary and dramatic output has merited national and international prizes, and includes numerous novels, works for the theater, a ballet, short story collections, and children's literature.

A precocious writer, Buitrago first dazzled readers with her controversial novel *El hostigante verano de los dioses* (1963; The Asphyxiating Summer of the Gods). Using innovative narrative techniques of multiple points of view, fragmentation, and collage, it advocated free love to a then deeply Catholic society. Buitrago was probably 18 or 19 years old when she wrote it. The novel's deep awareness of cultural, political, and social problems and its critique of age, gender, race, and class—well before such topics became part of 1970s intellectual discourse—are striking. Buitrago depicts both victims and victimizers of social and political violence in the cultural context following Colombia's infamous 1948 *Bogotazo. It forms an integral part of this novel and most of her subsequent works.

Her novel, *Bello Animal* (2002; Beautiful Animal), follows the rise to stardom of fashion model Gema Brunés through modeling agencies, publicity companies, TV programmers, slimy Internet people, and powerful commercial enterprises; all part of today's "trendy" Bogotá, shown to consist of women and men who imitate rock stars and TV celebrities, eagerly trying to be "beautiful animals."

Inca Molina Rumold

Work By:

Bello animal. Bogotá: Planeta Colombiana, 2002.

Señora Honeycomb. Trans. Margaret Sayer Peden. New York: Harper Collins, 1996.

Work About:

Utley, Gregory, "The Development of Subjectivity in Fanny Buitrago's *Señora de la miel*." *Hispanic Journal* 25.1–2 (2004): 131–44.

Bullrich, Silvina (1915–1990)

This novelist, storyteller, essayist, translator, journalist, and screenwriter born to a prominent family in Buenos Aires, Argentina, enjoyed the benefits of private education with frequent travel to Europe. Bullrich taught French literature at the Universidad Nacional de La Plata and translated works of Graham Greene, Simone de Beauvoir, and Louis Jouvet. In 1945, she collaborated with acclaimed writer Jorge Luis *Borges on the anthology collection *El compadrito*.

Bullrich's works revolve around two distinctive topics: the repressive condition of bourgeois women restrained by patriarchal and religious mores (as in *Bodas de cristal* [1951; Crystal Wedding] and *La Mujer Postergada* [1982; The Postponed Woman]), and the social and political division between upper and lower classes (in *Los burgueses* [1964; The Bourgeois], *Los salvadores de la patria* [1965; Homeland Saviors], and *Los Monstruos Sagrados* [1966; Sacred Monsters]). For years, her novels remained at the top of the best-seller lists and were translated into several languages. She died in Switzerland.

María Claudia André

Work By:

Tomorrow I'll Say, Enough. Trans. Julia Shurek Smith. Toronto: Hushion House, 1996.

Work About:

Lindstrom, Naomi. "Literary Convention and Sex-Role Analysis: Silvina Bullrich's 'Abnegation.' " *Denver Quarterly* 17.2 (Summer 1982): 98–105.
Stevens, James R. "*Los burgueses* of Silvina Bullrich: A Study of Generational Decadence." *MACLAS: Latin American Essays* 2 (1988): 35–39.

Burgos, Carmen de (1867–1932)

Also known as "Colombine," she was one of Spain's first feminists. Ill-married at 16, she soon realized that economic independence was the key to escaping her subordinate condition as housewife. As soon as she passed examinations to become a teacher, Burgos left her husband and moved to Guadalajara with her only daughter. Her literary career started with small collaborations for newspapers and magazines. In a time when divorce was illegal in Spain, her husband's timely death improved her social acceptance. Burgos's ambition to be a serious reporter led her to Melilla (Africa) during the Spanish–Moroccan war, becoming Spain's first female war correspondent in 1909. In time, her articles achieved tremendous popularity due to their controversial topics and the inclusion of readers' opinions. Her articles requested feedback on polemical issues, inspiring thousands of letters, including some from important political and cultural figures.

Burgos was also an accomplished novelist and public speaker. Most of her numerous short stories and novels dealt with the precarious life of Spanish women. Considering herself mainly an educator, her objective was to inform Spanish society, and especially women, of their unequal situation and rights, thereby hoping to improve women's lives.

Miryam Criado

See also Feminism in Spain: 1700 to Present; Women Writers in Spain: 1900 to Present.

Works By:

La flor de la playa y otras novelas cortas. Madrid: Castalia, 1989.

Work About:

Anja, Louis. *Carmen de Burgos, an Early Feminist*. Woodbridge, UK: Tamesis, 2005.

Bieder, Maryellen. "Carmen de Burgos: Modern Spanish Woman." *Recovering Spain's Feminist Tradition*. Ed., intro. Lisa Vollendorf. New York: Modern Language Association of America, 2001, 241–59.

de Burgos, Julia (1914–1953)

The life of this Puerto Rican feminist and poet was filled with challenges, including a family affected by poverty and illness and her own struggles with alcoholism and depression. She lived in New York City off and on from 1940 until her mysterious death in 1953. Suffering from cirrhosis of the liver, de Burgos collapsed on the street without identification and was buried in a common grave in Potter's Field, where she remained until her body was returned to Puerto Rico a month later.

De Burgos is known for challenging the social norms of her time and is considered a foremother for Puerto Rican feminists. One of her most studied poems is "A Julia de Burgos" from *Poema en veinte surcos*, in which the "you" described as a "cold doll of social lies" is contrasted with the more authentic, poetic "I." Rejecting the "prejudices of men," she chastises her public self because "everyone commands you." Other poems highlight female sexuality, a love of Puerto Rico's landscape, and her political convictions as an *independentista* who also argued for the rights of women, workers, and children.

Julia de Burgos as a cultural icon whose poetry is recited by Puerto Rican children often overshadows her literary importance. Nonetheless, she remains one of the most popular and most influential Puerto Rican poets of the 20th century.

Betsy A. Sandlin

Work By:

Song of the Simple Truth: Obra completa poética: The complete poems/Julia de Burgos. Ed., trans. Jack Agüeros. Willimantic, CT: Curbstone, 1997.

Work About:

Esteves, Carmen. "Julia de Burgos: Woman, Poet, Legend." *A Dream of Light and Shadow: Portraits of Latin American Women Writers*. Ed. Marjorie Agosín. Albuquerque: University of New Mexico Press, 1995, 221–36.

Zavala-Martínez, Iris. "A Critical Inquiry into the Life and Work of Julia de Burgos." *The Psychosocial Development of Puerto Rican Women*. Ed. Cynthia T. García Coll and María de Lourdes Mattei. New York: Praeger, 1989, 1–30.

C

Caballero Calderón, Eduardo (1910–1993)

Born in Bogotá, Colombia, to a patrician family, this influential writer, journalist, and diplomat produced a stylistic panoply of writings including the speculative essay, the chronicle, cultural history, and children's literature, but he is mostly remembered for realist, descriptive novels that reflect the many hardships of rural life in Colombia during the mid-20th century.

Written in a brisk, effective style, *El Cristo de espaldas* (1952; Christ Backwards) was the first of such works to receive widespread notoriety. The protagonist, a young priest who on his first assignment finds himself immersed in the fanatical struggle of the period in Colombian history known as la *Violencia*, illustrates the author's interest in personal redemption, religiosity, and socioeconomic conditions. These themes resurface in *Manuel Pacho* (1962), the story of a borderline mentally retarded young man who fights against the elements to take his father's corpse to a village where it may receive a Christian burial.

Caballero Calderón received Spain's prestigious Nadal Award for his novel *El buen salvaje* (1966; The Bon Sauvage), an experimental work that, combining essayistic prose with inner dialogue, narrates the misfortunes of a Latin American student and aspiring novelist living in Paris.

Héctor M. Hoyos

Work By:

El Cristo de Bogotá. 2nd ed. Bogotá: Panamericana, 1998.

Work About:

Iriarte Núñez, Helena. "Eduardo Caballero Calderón y la historia de los años cincuenta." *Literatura y cultura: narrativa colombiana del siglo XX*. Ed. María Mercedes Jaramillo, Betty Osorio, and Ángela Robledo. Bogotá: Ministerio de Cultura, 2000. I: 280–95.

Cabezas, Ómar (1950–)

Born in León, Nicaragua, this prose author studied law and was a revolutionary Sandinista who in 1979 helped overthrow the Somoza family political dynasty (roughly 1937–1979), supporting the Sandinista National Liberation Front (FSLN) of which he was an active member. As of 2009, Cabezas was the prosecutor general of the Office of Human Rights in Nicaragua, and continuing his membership in the FSLN.

His personal testimony, *La montaña es algo más que una inmensa estepa verde* (1982; *Fire from the Mountain: The*

Making of a Sandinista, 1985), describes the situation under Somoza, the activities of the National Guard, and the development of the resistance. Written in an informal style with fresh, direct Nicaraguan Spanish, it is the largest-selling book ever published in Nicaragua.

María José Luján

See also Testimonial Writing in Central America.

Work By:

Fire from the Mountain: The Making of a Sandinista. Trans. Kathleen Weaver. Intro. Carlos Fuentes. New York: Crown, 1985.

Work About:

Mantero, José María. "La mitificación de la revolución sandinista: El caso de Omar Cabezas y *La montaña es más que una inmensa estepa*." *Revista de Estudios Hispánicos* 30.2 (2003): 47–57.

Cabrera, Lydia (1900–1991)

A prolific chronicler of Afro-Cuban culture, this Cuban ethnographer blurred the lines between fiction and science. In 1936, she first published *Cuentos negros de Cuba (1940; Black Tales of Cuba, 2004)* in French translation while she lived in Paris. Inspired by the Négritude movement and French surrealism, with its rejection of rational Western culture, Cabrera penned and embellished the childhood stories that she had heard from her Afro-Cuban nanny in Cuba. Using a style resembling oral African narrative, a poetic prose with rhythmic repeating verses, she depicted a magical world of African animism.

Upon her return to Cuba in 1938, Cabrera dedicated her life to the study of Afro-Cuban culture. Her research, through Afro-Cuban informants and participant observation, resulted in an impressive bibliography, including the seminal work *El monte* (1954; *The Wilderness*), considered the Bible of Afro-Cuban religions. By highlighting Cuba's African heritage, often marginalized by the white hegemony, Cabrera's work rightly centers the African contribution to Cuban culture and identity.

Rebeca Rosell Olmedo

See also Afro-Hispanic Literature in Spanish America.

Work By:

Cabrera, Lydia. *Afro-Cuban Tales*. Trans. Alberto Hernández-Chiroldes and Lauren Yoder. Intro. Isabel Castellanos. Lincoln: University of Nebraska Press, 2004.

Work About:

Rodríguez-Mangual, Edna M. *Lydia Cabrera and the Construction of an Afro-Cuban Cultural Identity*. Chapel Hill: University of North Carolina Press, 2004.

Cabrera Infante, Guillermo (1929–2005)

One of the Spanish-speaking world's most accomplished novelists, he also worked as film critic, screenwriter, and prolific essayist. Born in Gibara, Cuba, he began writing short stories and film criticism for magazines and journal supplements like *Bohemia* (1908–) and *Carteles* (1919–1960), editing as well. When directing *Lunes de revolución* (1959–1961), the most important cultural supplement of the Cuban Revolution's first years, he and the journal fell from grace in 1962. After moving from Havana to Brussels that year, and then to Madrid, he settled in London in 1966, becoming a British citizen in 1979.

Cabrera Infante first began publishing short fiction in *Bohemia*; some of these appeared in his first collection *Así en la paz como en la guerra* (1960; *Writes of Passage*, 1993). Some stories brought him political trouble during the second Fulgencio Batista regime (1952–1959), and he spent several days in jail. His writing kept him in trouble with Castro's regime, forcing him to choose exile. In 1967, his masterpiece, *Tres tristes tigres* (*Three Trapped Tigers*, 1971), appeared, after receiving the 1964 Novela Breve Prize from Seix Barral. This canonical work of the so-called *Boom* is one of the finest novels ever written in Spanish.

Tres tristes tigres presents a nocturnal rhapsody on the city of Havana; its irregular form makes up an improvised, miscellaneous collection voiced by multiple narrative voices and incorporating various texts—letters, short stories, oral speech—all with a high dose of irony. Different sections, framed between the prologue and the epilogue, introduce a series of characters and scenes from Havana's night life in the late 1950s. The narrative voice switches from one character to another, giving the novel a choral feeling. Two characters are particularly relevant: Códac and Bustrófedon. The latter loves witticism and playing with words and language. It is also a novel of language, written in *cubano*, Cabrera Infante's own version of "Havana" Spanish. Some sections are meant to be read aloud, as in a performance. Witticism, intertextuality, hyperbole, and parody reference the baroque tradition (or neobaroque, as Severo *Sarduy wrote in 1972) that critics use to describe writings of such other contemporary Cuban writers as Alejo *Carpentier and José *Lezama Lima. The story constitutes a swan song to Havana's night life right before the triumph of Castro's revolution, and although there are no direct mentions of Castro or the revolution, the novel is subversive in its depiction of a society not fully aware of the pending changes that will lead the country to ruin.

Cabrera Infante's keen interest in language emerged after he moved to Havana as a teenager and studied English. He later learned French and Italian, and the conscious play with words and meanings became a hallmark of his writing, influencing other Cuban writers. His use of language and humor link him to James Joyce and William Sterne. Cabrera Infante dealt with adversity by turning it into a joke and covering pain and fear with humor.

Together with literature and language, film was another passion of this author. He wrote film scripts, film criticism, translated American films to be dubbed into

Spanish, and served as jury in film festivals. Besides film and language, numerous details of popular culture figure in his work technically and thematically. Some novels assemble fragments similar to the way comic strips work, and popular films and music—mostly *boleros*—become topics of his narratives. His love for tobacco inspired him write the book *Holy Smoke* (1985) in English.

Critical reaction to his work is disparate; some acknowledge his importance in Hispanic letters, others affirm that, after *Tres tristes tigres*, other writings fail to attain the high level of his masterpiece. Nonetheless, he received the Cervantes Literary Prize in 1997. Cabrera-Infante has influenced other writers, particularly Cubans, and especially, in recent times, Zoé *Valdés.

Miguel Ángel González-Abellás

See also Havana in Literature.

Work By:

Infante's Inferno. Trans. Suzanne Jill Levine with the author. New York: HarperCollins, 1984.

Three Trapped Tigers. Trans. Donald Gardner and Suzanne Jill Levine with the author. New York: HarperCollins, 1971.

Work About:

Nelson, Ardis L. *Guillermo Cabrera Infante: Assays, Essays, and Other Arts.* New York: Twayne, 1999.

Souza, Raymond D. *Two Islands, Many Worlds.* Austin: University of Texas Press, 1996.

CADA (1979–1985)

CADA, the Chilean Colectivo de Acciones de Arte (Activist Art Collective), was established just a few years after Augusto Pinochet's CIA-supported military coup in Chile. Its founders included sociologist Fernando Belcells, writer Diamela *Eltit, poet Raúl *Zurita, and visual artists Lotty Rosenfeld and Juan Castillo. The organization's primary goal was to revitalize national art by combining it with sociopolitical life. Participants aimed to create an activist artistic movement that would denounce Chile's contemporary social life. CADA achieved this goal by staging "happenings" that questioned the standard of living and the political atmosphere in the capital and throughout the country. These artists imagined society as a museum and life as a work of art that could be corrected and improved.

The group predominantly worked in an urban space of Santiago, the nation's capital. Their first happening, "Para no morir de hambre en el arte" (In order to not starve to death in art), was carried out in three stages. On October 3, 1979, hundreds of milk cartons were distributed to poor communities. This distribution of milk carried political connotations, since it referenced former Chilean president Salvador Allende's promise to provide milk to every child. When the empty cartons were returned, they were given to artists who used them to create works of art for an exhibition at the Galería Centro Imagen. The group also protested with a speech titled "No es una aldea" (It's not a village) in front of the ECLAC (The Economic Commission for Latin America and the Caribbean) building.

Another example of CADA happenings was the idea to write the following on walls throughout the city of Santiago: "No +." Throughout 1983 and 1984, unknown, anonymous people added their own words to the phrase, completing the sentence in ways like: "No + death," "No + disappeared," "No + torture," and so on, thereby creating a mass graffiti series expressing discontent with Chile's dictatorial regime. By these and similar actions, CADA artists intended to criticize Pinochet's oppressive dictatorship. Activist art, in their opinion, represented the best medium for social and political critique.

Ketevan Kupatadze

See also Chilean Women Writers: The *Ergo Sum* Project.

Work About:

Neustadt, Robert Alan. *CADA día: La creación de un arte social.* Santiago, Chile: Cuarto Propio, 2001.

Cadalso, José (1741–1782)

This Spanish author represents an early example of *romanticism in Spain. In his youth, he traveled around Europe, and then followed a military career, dying in an accident during the siege of Gibraltar (1779–1783), when Spain and France joined forces to wrest control of Gibraltar from the British.

Although Cadalso also wrote drama and poetry, he is remembered for two prose texts. *Cartas marruecas* (1789; Moroccan Letters) is a collection of fictive letters, unpublished during his life. The senders/recipients are three friends, two Moroccans and one Spaniard, and in these letters they discuss Spain's identity and history of their time and of the past. The epistolary structure allows Cadalso to include different topics related to Spanish identity. Although he tries to stay objective and acknowledge that nations have virtues and vices, criticism sometimes transpires as the character Nuño observes that Spain's glory remains in the past. This text recalls the type of national description and criticism found in later *costumbrista* aspects of Spanish romanticism.

Noches lúgubres (1789; *Lugubrious Nights*, 2008) is considered an early example of romantic texts. A desperate man, hoping to accompany his deceased bride for eternity, decides to unearth her corpse, lay her in bed beside him, and burn down the house. The plot, themes, and descriptions of the cemetery and the protagonist's psychological state, added to the angst and somber ambiance, advance the kind of romanticism later found in José de *Espronceda or José *Zorrilla y Moral.

Vicente Gomis-Izquierdo

Work By:

Cartas marruecas. Ed. Santiago Fortuno Llorens. Barcelona: Hermes, 2000.
Lugubrious Nights: An Eighteenth-Century Spanish Romance. Trans.

Russell Sebold. Albuquerque: University of New Mexico Press, 2008.

Work About:

Barnette, Linda-Jane. "Woman as Mirror in Cadalso's *Cartas Marruecas*." *Mountain Interstate Foreign Languages Conference Review* 7 (1997–1998): 102–12.

Scarlett, Elizabeth. "Mapping out the *Cartas Marruecas*: Geographical, Cultural and Gender Coordinates." *Revista de Estudios Hispánicos* 33.1 (1999): 65–83.

Calderón de la Barca, Pedro (1600–1681)

Unquestionably the most important playwright of the Spanish Golden Age (roughly 1500–1700), he studied at the Colegio Imperial of the Jesuits before subsequently registering at the University of Alcalá in 1614. He studied canon law in Salamanca until 1620, but then abandoned the ecclesiastical calling and returned to Madrid. The next year, he and his brother were implicated in a homicide. Despite brushes with the law and the church, Calderón enjoyed the king's favor, and was knighted by him in the Order of Santiago in 1637. After a few years, he abandoned the military and began service to the Duke of Alba. In 1651, he was ordained a priest and appointed chaplain of Toledo Cathedral's Capilla de los Reyes Nuevos. After that, Calderón kept closer to the court than to the popular atmosphere.

In comparison to Lope de *Vega's dramatic art, Calderón typically structures the plot with more coherence and a greater abundance of characters with diverse, complex natures, in careful accord with philosophical terms and axioms of his day. Learned expressions and an extensive use of conceits are intertwined in his baroque language.

Four numbered *Partes* (collections of his plays) were published during Calderón's life, each supervised by a trusted friend or relative, but he rejected authorship of some plays in the final collection. In 1677, 12 *autos sacramentales*, or allegorical religious plays, were published in a *Primera parte*. In this entry, dates given for individual plays generally refer to composition or performance years.

Before Calderón was 30, he already had written two important comedies: *La dama duende* (1629; *The Phantom Lady*, 1975) and *Casa con dos puertas, mala es de guardar* (1629?; *A House with Two Doors Is Difficult to Guard*, 1963), where the use of deceptive appearances is prominent. Almost simultaneously, he opened several other major plays, including *El príncipe constante* (1629; The Constant Prince), *La devoción de la Cruz* (1623–1633; *Devotion to the Cross*, 1996), and the complex drama *La cisma de Inglaterra* (1627?; *The Schism in England*, 1990). Several of these plays share marked resemblances, particularly in the treatment of love intrigues, as in *A secreto agravio, secreta venganza* (1635; *Secret Vengeance for Secret Insult*, 1996) and *El pintor de su deshonra* (1640–1644; *The Painter of His Dishonour*, 2000).

Two modalities dominate in Calderón's use of language: some dramas tend to highlight human cruelties (c. 1628; *Luis Pérez el Gallego* [L. P. the Galician], *La devoción de la Cruz*; *Las tres justicias en una* [1636–1637; Three Justices in One]). Others feature characters that join a system of power: antithetical structures represent the polarization of the individuals who enact them (c. 1642; *El alcalde de Zalamea* [*The Mayor of* Zalamea, 1990], *El gran teatro del mundo* [1635; *The Great Theater of the World*, 1990]).

Calderón's work exhibits great variety, including cloak-and-dagger comedies (1633; *La dama duende*, 1635; *Mañanas de abril y mayo* [Mornings of April and May]); dramas based on jealousy (*El médico de su honra* [1635; *The Physician of His Honour*, 1982]), philosophical plays (*La vida es sueño* [1635; *Life Is a Dream*,1970]); musicals (1658; *El laurel de Apolo* [1658; The Laurel of Apollo]); and operas (*La púrpura de la rosa* [1660; The Blush of the Rose], *La estatua de Prometeo* [1673?; Prometheus's Statue]).

El príncipe constante presents an interesting case of Christian tragedy: the protagonist is a member of the upper nobility, surrounded by suffering and disaster, who wills his own sacrifice. This piece represents the sacrifice of a martyr while offering insight into the potential of a humankind that has fallen into acquisitive materialism.

Considered a masterpiece for its beautiful verse, double plot strands, and profound messages, *La vida es sueño* includes love stories, religious and sociological commentary, and piercing psychological observations. Rosaura, accompanied by the *gracioso* (comic servant) Clarín, returns to her homeland, Poland, dressed as a man and with a sword from her father, whom she does not know. They meet a character covered with fur, Segismundo, who, unknowingly, is heir to the throne. He has been subjected to this condition by his father, the king Basilio. During the play the unruly, violent Segismundo is transformed into a respectful, civilized human being who uses reason to prevail over instinct.

Some of Calderón's plays are traditional comedies, such as *La dama duende*, *Guárdate del agua mansa* (*Beware of Still Waters*, 1984), or *Casa con dos puertas, mala es de guardar*. Others, even though they contain comic scenes and characters, like *La vida es sueño* or *El mágico prodigioso* (1637; *The Prodigious Magician*, 1982), have been classified as tragedies, because a play's genre is determined by its structure, not by its resources of humor (identity confusions, ridiculous figures, and so on). The characteristic elements of comedies include self-consciousness, play as a constitutive element, and commentaries on the action by the *gracioso*. The Calderonian classical ideal consists of a search for unity, sporadic use of secondary plots, strong dramatic economy, unity of scenic effects, and coherence in imagery and dramatic development.

In Hispanic theater, Calderón's expressive richness and variety of themes make him comparable to Shakespeare. Many editions of his complete works exist, including the facsimile edition published by D. W. Cruickshank y J. E. Varey; the ongoing project of Kurt and Roswitha

Reichenberger to edit the *comedias* and the *autos sacramentales* deserves special consideration.

Daniel Altamiranda

See also Theater in Spain: Beginnings to 1700.

Work By:

Eight Dramas of Calderón. Trans. Edward Fitzgerald. Foreword Margaret R. Greer. Champaign: University of Illinois Press, 2000.

Life's a Dream. Prose translation, intro. Michael Kidd. Boulder: University Press of Colorado, 2004.

Three plays. Trans. Adrian Mitchell and John Barton. Bath, England: Absolute Classics, 1990.

http://www.cervantesvirtual.com/bib_autor/calderon/.

Work About:

Benau, Isaac. *Reading for the Stage: Calderón and His Contemporaries.* Woodbridge, UK: Tamesis, 2003.

McGaha, Michael D., ed. *Approaches to the Theater of Calderón.* Lanham, MD: University Press of America, 1982.

Parker, A. A. *The Mind and Art of Calderón. Essays on the Comedias.* Cambridge: Cambridge University Press, 1989.

Suscavage, Charlene E. *Calderón. The Imagery of Tragedy.* New York: Peter Lang, 1991.

Cambaceres, Eugenio (1843–1889)

A native of Argentina, this realist writer's critical perspective on Argentine society clearly informs his novels. Cambaceres traveled through Europe extensively. He became a politician but later gave up his office due to corruption within his own party.

His first novel, *Pot pourri, silbidos de un vago* (1881; *Pot Pourri: Whistlings of an Idler*, 2003), satirizes Argentine society through a naturalistic attack of social vices, with the aim of righting the woes he observed.

Cambaceres's best-known text, *Sin rumbo* (1884; Without Direction), offers a bitter, depressing naturalistic view of the nation's ruling classes. Protagonist Andrés has lost all direction in life, drawing pleasure only from the most decadent habits like squandering money, womanizing, and drinking. The novel's rural and urban settings allow Cambaceres to reveal, with determinist perspective, a more complete picture of what he considered a decadent Argentina, a nation without a clear future as reflected in the protagonist's life.

Vicente Gomis-Izquierdo

Work By:

Pot Pourri: Whistlings of an Idler: A Novel of Argentina. Trans. Lisa Dillman. Ed. Josefina Ludmer. New York: Oxford University Press, 2003.

Sin rumbo. Ed. Juan Pablo Spicer-Escalante. Buenos Aires: Stockcero, 2005.

Work About:

Spicer-Escalante, Juan Pablo. "Civilización y barbarie: Naturalism's Paradigms of Self and Nationhood in Eugenio Cambaceres' *Sin rumbo.*" *Excavatio* 13 (2000): 299–309.

Campo, Estanislao del (1834–1880)

This Argentine politician, writer, and poet of the 1880s' generation was appointed congressman for the liberal Mitrista Party, and at the end of his term, he served as a government official in the Ministry of Political Affairs. He started his literary career in 1857 with a series of *gaucho* poems edited under the pseudonym Anastasio el Pollo.

Del Campo, however, is mostly known for *Fausto* (Faust), a groundbreaking literary piece edited in a local newspaper in 1866. After attending a performance of Gounod's opera—based on Goethe's seminal play of the same name—Del Campo felt inspired to write this humorous poem about a *gaucho*'s impressions of his evening at the Colón theater. Unable to distinguish between reality and fiction, Anastasio, the narrator, speaks in bewilderment of the Devil's influence over Dr. Fausto and his beloved Margarita. Although the poem was criticized for its many misrepresentations of rural lexicology, it remains one of the best examples of Argentine *gaucho* literature.

María Claudia André

See also Gaucho Literature.

Work By:

Faust. Eng. verse adaptation Walter Owen. Buenos Aires: Owen, 1943.

Work About:

Ludmer, Josefina. "En el paraíso del infierno. *El Fausto* argentino." *Nueva Revista de Filología Hispánica* 35.2 (1987): 695–719.

Page, Frederick. "*Fausto*, a Gaucho Poem." *PMLA: Publications of the Modern Language Association of America* 11.1 (1986): 1–62.

Campo Alange, Condesa de (1902–1986)

Despite her patrician, conservative roots, Spaniard María de los Reyes Laffite y Pérez del Pulgar became a post–civil war feminist writer. Born in Seville, she was raised in a very protective environment, in accord with the social norms of her day; Campo Alange always resented this lack of a formal education. During the Second Republic she left Spain with her husband and resided in France until the end of the war (1939). Paris afforded her a more independent life, and she attended art school. Upon returning to Spain, she published her first book about art, a biography of Spanish painter María Blanchard, and joined *La Academia Breve de las Artes*, being the only woman among 10 men.

Laffite devoted herself to feminist studies in the inauspicious postwar period. Her view of gender as a cultural construct remains valid. In 1948, she published one of her most polemical books, *La guerra secreta de los sexos* (The Secret War of the Sexes), which analyzes women's invisibility as the product of patriarchal domination in Western civilization. Other works on the same subject, based on anthropological and historical readings, followed this one. In 1960, she founded the Women's Studies

Sociology Seminar (SESM) devoted to researching women's role in Spanish society. The group existed for some 25 years, providing like-minded women with a venue for discussion and support.

Liliana Dorado

See also Feminism in Spain: 1700 to Present.

Work By:

La mujer en España: cien años de su historia, 1860–1960. Madrid: Aguilar, 1964.
Mi niñez y su mundo. Madrid: Revista de Occidente, 1956.

Campobello, Nellie (1900–1986)

This Mexican writer, the first woman to write about the 1910 Mexican Revolution, was born Francisca Luna. Some believed that Campobello's father was Pancho Villa, whom she strongly admired.

In 1929, Campobello published *Yo Francisca* (I, Francisca), a novel she had written at age twelve. She caught public and critical attention with *Cartucho* (1931; Eng. trans., 1988), with its innovative testimonial-autobiographical vignettes wherein a young girl candidly presents the horrors of the revolution. Mexican author Elena *Poniatowska considers it the only true depiction of that conflict. With documents acquired from one of Villa's wives, she wrote *Apuntes sobre la vida militar de Francisco Villa* (1940; Notes on the Military Life of Francisco Villa), aiming to set the record straight on his good character. As homage to her mother, who died of sadness after the death of Nellie's youngest brother, she published *Las manos de mamá* (1937; *My Mother's Hands*, 1988), illustrated by muralist José Clemente Orozco. Also a dancer and choreographer, Campobello cowrote with her half-sister Gloria *Ritmos indígenas de México* (1941; Indigenous Rhythms of Mexico), emphasizing dances of northern Mexico. Kidnapped in 1985, possibly to strip her of her Orozco collection, she died while held captive, but details remain a mystery. Authorities found her remains 12 years later.

Susana Perea-Fox

See also Documentary Narrative in Spanish American Literature; Novel of the Mexican Revolution.

Work By:

Cartucho. My Mother's Hands. Trans. Doris Meyer and Irene Matthews. Austin: University of Texas Press, 1988.

Work About:

Linhard, Tabea A. "Dancing with Pancho Villa's Head." *Fearless Women in the Mexican Revolution and the Spanish Civil War*. Columbia: University of Missouri Press, 2005. 161–85.
Poniatowska, Elena. "Nellie Campobello." *Las siete cabritas*. México: Era, 2000. 145–77.

Campos, Julieta (1932–2007)

Born in Havana, she actively worked as translator, university professor, and editor; as a writer, she cultivated almost all literary genres, and thereby contributed to a reflection of the creative process and the reader's role in the text. After studying literature in Cuba and France, she moved to Mexico in 1955. Her earlier creative works appear in *Reunión de familia* (1997; Family Reunion). Similarities between Campos's first fictional works and the French "new novel" of minimal action, characters who are articulated through internal monologues, and banal dialogues have repeatedly been noted. Nonetheless, Campos included herself within a Mexican generation of writers born in the 1930s who view the text as an independent space, with a logic that is not controlled by historic causality.

Tiene los cabellos rojizos y se llama Sabina (1974; *She Has Reddish Hair and Her Name Is Sabina*, 1993) is the best known of her narratives. Envisaged as a work in progress, it is the apotheosis of an open work, allowing for multiple readings. The open, polyphonic (multiple narrator) structure continues in her two last novels. Campos recently published *La Forza del Destino* (2004; The Force of Destiny), a encompassing Cuban saga stretching from 1942 to the present, which adds a historical dimension to her fiction.

Campos also participated in projects to improve the living conditions of Mexico's indigenous population; this interest led her to publish a collection and analysis of oral Nahuatl stories and books on indigenous history, art, myth, and traditions. She also published a book addressing poverty among Mexican peasants and small entrepreneurs.

Mercedes Guijarro-Crouch

Work By:

Reunión de familia. México, DF: Fondo de Cultura Económica, 1997.

Work About:

Garfield, Evelyn Picón. *Women's Voices from Latin America: Interviews with Six Contemporary Authors*. Detroit: Wayne State University Press, 1985.

Torres·Fierro, Danubio. "Julieta Campos." *BOMB* 94 (Winter 2006). http://www.bombsite.com/issues/94/articles/2795.

Canary Islands Writers

Historically speaking, Spanish literature critics tend to disregard the exemplary literature produced outside the mainland territory. In this regard, one must ask, do the Canary Islands have a distinct literary tradition, or should their literary output be conceived as a secondary or minor phenomenon within Spanish literature? Moreover, is it fair to limit such study solely to the rich poetic tradition, ignoring the impact of its abundant historical, fictional, and journalistic prose? Five hundred years of prolific literary production demonstrate the legitimacy and stature of writing by Canary Islands authors.

Such critics as Andrés Sánchez Robayna speak of a "literary micro-tradition" in the islands with distinct psychological and geographic characteristics (insularity, the sea, the landscape) dating to the 15th century and coinciding with the islands' first literary piece in Spanish, an *endecha* (song of grief) titled *Endechas a la muerte de Guillén Peraza* (*Endecha* on the Death of Guillén Peraza). The founding father of Canary Islands literature is Bartolomé

Cairasco de Figueroa (1538–1610), creator of the renowned island myth, "Doramas's Forest." Antonio de Viana (1578–1650), the other foundational Canaries poet, penned a monumental *Antigüedades de las Islas Afortunadas* (1604; Antiquities of the Fortunate Islands) that represents the epitome of *epic poetry of the islands. Two additional founding poets, José de Anchieta (1534–1597), first literati of Brazil, and Silvestre de Balboa (1513–1620), founder of Cuban poetry, also count among the prolific Canary Islands authors.

Two poets from La Palma, Juan Bautista Poggio Monteverde (1632–1707) and Pedro Álvarez de Lugo y Usodemar (1628–1706), exemplify the islands' baroque period. Poggio Monteverde cultivated heroic and romantic poetry while Álvarez de Lugo y Usodemar excelled in prose and has recently received new recognition for his 17th-century *Ilustración al Sueño* (Elucidation of the Dream), the only literary commentary of the day on Sor Juana Inés de la *Cruz's (1648?–1695) *Primero Sueño*. Other important figures of the period include Andrés de Abreu (1647–1725), Cristóbal del Hoyo, andVizconde del Buen Paso (1667–1762). The leading Canaries exponent of neoclassicism is historian and botanist José de Viera y Clavijo (1731–1813), whose prodigious output includes *Noticias de la Historia General de las Islas Canarias* (1783; Notes on the General History of the Canary islands) and *Diccionario de Historia Natural de las Islas Canarias* (1866; Dictionary of Natural History in the Canary Islands). José Clavijo y Fajardo (1726–1806), a founder of Spanish journalism, earned great renown for his writing in *El Pensador* newspaper.

Nineteenth-century literary production in the islands exhibits many such artistic tendencies as *romanticism and *realism that merge with new scientific discourse (Darwinism, positivism, etc). Journalism also flourishes with periodical and magazine publications like *El Atlante* (1837–1839) and the positivist journal *La revista de Canarias* (1878–1882). Canary Islander Benito *Pérez Galdós is the best-known author of 19th-century Spain; his life and work have been widely studied nationally and internationally. The works of two brothers, Agustín (1861–1935) and Luis (1863–1925) Millares Cuba stand as distinguished precursors of the islands' regional novel tradition.

Modernismo (the cultural movement aspiring to renovate artistic practices in the late-19th and early 20th century) finds its islands' voice in the poetry of Tomás Morales (1885–1921); his work *Las rosas de Hércules* (1919; Hercules's Roses) is a forerunner of contemporary poetry in the Canary Islands. Other consummate modernist authors are Alonso Quesada (1886–1925) and Saulo Torón (1885–1974). The avant-garde artistic movement was also well received in the islands, with publication of *Gaceta de Arte* (1932–1935), *La Rosa de los vientos* (1927–1928) and similar literary magazines. Agustín Espinosa (1897–1934), member of Spain's *Generation of 1927 and author of the prose work *Crimen* (1934; Crime), is the leading exponent of surrealism in the islands. Pedro García Cabrera (1905–1981), another Generation of 1927 member, is the second great surrealist poet. Other noted authors are Claudio de la Torre (1895–1973) and Agustín Millares Carlo (1893–1980), the noted 20th-century islander paleographer.

The Spanish Civil War (1936–1939) hindered progress of the avant-garde movement. After the war, literary production tended to abandon surrealism and experimentation, moving toward existentialism and social compromise. The prose of Agustín Millares Sall (1917–1989), texts by narrator and playwright Pedro Lezcano (1920–2002), and publication of the magazine *Antología Cercada* (1947), constitute the most relevant literary events of this period. In the 1950s and 1960s, the poetic, pictorial and editorial work of Manuel Padorno (1933–2002), founder of *Astil* magazine, deserves special mention. Poetry regained strength in the 1960s as indicated by publication of the anthology *Poesía canaria última* (1966; Recent Poetry of the Canary Islands).

The 1970s saw Canary Islands literature undergo a singularly successful social and literary phenomenon in which authors and readers conspired to give birth to a narrative boom. Authors of this intergenerational group (novelists born in the 1920s and others in the 1940s) sought to recover the islands' historical memory and identity and provide a personal image of their reality through realistic, experimental, historical, and even surrealist tendencies. An uncontrolled and unregulated publishing market, the birth of several private- and government-sponsored publishing houses, and the establishment of multiple literary prizes all contributed to this unprecedented islands literary boom. The most well-published authors and their work include Isaac de Vega, author of *Fetasa* (1957–1973; name given to a group of writers); *Mararía* (1968)—Rafael Arozarena's classic Canarian novel; Alfonso García Ramos's *Guad* (1970; Water)—winner of the Benito Pérez Armas Award; *Crónica de la nada hecha pedazos* (1971; Chronicle of Nothingness Smashed to Pieces), by Juan Cruz Ruiz; *El camaleón sobre la alfombra* (1974; The Chameleon on the Rug), penned by J. J. Armas Marcelo—winner of the Pérez Galdós Award; and Víctor Ramírez's *Cada cual arrastra su sombra* (1971; Everyone Carries Their Shadow Along), to mention a few. Unfortunately, this boom lasted but a few years due to the publishing industry monopoly, the discontinuance of literary magazines, and a general cultural disinterest. Many authors from the 1970s continue to publish, such as Fernando García Delgado, Planeta Prize–winner for *La mirada del otro* (1995; The Look of the Other).

Literary production in the 1980s and 1990s was driven by an individualistic, introspective approach to social reality. One paradigmatic characteristic was proliferation of the short story, as exemplified by a generation of authors born in the 1950s (Roberto Cabrera, Lorenzo Croissier, Juan José Delgado, José Zamora, Sabas Martín, etc.), whose works appear in *Narrativa Canaria Última* (2001; Latest Canaries Narrative).

Five hundred years of Canary Islands literary production should be sufficient to justify a thorough critical study of the islands' literature. This literary corpus has influenced Spanish mainland poetry, prose, and journalism. Unfortunately, excepting such authors as Pérez Galdós, who made their literary careers on the mainland, Canary Islands literature remains relatively unknown outside the islands, still awaiting widespread recognition.

Juan Carlos Martín

See also Insularismo.

Work By:

Delgado, Juan José. *El cuento literario del siglo XX en Canarias*. Santa Cruz de Tenerife: Cuadernos de Literatura Ateneo de La Laguna, 1999.

Nuez Caballero, Sebastián de la. *Poesía Canaria 1940–1984*. Santa Cruz de Tenerife: Interinsular Canaria, 1986.

Sánchez Robayna, Andrés. *Museo Atlántico: antología de la poesía canaria*. Santa Cruz de Tenerife: Interinsular Canaria, 1983.

Work About:

Bohn, Willard. *Marvelous Encounters: Surrealist Responses to Film, Art, Poetry, and Architecture*. Lewisburg, PA: Bucknell University Press, 2005.

Contemporary Poetry from the Canary Islands. Trans. Louis Bourne. Sel. and intro. Sebastián de la Nuez Caballero. London and Boston: Forest Books, 1992.

Merediz, Eyda M. *Refracted Images: The Canary Islands through a New World Lens: Transatlantic Readings*. Tempe: Arizona Center for Medieval and Renaissance Studies, 2004.

Cancionero **Poetry in Spain**

Written to and by the 15th-century Spanish aristocracy, this type of poetry, which was eventually collected into large volumes called *Cancioneros* (Songbooks), faithfully follows lyrical models inherited from the Galician-Portuguese and Provenzal traditions. It also adapts such select contemporary features as the Italian *stilnovisti* or models of contemporary French authors. Because court language had begun evolving from Galician-Portuguese to Castilian during the previous century, *cancionero* poems are in Castilian rather than Galician-Portuguese.

Cancionero texts are of two distinct types: the *canción* (song) and the *decir*. The *canción* differs in two ways from the Galician-Portuguese *cantiga de amor* and the Provencal *canço*: first, the Castilian poems are arranged in the songbooks according to stylistic criteria, rather than by subject matter, and second, the musical element is suppressed.

The *decir* is a type of text that, despite its lyrical nature, is inserted in a narrative frame that is often allegorical (through dream or vision) and ethical, didactic, or political in tone. Formally, the alternation between description and narration, direct and indirect speech and, above all, the presence of a narrative subject, distinguish it from the *canción*. Love is the main topic, and it is dealt with solemnly. The three main 15th-century *cancioneros* are the result of intense activity in three important courts: the Castilian court, which produced the *Cancionero de Baena*, the Napolitan court, with its *Cancionero de Estúniga*, and the Valencian court, source of the *Cancionero General*.

María Gimena Del Río Riande

Work By:

Cancionero [sound recording]: Music for the Spanish Court (1470–1520). Performed by the Dufay Collective. Wembley, Middlesex: Avie, 2002. [Program notes, English, Spanish, and French. Liner Texts in Spanish, French, and English].

Poetry at Court in Trastamaran Spain: From the Cancionero de Baena *to the* Cancionero General. Ed. E. Michael Gerli and Julian Weiss. Tempe, AZ: Medieval & Renaissance Texts & Studies, 1998.

Work About:

Macpherson, Ian Richard. *The Invenciones y Letras of the Cancionero General*. London: Queen Mary and Westfield College, 1998.

Cané, Miguel (1851–1905)

This Argentinean writer, best known for the remarkable memoir *Juvenilia* (1882), was born in Montevideo, Uruguay, where his family lived in exile during Juan Manuel de Rosas's dictatorship. As part of a wealthy family, he attended the prestigious Colegio Nacional de Buenos Aires. His childhood and adolescent experiences at this school between 1863 and 1868 became the subject of *Juvenilia*. An autobiographical account (the most characteristic genre used by Argentine Generation of 1880 writers), the text is considered a "collective memoir," the portrayal of a group of upper-class individuals educated in the Colegio Nacional. Central to the book are xenophobic remarks against immigrants, foreign literary references, upper-class bonding, and an aristocratic interpretation of Argentina's social conflicts. Thanks to its narrative fluidity and depiction of schoolboy life, Cané's text is still read in schools across Argentina.

Other writings by Miguel Cané like *Ensayos* (1877; Essays), *En Viaje* (1884; On My Travels), or *Notas e Impresiones* (1901; Notes and Impressions), mostly the product of his journalistic work and travel as Argentina's ambassador in Venezuela, Colombia, and Europe, highlight the constant representation of an elitist group in Cané's texts and distinguish his testimonial style. As part of his cultural agenda, he became a founding member of the College of Philosophy and Letters at the University of Buenos Aires.

Marcos Campillo-Fenoll

Work By:

Cané, Miguel. *Juvenilia y otras páginas argentinas*. Intro. Josefina Ludmer. Buenos Aires: Espasa Calpe, 1993.

Work About:

Foster, David William. "Miguel Cané's *Juvenilia:* Autobiography and the Ideologizing of Adolescence." *Symposium* 41.4 (1987/1988): 267–77.

Canetti Duque, Yanitzia (1967–)

Born in Havana and currently living in the United States, Canetti mostly produces children's literature in English and Spanish, but her fame is due to two novels written for adults: *novelita Rosa* (1997; through Rose-Colored Lenses), and *Al otro lado* (1997; To the Other Side). The *novelita Rosa* reveals the dangers of the false world of television for the lonely and uneducated and criticizes the excessive consumerism of American lifestyles. *Al otro lado* uses a lyrical, carefully elaborated prose, subtle humor, and abundant eroticism to tell the story of a woman who attends confession in a church that may exist only in her imagination. The novel explores loneliness, love, identity, and death, themes that obsess Canetti. Unlike most contemporary Cuban letters, her narratives do not address today's issues and conflicts of Cuba. Nonetheless, this novel has been praised as an extremely important work of contemporary Cuban fiction.

Miguel Ángel González-Abellás

See also Children's Literature in Spanish in the United States.

Work By:

Al otro lado. Barcelona: Seix Barral, 1997.
novelita Rosa. Andover, MA: Versal, 1997.

Work About:

Fuentes, Yvette. "En medio de dos aguas: Yanitzia Canetti y la literatura cubana en Estados Unidos." *Guayaba Sweet: Literatura cubana en Estados Unidos*. Eds. Laura P. Alonso Gallo and Fabio Murrieta. Cádiz, Spain: Aduana Vieja, 2003, 197–216.

Yanitzia Canetti (author's Web page). http://www.yanitziacanetti.com.

Cantar de Mío Cid

Also known as the *Poema del Cid (Song of the Cid*, 2009), it is considered the oldest medieval text in Spanish. Probably written by 1140, it represents the 11th- and 12th-century social and cultural values of Castile. A version from 1207 makes reference to Per Abbat as its author, but, most scholars agree that it is an anonymous work. It contains approximately 3,730 lines, depending on the version. It was transmitted orally by *juglares* (jongleurs) who would recite this long poem to townspeople where they traveled, with the purpose of educating while they entertained. The *Cantar* is different from any other text of the period because its protagonist, Rodrigo Díaz de Vivar (1043–1099) actually existed. His 1074 marriage to Ximena, daughter of the Count of Oviedo, in 1074 produced two daughters, María (doña Sol in the poem), Cristina (doña Elvira), and a son, Diego Díaz, who died in the battle of Consuegra in 1097. Also known as El Cid (derived from the Arabic *sayyid*, which means "lord"), Rodrigo fought against the Moors in Valencia and was the first Christian to defeat the Almorávid Berbers then occupying much of the peninsula.

An epic narrative designed to celebrate the deeds and virtues of its protagonist, the poem vividly describes the key events and battles of Rodrigo's adult life, closely following the historiography of el Cid.

Divided into three sections called *cantares* or songs, the first, "Cantar del destierro" (Banishment of the Cid), explains the protagonist's sentence of exile from Castile by King Alfonso VI of León, Castile, in 1081. The second part, "Cantar de las bodas de las hijas del Cid" (Marriage of the Cid's Daughters), recounts the wedding of Rodrigo's daughters to the Infants (royal heirs) of Carrión. The concluding "Cantar de la afrenta de Corpes" (The Affront of Corpes) expresses the Cid's request for justice for his daughters, doña Sol y doña Elvira, who have been severely abused by their husbands. The work concludes happily when the Cid's daughters are remarried, this time to princes from Navarre and Aragon. El Cid is a medieval Spanish hero who became famous, respected, and admired for his honor and exemplary behavior as husband, father, and friend, and for his military prowess and bravery.

Martha García

See also Chivalry Literature in Spain and the New World.

Work By:

Cantar de mio Cid. http://bib.cervantes virtual.com/bib_obra/Cid/.

The Song of the Cid. Trans. Burton Raffel. Intro. María Rosa Menocal. New York: Penguin, 2009.

Work About:

Barton, Simon, and Richard Fletcher. *The World of El Cid: Chronicles of the Spanish Reconquest: Selected Sources.* Manchester: Manchester University Press, 2000.

Capetillo, Luisa (1879–1922)

A Puerto Rican anarchist, labor activist, journalist, writer, and early feminist, she fought tirelessly for workers' and women's rights in Puerto Rico and the United States. Homeschooling by her parents implanted the seeds of liberal philosophical and political ideologies. After the first of her two out-of-wedlock children was born (1898), Capetillo found employment as a reader in an Arecibo cigar factory and there was introduced to the Puerto Rican Union movements of the day. As a result, Capetillo began penning opinionated essays on working conditions that were published in radical and union newspapers.

During Puerto Rico's 1905 tobacco worker strikes, Capetillo organized workers, wrote strike propaganda, and became the leader of the Puerto Rican American Federation of Labor. She also founded the newspaper *La Mujer* in 1910. The year 1911 saw publication of *Mi opinión acerca de las libertades, derechos y deberes de la mujer* (*A Nation of Women; An Early Feminist Speaks Out*, 2004). This collection of Capetillo's essays, letters, pamphlets, and speeches presents an eloquent, at times radical, case for women's liberation, and also deals with such practical issues as women's nutrition, hygiene, spiritual dimension, and need for education. Some five years later, *Influencias de las ideas modernas* (1916; The Influences of Modern Ideas) appeared. Written while she advocated for women and workers in New York City, Tampa, and Cuba (where she was arrested for wearing trousers, and expelled for political activism), it reflects increasing maturity in her feminist thought.

Amarilis Hidalgo de Jesús

Work By:

A Nation of Women. An Early Feminist Speaks Out. Ed., intro. Félix V. Matos Rodríguez. Trans. Alan West-Durán. Houston: Arte Público, 2004.

Work About:

Sánchez Gonzales, Lisa. "For the Sake of Love: Luisa Capetillo, Anarchy and Boricua Literary History." *Writing Off the Hyphen: New Perspectives on the Literature of the Puerto Rican Diaspora.* Ed, intro. José L. Torres-Padilla and Carmen Haydée Rivera. Seattle: University of Washington Press, 2008, 52–80.

Suárez Findlay, Eileen. *Imposing Decency: The Politics of Sexuality and Race in Puerto Rico, 1870–1920.* Durham, NC: Duke University Press, 2008, 158–66.

Caro y Cuervo Institute

Established in 1942 by the Colombian government, the initial charge of this internationally respected organization was to continue and publish the philological research initiated by Miguel Antonio Caro (1843–1901) and Rufino José Cuervo (1844–1896). The resulting *Diccionario de construcción y régimen de la lengua castellana*, edited annually, is quite unlike traditional dictionaries. As a tool for specialists rather than the general public, its focus is restricted to standard Spanish vocabulary that exhibits syntactic (word order) irregularities in usage; it incorporates extensive quotes from Spanish language literary texts to exemplify points and includes the etymology (origins) and history of usage for words. From 1945 to 1999, the Institute also published *Thesaurus*, a scholarly journal devoted to the study of Spanish and American indigenous languages, literatures, and cultures. In collaboration with Spain's Instituto Cervantes, the entire 54 volumes have recently been digitized and made available for scholarly research.

Housed at three locations in Bogotá, the Institute's range of activities has expanded over the years to presently include supporting and publishing scholarly study of languages, dialects, and cultures of Colombian peoples and those of Latin America; producing critical editions of literary texts; providing postgraduate study through the Seminario Andrés Bello, which offers two-year MA degrees in Spanish linguistics and Hispanic literature; collaborating with universities and international organizations with similar goals; supporting activities related to the history, use, and dissemination of the Spanish language and of Spanish-language literature; and promoting literacy and reading in Colombia. The Institute's library contains over 180,000 volumes, and its initiatives have been honored through such awards as the Prince of Asturias Award and the Bartolomé de las Casas Prize.

Maureen Ihrie

Work About:

Arrington, Teresa. "The 'Academia Colombiana de la Lengua' and the 'Instituto Caro y Cuervo': History, Organization, Mission." *Global Demands on Language and the Mission of the Language Academies.* Lexington: University of Kentucky, 1988, 47–55.

La lenga española, hoy. Ed. Manuel Seco and Gregorio Salvador. Madrid: Fundación Juan March, 1995, 309.

Carpentier, Alejo (1904–1980)

Undoubtedly one of the most influential figures of 20th-century Latin American arts, Carpentier's narrative earned him such prestigious literary awards as the Miguel de Cervantes Saavedra Prize in 1978. First known as a journalist, critic, musicologist, and radio personality, Carpentier was born in Cuba to a French father and Russian mother. His father's French library nurtured a bilingual and bicultural Carpentier, who spent many years in France and traveled widely. His trips to Spain, Venezuela, and Haiti as well as his vast musical and historical research impregnate his prose. In Spain, he encountered the baroque, an aesthetic concept that he developed and employed.

Early in his life, Carpentier became interested in the African presence in Cuba and its contribution to Cuban culture. Works such as his first novel, *¡Écue-Yamba-O!* (1933; Lord, Praised Be Thou), written in an Afro-Cuban language, and a history of music in Cuba (1946; *La música en Cuba,* [1946; *Music in Cuba,* 2001]) combine an affirmation of his Latin American roots and a search for origins that imbue all his work. His appreciation of the Afro-Caribbean appears in these formative works as well as in *El reino de este mundo* (1949; *The Kingdom of This World,* 1957), whose prologue contains his significant theory of *lo real maravilloso americano* (marvelous American reality), sometimes translated as, but not always conflated with, "*magical realism."

For Carpentier, the marvelous, which he attributes to Latin American nature, its history, and its people, constitutes the essence of Latin America, a continent where the unusual, strange, and unexpected are common. In the 1964 essay collection, *Tientos y diferencias* (Attempts and Differences), Carpentier elaborates on *lo real maravilloso americano*, which he believes the writer perceives and transforms into a work of art. The Latin American writer should not copy European movements, but rather generate a work that expresses the marvelous American reality of the New World.

The most appropriate tools for the above task are a baroque language and style because, according to Carpentier, America has been baroque since its beginnings. Thus Carpentier's writing evolves into a mature style classified as baroque. One of his last novels, *Concierto barroco* (1974; Eng. trans., 1988), mirrors the baroque in its title, theme, lexical density, and other formal stylistic devices. All Carpentier's baroque novels contain abundant figurative language, uncommon or archaic words, and a long, complex sentence structure.

The use of time, both as theme and narrative technique, characterizes Carpentierian prose. The short narrative "Viaje a la semilla" (1944; Journey Back to the Source) presents a reversal of time from the protagonist's death to his birth. In *Los pasos perdidos* (1953; *The Lost Steps*, 1971), his most famous novel, the protagonist-narrator undergoes self-discovery as he travels from a big city through a Spanish American jungle. The voyage, which becomes a journey through space and time, suggests the coexistence of different historical epochs, and communicates a yearning to transcend time.

Rebeca Rosell Olmedo

See also Afro-Hispanic Literature in Spanish America

Work By:

Music in Cuba. Ed., intro. Timothy Brennan. Trans. Alan West-Durán. Minneapolis: University of Minnesota Press, 2001.

Work About:

Shaw, Donald L. *Alejo Carpentier*. Twayne: Boston, 1985.

Carranza, María Mercedes (1945–2003)

Born in Bogotá, this Colombian poet, journalist, and cultural advocate belonged to the *Generación desencantada* (Disenchanted Generation) poetry group. She directed the literary supplements of *El Siglo* and *El Pueblo* newspapers, worked as an editor for the *Nueva Frontera* political magazine, and later wrote a literary column for *Semana* magazine.

In her first book, *Vainas y otros poemas* (1972; A Pain in the Ass and Other Poems), her irony and frankness regarding Colombia's society stand out. Carranza's writing rejects emotion and rhetorical flourishes and employs colloquial language to express contempt toward social conventions, patriotism, and stereotypes about women. Later poetic works *Tengo miedo* (1983; I Am Afraid), *Hola soledad* (1987; Hello Loneliness), and *Maneras del desamor* (1993; Ways of Lost Love) explore the trials of love and the uncertainty of life in a violent country.

From 1986 until her death, she directed the Casa de Poesía Silva foundation. Carranza was also elected to the assembly that drafted Colombia's 1991 Constitution. In 1997, she published her masterpiece, *El canto de las moscas* (Song of the Flies). This poetry collection offers witness to the massacres that took place during the 1990s as a result of the intensified armed conflict in Colombia. On June 10, 2003, she committed suicide after suffering a profound depression brought on by the kidnapping of her brother Ramiro, who died while being held captive by the FARC guerillas.

Yohainna Abdala-Mesa

Work By:

Poesía completa y cinco poemas inéditos. Ed. Melibea Garavito. Bogotá: Alfaguara, 2004.

Work About:

Kearns, Sofia. "Political and Toxic Discourse in María Mercedes Carranza's Latest Poems." *Ciberletras* 5. May 15, 2001. http://www.lehman.cuny.edu/ciberletras/v05/kearns.html.

Carrasquilla, Tomás de (1858–1940)

Novels by this talented Colombian regionalist writer depict life in Antioquia, a central northwestern department (i.e., state) of Colombia. Born and raised in Santodomingo pueblo, the second half of Carrasquilla's schooling took place in Medellín, the department capital. The 1876 civil war interrupted his studies toward a career in law, and he returned to Santodomingo, working variously as a tailor, a storekeeper in a mine, and in similar jobs, but always engaging seriously with the intellectual life of his day, particularly as a member of Medellín's Casino Literario (Literary Club).

Carrasquilla's first novel, *Frutos de mi tierra* (1896; Fruits of My Homeland) is a realist text set in late 19th-century Medellín with two parallel plot lines involving love stories. A primary theme is the sharp critique of an acquisitive, nouveaux riche Antioquia society in which the desire for economic gain has become the motivating force of relationships between individuals. This work, as does all his writing, includes much local color and use of colloquial dialects.

Carrasquilla's finest novel, *La marquesa de Yolombó* (1935; The Marchioness of Yolombó) is set in the late 18th-century town of Yolombó. Known for its gold mining industry, the city is now in decay and dominated by a corrupt upper class and equally acquisitive Catholic Church, both of whom are mercilessly depicted. His last novel, the three-volume *Hace tiempos: memorias de Eloy Jamboa* (1935–1936; Long Ago: Memoirs of Eloy Jamboa) tracks Colombia's evolution from a 19th-century mining economy to one based on commerce and agriculture.

Maureen Ihrie

Work By:

La marquesa de Yolombó. Bogotá: El Áncora, 1997.

Work About:

Avelar, Ildeber. "*Frutos de mi tierra*, o la fabulación del valor de cambio." *Estudios de Literatura Colombiana* 23 (July 2008): 15–26.

Levy, Kurt. L. *Tomás Carrasquilla*. Boston: Twayne, 1980.

Neira Palacio, Edison. "El contexto regional de Tomás Carrasquilla." *Hispamérica* 30.89 (August 2001): 87–93.

Carrera Andrade, Jorge (1902–1978)

Born in Quito, Ecuador, this innovative poet, translator and essayist is one of the most influential poetic voices of Ecuador and Latin America's avant-garde. A master of the metaphor, he continuously searched for the essence of existence and of language. He considered himself a poet of the Americas, as he dealt with all aspects of human life. His generation broke from *modernismo*'s conventions and employed and joined the vanguard through experimental language and forms of the avant-garde.

His first poetry collection of poetry, *Estanque inefable* (1922; Ineffable Pond), uses a bucolic scene and simple elements of nature to search for life's meaning. *La guirnalda del silencio* (1926; Garland of Silence) employs a less intimate, more engaged tone to display concern for contemporary world politics. *Boletines de mar y tierra* (1930; Bulletins from the Sea and the Earth) marks a change of voice as he adapts avant-garde aesthetics. Its more mature poetic voice proclaims a cosmic universalism. Following this work was *Microgramas* (1940; *Micrograms*, 2007). These poems demonstrate the influence of the Japanese *haiku*, which captures the essence of language as it deciphers "the bird's alphabet" and similar signals of the planet's spiritual order. *Hombre planetario* (1959; Planetary Man) collects 20 poems that address aspects ranging from the most insignificant to the most important of the universe. This book shows the poet's worldview as he identifies himself as a Latin American and a man of the world, and celebrates the beauty of things with calls for social justice. Andrade's profound essays deal with his travels and views of injustice as in *Latitudes* (1934) and *Cartas de un emigrado* (1983; Letters from an Emigrant). Among other themes, the latter collection strongly criticizes the exploitation of Ecuador's indigenous population. Also a career diplomat, he served as Ecuador's ambassador to France. Carrera Andrade was nominated for the *Nobel Prize in 1975.

Ivonne Gordon-Vailakis

See also Avant-Garde Poetry in Spanish America; *Modernismo* in Hispanic Literature.

Work By:

Andrade, Jorge Carrera. *Century of the Death of the Rose.* Ed., trans. Steven Ford Brown. Montgomery, AL: New South Books, 2002.

Obra Poética. Ed. Raúl Pacheco and Javier Vásconez. Quito: Acuario, 2004.

Work About:

Gleaves, Robert M. "The Reaffirmation of Analogy: An Introduction to Jorge Carrera Andrade's Metaphoric System." *Confluencia: Revista Hispánica de Cultura y Literatura* 10.1 (Fall 1994): 33–41.

Muñoz, Gabriel Trujillo. "Aurosia, the Utopian Planet: Jorge Carrera Andrade's Latin American Vision." *New York Review of Science Fiction* 17.1 (September 2004): 1, 4–6.

Carreras, Roberto de las (1875–1963)

This Uruguayan poet and prose writer was strongly influenced by *modernismo* literary tenets and, more specifically, *decadentismo* (bizarre subjects, inversion of accepted norms, ennui, and so on). Along with Horacio *Quiroga, José Enrique *Rodó, Delmira *Agustini, Florencio *Sánchez and others, he was a member of the Generation of 1900, the first generation of Uruguayan writers, born on the brink of the 20th century. His fame stems more from his eccentric attitudes than his writings. After spending some three years in Europe, he returned personifying the figure of the *dandy*. An anarchist and cultivator of free love, he enjoyed scandalizing village-like Montevideo with his works and, especially, his conduct. Carreras declared himself a bastard son and was in the habit of roaming the streets in a waistcoat sporting a bullet hole received from a jealous husband. Having spent the fortune inherited from his father, in 1906 he began to suffer the first symptoms of the mental illness that forced him to live in seclusion for over 50 years.

Carreras's poetry reflects his uncontrollable passions, like that which he felt for Italian actress Lina Cavalieri, to whom he dedicated his famous "Psalmo" (1905; Psalm). A skilled versifier, he attempted to reform antiquated poetry in Spanish under the influence of French symbolism. In his prose, an inventive cleverness distinguished his texts, as exemplified in *Amor libre: Interviews voluptuosos con Roberto de las Carreras* (1902; Free Love. Sensual Interview with Roberto de las Carreras), where he introduced himself as a cuckold and a master of sensuality.

Liliana Dorado

Work By:

Amor libre: Interviews voluptuosos con Roberto de las Carreras. Montevideo, 1902.
Por el mundo: crónicas de viaje. Ed. Electra de las Carreras and Susana de Jaureguy. Montevideo: El Galeón, 2008.

Work About:

Domínguez, Carlos María. *El bastardo: la vida de Roberto de las Carreras y su madre Clara.* Montevideo: Cal y Canto, 1997.

Carreta, La (1952; The Oxcart, 1969)

Written by Puerto Rican author René *Marqués, this iconic play centers on the Puerto Rican emigration to the U.S. mainland. It follows the emigration saga of a poor family that migrates first from the rural mountains of Puerto Rico to the slums of the island's capital city, San Juan, and from San Juan to the Spanish ghettos of New York City. Luis, the oldest son, convinces the family to move to the city in search of better economic possibilities. Marqués connects those possibilities with Puerto Rico's accelerated industrialization during the 1930s and 1940s. The emigration process causes the family to face unhappiness stemming from moral and social degradation. Through the play, Marqués constantly opposes the ideological views of the old generation (Don Chaguito) with the elusive progressive vision of his son, Luis, during the three acts set respectively in the island's countryside, the slums of San Juan, and New York's Spanish ghetto.

Some 30 years later, Tato *Laviera's poem collection *La Carreta Made a U-Turn* (1976) revisits Marqués's play and, as Waldron demonstrates, uses parody to undermine the essentially colonialist situation of the canonical work.

Amarilis Hidalgo de Jesús

Work By:

The Oxcart (La carreta). Trans. Charles
Pilditch. New York: Charles Scribner's
Sons, 1983.

Work About:

Waldron, John. "Tato Laviera's Parody of
La carreta: Reworking a Tradition of
Docility." *Writing Off the Hyphen.*
*New Perspectives on the Literature of
the Puerto Rican Diaspora.* Ed. José
L. Torres-Padilla and Carmen Haydée
Rivera. Seattle and London: University
of Washington Press, 2008, 221–36.

Carrión Mora, Benjamín (1897–1979)

This writer and founder of Ecuador's Casa
de la Cultura in 1944 embodies that country's cultural history during most of the
20th century. A tireless defender of social
justice for all Latin Americans, he
received Mexico's Benito Juárez Prize in
1968, a one-time award that ensured his
stature as an intellectual force throughout
the continent. For most of his adult life,
Carrión promoted Ecuadorian and Latin
American writers and artists through his
publications, diplomatic posts, and many
travels abroad. Without ignoring the
esthetic aspects of art, Carrión belonged
to a long tradition of Latin American intellectuals who believed that an appreciation
of beauty would necessarily lead to ethical
behavior. It is not surprising that he was
one of the founders of Ecuador's Socialist
Party in 1926 and never wavered in his
support of the 1959 Cuban Revolution.

Among his many noteworthy publications is *Cartas al Ecuador* (1943; Letters
to Ecuador), an essay collection written
shortly after Ecuador lost much of its
national territory to Peru in 1941. Confronted with a demoralized nation, Carrión
celebrated Ecuador's potential and
insisted that a small country could achieve
greatness through its cultural production.
Although his idealism has often been criticized as naïve and simplistic, his call to
Ecuadorians to reconstruct and to recom-
mit to their country (*volver a tener patria*)
continues to resonate.

Michael Handelsman

Work By and About:

Handelsman, Michael, ed. *Benjamín Carrión. Pensamiento fundamental.* Quito:
Corporación Editora Nacional y Universidad Andina Simón Bolívar, 2007.

Casal, Julián del (1863–1893)

Born in Havana, Cuba, this leading poet of
early *modernismo* suffered from poor
health most of his life, coupled with a generational, "end-of-the-century" malaise.
He made a brief trip to Europe but returned
home before visiting Paris, fearing that the
city would fail to measure up to how he
imagined it.

In his life and work, Casal closely
adhered to the *modernismo* aesthetic. He
published two volumes of poetry during
his lifetime, *Hojas al viento* (1890; Leaves

in the Wind), and *Nieve* (1892; Snow). *Bustos y rimas* (1893; Busts and Rhymes), a collection of prose sketches and verse, was published posthumously. Cosmopolitanism, pessimism, and cultivation of the morbid and grotesque dominate these writings.

Casal played a principal role in introducing Orientalism, a fascination with Eastern culture, into *modernismo* poetry. A reclusive figure, he sought to escape mundane reality by decorating his living quarters with Chinese and Japanese artifacts, and transformed these artifacts into poetic motifs. *Kakemono* (Japanese scroll painting) and *Sourimono* (Japanese postcard) illustrate his taste for the exotic. "Neurosis," which depicts the prostitute Noemí, highlights the decadent strain in his poetry. Casal's elitism and escapism represent the antithesis of fellow Cuban José *Martí's socially and politically committed writings.

Melvin S. Arrington Jr.

Work By:

The Poetry of Julián del Casal: A Critical Edition. Ed. Robert Jay Glickman. Vol. 1. Gainesville: University Press of Florida, 1976.

Work About:

Clay Méndez, Luis Felipe. "Julián del Casal and the Cult of Artificiality: Roots and Functions." *Waiting for Pegasus*. Ed. Roland Grass and William R. Risley. Macomb: Western Illinois University, 1979, 155–68.

Jiménez, Luis A., ed. *Julián del Casal en el nuevo milenio*. Managua, Nicaragua: PAVSA, 2005.

Casona, Alejandro (pseudonym of Alejandro Rodríguez Álvarez) (1903–1965)

Upon completing his formal education, this popular Spanish dramatist taught in the Arán Valley, founded a children's theater, and discovered his passion for drama. By 1934, he had spent five years leading acting groups on tours to over 300 towns throughout Spain.

A political exile during and after the Spanish Civil War (1936–1939), Casona traveled to France and throughout Latin America, eventually settling in Buenos Aires. There, he thrived as a dramatist, delighting Spanish-speaking audiences with his ability to integrate serious themes like death and existential ponderings with stories of love and fantasy, all with gentleness and humor. A didactic intent pervades his drama, yet what distinguishes it is a skillful weaving of the real and surreal against a backdrop of folklore and regional traditions.

His first major play, *La sirena varada* (1934; Mermaid Aground), a love fantasy set in a community whose inhabitants escape the pain and tedium of reality by allowing themselves to be governed not by common sense, but by the imagination, premiered in Madrid in 1934. The following year, Casona's only true social drama, *Nuestra Natacha* (1935; Our Natacha), became Spain's most successful play; however, its appeal for societal and educational reforms instead of conformity later led the government to ban his works. Other immensely popular plays include the surrealistic *Prohibido suicidarse en primavera* (1937; *Suicide Prohibited in Springtime*, 1968), in which an institution ostensibly established to encourage suicidal individuals to end their lives is instead revealed to be a haven where they obtain a purpose for living, and *La dama del alba* (1944; *The Lady of the Dawn*, 1972), which incorporates traditions and superstitions of Spain's Asturias region into a tender story about death.

La barca sin pescador (1945; *The Boat without a Fisherman*, 1970), *Los árboles mueren de pie* (1949; Trees Die Standing), and *Siete gritos en el mar* (1952; Seven Shouts on the Sea) all premiered in Latin America. Casona returned to Spain in 1962, where his final drama, *El caballero de las espuelas de oro* (1964; The Knight with the Golden Spurs), based on the complex life of baroque Spanish satirist and poet Francisco de *Quevedo, enjoyed over 1,000 performances.

Charles Maurice Cherry

Work About:

Moon, Harold K. *Alejandro Casona*. Boston: Twayne, 1985.

Thomas, Katherine M. "Mythic Archetypes in Casona's *La dama del alba.*" *Text and Presentation: The Journal of the Comparative Drama Conference* (1992): 77–82.

Castellanos, Rosario (1925–1974)

An essayist, poet, and novelist, she was born in Mexico City to a family of means.

After graduating with a master's degree in philosophy from Mexico's National University, she received a fellowship from the Rockefeller Foundation that allowed her to write her first novel, *Balún-Canán* (1957; *The Nine Guardians*, 1992), a narrative on women's marginal position within Mexican society, based on personal experiences. Through the years, Castellanos wrote for several journals and magazines and held visiting professorships in Latin American literature. In 1967, she lectured at several universities in the United States, and in 1971, was appointed Mexico's ambassador to Israel, where she also taught at Jerusalem's Hebrew University.

Heavily influenced by French feminist Simone de Beauvoir's views on maternity and marriage, Castellanos's essays, poetry, and narrative writing render an account of her own life while reflecting on the ways in which the myth of femininity has suppressed most Mexican women of her generation.

María Claudia André

See also Feminism in Spanish America.

Work By:

A Rosario Castellanos Reader: An Anthology of Her Poetry, Short Fiction, Essays, and Drama. Ed. and trans. Maureen Ahern et al. Austin: University of Texas Press, 1990.

Meditation on the Threshhold: A Bilingual Anthology of Poetry. Ed., trans. Julian Palley. Tempe AZ: Bilingual, 1988.

Work About:

Bonifaz Caballero, Óscar. *Remembering Rosario, a Personal Glimpse into the*

Life and Works of Rosario Castellanos. Trans. Myralyn F. Allgood. Potomac, MD: Scripta Humanística, 1990.

Friis, Roland. "The Fury and the Mire of Human Veins. Rosario Castellanos and Frida Kahlo." *Hispania* 87.1 (2004): 53–61.

Castillo, Amelia del (1923–)

Born in Matanzas, Cuba, this poet, musical composer, and short story writer has resided in Miami, Florida, since November 1960, when she left the island. Castillo is a cofounder of the *PEN Club de Escritores Cubanos en el Exilio*, an important literary organization dedicated to expanding and promoting Cuban artists in exile. Her poetry often uses images and expressions that evoke her passion for Cuba; many poems contrast past and present, the tangible and the intangible, or the inner voice and dialogue.

As a composer, Castillo has written several songs—music and lyrics—for the guitar. Her prose masterfully employs the technique of silence as a valuable narrative tool for artistic purposes. The reader will perceive lapses, omissions, and inconsistencies between the dialogue, content, or narrative information, and will experience a sensation that something is missing or incomplete; consequently, the silence becomes the untold discourse. The short story collection *De trampas y fantasías* (2001; Of Traps and Fantasies) explores many complex aspects of human nature such as emotions, loss, feelings, actions and reactions, faith, relationships, and

consequences of the decision making process. In each of her poems, songs, and short stories, readers will find an intrinsic characteristic: the presence of a female voice *yo* (I) in harmony with the *tú* (you, second person, singular) throughout the artistic encounters and interactions. Castillo has been recognized nationally and internationally for her extensive creative work.

Martha García

See also Cuban American Writers; PEN Club in the Hispanic World.

Work By:

Agua y espejos. Miami: Universal, 1986.
De trampas y fantasías. Miami: Universal, 2001.

Work About:

Jiménez, Luis A. "Hacia una ecocrítica de la novísima poesía de Amelia del Castillo." *South Eastern Latin Americanist* 44.4 (Spring 2001): 32–42.

Castro, Rosalía de (1837–1885)

This Galician prose and verse writer was born in Santiago de Compostela, Spain, to Teresa de Castro y Abadín and priest José Martínez Viojo. Many critics have given excessive weight to this fact when analyzing her work. Her biographers do note that Castro's first years were spent with her father's family and she was subsequently very close to her mother. In fact, Castro published *A mi madre* (1863; To My Mother) in homage to her mother. Castro married literary critic and historian

Manuel Martínez Murguía in 1858; together, they form part of the Galician *Rexurdimento*, or renaissance of culture in that language.

A bilingual writer, Castro's first volumes were in Spanish: *La Flor* (1857; The Flower), collected poems; and the novels *La hija del mar* (1859; Daughter of the Sea) and *Flavio* (1861). Yet it was her verse collection *Cantares Gallegos* (1863; Galician Songs) that gave rise to that renaissance, because it was the first Galician-language book to be published in four centuries. In this sense, Rosalía's work became the continuation of verse by medieval King of Castile *Alfonso X el Sabio whose *cantigas*—written in Galician-Portuguese—had been considered the peninsula's highest cultural form during the 13th century. To commemorate the May 17 publication of *Cantares Gallegos*, in 1963 that date became the official Day of Galician Letters. To this day it is celebrated annually.

Castro subsequently published in Spanish the following texts: her novels *Ruinas* (1866; Ruins), *El caballero de las botas azules* (1867; The Gentleman in the Blue Boots), and *El primer loco* (1881; The First Madman); and the shorter prose pieces "El cadiceño" (1863; The Man from Cadiz), "Las literatas" (1866; Bluestockings), "El domingo de Ramos (1881; Palm Sunday), and "Padrón y las inundaciones" (1881; Padrón and the Floods). Her last poetry volume, *En las orillas del Sar* (1884; On the Banks of the Sar River), also was composed in Spanish. While the latter is perhaps Castro's best-known work for non-Galician readers, both *Cantares Gallegos* and her other extensive volume of Galician verse, *Follas Novas* (1880; New Leaves), constitute major accomplishments of her literary career and are necessary for understanding Castro's reasons and sources for writing.

As a 19th-century woman dedicated to a literary profession, Castro encountered barriers inside and outside Galicia. Her earliest critics quickly praised her lyrical talent, but did not easily recognize her views on Spanish politics and—especially—her views on the exploitation and marginalization of Galicians. As a bilingual writer, she was also caught between those who valued the sincerity and ability to write verse based on popular forms of oral culture in the vernacular language and those who failed to perceive to see a harsh criticism of contemporary society in her Spanish-language novels.

Since the centennial of Castro's death in 1985, scholars have begun a serious and much-deserved revision of her writing and objectives. Her work as a whole is finally being considered, requiring the study of Spanish and Galician writings, as well as her prose (novel and shorter texts) and poetry. After decades of being relegated to the periphery, Castro has emerged as a nationalist and feminist writer, with a clear vision of her regional conditions, of women's difficulties in being taken seriously as writers, and of her role as an advocate for the language of the people. It is no longer possible to overlook her lucid portrayals of the hunger and unemployment that forced thousands into Castile and even to the Americas for survival. Similarly, her depiction of Galician women as "widows of the living," desirous of healthy, just, sexual relation-ships with men, has become more than evi-dent. The traditional image of "Santa Rosalía" (Rosalía the Saint) as a woman writer with vague sense of social problems expressed existentially in references to a *negra sombra* (black shadow), who endured a painful cancer in the final stages of her life, can no longer be sustained. Precisely because of the last two decades of scholarly work, using nationalist and feminist theory, the body of Castro's writing continues to be as alive as when she revolutionized Gali-cian letters on May 17, 1863.

Kathleen March

See also Feminism in Spain: 1700 to Present.

Work About:

Small, Elizabeth. "Tropo y locus: Árboles en la poesía de Rosalía de Castro." *His-pania* 90.2 (May 2007): 205–14.

Tolliver, Joyce. "Rosalía between Two Shores: Gender, Rewriting, and Trans-lation." *Hispania* 85.1 (March 2002): 33–43.

Castro Quesada, Américo (1885–1972)

This historian, literary critic, and philologist was born in Brazil to Spanish parents. In 1889, the family returned to Spain, where he later studied at the University of Gra-nada, graduating in 1904. In 1915, soon after earning his doctorate from Madrid's Central University, he began lecturing at various universities, and collaborated with eminent scholar Ramón Menéndez Pidal at the Center for Historical Studies, where he directed the Office of Lexicography. Castro's critical editions of such Spanish classic authors as Lope de *Vega represent the best testimony of his work as philologist and his expertise in the Spanish language.

Castro's intellectual life was influenced by his political association with the government of the Spanish Republic (1931–1936), which named him Spain's ambassador to Berlin in 1931, a position he left one year later. At the beginning of the Spanish Civil War (1936–1939), Castro went into exile in the United States, holding chairs in Spanish Literature at uni-versities in Wisconsin, Texas, and, for 13 years, at Princeton.

In the United States, his work sparked an authentic revolution in Spanish histori-ography, through his exploration of the distinctive historical and cultural roots of Spanish and Spanish American identity. Against the widespread notion of Spain as a nation that evolved from a single eth-nic group, Castro deconstructed Spanish identity by developing the notion of *hispa-nidad*. This concept was understood as a product of the long dialogue and inter-changes of cultural practices and knowl-edge among the three medieval Iberian cultures and religions: Christianity, Juda-ism, and Islam. Castro's position was countered by Claudio Sánchez Albornoz, who stressed that the Germanic compo-nent dominated over the Semitic element in forming Spanish identity. Castro received numerous prizes and honorary degrees for his original thought. Today, his work continues to impact such scholars and writers as Juan *Goytisolo.

Enric Mallorquí-Ruscalleda

Work By:

The Spaniards: An Introduction to Their History. Trans. Willard F. King and Selma Margaretten. Berkeley: University of California Press, 1971.

Work About:

Surtz, Ronald E., Jaime Ferrán, and Daniel P. Testa, eds. *Américo Castro: The Impact of His Thought.* Madison: Hispanic Seminary of Medieval Studies, 1988.

causa por la raza, la (The Cause for the Mexican Race)

This concept of requiring equity and respect for the lives of Mexican migrant workers motivated César Chávez and cofounder Dolores Huerta to establish the Farm Workers of America labor union (1962) to obtain better wages and improved working and living conditions for these laborers. The concept provided crucial underpinnings for the four-year strike against California grape growers, which moved the conflict beyond the parameters of a routine labor strike by focusing on social justice and dignity for these workers. The dispute engaged sympathies nationally, inspiring the boycott of table grapes. Later in the decade, *la causa*'s concern for equity and dignity spread to inform the Chicano civil rights struggle.

During this same period, Dolores Huerta originated the slogan *Sí se puede* (Yes we can) during the farm worker marches; it has later been used by other strikers, immigration reform groups, and more recently, in the English adaptation, by President Barak Obama.

Maureen Ihrie

See also Chicano Movement Literature and Publishing.

Work About:

Levy, Jacques E., and Fred Ross, Jr. *César Chávez: Autobiography of La Causa.* Minneapolis: University of Minnesota Press, 2007.

Cela, Camilo José (1916–2002)

Winner of the 1989 Nobel Prize in Literature, this Galician-born Spaniard founded the Spanish literary style of *tremendismo*—novels emphasizing the repulsive, the grotesque, and the violent. He fought in the Spanish Civil War (1936–1939) on the Nationalist side (rebels led by Francisco Franco) but was discharged after being wounded. Later, he would publish the journal *Papeles de Son Armadans* (1956–1979), which served as a print venue for young antifascist writers.

La familia de Pascual Duarte (1942; *Pascual Duarte's Family*, 1946) is the first *tremendista* novel, in which Pascual's father dies of rabies; a pig bites off the ear of Pascual's infant brother, and Pascual himself commits several murders, including knifing his own mother. Another important novel by Cela is *La colmena* (1951; *The Hive*, 1953), which combines realism (depicting life as it is rather than idealizing it) with the more experimental style of stream of consciousness (transcribing thoughts as they occur with scarce attention to grammatical structure or coherency). The novel contains little action and, in large part, presents the poor people of Madrid's literary cafés in the early post–civil war years.

Cela's work became increasingly experimental: *San Camilo, 1936* (1969; Eng. trans., 1991) offers a surrealist description of the day the Spanish Civil War began; *Cristo versus Arizona* (1988; *Christ versus Arizona*, 2007) is a 100-page, one-sentence-long story of a duel at the OK Corral in the U.S. Wild West.

Elected a member of the *Real Academia Española in 1957, Cela was also a member of the Constitutional Convention that wrote the Spanish Constitution of 1978 after the death of dictator Francisco Franco. In all, Cela authored 13 novels, several books of poetry and drama, short stories, travel books, and even a dictionary of vulgarisms. His standing as one of the most important writers of 20th-century Spain is further evidenced by his winning Spain's most prestigious literary award, the Cervantes Prize, in 1995. Cela died in Madrid.

Jeffrey Oxford

See also Censorship and Literature in Spain; Francoism, Fascism, and Literature in Spain; Nobel Prize Literature in Spanish; Novel in Spain: 1900 to Present.

Work By:

Christ versus Arizona. Trans. Martin Sokolinsky. Rochester, NY: Dalkey Archive, 2007.
San Camilo, 1936. Trans. J. H. R. Polt. Durham, NC: Duke University Press, 1991.

Work About:

Camilo José Cela Number. The Review of Contemporary Fiction 4.3 (Fall 1984). Special Issue.
Cela Conde, Camilo José, *Cela, mi padre*. 3rd ed. Madrid: Temas de Hoy, 2002.
Charlebois, Lucile C. *Understanding Camilo José Cela*. Columbia: University of South Carolina Press, 1998.
Pérez, Janet. *Camilo José Cela Revisited: The Later Novels*. New York: Twayne, 2000.

Celaya, Gabriel (1911–1975)

This popular poet played a decisive role in the development of social poetry in Spain. While most of his predecessors evaded the suffocating reality imposed by Franco's regime, focusing on religious and abstract themes expressed in highly crafted verses, Celaya poetized the day-to-day reality of the common man, using colloquial language. He emphasized communication over verse ornamentation, but knew how to bring out the poetic value of everyday language.

Celaya studied engineering in Madrid, and there met many members of the poetic *Generation of 1927, which greatly influenced the poets of the 1950s Spain. Addressing the theme of Spain from a political perspective, he depicted the injustices of the working world. He introduced a new concept of the poet and poetry: "The poet is a man, and no man can be neutral in the face of injustice and social conflicts." Celaya conceived poetry as an instrument to change the world through human solidarity.

His writing extends far beyond social poetry, including more than 40 volumes of poetry, essays, novels, and a children's book. His work synthesizes almost all styles and concerns of the 20th-century Spanish poetry panorama, including romantic, neovanguard, experimentalist, surrealist, and existentialist writings.

In a time when most writers remained silenced, Celaya demanded liberty. The sincere tone of his verse, which derives from his rationality as well as his emotions, continues to move modern readers. Celaya wrote "the poetry of us," trying to understand a world that encompasses death and life, love, happiness, and suffering.

María-Cruz Rodríguez

Work By:

The Poetry of Gabriel Celaya. Trans. Betty Jean Craige. Lewisburg, PA: Bucknell University Press, 1984.

Work About:

Ugalde, Sharon Keefe. *Gabriel Celaya.* Boston: Twayne, 1978. www.gabriel celaya.com.

Celestina, La in Spain and the New World

This fatalistic Spanish story of love and seduction, written in dialogue form at the end of the 15th century, stars an outstanding archetype, the female "go-between," or "yentl." The exposition is straightforward: Advised by his servants, nobleman Calisto hires Celestina, an old go-between, witch, healer, and bawd, to help him seduce Melibea, an upper-class maiden. Both Calisto's and Celestina's servants hope to profit as much as possible from Calisto's sexual passion. The love story is overshadowed by the cynical attitude of the lower-class characters (servants and prostitutes), and by the lovers' hypocritical code of conduct. The latter's unrestrained passion and the servants' insatiable greed lead all to a tragic end.

Celestina's presence dominates the text to the point that her character's name became the most widespread title for the work by the beginning of the 16th century. In 1569, the work was first published in Spain with this title. Just as the text's title changed over time, the content also varied. The first edition, titled *Comedia de Melibea* (1499; Melibea's Play), had only 16 acts. Subsequent editions included 21 acts, and a title change from *Comedia de Calisto y Melibea* (1501; Play of ...) to *Tragicomedia de Calisto y Melibea* (1502; Tragicomedy of ...). Variations in these earlier editions and questions as to authorship have provoked endless controversies. Nevertheless, scholars have identified Fernando de Rojas, a converted Jewish lawyer, as author of the text.

Another puzzling question deals with *La Celestina*'s genre; whether it is a play or a novel is still debated. This generic ambiguity has not prevented Rojas's work from being considered a masterpiece and precursor to the picaresque novel. Despite very different structures, the crude representation of urban slums inhabited by marginal, corrupt characters marked by materialist and egotistic motivations and a hypocritical concept of honor links these cynical novels to *La Celestina*. Furthermore, *La Celestina*'s lively dialogue of multiple registers, developed as an interchange of different points of view among individuals aiming to influence each other, inaugurated the multiple perspective dialogue that Miguel de *Cervantes masters in *Don Quijote de la Mancha*.

Interpretations of the author's intentions have similarly provoked unresolved debate. Regarded by some scholars as an heir of medieval literature of moral admonition, detractors of this didacticism consider *La Celestina* to be nihilistic and fatalistic, expressing Rojas's pessimistic views as a *converso* (converted Jew) living in anti-Semitic 15th-century Spain. *La Celestina* has been valued for its historical relevance, as it dramatizes social transformations generated by the transition from a medieval world to one in crisis, which characterizes modernity. Transformation has been inherent to Rojas's artistic intention, since he transformed the medieval and Latin sources he started from, inaugurating Spanish modern literature and announcing development of a new genre, the novel.

Just as *La Celestina* has generated extensive critical research, its eponymous protagonist and plot have become a generative force for Spanish artistic imagination. Celestina's precursor is the character Trotaconventos (Convent Trotter), from the *Arcipreste de Hita's *El libro de Buen Amor* (manuscript c. 1330; The Book of Good Love) whose source can be traced to the *Pamphilus de amore*, attributed during the Middle Ages to Latin poet Ovid. Celestina became a Spanish literature prototype, inspiring a long tradition of old, wise witches and bawds whose seductive powers manipulate human destiny.

From the very beginning of Spanish colonization in the New World, despite the Crown's efforts to ban exportation of frivolous literature, *La Celestina* was a leading favorite of 16th-century books in New Spain, quickly inspiring Celestinesque elements in early Spanish American literature. *La Celestina*'s presence has been observed in *El carnero* (1636–1638; The Ram) by Colombian Juan Rodríguez Freile. This historical fiction squeals of vice and passions in recently founded cities, and is replete with misogynist digressions that mimic the negative representation of Celestinesque characters. Moreover, such characters as the witch and midwife, Juana García, also form part of Celestina's brood.

For three centuries *La Celestina* has also had its detractors. The *Inquisition in Spain minimally censored the work during the 16th century; in 1640, 50 lines were expurgated, and in 1793 the Inquisition banned the work, considering Rojas's text inappropriate for a time when moral relaxation was the norm. Nevertheless, *La Celestina* remained influential in Spanish literature. The 19th-century urban slums of realism's novels recall Rojas's masterpiece. Such Spanish authors from the *Generation of 1898 as *Azorín and Ramiro de *Maeztu returned directly to *La Celestina* to explore Spanish literary myths and origin. During the second half of the 20th century, *La Celestina* appeared in works of such Latin American writers as Carlos *Fuentes's *Aura* (1962; English trans., 1965) and *Terra nostra* (1975; Eng. trans., 1987); Gabriel *García Márquez's *Cien años de soledad* (1967; *One Hundred Years of Solitude*, 1970) and "La increíble y triste historia de la cándida Eréndira y su abuela desalmada" (1973; "The Incredible and Sad Tale of Innocent Erendira and Her Heartless Grandmother," 1979); and Severo *Sarduy's *Cobra* (1972; Eng. trans., 1995). *La Celestina* is also present in Laura *Restrepo's *La novia oscura* (1999; The Dark Bride, 1999). In a search for origin, *La Celestina* represents a literary ancestor of the urban, irreverent, subversive novels by Latin American *Boom* writers.

Celestina has transcended literary representations and influenced all aspects of Hispanic culture. The name has become an everyday Spanish word to define those who act as go-betweens. Celestina is present in paintings by Francisco de Goya (1746–1828) and Pablo Picasso (1881–1973).

Mercedes Guijarro-Crouch

See also *Converso* Literature in Spain; Novel in Spain: Beginnings to 1700; Picaresque Literature in the Hispanic World.

Work:

Celestina. Intro., notes Dorothy Severin Sherman. Trans. James Mabbe. Warminster, UK: Aris and Phillips, 1987.

Fernando de Rojas *La Celestina.* http://mgarci.aas.duke.edu/cgi-bin/celestina/sp/index-dq.cgi?libroId=1001.

Work About:

Gónzalez Echeverría, Roberto. *Celestina's Brood: Continuities of the Baroque in Spanish and Latin American Literatures.* Durham, NC: Duke University Press, 1993.

Censorship and Literature in Spain

Defined as the prohibition and rigorous suppression of information from the public by a ruling authority or political power, censorship generally is carried out by government leaders, religious groups, or the mass media together with members of law enforcement. The term connotes inappropriate, unnecessary, or repressive secrecy that directly clashes with such freedoms normally coveted in democracies as the freedoms of speech and expression. Although censorship has taken various manifestations during Spain's history, from the period of the Catholic Monarchs and the reign of Charles IV, scholars most associate state-mandated censorship in Spain with the Spanish Civil War (1936–1939) and the period of dictatorship (1939–1975) that directly followed. Together with the help of the military, the conservative Catholic Church, and the Guardia Civil (police force)—all close allies of the Falangist nationalist movement—Generalísimo Francisco Franco (1892–1975) authorized and enforced censorship of all public communication media, including literary publications, newspapers, magazines, television, radio, and cinema, until his death.

At the start of the war, Nationalist leaders established the 1936 Press and Propaganda Office in Salamanca. The Office's popular slogan, "Death to Intelligence," compelled authors and other artists who had previously supported the movement to abandon it, among these Miguel de *Unamuno (1864–1936). By 1937, the task of censorship passed to the Press and Propaganda Delegation located in Burgos. The Delegation instituted film censorship offices in other cities, particularly La Coruña and Seville. By 1938, radio communication came under greater scrutiny, as it became the easiest way to quickly transmit information to the public and a chief means of gaining popular support. The retroactive 1939 Law of Political Responsibilities furthered Franco's overall mission of controlling information by dismissing "subversive" journalists from their positions and putting the press at the service of the state.

In the literary publishing world, early censorship was harsh. *Juntas de censura*, special committees made up of individuals that maintained the regime's stringent ethical code, regularly met to review, edit, and repress publication of texts deemed contrary to the ideals of the dictatorship. The 1945 Fuero de Españoles, a set of laws that took the place of a national constitution, declared that "All Spaniards may express their ideas freely provided they do not contravene the fundamental principles of the state."

Censors, whose job it was to guarantee that the state's political agenda be upheld, came from various walks of life, from the military and clergy to civilian personnel. Care was taken to assure the anonymity of censors, keeping their identities largely unknown to the public. When censors could not arrive at a resolution as to the propriety of a text, it was often sent to Franco himself for approval. Even after censors approved a work, there was no guarantee that the work would not be censored; books permitted by the Juntas might be secretly confiscated by the military or otherwise denounced by Church leaders as sinful. Subjects deemed inappropriate for publication included the Second Republic (the government that immediately preceded the civil war), noted Republican individuals, seizure of resistance members, court tribunals, torture, capital punishment, unionization, devaluation of the *peseta*, overall weakening of the economy, food or housing shortages, and the monarchy. *Children's literature was reviewed by an office of the Church, and comics likewise fell under censorship rules. In the early years of the regime, Nationalist sympathizers celebrated censorship activities by burning censored materials at annual book fairs.

Renowned authors fled Spain during the Spanish Civil War and its aftermath, demonstrating their opposition to Franco and the loss of individual freedoms that accompanied the dictatorship. Among those who successfully fled, poets Luis *Cernuda (1902–1963) and Pedro *Salinas (1891–1951) continued to speak publicly and write and teach at colleges and universities around the world, while Rafael *Alberti (1902–1999) largely dedicated himself to writing and painting until finally returning to Spain in 1977.

Other writers were not so lucky and succumbed to persecution by Franco's henchmen. Perhaps the most famous case is that of poet, playwright, and essayist Federico *García Lorca (1898–1936). A Republican sympathizer and known homosexual, Lorca was deemed a threat to the Nationalists and ordered put to death by one of Franco's generals in the first year of the civil war. Poet Miguel *Hernández (1910–1942), who attempted to escape Nationalist Spain in 1939, was similarly mistreated. While fleeing to Portugal, Civil Guard officers had Hernández detained, arrested, and beaten. Although initially freed, Hernández was later imprisoned again for three years and eventually died of tuberculosis.

A few writers either remained in Spain during the dictatorship or were born into it. While Dámaso *Alonso (1898–1990) bitterly put up with the new authoritarian rule, others, for example, Gerardo *Diego (1896–1987), supported Nationalist values, including censorship. Some born during the dictatorship chose self-exile to demonstrate their opposition. Juan *Goytisolo (1931–), whose mother was killed in a civil war air raid and whose father was imprisoned as a Republican dissenter, chose to emigrate to France in the 1950s and currently lives in Morocco. Despite democratization, he continues to speak out against Spain's history of sexual and religious repression.

Certain cases, however, somewhat defy explanation. Camilo José *Cela (1916–2002), who fought as a Nationalist during the civil war and worked as a magazine censor from 1941 to 1945, wrote the *tremendista* novel *La familia de Pascual Duarte* (1942; The Family of Pascual Duarte, 2004), which was harshly critical of the regime. Although the novel was deemed excessively violent and was originally banned from publication in Spain, the very fact that Cela continued to prolifically produce literature and live in Spain during the dictatorship demonstrates the arbitrary, unpredictable nature of its administrators.

Female authors, like male authors, were subject to rigorous scrutiny. Nonetheless, their position may have been particularly challenging due to their second-class status under the dictatorship. Censors banned Ana María *Matute's (1926–) *Luciérnagas* (1953; Fireflies) and suppressed publication of 19 pages of *Los hijos muertos* (1958; The Dead Children), even though the latter somewhat curiously won Spain's National Literature Prize that same year. Other women's novels inexplicably seemed to evade censorship laws. Carmen *Laforet (1921–2004) successfully published *Nada* (1944; *Nada*, 2007) though it depicted the feelings of alienation so common in the postwar period. Likewise, Elena *Quiroga (1921–1995) and Carmen *Martín Gaite (1925–2000) published narratives concerning women's struggles and experiences. Some scholars suggest that these authors' emphasis on developing women's interior lives and friendships safeguarded their works from appearing particularly threatening to censors.

Foreign and Latin American texts were also subject to censorship. In the case of foreign literature, such taboo subjects as communism, abortion, divorce, and sex remained forbidden. Literary texts printed in less popular languages remained unpublished in Spain because censors fluent in those languages could not be found to review their propriety. Latin American authors faced fewer obstacles, since publication of their works ultimately increased exports from Spain.

The cultural policy of censorship relaxed with time, first in the late 1940s and most notably in the late 1960s and early 1970s. For example, in a 1941 decree, the state prohibited the use, teaching, and diffusion of minority languages, thereby outlawing publication and even public use of Catalan, Galician, Basque, and all other minority languages. Additionally, it imposed "hispanizing" of regional Christian names and places, and banned borrowed words, songs, and films using foreign languages. By the late 1940s, strict application of this decree was lifted, allowing for publication of minor language texts deemed less "threatening" to the objectives of the dictatorship, namely, literature dealing with religious teachings and less popular genres, such as poetry.

A major shift in legislation occurred with the 1966 Ley Fraga (Fraga Law), named after Manuel Fraga Iribarne (1922–present), the minister of information and tourism at that time. Fraga's Law represented a restrained broadening of the 1938 Press Law, although it appeared more lenient. The new law eliminated advance censorship, making it unnecessary to receive the explicit permission of committees to publish a work. Rather, the onus was placed on authors, editors, journalists, and others to ensure that nothing published would be offensive to the state. Authors were still obliged to deliver their published works to the Ministry of Information and Tourism offices, and the office retained the right to sanction or fine individuals, suspend the publication of literature, or close newspapers and publishing houses. Those found in violation of the law were often accused of plotting against Franco's regime.

The most significant change in censorship rules resulted from the ratification of the 1978 Spanish Constitution, about three years after Franco's death. Article 20 of the Constitution permits Spanish citizens the explicit right to freely express themselves and defends the right of authors to publish in languages other than Spanish.

Looking back on the period of dictatorship, scholars suggest that state-mandated censorship created an acutely discerning public that was likely to read the political into any cultural text. Writers also subverted the authority of censors by using such literary tropes as allegory, symbolism, and metaphor or borrowing cinematic strategies like flashbacks and parallel scenes. Ironically, critics also suggest that censors occasionally permitted publication of questionable texts, banking on the fact that the general public would either not comprehend the oppositional nature of such works or simply fear publicly responding to them.

Maria DiFrancesco

See also Civil War Literature in Spain; Francoism, Fascism, and Literature in Spain; Inquisition and Literature in the Hispanic World.

Work About:

Abellán, Manuel L. *Censura y literaturas peninsulares*. Amsterdam: Rodopi, 1987.

Herrero-Olaizola, Alejandro. *The Censorship Files: Latin American Writers and Franco's Spain*. Albany: State University of New York Press, 2007.

Cepeda Samudio, Álvaro (1926–1972)

This Colombian journalist, novelist, short story writer, and filmmaker, born in the coastal city of Barranquilla, became the principle modernizer of mid-20th-century Colombian narrative. The stark prose of his first and only novel, *La casa grande* (1962; Eng. trans., 1991) recalls William Faulkner and features a singular, unmediated narrator. The novel's 10 distinct sections require readers to actively participate in deciphering connections between the disjointed parts and uncovering the implied sociopolitical critique. The story addresses the 1928 Santa Marta Massacre of United Fruit Company's striking banana workers. With groundbreaking novelty, instead of relating an expository account, the violent event itself is withheld from the narrative and presented exclusively through the psychological reactions of townspeople and family members (the unnamed older sister, the brother, father, etc.) of the Big House, *la casa grande*. This novel constitutes an important forerunner of Gabriel *García Márquez's *One Hundred Years of Solitude* (1967), and

significant contribution to the novel in Latin America.

Inca Molina Rumold

See also Cien años de soledad (1967; *One Hundred Years of Solitude*, 1970).

Work By:

La casa grande. Trans. Seymour Menton. Austin: University of Texas Press, 1991.

Work About:

Bastasi, Elena. "Del odio de la casa caribe a la tragedia de la casa andaluza: *La casa grande* de Alvaro Cepeda Samudio y *La casa de Bernarda Alba* de Federico García Lorca." *Estudios de Literatura Colombiana* 18 (Jan.–June 2006): 61–77.

Tittler, Jonathan. "Alvaro Cepeda Samudio: Neo-Colombian Literature's Source?" *Readerly/Writerly Texts: Essays on Literature, Literary/Textual Criticism, and Pedagogy* 3.1 (Fall–Winter): 151–60.

Cerda, Martha (1945–)

Born in Guadalajara, Mexico, she received the Jalisco Literary Award in 1998 for her second novel, *Toda una vida* (1998; A Lifetime). Soon after its first edition in Spanish, the novel was translated into Italian and Norwegian and received high acclaim in those countries. Cerda is currently Director of the Guadalajara Writers School (SOGEM) in Guadalajara and president of Guadalajara's PEN Women Writers Committee. Her first major literary achievement was *La señora Rodríguez y otros mundos* (1992; *Señora Rodríguez and Other Worlds*, 1997), which attracted international interest by being immediately translated into several languages. Like other women authors, she revises Mexico's history from a feminine point of view that displaces the phallocentric orientation and uncontested assumptions of the past. Cerda's style is consistently intertextual and thus often catalogued as postmodernist. She draws freely from the daily conflicts that society confronts that have immediate impact on culture; for example, her prose addresses Mexico City's catastrophic 1985 earthquake in *A Lifetime*, as well as the disastrous 1992 gas leak in the Guadalajara sewer system in *Y apenas era miércoles* (1993; And One Wednesday). In both texts, Cerda employs a myriad of techniques: documentary fiction, local reports from newspapers, television, and radio. Being a committed member of the PEN club that promotes literature and defends freedom of expression, she does not shy away from using real names of public figures as well as imaginary characters representing different sectors of the stratified Mexican society.

María Teresa Martínez-Ortiz

See also Feminism in Spanish America; PEN Club in the Hispanic World.

Work By:

Señora Rodríguez and Other Worlds. Trans. Sylvia Jiménez-Andersen. Durham, NC: Duke University Press, 1997.
Toda una vida. Barcelona: Ediciones B, 1998.

Work About:

Duncan, Patricia. "*A Lifetime*: The Fetus Speaks." *Hopscotch: A Cultural Review* 2.2 (2001): 114–19.

Cernuda, Luis (1902–1963)

A member of the elite *Generation of 1927 and one of Spain's most important 20th-century poets, Cernuda was born in Seville. The child of an authoritarian father, he experienced a strict upbringing and pursued a conventional career in law at the University of Seville until he met famed poet Pedro *Salinas, one of his professors and first mentors. He soon abandoned his legal studies to work exclusively as a poet, literary critic, and teacher. His book *Perfil del aire* (1927; Air's Profile) examines themes that would haunt him throughout his life, including the clash between erotic desire and reality, and one's ability to rise above actuality through poetic, often surreal, imagination.

Unlike many of his contemporaries, Cernuda accepted and publicly addressed his homosexuality in *Los placeres prohibidos* (1931; Forbidden Pleasures), a collection that borrows techniques from avant-garde and surrealist artists to self-reflectively discuss same-sex desire through unconventional syntax. Cernuda minimized his regard for the avant-garde in *Donde habite el olvido* (1934; Where Forgetfulness Lives), a verse collection that pays homage to Spanish *romanticism, especially Gustavo Adolfo *Bécquer (1836–1870). Like many supporters of the republic during the Spanish Civil

War (1936–1939), Cernuda fled Spain to live in exile in 1938. He moved first to England and then to Scotland, where he lectured at Cambridge University and the University of Glasgow. Between 1947 and 1952, he taught at Mount Holyoke College. In 1952, Cernuda moved to Mexico to spend the remainder of his life with his longtime partner, dying of a heart attack in Mexico City.

Maria DiFrancesco

See also Censorship and Literature in Spain; Poetry in Spain: 1900 to Present; Queer Literature in Contemporary Spain.

Work By:

Selected Poems of Luis Cernuda. Trans. Reginald Gibbons. Riverdale-on-Hudson: Sheep Meadow, 1977.
Written in Water: The Prose Poems of Luis Cernuda. Trans. Stephen Kessler. San Francisco: City Lights Books, 2004.

Work About:

Logan, Aileen. "Memory and Exile in *Las nubes*, *Como quien espera el alba* and *Vivir sin estar viviendo* by Luis Cernuda." *Forum for Modern Language Studies* 42.3 (July 2006): 298–314.
McKinlay, Neil C. *The Poetry of Luis Cernuda: Order in a World of Chaos.* London: Tamesis, 1999.

Cervantes, Miguel de (1547–1616)

The son of an itinerant surgeon, Miguel de Cervantes Saavedra was born in the Spanish university town of Alcalá de Henares. Relatively little is known of his early years and education; it is believed he was trained in the humanities before leaving for Italy in service to a church official. In 1571, Cervantes took part in the Battle of Lepanto, a major Christian triumph, and was gravely wounded in his left shoulder and arm. Subsequently known as *el manco de Lepanto* (the cripple of Lepanto), he considered his participation in the victory over the Muslim enemies to be his most glorious moment. Soon a decorated soldier en route to Spain with letters of recommendation, his ship was overtaken by corsairs, and he spent five years as a captive in the prisons of Algiers. Finally ransomed, he found it difficult to acquire a professional position. He had a variety of jobs, none prestigious or satisfying. He married Doña Catalina de Salazar y Palacios, 19 years his junior, and by all reports it was not a happy union.

His first novel, a pastoral romance titled *La Galatea*, appeared in 1585. Cervantes also tried his hand at the theater and claims to have had some success. Only two plays, *La Numancia* (1580s; *Numantia*, 1885) and *Los tratos de Argel* (1580s; *The Commerce of Algiers*, 1870), are conserved from the first period. When he published eight full-length plays (*comedias*) and eight comic interludes (*entremeses*) in 1615, he underscored that none had thus far been performed on stage. As an aspiring playwright, Cervantes was totally overshadowed by his contemporary Lope de *Vega, whose model for dramatic composition defined early modern Spanish theater. *Don Quijote*, published in two parts in 1605 and 1615, was an immediate best seller, finally bringing Cervantes the fame that had eluded him. He was 58 years old when Part I was published and 68 when Part II appeared. His last novel, *Los trabajos de Persiles y Sigismunda* (1619; *The Trials of Persiles and Sigismunda*, 1989), which he called an epic in prose, was published posthumously, in 1617.

In conceiving *Don Quijote*, which starts out as parody, Cervantes came upon the idea that madness could be humorous. In this case, his knight errant (or errant knight) suffers from a literature-induced malady that brings readers, writers, and fiction making into the frame. Don Quijote, accompanied by his somewhat reluctant squire Sancho Panza, has the best of intentions, if not the most practical of agendas: to correct injustices and to serve the lady he has created in his mind, Dulcinea del Toboso, modeled after the neighboring farm girl Aldonza Lorenzo. His anachronistic plan and his eccentricities give the exploits a special cast. Don Quijote ultimately shares the stage with the author himself and a band of narrators who undertake adventures of their own. At the beginning of the 17th century, when Cervantes produced *Don Quijote*, the novel genre was new and in the process of inventing itself. Cervantes breaks away from the idealism of chivalric, pastoral, and sentimental romance as he helps to develop narrative realism. At the same time, he moves in an entirely different direction by calling attention to the act and the trials of composition. *Don Quijote* announces itself as a "true history," but its fictional devices clearly show through. Spanish society is on display, but so are the literary forms of the day, to be acknowledged and often satirized.

In 1614, a writer using the pseudonym Alonso Fernández de Avellaneda published a "false" second part of *Don Quijote*, an action that enraged Cervantes but forced him to come to terms with the sequel in his own Part II. The result is magical, as the "real" Don Quijote and his author defend themselves against the unwelcome intruders. *Don Quijote* is, thus, a novel and a theory of the novel, brilliantly comic, but profound as well. It serves as a type of template for future novels and, accordingly, for future experiments, as subsequent literary texts engage and challenge tradition. Over 400 years after its publication, it continues to inspire scholars, students, and readers of all persuasions. Even those who have not read the novel have a sense of Don Quijote, from the images of the elongated knight and the rotund squire to the famous scene of tilting at windmills, subjects of innumerable works of art.

After *Don Quijote*, Cervantes's most read and studied narratives are the *Novelas ejemplares* (1613; *Exemplary Stories*, 1972), 12 novellas on a variety of topics. Some are oriented toward realism and others toward idealism, and still others fit neither mold; the author claims that each is, in its own way, instructive or exemplary, as well as entertaining. To cite several cases: *El licenciado Vidriera* (*The Glass Licenciate*) tells the ironic story of a man who loses contact with reality— thinking that he is made of glass and fearful of being broken—after being given a love potion. He becomes an outspoken critic of human shortcomings and is consulted as a sage, until he is cured and returns to his former state. *Rinconete y Cortadillo* follows the *picaresque adventures of two young boys who end up in Seville's criminal circles. As the name suggests, *El coloquio de los perros* (*The Dogs' Colloquy*) features talking canines. The cast of characters of *La española inglesa* (*The Spanish Lady in England*) includes Queen Elizabeth I of England. The title figure of *La gitanilla* (*The Little Gypsy Girl*) is proven to be a noblewoman. *El celoso extremeño* (*The Jealous Extremaduran*) offers a variation on the theme of the old man who marries a young bride, with less than positive results. The *Novelas ejemplares* are worthy complements to *Don Quijote*, which has a status all its own. Cervantes felt that *Persiles* would make him immortal, but fate made *Don Quijote* the primary vehicle of his renown in Spanish letters and in world literature.

Edward H. Friedman

See also Chivalry Literature in Spain and the New World; *Don Quijote de la Mancha* in Spanish American Literature and Culture; Novel in Spain: Beginnings to 1700.

Work By:

Don Quixote. Trans. Edith Grossman. New York: Ecco, 2003.

Don Quixote. Trans. Tom Lathrop. Newark, DE: Juan de la Cuesta, 2005.

Exemplary Stories. Trans. Lesley Lipson. Oxford: Oxford University Press, 1998.

The Trials of Persiles and Sigismunda. Trans. Celia Richmond and Clark A. Colahan. Berkeley: University of California Press, 1989.

Work About:

Boyd, Stephen, ed. *A Companion to Cervantes's* Novelas ejemplares. Woodbridge, Suffolk: Tamesis, 2005.

Cascardi, Anthony J., ed. *The Cambridge Companion to Cervantes*. Cambridge: Cambridge University Press, 2002.

Childers, William. *Transnational Cervantes*. Toronto: University of Toronto Press, 2006.

Gonzales Echevarría, Roberto, ed. *Cervantes' Don Quixote: A Casebook*. Oxford: Oxford University Press, 2005.

Johnson, Carroll J. *Don Quixote: The Quest for Modern Fiction*. Long Grove, IL: Waveland, 2000.

Mancing, Howard. *The Cervantes Encyclopedia*. 2 vols. Westport, CT: Greenwood, 2004.

Proyecto Cervantes. http://www.csdl.tamu.edu/cervantes/.

Cervantes de Salazar, Francisco (1514/1518?–1575)

This New World historian was born in Toledo, Spain. After studying humanities and law, he served Cardinal Loaisa, archbishop of Seville and president of the Council of the Indies. He immigrated to Mexico in 1550, there improving his social and economic position dramatically. Ordained as a priest in 1554 and later awarded the title of doctor of theology, by 1557 he was rector of the University of Mexico, then the acting cantor of the metropolitan cathedral (1560–1562), and finally a church canon. In 1572, he became the official chronicler of New Spain.

Cervantes de Salazar is best known for the incomplete *Crónica de la conquista de la Nueva España* (Chronicle of the Conquest of the New Spain). Although he wrote it some time after 1560, the *Crónica* was not published until 1914. Using eyewitness accounts of the first conquerors and their historians, such as Francisco López de Gómara (1511–1564?), this chronicle is not only a testimony of pre-Colombian cultures, but also a detailed description of the process of conquest headed by Hernán Cortés (1485–1547).

Enric Mallorquí-Ruscalleda

See also Discovery and Conquest Writings: Describing the Americas.

Work By:

Life in the Imperial and Loyal City of Mexico in New Spain . . . as Described in the Dialogues for the Study of the Latin Language. Facs. reproduction, trans. (Latin to English) Minnie L. Barrett Shepard. Westport, CT: Greenwood, 1970.

Work About:

Bono, Dianne M. "The Contemporary Critics and the Native American in Colonial New Spain in the Works of Francisco Cervantes de Salazar." *Confluencia: Revista Hispánica de Cultura y Literatura* 5.1 (Fall 1989): 65–71.

Chacel, Rosa (1898–1994)

Born in Valladolid, Spain, into an intellectual family, this distinguished writer was constantly stimulated and exposed to literature, theater, and the fine arts. In 1915, she entered Madrid's San Fernando Academy of Fine Arts, where she met her future husband, painter Timoteo Pérez Rubio. The influence of fine arts became a constant in her writing. In 1918, Chacel left the Academy to pursue a writing career and started frequenting the most famous intellectual and literary enclaves of Madrid. There, she became acquainted with the aesthetic dictates of Spanish philosopher and cultural critic José *Ortega y Gasset. As a member of the *Generation of 1927, Chacel was deeply influenced by Ortega's ideas on literature and art; however, she departed drastically from Ortega's misogynist views about women, which reflected the prevailing discourse about gender during that period. Chacel especially opposed the thesis of absolute opposites, which she viewed as an excuse to exclude women from the realm of cultural creation.

Chacel's works are deeply influenced by existentialism and her position is akin to that of Simone de Beauvoir. As a writer, she published articles, essays, and short stories in prestigious literary journals and numerous novels, many of which are autobiographical. *Estación. Ida y vuelta* (1930; Station. Round Trip) constitutes a good example of avant-garde artistic principles as well as Ortega's aesthetics. It explores a couple's relationship in which both characters are psychologically fused. The narrator's stream of consciousness allows readers to experience his psychological, emotional, and intellectual journey toward a more balanced, meaningful existence. *Memorias de Leticia Valle*

(1945; *Memoirs of Leticia Valle*; 1994) represents Chacel's response to one of Dostoevsky's novels in which a young girl commits suicide after being seduced by her teacher. In her version, however, the teacher commits suicide after being seduced by Leticia, the young protagonist. Through her writing, Leticia resists her father's version of events and criticizes the lack of meaningful education for women in Spain and the subordinate role expected of them. Chacel lived in Brazil and Argentina with her husband and son during Francisco Franco's dictatorship, returning to Madrid in 1978.

María A. Zanetta

See also Feminism in Spain: 1700 to Present.

Work By:

Memoirs of Leticia Valle. Trans. Carol Maier. Lincoln: University of Nebraska Press, 1994.
The Maravillas District. Trans. D. A. Démers. Intro. Susan Kirkpatrick. Lincoln: University of Nebraska Press, 1992.

Work About:

Johnson, Roberta. *Gender and Nation in the Spanish Modernist Novel*. Nashville, TN: Vanderbilt University Press, 2003.

Champourcin, Ernestina de (1905–1999)

Arguably the most celebrated woman poet of Spain's *Generation of 1927, Champourcin went into exile in Mexico at the conclusion of the civil war (1936–1939) with her husband, poet Juan José Domenchina. She lived there until her 1972 return to Spain.

Champourcin's poetry evolves from the emphasis on emotions and formal experimentation to mysticism and the remembrance of her past. Her first book, *En silencio* (1926; In Silence), contains poems clearly influenced by *romanticism and modernism. Subsequent poetry collections, such as *La voz en el viento* (1931; The Voice in the Wind), follow avantgarde tendencies and present a conceptual, pure poetry that underlines the poet's self-determination and creative liberty.

During exile, Champourcin finds in religion a solution to her existential agony. After a 16-year lapse, in poem collections like *Presencia a oscuras* (1952; Presence in Darkness), the poet dialogues with God and yearns for spiritual union with Him.

Primer exilio (1978; First Exile) initiates Champourcin's last and retrospective poetry with memories of the Spanish Civil War and her trip into exile. Her final works suggest that human loneliness can be surmounted by faith in life after death.

Iker González-Allende

See also Civil War Literature in Spain; Poetry in Spain: 1900 to Present.

Work By:

Poesía a través del tiempo. Ed. José Ángel Ascunce. Barcelona: Anthropos, 1991.

Work About:

Bellver, Catherine G. "Ernestina de Champourcin: A Poet and Her Poetics." *Hispanic Review* 69.4 (2001): 443–65.

Landeira, Joy. *Ernestina de Champourcin: Vida y literatura*. Ferrol, Spain: Sociedad de Cultura Valle-Inclán, 2005.

Wilcox, John C. "Ernestina de Champourcin and Concha Méndez." *Women Poets of Spain, 1860–1990: Toward a Gynocentric Vision*. Urbana: University of Illinois Press, 1997, 87–133.

Changó, el gran putas (1983; *Changó, the Biggest Badass*, 2010)

A product of 20 plus years of research by Afro-Colombian novelist Manuel *Zapata Olivella (1920–2004), the novel *Changó el gran putas* (1983; *Changó, the Biggest Badass*, 2010) serves as an important reminder of Latin America's African heritage and the region's connection to other African populations in the New World. Its references to Africa, Colombia, Haiti, and the United States demonstrate a connection among dispersed African-descended populations and their shared historical background. The text is divided into five sections that relate the universal black experiences of slavery, racism, and social upheaval. The first part, "The Origins," narrates the beginnings of the Afrian population dispersal throughout the Americas. The second part, "The American Muntu," captures the experience of slavery in the Americas, specifically the African's enslavement in Cartagena, Colombia. Part III, "The Rebellion of the Voodoos," focuses primarily on the Haitian Revolution (1791–1804) under the leadership of Bouckman, a Jamaican-born slave who spearheaded the rebellion. Next, the fourth part, "Conflicting Bloodlines," deals with 19th-century Spanish American Independence and the blacks who fought in these wars, such as Mexican José María Morelos y Pavón (1765–1815). Although Morelos is known nationally as a Mexican revolutionary, Zapata Olivella focuses on the leader's lesser-known African heritage, which becomes the character's most important aspect. Part V, "The Combative Ancestors," completes the cycle of black exploitation in the United States and portrays the civil rights movement (1955–1968). These events explicate the history of the black experience in Colombia and the Americas and position this novel to be an Afro-American saga similar to the novel *Roots* (1976) by Alex Haley (1921–1992).

Sonja Stephenson Watson

See also Afro-Hispanic Literature in Spanish America.

Work:

Zapata Olivella, Manuel. *Changó, the Biggest Badass*. Trans. Jonathan Tittler. Intro. William Luis. Lubbock: Texas Tech University Press, 2010.

Work About:

Tillis, Antonio D. *Manuel Zapata Olivella and the "Darkening" of Latin American Literature*. Columbia: University of Missouri Press, 2005.

Watson, Sonja Stephenson. "*Changó, el gran putas:* Contemporary Afro-Hispanic Historical Novel." *Afro-Hispanic Review* (2006): 67–86.

Chaviano, Daína (1957–)

Born in Havana and currently living in Miami, this Cuban novelist and poet numbers among the best science fiction writers in Hispanic letters. Her first novel, *Fábulas de una abuela extraterrestre* (1988; Fables from an Extraterrestrial Grandmother) became a classic in Latin American science fiction. Chaviano employs a mythological as opposed to technological approach. Her work, which incorporates new ideas in quantum physics and string theory, has played a fundamental role in opening Latin American letters to high quality science fiction.

Recently, she began to explore a new direction, combining fantastic realism with science fiction in Cuba at the end of the 20th century. The result was "La Habana oculta" (The Occult Side of Havana), a series of four novels where Havana serves as a point of departure for journeys into other dimensions. One, *El hombre, la hembra y el hambre* (1998; Men, Woman, and Hunger), won Spain's Premio Azorín for best novel, and its success led to publication of the other works in the series, establishing Chaviano as a major author.

Miguel Ángel González-Abellás

See also Havana in Literature; Science Fiction in Spanish America.

Work By:

El hombre, la hembra y el hambre. Barcelona: Planeta, 1998.
Fábulas de una abuela extraterrestre. Havana: Letras Cubanas, 1988.

Works About:

Chaviano, Daína. *Daína Chaviano* (author's Web page). http://www.dainachaviano.com/.
Whitfield, Esther. "The Novel as Cuban Lexicon: Bargaining Bilinguals in Daína Chaviano's *El hombre, la hembra y el hambre.*" In *Bilingual Games: Some Literary Investigations.* Ed. Doris Sommer. New York: Palgrave Macmillan, 2003, 193–201.

Chicano

This term denotes a Mexican American born or raised in the United States who self-identifies as Chicano by integrating a cultural, historical, and political consciousness into a binational identity. Most scholars agree that the term derives from the Mexica (Meshicano) Indians of pre-Columbian Mexico, emphasizing the indigenous roots of Chicanos.

As an academic discipline, Chicano studies was born during the *Chicano movement during the late 1960s and early 1970s, specifically during meetings held at the University of California at Santa Barbara in 1969, and includes the literature, arts, history, and other disciplines related to Mexican Americans, Chicanos, Chicanas, Latinos, and Latinas. That same year, the University of California at Los Angeles established the Chicano Studies Research Center Library, the first library dedicated specifically to collecting, housing, and disseminating such materials.

Spencer R. Herrera

Work About:

http://www.chicano.ucla.edu/.

Chicano Movement: Literature and Publishing

In the mid- to late 1960s, in what is often considered a Chicana/o Renaissance, young poets, novelists, and playwrights began to publish an astonishing number of literary works. These texts expressed several prominent themes, including cultural pride, resistance to assimilation, assertion of indigenous identity, challenges to historical narratives, and the importance of personal and collective expression. Authors utilized several languages—English, Spanish, caló (Mexican Spanish slang)—and employed high rates of "code-switching," or using English and Spanish words and phrases within one sentence or paragraph. Dozens of literary journals and presses supported these publications, and some continue to publish today; these writings were devoured by a generation of youth eager to see themselves and their communities reflected in cultural works.

No poem is more associated with the Chicano movement than Rodolfo "Corky" Gonzales's epic "Yo soy Joaquín" (1965; I Am Joaquin). Written primarily in English, the work traces Chicana/o identity through such important Mexican leaders as Cuauhtémoc, Emiliano Zapata, Benito Juárez, and Father Hidalgo. Noticeably absent from the poem are references to any specific women. Gonzales stresses that the legacy of the Chicano is that of both conquered and conqueror, *indio* and Spaniard, victim and oppressor. In a manner consistent with Chicano movement literature, "Yo soy Joaquín" stresses the endurance of the Chicana/o people and culture and highlights indigenous identity.

The 1969 Youth Conference organized by Gonzales marked the debut of the young poet Alurista (pen name of Alberto Baltazar Urista Heredia). Reading his text, Alurista captured the idea that a new group of people was emerging, *La Raza de Bronce* (Bronze Race), united by a history of oppression and a future of revolutionary nationalism. His poem's first stanza was adopted as the preamble to El Plan Espiritual de Aztlán (the movement's defining manifesto), and Alurista became known as the "poet laureate of Aztlán." In addition to Gonzales and Alurista, such Chicana/o poets as raulsalinas, Ángela de Hoyos, Miriam Bornstein-Somoza, Carmen Tafolla, and José Montoya published their first works in the late 1960s and early 1970s. These authors and their works emphasized Chicano identity, collective consciousness, and rebellion against oppressive state structures.

Several important prose works, written in both English and Spanish, were also published during this time period. Tomás Rivera's * . . . y no se lo tragó la tierra . . . (1971; . . . And the Earth Did Not Devour Him, 1987) and José Antonio Villarreal's *The Plum Plum Pickers* (1971) emphasized issues of migration and labor within Chicano communities, while other works, such as Rodolfo Anaya's *Bless Me, Última*

(1972) and Ernesto Galarza's *Barrio Boy* (1971), detailed the search for identity by young men. The 1970s also saw publication of texts that directly reflected and responded to movement politics, such as Oscar Zeta Acosta's *Autobiography of a Brown Buffalo* (1972) and *The Revolt of the Cockroach People* (1973); short story collections like Estella Portillo-Trambley's *Rain of Scorpions* (1975); and works that combined such genres as Ricardo Sánchez's *Canto y Grito Mi Liberación* (1971; I Sing and Shout My Liberation).

Dramatic performances represented a particularly important part of movement literature, culture, and political organizing. Small theater groups, or *teatros*, composed of both professional actors and writers and community members sprung up on picket lines, in migrant camps, and on university campuses. Performances often served multiple purposes: they helped raise consciousness about relevant issues, they allowed actors and audience members to experience different power relationships (for example, by assuming the role of the *patrón* or winning a struggle), and they provided entertainment to workers and strikers. Luis Valdez's **Teatro campesino* is the most well-known *teatro* from the movement era, but several (women's) Chicana-led groups also formed during this time period, including *Teatro a la Brava*, *Teatro de las Chicanas*, *Teatro Laboral*, and *Teatro Raíces*.

Without supporting journals, presses, and publication houses, Chicana/o movement writers would not have been able to disseminate their work to a large audience or contribute to the historical record of Chicana/o literature. Early magazines that published Chicana/o writing included *Caracol*, *Con Safos*, *El Grito*, *De Colores*, *El Pocho-Che*, and *Revista Chicano-Riqueña*. Presses committed to publishing work by such Chicano and Latino writers as Ediciones Pocho-Che and Quinto Sol Publications, also made significant contributions to the growth and dissemination of Chicana/o literature. The scholarly journal *Aztlán*, which began appearing during this time period, continues to publish today.

Ariana E. Vigil

See also Aztlán; Chicano Writers; Cultural Icons of Chicanos; Latinos and Latinas in the United States: History, Culture, and Literature; Latino Theater in the United States: Social Cohesion and Activism; Recovering the U.S. Hispanic Literary Heritage Project.

Work About:

Allatson, Paul. *Key Terms in Latino/a Cultural and Literary Studies*. Malden, MA: Wiley, Blackwell, 2007.

Broyles-González, Yolanda. *El Teatro Campesino: Theater in the Chicano Movement*. Austin: University of Texas Press, 1994.

Bruce-Novoa, Juan. *La literatura chicana a través de sus autores*. México: Siglo Veintiuno, 1983.

Garcia, Laura E., Sandra M. Gutierrez, and Felicitas Nuñez. *Teatro Chicana: A Collective Memoir and Selected Plays*. Austin: University of Texas Press, 2008.

Mariscal, George. *Brown-Eyed Children of the Sun: Lessons from the Chicano Movement, 1965–1975*. Albuquerque: University of New Mexico Press, 2005.

Rebolledo, Tey Diana, and Eliana S. Rivero. *Infinite Divisions: An Anthology of*

Chicana Literature. Tucson: University of Arizona Press, 1993.

Tatum, Charles. *A Selected and Annotated Bibliography of Chicano Studies.* Manhattan, KS: Society of Spanish and Spanish American Studies, 1976.

Chicano Writers

Many Chicano authors write exclusively or primarily in English, including Rudolfo Anaya, Richard Rodriguez, Oscar Acosta, Denise Chávez, Sandra Cisneros, and Pat *Mora, although some of their works have been translated into Spanish. Other Chicano writers of various genres poetically mix Spanish and English, particularly Luis *Valdez, Alurista, Gloria *Anzaldúa, Alicia Gaspar de Alba, Lucha *Corpi, and José Montoya. A third group of Chicano writers established themselves by composing only in Spanish. Highly recognized and celebrated Chicano authors employing Spanish include Tomás Rivera, Sabine *Ulibarrí, Miguel Méndez, Aristeo Brito, Rolando *Hinojosa Smith, Margarita *Cota Cárdenas, and José Antonio Burciaga.

Although much contemporary Chicano literature uses English, it is nonetheless rooted in Spanish-language culture, beginning with folktales, legends, and myths passed down through generations, and *corridos* (border ballads) that first appeared at about the time of the Mexican–American War (1846–1848). It is significant to recognize the strong, unwavering presence of a bilingual voice, written and embedded, in Chicano writing because language and identity are major themes within this literature. The centuries-long struggle of living between two worlds (Mexico and the United States) with two cultures, constitutes a unique cultural phenomenon that has inspired many to pen their stories.

Chicano literature has five major periods: Spanish Mexican, Mexican American, Annexation, Chicano Renaissance, and modern. The first begins with Álvar Núñez Cabeza de Vaca's *La relación* (1542; *Relation*, 2003), which narrates his experiences of eight years of travel and survival in present-day Texas, New Mexico, and northern Mexico. The Mexican American period begins during Texas's independence from Mexico in 1836 and concludes in 1848 with the Treaty of Guadalupe Hidalgo, when Mexico cedes half of its territory to the United States following the Mexican–American War (1846–1848). Juan Seguín's representative text, *The Personal Memoirs of John N. Seguín* (1858), describes the difficulties he endured after fighting for Texas's independence and suffering rejection by Anglos and Mexicans.

The Annexation period begins in 1912, when New Mexico officially becomes the 47th state of the Union and many Mexican Americans lament their cultural fate and forever-changed lives with the arrival of U.S. customs and English-language dominance. Cleofas Jaramillo's *Romance of a Little Village Girl* (1955) provides an insightful look into the tremendous impact such changes wrought in rural New Mexico.

The Chicano Renaissance during the late 1960s and 1970s witnessed a literary explosion and established a Chicano literary canon. Much literary production of that time showed influence of the ongoing civil rights movement. Although much of the movement's success was credited to Martin Luther King Jr. in the South, Chicanos led by César Chávez, Dolores Huerta, and others in the Southwest fought their own battles for equality. Rodolfo "Corky" Gonzales, a Chicano activist who formed the Crusade for Justice, dedicated himself to Chicano civil rights issues and inspired many to continue the struggle with his epic poem *Yo soy Joaquín* (1967; I Am Joaquín), which strives to overcome a sense of loss by embracing the history, culture, and bloodlines of Chicano identity.

Since the mid-1980s, modern Chicano literature has been mostly defined by women writers who have validated Chicano literature as part of a broader American canon. Although most Chicano writers have roots in the Southwest, Mexican migration to the Midwest produced prominent Chicago-born writers Sandra Cisneros and Ana Castillo. With this move from masculine to feminine and rural to urban, Chicano literature has broadened its scope to include more themes and experiences, provoking the emergence, for example, of Richard Rodriguez, who writes about identity issues as a conservative, gay, Catholic Mexican American opposed to bilingual education and affirmative action; and Gloria *Anzaldúa, who as a feminist lesbian, broadens the scope of what it means to write and live in the borderlands. These changes demonstrate that Chicano literature represents a broad spectrum of themes and perspectives that

stem from many very individual experiences, enriching what it means to be Chicano today.

Spencer R. Herrera

See also Gonzales-Berry (1942–), Erlinda; Latinos and Latinas in the United States: History, Culture, and Literature; Latino Theater in the United States: Social Cohesion and Activism.

Work About:

Kanellos, Nicolás, ed. *Herencia: The Anthology of Hispanic Literature of the United States*. Oxford: Oxford University Press, 2002.

Tatum, Charles M. *Chicano and Chicana Literature: Otra Voz del Pueblo*. Tucson: The University of Arizona Press, 2006.

Children's Literature in Spain: 1900 to Present

The birth of a market for children's literature in Spain can be tracked back to the last quarter of the 19th century when Saturnino Calleja established a publishing empire that flourished in large part because of the classic fairy tales he printed in editions economical enough for many households. As demand grew, adaptations and translations of texts by such well-known authors as Charles Perrault, the Brothers Grimm, and Hans Christian Andersen were published alongside an increasing number of original stories, without reference to either an author or translator. In later years, some of the greatest innovators of fiction for children, like Salvador Bartolozzi, would join Calleja

Publishing House. In 1925 Bartolozzi became director of Calleja's magazine, *Pinocho*. Best known for his adaptations of Carlo Collidi's Pinocchio and "Las aventuras de Pipo y Pipa" (Adventures of Pipo and Pipa) later published in the journal *Estampa*, Bartolozzi revolutionized the comic strip form in Spain. He also worked closely with his wife, Magda Donato (Carmen Eva Nelken) to renovate children's theater in Spain, emphasizing the need to amuse in opposition to more conservative playwrights Cristina Aguilá, Pilar Contreras de Rodríguez, Micaela Peñaranda, and Matilde Ribot, who scripted plays as a means of using the stage to impart lessons on morality and proper behavior.

The years prior to the Spanish Civil War (1936–1939) yielded a much higher level of original works for children in Spain than had been seen before. In the 1920s, in addition to magazines specifically for children, such as *Pulgarcito* (Tom Thumb), a number of important journals and newspapers began to include supplements for young readers. Such was the case for *El Imparcial*, which dedicated sections of its literary supplement *Los lunes del Imparcial* to fiction for children, and *ABC*, with its supplement *Gente Menuda*. Elena *Fortún, one of the authors who published in this newly established children's supplement, enjoyed great success with her *Celia* series (1929; *Celia, lo que dice* [1929; Celia, What She Says], *Celia en el colegio* [1932; Celia at School], *Celia novelista* [1934; Novelist Celia], *Celia en el mundo* [1934; Celia in the World], 1935; *Celia y sus amigos*

[1935; Celia and Her Friends]), so much so that the stories moved out of journals and into book format with Aguilar publishers. These tales follow an irreverent little girl whose comments often served to mock the values of the bourgeoisie and even of a Catholic education. Another great author from the prewar period was Antoniorrobles (Antonio Joaquín Robles Soler), creator of *Ocho cuentos de niñas y muñecas* (1930; Eight Tales of Girls and Dolls), *Cuentos de los juguetes vivos* (1931; Tales of Live Toys), *Cuentos de las cosas de Navidad* (1931; Tales of Christmas Things), and *Hermanos monigotes* (1935; The Wimpy Brothers). He also authored adaptations of fairy tales for the Communist Party's *Estrella*, its publishing arm for the young. In his version of Cinderella, the protagonist refuses to marry the prince unless he gives up the throne and adopts a more egalitarian lifestyle.

As was the case for the arts in general, the outcome of the civil war struck a deadly blow to the production of children's literature in Spain, with many of the best-loved writers going into exile and having their books censored. This was the case for Bartolozzi, Donato, Fortún, and Antoniorrobles, among others. Fortún's work was again published at the end of the war in 1939, but with a very different tone: in *Celia madrecita* (Celia the Little Mother), at age 15, Celia becomes the perfect housewife and mother to her younger siblings after the death of their mother.

Bruguera publishers led the charge in resurrecting a market of children's literature in postwar Spain. They primarily published traditional fairy tales and adulterated versions of Jules Verne and Emilio Salgari. Another staple in any child's readings were the hagiographies recommended by the Catholic Church, especially those saints whose stories emphasized the suffering and privation endured by holy children with the thought that they would help children better endure the hardships of life in postwar Spain. During these difficult times, many children received their steady dose of children's literature from magazines. In 1947, the regime began to reach children through *Bazar: Revista de la sección femenina de F.E.T. y de las J.O.N.S. para las juventudes. Bazar* had the surprising characteristic of being aimed at both boys and girls during a period when the sexes were separated for all social and educational purposes. The serial was openly used as a tool for political indoctrination, as in the January 1948 issue that featured the heroic biography of the founder of Spain's Falange Party. The comic strip "José Antonio Primo de Rivera, Capitán de la Juventud," was a continuation of the simplified explanation for children of the Falange's dogma in the November 1948 hagiography, "José Antonio, niño." *Bazar* also published stories and plays for girls with the obvious intention of imparting lessons on home economics. Although less obviously propagandistic, the magazines *Mis chicas* (My Girls)—later *Chicas* as readers became teens—and *Chicos* (Boys) served much the same purposes. Alongside modernized versions of classical literature and medieval *romances*, *Chicos* published the adventures of

Cuto, the incarnation of the winning ideology, and *¡Franco! Al muchacho español!* (Franco! Here's to the Spanish Boy!) by L. Quintana. Yet, even in this period of heavy censorship, when children's literature was blatantly used for political indoctrination, there were such occasional sparks of interest and creativity as Manuel Gago's popular series *El guerrero del antifaz* (1944–1966; The Masked Warrior) and *El Capitán Trueno* (1956–1968; Captain Thunder) by Víctor Mora (Eugenio Roca), with illustrations by Miguel Ambrosio.

Before moving into print format in *Chicas* in 1947, Borita Casas created the character *Antoñita la Fantástica* for a radio audience. A year later the series would begin a run of 12 books with Gilsa publishers that concluded in 1958. Not as openly critical of bourgeois society as the earlier *Celia*, Antoñita is the proper sort of girl on the surface, but her not-so-innocent comments often point out that even the privileged suffered food shortages, and constantly worried about the health of their children. At the international level, the best-known Spanish author of children's fiction is José María Sánchez Silva, the only Spanish author to receive the Andersen Prize, whose 1953 novel *Marcelino, Pan y Vino* (Marcelino, Bread and Wine) was the basis for one of the most popular Spanish films of all time. To stimulate the production of children's literature in Spain, in 1958 the Instituto Nacional del Libro Español created the Premio Lazarillo award, with recognition for individual authors and publishing houses.

Some of the greatest writers for adults have also contributed to children's literature in Spain. Carmen Kurtz (Carmen de Rafael Marés) wrote the series that started with *Óscar, cosmonauta* (1963; Oscar the Cosmonaut) in which Oscar, together with his pet goose, Kina, has 15 more adventures traveling to Africa, being a spy, and so on. Starting in 1980, Kurtz also penned the life of the talking infant Veva that resulted in seven books over the next decade. Gloria *Fuertes published 15 very popular poetry books for children as well as four plays. Fuertes may be best known to the generation of Spaniards who were children during the transition to democracy as creator of the highly innovative television program *Un globo, dos globos, tres globos.* (One Balloon, Two Balloons, Three Balloons) that aired from 1974–1979. The show introduced young audiences to what at the time were highly innovative techniques that combined learning with poetry, and often nonsensical fun that stimulated the imagination. The opening sequences compared the earth to a balloon that would carry children on voyages of exploration.

The influence of exiled Republican writers lingered during the Francoist regime as well. Carmen *Martín Gaite cites both Antoniorrobles and Fortún as inspirations for her own writing. Martín Gaite wrote literature for children with titles like *El castillo de las tres murallas* (1981; The Castle with Three Walls), *El pastel del diablo* (1985; The Devil's Cake), and *Caperucita en Manhattan* (1990; Little Red Riding Hood in Manhattan) and she adapted Fortún's Celia into a character for a film based on the books. Citing Hans Christian Andersen as one of her main influences, Ana María *Matute also wrote prizewinning children's books like *El polizón del Ulises* (1965; A Stowaway on the Ulysses), *Paulina* (1966), *Sólo un pie descalzo* (1983; One Shoeless Foot), and *El verdadero final de la Bella Durmiente* (1995; The Real Ending to Sleeping Beauty). Like much of her fiction for adults, Matute creates child protagonists to denounce society's injustices. Issues of how children survive in less-than-ideal circumstances also provide the background for the much more humorous tales of Elvira Lindo's *Manolito Gafotas* series that began in 1994 with the first book titled after the working-class protagonist; it has evolved into six more print titles, two films, and a television series.

More recently, there is a significant production of works for children in the regional languages of the Peninsula. Among those writing in Catalan, Miguel Rayó stands out with *La bella ventura* (1986; Beautiful Luck), *Les ales roges* (1987; The Red Wings), and *Les muntanyes de foc* (1999; Fire Mountains), among others. In Galician, one example is Agustín Fernández Paz, author of *O único que queda é o amor* (2007; The Only Thing Left Is Love). Greater creativity in children's theater has also returned with such companies as Teatro Paraíso (from Vitoria), Teatre de la Resistencia (Barcelona), and La Machina (Cantabria).

María Elena Soliño

See also Censorship in Spain; Children's Literature in Spanish in the United States; Francoism, Fascism, and Literature in Spain.

Work About:

Guerrero Ruiz, Pedro, ed. *Words Toward the Future: Theory and Practice of Children's and Youth Literature in Spain*. Letras Peninsulares 20.1 (Spring 2007). Special Issue.

Premio Lazarillo. http://www.oepli.org/pag/cas/lazarillo.php

Saíz Ripoll, Anabel. "La literatura infantil española en el siglo XX." *Revista de literatura* 205 (2004): 17–24. Also available online: www.islabahia.com/Culturalia/04literatura/laliteraturainfantil1.shtml.

Children's Literature in Spanish in the United States

Within the United States, publication of Spanish-language literature for children gained momentum only late in the 20th century, closely paralleling the improvements in civil rights for minorities and new approaches to diversity in the educational system that began to take hold in the 1960s and 1970s. Before this time, Spanish-speaking children in the United States had access to printed literature in the form of translations, imports, and selections published in periodicals. In addition, families nurtured a rich oral tradition of songs, stories, and nursery rhymes, which had been collected in picture books by Lulu Delacre and José Luis Orozco, among others.

An influential yet short-lived early periodical for Spanish-speaking children was *La Edad de Oro*, a children's magazine published by Cuban poet José *Martí while exiled in New York in 1889. The stories, poems, and nonfiction texts collected in the four issues remain in print throughout the Americas more than a century after their creation. The founding mother of U.S. Spanish-language children's literature was New York City librarian Pura *Belpré, a native Puerto Rican who developed programs and wrote books for Spanish-speaking children from the 1920s through the 1960s.

The civil rights and Chicano movements in the 1960s brought new attention to educational inequities, including the severe lack of cultural and ethnic diversity in U.S. children's literature. Such intellectuals as Ernesto Galarza began to establish a body of work that would speak to and about young Chicanos. Following the 1974 Bilingual Education Act, the growing demand for bilingual materials in schools and the availability of federal funding encouraged the formation of such new publishers as Children's Book Press.

Throughout the 1980s and 1990s, as the U.S. Spanish-speaking population grew, the realities of bilingualism and diversity continued to open the market for Spanish-language children's literature. As the 21st century began, an exponentially increasing number of writers and illustrators sought to engage the experiences of Spanish-speaking children living in the United States, often collaborating with such specialized publishers as Piñata Books and Cinco Puntos. A few of the writers behind this relative boom were Alma Flor *Ada, Francisco X. Alarcón, Pat *Mora, Jan Romero Stevens, and Ofelia Dumas Lachtman.

Some aspects of this newly thriving body of literature suggest the potential for further growth: male writers and characters are underrepresented, and works directed toward older children are scarce. In the 1990s, the Pura Belpré Award, the Américas Book Award, and the Tomás Rivera Award were established to recognize outstanding U.S. children's works representing the Spanish-speaking world. Given the substantial portion of these honors awarded to English-language books, Spanish works seem to occupy a marginal position within this canon. Self-translation and bilingual collaboration are growing increasingly common, however, complicating the classification of Latino children's literature by language.

Laura Kanost

See also Children's Literature in Spain: 1900 to Present; Latinos and Latinas in the United States: History, Culture, and Literature.

Work About:

Barahona Center for the Study of Books in Spanish for Children and Adolescents. http://www.csusm.edu/csb/

Gonzalez-Jensen, Margarita. "The Status of Children's Fiction Literature Written in Spanish by U.S. Authors." *Bilingual Research Journal* 21.2 (1997).

Chile: History, Culture, and Literature

History

The discovery of Chile in 1535 by Diego de Almagro (1475–1538) and his troops set in motion a historical process characterized by the confrontation between power and resistance. The Spanish explorers did not find the riches so desired; they suffered instead a horrendous expedition across the Andes as well as attacks by indigenous tribes, especially the Mapuches (also referred to as Araucanos), who for three centuries resisted the colonial Spaniards in the War of Arauco. In 1536, the defeated expeditionary forces returned to Peru where, in 1540, a second excursion was organized under the command of Pedro de Valdivia (1497–1553). This expedition initiated the period of the conquest of Chile. On February 12, 1541, Valdivia founded Santiago, the country's capital, and a few months later was proclaimed governor of Chile. The new governor launched a military campaign in Chile's southern territories but was killed in an ambush planned by the Mapuche leader Lautaro (1534–1557) during the Arauco War.

The 17th century marked the beginning of the colonial period; it lasted for two centuries, during which the Spaniards consolidated their power. Spanish domination was resisted intermittently by surges of indigenous rebellion. In 1810, the first regional government was established and a movement toward autonomy was initiated by the Creoles Bernardo O'Higgins (1778–1842), José Miguel Carrera (1785–1821), and Manuel Rodríguez (1785–1818). These men helped to usher in the period of the *Patria Vieja*, or the Old Fatherland, which lasted until the Disaster of Rancagua in 1814, in which the Spanish army reconquered the Chilean territory.

While seeking refuge in Mendoza following the disaster, the advocates of independence would constitute, along with Argentine patriots, the Army of the Andes commanded by General José de San Martín (1778–1850). After its victory at the battle of Chacabuco in February of 1817, this army would advance the freedom cause and one year later, O'Higgins would be confirmed as supreme director of Chile. The troops led by San Martín and O'Higgins triumphed at the battle of Maipú in April of 1818; in this same year the "Patria Nueva" was declared and Chile gained its independence.

The tension between power and resistance escalated once independence was proclaimed, as the liberal and conservative Creoles fought to institute different national projects. The Revolution of 1829 established the Conservative Republic; its leader, Diego Portales (1793–1837), would become a central proponent of the Constitution of 1833, which would organize the country during the 19th century. In 1861, under the rule of the Liberal Faction, the country entered into a period of economic wealth due to the exploitation of potassium nitrate in Antofagasta. In 1891, conflicts between President José Manuel Balmaceda (1840–1891) and Congress led to civil war, after which the triumphant Congress faction inaugurated a Parliamentary Republic. Despite economic growth, the unequal distribution of wealth generated political instability and retaliation from the proletariat movement. President Arturo Alessandri (1868–1950) attempted to mediate between the oligarchy and the proletariat, instituting the Constitution of 1925 that originated a presidential republic.

The economic crisis during the first decades of the 20th century required the intervention of groups that demanded greater social transformations. In this context, Pedro Aguirre Cerda (1879–1941) assumed the presidency in 1938, aided by a political group opposed to rule by the Chilean elite. Aguirre Cerda's election inaugurated a period ruled by the Radical party factions. To combat poverty, Aguirre Cerda created the Production Development Corporation and promoted school education by founding schools and improving labor conditions for teachers.

Following the period of Radicalism, the rightist independent government of Jorge Alessandri (1896–1986) and of Christian Democrat Eduardo Frei Montalva (1911–1982), Socialist president Salvador Allende (1908–1973) was elected in 1970, which complicated the sociopolitical scene. The Popular Unity Coalition headed by the socialist leader faced a deep economic crisis and intense internal resistance that was supported by the U.S. government. On September 11, 1973, a military coup d'etat led by General Augusto Pinochet (1915–2006) overthrew the Popular Unity Coalition and installed an authoritarian military regime in its place.

The new government quickly suppressed all opposition and committed atrocious human rights violations that resulted in more than 3,000 deaths, some 35,000 incidents of torture, 1,000 disappeared prisoners and roughly 200,000 individuals who fled to exile. As a result of the 1988 plebiscite favoring the dictatorship opposition, Pinochet was ousted in March of 1990. That same year, Patricio Aylwin (1918–) assumed the presidency, initiating the period known as the "transition," which restored a democratic government system, reduced poverty levels, and officially recognized the human rights abuses committed during the military dictatorship. Aylwin's successor, Eduardo Frei Ruiz-Table (1942–), was elected in 1994 and succeeded in expanding Chile's economic development by opening up to foreign markets.

In 2000, Ricardo Lagos (1938–) became the third president of the transition. During his presidency, the country became increasingly incorporated into the international league by participating in the United Nations Security Council and rejecting the invasion of Iraq. In 2006, socialist candidate Michelle Bachelet (1951–) became the first woman president in the history of Chile. Bachelet implemented policies that favor gender equality as her central tasks while in office. She also instituted free public health care to senior citizens over 60 years of age, and in 2007 established the highest fiscal budget in the country's history. Following the election on January 17th, 2010, Chilean billionaire candidate of the newly formed "Coalition for Change," Sebastián Piñera, assumed control of the country's nearly 17 million inhabitants (July 2011 estimate), becoming the first rightist president since 1990.

Culture

The culture of the Republic of Chile developed from the encounter between the first Spanish conquistadors and the indigenous tribes, particularly the Mapuches. White immigrants, Creoles and Mestizos constitute the majority of Chile's population and have contributed extensively to the country's cultural development. The first colonizers arrived as part of the 16th-century Spanish immigration; immigrations beginning in the 18th century involved groups from Germany, Great Britain, France, Ireland, and Yugoslavia. The mestizo population originated as the mix between Spaniards and indigenous people.

The Spanish conquistadors introduced a written and spoken language. Spanish, or Castilian, became Chile's official language, although various native tongues still exist today. In northern Chile, the Aimara people speak the language that shares the name of their tribe; on Easter Island, the habitants communicate in Rapa Nui, a Polynesian tongue; and in southern Chile, more than half a million Mapuches speak Mapudungun. The conquest fomented a conversion from a polytheistic religious system to monotheistic Christianity. Presently, approximately 80 percent of the population adheres to Catholicism, although Evangelical Protestantism has grown increasingly popular. However, there is currently no official religion, due to the separation of Church and state, and many indigenous tribes continue to practice their native religious traditions. In the northern areas of the country, native tribes celebrate the carnival of the Fiesta de la Tirana, a tradition that mixes aspects of Catholicism with indigenous practices.

The Spanish influence was also expressed in the physical subsistence, as the cultural contact altered the customs of food production and consumption. The original predominance of corn gave way to cultivation of wheat and beans, and Spaniards introduced the breeding of fowl, swine, cattle, and horses. Over time, traditional Chilean cuisine began to expand, reflecting the country's diverse topography. Major food groups include fish and seafood, beef, and fresh fruits and vegetables. One typical dish is "poor man's steak," which consists of a portion of beef with two fried eggs placed on the meat, accompanied by a large serving of fried potatoes and onions. Another traditional dish is *curanto*, a stew prepared with fish, shellfish, chicken, pork, lamb, beef, and potatoes. Chilean wine is regarded as among the best in Latin America, and is the beverage of choice at cultural and family celebrations.

Besides its economic and military uses, the horse in Chile constituted a pillar of the "Huasa" culture that flourished in the central area of the country. Because a majority of the population is concentrated in this geographic region, "Huasa" culture is considered the primary source of Chilean cultural identity. A main activity of this culture is the rodeo, which has become one of the most popular national sports after *soccer. British immigrants introduced soccer to the nation in the 19th century, and it is the nation's most important sport.

The "Huasa" culture is also associated with such significant artistic expressions in Chile as folkloric music and dance. Chile's folkloric music fuses traditional aborigine sounds with those brought from Spain, as seen in the music of the Cueca. This music requires a guitar, a harp, and an accordion and it accompanies Chile's traditional dance, also called the Cueca. Although it has been a prominent artistic form since the latter half of the 19th century, the Cueca was not acknowledged as the national dance until 1979. Cueca performances take place especially during Chile's patriotic celebrations, particularly Independence Day, which is observed in mid-September.

Folkloric music was revitalized during the 1960s through what was called the New Chilean Song, a musical movement in which artists researched the country's musical roots and created their own interpretations based on their findings. Artists included in this movement are Violeta Parra (1917–1967) and Víctor *Jara (1932–1973), as well as the musical groups Quilapayún and Inti-Illimani. During the later decades of the 20th century, the lyrical and musical compositions of this artistic movement inspired a form of cultural resistance for the victims of the military dictatorship that ruled from 1973 to 1990.

Along with creators of the New Chilean Song, work by other artists throughout the 20th century has been a source of national pride. They include such composers and interpreters of classical music as pianist Claudio Arrau (1903–1991) and tenor Ramón Vinay (1912–1996); surrealist painter Roberto Matta (1911–2002); and poets Gabriela *Mistral (1889–1957) and Pablo *Neruda (1904–1973), both of whom were awarded the *Nobel Prize for Literature in 1945 and 1971, respectively.

Literature

Chilean literature is intimately linked to the nation's historical and social conflicts. Literature developed in the 16th century during the Spanish conquest and colonization. The epic poem *La Araucana* (1569) is considered the inaugural text of Chilean literature. In it, Alonso de *Ercilla (1533–1594) describes the contentious issues between the Spanish and the Mapuche nation. Pedro de Oña (1570–1643), the first poet born in Chile, follows the epic model in *Arauco Domado* (1596), in which he describes the Arauco War. A major figure during the 17th century is Alonso de Ovalle (1603–1651); his chronicles, titled *Histórica relación del Reyno de Chile* (1646; Historical Relation of the Reign of Chile), depict the conquest and the Arauco War.

During the period of Independence and the framework of *romanticism, José Victorino Lastarria (1817–1888) founded the Literature Society of 1842, whose purpose was to spread *Enlightenment ideals and promote the national literature. Lastarria is recognized for initiating the short story in Chile with his work "El mendigo" (1843; The Beggar) and the short novel, with *El Alférez Alonzo Díaz Guzmán* (1848; Second Lieutenant Alonzo Díaz Gúzman). This support for a national literature was enriched by the participation and work of foreign intellectuals who came to Chile, including Andrés *Bello (1781–1865) and Domingo Faustino *Sarmiento (1811–1888).

An active literary generation influenced by the Realism aesthetic emerged during the latter decades of the 19th century. Alberto *Blest Gana (1830–1920), one of this generation's most prominent representatives, earned the designation of father of Chile's historical novel with the publication of *Martín Rivas* (1862). This novel presents a detailed portrayal of Chilean society of the mid-19th century and reaffirms the Liberal democratic project that Lastarria had envisioned for Chilean literature.

As in many Latin American countries, Chilean literature underwent extensive and heterogeneous development throughout the 20th century. The most recognized writers during the initial decades of this century, influenced by *criollismo* and naturalism, include Mariano *Latorre Court (1886–1955), with his novel *Zurzulita* (1920), and Baldomero Lillo (1867–1923), with his short story volumes *Sub terra* (1904; [Latin for] Under the Soil) and *Sub sole* (1907; [Latin for] Under the Sun). In part of his work, Augusto D'Halmar (1882–1950) adopts an allegorical and fantastic discourse as an alternative to *criollismo* and naturalism, inaugurating the *imaginismo*, the use of precise vocabulary and an unsentimental focus, with such texts as *La lámpara en el molino* (1915; The Light in the Mill) and *La sombra del humo en el espejo* (1918; The Shadow of Smoke in the Mirror). Pedro Prado (1886–1952) subscribes to this model in his novel *Alsino* (1920). María Luisa *Bombal (1910–1980) emphasizes surrealism in her novels *La última niebla* (1935; *The Final Mist*, 1982) and *La amortajada* (1938; *The Shrouded Woman*, 1948). Also popular during the same period was a new version of neorealism that reasserted the defense of society's subordinate sectors. The novels *Los hombres oscuros* (1939; The Dark Men) and *La sangre y la esperanza* (1943; Blood and Hope) by Nicomedes Guzmán (1914–1964) constitute two clear representatives of this literary tendency, which is also identified as the Chilean social novel.

In the second half of the 20th century and the beginning of the 21st, Chilean literary production has assumed greater prominence within the panorama of Latin American literature and has appropriated the ideological and aesthetic tendencies of modern and postmodern literatures. Fragmented narration substitutes the cause–effect principle; similarly, simultaneity and a discontinuous plot replace the ordered sequence. The literature exhibits in a rather eclectic way such ideas inspired by modern thought as psychoanalysis, existentialism, relativism, and cultural anthropology, all of which become tools for critiquing society from multiple perspectives. One paradigmatic text that represents a transition between the social novel and contemporary literary tendencies is *Hijo de ladrón* (1951; Thief's Son), written by Manuel Rojas (1896–1973).

Chilean literature continues to be developed by authors who in recent decades have achieved international recognition. Several writers have received such prestigious literary awards as the Nobel Prize for Literature, the Cervantes Prize, the Rómulo Gallegos Prize, the Biblioteca Breve Prize, the Juan Rulfo Prize, the Casa de las Américas Prize, the Planeta Prize and the National Prize for Literature; additionally, they enjoy acclaim from specialized critics and the reading public. These prominent writers include novelists José *Donoso (1924–1996), Jorge *Edwards (1931–), Antonio *Skármeta (1940–), Ariel *Dorfman (1942–), Isabel *Allende (1942–), Diamela *Eltit (1949–), Marcela *Serrano (1951–), Roberto *Bolaño (1953–2003), and Mauricio Electorat (1960–); poets Gabriela *Mistral (1889–1957), Pablo *Neruda (1904–1973), Nicanor *Parra (1914–), Gonzalo *Rojas (1917–2011), Enrique Lihn (1929–1988), and Raúl *Zurita (1950–).

Guillermo García-Corales

See also Appendix B for other entries related to Chile.

Work About:

Collier, Simon, and William F. Sater. *A History of Chile, 1808–1994*. New York and Cambridge: Cambridge University Press, 1996.

Promis, José. *La literatura del reino de Chile*. Chile: Universidad de Playa Ancha de Ciencias de la Educación, 2002.

Chilean Colectivo de Acciones de Arte. *See* CADA (1979–1985)

Chilean Theater: 1900 to Present

The first decade of Chile's 20th-century theatrical activity was largely dominated by romantic melodramas performed by foreign troupes that made stops in the city of Santiago on their Latin American tours. A growing middle-class concerned with the construction of a national identity in the face of an increasing immigrant population called for a change in the character and nationality of theatrical productions. In 1913, the National Drama Company emerged, followed shortly by Luis Emilio Recabarren's founding of the Worker's Theater in 1917. At this same time, Armando Moock Bousquet (1894–1942) initiated his dramatic career with pieces that combined psychological analysis with traditional *costumbrismo* (depiction of everyday customs and mores), focusing on marginalized Chilean communities and peoples, as in *Crisis económica* (1914; Economic Crisis), *Pueblecito* (1918; Little Town), and *La serpiente* (1920; The Serpent).

A contemporary of Moock, Germán Luco Cruchaga (1884–1936) is best recognized for his creole-naturalist play *La viuda de Apablaza* (1928; *The Widow of Apablaza*), oftentimes called the best Chilean play of that time for its tragic representation of social dichotomies present in the transition from feudalism to a more modern, capitalist society. During this same time period, the so-called father of Chile's National Social Theater, Antonio Acevedo Hernández (1886–1962) initiated his career with *Almas perdidas* (1917; Lost Souls) and achieved his greatest success a few decades later with *Chañarcillo* (1936).

The momentum initiated by Moock, Luco, and Acevedo in the first quarter of the 20th century surged in following decades, helped by the foundation of university theater groups that primarily aimed to promote and nurture national drama by traveling throughout Chile's provinces and staging productions. Aided by Pedro Aguirre Cerda's left-wing coalition government, the Popular Front (1936–1941), whose motto was "to govern is to educate," the University of Chile's Experimental Theater (TEUCH; renamed ITUCH in 1959) opened its doors at the Teatro Imperio in 1941, headed by Chilean dramatist Pedro de la Barra (1912–1976). Two years later, Pedro Mortheiru founded the Teatro de Ensayo at the Catholic University of Chile (TEUC).

This movement initiated by Santiago university groups soon extended outside the capital, reaching such important cities as Concepción (1947), Valparaíso (1958), and Antofagasta (1962). Providing professional training for actors, directors, and technicians, the university groups introduced European practices and plays, showcased national playwrights, and fueled one of Chilean theater's most prolific periods, the movement known today as the Generation of 1957.

Notable, recognized dramatists and plays that emerged out of the Generation of 1957 include María Asunción Requena (1915–1986), whose *Fuerte Bulnes* (1955; Fort Bulnes) offers a nationalist depiction of colonization in Chile's southern territories, and *Versos de ciego* (1961; The Blind Man's Verse), a transcendental work by Luis Alberto Heiremans (1928–1964) that incorporates elements of medieval sacred plays and local folkloric realism. Other plays belonging to the same vein of critical realism with emphasis on contemporary socioeconomic issues include *Mi hermano Cristián* (1957; My Brother, Christian) by Alejandro Sieveking (1934–), *Mansión de lechuzas* (1958; The House of Owls), by Egon *Wolff (1926–), *Deja que los perros ladren* (1959; Let the Dogs Bark), by Sergio *Vodanovic (1926–2001) and the musical comedy *La pérgola de las flores* (1960; The Flower Market), by Isidora Aguirre (1919–2011).

By the mid-1960s to early 1970s, independent theater groups began to emerge as a result of changes in university structuring and the national political climate. In reaction to the tendency to associate academics with bourgeois authoritarianism, such groups as El Aleph, El túnel, Compañía de los cuatro, and Ictus teamed up alongside Argentinean-born playwright Jorge Díaz (1930–2007) and began to explore and incorporate existentialist and absurdist influences of European theater movements initiated by France's Antonin Artaud (1896–1948) and Eugène Ionesco (1909–1994) and Ireland's Samuel Beckett (1906–1989), among others. Aided by a national law that required the performance of one Chilean play per year, the Ictus group and Díaz successfully staged numerous plays of a collaborative nature, including *El cepillo de dientes* (1961; The Toothbrush) and *El velero en la botella* (1962; The Sailboat in the Bottle), which satirized the affluence and consumerism in Chilean society and the absurdity of the human condition. In general, however, the successful Chilean theater of the 1950s waned as those who had previously supported university theaters stayed home to watch increasingly popular television

programs, or frequented movie houses to watch films made by the newly emerging and energetic Chilean cinematographic industry.

Reflective of the political and social polarization at the core of all artistic and political movements of the early 1970s, Egon Wolff's most recognized play, *Flores de papel* (1970; *Paper Flowers*, 1971) directly addressed the animosity and dependency between social classes through the representation of Eva, an established woman of society, and her desire for the vagabond Merluza. Similarly critical in nature, two theater groups began new and interesting work in the early 1970s: Ángel's Theater, led by dramatist Alejandro Sieveking (1934–) and his actress wife Bélgica Castro, and the New Popular Theater, a group formed by graduates from the University of Chile theater school who presented their productions in union halls across the country. After the 1973 coup d'etat, most independent and university-related theatrical activity came to a halt, as many playwrights, actors, and technicians were detained or disappeared; fled into exile, such as Sieveking's group, which relocated to Costa Rica for 10 years; or suffered the direct effects of the unofficial censor—a high 22 percent value added tax was imposed on box office proceeds for plays not approved by the government.

By 1975, a few courageous theatrical companies had emerged, invigorated by the various stylistic works of up-and-coming dramatists categorized as the Generation of 1972, a group who attempted to work within the constraints of the military dictatorship. Alongside Ictus and Taller de Investigación Teatral (TIT), David *Benavente (1941–) composed *Pedro, Juan y Diego* (1976; Peter, John and James) and *Tres Marías y una Rosa* (1979; Three Marys and a Rose), which reached wide audiences after narrowly avoiding closure due to their defense of the preservation of human dignity in the face of widespread economic hardship. Teatro Imagen began performing abstract plays by Marco Antonio de la *Parra (1952–) that indirectly pertained to violence and basic human rights, including *Matatangos* (1978; Killer Tangos) and *Lo crudo, lo cocido, lo podrido* (1979; The Raw, the Cooked, the Rotten), ultimately banned the day before opening due to its controversial language. Teatro de Comediantes performed the earliest theatrical piece by Juan Radigán (1937–), *Testimonios de la muerte de Sabina* (1979; Testimonies of Sabina's Death); it was the first in a prolific career that included *El loco y la triste* (1979; The Crazy Man and the Sad Woman), *Hechos consumados* (1981; Consumed Facts), and *Informe para indiferentes* (1982; Report for the Indifferent).

By the mid- to late 1980s, Chilean theater again flourished with new plays, festivals, and such experimental theater groups as El Gran Circo Teatro and El Troley, as previously imposed government restrictions were loosened. In 1984, the government reduced the list of people banned from reentering Chile, encouraging the return of such exiled playwrights and artists as Jorge Díaz, Antonio *Skármeta (1940–), and Ariel *Dorfman (1942–). Their key plays tackled issues presented by the return process,

understood either as coming back physically or as resuming a state of democracy, as seen in Skármeta's *Ardiente paciencia* (1982; *Burning Patience*, 1985) and Dorfman's *La muerte y la doncella* (1991; *Death and the Maiden*, 1991).

In the last decade of the 20th century, under democratically elected governments, Chilean theatrical productions witnessed the resurgence of female playwrights in the vein of Requena and Aguirre, seen in the significant productions *Cariño malo* (1990; *Bad Love*) and *Malinche* (1993), by Inés Margarita Stranger (1957–).

Laura Senio Blair

See also Theater in Spanish America: 1900 to Present.

Work About:

Boyle, Catherine M. *Chilean Theatre, 1973–1985. Marginality, Power, Selfhood*. Teaneck, NJ: Fairleigh Dickinson University Press, 1992.

Dirección de bibliotecas, archivos y museos (dibam). "Memoria Chilena: Teatro chileno." http://www.memoria chilena.cl/artes_visuales/teatro.asp.

Piga, Domingo. "El sexagésimo aniversario del Teatro Experimental de la Universidad de Chile." *Latin American Theatre Review* 34.2 (2001): 189–97.

Chilean Women Writers: The *Ergo Sum* Project

Founded in 1977 by Chilean author and activist Pía *Barros, this project evolved from a clandestine creative writing workshop for aspiring women writers into a multifaceted political and literary experiment involving hundreds of authors and graphic artists. Barros began the project in the midst of the Augusto Pinochet military regime (1973–1990), a political situation that prompted her to create the literary innovations for which *Ergo Sum* is known.

In 1985, she opened the underground press, Ediciones Ergo Sum, to publish political literary works, primarily short and mini-short story anthologies consisting of collectively written short stories created in the *Ergo Sum* workshops. The publications for which the Ergo Sum press and workshops are most famous, handmade publications called book-objects, constitute an inventive publication form designed to highlight the collaborative, feminist, and activity-based structure of the Ergo Sum workshops and the context of military censorship that inspired the first workshops and book-objects. The project continues to figure prominently in the Chilean literary scene even though the regime that so conditioned it has been deposed.

When Barros initiated the project, a culture war known as the Cultural Blackout (*Apagón cultural)* was being waged in Chile. Promptly after the coup d'état, the government declared a state of siege and assumed the authority to govern through military edicts. The military assassinated, incarcerated, and exiled intellectuals, prohibited publication of uncensored literary texts, banned "subversive" literature, and took over the mass media. A curfew banning unsupervised gatherings of four or more people was implemented to prohibit the free exchange of ideas. Concurrently, the government encouraged, and at times violently enforced, a return to traditional gender roles. These policies unwittingly produced a prolific artistic counterculture known as the Generation of 1980. Additionally, Chile experienced its greatest growth of feminist activism and the largest boom in women writers. The *Ergo Sum* project emerged as part of this countercultural movement and is one of the best examples of literary experimentation and intellectual activism associated with the Generation of 1980 writers.

The *Ergo Sum* project has marked Chilean literature and social life by including the participation of hundreds of prose authors and graphic artists; developing a neo-avant-garde publication form called the book-object, which fused literary and visual media; creating Chile's first collective feminist literary movement; and contributing to the early formation of numerous contemporary authors including Alejandra Basualto, Teresa Calderón, Alejandra Costamagna, Lilian Elphick, Nona Fernández, Astrid Fugellie, Sonia González Valdenegro, Sonia Guralnik, Elvira Hernández, Luz Larraín, Pedro Lemebel, Andrea Maturana, Jorge Montealegre, Ana María del Río, Susana Sánchez, Digna Tapia, Emilio Torrealba, Virginia Vidal, and Lyuba Yez, among others. The workshop also provided a venue for censored graphic artists to publish hand-in-hand with censored writers. Among the more known participants are Luis Albornoz, Anita, Eduardo de la Barra, Máximo Carvajal, Hervi (Hernán Vidal), Palomo

(José Palomo), Rulfino (Alejandro Montenegro), Hernan Venegas, and Guillo (Guillermo Bastías).

A bastion of feminist activity since their inception, in the Ergo Sum workshops Barros includes participants of differing socioeconomic and literary backgrounds and engages them in a myriad of literary and social activities. The predominantly female group works together to form social and professional alliances, develop skills as writers, discuss issues of feminist concern, and publish their work.

The workshops have always welcomed male participation, even though they are primarily intended to empower women. Most male collaborators take part in the graphic illustration and design of book-object anthologies. Barros believes that the inclusion of men supports the project's feminist principles, which stress art as collective action, and demonstrates the vitality and desirability of social and gender equality, comprehensive political participation, and freedom of expression.

The dictatorship-era workshops have left an indelible mark on Barros's approach. Her activity-based style engages students in relevant literary and extraliterary tasks to create writers conversant in all facets of literary production and cognizant of women's marginality in social, political, and literary life. From the start, in regularly scheduled meetings participants would compose, edit, recite, and critique their short stories. Eventually they organized, published, and marketed the handmade collaborative anthologies. All the while, a relationship between their literary activities and women's work was under-

scored, and a clear feminist agenda was advanced.

The early workshops generated short story writings side-by-side with handcrafted artisan anthologies and literary pamphlets made from inexpensive and recycled materials. Participants distributed and performed short story texts on city buses and on bustling corners; they published a feminist magazine called *Nos = otras* (We = the Others [Women]); they held creative writing workshops in slums, prisons, and the countryside; and they dispersed book-objects to raise funds for church-sponsored soup kitchens, one of many popular sites of resistance against military authority.

In 1985, the press published its first literary artifact, the original anthology that has since grown to include an array of books-in-disguise, which include boxes for handkerchiefs, shoes, matches, and wine; burlap and recycled bags; tarot cards; packages of women's undergarments; mini-hope chests; books of postcards; suitcases; subway tickets; letters; and pairs of miniature blue jeans. Since its first object, Ediciones Ergo Sum has published at least one new artifact each year, producing a collection of well over 30 illustrated short and mini-short story collections, poetry anthologies, and loose leaflets. Each book-object makes a visual commentary either about its historical moment or about being a woman writer.

Many publications in the collection deserve mention. The initial *Ergo sum* (1985; Therefore, I Am) anthology contains illustrated short stories gathered together in a handkerchief box. It contains writings from the earliest workshop participants and a manifesto outlining Barros's goals, approach, and philosophy. The book-object *Incontables* (1986; What Can't Be Told), a short story collection contained in an oversized envelope, is the first published work of now famous writer and performer Pedro Lemebel. Such pamphlets as the illustrated feminist poem "Mujeres del mundo, unidos," (1985; Women of the World, United) by Teresa Calderón became cult items that decorated homes throughout Santiago's slums during the years of military hegemony.

Book-object designs released after Pinochet was deposed visually represent events of the transition from dictatorship to democracy, such as *Desaforados* (2000; Let Loose), which visually connotes Pinochet's house arrest. Objects published in the new millennium include a miniature pair of blue jeans titled *Tenemos pantalones* (2006; We Too Wear the Pants), in support of President Michelle Bachelet's feminist politics. As of 2008, Barros continues to direct workshops and publishes a yearly book-object.

Resha Cardone

See also CADA (1979–1985); Chile's Generation of 1980: The New Scene; Feminism in Spanish America.

Work About:

Barros, Pía. Preface. *Ergo Sum*. Santiago: Ergo Sum, 1985.

Trevisan, Liliana. "Pía Barros." *Escritoras chilenas: novela y cuento*. Ed. Patrícia Rubio. Santiago: Cuarto Propio, 1999, 579–93.

Chile's Generation of 1950

Chilean author and critic Enrique Lafourcade originally named this literary movement in the prologue to his 1954 *Antología del nuevo cuento chileno*, a short story collection featuring the generation's first participants. A short-lived controversy followed Lafourcade's compilation: when the anthology was published in 1954, the major works of the generation were still unwritten and some critics considered Lafourcade's announcement premature. The writers selected nevertheless earned their position in national letters throughout the 1950s and 1960s, thanks to Lafourcade and the existence of Chile's Zig-Zag, then South America's largest publishing house and the principal publisher of the Generation of 1950 authors.

These writers abandon the socially conscious propensities characterizing their Generation of 1938 predecessors, a group known for enlisting literature in the struggle to emancipate the Chilean proletariat in the 1930s and 1940s. Disillusioned with the artless socialist realism of these forbearers, Generation of 1950 writers imbued cosmopolitan views in their writing, hoping to situate Chile within the international literary arena. They were influenced by French existentialism and feminism, Russian nihilism, and European experimentation, and endeavored to create a highly intellectual and artistic generational *oeuvre* that focused on the Chilean bourgeoisie rather than the worker. Lafourcade characterized the group as individualistic, antirevolutionary, hermetic, and elitist. These postwar writers in fact lacked the faith in humanity needed to produce a socially or politically engaged art; they did, however, host Chile's first boom in women writers, a feature that would characterize the national literary scene thereafter. Many of these female authors became best-selling writers and constituted the first group of women writers to import international feminist thought to Chile through the literary medium. The most known figures of this generation include prose authors Margarita Aguirre, Guillermo Blanco, José *Donoso, Jorge *Edwards, María Elena Gertner, Claudio Giaconi, Enrique Lafourcade, Elisa Serrana, and Mercedes Valdivieso; poets Miguel Arteche, Enrique Lihn, and Jorge Tellier; and dramatists Isadora Aguirre, the earlier mentioned María Elena Gertner, and Egon *Wolff.

Resha Cardone

Work About:

Dorfman, Ariel. "Notas para un análisis marxista de la narrativa chilena de los últimos años." *Casa de las Américas* 69 (1971): 65–83.

Godoy Gallardo, Eduardo. *La generación del 50 en Chile: historia de un movimiento literario*. Santiago, Chile: La Novia, 1992.

Lafourcade, Enrique, comp., ed. *Antología del nuevo cuento chileno*. Santiago, Chile: Zig-Zag, 1954.

Chile's Generation of 1980: The New Scene

This movement appeared in Chile in about 1976 when groups targeted by Augusto Pinochet's military government—students, artists, intellectuals, women, homosexuals, and the poor, among others—began to meet clandestinely to create art opposing the military attempt to disassemble the counterculture. Promptly after the 1973 coup d'état, the military declared a culture war known as the Cultural Blackout (*Apagón cultural*): it murdered, tortured, incarcerated, and exiled the aforementioned dissidents, instituted a curfew, censored all forms of expression, and prohibited gatherings where ideas could be exchanged.

This emergency situation produced a dynamic underground art scene known variously as the Generation of 1980, the *Nueva escena*, the *Avanzada*, the Generation of 73 and 87, the Post-Coup Generation, the Generation NN, and the Marginal Generation. A neo-avant-garde movement, it was characterized by an intricate formal experimentation with language and visual media aimed at dismantling the authoritarian features inherent in art, society, and politics. Censorship strengthened aesthetic innovation as artists concealed messages in word plays, double entendres, metaphors, and mythological and literary allusions. Further, the artists of the Generation of 1980 tended to collaborate in literary happenings and alternative, self-edited, artisan publications; to cross boundaries that traditionally separate genres; to juxtapose visual and textual elements; and to reveal the relationship between art and politics. The era became the apogee of women's writing in Chilean literary history. Many women authors (such as Pía *Barros, Heddy Navarro, and Ana María del Río, among others) composed erotic literature in which the female body—silenced, tortured and sexualized—became a metaphor for the nation under siege and the repressive structures defining human relationships.

A variety of collective projects within this generation merit particular mention, such as the Arpillera workshop, the Colectivo de acciones de arte—known as *CADA, the *Ergo Sum* group, and the Yeguas del apocalipsis. The major figures of the generation included Barros, Teresa Calderón, Gregory Cohen, Eugenio Dittborn, Diamela *Eltit, Ramón Díaz Eterovic, Ramón Griffero, Elvira Hernández, Pedro Lemebel, Jorge Montealegre, Diego Muñoz Valenzuela, Rosabetty Muñoz, Esteban Navarro, Heddy Navarro, Marco Antonio de la *Parra, Clemente Riedemann, Ana María del Río, Lotty Rosenfeld, Bruno Serrano, Leonora Vicuña, and Raúl *Zurita, among others.

Though the dictatorship that so defined the movement ended in 1990, many members of the Generation of 1980 remain active in Chilean art and politics. The emerging group of writers, known as the Generation of 1990, the *McOndo group, and the Group of Cultural Industry, has not yet achieved the national and international acclaim of earlier generations.

Resha Cardone

See also Chilean Women Writers: The *Ergo Sum* Project; Southern Cone Writing: Literature of Transition from Argentina and Chile.

Work About:

Del Río, Ana María. "Literatura chilena: generación de los ochenta. Detonantes y rasgos generacionales." *Literatura chilena hoy. La difícil transición*. Ed. Karl Kohut and José Morales. Frankfurt: Iberamericana-Vervuert, 2002.

Nelson, Alice. *Political Bodies: Gender, History and the Struggle for Narrative Power in Recent Chilean Literature*. Lewisburg, PA: Bucknell University Press, 2002.

Richard, Nelly. *La insubordinación de los signos (Cambio político, transformaciones culturales y poéticas de la crisis)*. Santiago, Chile: Cuarto Propio, 1994.

Chivalry Literature in Spain and the New World

Associated primarily with medieval and Renaissance Europe, chivalry literature emerged from an admixture of fictional and factual sources, including legends of Greco-Roman heroes, Arthurian romances, French *chansons de geste*, Crusade narratives, and the troubadour songs of courtly love. Versions of these texts enjoyed popularity in the oral tradition of Spanish Christians who, while challenging Muslim control of the Iberian Peninsula during the Reconquest (718–1492), established kingdoms with strong ties to other European courts with vibrant chivalric traditions. By the mid-13th century, written *epics, chronicles, and other chivalric texts emerged in Spain from this synergy of experiences and trends. Centuries later, with the rise of the printing press and literacy during Spain's *Renaissance, chivalry literature encompassed a variety of literary genres, particularly prose books of chivalry (*libros de caballerías*), appealing to *bourgeois* and aristocratic readers alike.

In Spain, as elsewhere in medieval Europe, the scope and nature of chivalry literature developed in tandem with the emergence of a military caste of horsemen or knights (*caballeros*) governed by a complex code of personal and public conduct. This protocol, known as chivalry (*caballería*), guided the beliefs, decisions, and actions of knights and eventually provided the basis of interaction for court culture and polite society in general. At first an expression and celebration of bravery, honor, and service specific to Spain's warrior class, chivalry literature gradually became an important vehicle of aristocratic values. Chivalry literature typically emphasizes the quest of a knightly hero who struggles with adversity and grows spiritually as he attempts to attain a military or social goal. This plot structure, intimately connected to such ancient narratives as the legends of the Holy Grail, continues to influence literature, music, and other media.

Among the first examples of chivalry literature to emerge from Spain's oral tradition were epics: verse narratives that recount the trials, adventures, and feats of brave and noble men. The **Cantar de Mío Cid* (c. 1207; *The Poem of the Cid*, 1957), for example, narrates the political, military, and personal struggles of the Castilian knight Rodrigo Díaz de Vivar (*El Cid*) within the context of courtly protocol, interpersonal intrigues, and the Christian reconquest of Iberia. Another seminal epic, the *Poema de Fernán González* (mid-13th century), recounts the campaigns of Fernán González, Count of Castile, against the Moors to the south as well as the Christians of Navarra to the east. Other important medieval Spanish epics feature such heroic figures as Bernardo del Carpio and the Seven Princes of Lara.

Medieval Spain also saw the rise and development of ballads (*romances*) and other songs associated with chivalry. Though many ballads refer to Spanish epic material as well as matters of Rome, France, and Britain, many *romances* incorporate themes and imagery linked to the chivalric tradition of courtly love. The first-known printed collections of Spanish ballads (*romanceros*) date from the early 16th century, but it is known that written ballads circulated decades earlier. Chivalric ballads, in fact, continue to form a part of Hispanic culture. During the Mexican Revolution, for example, epic ballads (*corridos épicos*) were composed to glorify leaders of humble origins.

The first full-length prose work of Spanish chivalry literature, the *Libro del Cavallero Zifar* (14th century; *The Book of the Knight Zifar*, 1983), narrates the adventures of the knight Zifar and his family. However, the apogee of Spanish chivalric prose fiction occurred in the 16th century, as books like Garci Rodríguez de Montalvo's *Amadís de Gaula* (1508; *Amadis of Gaul*, 2003) and Francisco Vázquez's imitation, *Palmerín de Oliva* (1511) reworked traditional chivalric themes for a mass readership. By minimizing didacticism and emphasizing such features as magicians, giants, and dragons, both books became very popular and spawned numerous imitations and continuations. Chivalry books translated from other languages, such as Joanot Martorell and Martí Joan de Galba's Valencian-language *Tirant lo Blanch* (15th century; *Tirant lo Blanc*, 1984), also captivated readers. Prose manuals of chivalry, written by figures such as Don *Juan Manuel and Ramon Llull, typically used fictional accounts to instruct readers in chivalric conduct.

Many Church leaders linked books of chivalry with a perceived moral corruption in society, but the genre's popularity persisted throughout the 16th century. Even after their success waned, books of chivalry continued to exercise influence in Spanish culture. Miguel de *Cervantes's *Don Quijote de la Mancha* (Part I, 1605 and Part II, 1615; *Don Quixote*, 2003) famously parodies books of chivalry, particularly those of the *Amadís* and *Palmerín* cycles.

Chivalry literature, especially books of chivalry, played a key role in conditioning the mind-set and actions of Spanish *conquistadores* in the New World. Such oral traditions as *romances* traveled with these men and with colonizers throughout the Americas, and as a result, chivalric themes are still evident in Latin American folklore and music. The Americas also played an important role in the creation of written texts with chivalric themes. Spain's most celebrated Renaissance epic, Alonso de Ercilla's *La Araucana* (1569, 1578 and 1589; *The Araucaniad*, 1945), uses chivalric themes and codes in its depiction of the battles between the Araucanian Indians of Chile and the victorious Spanish conquerors. Though chivalry literature lost favor in Spain and the New World during the 17th and 18th centuries, the romantic movement of the early 19th century and the *Generation of 1898 briefly revived interest in chivalric heroes and themes.

R. John McCaw

See also Romance (Ballad) Tradition in the Hispanic World.

Work About:

Eisenberg, Daniel. *Romances of Chivalry in the Spanish Golden Age*. Newark, DE: Juan de la Cuesta, 1982.

Cien años de soledad (1967; One Hundred Years of Solitude, 1970)

In 2007, with the publication of a 40th anniversary commemorative edition, the *Real Academia Española (Royal Spanish Academy) paid homage to this world literature masterpiece, and honored its Colombian author Gabriel *García Márquez on his 80th birthday. Earning him a Nobel Prize in literature in 1982, this superbly crafted novel, while humorous and entertaining, reflects on the nature of reality, the human condition, and Latin American history.

Featuring a suspenseful plot with numerous events and characters, *One Hundred Years of Solitude* tells the story of six generations of Buendías who live in the fictional town of Macondo, a symbol for Colombia and Latin America in general. Replete with biblical allusions, the novel begins in a narrative style resembling the book of Genesis. After killing a man, patriarch José Arcadio Buendía, his wife Úrsula, and a group of friends leave their home in search of an unpromised land where they found the city of Macondo. Because she and José Arcadio are cousins, Ursula fears giving birth to a child with a pig's tail. Incest and solitude threaten each generation of Buendías until the last couple, who are nephew and aunt, engenders the dreaded child. An apocalyptic wind destroys Macondo as Aureliano Buendía deciphers a manuscript which, he discovers, is in fact the written history of his family. Another character, the family's alchemist friend Melquíades, has written this story, which will end with Aureliano's death at the conclusion of his reading. Thus forced to confront the fictionality of the text, the reader compellingly considers the illusion of boundaries between life and fiction.

Although myth pervades the world of Macondo, the town also incarnates the sociopolitical reality of Latin Americans' past and present. García Márquez uses the narrative technique of *magical realism to vividly interpret Latin American culture and history. The novel abounds in hyperbole and impossible events reported with objective detachment, as if commonplace. Readers familiar with Latin America recognize the historical fidelity that novelistic accounts of political violence, civil wars, rigged elections, and portrayals of liberals and conservatives present. These narrative events reveal both the general historical tradition of Latin America, and very specific proceedings such as the banana strike and massacre that took place in Ciénega, Colombia in 1928.

Among the many themes of this novel, time and intertextuality predominate. Arranged in episodic fashion, *One Hundred Years of Solitude* confounds the reader with its puzzling notions of time. In the unspecified century that the novel unfolds time is linear and sequential, but may also retreat, circle, and stop. Clearly influenced by Kafka, Jorge Luis *Borges, William Faulkner and Miguel de *Cervantes, García Márquez has in turn renovated Western literary tradition in writing a novel that critics have acclaimed as Latin America's *Don Quijote*.

Rebeca Rosell Olmedo

See also Don Quijote de la Mancha in Spanish American Literature and Culture; Nobel Prize Literature in Spanish.

Work:

García Márquez, Gabriel. *One Hundred Years of Solitude*. Trans. Gregory Rabassa. New York: Perennial Classics, 1998.

Work About:

Bell-Villada, Gene H., ed. *Gabriel García Márquez's* One Hundred Years of Solitude. New York: Oxford University Press, 2002.

Cisneros, Luis Benjamín (1837–1904)

A Peruvian statesman and novelist, Cisneros participated in the cultural and economic reinvention of Peru that occurred when civil reformists ascended during the military state's free-trade liberalism (1852–1871). When he was consulgeneral in France, Cisneros published *Julia* (1861) and *Edgardo* (1864), two brief novels that, like other romance literature of the period, resorted to sentimental romanticism, *costumbrismo* (depiction of local speech, customs, and dress), and some realist elements to propose a "regeneration" of Lima's society, then plagued by consumerism and civil wars. Focusing on middle-class domestic life, Cisneros combined didacticism and an idealization of European bourgeois domesticity to define a modern, virtuous femininity for Lima's women that would inspire men to embrace civic life. These novels foreshadow his industrial proposal of 1866, which recommended state-sponsored industrialization and a reduction in foreign imports. Back in Lima, Cisneros served as vice president for Manuel Pardo, Peru's first civilian president (1872–1876). Later afflicted with paralysis, Cisneros left government and returned to his literary production. The epic poem *Aurora amor* (1885; Dawn Love) sings to nature, progress, and Christian reason to welcome the 20th century. *De libres alas* (1900; Of Free Wings) collects his lyric poetry.

Soledad Gálvez

See also *Costumbrismo* in Spanish America.

Work By:

Edgardo, o Un joven de mi generación. Romance americano español. http://www.cervantesvirtual.com/servlet/SirveObras/35759731214026384122202/index.htm.

Julia, o Escenas de la vida en Lima. Romance. http://www.cervantesvirtual.com/servlet/SirveObras/56818406542381662843457/index.htm.

Work About:

Denegri, Francesca. *El abanico y la cigarrera. La primera generación de mujeres ilustradas.* Lima: Flora Tristán, 1996, 33–39.

Gootenberg, Paul. "Luis Benjamín Cisneros: Neoprotectionist Turn." *Imagining Development: Economic Ideas in Peru's "Fictitious Prosperity" of Guano, 1840–1880*. Berkeley: University of California Press, 1993, 111–30.

Civil War Literature in Spain

A well-known and controversial topic, the body of literature regarding (partially or completely) this conflict from the war's beginning in 1936 until today is extremely large. In the last decade, literature relating to the civil war has regained significant sociopolitical, cultural, and emotional interest. In 2006, the Socialist government declared that year as "Year of the Historical Memory" to vindicate and restore the memory of victims who tragically lost their lives during or after the civil war. Nevertheless, the majority of the Spanish political right wing, normally linked with fascist and rebel forces, insists on avoiding the past, arguing that one should leave old wounds untouched and that the past must be forgotten. However, the defeated forces, the legal democratic government at the time of the war, and their descendents claim still today the right to vindicate the past and come to terms with a wound that has never healed completely.

During the war (1936–1939), literature functioned as political propaganda at the service of two distinct forces: the Republicans; and the Nationals, representing the fascist military revolt. *Hora de España* (Hour of Spain) and *El Mono Azul* (The Blue Overalls) in the Republican zone, and *Jerarquía* (1936–1938; Hierarchy), in the National zone, represent three important wartime publications. Also of importance is the alliance of antifascist intellectuals formed by many Spanish and international artists; from this came important works like *Romancero de la Guerra de España* (1937; Ballads of the Spanish War), dedicated to the memory of Federico *García Lorca. It collects 300 poems by more than 80 authors, with Rafael *Alberti at the head.

After the war, political and ideological distinctions between the two forces were maintained by the literature written by the Nationalist victors and defeated Republicans. Dionisio Ridruejo's *Poesía en armas: Cuadernos de la Guerra Civil (1936–1939)* (1940; Poetry at Arms: Notebooks of the Civil War [1936–1939]) represents an essential example of fascist poetry. On the other hand, Dámaso *Alonso's *Hijos de la ira* (1944; *Children of Wrath*, 1971) offered a change from fascist poetry production in the 1940s. Idealization and exaltation of the war characterizes much narrative written by the victors, including Rafael García Serrano's *La fiel infantería* (1943; The Faithful

Infantry). Agustín de Foxá Torroba's novel *Madrid, de Corte a checa* (1938; Madrid, from Royal Court to Kangaroo Court) possesses a distinct fascist tone as it tells a remarkable tale concerning the first turbulent, horrific years of the civil war as seen through the eyes of young fascist José Félix. Another paradigmatic author, Josep Maria Gironella, winner of Nadal and Planeta Prizes, penned *Los cipreses creen en Dios* (1953; *The Cypresses Believe in God*, 1955)—probably the most-read novel in 20th-century Spain—as part one of a successful, high-quality civil war trilogy. *Un millón de muertos* (1961; *One Million Dead*, 1963) and *Ha estallado la paz* (1966; *Peace after War*, 1969) complete the series.

The narrative produced by those defeated in the conflict tended to be more concerned with the existential reality of the individual. Censorship and persecution forced established authors to flee Spain and produce much of their most successful, important work in exile. Key examples of distinguished exile narratives include Ramón J. *Sender's novel *Réquiem por un campesino español* (1960; *Requiem for a Spanish Peasant*, 1960) and his novel collection *Crónica del alba* (1942–1966; *Chronicle of Dawn*, 1944), Max *Aub's novel cycle *El laberinto mágico* (1943–1967; The Magical Labyrinth), and Arturo *Barea trilogy *La forja de un rebelde* (1951; *The Forging of a Rebel*, 1941–1946).

In Spain, censorship was particularly harsh in the theater, yet some playwrights, such as Antonio *Buero Vallejo, still denounced the political and social situation;

others, such as Alfonso *Sastre, condemned militarism, as in *Escuadra hacia la muerte* (1951; *The Condemned Squad*, 1961). Rafael Alberti's *Noche de guerra en el museo del Prado* (1956; *Night and War in the Prado Museum; An Etching in a Prologue and One Act*, 1968), is one of the most well-known examples of civil war theater produced in exile.

The 1966 Press Law decreased censorship, facilitating an increase of civil war literature from the perspective of those who lost the war. Ángel María de Lera's novel *Las últimas banderas* (1967; *The Last Flags*) portrays the first protagonist to fight under the Republican forces. The law also coincided with the publication of works by exiled writers (Alberti, Sender, among others). In 1975, coinciding with the end of censorship, many authors approached the civil war from a more intimate, memorial and historical perspective. Particularly notable are Carmen *Martín Gaite's novel, *El cuarto de atrás* (1975; *The Back Room*, 2000); and Carlota O'Neill's *Una mujer en la guerra de España* (1964 [México], 1974 [Spain]; *Trapped in Spain*, 1978), an appalling tale of dreadful conditions suffered by imprisoned women during and after the war.

Bertrand de Muñoz has noted that in the 1980s, literary treatment of the civil war became somewhat mythical, as exemplified by some novels, such as Jesús *Fernández Santos's *Los jinetes del alba* (1984; Riders of the Dawn) or Julio Llamazares's *Luna de lobos* (1985; Wolves' Moon). Moreover, such exemplary theatrical productions as *Las bicicletas son para el verano* (1978; Bicycles Are for the Summer), by Fernando *Fernán-Gómez, and José Sanchís Sinisterra's *¡Ay Carmela!* (1987) revisited the topic of the civil war. In the 1990s, literature about civil war themes continued to provide editorial success to many authors. Antonio *Muñoz Molina's *El jinete polaco* (1991; The Polish Rider), winner of the Planeta Prize, is a paradigmatic example.

Literary fictions continue to broach the Spanish Civil War topic in the new millennium. From 2001 to 2007, there has been a narrative "boom" with dozens of titles, some of which have enjoyed tremendous social and editorial impact, including Javier Cercas's *Soldados de Salamina* (2001; *Soldiers of Salamis*, 2003) and Alberto Méndez's novel *Los girasoles ciegos* (2004; The Blind Sunflowers). Paradoxically, literature concerning the defeated in the civil war has been somewhat self-critical, acknowledging the accountability of democratic forces and their wrongdoings in the war. However, except for very few exceptions, such as Gironella's earlier mentioned trilogy, literary works produced by victors have tended to minimize or discount their role in the conflict, despite thousands of unaccounted-for dead on the Republican side.

Outside Spain, such authors as Arthur Koestler, Graham Greene, John Dos Passos, Ernest Hemingway, and George Orwell have novelized the Spanish Civil War successfully. Hemingway's *For Whom the Bell Tolls* (1940) and Orwell's *Homage to Catalonia* (1938) represent iconic examples of the conflict from the standpoint and ideology of each author.

Juan Carlos Martín

See also Censorship and Literature in Spain; Exile Literature by Spanish Civil War Émigrés; Francoism, Fascism, and Literature in Spain; Neohistoricism in the Contemporary Spanish Novel.

Work About:

Bertrand de Muñoz, Maryse. "The Civil War in the Recent Spanish Novel, 1966–1976." *Red Flags, Black Flags: Critical Essays on the Literature of the Spanish Civil War.* Ed. John Beals Romeiser. Madrid: Porrúa Turanzas, 1982, 199–252.

Gareth, Thomas. *The Novel of the Spanish Civil War* (1936–1975). New York: Cambridge University Press, 1990.

Rosenthal, Marilyn. *Poetry of the Spanish Civil War.* New York: New York University Press, 1975.

The Spanish Civil War in Literature. Ed. Janet Pérez and Wendell Aycock. Lubbock: Texas Tech University Press, 1990.

Clarín (pseudonym of Leopoldo Alas) (1852–1901)

Author of the Spanish novelistic masterpiece *La Regenta*; (1884–1885; Eng. trans., 1984), Clarín's writing career started early—as a young man he founded, edited, and published the newspaper *Juan Ruiz.* Later in Madrid, inspired by *tertulias* (literary salons) with like-minded men, he pursued journalism in earnest, composing essays and reviews for newspapers and magazines. In an 1875 review, he used his pseudonym for the first time: Clarín, Spanish for clarion—a medieval trumpet—and also the name of a character in 17th-century dramatist Pedro *Calderón de la Barca's *La vida es sueño.* In Oviedo, he wrote influential literary reviews and essays for the national press, often in an acerbic tone that earned him many enemies and for which he was well remunerated. Clarín corresponded with many authors of the time, reviewing their works as critic and reflecting their influence in his own work.

Clarín also continued to publish short stories. In "Adiós, Cordera" (1893; Goodbye, Little Lamb) readers see the havoc brought on by increasing urbanization through the eyes of a cow. Religion also figures thematically in Clarín's writing. Although some texts are anticlerical, they are not antireligious. "El frío del Papa" (1895; "The Cold and the Pope," 1988) shows the faith of common Spaniards to be rooted in tradition, not doctrine.

In 1884–1885, Clarín published *La Regenta*, his masterpiece, followed by the novel *Su único hijo* (1890, *His Only Son*, 1981), and the drama *Teresa* (1894). Key influences of his writing include naturalism (a realism subtype that focuses on negative influences of environment and heredity) and *Krausism (a Kantian ethics-based philosophy) as well as fiction by Miguel de *Cervantes, Benito *Pérez Galdós, Leo Tolstoy, Emilia *Pardo Bazán, and others.

La Regenta follows Ana Ozores, the regent's wife, who lives in the imaginary provincial capital that is undeniably Clarín's Oviedo. Víctor Quintanar, the town's regent, is more father than husband to her. Fermín de Paz, canon of the town cathedral who serves as Ana's confessor and spiritual advisor, falls in love with her just when the city's womanizer, Álvaro Mesías, attempts to seduce Ana. After Ana becomes aware of Fermín's feelings, she surrenders to Álvaro. Both Fermín and the regent discover Ana's betrayal. In the end, the regent dies during a duel with Álvaro, and Fermín rejects Ana's attempt to repent. The novel skillfully deals with many themes, such as the stifling atmosphere of a provincial capital, the petty jealousies found there, and, most importantly, the subservient, passive roles women were supposed to play and the punishment meted out to those who transgressed traditional boundaries.

Matthew A. Wyszynski

See also Novel in Spain: 1700–1900.

Work By:

His Only Son. Trans. Julie Jones. Baton Rouge: Louisiana State University Press, 1981.
La Regenta. Trans. John Rutherford. Harmondsworth: Penguin, 1984.
The Moral Tales. Trans. Kenneth Stackhouse. Fairfax, VA: The George Mason University Press, 1988.

Work About:

Jaffe, Catherine. "In Her Father's Library: Women's Reading in *La Regenta*." *Revista de Estudios Hispánicos* 39 (2005): 3–25.
Valis, Noël. "Hysteria and Historical Context in *La Regenta*." *Revista Hispánica Moderna* 53 (2000): 25–51.
Valis, Noël. "Order and Meaning in Clarín's *La Regenta*." *Novel: A Forum on Fiction* 16.3 (Spring 1983): 246–58.

Clavel, Ana (1961–)

Part of an exciting new breed of Mexican writers, her short stories and novels focus on women's sociohistorical marginalization and female sexuality, similar to other Mexican women writers. However, Clavel's writing breaks with traditional themes, narrative genres, and techniques. Her short story collections include *Fuera de escena* (1984; Out of the Picture), *Amorosos de atar* (1992; Mad Lovers), and *Paraísos trémulos* (2002; Trembling Paradise). Her first novel, *Los deseos y su sombra* (1999; *Desire and Its Shadows*; 2006) was followed by *Cuerpo náufrago* (2005; *Shipwrecked Body*, 2008), and *Las Violetas son flores del deseo* (2007; Violets Are Flowers of Desire). The last two works are particularly innovative in terms of themes and the inclusion of a "multimedia" element. *Cuerpo náufrago* tells the story of Antonia, who one morning awakens transformed into a man, leading to his/her uninhibited sexual exploits. *Las Violetas son flores del deseo* explores the incestuous desires of protagonist Julián Mercader for his daughter Violeta. Instead of committing the heinous crime, Julián, who owns a doll factory, creates a set of dolls called las Violetas that he then sells to male clients. Most uniquely, both novels from inception were conceived as the basis of wider "multimedia projects." In these, Clavel collaborated with various artists, photographers, and performers to create art installation, video-performance, and photographic exhibitions that have been displayed in various cultural centers of Mexico City.

Jane Elizabeth Lavery

Work By:

Desire and Its Shadows. Trans. Jay Misko-wiec. Minneapolis: Aliform, 2006.

Shipwrecked Body. Trans. Jay Miskowiec. Minneapolis: Aliform, 2008.

http://anaclavel.com/.

http://www.violetasfloresdeldeseo.com/.

Work About:

Lavery, Jane. "Beyond the Shadows of Silence: Self, Desire and (Dis)embodiment in *Los deseos y su sombra* by Ana Clavel." *Modern Language Review* 102: 4 (2007): 1055–70.

Codorniz, La Literary Magazine (1941–1978; The Quail)

This Spanish graphic humor publication sprang from the successful civil war comic magazine *La Ametralladora* (1937; The Machine Gun). It is worth noting that, in times of hunger, the quail represented sustenance for the soul. In postwar Spain, *La Codorniz* served as inspiration to such other satirical, highly critical magazines as *El Papus* (1972–1987), *Hermano Lobo* (1972–1976), *Por favor* (1974–1978), and *El Jueves* (1977). Founded by writer Miguel *Mihura, it initially displayed an absurd, avant-garde humor for which society was not ready yet (1941–1944). Such writers as Tono, Ramón *Gómez de la Serna, Edgar Neville, and Enrique *Jardiel Poncela contributed during this period. Later (1956–1965), Álvaro de Laiglesia directed the magazine; under his command, the publication's social satire and realistic humor, laced with irony and parody of manners, offered a more critical glimpse into Francisco Franco's repressive regime. The most popular of its humor and illustration collaborators at this time were Mingote, Gila, Chumy Chúmez, Perich, and Forges. During its final years, the magazine encountered problems with *censorship and received multiple fines, warnings and, finally, suspensions in 1973 and 1975. When Franco's regime ended and the magazine competed freely with other, more combative publications, *La Codorniz* failed to appeal to a wider audience. That fact, plus economic limitations, forced its closure in 1977.

Judith García-Quismondo García

See also Civil War Literature in Spain; Francoism, Fascism, and Literature in Spain.

Work By:

La Codorniz: Antología, 1941–1978. Comp. Ángel Antonio Mingote, Chumy Chúmez et al. Madrid: Edaf, 1998.

Work About:

Llera Ruiz, José Antonio. *El humor verbal y visual de 'La Codorniz.'* Madrid: Instituto de la Lengua Española del Consejo Superior de Investigaciones Científicas, 2003.

Collazos, Óscar (1942–)

This novelist, journalist, and essayist was strongly influenced by childhood years spent in Bahía Solano, one of Colombia's most neglected areas. The years he lived in this Pacific region form an important part of his literary production; there he was exposed to the social injustices suffered by most of its inhabitants for many years. Upon moving to Bogotá in the early 1960s, he became acquainted with important cultural figures like Germán Vargas, Marta *Traba, and Germán Espinosa. During this time, Collazos publishes his first innovative narratives, in which characters struggle with a loss of connection to their homeland and the institutions of family and government. These topics become the core of his narrative.

One of his most recognized novels, *Fugas* (1990; Escapes) presents a modern *picaresque tale. Born to a lowly prostitute, protagonist Fabricio Ele manages to ascend the social ladder and become rich and famous by selfishness, lying, and exploiting other people. Through Fabricio, Collazos delivers a scathing critique of today's ruthless social climbers.

Collazos has also worked as a journalist for important Colombian newspapers like *El Espectador* and *El Tiempo*. His articles express the same criticisms that characterize his narrative.

Jaime A. Orrego

Work By:

Fugas. Bogotá: Planeta, 1990.

Work About:

Herrera, Marcos Fabián. " 'Ni héroe ni villano: Simplemente, un escritor con conciencia de época.' Entrevista con Oscar Collazos." *Espéculo: Revista de Estudios Literarios* 33 (July 2006): no pagination. http://www.ucm.es/info/especulo/numero33/ocollazo.html.

Colombia: History, Culture, and Literature

Situated in northwestern South America, Colombia is one of two Latin American countries with land touching both the Atlantic and Pacific Oceans. Its population of roughly 45,644,000 occupies a total area of 707,682 square miles. The nation shares borders with Ecuador and Peru to the south, Venezuela and Brazil to the east, and Panama to the west. Tropical and mountain regions provide a diverse climate. Santafé de Bogotá is the official full name of the capital city. The country's most recognized agricultural products are flowers and coffee; natural resources include emeralds, gold, coal, nickel, and petroleum.

Before Spanish colonization commenced (1510), different indigenous communities inhabited the territory, the Chibchas being the largest group. During the Spanish colonial period, Colombia, Ecuador, and Venezuela constituted the Viceroyalty of Nueva Granada, established in 1740. Colombia's independence from Spain was initiated by Antonio Nariño on July 10, 1810. Even though this date is still celebrated, independence was not officially declared until after the 1819 Battle of Boyacá, led by Simón *Bolívar.

A legacy of civil confrontations and uprisings that marked the postindependence period seems to endure even today in conflicts with neighboring countries. During the past several decades, Colombia's complex sociopolitical situation has also contended with such national subversive groups as FARC (Revolutionary Armed Forces of Colombia) and AUC (United Self-Defense Forces of Colombia), among others. The former, a self-described Marxist–Leninist revolutionary organization, is the nation's largest guerrilla group; the latter was a civilian-established, right-wing paramilitary organization that surrendered its weapons in 2008.

Colombians display great passion for cuisine, sports, music, art, and literature. Gastronomy changes from region to region; Santafé de Bogotá's signature dish, the *ajiaco santafereño*, is considered the national dish. This soup consists of three types of potato, chicken, corn, capers, and *guascas* (an aromatic herb), and is usually served with rice, avocado, and heavy cream on top. The Atlantic coast originated the *sancocho*, another hearty soup made of different vegetables, plantains, yucca, potatoes, and either beef, chicken, or fish. Another celebrated Colombian specialty is *bandeja paisa*, a filling meat, bean, vegetables, egg, avocado, bacon, and rice dish from the Antioquia region.

With regard to music, such internationally acclaimed singers as Shakira, Carlos Vives, Juanes, Juan Fernando Fonseca, and Andrés Cabas have developed new musical styles that combine rhythms from sources ranging from Colombian folk music to pop. Vives's and Fonseca's songs exhibit different styles, but most form part of new genre of *vallenato* (a type of folk music) known as ethnic fusion period. Cabas's songs are classified as *cumbia*, *fandango*, and Latin rock. Shakira's and Juanes's songs have been classified as

Latin pop. These singers celebrate their Latino roots and communicate Colombian culture in music.

Outstanding sports figures include Santiago Botero Echeverry, world champion cyclist in the 2002 individual time trials; weightlifter María Isabel Urrutia, 2000 Summer Olympics gold medalist in the women's 75 kilograms; Carlos "El Pibe" Valderrama, a *soccer player who was captain of the national team in three World Cups (1990, 1994,1998) and played for 13 years (1985–1998) on different national teams.

In art and literature, 19th-century Colombian cultural representations exhibited great concern with ancestral roots and the nation's future. *El Caballero de Rauzán* (1887; The Gentleman from Rauzán) by Felipe Pérez (1836–1891) portrayed relationships between masters and slaves, particularly on the Atlantic coast. In similar fashion, Juan José Nieto (1805–1866), in the novel *Ingermina* (1844), showed the indigenous man as noble savage and the conqueror as brave warrior. *Episodios novelescos . . . la insurrección de los comuneros* (1887; Novelistic Episodes . . . the Comuneros's Insurrection) and the drama *Las víctimas de la guerra* (1884; The Victims of War), both by Soledad Acosta de Samper (1833–1913), exemplify concern with 19th-century events and remain central to understanding today's political conflicts. José María Vargas Vila (1860–1933) openly opposed Catholic Church influences on government ideology and criticized U.S. imperialism in essays included in his book *Ante los bárbaros: el yanki; he ahí el enemigo* (1917; Against the Barbarians; the

Yankee; Here's the Enemy). Finally, writings by Miguel Antonio Caro (1843–1909) provided the basis for the national Constitution of 1886, which remained valid for over a century.

Political affairs figure prominently in works by 20th- and 21st-century authors and artists. Among excellent Colombian writers towers Gabriel *García Márquez (1927) and his novels *La mala hora* (1952; In the Evil Hour), *El Coronel no tiene quien le escriba* (1958; No One Writes to the Colonel), *Cien años de soledad* (1967; *One Hundred Years of Solitude*, 1970), which in different ways parody and sarcastically expose the problems of peasants who used to work for international banana companies, and of soldiers or colonels retired from the national army and waiting endlessly for their retirement pension. Numerous other authors voice concern with the sociopolitical situation and, like García Márquez, use humor to present national conflicts and portray individuals who exalt cultural heritage. Such writers include Germán Espinosa (1938–2007), with such novels as *La tejedora de coronas* (1982; The Weaver of Crowns) and *El signo del pez* (1987; The Sign of the Fish); Álvaro *Mutis (1923–) in such novels as *La nieve del Almirante* (1986; The Snow of the Admiral); Laura *Restrepo (1950–), with novels like *La multitude errante* (2001; A Tale of Dispossessed); and Santiago Gamboa (1965–), in *Perder es cuestión de método* (1997; Losing Is a Question of Method).

Painters including D'bora Arango (1907–2005), Rafael Sáenz (1910–1998) and Pedro Nel Gómez (1899–1984) all titled one of their paintings *La República* (The Republic), aiming to present different visions of Colombia. In Arango's painting (1960), the nation is seen as a woman being destroyed by vultures that devour her internal organs. This most probably continues *Sáenz's work; in 1953, he depicted the nation as a depressed, solitary woman. Gómez initiated the idea in 1934 in his portrayal of different citizens, organized by ethnic groups, immersed in a chaotic situation in which postindependence conflicts have not ended.

This concern with in national conflicts is evident throughout the 20th century and at the beginning of the 21st century. Among the century's remarkable works figure paintings like Alejandro Obregón's *Estudiante muerto* (1956; The Dead Student), which illustrates how students and popular leaders lost their lives during political and social activism in public universities. Another notorious painter, Fernando Botero (1932–), has used his paintings to express his concern with national problems, as in his painting in 1999 of FARC leader Manuel Marulanda (c. 1930–2008), alias *el Tirofijo*, "Sure-Shot." This painting symbolizes the national conflict: Botero's shows its traces by putting a red towel upon Marulanda's shoulders to subtly reclaim the blood of the many civilians who have died at the hand of subversive groups.

Today, Colombian artists focus on the contemporary crises of social violence, displacement of citizens, subversive groups, internal wars, and the victims of drug dealers. The current crisis appears also in the work of Jaime Abril (1968–), as in *Homenaje a los nacidos en combate* (1998; Homage to Those Born in Combat), which demonstrates the artist's sensitivity to historical and present-day conditions that mark the national situation. Finally, some contemporary artists not only use paintings and sculptures to reflect national conflicts, they also employ sound and light to create the illusion of warfare, or of drug dealer refugees, thereby exposing and rejecting these conflicts. Such work is presented by means of *instalaciones* (installations) staged in galleries, national museums, and public spaces.

Yudis Contreras

See also Appendix B for other entries related to Colombia.

Work About:

Safford, Frank, and Palacios, Marco. *Colombia*. New York: Oxford University Press, 2002.

Williams, Raymond. *The Colombian Novel, 1844–1987*. Austin: University of Texas Press, 1991.

Colombian Exile Writers

Like millions of their compatriots, writers leave Colombia for varied reasons ranging from a search for professional advancement (literary or otherwise) to concerns for personal safety amid the country's recurring armed conflicts. This heterogeneous group of authors thus differs from those who fled dictatorships in other Latin American nations. However, as one could argue about Latin American literature in general, many of the canonical works of Colombian literature have been written either outside the country or by authors who have spent a significant portion of their lives abroad.

The itinerant, ill-fortuned Porfirio Barba Jacob (born Miguel Ángel Osorio Benítez, 1883–1942) epitomizes the life of an exiled writer. Barba left Colombia at age 23, and spent 20 years in over a half-dozen countries, working as a journalist and influencing numerous literary circles. Not surprisingly, his work elaborates on the idea of journey, as in his famous poem "Futuro" (no date; Future), where the poetic voice assimilates itself to a flame in the wind. In 1930, he took up permanent residence in Mexico.

Many Colombian writers have been drawn to New York. Rafael Pombo (1833–1912) lived in the city for 17 years, a decisive period for his literary creation. A romantic poet, he cultivated his interest in children's literature when Appleton & Co. hired him to translate nursery rhymes into Spanish. Generations of Colombian children since have recited his popular poems on the adventures of such stock characters as "Rin Rin Renacuajo" (Rin Rin, the Tadpole) and "Michín, el Gato Bandido" (Michin, the Bandit Cat).

After an initial exile in Venezuela, bestselling author and polemicist José María Vargas Vila (1860–1933) lived in New York for 15 years. Internationally renowned for the woeful love story of *Aura o las violetas* (1887; Aura, or, the Violets), while in the city he befriended Cuban revolutionary writer José *Martí; founded the literary magazine *Némesis*; and published *Ante los bárbaros* (1902; Before the Barbarians), a fierce diatribe against U.S. imperialism. In 1905, he settled definitively in Spain.

Alirio Díaz Guerra (1862–? after 1933?) followed a similar path. An acquaintance of poet José Asunción *Silva, he enjoyed a privileged position in the intellectual milieus of Bogotá and, later, Caracas. Ultimately, he lived in New York for more than 30 years in relative anonymity. He wrote the earliest known Spanish-language novel of immigration to the United States, the semi-autobiographical *Lucas Guevara* (1914; Eng. trans., 2003), which narrates the misfortunes of an immigrant whose American dream turns into nightmare.

Such a motif appears in more recent work. *Paraíso Travel* (2001; *Paradise Travel* 2006) by Jorge Franco (1962–) follows a couple of hopefuls who, seeking opportunities, become separated and face the adversities of living as undocumented immigrants in the United States. Jaime Manrique (1949–), the most prominent Latino writer of Colombian origin, gives a comical turn to the theme in the English-language *Latin Moon in Manhattan* (1992), which tells the story of a transplanted gay *bogotano* poet trying to find his place in the city.

Various European cities inspire similar narrations. Decades apart, both *El buen salvaje* (1966; The Bon Sauvage) by Eduardo *Caballero Calderón (1910–1993) and *El síndrome de Ulises* (2005; Ulysses Syndrome) by Santiago Gamboa (1965–) recount the lives of young Colombians in Paris who struggle with their literary aspirations. Representing a different aspect of the broad spectrum of experiences of Latin Americans abroad, *Nada importa* (2000; Nothing Matters) by Álvaro Robledo (1977) offers a light-hearted story on the European road trip of a Colombian and his two Danish friends.

The precariousness of life in a foreign land translates into unique imagery in the short story collection *Doce cuentos peregrinos* (1992; *Strange Pilgrims* 1993) by Gabriel *García Márquez (1928), the country's foremost writer. In "The Trail of Your Blood in the Snow," a young woman from Cartagena pinches her finger with a rose while on her honeymoon trip. She eventually dies as, inexplicably, her finger bleeds continuously from Madrid to Paris, leaving behind the trail that gives occasion to the story's title.

García Márquez lives abroad himself, having settled in Mexico City in the 1970s. An important hub for Colombian writers, Mexico also hosts Álvaro *Mutis (1923–), Fernando *Vallejo (1942–), and Laura *Restrepo (1950–), who have all explored the theme of exile in different ways. Mutis elaborates on the topic through his character "Maqroll the Lookout," a sailor whose wanderlust has philosophic overtones and whose adventures span many of the author's novels. Vallejo's multivolume autobiography, *El río del tiempo* (1987–1993; The River of Time), narrates his years abroad, while his most famous novel to date, *La virgen de los sicarios* (1994; *Our Lady of the Assassins*, 2001), recounts the story of a grammarian who, after years in exile, returns to Medellín and falls in love with a teenage hitman. Restrepo's historical novel *La isla* *de la pasión* (1989; *Isle of Passion*, 2005) follows Mexican settlers who all but perished during the Mexican Revolution (1910–1920) when they were abandoned on a remote island in the Pacific Ocean.

Other prominent writers who have spent significant portions of their lives abroad include Marvel *Moreno (1939–1995), Héctor Abad Faciolince (1958–), Luis Fayad (1945–), Tomás González (1950–), and Juan Gabriel Vásquez (1973–). Long before globalization as it is known today, the wealth of experiences of these writers and their literary reflections on exile speak to the reach of Colombian literature beyond national borders.

Héctor M. Hoyos

Work By:

Barba Jacob, Porfirio. *Poemas*. Bogotá: Procultura, 1985.

Díaz Guerra, Alirio. *Lucas Guevara*. Trans. Ethriam Cash Brammer. Houston: Arte Público, 2003.

Franco, Jorge. *Paradise Travel*. Trans. Katherine Silver. New York: Farrar, Straus and Giroux, 2007.

Work About:

Browitt, Jeff. "Sexual anxiety in Alirio Díaz Guerra's *Lucas Guevara*." *Hispania* 88.4 (2005): 677–86.

Márceles Daconte, Eduardo. "Narradores colombianos en Estados Unidos." *Literatura y cultura: narrativa colombiana del siglo XX*. Ed. María Mercedes Jaramillo, Betty Osorio and Ángela Robledo. Vol. 2. Bogotá: Ministerio de Cultura, 2000, 617–31.

Colombian Modernist Writing: 1885–1915

Literature of this period presents a mixture of elements that reflects the tumultuous intellectual discussions being held at the end of the 19th century, a time of rupture and antagonism. The new literature reflected the strong impact of the industrial revolution in a country where modernity was mostly a dream; modernist writing was a personal, historical, and literary search. In Colombia, most fiction writers at that time represented very traditional literary trends, such as romanticism; these authors often were philologists or grammarians, closely attached to classical styles. Modernist writing aimed to challenge this literature, which also meant defying the representatives of the most powerful political and cultural currents.

Modernist ideas opened up new possibilities in every field of writing. Writers rebelled against fixed criteria, undermined the dominant rhythms, and popularized new poetic forms where free verse dominated; their writings renewed language. Along with the most traditional Spanish forms, there appeared neologisms (invented words), gallicisms (French-derived words), and anglicisms (words adapted from English). Literary critics battled the new movement because it subverted punctuation and grammar rules. Poems and novels preferred cosmopolitan over local settings. Authors questioned their role as intellectuals vis-à-vis the sociopolitical independence of their nations and any kind of traditional political, religious, or sociocultural power. The mass popularization of newspapers also influenced these writers, making them care more about readers' perceptions of their work. Modernists demanded to be considered professionals, and local intellectuals began to question their personal situation in relation to the local and global environment. With growing concern that the technological advances achieved by other nations were not reaching Latin America, and worry regarding the increasing U.S. influence, modernists asserted their role as global leaders. All these aspects were discussed and analyzed in their literary production.

José Asunción *Silva (1865–1896) was the first Colombian writer to adopt the modernist style. His poetry is considered a precursor of the *modernismo* popularized some years later by Nicaragua's Rubén *Darío. Silva's *Nocturno* (Nocturnal) poems opened a magical perception of sensorial combinations never produced before by any Colombian writer, gaining him recognition as one of the finest Spanish-language poets. His poetic work was complemented by *De sobremesa* (1925; *After-Dinner Conversation*, 2005), the most representative novel of Latin American decadence, a modernist prose style. The novel follows typical characteristics of this style, including aestheticism, dandyism, and necrophilia. Silva's text transcended European decadent novels by adding two new characteristics: an oral element, through which protagonist Juan Fernández reads his own adventures while in Europe; and a particular passion for life. Almost a century passed before the novel, written in 1896 (almost 30 years before its publication), was officially accepted in the modernist canon.

Prose author José María Vargas Vila (1860–1933) produced short novels that became the first Latin American best sellers; his literary writings influenced most popular political movements of his day, including the Mexican Revolution (1910–1920). His most widely known writings were political pamphlets defending liberal ideas and attacking tyranny and its representatives. His novel *Aura o las violetas* (1892; Aura or the Violets) was adapted for the theater; *Ibis* (1889), however, guaranteed his inclusion in the modernist movement. Also known as the "Suicidal Bible" due to many suicide stories indirectly related to its reading, it is the first novel Vargas Vila truly liked. A subversive work, it questions the powerful influence of both the Catholic Church and the Colombian conservative political party ruling the country, and even the representation of women at the time, constituting a clear transition to what was considered modernism in other Western traditions.

Other important representatives of Colombian modernism include essayist and literary critic Baldomero Sanín Cano, prose author José María Rivas Groot, and poets Guillermo León *Valencia and Porfirio Barba Jacob (1883–1942), best remembered for his immortal poem *Canción de la vida profunda* (1907; Song of the Deep Life).

Cenaida Alvis Barranco

See also Modernismo in Hispanic Literature.

Work About:

Fernández-Medina, Nicolás. "The Modern Self as Subject: The Structure of Crisis in José Asunción Silva's *De sobremesa*." *Latin American Literary Review* 34.68 (July 2006): 59–82.

Jrade, Cathy L. *Modernismo, Modernity, and the Development of Spanish American Literature.* Austin: University of Texas Press, 1998.

Molloy, Sylvia. "Voice Snatching: *De sobremesa*, Hysteria, and the Impersonation of Marie Bashkirtseff." *Latin American Literary Review* 25.50 (1997): 11–29.

Pérez, Rolando. "Irony, Love, and Political Economy in José Asunción Silva's *De Sobremesa*." *Hispanófila* 150 (May 2007): 87–102.

Colombian Women Writers: 1950 to Present

Women writing during the 1950s in Colombia could look to only a very few precursors, for conditions during the nation's period of la *Violencia* (1948–1957) and the misogyny and paternalism among intellectuals strongly inhibited development of a tradition of women novelists. One important model, Elisa Mújica (1916–2003), incorporated avant-garde techniques in her first novel, *Los dos tiempos* (1949; Two Times). Despite these conditions, during the 1940s and 1950s a generation of women poets unabashedly developed among themselves an intimate and sentimental poetry. Known as the neoromantics, the principle members of this group include Matilde Espinosa (1910–2008), Meira Delmar (1922–2009), Maruja Vieira (1922–), and Dora Castellanos (1924–).

The 1960s and 1970s constituted a seminal period that nurtured several thematic tendencies in women's narrative along with consolidation of the novel. Mújica's *Catalina* (1963) and *La cisterna* (1971; The Cistern) by Rocío Vélez de Piedrahita (1926–) question women's role in patriarchal society and experiment with temporal relativity and oneiric narration. A second tendency emerges with a new generation of authors who capture the free spirit of these years; the novel *El hostigante verano de los dioses* (1963; The Harassing Summer of the Gods) by Fanny *Buitrago (1943–) scandalized conservatives for its frankly depicted treatment of sexuality among a group of young artists (which many identify with the Nadaista poetry group). Albalucía *Ángel's (1939–) *Los girasoles en invierno* (1970; Sunflowers in Winter) narrates the adventures of a Colombian singer in Europe, free from family ties. Ángel also wrote *Dos veces Alicia* (1973; Alice Twice Over), an experimental metafictional novel that interweaves the detective genre, the writing of a novel, and the *Alice in Wonderland* tale.

In the same spirit, Mújica's earlier-mentioned *Los dos tiempos* combines a discourse of political awakening, the history of violence racking Colombia, and the denunciation of social inequality that will become the third general subject in women's writing. Buitrago's play *El hombre de paja* (1964; The Straw Man) tells the story of a civil war refugee; Flor Romero (1933–) portrays the story of a guerrilla in the novel *Mi Capitán Fabián Sicachá* (1967; My Captain Fabián Sicachá); and Ángel's *Estaba la pájara pinta sentada en el verde limón* (1975; The Painted Bird Perched on the Green Lemon Tree) depicts a woman's search for identity in the aftermath of *la Violencia* while reinterpreting Colombia's history.

In poetry, authors broke with the sentimentalism of the previous generation; *Vainas y otros poemas* (1972; A Pain in the Ass and Other Poems) by María Mercedes *Carranza (1945–) is marked by disillusion while *La mujer del esquimal* (1980; The Eskimo's Wife) by Anabel Torres (1948–) employs detached humor.

The 1980s witnessed a literary explosion of works by women: Ángel's experimental narrative poem *Las andariegas* (1984; Women Wayfarers) received international critical acclaim for its mythical celebration of women as a collective and the deep influence of French feminism. Playwright Patricia Ariza (1945–), who since the 1960s had participated in the collective work by La Candelaria Theater, wrote her first plays during this period. Ariza's theater questions established cultural, historical, and political notions and reflects Colombia's social degradation. In *El viento y la ceniza* (1986; Ashes and Wind) she redefines the conquest by portraying a failed conquistador obsessed with finding El Dorado.

The short story *Algo tan feo en la vida de una señora bien* (1981; Something So Ugly in the Life of a Well-Bred Woman)

by Marvel *Moreno (1939–1995) stands out for its construction of an alternative Caribbean imaginary; Carmen Cecilia Suárez's (1946–) collection *Un vestido rojo para bailar boleros* (1987; A Red Dress for Dancing Boleros) caused a stir for portraying sex from the perspective of a sexually liberated woman.

In 1985, poet Agueda Pizarro (1941–) founded an important venue for Colombia's women poets: the Encuentro de Poetas Colombianas. Each year, renowned poets have participated, including Guiomar Cuesta (1950–), known for her feminist poetic voice in *Cábala: círculo, madre tierra* (1989; Cabbala: Circle, Mother, Earth), and Renata Durán (1950–) whose inward, erotic expression excels in *Muñeca Rota* (1981; Broken Doll).

The most important novel from this period is Moreno's *En diciembre llegaban las brisas* (1987; In December When the Winds Began to Blow), a neobaroque retrospective portrayal of three generations of Barranquilla women and their violent struggle to survive in a male world. The novel *Fiesta en Teusaquillo* (1981; A Party in Teusaquillo) by Helena Araújo (1934–) depicts the decadence of Bogotá's high society and evokes the political and social history of party rivalry and civil war in the nation. Both Araújo and poet Montserrat Ordóñez (1941–2001) later became pioneers in criticism of women's literature.

The 1990s in Colombia saw significant social, political, and cultural changes, including the acceptance of the nation's multiculturality. In this decade, poet and playwright Piedad Bonnet (1951–) stands out. Bonnet's poetry collection *El hilo de* *los días* (1995; The Thread through the Days) is a meditation on the poetic reality of daily life. Regarding the novel, Ana María Jaramillo (1956–) in *Las horas secretas* (1990; The Secret Hours) and Laura *Restrepo (1950–) in *La multitud errante* (1999; A Tale of the Dispossessed) return to the recent history of violence and its consequences, confirming that sociopolitical conditions have been a primary influence on women's writing in Colombia.

During the first decade of the 21st century, Colombian women writers have gained international recognition. Restrepo's novel *Delirio* (2004; *Delirium*, 2007), which combines mystery novel, love story, and family saga against a backdrop of the illegal drug trade subculture, won the Alfaguara Prize. Finally, Ángela Becerra (1957–), author of *Ella que lo tuvo todo* (2009; She Who Had Everything), earned the Planeta–Casa de América Prize in 2009.

Yohainna Abdala-Mesa

Work About:

Araújo, Helena. "Oppression, Tradition, Transgression in some Colombian Female Novelists." *Splintering Darkness: Latin American Women Writers in Search of themselves*. Ed. Lucía Guerra Cunningham. Pittsburgh: Latin American Literary Review Press, 1990, 131–42.

Ordóñez, Montserrat. "One Hundred Years of Unread Writing: Soledad Acosta, Elisa Mújica, Marvel Moreno." *Knives and Angels. Women Writers in Latin America*. Ed. Susan Bassnett. London: Zed, 1990, 132–44.

Osorio, Myriam. "Retracing Genealogy: Mothers and Daughters in *Las andariegas* by Albalucía Ángel." *Relocating Identities in Latin American Cultures*. Ed. Elizabeth Montes. Calgary: University of Calgary Press, 2006, 99–116.

Utley, Gregory. "The Development of Subjectivity in Fanny Buitrago's *Señora de la miel*." *Hispanic Journal* 25.1–2 (2004): 131–43.

Colón, Jesús (1901–1974)

This self-taught Puerto Rican intellectual chronicled the racism, injustice, degrading living conditions, and consumerism that Puerto Ricans encountered in New York City. His poems and prose vignettes belong to the testimonial genre, and his analysis of Puerto Rican identity in that context represents an important early contribution to the concept of *Nuyorican identity. Although he published only one prose collection, his many articles and columns in Spanish- and English-language newspapers span over 40 years.

During his childhood on the island—hours he spent at the nearby cigar factory, listening through a window to the *lector* (individuals hired to read newspapers and books to factory workers as they rolled cigars)—taught Colón about a world beyond the island. At age 16, he stowed away on a ship bound for New York City, where he came face to face with discrimination, exploitation, and deplorable working and living conditions.

Padilla Aponte observes three stages in Colón's writing. He first appeared in

Spanish-language newspapers like *Gráfica*, read by semieducated Puerto Rican immigrants. Writings of the first period (1927–1935) use such pseudonyms as Miquis Tiquis and express resentment and outrage over unjust treatment, particularly in poems in colloquial Spanish, incorporating Anglicisms. During the second period, from roughly 1943 to 1946, Colón's belief in socialism's is seen in his efforts to educate workers and organize the Puerto Rican community. These writings, still in Spanish, are more serious in nature, use more formal language, and appear under his real name.

From 1955 to 1971, Colón began publishing in the English-language communist newspaper *Daily Worker*. The scope of his subject widened to include concerns of minorities beyond U.S. borders. This period also saw publication of *A Puerto Rican in New York and Other Sketches* (1961), 55 stories of pivotal moments in his life. Posthumously, a second English-language volume of Colón's published and unpublished writings appeared under the title *The Way It Was, and Other Writings* (1993).

Maureen Ihrie

Work By:

"Lo que el pueblo me dice . . ." Crónicas de la colonia puertorriqueña en Nueva York. Ed., intro. Edwin Karli Padilla Aponte. Houston: Arte Público, 2001.

Work About:

Irizarry Rodríguez, José M. "Evolving Identities." *Writing Off the Hyphen. New Critical Perspectives on the Literature of the Puerto Rican Diaspora*. Ed. José L. Torres-Padilla and Carmen Haydée Rivera. Seattle and London: University of Washington Press, 2008, 31–51.

Colonial Baroque Writing in Spanish America

The baroque literary style in colonial Spanish America, known also as *barroco de indias* (baroque of the Indies), was imported from 17th-century Spain, when baroque aesthetics flourished. One can only understand the phenomenon in Spanish America by first acknowledging its origins: the poetry of Luis de *Góngora, master of the Spanish baroque. His literary style, filled with neologisms, word play, elegant wit, and striking erudition, inspired the term *gongorismo* (gongorism) to characterize this mode of writing, which was adopted by other Spanish poets of the time.

While baroque writing tends to align itself with poetry, it can apply to prose. The baroque favors style over subject matter and reflects duality: it is cerebral yet sensual; it highlights beauty in ugliness. Its form revels in exaggeration and complexity; its tone reflects bitterness, desperation, and tension; thematically, it prefers obscure allusions and contrasts. The predominant theme that deception masks all reality consequentially makes earthly life an illusion. Truth is only discovered in death. As a result, the poetic voice frequently laments, suffers, and criticizes the world he inhabits or the woman he loves. The poet frequently uses metaphor, hyperbole, and repetition to express these frustrations.

Prominent colonial baroque writers include Mateo Rosas de Oquendo, Juan del Valle y Caviedes, and Carlos Sigüenza y Góngora. Rosas de Oquendo's *Sátira hecha por Mateo Rosas de Oquendo a las cosas que pasan en el Pirú año de 1598* (1598; Satire Written by Mateo Rosas de Oquendo about Things Happening in Peru in the Year 1598) presents a double entendre poetic critique of Peruvian social structures. Juan del Valle y Caviedes, although born in Spain, lived in Peru during his formative years and, like Rosas de Oquendo, was a formidable satirist. His *Diente del Parnaso* (1683; Tooth of Parnassus), a collection of some 47 poems, criticizes medical doctors of the time. Unlike the two aforementioned authors, Sigüenza y Góngora is primarily a prose writer. *Los Infortunios de Alonso Ramírez* (1690; *The Misadventures of Alonso Ramirez*, 1962), his most outstanding text, narrates a picaresque-like tale about a Puerto Rican boy aspiring to a better life who is instead captured by pirates.

Colonial baroque writing reaches its zenith with Sor Juana Inés de la *Cruz. Her most noteworthy baroque pieces include *Primero Sueño* (1692; *First Dream*, 1988), *Respuesta a Sor Filotea* (1691; *The Answer*, 1994), and the renowned poem "Hombres necios" (1680; "Foolish Men"). Today, Sor Juana is considered the most recognizable figure of the colonial baroque. At a time when women did not traditionally produce literature, she used baroque style to develop philosophical essays, feminist

poems, and religious and secular plays that now represent the cornerstone of the Hispanic literary canon.

Bonnie L. Gasior

Work About:

Spadaccini, Nicholas and Luis Martín-Estudillo, eds. *Hispanic Baroques: Reading Cultures in Context*. Nashville: Vanderbilt University Press, 2005.

Colonialism and Anticolonialism in Spanish American Literature

Colonization of Latin America constitutes an essential component of its condition today. A large body of heterogeneous texts, in the form of chronicles, histories, and letters, has been written over the centuries that attests to the events of colonization. One of the earliest texts, *Relación acerca de las antigüedades de los indios* by Fray Ramón Pané (1498; *An Account of the Antiquities of the Indians*, 1999) records the extermination of the Taíno people, the original inhabitants of Hispaniola (present-day Haiti and Dominican Republic). Texts that deal with the events of the Spanish conquest in the Meso-American region include Hernán Cortés's *Cartas de relación* (written c. 1519–1925; *Letters*, 1986); Bernal *Díaz del Castillo's *Historia verdadera de la conquista de la Nueva España* (1639; *The Conquest of New Spain*, 1963); and the monumental work of Fray Bernardino de *Sahagún, the *Historia General de las Cosas de la Nueva España* (1547–1558; *General History of the Things of New Spain*,

1950–1982), also known as the *Florentine Codex*—which is based on the knowledge of indigenous informants. Mestizo chronicle writers have also composed such histories as Fernando de *Alva Ixtlilxóchitl's *Historia Chichimeca* (1610–1640; Chichimeca History). Bartolomé de las Casas, the "defender of the Indians," authored *Brevísima relación de la destrucción de las Indias Occidentales* (1539–1542; A Very Short Account of the Destruction of the Western Indies), which denounces the mistreatment of indigenous peoples.

In South America, the best-known chronicles are Pedro de Cieza de León's *Crónica del Perú* (1554; Peru's Chronicle), mestizo author el Inca *Garcilaso de la Vega's *Comentarios Reales de los Incas* (1609; trans. as *Royal Commentaries*, 2006, and *General History of Peru*, 2006), and Amerindian Guamán Poma de Ayala's *Primer nueva corónica y buen gobierno* (1615; First New Chronicle and Good Government), which is unique because it contains 398 drawings. These texts chronicle the events of the conquest and subsequent colonization, and the establishment of viceroyalties—administrative structures that governed the colonies. Some writings, particularly those by indigenous or Mestizo authors, address the indigenous resistance to colonization that surfaced immediately. Thus, resistance literature has a long tradition in Latin America, because the efforts of decolonization started during colonization.

Anticolonial works acquired a new impetus during the period of independence in the early 19th century, as seen in Venezuela-born Simón Bolívar's "Carta de Jamaica" (1815; "The Letter of Jamaica," 1818?); poetry by Ecuadorian José Joaquín *Olmedo, "Victoria de Junín" (1848; "Victory of Junín," 1920) and "Canto a Bolívar" (1826; "Song to Bolívar," 1920); and Venezuelan Andrés *Bello's poetry and essays. Cuban José *Martí's poetry, extensive collection of journalistic writing, and the renowned essay *"Nuestra América" (1891; "Our America," 1977) are similarly emblematic of the era. The voice of otherness (marginalized groups) also emerges in this period in the publication of *Autobiografía* (1837; *Autobiography of a Slave*, 1996) by Cuban freed slave, Juan Francisco *Manzano.

It is important to note that colonialism in the 19th century underwent a change of meaning. During the previous three centuries, American territories existed as part of the Spanish Crown's patrimony and fell under its direct control. After Spanish America's independence was secured, European countries and the United States became increasingly interested in controlling the means of production in these fledgling nations, especially mining, agriculture, and the development of new technologies like railways and the telegraph. The United States invaded some countries, leading to such changes as Mexico's loss of territory from New Mexico to California and the creation of a new country like Panama, using territory that was formerly part of Colombia.

In the following century, the essay collection by Peruvian José Carlos Mariátegui, *7 ensayos de interpretación de la realidad peruana* (1928; *Seven Interpretive Essays on Peruvian Reality*, 1984) openly blames colonization for the deplorable conditions suffered by the indigenous population, much like *indigenista* novels do, although they were written by authors of European descent. Writers of Latin America's *Boom* generation have published a variety of narrative works that variously 1) display resistance to European colonization, as in Cuban Alejo *Carpentier's *El reino de este mundo* (1949; *Kingdom of this World*, 1989); 2) depict the horrors of Latin American dictatorships, which mirror the power structure imposed earlier by the colonizers, as seen in Paraguayan Augusto *Roa Bastos's *Yo, el supremo* (1974; *I, the Supreme*, 2000) and Colombian Gabriel *García Márquez's *El otoño del patriarca* (1975; *The Autumn of the Patriarch*, 1999); or 3) deal with European or hemispheric neocolonization, in which powerful nations use political and economic influence to control less powerful countries. This perspective is developed in Peruvian José María *Arguedas's last novel, *El zorro de arriba y el zorro de abajo* (1970; *The Fox from Up Above and the Fox from Down Below*, 2000), and Mexican Carlos *Fuentes's *La muerte de Artemio Cruz* (1962; *The Death of Artemio Cruz*, 1991). Similar works authored by indigenous or Mestizo authors do not appear until the late 20th century; two such examples are 1992 Guatemalan Nobel Peace Prize–winner Rigoberta *Menchú's *Me llamo Rigoberta Menchú y así me nació la conciencia* (1983; *I, Rigoberta Menchú. An Indian Woman in Guatemala*, 1984) and Chilean poet Elicura Chihuailaf's *Recado Confidencial a los Chilenos* (1999; Confidential Message to the Chileans).

As detrimental aspects of colonization are exposed in the fifth centenary of the "discovery" in 1992, writers tend to demystify those events through irony and carnivalization (overturning traditional hierarchies), as does Argentine Abel Posse in *Perros del paraíso* (1983; Dogs in Paradise), and Cuban Reinaldo *Arenas in *El mundo alucinante* (1966; *Hallucinations*, 2001). The treatment of the "other" appears yet again with all of its controversies in *El entenado* (1983; The Stepson), by Argentine Juan José Saer and his compatriot Sylvia *Iparraguirre's text *La tierra del fuego* (1998; *Tierra del Fuego*, 2000). With globalization being considered by many as a form of neocolonization, works including that theme also become part of the on-going production of anticolonial writing. Chilean Roberto *Bolaño (1998; *Los detectives salvajes*, [1998; *The Savage Detectives*, 2007]), Bolivian Edmundo Paz Soldán (*El delirio de Turing* [2003; Turing's Ravings]), and Chilean Alberto Fuguet (*Mala onda* [1991; Bad Vibes]) have produced such texts; they are considered part of the *McOndo generation of writers, characterized by their irreverence and sarcasm. Irony that subverts the hegemonic discourse is becoming increasingly popular in Latin American narrative, as it deconstructs Eurocentric myths about colonization and, more recently, globalization.

Silvia Nagy-Zekmi

See also Bolívar, Simón in Contemporary Literature and Culture; Colonial Religious Chronicles in Spanish America; *Criollista* Novel in Spanish America; Discovery and Conquest Writings: Describing the Americas;

Indigenismo in Spanish American Literature; Slavery and Antislavery Literature in the Caribbean.

Work About:

Bolaños, Álvaro Félix, and Gustavo Verdesio, eds. *Colonialism Past and Present. Reading and Writing about Colonial Latin America Today.* Albany: State University of New York Press, 2002.

Verdesio, Gustavo, ed. *Race, Colonialism, and Social Transformation in Latin America and the Caribbean.* Gainesville: University Press of Florida, 2008.

Colonial Religious Chronicles in Spanish America

In the 16th century, the kings of Spain secured authority over the Church in America under the *Patronato Real* (Royal Patronage). Within its realm, missionaries became the emissaries of the Crown with extensive powers to establish the Catholic Church in the newly found lands. Missionaries who established Catholic hegemony in the New World came from the regular orders, that is, clerics who belong to organized religious orders and follow the rule of their order. The Franciscans were the first to arrive in New Spain in 1523; followed by the Dominicans in 1526, and then the Augustinians in 1533. The Jesuits established missions in areas neglected by other orders. The regular orders obtained a special bull, the *Omnimoda*, that granted them extraordinary apostolic powers. In addition to their missionary functions, they could administer the sacraments and establish monasteries and churches. Missionaries were interested in

influencing the Crown's opinions about the colonial subjects and the policies that would affect their missions' development.

During the colonial era, missionaries wrote thousands of letters, reports, histories, and yearly summaries. This discursive production can be divided in two parts. The first, completed in the 16th century, was characterized by an ethnographical interest in recovering natives' pre-Hispanic religious beliefs, history, and language and was interwoven with accounts of swift conversions and the missionaries' concrete suggestions regarding the Crown's obligations to ensure the Indians' well-being. The second part includes reports that chronicle the founding of new parishes and expansion of missions; these were written during the 17th and 18th centuries and served to show the missionaries' success in evangelizing native populations and justify further financial support.

Religious colonial chronicles were hybrid discourses that combined features of official and natural histories, legal defenses, and religious oratory. They used Biblical language and preaching images, and on occasion included supernatural narrations of miracles and instances of martyrdom.

The first group of texts from the viceroyalty of New Spain (possessions in North America and the Asian Pacific) includes Franciscan writings like Bernardino de Sahagún's *Historia general de las cosas de la Nueva España* (composed between 1560 and 1580; *General History of the Things of New Spain: Florentine Codex*, 1950–1982), based on questionnaires to native elders, as well as Toribio de Motolonía's *Historia de los Indios de la Nueva España* (completed in about 1541; *History of the Indians of New Spain*, 1951), which portrays the missionaries as defenders of the natives. Motolinía was among the first 12 Franciscan missionaries to arrive in New Spain. Gerónimo de Mendieta's *Historia eclesiástica indiana* (completed 1596, published 1870; Ecclesiastical History of the Indies) wielded particular influence in shaping the Crown's policies toward the natives. He described the Indians as weak and wretched, thereby hiding the project of domination behind a discourse of protection.

José de Acosta, a Jesuit who held the post of provincial in Peru wrote the *Historia natural y moral de las Indias* in 1590 (*Natural and Moral History of the Indies*, 2002), and catechisms in Quechua and Aymara. Among the Dominicans is the *Historia de las indias de Nueva España* (*The History of the Indies of New Spain*, 1994) composed sometime near 1588 by Diego Durán; and in the Guatemala and Yucatán region, in the early 18th century, Francisco Ximénez translated the *Popol vuh* (*Popol vuh: The Sacred Book of the Ancient Quiche Maya*, 1950) from Quiché, and wrote the chronicle of his province.

Later chroniclers combined their narrations of success in converting the Amerindians with territorial advances and foundations of churches and seminaries. The Jesuit Andrés Pérez de Rivas penned *Historia de los triunfos de nuestra santa fe* (1645; *History of the Triumphs of Our Holy Faith*, 1999). In Peru, the Franciscan Diego de Mendoza composed *Chrónica de la provincia de las Charcas* (1664; Chronicle from the Province of Charcas); and José de Santa Cruz compiled *Chrónica de la santa provincial de San Miguel* (1671; Chronicle from the Province of Saint Miguel). The *Chrónica apostólica y seráphica* (1746; Apostolic and Seraphic Chronicle) by Franciscan Félix de Espinosa recounted the revival of missionary fervor that led to the expansion of the Empire's frontier. He is known as the chronicler of the 18th century's missionary endeavor in what is now the state of Texas. Although America achieved its independence from Spain in the early 19th century, the various religious orders continued to chronicle their activities and the exemplary lives of their members. However, their purpose was to provide a historical account of their order's development and did not necessarily involve contributing to imperial expansion and control.

Mónica Díaz

See also Discovery and Conquest Writings: Describing the Americas; Mayan Literature.

Work About:

Díaz Balsera, Viviana. *The Pyramid under the Cross: Franciscan Discourses of Evangelization and the Nahua Christian Subject in Sixteenth-century Mexico*. Tucson: The University of Arizona Press, 2005.

O'Malley, John. *The Jesuits: Cultures, Sciences and the Arts, 1540–1773*. Toronto: University of Toronto Press, 1999.

Phelan, John Leddy. *The Millennial Kingdom of the Franciscans in the New World: A Study of the Writings of*

Gerónimo de Mendieta (1525–1604). Berkeley: University of California Press, 1956.

Colonial Theater in Spanish America

Spanning roughly 300 years (1492–1810), Spanish American colonial theater was influenced by the 17th-century Spanish baroque period. Critics tend to classify theatrical productions in three main groups: missionary, student, and Creole. Missionary theater, performed by Indians themselves in their own language, was a tool for religious conversion; student theater (*comedia escolar*) related allegorical dialogues for didactic purposes; and Creole theater, composed by nonindigenous colonial writers, frequently touched on social issues of the time. Despite their distinct, defining characteristics, all ultimately reinforce the propagation of Christianity. While the quantity of colonial theater pales in comparison to that which Spain produced during those years, the quality of many New World plays does compare favorably. Two of the era's most outstanding playwrights, Juan *Ruiz de Alarcón and Sor Juana Inés de la *Cruz, masterfully adapted the baroque style in original ways.

Even before the Spanish made landfall on New World soil, an embryonic theater tradition existed among many indigenous groups from Mexico to Chile, and these New World spectacles influenced the theater's development in the Spanish colonies. While pre-Columbian theater is only a distant relative of its Spanish cousin, elements that parallel those of Iberian theater deserve mention. Argentina's Araucano Indians, for example, developed a lyrical dance called the "areíto," and certain Mexican tribes produced short plays involving a strong dance element. Spanish writers and conquistadors including Hernán Cortés, El Inca *Garcilaso, and Fray Diego de Landa all make reference in their writings to theatrical elements they witnessed in these New World societies, confirming the importance of similar cultural products that they witnessed.

For the Spanish, theater was a national pastime; even today Spaniards continue their centuries-long love affair with theater. It is no surprise, then, that rudimentary stages were constructed in the colonies shortly after some of the first settlements were established. Given the Iberian goal of mass Christianization of the Indians, many of the early plays staged dealt with religious themes and conversion allegories. The first documented play in Spanish America reportedly took place in about 1543.

Sixteenth-century colonial theater was primarily concerned with propagating the Catholic faith among the Indians. It was also a building-block century, as the first traveling theaters appeared and the first *corrales* (outdoor theaters) were built. By the early 1600s, the Spanish baroque *comedia* (a term then used to denote Spanish plays in general) was in full force and invariably permeated the stylistic, linguistic, and thematic corpus of New World theater. Such playwrights as Alarcón, heavily influenced by Lope de *Vega, and

Sor Juana, undeniably inspired by Pedro *Calderón de la Barca, warmly embraced the baroque style in their *comedias*, *auto-sacramentales* (short, allegorical plays that expounded on the mystery of the Holy Eucharist), and *entremeses* (one act plays performed between acts of a larger play). Sor Juana's most-known theatrical work, *Los empeños de una casa* (1680; *The House of Trials*, 2002), examines honor compromised by love triangles, mistaken identity, and other twists and turns. Ruiz de Alarcón composed *La verdad sospechosa* (1634; *Love's True Lies*, 1997), a masterful play about love, lies, and the fallibility of sight and words. Because of their literary achievements, both Sor Juana and Alarcón's plays regularly appear in anthologies of Spain's Golden Age dramatists or in syllabi of Spanish Golden Age theater classes.

Arrom divides Spanish American colonial theater into two phases: the "dawn" of baroque theater (1600–1681, which coincides with Calderón's death and is considered the phase's apex) and its "dusk" (roughly the next 70 years). The second half of the 18th century, however, reflects a measurable resurgence of theater production in the Americas as a result of Bourbon reforms. In 1789, for example, Argentina staged its first American-themed play, Manuel José de Lavardén's *Siripo*, considered that decade's most important work.

Bonnie L. Gasior

See also Pastorela.

Work By:

Schmidhuber, Guillermo. *The Three Secular Plays of Sor Juana Inés de la Cruz:* *A Critical Study*. Trans. Shelby C. Thacker. Louisville: University Press of Kentucky, 2000.

Work About:

Arrom, José Juan. *Historia del teatro hispanoamericano*: *época colonial*. Mexico: Andrea, 1967.

Versenyi, Adam. *Theater in Latin America: Religion, Politics and Culture from Cortés to the 1980s*. Cambridge and New York: Cambridge University Press, 1993.

CONAIE (Confederación de Nacionalidades Indígenas del Ecuador)

Established in 1986, this grassroots organization of indigenous peoples advocates for indigenous rights and concerns in Ecuador. In addition to protecting such issues as land rights, potable drinking water, and sustainable ecological practices, the organization works to ensure the survival and health of indigenous cultures, music, and other traditions. In 1989, the organization signed a historic agreement with Ecuador's Ministry of Education, establishing a national program for bilingual and bicultural education to promote usage of indigenous languages and protect their diverse cultural heritage for future generations.

Maureen Ihrie

Work About:

CONAIE Web site. http://conaie.native web.org/index.html.

Conde Abellán, Carmen (1907–1996)

The first woman elected to Spain's *Real Academia de la Lengua (1978), Conde's work spans a large part of the 20th century, serving as a model for women's literature. Born in Cartagena, she authored collections of poetry, criticism, and editions of collected works, novels, plays, children's literature, memoirs, and translations. Her most widely known verse collection, *Mujer sin Edén* (1945; Woman without Eden), exemplifies her ability to focus on the truly feminine qualities of the poetic subject and to address the issue of women's subjugation through biblical references with political overtones. Her writing imbues a sense of intimacy associated with a personal perspective via themes of nature, human suffering, religion, and gender relations. Conde wrote under the pseudonyms Florentina del Mar and Magdalena Noguera. She died in Madrid.

Lisa Nalbone

See also Women Writers in Spain: 1900 to Present.

Work By:

Canciones de nana y desvelo. Madrid: Susaeta, 1985.

Work About:

Richards, Judith. "The World without End: Mythic and Linguistic Revision in Carmen Conde Abellán's *Mujer sin Edén*." *Monographic Review* 6 (1990): 71–80.

Wilcox, John C. *Women Poets of Spain: Toward a Gynocentric Vision*. Urbana and Chicago: University of Illinois Press, 1997, 137–72.

Contemporáneos Group

This avant-garde group of Mexico City writers thrived during the 1920s and 1930s. The name refers to a lavish literary journal edited by Jaime Torres Bodet between 1928 and 1931 under the protection of culturally sophisticated politicians like José *Vasconcelos. The group coalesced at Mexico City's National Preparatory School under the influence of professors like Pedro Henríquez Ureña and Antonio Caso. Members included Jorge Cuesta, Enrique González Rojo (son of modernist poet and professor Enrique González Martínez), José *Gorostiza, Bernardo Ortiz de Montellano, Carlos *Pellicer and Torres Bodet, and were later joined by the "Generation of Two," Salvador *Novo and Xavier *Villaurrutia.

These writers developed a universal literary movement opposed to the ultranationalism of the Mexican Revolution's official culture—that of the muralists or the stylized indigenous Mexico seen in what is now considered the "Golden Age" cinema of that day. The *Contemporáneos* followed cultural trends of the European avant-garde, U.S. movements like the Harlem Renaissance, and Spain's *Generación of 1927. Paris had served as an obligatory referent for Latin American cultural elites for almost a century, while Spain and the United States were taboo because they represented the colonial past and present. As politicians, journalists, playwrights, and cinematographers, they shaped Mexican middlebrow culture, aiming to provide a voice for Mexico's middle class, as opposed to the proletariat (subject of the muralists) or elite Mexicans (the audience of most avant-garde groups).

Primary influences of the *Contemporáneos* were baroque Spanish writers like Luis de *Góngora (1561–1627) and Francisco de *Quevedo (1580–1645); additionally, they promoted the development of Sor Juana Inés de la *Cruz (1651–1695) and Carlos de Sigüenza y Góngora (1645–1700) as icons of Mexican literature. Because they wanted to "write the city"—to capture the life of the capital's *flâneur*, the idle man in the city—they avidly read contemporary urban writers like Argentinean Leopoldo *Lugones and the United States' Edgar Allan Poe. This group also penned the first queer literature in Mexico.

Salvador A. Oropesa

See also Henríquez Ureña Family and Their Relation with the United States; Mexico City in Literature; Queer Literature in Spanish America.

Work About:

Oropesa, Salvador A. *The Contemporáneos Group. Rewriting Mexico in the Thirties and Forties*. Austin: University of Texas Press, 2003.

Contemporary Guatemalan Indigenous Authors

Since the 1940s, Guatemala has witnessed the gradual emergence of a group of indigenous intellectuals and writers who became influential in the 1980s and consolidated their literary importance in the 1990s. Their texts use Spanish and often a Mayan language, they include testimonial elements and a Mayan worldview, and they appropriate Western literary techniques. Although Mayans make up a clear majority of the population (61 percent), they have historically been the poorest, least-educated ethnic group; this new visibility of indigenous intellectuals indicates their growing political relevance.

The Spanish conquest (1524) started the systematic oppression of the Maya, and independence from Spain (1821) brought little change. During the Liberal rule (1871–1944), Guatemala shifted to a coffee economy; land expropriations and forced labor laws were applied, but later abolished by the revolutionary governments of Arévalo and Arbenz (1944–1954). Not long after a coup ended this democratic decade, leftist guerrilla movements organized and were supported by thousands of Guatemalans, including many Mayans. The 36-year civil war that ensued triggered a cruel counterinsurgent genocide by the army, yielding mostly indigenous victims (150,000 killed and 500,000 displaced civilians).

As a strategy of resistance and ethnic pride, members of the pan-Maya movement began promoting linguistic and cultural revitalization. Rigoberta *Menchú's significant testimony (1983), and the continental movement for indigenous rights in the 1990s drew international attention to Mayan literature and culture. Mayans also gained some political recognition and participated in the talks leading to the 1996 Peace Accords. In this context emerged such authors as Luis de Lión, Luis Enrique Sam Colop, Gaspar Pedro Gonzales, Víctor Montejo, Humberto Ak'abal, Calixta Gabriel Xiquín, Demetrio Cojtí Cuxil, Maya Cú, and Irma Otzoy. Out of 24 languages spoken in Guatemala, 21 are Mayan, the largest linguistic groups being K'iche,' Kaqchikel, Mam, and Q'eqchi.' All indigenous writers use Spanish—traditionally the language of schooling and power—to reach a multicultural audience; most of them also write in their Mayan language to address their native communities and to assert their cultural and political importance.

Although a few writers compose narratives and essays, poetry is the most practiced genre. Well-known and widely translated K'iche' poet Humberto Ak'abal has received several national and international awards; his precise Spanish is enriched by traces of K'iche.' Jakaltek narrator and anthropologist Víctor Montejo wrote a testimonial account of army violence in a village, re-creations of Mayan tales, and ethnographical studies. Kaqchikel writer and educator Luis de Lión authored a ground-breaking novel portraying male–female relations across the ethnic divide before he was kidnapped and killed by the army in 1984. Kaqchikel poet and spiritual guide Calixta Gabriel's texts combine the pain of exile, ideological analysis, and her experience of Mayan religious awakening. Others, like linguist Luis Enrique Sam Colop and social scientists Irma Otzoy and Demetrio Cojtí Cuxil, analyze historical, cultural, and racial issues in essays and newspaper columns.

Guatemalan indigenous writers play an important role advocating human rights, promoting literacy and education, and emphasizing Mayan cultural renaissance at a time when indigenous peoples across the Americas are being politically empowered. The recently held first literary contest in indigenous Guatemalan languages and the candidacy of the first indigenous woman in presidential elections suggest a more tolerant future, allowing for some optimism about these writers' struggle for true multiculturalism and acceptance.

Claudia S. García

See also Mayan Literature; Testimonial Writing in Central America.

Work By:

Ak'abal, Humberto. *Poems I Brought Down from the Mountain*. Trans. Miguel Rivera with Robert Bly. Minneapolis: Nineties, 1999.

Gabriel Xiquín, Calixta. *Tejiendo los sucesos en el tiempo/Weaving Events in Time*. Trans. Susan G. Rascón and Suzanne Strugalla. Rancho Palos Verdes, CA: Fundación Yax Te', 2002.

Montejo, Víctor. *The Bird Who Cleans the World and Other Mayan Fables*. Willimantic, CT: Curbstone, 1991.

Montejo, Víctor. *Testimony: Death of a Guatemalan Village*. Trans. Víctor Perera. Willimantic, CT: Curbstone, 1987.

Work About:

González, Gaspar Pedro. *Sq'anej maya.' Palabras mayas*. Rancho Palos Verdes, CA: Fundación Yax Te,' 1998.

Warren, Kay B. *Indigenous Movements and Their Critics. Pan-Maya Activism in Guatemala*. Princeton, NJ: Princeton University Press, 1998.

Contemporary Moroccan Literature Written in Spanish

The first literary works addressing the modern migration of African citizens from Morocco to Europe during the 1970s were written in Arabic or French by Mohamed Zafzaf, Abdallah Laroui, and Tahar Ben Jelloun, among others. On February 7, 1992, the first *patera* (a floating device used by smugglers to transport illegal immigrants from Africa) with 300 Maghrebis (inhabitants of northern Africa) shipwrecked by the coast of Almeria, in southern Spain, claiming 20 victims. The first Moroccan intellectual to react in Spanish to the modern and clandestine migratory process was Goncourt Prize–winner Tahar Ben Jelloun (1944–); he wrote a literary essay for Spain's *El País* newspaper titled *¿Cómo se dice 'boat people' en español?* (How do you say "boat people" in Spanish?).

After Ben Jelloun, Moroccan authors who had been writing poems and short stories in the Spanish supplement of Moroccan newspaper *L'Opinion* and in the cultural section of *La mañana* (1990–2006), Rabat's first and only Spanish-language newspaper produced by Moroccan nationals, began to denounce the onslaught of migrants who cross the Strait of Gibraltar in search of El Dorado (a mythical city of gold). Although such

Moroccan literati as Abdul Latif Jatib, Mohammad Tensamani, and Mohamed Ibn Azzuz Hakim have sporadically published literary works in Spanish since the time of the Protectorate (1912–1956) in such newspapers as *España*, *Marruecos*, *Unidad Marroquí*, *Diario Marroquí*, *Diario de África*, and *El Lukus*, the modern migration outburst produced a reawakening of Moroccan literature in Spanish.

One of Morocco's first contemporary intellectuals of Spanish expression to write about migration was Sephardic León Cohen Mesonero (1946–), in a literary essay entitled *Camisas mojadas* (1992; Wetbacks), published in Andalusia's *Europa Sur* newspaper. A year later, Mohamed Sibari (1945–) published *El caballo* (1993; *The Horse*), the first Moroccan novel written entirely in Spanish; its main character is a desperate young man who wants to migrate to Spain.

Since 1995, every year approximately 40,000 Moroccan and Sub-Saharan migrants land in the Canary Islands and the coasts of southern Spain. As a response to the harshening Spanish media reports of the modern migration phenomenon, which compare it to the Berber invasions of the 17th century, a new "fiction of resistance" arose in Morocco between 1995 and 2000. This new phase of Moroccan literature in Spanish employed irony, neosymbolism, and historical annals as it tracked the centuries-long North African presence in Spain as a way of validating the new migrant experience. During this period, 15 novels and short story collections sharing this agenda were produced in Morocco and Spain. A paradigmatic case is that of

Abderrahman El Fathi (1964–); known as "the poet of migration," he published six books: *Triana, imágenes y palabras* (1998; Triana, Images and Words), *Abordaje* (2000; Boarding), *África en versos mojados* (2002; Africa in Wetback Verse), *Primavera en Ramallah y Bagdad* (2003; Spring in Ramallah and Baghdad), *El cielo herido* (2003; Wounded Sky), *Desde la otra orilla* (2004; From the Other Shore), and a short play, *Fantasías literarias* (2000; Literary Fantasies). El Fathi unifies the subaltern (subordinate) voice of the *pateristas* (boat people), *harragas* (illegal immigrants), and refined lyricism, while denouncing the double standard of European politicians that falsely inculcate democratic processes of *convivencia* (living together) and free market as they validate new displacements (cultural and economic), and massive holocausts.

For his part, Mohamed Lahchiri (1950–)—the first editor in chief of *La mañana* newspaper throughout the 1990s—wrote three short story collections: *Pedacitos entrañables* (1994; Dearly Loved Pieces), *Cuentos ceutíes* (2003; Ceuta's Short Stories), and *Una tumbita en Sidi Embarek* (2006; A Little Tomb in Sidi Embarek). Lahchiri was born in Ceuta, one of Northern Africa's two Spanish enclaves; his writings narrate the transformations of territories and people from the former protectorate into unequal, antagonistic spaces of postindependence modernity.

The group of Moroccan writers that proliferated in the last eight years places Spanish-language Moroccan literature within the framework of a literature without borders. This writing, composed in Morocco by Moroccans, with Moroccan topics and characters, is developing a series of questions about using the language of the "Other" (Spanish); the aesthetic practices of Western literature; and a deeply critical consideration of Western media's influence in Morocco. These authors address the discussions of Madrid's 11M bombings (the March 11, 2004 terrorist attacks of trains at the Atocha station) and, at the same time, recreate the shadows of intolerance as represented in the darkest days of 15th-century Spanish *Inquisition activities and of Spanish dictator Francisco Franco's Fascist dictatorship (1939–1975). The "threat" of terrorism is answered in literary texts that, while writing Maghrebi immigrants' lives and arrival to Spain, are surrounded by the ghosts of Spain's Muslim past. Within this group, Moroccan writers like Ahmed Ararou (1953–), Ahmed El Gamoun (1950–), Larbi El Harti (1963–), and Mohamed Lahchiri are very conscious of the ontological and epistemological differences between both cultures and can cross from one side to the other (from West to East), criticizing both cultures, with no need to request a "visa" from any "academic guard," neither from the East nor from the West. Without apostatizing their Arab–African–Muslim culture, in many cases they know "the house of their neighbor" (Spain), better than their own, as El Harti has observed.

In the last few years (2004–present), Catalonian presses have published female Moroccan/Amazigh voices who write in Catalan and have lived in Catalonia since their childhood (Amazigh is the correct term for "Berber," the indigenous people of northern Morocco and Algeria whose main language is Tamazight, not Arabic). It is worth noting that among the 600,000 Moroccans living in Spain, 200,000 belong to this group. In 2008, the Ramón Llull Prize for Catalan authors was awarded to Moroccan/Amazigh immigrant Najat El Hachmi (1979–), the first time that the award has been won by a non-Catalonian Her novel, *L'ultim patriarca* (2008: The Last Patriarch) is narrated exclusively by the third—and only—daughter of Mimoun, a girl who announces at the story's onset the end of the family bloodline and her father's discriminatory, dictatorial ways. Once the eldest son in the family is born, the text highlights the excesses of paternal authority, as seen in the physical abuse and sodomy inflicted by the son's uncle. From that moment on, the fictional autobiography is told from the point of view of a grown woman, a textual move that subverts and perverts the status imposed by religious practices and traditions of a society (like many others—including European cultures) that encourage patriarchy. *L'ultim patriarca* was originally composed in Catalan, and then translated to Spanish by Maria Rosa Prats, under the author's supervision. The novel is now being translated into eight different languages, including French, English, German, Arabic, Italian, Portuguese and Swedish.

Today some 40 authors write in Spanish and Catalan, and publish their works in Morocco and Spain. Their texts have been ignored by scholars. Nonetheless, these writings possess the potential to reshape the landscape of postcolonial Spain. These works can help revitalize Spain's contemporary literature and contribute to a "South to South" dialogue between North Africans, Asians, Latin Americans, North American natives, and Chicanos who face modern imperialistic cultures.

Moroccan literature written in Spanish and Catalan should be placed within the ampler context of borderland studies, which relates to 19th-century Philippine literature in Spanish, and emerging diaspora literatures such as those by Tunisian, Algerian, sub-Saharan, and Latin American authors who study their intercultural experience in Europe. This cultural phenomenon has characteristics common to other world literatures, such as Chicano and Mexican American literature in relation to the pilgrimage of "modern" Aztecs to the mythical land of *Aztlán.

Finally, it must be noted that there is also a Saharawi (or Saharaui) literature in Spanish. This literature of the Western Sahara Desert region does not exhibit hybridizing processes; instead it reflects the Saharawis people's fight for independence from the Moroccan government. Most Saharawi writings depict the lonely people of the desert, their nomadic nature and unique identity. Representative poems, short stories, and novels are available online at the Saharawi website *Literatura saharaui*, http://literaturasaharaui .blogspot.com.

Cristián H. Ricci

See also Chicano Movement Literature and Publishing; Equatorial Guinea's *Generación del Silencio* (The Generation of Silence); Exile Writing in the Hispanic World; Islamic

Presence in Spain; Philippine Literature in Spanish; Transculturation in the Hispanic World.

Work By:

Cerezales, Marta, Miguel A. Moreta, and Lorenzo Silva, eds. *La puerta de los vientos. Narradores marroquíes contemporáneos.* Barcelona: Destino, 2004.

Daoudi, Ahmed. *El diablo de Yudis.* Madrid: Vosa, 1994.

El Fathi, Abderrahman. *Desde la otra orilla.* Cádiz: Quórum, 2004.

El Hachmi, Najat. *El último patriarca.* Barcelona: Planeta, 2008.

El Harti, Larbi. *Después de Tánger.* Madrid: Sial, 2003.

El Hassane, Arabi. *Cuentos del Marruecos español.* Madrid: Libros Clan, 1998.

Monleón, José, ed. *Cuentos de las dos orillas.* Granada: Junta de Andalucía, 2001.

Tazi, Aziz et al., eds. *Calle del agua. Antología contemporánea de literatura hispano-magrebí.* Madrid: Sial, 2008.

Work About:

Bouissef Rekab, Mohamed. *Escritores marroquíes de expresión española. Grupo de los 90-Antología.* Tetuán: Asociación Tetuán ASMIR, 1997.

Bounou, Abdelmouneim, ed. *Actas del Coloquio Internacional Escritura Marroquí en Lengua Española.* 1994. Fez: U Sidi Mohamed Ben Abdellah, 1998.

Chakor, Mohammad y Sergio Macías. *La literatura marroquí en lengua castellana.* Madrid: Magalia, 1996.

Ricci, Cristián H. "African Voices in Contemporary Spain." *New Spain, New Literatures.* Ed. Nicholas Spadaccini and Luis Martín-Santos. Knoxville: Vanderbilt University, 2010, 203–31.

Ricci, Cristián H. "El regreso de los moros a España: Fronteras, inmigración, racismo y transculturación en la literatura marroquí contemporánea." *Cuadernos de ALDEEU* 21 (2005): 1–12.

Ricci, Cristián H. "Morrocan Literature in Castilian: Borderland Literature—Literature without Borders." *Alternative Orientalisms in Latin America and Beyond.* Ed. Ignacio López-Calvo. Newcastle: Cambridge Scholars Publishing, 2007, 194–204.

Ricci, Cristián H. "Najat El Hachmi y Laila Karrouch: Escritoras marroquíes-imazighen catalanas en el marco del fenómeno migratorio moderno." *Revista EntreRíos* 6 (2007): 92–97.

Contemporary Puerto Rican Short Story Writers: 1980 to Present

During the 1970s, a group of writers that included Luis Rafael *Sánchez, Edgardo Rodrígues-Juliá, and Rosario *Ferré started to change the traditional paradigms in Puerto Rican literature. New themes were explored, and female writers started publishing avidly, especially short stories. Starting with an innovative language filled with colloquialisms, street slang, and Anglicisms, these authors exposed the lives of groups living in the margins of urban settings while presenting the popular culture of the masses in a parodic way. The tone, deeply humorous and ironic, serves to criticize the new, materialistic Puerto Rican society by raising consciousness regarding all forms of discrimination and the pitfalls of consumerism. This tendency continued in the 1980s and beyond, and expanded to include such discourses as gay issues, the erotic, the bizarre, and violence. A main difference between the 1970s writings and what has come since is that the earlier texts expressed a strong commitment to the island's political arena and continued the traditional search for Puerto Rican identity in its literature. After the 1980s, the latter concern has been generally absent. The current interest is to situate Puerto Rico as part of a Latin American and global community, and, in this context, as a society with problems belonging to a global trend.

Starting with a group of authors named by local critics as the "70s Generation," but who have mainly published after the 1980s, Ana Lydia *Vega (1946–) together with Carmen Lugo-Filippi (1940–) wrote *Vírgenes y mártires* (1981; Virgins and Martyrs), a critically acclaimed short story collection noted for its feminist discourse, use of popular culture and music, plus innovative language using street talk, sarcasm, and vicious humor. Vega also composed *Encancaranublado y otros cuentos de naufragio* (1982; Cloudy Skies and Other Shipwreck Stories), a Casa de las Américas Prize–winner that exposes what unites and differentiates Caribbean people; *Pasión de historia y otras historias de pasión* (1987; Passion for History and Other Passionate Stories), which plays

with detective stories; and *Falsas crónicas del sur* (1991; False Chronicles from the South), where she reinterprets the history of a southern town in Puerto Rico using traditional discourses and language. A collection of her stories has been translated and published in *True and False Romances* (1994).

Another member of this group, the award-winning short story writer Edgardo Sanabria-Santaliz (1951–), published *El día que el hombre pisó la luna* (1984; The Day Man Stepped on the Moon), *Cierta inevitable muerte* (1988; Certain Unavoidable Death), *Las horas púrpura* (1994; The Purple Hours), and *Peso pluma* (1996; Light Weight). From the dysfunctional family named in the title story of his first book, to the terrible deadly secrets guarded by a funerary family in the title story of his third text, the author explores love and death, family relationships, poverty, mass communication, and fantastic creatures like vampires.

A transition writer between the older generation and the next, novelist and short fiction author Luis López-Nieves (1950–) focuses mainly on reinterpreting history and rewriting it with humor and irony. His first published story, "Seva" (1983)—which was published as a book in 1994—narrates a government conspiracy to quell news about the extermination of the people of Seva who fought against American forces during the first (previously unknown) U.S. occupation of the island in 1898. Due to its documentary style, the public thought the story was in fact real, and it created an uproar on the island. López-Nieves's short story collection

La verdadera muerte de Juan Ponce de León (2000; The True Death of Juan Ponce de Leon) won the National Literature Prize. Short fiction in *Escribir para Rafa* (2006; Writing for Rafa) continues his fascination with history and the inclusion of journalistic interviews, confessions, letters, and police reports, and similar intertexts.

Humor, sarcasm, and parody figure prominently in Puerto Rican short fiction authors, but other characteristics also emerge, including the erotic. Daniel Torres (1961–) continued the trend of gay literature initiated by Manuel *Ramos Otero in the 1970s. He uses street slang and eroticism to shock readers. *Cabronerías o historias de tres cuerpos* (1995; Infidelities: Stories of Three Bodies) and *Mariconerías: escritos desde el margen* (2006; Things Gay: Writings from the Margin) recount gay and heterosexual relationships using erotic, popular, and lyrical language. Novelist, poet, and short story writer Mayra Santos-Febres (1966–) also employs sarcasm and acerbic wit to expose the hypocrisy of Puerto Rican society regarding race, gender, and sexual discrimination. Her two short story collections, *Pez de vidrio* (1996; Fish of Glass), and *El cuerpo correcto* (1998; The Correct Body), validate the culture of anonymous people by focusing on the city and exploring its marginal groups, dialects, and popular culture with erotic tones and feminism. A selection of her stories has been translated and published in *Urban Oracles* (1997).

Other authors explore improbable and fantastic worlds. José (Pepe) Liboy-Erba (1964–), a *PEN Club Award recipient, has been a cult figure since the 1980s, publishing his stories in local magazines and journals. Only in 2003 did he publish his collection *Cada vez te despides mejor* (Every Time You Say Good-Bye Better). Liboy-Erba's stories explore the bizarre, and instead of following a typical chronological account, they present snapshots of moments or feelings that sometimes repeat themselves. His humor and irony pinpoint the absurdity of life and its farcical quality. Similarly, Pedro Cabiya (1971–), who uses the pseudonym Diego Deni, pens humorous, fantastic tales that employ strange characters to explore absurd situations, as in *Historias tremendas* (1999; Dreadful Stories) and *Historias atroces* (2003; Appalling Stories). His concern is to present the uncommon as common. Characters that seem monstrous are shown to have the same feelings as everyone else; characters that suffer from sordid situations are presented in an innocuous and normal way. Lastly, José E. Santos (1963–) probes the world of the gothic, violence, and death. His collections include *Archivos de oscuridades* (2003; Archives of Obscurities), *Deleites y miserias* (2006; Delights and Miseries), *Los viajes de Blanco White* (2007; Blanco White's Travels), *Los comentarios* (2008; Commentaries), and *Trinitarias y otros relatos* (2008; Bougainvilleas and Other Stories). Although his stories begin from a literal place, what in fact emerges is a surreal world in which different alter egos fluctuate through temporal and spatial scenes, desperately seeking escape from reality, only to find that happiness remains elusive.

Other authors still tend to be more lyrical in their reflections. Historian and critic Mario R. Cancel (1963–) has produced two short fiction collections, *Las ruinas que se dicen mi casa* (1992; The Ruins That Call Themselves My Home) and *Intento dibujar una sonrisa* (2005; I Try to Draw a Smile). Using a nostalgic, poetic tone, he examines memories in all their forms: the history of Puerto Rico, country and urban life, historical and common people, plus modernity and metafiction. In his second short story collection, the main characters deal with solitude and with the process of writing and collecting books while trying to reconstruct the past of everyday people and their own. Finally, Yolanda Arroyo-Pizarro (1970–) has two collections to date: *Origami de letras* (2005; Origami of Letters) and *Ojos de Luna* (2007; Moon Eyes). Drawn to the compendium of the human experience, she delves into themes involving historical figures, different epochs, humanity and bestiality in all forms, religion, love, and nature and the universe, using both graphic and poetical language.

Other noted short story writers include Marta Aponte-Alsina, Zoé Jiménez-Corretjer, Ana María Fuster-Lavín, Elidio La Torre-Lagares, Eduardo Lalo, Daniel Nina, and Moisés Agosto.

Michele C. Dávila Gonçalves

Work By:

Bobes, Marilyn, Pedro Antonio Valdez, and Carlos R. Gómez Beras. *Los nuevos caníbales: antología de la más reciente cuentística del Caribe Hispano*. San Juan, Puerto Rico: Isla Negra, 2000.

Cancel, Mario R. *Literatura y narrativa puertorriqueña: la escritura entre siglos*. Colombia: Pasadizo, 2007.
López-Baralt, Mercedes. *Literatura puertorriqueña del siglo XX: Antología*. Río Piedras, Puerto Rico: Universidad de Puerto Rico, 2004.

Work About:

Mercado, Ivonne. *Rewriting Women: The Voices of Change in Puerto Rican Literature*. Austin: University of Texas at Austin, 1995.
Reyes, Israel. *Humor and the Eccentric Text in Puerto Rican Literature*. Gainesville: University Press of Florida, 2005.

Conti, Haroldo (1925–1976)

This Argentine author, screenwriter, teacher, and Latin professor, born in Chacabuco, Buenos Aires, was disappeared by the Argentine military junta in 1976. Winning the Fabril Prize for best novel, *Sudeste* (1962; Southeast), marked Conti as a prominent member of the *Contorno* generation of politically engaged intellectuals who felt alienated by Peronism. While his early work was largely descriptive and pastoral in nature, his style became increasingly politicized. In *Alrededor de la jaula* (1967; Around the Cage)—adapted for the film *Crecer de golpe* (1977)—Conti's allegorical representation of the Perón era critiques a society that is increasingly consumer oriented and superficial. A year before his disappearance, Conti received the Casa de las Américas Prize for *Mascaró, el cazador americano* (1975; Mascaró, the American Hunter), a symbolic novel that traverses the misery and abandonment of several towns while inciting the need for an awakening of sorts that could be interpreted as a call to revolution.

Conti chose to remain in Argentina and to continue writing despite his awareness that in 1975 the military held his name on a list of subversive agents. The day of his disappearance, May 5, is recognized annually in his honor as the "Día del Escritor Bonaerense" (Day of the Buenos Aires Writer). In 2008, the biopic *Haroldo Conti, Homo Viator*, directed by Miguel Mato, premiered in Buenos Aires.

Annette H. Levine

Work About:

López, María Pía. "Viajes al país del pueblo: Notas acerca de las novelas de Haroldo Conti." *Inti: Revista de Literatura Hispánica* 52–53 (Autumn 2000 Spring–2001): 335–44.

Convent Writing in Spain and the New World

Early modern religious women on both sides of the Atlantic produced hundreds of texts as an integral part of their spiritual lives. The practice of spiritual writing dates to at least the medieval period, when nuns wrote for convent musical and theatrical performances and confessants began jotting down notes about their interior lives for spiritual directors. But the works written by Santa *Teresa de Jesús (1515–1582) served as the catalyst for a boom in Hispanic religious women's writings and a codification of conventions for distinct textual genres, in particular visionary and mystical texts and life confessional accounts. Immediately following the publication of Teresa's works (*Libro de la vida* [1560; *Life of Teresa of Avila*, 1976]; *Las moradas* [1577; *Interior Castle*, 1976]; *Libro de las fundaciones* [1573–1576–1582; *Foundations*, 1979]), several of her Carmelite Sisters wrote spiritual accounts for their confessors. By the first half of the 17th century, the practice had spread to other religious orders in Spain and Latin America, where convent writing remained common until the mid-18th century.

By the time Teresa was writing her most influential works, the Counter-Reformation Church, through the decrees of the Council of Trent (1545–1563), had codified a new Catholic spiritual practice that discouraged individual manifestations of spirituality while emphasizing the importance of obedience to Church authorities and strict observance of the sacraments. Women were closely monitored through the practice of oral and written confession because they were considered by the Church to be more prone to emotional states than men. They were thought to be more easily influenced by the devil and, conversely, more open to serving as an instrument of divine will. Clergy searched for evidence of the two extreme limits set by the Church for Catholic behavior—the holy and the heretical—in an attempt to revitalize the Church with saintly models and to stamp out such unorthodox religious practices as Judaism, illuminism (*alumbradismo*), Protestant-ism, and religious fakery (*beatas falsas*). Many of the confessional writings are still in archives today, as few were published in their original format during the early modern period. If published at all after the Council of Trent, the spiritual texts by women were excerpted and printed within an official Church format, such as a hagio-graphic biography, prayer book, or sta-tions of the cross.

The term "convent writing" was coined by late 20th-century scholars who redis-covered the body of literature that this spiritual practice produced. The majority of the texts were written by nuns, who in general tended to be relatively well edu-cated and monitored closely by Church superiors. Some noncloistered religious women participated in this textual prac-tice; however, after the Council of Trent, religious women were increasingly dis-couraged from living outside of the con-vent because it was viewed as a danger to the spiritual well-being of both the indi-vidual woman and the community at large. The lay religious woman Rose of Lima (1586–1617) and her follower María Luisa Melgarejo, for example, wrote accounts of their visionary and mystical experiences for their confessors. While Rose was canon-ized as America's first saint, her followers were persecuted by the *Inquisition. Most lay religious women's writings have not survived or are only recently being redis-covered in the vast materials buried in the Inquisition archives.

Because convent writing includes a broad range of textual types and spans more than two centuries and all of Spain and Latin America, it is difficult to charac-terize the large body of writings produced. Nonetheless, the texts generally fall into one of three categories. The most preva-lent type are autobiographical spiritual accounts that include full-length (20 to 200 pages), general confessional accounts about the author's entire life (*vidas*) and shorter, theme- or incident-specific accounts (*cuentas de conscien-cia*). Written at the behest of a confessor, these accounts draw on confessional nar-rative strategies codified by Teresa de Jesús, such as the use of the rhetorical topics of women in particular being hum-ble, ignorant writers and being obedient to Church hierarchy. At the same time, the accounts attempt to justify the worthi-ness of the author's spiritual path by draw-ing on hagiographic conventions used to describe the lives of the saints, such as describing incidents of heroic virtue. Most of the nuns whose texts survive wrote at least one version of an autobiographical confessional account.

A second general category, often an outcome of the autobiographical account, is the didactic spiritual text, including mystical treatises and prayer books. Reli-gious women gifted with extraordinary visions and understanding of spiritual practices for prayer often recorded their experiences in a written form. After spiri-tual directors examined the texts, other Church authorities examined them as well. In search of orthodoxy as well as material to inspire the faithful, the Church some-time published these writings. The most notable authors of spiritual and mystical guides are Teresa de Jesús, Madre María de Ágreda (1602–1665), and María de San José Salazar (1548–1603) in Spain; and María Anna Agueda de San Ignacio (1695–1756), María de San José (1656–1719), and Madre Castillo (1671–1742) in Spanish America.

Lastly, a few nuns wrote in the more traditionally literary genres of poetry and drama. Although there are several cases of nuns writing secular verse for wealthy patrons, most nuns wrote about their spiritual reflections in popular verse forms or in response to civic and religious patrons requesting a play (*auto sacramental*) for the celebration of a religious feast day or carols (*villancicos*) to be sung during Mass. In this category, the most renowned authors are Marcela de San Félix (1605–1687), daughter of Golden Age Spain's famous dramatist, Lope de *Vega, and the Mexican, Sor Juana Inés de la *Cruz (1648–1695).

Kathleen Ann Myers

See also Autobiography in Spain: Beginnings to 1700; Autobiography in Spanish America; Biography in Spain: Beginnings to 1700; Biography in Spanish America; *Converso* Literature in Spain; Mysticism and Asceticism in Spain.

Work By:

Marcela de San Félix, *Coloquios del alma*. Ed. Susan Smith and Georgina Sabat de Rivers. Newark, NJ: Juan de la Cuesta, 2006.

María de San José Salazar, *The Book of the Hours of Recreation*. Ed. Alison Weber. Trans. Amanda Powell. Chicago: University of Chicago Press, 2002.

Mujica, Barbara, ed. *Women Writers of Early Modern Spain: Sophia's Daughters*. New Haven, CT: Yale University Press, 2004.

Myers, Kathleen A., and Amanda Powell, eds. and trans. *Wild Country Out in the Garden: The Spiritual Journals of a Colonial Mexican Nun*. Bloomington: Indiana University Press, 1999.

Myers, Kathleen A. *Word from New Spain: The Spiritual Autobiography of María de San José (1656–1719)*. Liverpool: Liverpool University Press, 1993.

Work About:

Bergmann, Emilie L., and Stacey Schlau, eds. *Approaches to Teaching the Works of Sor Juana Inés de la Cruz*. New York: Modern Languages Association of America, 2007.

Lavrin, Asunción. *Brides of Christ: Conventual Life in Colonial Mexico*. Palo Alto, CA: Stanford University Press, 2007.

McKnight, Kathryn Joy. *The Mystic of Tunja: The Writings of Madre Castillo, 1671–1742*. Amherst: University of Massachusetts Press, 1997.

Myers, Kathleen Ann. *Neither Saints nor Sinners: Writing the Lives of Women in Spanish America*. Oxford and New York: Oxford University Press, 2003.

Weber, Alison, ed. *Approaches to Teaching Literature: Teresa of Avila*. New York: The Modern Languages Association of America, 2009.

Converso Literature in Spain

The abundant literature by *conversos* (Jewish converts to Christianity, or their descendants) has strongly influenced

Spain's culture. Two distinct periods of *converso* literature production were created by the monarchy's momentous 1492 Edict of Expulsion, which invited all Jews to convert to Christianity and required expulsion for all who refused to do so. Writings before 1492 were produced when, for the most part, observing Jewish traditions did not seriously threaten one's safety; *converso* literature composed after 1492 is intertwined with *Renaissance and Golden Age Spanish literature and may be considered crypto-Jewish, that is to say, informed by a secret adherence to Jewish customs and beliefs.

During the first, medieval period, such authors as Pedro Alonso (1162–1210) converted to Christianity and produced literature that dealt openly with such religious issues as *Diálogo entre un judío y un cristiano* (12th century; Dialogue between a Jew and a Christian), and writings in Latin that mix Jewish folk tradition with Catholic medieval ideas and customs, as in *Disciplina Clericalis* (12th century; Ecclesiastical Discipline), a collection of racy short stories intended to educate young men who become ordained priests. After the 1391 pogrom and its massacres and the destruction of many Jewish neighborhoods in Andalusia, Castile, and Catalonia, the situation changed and the *conversos*, also known as "new Christians," assimilated as much as possible into an increasingly intolerant Christian society. Before Ferdinand and Isabella assumed control of the Spanish Crown, the situation deteriorated, prompting many more conversions, and new Christians aggressively self-assimilated and erased all signs that would differentiate them from the rest of society. Authors of this period include Alonso de Cartagena, with his *Discurso* (1436; Discourse) and *Defensorum Unitatis Christianae* (1450; In Defense of Christian Unity), Diego de Valera, composer of *Espejo de la verdadera nobleza* (1452; Mirror of True Nobility) and possibly Juan de Mena, who produced *Laberinto de Fortuna* (1444; Labyrinth of Fortune). These texts exposed the need for social acceptance and highlighted the social value of good character above a long lineage of Christian ancestry.

The very moment that the 1492 Edict of Expulsion made the practice of Judaism in Spain illegal, Antonio de Torquemada, himself a descendant of *conversos*, became inquisitor general. Torquemada became an overzealous persecutor of *conversos*. After this moment, no writers openly declared themselves *conversos*.

Scholarly research of genealogy and textual clues has unearthed the Jewish ancestry of many seminal writers of later generations, particularly between the 16th and 18th centuries; they are now considered *conversos*. One of the earliest post-1492 *converso* authors is Fernando de Rojas, composer of *La *Celestina* (1499; Eng. trans., 1987). Many of the best-studied writers in the 16th and 17th centuries were *conversos* or descendants of *conversos*, such as Juan de Mena, Santa *Teresa de Jesús, San *Juan de la Cruz, and Miguel de *Cervantes. Fray Luis de *León, one of the translators and poets of that day, composed Spanish translations of Horace's *Odes*, *Commentaries on the Book of Job* and *Song of Songs*; because of this last work he was denounced to the

*Inquisition and, from 1572 to 1576, imprisoned. His *De los nombres de Cristo* (1583–1585; *The Names of Christ*, 1984) was written in jail. Fray Luis also penned the prose instruction model *La perfecta casada* (1583; *The Perfect Wife*, 1943).

Noted Carmelite mystic Santa Teresa de Jesús (1515–1582) reformed the Order of the Carmel and composed her autobiography, *Libro de la vida* (1567; *The Life of Teresa of Jesus*, 1960), *Camino de perfección* (1567; *The Way of Perfection*, 1964), and *El castillo interior* (1577; *Interior Castle*, 1961), among other texts. Her reform initiatives provoked an investigation by the Inquisition in 1576 but the process was ultimately dropped several years later. Another notable mystic of the Catholic Church, San Juan de la Cruz (1542–1591), served as friend and spiritual counselor to Santa Teresa. Reformer of the Discalced Carmelites, his poems *Cántico Espiritual* (1618; *Spiritual Canticle*, 1996) and *Noche Oscura del Alma* (1618; *Dark Night of the Soul*, 1996) took inspiration from the Old Testament *Song of Songs*.

The case of philosopher and educator Juan Luis *Vives (1492–1540) as a *converso* is quite clear, as his parents were executed by the Inquisition when he was a boy. In 1509, he began studies at the Sorbonne in France, and never returned to Spain. His friendship with Erasmus of Rotterdam and Catherine of Aragon (wife of England's King Henry VIII) allowed him to live in England, where he was a professor at Oxford, and also to teach at Louvaine in Belgium. In 1529 Vives wrote, in Latin, one of Europe's first books about the importance of women's education (later translated to English as *The Education of a Christian Woman* (2000). He also advocated the improvement in living conditions of the poor in *De Subventione Pauperum* (1526).

Francisco Delicado (1480–1535) composed *La Lozana Andaluza* (1528; The Lusty Andalusian Woman). This novel in dialogue, unknown in Spain until the 19th century, gives examples of traditions and social networking of *conversos* outside of Spain. Delicado died in Venice.

By the 1600s, the Inquisition and civil authorities demanded a *Certificado de Limpieza de Sangre* (Certificate of Purity of Blood) documenting an individual's genealogy for eight generations in order to receive full privileges of citizenship. It is possible that this document was what prevented Miguel de *Cervantes from traveling to America as a colonist, as some scholars believe that the author of *Don Quijote* was a *converso*.

María Luisa García-Verdugo

See also Judeo-Spanish Writing in Spanish America; Sephardic Literature in Spain.

Work About:

Kaplan, Gregory. *The Evolution of Converso Literature*. Gainesville: University of Florida Press, 2002.

Kamen, Henry. *The Spanish Inquisition*. London: Yale University Press, 1997.

Coronado, Carolina (1823–1911)

Since her childhood, spent in Extremadura province, this Spanish poet experienced the limited education available to women when her mother forbade her to read and write poetry. Despite such limitations, she began composing verses, and at age 13 wrote "A la palma" (To the Palm), which was celebrated by writer Mariano José de *Larra in a laudatory poem. Dramatist Juan Eugenio *Hartzenbusch became her mentor and wrote the prologue to her first book, *Poesías* (1843; Poems). Letters she sent him show her trust in his guidance, corrections, and occasional censorship of compositions. Once famous, Coronado similarly encouraged and promoted other women writers' work. She also published a newspaper series, the "Galería de poetisas españolas" (1857) on women poets and related issues. Kirkpatrick observes that this series allowed her to establish a literary sisterhood that became the first romantic Spanish women poets' generation.

Two other poetry collections, identically titled (1852, 1872), were followed by isolated compositions published in newspapers. In addition to poems on nature, Coronado's themes involved historical and political topics, social issues, and metalyrical reflections. The poems "A la abolición de la esclavitud en Cuba" (To the Abolition of Slavery in Cuba) and "El marido verdugo" (The Executioner Husband) demonstrate her concern regarding oppression and domestic abuse. Disregarding the compliant tone expected of 19th-century women writers, she also expressed humor, irony, and sarcasm; thus the feisty nuances in "Ya Neira, despedí a la golondrina" (I Have Already Said Goodbye to the Swallow, Neira) reveal her annoyance with male criticism.

Once her family moved to Madrid, Coronado was invited to literary gatherings and aristocratic salons. Her interest in theater led her to produce plays that remain lost, except for *El cuadro de la Esperanza* (1849 debut; The Painting of Hope). In it, two men fight for Esperanza's love by painting competing portraits of her. Archived with Hartzenbusch's papers, it is now kept in Madrid's National Library. Her prose remains less studied, even though she published *Jarilla* (1850) and *La Sigea* (1854), historic novels influenced by *romanticism, in which cruelty, male domination, corruption, and greed among aristocrats are intertwined with oppositions and the author's reflections.

Coronado continued naming her works after her female progatonists, as in the novel *Luz* (1851), the short piece *Adoración* (1850), and the novella *Paquita* (1850). The latter text offers a parody of pastoral literature when the poet complains about the protagonist's prosaic name—so common that it hinders his creative inspiration. Her novel *La rueda de la desgracia* (1873; The Wheel of Misfortune) followed by the novella *El oratorio de Isabel la Católica* (1886; Queen Isabelle the Catholic's Oratory) share similarities, although the first one also criticizes materialism as well as compulsive gambling, and its consequences.

The feminist stance taken in some of Coronado's writing abated after she married U.S. diplomat Horace Perry in 1852 and began a family. The loss of two children in 1854 and 1873 exacerbated her eccentricities and prompted her isolation.

Mayte de Lama

Work By:

Obra en prosa: Carolina Coronado. Ed., intro. Gregorio Torres Negrera. Mérida, Spain: Editora Regional de Extremadura, 1999.

Poesías. Ed., intro. Noël M. Valis. Madrid: Castalia, 1991.

Work About:

Kirkpatrick, Susan. "Irony in Carolina Coronado's *Paquita*: The Voice of the Female Subject in Spanish romanticism." *Letras Peninsulares* 10.1 (Spring 1997): 169–83.

Surwillo, Lisa. "Poetic Diplomacy: Carolina Coronado and the American Civil War." *Comparative American Studies: An International Journal* 5.4 (2007): 409–22.

Valis, Noël M. "Autobiography as Insult." *Culture and Gender in Nineteenth-Century Spain*. Ed. Lou Charnon-Deutsch and Jo Labanyi. Oxford: Clarendon, 1995, 27–52.

Coronel Urtecho, José (1906–1994)

A great poet, prose author, essayist, playwright, historian, and disseminator of his country's culture, he was born in Granada, Nicaragua. In 1931, he and several other writers founded the *Grupo de Vanguardia*, an avant-garde literary movement that opposed classical literary models in order to experiment with modern forms. Coronel Urtecho also held diplomat posts in the United States and Spain and served as an official in the Somoza's administration, although he became a strong critic of it after he began writing about Nicaraguan history.

His poem "Oda a Rubén Darío" (1927; Ode to Rubén Darío) has been considered Nicaragua's first avant-garde aesthetic writing: using a new discourse that combined colloquial style, dialogue, and free verse, it rejected *modernismo*'s "inauthentic" and "dated" topics. Most of his poems are collected in the volume, *Pol-La D'Ananta Katanta Paranta*, taken from a verse by Homer that means, "Ever upward, downward, sideward and aslant they fared." This book includes odes, folk songs, and such avant-garde expressions as neologisms and words of classical origin. His narrative work, primarily published in literary journals, was later collected in the volume *Prosa de José Coronel Urtecho*.

María José Luján

Work About:

Oviedo, José Miguel. "Nicaragua Voices in Conflict." Trans. Lori M. Carlson. *Latin American Literature and Arts* 31 (1982): 19–25.

Corpi, Lucha (1946–)

Born in Jaltipán, Mexico, this U.S. Latina author is best known for her poetry and a detective series featuring a Chicana investigator. Her first poetry collection, *Fireflight* (1976), expresses her conflicting feelings as a Catholic Mexican living as a single mother in the United States, unable to fully identify with either culture. Corpi's writings echo the experiences of many women of color: oppressed because of race, class, and gender, they also fight the dominant culture and their families and community for their right to autonomy. In 1989, she published the autobiographical novel *Delia's Song*; in it the protagonist, a housewife and later a writer living in 1960s Berkeley, witnesses the violent repression during the Third World student strike.

Corpi's first detective novel, *Eulogy for a Brown Angel* (1992), features investigator and activist Gloria Damasco. The novel begins with the aftermath of the August 1970 incident at the National Chicano Moratorium, where police attacked protesters and peaceful families picnicking in the park. Gloria becomes a series detective whose cases usually involve issues of social justice affecting women and Chicanos. She reappears in *Cactus Blood* (1995), *Black Widow's Wardrobe* (1999), and *Crimson Moon* (2004). Corpi's bilingual work includes two collections of poetry, *Palabras de mediodía/Noon Words* (1980) and *Variaciones sobre una tempestad/Variations on a Storm* (1990), both translated by Catherine Rodríguez-Nieto, and *Where Fireflies Dance/Ahí, donde bailan las luciérnagas* (1997), a children's book for which Corpi wrote the English and the Spanish versions.

Gianna M. Martella

See also Chicano Writers; Chicano Movement Literature and Publishing; Latinos and Latinas in the United States: History, Culture, and Literature.

Work By:

Crimson Moon. Houston: Arte Público, 2004.
Palabras de mediodía. Noon Words. Houston: Arte Público, 2000.

Work About:

Armstrong, Jeanne. *Demythologizing the Romance of Conquest*. Westport, CT: Greenwood, 2000, 85–111.
Martella, Gianna M. "Family, Identity and the Latina Private Investigator." *Hispanic and Luso-Brazilian Detective Fiction*. Ed. Craig-Odders, Renée et al. Jefferson, NC: McFarland, 2006, 204–18.

Correa, Miguel (1956–)

Born in Placetas, Cuba, this novelist and critic has become an important voice among Cuban writers who arrived in the United States during the 1980 Mariel exodus. Correa has resided in New Jersey since his arrival, earning a Ph.D. in 2002 in Hispanic literatures from the City University of New York, in which system he is currently a professor. A collaborator for the literary journal *Mariel*, Correa is best known for his opposition to the Castro regime and his award-winning fiction.

First published in 1983 but then reworked in 2002, *Al norte del infierno* (*North of Hell*, 2008) is Correa's most important publication. Composed of 24 fragments that creatively and polyphonically narrate and reflect the years between the 1959 Cuban Revolution and the text's first appearance, the work offers a panoramic exposé of pre-Mariel life in Cuba and post-Mariel life in the United States, while connecting autobiographically to Correa's personal experience. A second novel, *Furia del discurso humano* (2006; The Avenging Goddess of Words), again employs a polyphonic voice and revolves around Regino, an apparent homosexual who, amidst the Cuban Revolution's *machismo*, is writing a novel chronicling life in Cuba. Aside from these texts, Correa has also penned several short stories and dramatic pieces.

Raúl Rosales Herrera

See also Cuban American Writers; *Mariel* Writers Generation.

Work By:

Furia del discurso humano. Los Angeles: Pureplay, 2006.

North of Hell. Trans. Alexis Romay. Los Angeles: Green Integer, 2008.

Work About:

García Ramos, Reinaldo. "Las voces del infierno." *Espéculo: Revista de Estudios Literarios* 24 (2003): 1–8.

Cortázar, Julio (1914–1984)

This seminal figure of Argentine and world literature was born in Brussels, Belgium, to Argentine parents. Throughout his prolific career, he wrote novels, short stories, literary and critical essays, and theatrical pieces, and translated authors like John Keats and Edgar Allan Poe. Cortázar studied at the University of Buenos Aires and taught French literature

at the University of Cuyo. In 1951, with a scholarship from the French government, he left Argentina, intending to never return due to his hatred of President Juan Domingo Perón and his regime. In France, Cortázar worked as a translator with UNESCO, and in 1981, the French government awarded him citizenship.

Inspired by the Cuban Revolution, he traveled to Cuba in 1961. Cortázar became actively involved in world politics and his writing was often politically charged. As an intellectual, writer, and politician, he visited Nicaragua, Chile, Mexico, and the United States, lecturing at the University of California, Berkeley. In 1967, Cuban journal *Casa de las Américas* published Cortázar's essay *Acerca de la situación del intelectual latinoamericano* (Regarding the Situation of the Latin American Intellectual). In it he confesses that, for the first time since leaving Argentina, he feels proud to be a Latin American author because the Cuban Revolutions placed the continent in the forefront of modern politics.

Cortázar's physical return to South America coincided with his ideological journey as a politically committed writer. Diagnosed with leukemia in 1981, Cortázar returned to Argentina to visit his mother a year before dying. Ignored by the Argentine government, his compatriots greeted him warmly. After his burial in Montparnasse, Alfaguara Press published his complete works, including previously unpublished writings.

Cortázar started writing as a young boy and continued throughout his life. One of his most famous works, the novel *Rayuela* (1963; *Hopscotch*, 1966) exhibits a noteworthy experimental structure. The author proposes that some chapters may be read or disregarded by readers, and that the suggested sequence of chapters can also be altered arbitrarily by readers. This reading as if one were playing hopscotch, jumping from chapter to chapter, marks two major characteristics of Cortázar's writing: its spontaneously playful nature and the writer's insistence on educating an active reader who participates in the creation of the literary work instead of passively enjoying it.

Cortázar is considered a master of the short story. Written in surrealistic style, his short fiction presents intriguing examples of the thin line that separates reality from fiction, and the real world from the fantastic one. He often surprises readers at the very end of a story that had started with the realistic depiction of characters and environment, and then discreetly introduced fantastic elements into the plot. *Continuidad de los parques* (1956; *Continuity of Parks*, 1967), one of his best-known tales, features a protagonist who returns home, sits in an armchair and starts reading a novel in which two characters plot to kill a man; at the novel's end, their victim appears to be the very protagonist who is reading the novel. Another example of Cortázar's technique that conflates reality with fantasy is his well-known story "Casa tomada" ("The House Taken Over"), included in *Bestiario* (1951; Bestiary). In it unidentifiable creatures invade the house of a brother and sister. The seemingly realistic world of the family is completely overtaken by the fantastic.

In "Las babas del diablo" ("Blow Up," 1967), from the collection *Las armas secretas* (1959; The Secret Weapons), Cortázar reflects upon the (un)reliability of narrative experience. The author switches narrative voices in the text, making it impossible for readers to determine the truth, and by doing so, gives readers the power to become creators of the story.

Ketevan Kupatadze

See also Novel in Spanish America: *Boom* Literature: 1950–1975.

Work By:

All Fires the Fire and Other Stories. Trans. Suzanne Jill Levine. London: Marion Boyars, 1973.

Blow Up and Other Stories. Trans. Paul Blackburn. New York: Pantheon, 1967.

Final Exam. Trans. Alfred Mac Adam. New York: New Directions, 1999.

A Manual for Manuel. Trans. Gregory Rabassa. New York: Pantheon, 1978.

Work About:

Critical Essays on Julio Cortazar. Ed. Jaime Alazraki. New York: Hall, 1999.

Julio Cortázar (Modern Critical Views). Ed. Harold Bloom. New York: Chelsea House, 2005.

Cossa, Roberto (1934–)

One of Argentina's most popular and renowned contemporary playwrights, Cossa's dramatic canon uniquely enacts Argentine portrayals of family, middle class, and immigration. Raised on the out-skirts of Buenos Aires, he first became involved in theater in 1957 when he began acting and directing with the San Isidro In-dependent Theater Group. Until 1976, Cossa also worked as a journalist for sev-eral Buenos Aires newspapers. He has written and premiered more than 25 plays and received national and international drama awards, including Argentina's National Prize for Theater.

Though consistently hailed as a realist, as demonstrated most emblematically in the major success *Nuestro fin de semana* (1964; Our Weekend), several later works reflect the heritage of the *sainete* and the *grotesco criollo*, early 20th-century Argentine genres documenting the experi-ence of recently arrived immigrants, first through parody, and later through more sober portrayals of urban alienation and the disillusion of the American dream. This influence is particularly rich in *La Nona* (1977; The Nona), perhaps Cossa's most famous work, featuring a narcissistic grandmother whose ravenous appetite leaves her family destitute and ultimately leads to its demise. Co-authored with playwrights Germán Rozenmacher, Carlos Somigliana, and Ricardo Talesnik, Cossa's experimental *El Avión Negro* (1970; The Black Plane) introduces a political vein to anticipate diverse societal reactions to Per-ón's mythic return. In 1981, Cossa partici-pated as a key organizer of **Teatro abierto* for a theatrical event widely considered one of the most significant acts of collec-tive resistance against the military dicta-torship (1976–1983). That first year, he premiered his play *Gris de Ausencia*

(1981; The Grayness of Absence), a play examining the sense of alienation and reverse nostalgia experienced by an Argentine family exiled in Europe.

Brenda Werth

See also Discépolo, Armando (1887–1971); *Género Chico Criollo and the* Río de la Plata *Saineteros* (*Sainete* Composers).

Work By:

Gris de ausiencia. Teatro III. Buenos Aires: de la Flor, 2000: 65–78.

La Nona. Teatro II. Buenos Aires: de la Flor, 2004: 67–137.

Nuestro fin de semana. Teatro I. Buenos Aires: de la Flor, 2005: 16–84.

Work About:

Woodyard, George. "The Theater of Ro-berto Cossa: A World of Broken Dreams." *Bucknell Review* 40:2 (1996): 94–108.

Costa Rica: History, Culture, and Literature

On September 18, 1502, during his fourth and final voyage to the New World, Chris-topher Columbus became the first Euro-pean explorer to visit Costa Rica. The name given to the lush land is owed to the native "Indians" who paddled out in canoes to greet the crew. Their gold body piercings and bands around their forearms conjured a "rich" coast to Spaniards. How-ever, during the early colonial era, Costa Rica's difficult access and lack of exploit-able resources caused Spaniards to bypass the region, lured instead by the readily available treasures of Mexico and Peru.

The first successful colonial city, Cartago, was erected in 1562.

Now recognized as one of the world's most biodiverse regions, evidence of human occupation in Costa Rica dates back 10,000 years. An early civilization left behind a vast array of perfectly spherical granite mounds ranging from the size of a hand to that of an SUV. Although archaeologists continue to study the spheres for their uses in astronomy, navigation, and the calendar, the site—located in the west, near the Pacific Ocean—is also a public park. Near the present capital city of San José, there exist ruins of a large, ancient city complete with aqueducts. In the southwestern region, fine artistic works and gold and jade jewelry date back more than 1,000 years. Ancient sites in the central highlands and the Nicoya peninsula on the Pacific side demonstrate the influence of early Mexican Olmec and Nahuatl civilizations.

Of the estimated 500,000 who resided in Costa Rica at the time of discovery contact, the principal indigenous groups were the so-called "Caribs" on the eastern coast, and the Borucas, Chibchas, and Diquis in the Southwest. Smaller groups inhabited the central highlands. The region along the current border with Panama housed the Chiriquí. The native population was greatly decimated by European diseases and enforced labor. Currently, about 1 percent of the population is of indigenous ethnicity. The now nearly extinct Chorotega culture, which arrived from Mexico's central valley some 1,000 years before the Spanish, is the best-known indigenous group. The name means "the people who move away." Chorotega sculptures and vases discovered in Guanacaste and Nicoya attest to a highly sophisticated culture.

Although little documented, during the mid- and late-colonial era, African slaves were brought to Costa Rica. Others, escaping slave labor on Caribbean islands, found refuge in coastal communities, where they mixed with indigenous populations. In the late 19th and early 20th centuries, laborers were brought in from Jamaica and other islands to work the banana plantations. Recent census cites a total of 70,000 persons of African heritage.

Costa Rica gained independence in 1821, as part of Mexico; two years later a civil war established its autonomy. Following years of an entrenched elite colonial system, land reforms were initiated. They were immediately contested, first by coffee barons, who overthrew the nation's first president, José María Castro, and by U.S. citizen William Walker, who invaded Mexico and several other Central American nations, intending to establish a slave state and declare himself ruler. After civil war erupted in 1848, the legislature abolished its national army, and has experienced no civil war since; this is now considered a distinguishing trait of Costa Rica. The 19th century's most notable president, Tomás Guardia, assumed power in 1870 and instituted progressive reforms.

Despite being the second-smallest nation in Central America, Costa Rica's ecotourism industry thrives. Additionally, the nation, whose population number close to 4,600,000 (July 2011 estimate), is attractive to U.S. companies involved in technological production, beginning with Intel. In 1987, Costa Rican President Oscar Arias was honored with the Nobel Peace Prize for his mediation between the Nicaraguan Sandinista government and its "Contra" rebels. Arias brought all Central American presidents to the table to sign the peace accord.

Costa Rica's significant literary production began with two tendencies in the late 19th century, the regional *costumbrista* style, and modernist–symbolist influence. The subsequent realism tendency sought to reflect genuine Costa Rican life; an excellent early example is Jenaro Cardona's *La esfinge del sendero* (1914; The Sphinx from the Path). Carmen Lyra (1888–1949), an early female writer-activist, founded the first Montessori school in San José. Active in the socialist movement, her novel *Bananos y hombres* (1931; Banana Trees and Men) denounces social injustice and the treatment of workers on Chiquita banana plantations. Also a folklorist, her *Cuentos de mi Tía Panchita* (1920; Stories of My Aunt Panchita) captures rural wisdom, humor, and traditions. Lyra suffered ostracism, and her work was banned until after her death.

In the next generation, award-winning novelist and short story writer Julieta Pinto (1922–) described the worker class and high society's lack of regard for them. Another prolific writer, Carmen Naranjo (1930–), served as ambassador to Israel and worked with international organizations for the betterment of Third World children's lives. Her award-winning novel *Los perros no ladraron* (1967; The Dogs Did Not Bark) stresses a sense of alienation in the urban environment, particularly for women, and the National Prize for Novel *Diario de una multitud* (1986; Journal of a Multitude) features an urban setting where individual reflections converge in a public space, opening to social revolt.

More recent writers of note include Fernando Contreras Castro (1963–), whose novel *Única mirando al mar* (1993; Única Contemplating the Sea) features a strong woman character and describes the effects of a consumer society; and Rafael Ángel Herra (1943–), author of *La guerra prodigiosa* (1986; The Prodigious War), who employs strategies of intertextuality to explore contemporary culture and society. During the 1980s, Costa Rican writers focused on themes of cultural identity, most notably in *Los estirpes de Montanchez* (1992; The Montanchez Pedigree) by Fernando Durán Ayanegui (1939–) and *Asalto al paraíso* (1992; Assault on Paradise*, 1998) by Tatiana *Lobo (1939–). The breathtaking poetry of Ana Istarú (1960–) portrays contemporary Costa Rican reality, especially her 1985 poem, "El hambre ocurre" (Hunger Occurs), in which death is chillingly personified as an uninvited guest who, feigning friendship, stealthily invades, violently nourishing itself upon the human body.

Costa Rican poets of African heritage include Eulalia Bernard (1935–), who uses innovative linguistic techniques, including neologisms combining Spanish, English, and indigenous and African Creole vocabulary. Her poems bring into focus the African-origen contributions to the formation of "Latin" American society.

Delia McDonald Woolery (1965–) aptly captures sensations and beauty in everyday objects, and Shirley Campbell (1965–) affirms female and African identity in passionate verse; her book-poem, *Rotundamente negra* (1994; Categorically Black), defines an existence between two opposite poles.

Elizabeth Coonrod Martínez

See also Appendix B for other entries related to Costa Rica.

Work About:

Helmuth, Chalene. *Culture and Customs of Costa Rica*. Westport, CT: Greenwood, 2000.

Mosby, Dorothy E. *Place, Language, and Identity in Afro-Costa Rican Literature*. Columbia: University of Missouri Press, 2003.

Palmer, Steven Paul, and Iván Molina Jiménez. *The Costa Rican Reader: History, Culture, Politics*. Durham, NC: Duke University Press, 2004.

Costumbrismo in Spanish America

This artistic style that produced literary and pictorial interpretations of local everyday life, mannerisms, and customs first developed as a genre in Spain between 1820 and 1870. *Literatura costumbrista* (literature of manners) manifested itself in the *cuadro* or *artículo de costumbres* (vignette of everyday life), a short prose piece. Spanish *costumbrismo* began before *romanticism, and influenced romanticism and the later realism movement through its realistic prose. These writings were normally restricted to descriptive text, keeping argument to a minimum. They described the lifestyle of the era, a popular local custom, or an individual stereotype. In many cases, as in the *artículos de costumbres* of Mariano José de*Larra, the pieces contained considerable satire. This literary style quickly expanded to America and was adopted by many writers, including Argentine Juan Bautista *Alberdi, Peruvians Felipe *Pardo y Aliaga and Manuel *Ascensio Segura, Guatemalan José Milla y Vidaurre, Venezuelans Rafael María Baralt and Abigail Lozano, an entire generation of Colombian authors writing for El Mosaico newspaper, and various other authors throughout Spanish America.

Costumbrista vignettes focused on generic descriptions of personality types (bullfighter, chestnut seller, water carrier, and so on) or scenes like a *romería* (pilgrimage) and market day. Large anthologies of such vignettes were compiled, such as *Los españoles pintados por sí mismos* (Spaniards Depicted by Themselves), which was first published in two volumes in 1843–1844. Spanish America soon followed with *Los cubanos pintados por si mismos* (1852; Cubans Depicted by Themselves) and two years later, *Los mexicanos pintados por sí mismos, tipos y costumbres nacionales* (1854; Mexicans Depicted by Themselves, National Types and Customs).

In Colombia, the discursive techniques and devices used in *costumbrismo* were put into effect by the intelligentsia to create a sense of national identity. Descriptions of customs and manners both from the capital city of Bogotá and the outlying provinces were used to portray Colombians to the outside reading public. Authors like Ricardo Silva, José Caicedo Rojas, José David Guaran, Ignacio Gutiérrez Vergara, Eugenio Díaz, Juan de Dios Restrepo, José María Vergara y Vergara, Jorge *Isaacs, José Manuel Marroquín, Tomás de *Carrasquilla, and José Eustacio Rivera became detailed observers that sometimes criticized and at other times just described customs and manners of different social classes and institutions.

The *cuadro de costumbres* and *artículo de costumbres* soon changed from a literary genre to a literary style. *Costumbrista* scenes appeared in most of the well-known 19th-century romantic and realist novels of Spanish America, such as Chilean Alberto *Blest Gana's realist novel *Martín Rivas* (1862); the romantic novel *María* (1867) by Colombia's Jorge *Isaacs; and *Cecilia Valdés* (1882), the important antislavery novel by Cuba's Cirilio *Villaverde, who used *costumbrista* scenes profusely to depict the lives of freed slaves. At the beginning of the 19th century, José Joaquín *Fernández de Lizardi's novel, *El periquillo sarniento* (1816; *The Mangy Parrot*, 2005), although written in the *picaresque mode, introduced many *costumbrista* scenes into the Latin American literary scenario.

Similar scenes appeared also in *costumbrista* theater in Peruvian plays like Manuel Ascensio Segura's *El Sargento Canuto* (1839) and Felipe*Pardo y Aliaga's *Frutos de la educación* (1830; Fruits of Education), and in Colombia in works by José María Samper. His play *Un alcalde a la antigua y dos primos a la moderna* (staged 1856; An Old-Fashioned Mayor and Two Modern Cousins) presents a common topic in *costumbrista* literature: the contrast between traditional values and modernity. Samper tells the story of a romance between two cousins, one a country girl and the other a modernized city dandy. While the playwright does not prescribe remedies, the author clearly brings his progressive political philosophy to the Colombian stage.

Costumbrismo influenced the visual art of the 19th century and was in turn influenced by that art. *Costumbrista* writers often composed literary sketches inspired by lithographs or pictures like the types that appeared in the earlier-mentioned *Los mejicanos pintados por si mismos*. *Costumbrista* art became particularly popular in 19th-century Perú, as seen in paintings by Pancho Fierro; in Colombia, in paintings and drawings by José María Espinosa and Ramón Torres Méndez; and in Mexico, in the art of José Agustín Arrieta.

Maida Watson

Work About:

Segre, Erica. *Intersected Identities: Strategies of Visualization in Nineteenth- and Twentieth-Century Mexican Culture*. New York: Berghahn, 2007.

Watson, Maida. *El Cuadro de costumbres en el Perú decimonónico*. Lima: Pontificia Universidad Católica del Perú, 1980.

Cota Cárdenas, Margarita (1941–)

A pioneer Chicana poet, novelist, and professor emeritus from Arizona State

University, she was born to Mexican migrant workers in California. From an early age, she showed a talent for writing. Initially, her writing voiced personal issues but later focused on social and feminist justice. As one of the very few Chicano writers who publish in Spanish, she has pioneered switching between two linguistic codes (Spanish and English).

Cota Cárdenas's poetry explores Chicana women's identity and portrays liberated women who question traditional cultural roles. In the poem "Nostalgia" she recalls her childhood desire to become a nun and ride away, as in a movie she had seen. *Noches despertando inConciencias* (1975; Nights Awakening UnAwareness) subverts patriarchal rule and myth as women become redeemers and the vital force.

In her first novel, *Puppet* (1985; Eng. trans., 2000), Spanish professor Petra Levya denounces the police's murder and cover-up of a 19-year-old Chicano laborer. In *Sanctuaries of the Heart/Santuarios del corazón* (2005; bilingual edition), narrator Petra Leyva explores the meaning of sanctuary (a safe place for personal growth; e.g., a university) for Chicanas after learning that her drunken father burned down his house.

With a grant from the National Endowment for the Arts, she and Eliana *Rivero cofounded Scorpion Press, which publishes bilingual texts by women.

Fabiola Fernández Salek

See also Chicano Writers; Chicano Movement Literature and Publishing.

Work By:

Puppet: A Chicano Novella. Trans. Barbara Riess and Trino Sandoval. Albuquerque: University of New Mexico Press, 2000.

Work About:

Rebolledo, Tey Diana. "The Bittersweet Nostalgia of Childhood in the Poetry of Margarita Cota-Cárdenas." *Frontiers* 5.2 (1980): 31–35.

Cotto-Thorner, Guillermo (1916–1983)

Born in Juncos, Puerto Rico, this author and Baptist minister is best known for two novels of immigration: *Trópico en Manhattan* (1951; Tropics in Manhattan) and *Gambeta* (1971). Each text chronicles Puerto Rican life in New York City's Spanish Harlem based on his personal observations during his years of ministering to *Spanish Harlem's Hispanic community. Filled with richly intimate details of daily life, both texts examine Puerto Rican migration to the United States within the frame of the Anglo-American immigration influence.

Cotto-Thorner also penned local columns for local New York City newspapers and numerous religious essays for Protestant periodicals. In 1945, a collection of 10 sermons was published as *Camino de victoria (sermones)* (Road of Victory [Sermons]).

Amarilis Hidalgo de Jesús

Work By:

Flores, Juan, ed. *Puerto Rican Arrival in New York: Narratives of the Migration, 1920–1950*. Princeton, NJ: Markus Weiner, 2005, 125–61.

Gambeta. San Juan, Puerto Rico: Cordillera, 1971.

Trópico en Manhattan. San Juan, Puerto Rico: Cordillera, 1951.

Criollista **Novel in Spanish America**

Also labeled "regionalist novels" or *novelas de la tierra* (novels of the land) because of their local color content, *criollista* texts appeared between the 1910s and 1940s. Central to them is man's connection and struggle with nature and his physical environment. Allegory plays a frequent role in depicting the man–nature relationship and its links to national foundations.

These novels surfaced throughout Latin America in reaction to external forces and as an expression of cultural unity, as the United States sought to promote a pan-American agenda throughout the continent to extend and cement its influence there. In response, literature became a vehicle for collectively affirming the continent's unique essence and distinctive reality, as Latin Americans used *criollista* narratives to articulate their distinct cultural, geographic, and historical identity. In 1910, Latin America's 100-year anniversary of the continent's independence movement from Spain also helped solidify the unified response.

Novels of this period exhibit a preoccupation with indigenous elements. Representations of these autochthonous national identities in terms of peoples and geography are commonplace, as in the *gaucho*'s popularity and use of the *pampa* (prairie) as a national territory in Argentina *criollista* narratives. These indigenous aspects deliberately emphasize and affirm elements of national identity.

National or continental territory is depicted in direct connection with its human inhabitants; consequently, these narratives accord geographic space the relevancy of a main character. Natural forces of the nation and continent—its landscape and diverse environments—are depicted as having generated Latin American and national identity. Ironically, individual pursuits to define and affirm cultural identity are also challenged by natural forces; indeed, many novels portray nature as a destructive force. Through this paradoxical dynamic of a physical environment that helps define Latin American identity but also stands as an obstacle to its affirmation, *criollista* novels garner their complexity and allegorical potential.

These texts enjoyed tremendous popular and international success. Three novels stand out as most prominent. *La vorágine* (1924; *The Vortex*, 1935), by Colombian José Eustasio Rivera, presents nature as an agent of death and destruction. Its sensitive protagonist Arturo Cova enters the Colombian jungle with a group of men in hopes of rescuing his kidnapped lover. The group soon gets lost in the rainforest and faces the full wrath of nature, from deadly insects to dangerous torrents. The jungle brings the group peril, disease, and the certainty that no one can escape nature's fury.

Don Segundo Sombra (1926; Eng. trans., 1948), by Argentine Ricardo *Güiraldes, celebrates *gaucho* life in the *pampa*. A young orphaned protagonist encounters Don Segundo, learns from him the essence of the *gaucho* way of life and its special connection to the land, and becomes enlightened in the process. Eventually, the young man discovers that he is a landowner and must therefore abandon his *gaucho* existence. Nevertheless, what he has learned from Don Segundo will inform and favorably impact his new position as a land-owning master.

Doña Bárbara (1929), by Venezuelan Rómulo *Gallegos, can be interpreted as an allegorical narration of the civilization versus barbarism dichotomy. The young Santos Luzardo travels from the city to his property in the plains and discovers it has been taken over by Doña Bárbara, a ruthless woman intent on asserting her will and control. The modernization and enlightenment personified by Luzardo plays out—and wins—against their antithetical incarnations in Doña Bárbara. The character of Doña Bárbara best illustrates the complexity and inherent contradictions of the *criollista* project, as she simultaneously represents the autochthonous land evocative of Latin American identity, while also acting as a destabilizing force that must be confronted and overcome in order to enable progress.

Other *criollista* novels include Cuban Luis Felipe Rodríguez's *Ciénaga* (1937; The Swamp), which explores *guajiro* (Cuban farmer) life amidst the rural landscape and abusive local landowners; Chilean Mariano *Latorre Court's *Zurzulita* (1920), a tragic love story, conditioned by nature, between a provincial man and a school teacher; and Puerto Rican Enrique *Laguerre's *La llamarada* (1935; The Blaze), featuring a young man's confrontation with social injustices on a sugar cane plantation. Finally, Chilean Pedro Prado's *Alsino* (1920; Eng. trans., 1995) follows the ordeal of a peasant boy after he magically grows wings following a fall, blending local color and realism with the poetic, philosophical symbolism of the modernist tradition.

Raúl Rosales Herrera

See also Amazon Theme in Spanish American Literature; Gaucho Literature; *Indigenismo* in Spanish American Literature.

Work About:

Alonso, Carlos. *The Spanish American Regional Novel: Modernity and Autochthony.* Cambridge: Cambridge University Press, 1990.

Cruz, Ramón de la (1731–1794)

Born in Madrid, this successful Spanish playwright participated in the dispute between those who defended French cultural influence in the peninsula and those who reacted against it. De la Cruz modeled neoclassic patterns to make them compatible with autochthonous genres inherited from Spain's baroque era. In particular, he reworked the *sainete*, a short one-act play of humorous and popular themes; he supposedly wrote more than four hundred. In addition to *sainetes*, his enormous theatrical *oeuvre* included **zarzuelas* (operettas), operas, *tonadillas escénicas*, *loas*, *introducciones*, and adaptations of French and Italian plays. Of note are *La Briseida* (1768) and *Las labradoras de Murcia* (1769; The Farmers from Murcia), both with music by Rodríguez de Hita; *El buen marido* (1770; The Good Husband), with music by García Pacheco; and *La Clementina* (1786) with music by Boccherini. De la Cruz's hybrid aesthetics, which fused aristocratic and popular tastes and conventions, were largely criticized by such contemporary authors as Tomás de *Iriarte, Gaspar Melchor de *Jovellanos, and Leandro *Fernández de Moratín.

Rafael Lamas

See also Enlightenment in Spain: 1700–1800.

Work About:

Bussey, William. *French and Italian Influence on the Zarzuela 1700–1770*. Ann Arbor, MI: UMI Research Press, 1982.

Gallego, A. *La música en tiempos de Carlos III*. Madrid: Alianza, 1988.

Cruz, Sor Juana Inés de la (1648–1695)

She is considered the most outstanding figure of 17th-century colonial Latin America, as well as one of the best poets of Spain's *Golden Age. Until recently, there were no specific data on Sor Juana's life other than her autobiographical letter *Respuesta a Sor Filotea de la Cruz* (written 1691; Response to Sor Filotea de la Cruz). Her recently discovered baptismal certificate states that Juana Inés Ramírez de Asbaje was born in San Miguel de Nepantla, Mexico. Juana was raised in the house of her maternal grandparents, where she secretly learned to read at age three.

When she was about seven and already completely literate, she wanted to study at the University in Mexico City; upon her mother's refusal, Juana quenched her thirst for learning by reading a variety of books borrowed from her grandfather's library. Several years later, she was sent to the city under the care of wealthier relatives. There, she devoted herself to studying Latin, a language she mastered in only 20 lessons. Her beauty and intelligence gained her a position as lady-in-waiting in the viceroyal court under the patronage of the Marquise of Mancera. At age 17, Juana brilliantly proved her intellectual genius by successfully passing a public oral examination conducted by several Mexican scholars of her time.

On August 14, 1667, determined to pursue her academic interests, Juana entered the Convent of the Discalced Carmelites of Saint Joseph. Unable to adapt to the rigorous confinement and highly restrictive rules of convent life, she left the order three months later to rejoin the court. On February 21, 1669, Juana entered the Convent of the Order of St. Jerome, where she adopted the name Sor Juana Inés de la Cruz. Her intellectual and scientific curiosity gained her the admiration of the most outstanding scholars and writers of the

New World. At a time when few men could read and write, Sor Juana owned a vast personal library exceeding 4,000 volumes. Members of the viceroyal court constantly commissioned her to write poetry and drama, which she did with great success.

Despite her fame as a poet and playwright, Sor Juana had to constantly defend her intellectual vocation within a society where the Spanish Inquisition was still active in the colonies and the realm of academia was strictly reserved for men. In 1690, an anonymous person commissioned her to compose a critique on a sermon delivered in 1650 by Portuguese Jesuit Antonio de Vieyra. In this essay, later published under the title of *Carta Atenagórica* (Athenagoric Letter), Sor Juana questioned and challenged Father Vieyra's theological views. The bishop of Puebla, Manuel Fernández de Santa Cruz, replied to Sor Juana's letter with one of his own, signed under the pseudonym Sor Filotea de la Cruz. The letter reveals his admiration of the nun's erudition and rhetorical dexterity, but it aims to discourage her interest in profane literature. This attack resulted in Sor Juana's famous autobiographical essay, *Respuesta a Sor Filotea de la Cruz* (c. 1692; Response to Sor Filotea). Here, the Mexican nun tactfully, yet sarcastically, justifies her scholarly vocation as a natural impulse God laid upon her, while at the same time admitting that convent life was the most decent path she could follow since she felt total abhorrence toward marriage.

In this firsthand account, Sor Juana reveals several aspects of her personality as she vehemently defends women's right to receive an education. In 1692, the first edition of the second volume of her works was successfully published in Seville; however, the Mexican nun had already decided to give up her studies and writing and devote herself completely to religious life. She disbursed all her possessions, forsaking a life-long pursuit to attain universal knowledge, and finally entered the spiritual path. She sold her books and her musical and scientific instruments, donating all proceeds to charity. A year later, she contracted cholera in an epidemic that plagued Mexico, and died on April 17.

Sor Juana's work reflects the influence of the main literary, philosophical, theological, and scientific tendencies of 17th-century European intellectual thought. Her work embraces a wide variety of poetic styles and encompasses a diverse array of such literary genres as carols, eulogies, essays, comedies, and secular and religious plays. Each of her writings offers a genuine example of the linguistic, rhetorical, and mental games typical of euphuism and conceptism (17th-century literary movements that often used such stylistic literary devices as riddles, euphemisms, conceits, and puns). In her excellence, Sor Juana joins the Spanish Golden Age's greatest writers, including Lope de *Vega, Francisco *Quevedo, Luis de *Góngora, and Pedro *Calderón de la Barca.

María Claudia André

See also Convent Writing in Spain and the New World; Feminism in Spanish America; Inquisition and Literature in the Hispanic World.

Work By:

Pawns of a House/Los empeños de una casa. Ed. Susan Hernández Araico. Trans. Michael McGaha. Tempe, AZ: Bilingual Review, 2005.

The Three Secular Plays of Sor Juana Inés de la Cruz. Ed., trans. Guillermo Schmidhuber and Olga Martha Peña Doria. Lexington: University Press of Kentucky, 1999.

Work About:

Merrim, Stephanie, ed. *Feminist Perspectives on Sor Juana Inés de la Cruz*. Detroit: Wayne State University Press, 1991.

Paz, Octavio. *Sor Juana, or, the Traps of Faith*. Trans. Margaret Sayers Peden. Cambridge, MA: Belknap, 1988.

Salazar, Norma. *Foolish Men! Sor Juana Inés de la Cruz as Spiritual Protagonist, Educational Prism, and Symbol for Women*. DeKalb: Northern Illinois University, 1994.

Sor Juana Inés de la Cruz Project. http://www.dartmouth.edu/~sorjuana/.

Cruz Varela, María Elena (1953–)

Born in rural Colón, Matanzas, this Cuban poet and human rights activist was largely self-educated. She began both activities in the mid-1980s. In 1990, she founded the peaceful opposition group *Criterio Alternativo* (Alternative Criteria), penning its "Manifesto" (1991), for which she was attacked, imprisoned, and expelled from the National Union of Cuban Writers and Artists. While incarcerated, she was nominated for two prizes (the Nobel Peace Prize and Spain's Prince of Asturias Prize), and awarded the Liberty International Prize for Freedom (1992) and the Poetry International Award, Rotterdam Poetry Festival (1993). Ruth Behar included her writing in *Bridges to Cuba* (1994), Mari Rodríguez-Ichaso featured her in the documentary, *Branded by Paradise* (1999), and Nilo Cruz's *Two Sisters and a Piano* (1998) is partially inspired by her life.

Nourished by her activism, Cruz Varela's free-form poetry is notable for its testimonial qualities and biblical imagery, bringing to light social and gender injustices in a style reminiscent of Russian poet Anna Akhmatova. Through her poetic convocation, she exhorts her fellow-citizens to assert their dignity and to enunciate their shared moral principles. In the novelized testimonial *Dios en las cárceles cubanas* (2002; God in Cuban Jails), she fictionalizes her own experience and that of other women, through whose voices she critiques inhumane prison conditions while highlighting female spiritual strength in resisting oppression. This text marks a transition to her 21st-century historiographic metafiction, in which she recreates the lives of Joan of Arc and Gertrudis *Gómez de Avellaneda, figures who exemplify the activism portrayed in her poetic themes. Exiled in 1994, she has lived in Puerto Rico, Spain, and Miami.

Elizabeth Espadas

See also Exile Writing in the Hispanic World; Testimonial Writing in Central America; Women Writers in Cuba: 1959 to Present.

Work By:

Ballad of the Blood/Balada de la sangre: The Poems of María Elena Cruz Varela. Ed., trans. Mairym Cruz-Bernal and Deborah Digges. New York: Ecco, 1995.

Work About:

Cámara, Madeline. *Vocación de Casandra: Poesía femenina cubana subversiva en María Elena Cruz Varela.* New York: Peter Lang, 2001.

Serrano, Pío. "La poesía de María Elena Cruz Varela." *Revista Hispano Cubana* (2002): 83–85.

Cuadra, Pablo Antonio (1912–2002)

Born in Managua, Nicaragua, this essayist, literary critic, playwright, and renowned poet also cofounded (1931) the *Grupo de Vanguardia*, an avant-garde literary movement that opposed classical literary models in order to experiment with modern forms. He became president of Nicaragua's Academy of Language (1945), codirector of *La Prensa* newspaper (1954), and editor of the important *El Pez y La Serpiente* literary journal (1961).

Cuadra's writing does not belong to any particular literary group; instead, his books represent a national, poetic response to foreign meddling of any kind. *Poemas nicaragüenses, 1930–1933* (1934; *Nicaraguan Poems*) expresses strong concern for Nicaraguan identity, and that of Latin America, and offers affirmation of Nicaraguan customs, speech, and daily life. The collection constitutes the country's first published literature using the new, avant-garde writing.

La tierra prometida (1952; *The Promised Land*) consists of mature poems that combine a personal, symbol-laden expression rooted in such pre-Columbian elements as the jaguar, the serpent, and the moon, and influenced by indigenous writings. Cuadra's full-bodied yet unadorned style sharply opposes the stylized, cerebral expression of *Modernismo.

María José Luján

Work By:

Songs of Cifar and the Sweet Sea: Selections from "Songs of Cifar, 1967–1977." Trans. Grace Schulman and Ann McCarthy de Zavala. New York: Columbia University Press, 1979.

The Birth of the Sun: Selected Poems, 1935–1985. Trans. Steven F. White. Greensboro, NC: Unicorn, 1988.

Work About:

Simon, Greg. "Horizons: Nicaragua and Pablo Antonio Cuadra." *Northwest Review* 26.3 (1988): 58–64.

White, Steven. "Poetry Is the Plenitude of Humanity's Word: An Interview with Pablo Antonio Cuadra." *Literature and Arts of the Americas* 67 (Fall 2003): 28–31.

Cuba: History, Culture, and Literature

Christopher Columbus discovered Cuba, the largest island in the Caribbean and the westernmost island in the Antilles, on his first expedition to the New World in 1492. The native Taíno and Ciboney populations declined rapidly after the Spanish discovery, resulting in an increased demand for and importation of African slaves. At the height of the slave trade, Havana became the port of departure for all fleets carrying treasure to Spain. The motherland tightened its administrative grip following a brief British occupation of *Havana (1762–1763). Despite a boom in sugar production and exportation, the mounting interventionism sparked a cycle of independence movements, rebellions, and oppression throughout the 1800s. The unsuccessful first war of independence (1868–1878) resulted in a particularly oppressive backlash. Only when the United States aided Cuba in a second war (1895–1898) did Cuba win its independence from Spain. Slavery was abolished in 1886.

Although the Treaty of Paris officially granted freedom from Spain on December 10, 1898, the United States directly administered the island's government until May 20, 1902, when the Cuban republic was officially instated. The republic (1902–1958) was characterized by cycles of economic booms and recessions linked to the sugar industry's ups and downs. The trend of democratically elected presidents of the republic was interrupted by the presidencies of Gerardo Machado (1925–1933) and Fulgencio Batista (1940–1944). At the end of his four-year term, Machado refused to cede power after the prescribed term of four years, and responded to the ensuing protests, debates, and demonstrations with violence and oppression. Following a 1933 coup, Batista assumed command of the military. He served as president from 1940 to 1944. After running unsuccessfully for the presidency in 1952, Batista staged another coup and took power forcibly, remaining in office until his exile from the island in December 1958. The backdrop of intense corruption, economic woes, an unpredictable sugar industry, and the oppressive Batista regime set the stage for Fidel Castro's ascent to power on January 1, 1959.

Cuba was not a Marxist state at the start of the revolution. The United States' increasingly closed political stance toward Cuba in the early 1960s culminated in enactment of a trade embargo (1961–present). The loss of U.S.-owned land on the island forced Cuba to seek support from the Soviet Union. With Castro's leadership came an upper- and middle-class exodus to South Florida, the Miami neighborhood of Little Havana being the most salient Cuban immigrant/exile community in the United States. Castro declared Cuba a socialist state in 1961 following the unsuccessful Bay of Pigs invasion, an attack that was sponsored by the United States and involved aerial attacks on Cuban air force bases by recent exiles. The backdrop of the Cold War and increasing tension between the U.S. and the USSR set the stage for the Cuban Missile Crisis (October 1962), a brief conflict surrounding the presence of Soviet nuclear weapons on Cuban soil. The 1960s and 1970s saw expanding bureaucracies and institutions of the Communist government and massive programs aimed at increasing sugar production. The constitution, enacted on

February 24, 1976, has been amended twice: July 1992 and June 2002. The 1992 revisions came about in reaction to a time of economic upheaval and social unrest, now known as the "special period." After worsening economic and human conditions in the 1980s, waves of immigrants began leaving Cuba for the United States, many using a makeshift raft (*balsero*) to make the 90-mile crossing to Florida. The trend continues today.

Cuba is divided into 14 provinces and one special municipality (The Isle of Youth). Havana, the capital, is the cultural, administrative, and population center. Primary agricultural products include sugar, tobacco, citrus, coffee, rice, and livestock. Natural resources consist of cobalt, nickel, iron ore, and chromium. Although Cuba produces some 72,000 barrels of oil per day, it relies on oil from Venezuela, its largest import partner.

Cuba's involvement in the slave trade profoundly impacted the island's racial composition. Of the country's 11,087,330 inhabitants (July 2011 estimate), 62 percent are mixed race or black, 37 percent are white and 1 percent is Chinese. Prior to the Castro regime, 85 percent of Cubans classified themselves as Roman Catholic, with other religions including Protestant, Jehovah's Witnesses, Judaism, and *Santería*. Cuba boasts the highest rate of literacy in the world: 99.8 percent.

The Cuban Ministry of Education subsidizes education for all citizens. Schools and universities are public; private institutions are prohibited. An established university culture notwithstanding, the education system is infiltrated by pro-Castro and procommunist agendas. Cuba has three national newspapers: *Granma*, the Communist Party's principal outlet; *Juventud Rebelde*, a publication of the Young Communists Union; and, the Cuban Workers Center's *Trabajadores*. Various regional newspapers exist. The national sport is baseball; *soccer is also popular.

Cuba's rich literary tradition began to flourish in the 19th century with such figures as novelist and poet Gertrudis *Gómez de Avellaneda (1814–1873), novelist Cirilio *Villaverde (1812–1894), and two poets of African descent: freed slave Gabriel de la Concepción *Valdés, known as *Plácido* (1809–1844), and the slave Juan Francisco *Manzano (1797–1854). Avellaneda and Villaverde each authored canonical slave novels, *Sab* (1841; Eng. trans., 1994) and *Cecilia Valdés* (1882; Eng. trans., 2005), respectively. The most notable Cuban literate is without doubt the poet, journalist, essayist, and patriot José *Martí (1853–1895). His most important works include the nostalgic, emotive, and patriotic *modernismo* poetry typical of collections like *Ismaelillo* (1882; *Little Ishmael*, 2007), *Versos sencillos* (1891; *Simple Verses*, 1998) and *Versos libres* (1891; *Free Verses*, 1997). Martí's fervent criticism of U.S. interventionism in Cuba appears in his seminal essay *Nuestra América* (1891; *Our America*, 2001).

Noted 20th-century Cuban writers include Alejo *Carpentier (1904–1980), Nicolás *Guillén (1902–1989), José *Lezama Lima (1910–1976), Guillermo *Cabrera Infante (1929–2005), Severo *Sarduy (1937–1993), and José *Triana (1931–). Carpentier has become one of

Latin America's most prolific and respected prose writers, with such works as *Los pasos perdidos* (1953; *The Lost Steps*, 1957), *El reino de este mundo* (1949; *The Kingdom of This World*, 1956), and *El siglo de las luces* (1962; *Explosion in a Cathedral*, 2001). Guillén is a capital voice for Cuba's racially mixed population, and is largely responsible for popularizing African themes in literature during a time of heightened racism and disparity toward blacks. Texts like Lezama Lima's *Paradiso* (1966; *Paradise*, 2000), Cabrera Infante's *Tres tristes tigres* (1967; *Three Trapped Tigers*, 1997), and Sarduy's *De donde son los cantantes* (1967; *From Cuba with a Song*, 1994) challenge conventional notions of novelistic practice in a so-called "neobaroque" fashion. Lezama Lima also composed poetry. Finally, Triana has made notable contributions to Cuban theater. His *La noche de los asesinos* (1964; The Night of the Assassins) offers a key commentary on the need for social justice in revolutionary Cuba.

Jeremy L. Cass

See also Appendix B for other entries related to Cuba.

Work About:

Bethel, Leslie. *Cuba: A Short History*. Cambridge: Cambridge University Press, 1998.

Domínguez, Jorge I. *Cuba: Order and Revolution*. Cambridge, MA: Harvard University Press, 1978.

González Echevarría, Roberto. *Cuban Fiestas*. New Haven, CT: Yale University Press, 2010.

Pérez, Louis A. *On Becoming Cuban: Identity, Nationality, and Culture*. New York: HarperCollins, 1999.

Pérez Firmat, Gustavo. *The Havana Habit*. New Haven, CT: Yale University Press, 2010.

Thomas, Hugh. *Cuba or The Pursuit of Freedom*. New York: Da Capo, 1998.

Cuban American Writers

Due to the political ups and downs of Cuba, Cuban authors have long written literature both on the island and abroad. Since the 19th century, Cuban writers have published in the United States, producing writings commonly labeled as Cuban exile literature. Some critics claim that Cuban American literature production started in the 19th century, and that such writers in exile as José *Martí (1853–1895), Cirilo *Villaverde (1812–1894), and Anselmo *Suárez y Romero (1818–1978) can be part of both Cuban and Cuban American literary traditions.

As a result of the Cuban revolution (1959), another group of Cuban authors, including Lino *Novás Calvo (1905–1983), Lydia *Cabrera (1899–1991), José Sánchez-Boudy (1928–), and Enrique Labrador Ruiz (1902–1991), sought exile in the United States. Their works, written and published in Spanish, frequently criticize the Cuban Revolution and Marxism and idealize the old Cuba. Dissident Cuban writers like Heberto *Padilla (1932–2000), Belkis Cuza Malé (1942–), Reinaldo *Arenas (1943–1990), and César Leante (1928–) reached exile in the United

States in the 1970s and during the *Mariel boatlift of 1980. These writers, who may have supported the rise of the Revolution, were persecuted as they started expressing open dissatisfaction with the Castro regime.

Others use the term Cuban American writers to refer specifically to those writers of Cuban origin who arrived in the United States as children or adolescents after the 1959 Cuban revolution, thus being educated first as Cuban, and then immersed in the U.S. education system. These authors have been identified as the "one-and-a half" generation, a term popularized by Gustavo *Pérez Firmat (1949–), who is part of this group himself. Many of these writers, such as Eliana *Rivero (1940–), Omar Torres (1945–), Pablo Medina (1948–), Carlos Eire (1950–), Roberto Fernández (1951–), and Elías Miguel Muñoz (1954–), started publishing in Spanish, but later shifted to English. Others, such as Lourdes Gil (1951–), keep Spanish as the language of choice.

Another coined term, Cuban American ethnic writers, designates writers who came to the United States at a very early age, for example Cristina García (1958–), Achy Obejas (1956–), Ruth Behar (1956–), or who were born in the United States to Cuban parents, as was the case of José Yglesias (1919–1995), from an earlier generation. Although these writers share a bicultural condition, some of them may have never mastered Spanish, since the experiences of their formative years took place in the United States.

The generational distance between these writers and their relationship toward Cuba and the United States contributes to a richly varied literature regarding ideological perspectives, attitudes toward identity and assimilation, and representation and connection to Cuba and the United States. If nationalism and politics are key topics for Cuban exile writers, the "one-and- a half" generation focuses on childhood memories about a Cuba idealized as the locus of happiness and/or represented as a traumatic place of poverty, repression, and violence.

Cuban Americans' bicultural status, explored from contradictory views, is another recurrent topic among these writers. Depictions of the life and fragmentation within the Cuban community also provide a source of inspiration. Roberto Fernández, in *La montaña rusa* (1985; The Roller Coaster) and *Raining Backwards* (1988), opts for a parodic, satirical discourse to illustrate tensions between older Cuban exiles and their children and the south-Floridian Anglo hostility toward Cubans. Other such writers as Pablo Medina in *The Marks of Birth* (1994) and Margarita Engle in *Skywriting* (1995) portray the Cuban community's fragmentation and diaspora in tragic terms, and human rights issues are scrutinized. Despite the diversity within Cuban American literary production, these texts share a historical and political relevance to their different reconstructions of space, Cuba, and the United States.

Mercedes Guijarro-Crouch

Work About:

Álvarez Borland, Isabel. *Cuban-American Literature of Exile*. Charlottesville: University Press of Virginia, 1998.

Pérez Firmat, Gustavo. *Life on the Hyphen: The Cuban-American Way.* Austin: University of Texas Press, 1994.

Cuban Exile Writing outside the United States

Political circumstances of their nation have forced numerous Cuban writers to live and write abroad. Although proximity made many choose the United States, some have moved to other countries. Even before achieving independence, 19th-century Cuban writers with proindependence ideas were forced into exile in Latin America (José María de *Heredia [1842–1905], Juan Clemente Zenea [1832–1871]) and, ironically, even Spain (José *Martí [1853–1895] was deported to Spain at the beginning of the 1870s). With the Cuban Republic's birth in 1902, two main waves of exile writers can be considered. Before the triumph of Fidel Castro's revolution, especially during Fulgencio Batista's dictatorship in the 1950s, such canonical figures as Alejo *Carpentier (1904–1980) and Nicolás Guillén (1902–1989) lived in Latin America until 1959. Once Castro assumed power, many writers left the island for the United States or Western Europe (Guillermo *Cabrera Infante [1929–2005], Calvert Casey [1924–1969], Jesús *Díaz [1941–2002], Abilio *Estévez [1954–], César Leante [1928–], Eduardo Manet [1927–], Severo *Sarduy [1937–1993], Nivaria Tejera [1929–], Zoé *Valdés [1959–], René Vázquez Díaz [1952–]), to name a few); for Latin America (Antonio Orlando

Rodríguez [1956–], Andrés Jorge [1960–]); and even as far as South Africa (Mireya Robles [1934–]). Clearly, Cuban exile writing extends far beyond the Cuban American community, and encompasses the globe.

The large number of writers and the different places and dates of their exile experience inspire richly diverse topics in their writing; nonetheless, some common themes have emerged since the 19th century. Common Cuban exile literature themes that are seen in other cultural traditions include the nostalgia of exile, with its extensive list of farewells, memories, and recollections of the island; politics, especially denunciation, either subtly or overtly exposed, always criticizing whoever is in power (the Spaniards in the 19th century, then Batista, later Castro); reflection on the new country of residence, noting similarities and differences with Cuba, and at times falling into stereotypes. Recently, the urban quality has surfaced: most short stories and novels take place in a city; very few are rural. Although, unlike the exiles who have moved to the United States, a different language is not the reality they face (since in most cases their host countries are Spanish-speaking: Spain and most of Latin America); in some cases (such as France), choosing a language becomes a creative decision. The majority prefer to write in Spanish (from Cabrera Infante to Valdés), but occasionally an author chooses to use the language of the host country (Eduardo Manet's narratives are all written in French and published by prestigious editorial houses, and even one of Cabrera

Infante's books, *Holy Smoke*, was originally written in English); this preference for Spanish allows for another topic, language, and especially the exploration of Cuban speech, or *hablar cubano*. Other typical topics of Cuban letters, such as the sea, Cuban identity, or race are common in most of these authors.

Besides literature, these exiles have been active in politics and the publishing world. Several Cuban writers have become publishers or directed collections in Spanish-speaking countries, such as Playor, Pliegos, and Verbum. Jesús Díaz also founded and directed until his death *Encuentro de la Cultura Cubana*, a journal that attempted to give voice to both sides of the political spectrum, and, like all things Cuban, was born and existed in a turbulent polemic. These authors went beyond producing works, and attempted to create a web of readers that included the citizens of the host country. This effort has paid dividends, as exile publications have recently initiated a boom in Cuban literature outside the island, mostly in Western Europe. Publication of Zoé Valdés's highly influential novel *La nada cotidiana* (1996; *Yocandra in the Paradise of Nada*, 1997) and its success in France, Germany, and Spain gave way to several other award-winning works by different Cuban authors—some living on the island, but publishing abroad—during the second half of the 1990s, showing that the Cuban diaspora is very much alive in creative terms at the beginning of the 21st century.

Miguel Ángel González-Abellás

Work About:

Espinosa Domínguez, Carlos. *El peregrino en comarca ajena*. Boulder, CO: Society of Spanish and Spanish American Studies, 2001.

Smorkaloff, Pamela Maria. *Cuban Writers on and off the Island*. New York: Twayne, 1999.

Cuban *Special Period* Fiction

This label designates a number of novels and short stories published between 1990 and 2005, written by Cubans living on the island or abroad, and having as their subject matter the peculiar situation in Cuba during those years. In 1990, Fidel Castro, then president of Cuba, declared it a "special period in times of peace," referring to the new era brought on by the fall of the Soviet Bloc, which triggered the withdrawal of Soviet subsidies to Cuba's economy. By 1993, Cubans had lost 70 percent of their purchasing power and were suffering severe shortages of food, medicine, and gasoline. To salvage the economy, the Cuban government introduced several reforms in this period, including legalization of the use of U.S. currency, acceptance of certain private initiatives, and the active promotion of tourism; these measures have been mostly rolled back since then. In the summer of 1994, the dire situation on the island motivated hundreds of people to begin leaving in makeshift rafts. Finally, in 2005, Castro stated in a speech that the special period had ended, which in effect meant that the worst of the economic crisis was over even though shortages continue.

Publication Abroad

Changes stemming from the Special Period in Cuba were reflected in the publishing process. Because of a tremendous paper shortage on the island, only short books of poetry and textbooks could be printed. For the first time, the Cuban government allowed writers to publish their books abroad, which sparked a veritable boom of Cuban books, especially in Spain and France. The fact that Cuban books were suddenly marketable had a significant impact on their subject and style, as it became clear that opposition to the Cuban regime, the depiction of vulgarity, and sexually explicit scenes were of interest to readers abroad. Some critics charge that Cuban writers exploited the exotic appeal of Cuba abroad for personal gain; others state that writers adopted an exotic outlook ironically, to expose that foreigners have a morbid interest in Cuba's downfall. Whatever their intentions toward readers were, most writers recognized that there was a parallel between the increasingly more common depiction of vulgarity, near-pornographic scenes and controversial issues in literature and the spread of corruption and decadence of ideological principles in daily life in the island.

Common Themes

Writers of the Special Period became known as "the iconoclastic generation,"

because they challenged social taboos and dealt with subjects that had hardly appeared in such open fashion in Cuban literature before, such as homosexuality, prostitution, drugs and gang culture, and abject poverty. Publication of these texts in foreign countries facilitated free expression, but after the worst years of the Special Period (1990–1994), even short stories and novels published in Cuba exhibited these characteristics. Due to such extensive publication abroad and the massive exile of Cuban writers, the term "Cuban" is used to designate both the authors who live abroad as well as those living on the island.

Special Period Writers and Texts

Zoé *Valdés has been acknowledged as the first writer of Special Period fiction, beginning with her two novels *La nada cotidiana* (1995; *Yocandra and the Paradise of Nada*, 1997) and *Te di la vida entera* (1996; *I Gave You All I Had*, 1999). Valdés was living in Paris when the latter was published. She employs humor and a sexually charged language to expose the desperate situation of Cubans during the Special Period.

Pedro Juan Gutiérrez's novel *Trilogía sucia de La Habana* (1998, *Dirty Havana Trilogy*, 2002) and others by him have earned the title of "dirty realism" for representing the lives of people in *solares* (tenement buildings) as mired in extreme poverty, promiscuity, and degradation. Gutiérrez's brutal realism includes no moral commentary or clear denunciation in these texts; characters' actions are presented matter of factly.

Ena Lucía Portela's *El pájaro, pincel y tinta china* (1997; The Bird, the Brush and India Ink) displays an opaque, difficult-to-understand style, challenging all conventions and morals and criticizing intellectual institutions in Cuba. Leonardo Padura is credited with introducing a counterpoint to the previous "socialist detective story," with a series of four books in which an inspector uncovers the wrongdoings of Cuban officials who were thought to be flawless revolutionaries. He denounces corruption at all levels of the revolutionary bureaucracy and exposes the disillusionment of the generation of people who spent their youth working for the revolution's future.

Paper shortages in the Special Period also promoted publication of short story volumes; many of them anthologized the work of such women writers as *Estatuas de sal* (1996; published in abbreviated form as *Cubana: Contemporary Fiction by Cuban Women*, 1998) and *El ojo de la noche* (1999; The Night Eye). Renowned Cuban short story writers include Aída Bahr, Marilyn Bobes, Pedro de Jesús, Ronaldo Menéndez, Achy Obejas, Antonio José Ponte, José Manuel Prieto, Karla Suárez, Anna Lydia *Vega and Mirta Yáñez, among many others. Of note, Antonio José Ponte's short story anthology *Un arte de hacer ruinas y otros cuentos* (2005; The Art of Making Ruins and Other Stories) and his novel *Contrabando de sombras* (2002; Smuggling Shadows) explore the ruins in contemporary Havana,

a topic that has found extensive echoes in essay and fiction writing.

Ana Serra

See also Balsero ("Rafter"); Havana in Literature.

Work By:

Whitfield, Esther, and Jacqueline Loss, eds. *New Short Fiction from Cuba.* Evanston, IL: Northwestern University Press, 2007.

Work About:

Álvarez, José B. *Contestatory Short Story of the Cuban Revolution.* Lanham, MD: University Press of America, 2002.

Hernández Reguant, Ariana. *Cuba in the Special Period. Culture and Ideology in the 1990s.* New York: Palgrave, 2009.

Quiroga, José. *Cuban Palimpsests.* Minneapolis: University of Minnesota Press, 2005.

Serra, Ana. *The "New Man" in Cuba. Culture and Identity in the Revolution.* Gainesville: University Press of Florida, 2007.

Whitfield, Esther. *Cuban Currency. The Dollar and Special Period Fiction.* Minneapolis: University of Minnesota Press, 2008.

Cueto, Alonso (1954–)

Born in Lima, Peru, Cueto has authored novels, short fiction books, essays and plays. Such early works as *La batalla del pasado* (1983; Battle of the Past), *El tigre blanco* (1985; White Tiger), and *Amores de invierno* (1996; Winter Love) pay tribute to the writings of Henry James and explore the melancholic psychology of characters mostly belonging to the Peruvian middle class. Detective fiction can be found in *Deseo de noche* (1993; Night Desire) and *El vuelo de la ceniza* (1995; Ashen Flights).

Demonio del mediodía (1999; The Devil at Noon), Cueto's lengthiest novel to date, depicts a love triangle in upper-class Peruvian society. Other works examine Peru's social and political turmoil of the 1980s, particularly the violence of the *Sendero Luminoso* (Shining Path) insurgency group, as in *Pálido cielo* (1998; Pale Sky) and *La hora azul* (2005; The Blue Hour); and the dictatorship of Alberto Fujimori's regime (1990–2000), as in *Grandes miradas* (2003; Daunting Looks). In *El susurro de la mujer ballena* (2007; The Whisper of the Whale Woman), Cueto dwells on feminine social identity in contemporary Peru.

César Ferreira

Work About:

Camacho Delgado, José Manuel. "Alonso Cueto y la novela de las víctimas." *Caravelle* 86 (2006): 247–64.

Navarro Santos, Marianela. "La narrativa de Alonso Cueto: limeños ofendidos." *Cuadernos hispanoamericanos* 608 (2001): 126–28.

Oviedo, José Miguel. "La hora de la violencia." *Letras libres* (June 2006): 91–92.

Cultural Icons of Chicanos

Many cultural icons populate the legends and myths of Chicano folklore and literature, but only a handful consistently maintains cultural significance. The most important, enduring Chicano and Mexican icon is the Virgin of Guadalupe. Her feast day, celebrated on December 12, commemorates her revelation in 1531 to a local Indian peasant, Juan Diego Cuauhtlatoatzin, on the hill of Tepeyac near present-day Mexico City. Her use of Nahuatl (the Aztec language) and her appearance before a humble native, recently canonized a saint by Pope John Paul II, facilitated a transition from local religions to Catholicism for indigenous populations, and also lent legitimacy to Spanish colonization there.

Another historical icon, *La Malinche* (1496?–1529?), also known as Malintzín and Doña Marina, served as interpreter, advisor, and mistress to Spanish conquistador Hernán Cortés. She bore him a son, making her the mother of all Mexicans—a mestizo race—and Chicanos. Historically branded a traitor for facilitating the Spanish conquest of the Aztecs, many scholars now believe she helped spare many lives. *La Llorona* (the weeping woman), whose legend dates back over 500 years, is said to have drowned her children in a river in retaliation for her husband's unfaithfulness and desertion. As punishment, God condemned her to search forever along the waters' banks for her children's lost souls.

More recently, Gregorio Cortez (1875–1916) became a hero and folk legend by defying Anglo law enforcement that wrongly accused him of horse theft. His legend was eventually immortalized in a *corrido* (border ballad), an artistic form that has sung the praises of many Chicano bandit heroes, and a film, *The Ballad of Gregorio Cortez* (1982). Finally, Chicano farm worker César Chávez (1927–1993) championed the civil rights of farm workers and Mexican Americans. With Dolores Huerta, he cofounded the National Farm Workers Association, which later became the United Farm Workers. He is remembered for values, his nonviolent advocacy, and his unwavering commitment to social justice and equity.

Spencer R. Herrera

See also Aztlán; Cultural Icons of Spanish America; Selena (stage name of Selena Quintanilla-Pérez) (1971–1995).

Work About:

Chicana Traditions: Continuity and Change. Ed. Norma Cantú and Olga Nájera-Ramírez. Urbana: University of Illinois, 2002.

Cultural Icons of Cuban Americans

Prominent icons are significant for Cuban Americans as cultural identity markers. Little Havana, Miami's Cuban enclave, symbolizes the geographic center of Cuban American culture. Spanish is the dominant language. Its main thoroughfare, *Calle Ocho* (Eighth Street), is lined with businesses serving as nostalgic connections to or representations of all things Cuban and Cuban American.

La Virgen de la Caridad del Cobre, or Virgin of Charity, is key to Cuban American religious and cultural heritage. Her feast day, September 8, commemorates her revelation in 1606 to two Cuban brothers whom she saved from a storm at sea. For Cuban exiles, she signifies their achieved freedom and hopes for a democratic homeland.

Celia Cruz (1925–2003) was the Grammy Award–winning, world-renowned Queen of Salsa whose inimitable style endeared her to millions. Cuban exiles saw fellow-exile Cruz as a cultural ambassador of their community. The same can be said of international superstar Gloria Estefan (1957–). Other icons include television's first Cuban American, Desi Arnaz (1917–1986); Cristina Saralegui (1948–), the Cuban Oprah; Hollywood actor Andy García (1956–); and writers and scholars of Cuban American culture, Gustavo Pérez Firmat (1949–) and Roberto *González Echevarría (1951–).

Raúl Rosales Herrera

See also Cultural Icons of Spanish America.

Work About:

Pérez Firmat, Gustavo. *Life on the Hyphen: The Cuban-American Way.* Austin: University of Texas Press, 1994.

Cultural Icons of Spain

The Spanish state possesses a lengthy history, and the symbols used to identify Spain and "Spanishness" have changed and evolved over this time. As it is customary in modern nationalism, a mixture of myths, historical figures, literary characters, and cultural appropriations form the pantheon of national icons.

In the Roman province of Lusitania, which occupied modern day Extremadura, Viriathus (?–139 BC), a local leader, defeated the Romans in several battles and became a symbol of the independent nature of the Iberian Peninsula. Once Romanized, Spain contributed two emperors to the Roman Empire, both from Itálica (near present-day Seville). Trajan (53–117 AD) and Hadrian (76–138 AD) are considered among the best emperors in Roman history and exemplify Hispania's importance to the Roman Empire. But it is the Roman philosopher Seneca the Younger (4 BC–65 AD) who became a symbol of "Spanishness": as a Stoic writer, he was Christianized and became one of medieval Europe's pre-Christian pillars.

Saint Isidore of Seville (c. 560–636) was the most cultured man of the Visigothic period. Isidore played an influential role in eliminating Arianism and therefore affirming the divinity of Christ. His accomplishments include writing the first medieval encyclopedia, the 20-volume *Etymologiae*; requiring all cathedrals in Spain to maintain a school to teach Latin, Greek, and the trivium and cuadrivium; and composing the first Laus Hispaniae, a eulogy on the greatness of Spanish territory and its inhabitants. Today, Isidore is the unofficial patron saint of the Internet in Spain. Following the Christian tradition of understanding woman as traitor, like Eve, Florinda or La Cava Rumia is both traitor and seductress. After she became the lover of Visigothic King Rodrigo, her father, count Don Julián, betrayed his king, and as governor of Ceuta, in northern Africa, allowed the Moors to cross over and invade Spain. The Visigoths, who were extremely debilitated by civil wars, were defeated in 711 in the battle of Guadalete and the Visigothic kingdom disappeared.

In Andalusia, in Muslim Spain, the Aristotelian philosopher Averroes (1126–1198) theorized the harmony of reason and faith. Born in Córdoba, he influenced the Jewish rabbi and philosopher Maimonides (c. 1137–1204), an Aristotelian expert also from Córdoba. Thanks to their influence, Aristotle became the most important pre-Christian philosopher in Europe during the Middle Ages. Averroes's *Mishneh Torah* belongs to the canon of Talmudic law. Maimonides and Averroes symbolize the myth of a Spain of three cultures—Jews, Muslims, and Christians—coexisting. El Cid (c. 1040–1099) is a Castilian lord who became legendary for using unorthodox military tactics in his fights against the Moors. He was crucial in the expansion of Castilian influence in the Spanish Levant. The epic poem "*Cantar de Mío Cid" is based on his life and considered one of Spanish literature's foundational texts.

The *Santiago de Compostela myth and the Camino de Santiago (Way of Santiago) are crucial formative elements of the idea of Spain and Europe. Santiago (Saint James the Greater) is the patron saint of Spain; different legends indicate that his remnants are buried in Santiago de Compostela in Galicia. Since the 10th century, pilgrims throughout Europe have traveled to the saint's tomb to receive plenary indulgence. Nowadays, Christians and non-Christians continue to be moved by a combination of religious, spiritual, and cultural manifestations to walk some or all of el Camino—the route across northern Spain that has been traveled by untold millions. Its main symbol is the scallop shell. As in the Middle Ages, the Camino is a place where cultures intersect and ideas are exchanged.

The second female cultural icon of Spain is the literary character *Celestina (1499), protagonist of the eponymous novel. A former prostitute, she takes in two younger prostitutes in her home and facilitates the illicit sexual activities of other townspeople. Although a negative character, modern Spaniards have seen in her a protofeminist and an entrepreneur.

In the 19th century, when modern Spanish nationalism took shape, Madrid's Prado Museum, which houses the royal painting collection, became instrumental in providing the idea of Spain sought by the liberal–conservative intellectual elite of the day. The first cornerstone of this project was El Greco (1541–1614), born on the island of Crete but artistically molded by his years in Venice and Rome. He became the most important painter of the Spanish Catholic Reform: his *The Burial of Count Orgaz*, housed in Toledo, is the most significant painting of Catholic soteriology—the doctrine of salvation. The most relevant protagonist of this Catholic Reform is Santa *Teresa de Jesús (1515–1582). She raised Spanish Catholicism to a new level of spirituality, and the number of convents she founded represents a mixture of religious zeal and business acumen.

Spain's most relevant symbol is Don Quijote, a character born in 1605 in the novel of the same name, written by Miguel de *Cervantes (1547–1616). He represents Spanish idealism; the difficulty of distinguishing between fiction and reality; and the idea that multiple perspectives must always be taken into account when discussing an issue. Spanish baroque produced the legendary character of *Don Juan. Tirso de *Molina (1571?–1648) created the first coherent manifestation of Don Juan in *El burlador de Sevilla y convidado de piedra* (1630; *The Trickster of Seville and the Stone Guest*, 1986). He represents the anxiety of modern society with regard to uncontrolled male sexuality and also symbolizes Spanish *machismo*.

If Don Quijote is the most important character to represent the Spaniard, Spanish complexity is best represented by paintings of official court painter Diego de Velázquez (1599–1660). Besides depicting the royal family, he produced portraits of beggars and court monsters (dwarves, midgets, unbalanced personalities) for the Royal Palace; in his youth he painted scenes of ordinary life—a water seller, an old woman frying eggs—expressing the importance of Spaniards of all social classes. At the heart of the Prado Museum is Velázquez's *Las Meninas*, a very complex painting. It is a self-portrait, representing the artist in the act of painting; it depicts the princess, her chambermaids, other members of her entourage, two dwarfs, and a dog; and it shows the king and the queen—who are visiting the painter's studio—reflected in a mirror. Finally, an open door at the back of the room and several open window panes provide the painting with unbelievable depth. Velázquez painted the atmosphere that his subjects inhabited; intellectuals have discussed this painting for centuries. The next master after Velázquez is Francisco de Goya (1746–1828). Also a royal painter, his *majas*—one dressed and one naked—his portrayal of the horrors of the war against Napoleon, and his monsters have become symbols of the beauty and the suffering of Spain and the coexistence of "two Spains," one modern and one mired in backwardness.

Spanish romanticism produced Carmen, the female Don Juan. A product of the imagination of French writer Prosper Mérimèe (1803–1870), she represents both the destructive power of female sexuality and the impossibility of representing Spanish ethnicity. Carmen is gypsy, Andalusian, and Basque. The 1875 opera *Carmen*, by France's George Bizet (1838–1875), and its "Spanish" music are universally known and helped propagate the stereotype of an exotic Spain of gypsies and bullfighters.

Alhambrismo refers to Spanish classical music with an Eastern touch that attempts to capture the soul of Spain; its main representatives include Isaac Albéniz (1860–1909)) with *Songs of Spain*, *Dances of Spain*, and the *Suite Iberia*; Manuel de Falla (1876–1946) with *Night in the Gardens of Spain*; Pablo Sarasate (1844–1908) with *Nine Spanish Dances*; Enrique Granados (1867–1916) with *Goyescas* and *Twelve Spanish Dances*; and Joaquín Turina (1882–1949) who composed *Gypsy Dances* and *Tales of Spain*. This formidable array of composers provides a soundtrack for the idea of Spain.

Barcelona has become synonymous with Catalan architect Antonio Gaudí (1852–1926). His Cathedral of La Sagrada Familia is now the most internationally well-known icon of Barcelona and/or Spain. *Time* magazine declared Pablo Picasso (1881–1973) the most influential artist of the 20th century. His mural *Guernica*, which condemns the bombardment of civilians in Guernica, a city of the Basque region, by the Nazi regime's German Luftwaffe, has become a symbol of Spain and the horrors of war worldwide.

*La *Movida* is the cultural movement that signaled Spain's return to democracy and freedom after Dictator Francisco Franco's death in 1975. It covered all the arts and the whole of Spanish geography. Barcelona, Valencia, Bilbao, and Vigo had their own *movidas*. Of particular note is *La Movida*'s impact on music, because it prompted the birth of a genuine Spanish pop that was not a mere translation of English and American pop and rock. Alaska y los Pegamoides, Radio Futura, Gabinete Caligari, Nacha Pop, Mecano, El Último de la Fila, and Siniestro Total are some of the movement's important groups. They cover genres as diverse as pop, rock, techno, and punk. In cinema, the colorful, daring movies of Pedro *Almodóvar (1949–) have enjoyed screenings worldwide; films of Bigas Luna (1946–) challenge Spanish sexuality and nationality. The *comedia madrileña* plays of Fernando Trueba (1955–) and Fernando Colomo

(1946–) explore how modernity has changed the mores of the middle class. In photography, Alberto García-Alix (1956–) and Ouka Leele (1957–) have achieved international fame. Agatha Ruiz de la Prada (1960–) has brought pop culture to the world of fashion. In painting, Guillermo Pérez Villalta (1948–) belongs to the new figurative school of Madrid; his works have reinterpreted classicism from a postmodern point of view. *La Movida* has become a symbol of postmodern Spain.

Millions of Spaniards follow *soccer every week. FIFA, the International Federation of Football, declared Real Madrid the best team of the 20th century. Real Madrid and FC Barcelona, or "Barça"—Barcelona's team—are the best ambassadors of modern Spain. The finest players in the world play on these teams and have followers all over the world. The two teams are also symbols of Spain's two most important cities.

The world of publicity has contributed one of modern Spain's most powerful icons. From time immemorial, the bull symbolized Spain; today the Osborne brand of liquors and wines has installed huge metallic silhouettes of these bulls along Spain's primary highways. Soccer fans have used the bull in flags of Spain, and the Osborne bull has become the unofficial national symbol. The Spanish government uses the letter "ñ" to promote Spanish culture, and the letter, pronounced "*eñe*," has entered popular culture: Spain's professional basketball league is known as the ÑBA. Finally, bullfighting and flamenco music still represent for many foreigners the main symbols of Spain, although Spaniards prefer more modern, dynamic icons of culture.

Salvador A. Oropesa

See also Don Quijote de la Mancha in Spanish American Literature and Culture.

Work About:

Stanton, Edward F. *Culture and Customs of Spain*. Westport, CT: Greenwood, 2002.

Cultural Icons of Spanish America

The unique, eclectic mixture of cultures and races in Latin America has produced since pre-Columbian times a vast gallery of popular icons that represent and embody its people's traditions, ideologies, and beliefs. Either religious or secular, icons are crucial to the formation of a national identity as well as a way to erase demarcations of race, class, and gender. Symbols, myths, and popular iconography are based on a series of cultural referents, and are articulated in a wide variety of ways according to the country's social and racial makeup. Rubén Dri maintains that symbols are fundamental for building our subjective identities. The icon, a symbolic subject, must not only serve as a role model, but also satisfy individual spiritual or emotional needs. Furthermore, icons must promote a social and a national identity.

While some religious icons correspond to the *santoral*—or saints—of the Catholic tradition, others, such as the Virgen de Guadalupe—the mestizo virgin and Mexican patron saint and protector—are the product of the syncretism (blending of common aspects) of Catholicism with local folklore. Other mestizo icons include María Lionza in Venezuela and El Gauchito Gil (Little Gil Cowboy) or La Difunta Correa (Deceased Correa) in Argentina. In countries with a large population of African heritage, like Brazil, Cuba, Dominican Republic, and Puerto Rico, religious iconography strictly relates to the gods and deities of the Yorubá religion. Yemayá, Oxalá, Olodumaré, Obatalá, and Xangó are only a few examples of these figures who give hope and spiritual guidance to those in need.

Latin American history has also produced a large pantheon of historical figures that incarnate values and ideals of freedom, standing as symbols of resistance against oppression and corruption. Ernesto "Che" *Guevara (1928–1967), Benito Juárez (1806–1872), José *Martí (1853–1895), and Simón *Bolívar (1783–1830) belong to the elite of historical figures who gave their lives fighting for Latin America's independence and ideological freedom.

Over the last several decades, with the advance of globalization, capitalism, and film, the lives and accomplishments of several personalities—religious and secular—have become iconographic symbols of popular consumption in Latin America and around the world. For many in the United States and Latin America, in particular, "Evita," Eva Duarte de Perón (1919–1952); Doña Marina, "La Malinche (16th c.);" Sor Juana Inés de la *Cruz (1648–1695); María Félix (1914–2002); and Frida *Kahlo (1907–1954) have the status of role models, cult figures, and

martyrs venerated to the point of sanctity as symbols of physical pain, social struggle, and gender or political oppression. Their lives have been represented in films, novels, plays, magazines, and in a wide variety of such marketable commodities as clothing, postcards, and even the national currency (as in the case of Mexican nun and poet Sor Juana).

María Claudia André

See also Cultural Icons of Chicanos; Cultural Icons of Cuban Americans; Gaucho Literature; Selena (stage name of Selena Quintanilla-Pérez) (1971–1995).

Work About:

André, María Claudia, ed. *Iconos latinos e hispanoamericanos*. Mountain View, CA: Floricanto, 2006.

Dri, Rubén, ed. *Símbolos y fetiches religiosos*. Buenos Aires: Biblos, 2006.

Cultural Institutions for Hispanism in the United States

According to the Merriam-Webster online dictionary, "hispanism" is a movement to reassert the cultural unity of Spain and Latin America. Hispanism as a discipline in U.S. universities began after the 1898 Spanish American War.

Institutions Promoting Hispanism

One of the oldest cultural institutions for hispanism in the United States is the Hispanic Society of America (HSA), founded in 1904 by Archer Milton Huntington and Anna Hyatt Huntington in

New York City. Their collection of art, ethnographic artifacts, and books, opened to the public in 1908, influenced scholarly study for the first part of the 20th century. HSA's art collection gathers more than 6,000 paintings and watercolors, 15,000 prints, and 1,700,000 photographs. The library holds more than 250,000 books and 200,000 manuscripts from the 12th century to the present. Since 1970, the HSA offers the Hispanic Seminary of Medieval Studies and publishes copies of medieval manuscripts and books for researchers (http://www.hispanicsociety.org/).

In 1991, the Instituto Cervantes was created by the Spanish government to promote Spanish language and culture worldwide. With a central site in Madrid, Spain, and satellite locations throughout the world, there are U.S. offices in New York, Chicago, Seattle, and Albuquerque. The institute's *Portal del Hispanismo* represents an important online source of information contacts and useful tool of research for the study of Spanish language, culture, and literature. It offers directories of professional associations, Hispanists, and events around the world as well as links to other resources. The sites in the United States offer classes, conferences, and art exhibitions by professionals from the Spanish-speaking world. Also part of the Instituto Cervantes, the Biblioteca virtual Miguel de Cervantes is an online library; users may read some of the books online if they are a part of the system or may be directed to other links (http://www.cervantesvirtual.com).

The Asociación Internacional de Hispanistas was founded in 1962 in Oxford, England. As the largest association of Hispanists in the United States, it organizes international conferences and offers a directory of institutions, associations, and academic institutions for Hispanists. The AIH publishes the *Boletin* with information about AIH members, conferences, and news important in the field (http://asociacioninternacionaldehispanistas.org/info.htm).

In 1917, the American Association of Teachers of Spanish and Portuguese was founded in New York City. In turn, the AATSP became a founding member of the Joint National Committee for Languages and the National Council for Language and International Studies (NCLIS) in the United States. NCLIS lobbies for languages at the national level. The executive director of each group maintains an office in Washington, D.C., to support the promotion of languages in the nation. Currently, the AATSP sets standards for foreign-language teaching in the United States and offers guidelines and resources for professionals. *Hispania*, its official publication, is one of the most important points of reference for scholars and teachers in the United States (https://www.aatsp.org/?page=Hispania).

Electronic Resources That Promote Hispanism

At the present time, access to Internet resources has opened immense possibilities for information searches. By visiting Web sites, researchers can locate cultural institutions and academic departments, enter blogs and professional chat rooms and, in some cases, download entire books that otherwise would be very difficult to locate.

Some currently available Internet resources include the following:

1. Latin American Network Information Center at University of Texas, Austin. *LANIC* is a center for Internet information intended for scholars and the general public on Latin America. It offers Internet links and information on institutions and investigation projects and on news in general. http://www1.lanic.utexas.edu/.

2. *Latin America Data Base* is an on-line center of information regarding current issues on the Spanish-speaking world. It originates from the University of New Mexico. http://ladb.unm.edu/.

3. The U.S. Library of Congress has a Hispanic Section with very useful documents for research, particularly on Spain in the 19th century and Latin America. http://www.loc.gov/rr/hispanic/

4. The Newberry Library in Chicago represents a tremendous source of material for researchers on colonial Latin America and cartography. http://www.newberry.org/.

5. For an extensive guide to Internet resources for hispanists, José Enrique Laplana's article is very informative: www.dartmouth.edu/~aih/pdf/aprox.pdf.

6. The Hispanic American Periodical Index, HAPI Online, is an international periodical index providing access to authoritative information and social sciences and humanities research on Latin America, focusing on such fields as anthropology, Latin American Indians and indigenous issues from all time periods, politics and government, foreign relations, business and industry, African diaspora issues, gender studies, history, art, literature, film, environmental issues, and social movements. Some coverage of U.S. Latino journals is also included. HAPI Online contains bibliographic citations to articles, reviews, original literary works, and other materials appearing in more than 400 social science and humanities journals published throughout the world. Most articles are in Spanish, English, or Portuguese; coverage is 1970–present (as defined by the Library of Iowa State University).

7. EBSCO Publishing and Arte Público Press are collaborating to produce a digitized collection of U.S. Hispanic written materials dating from colonial times until 1960. These materials, located through the University of Houston's *Recovering the U.S. Hispanic Literacy Heritage Project, will initially include approximately 60,000 historical articles and 1,100 books. About 80 percent of the materials are in Spanish. The collection is scheduled to be available in the second half of 2009 (as announced by EBSCO in November 2008).

Periodical publications in the United States have played a vital role for disseminating scholarship, and some of these publications can also be found online. Some of the oldest and best known in paper and electronic form include the earlier mentioned *Hispania*, published by the AATSP, at http://www.hispaniajournal .org/; *Hispanic Review*, from the University of Pennsylvania, at http://hr.pennpress .org/; *Romance Philology*, published by the University of California, Berkeley, at http://socrates.berkeley.edu/~rescent/ rph.html; *Espéculo*, from the Universidad Complutense de Madrid, at http://www .ucm.es/info/especulo/; and, *Parnaseo*, from the Universidad de Valencia, at http:// parnaseo.uv.es/.

Older institutions located in other countries are digitizing their holdings, which will open great possibilities for the future. E-Journal, at www.ejournal.unam.mx, is sponsored by UNAM, the Universidad Nacional Autónoma de México; it provides the full text of selected articles published by the university. One important collection for research in Spain is Dialnet, at http:// dialnet.unirioja.es/; sponsored by the Universidad de La Rioja, it includes over 1,100 open access journals covering arts, humanities and sciences. Three noteworthy Madrid-based efforts involved in this process are *Real Academia Española de la Lengua, at http://www.rae.es/; the Consejo Superior de Investigaciones Científicas, at http://www.csic.es/index.do and the Biblioteca Nacional, at http://www.bne.es/esp/ catalogos/coleccionesdigitales.htm.

María Luisa García-Verdugo

See also the Selected List of Publicly Available, Free Electronic Sources Related to Hispanic Literature and Culture

Work About:

Greer, Margaret: Hispanism and its *Disciplina*. http://spanport.cla.umn.edu/publications/ HispanicIssues/pdfs/greer.pdf.

Curanderismo and *Brujería*

Traditional practitioners known as *curanderos* (*-as*) provide fundamental health care services to rural communities. These services encompass a wide range of skills, including midwifery (*parteras*), traditional herbalism (*yerberos/-as, médicos/- as*), and physical therapy (*sobadores/-as*). *Curanderos* often rely on local herbal remedies and osteopathic manipulations as well as divine intervention through prayer and the laying-on of hands. Geographic isolation prohibits many communities in Latin America from having medical professionals or hospitals, making *curanderos* often the only available health care providers to rural dwellers.

Conversely, *brujería* refers to the malevolent, dark arts practiced by sorcerers (*brujos/-as*). These practices generally rely on belief in the supernatural and prey upon the superstitious nature of recipients. The bewitchments, curses, and other machinations of *brujería* practitioners are often countered by spiritual purifications (*limpias*) of skilled *curanderos*.

John P. Campiglio

Work About:

Flys-Junquera, Carmen. "Detectives, Hoodoo, and *Brujería*: Subverting the Dominant U.S. Cultural Ethos." *Sleuthing*

Ethnicity: The Detective in Multiethnic Crime Fiction. Ed., intro. Dorothea Fischer-Horning and Monika Mueller. Madison, NJ and London: Fairleigh Dickinson University Press and Associated University Presses, 2003.

Trotter, Robert T., II and Juan Antonio Chavira. *Curanderismo: Mexican American Folk Healing*. 2nd ed. Athens: University of Georgia Press, 1997.

D

Dalton, Roque (1935–1975)

One of El Salvador's most celebrated writers, during his brief life he published six poetry books, a novel, essays, and two chronicles; one, the historic treatise *Miguel Mármol* (1972; Eng. trans., 1982), documented the 1932 massacre of thousands of Salvadoran peasants. Dalton was studying law when he traveled to Moscow in 1957. Upon his return, he helped found the Salvadoran Communist Party and changed careers, dedicating himself to writing and poetry. Always critical of authoritarian rule, he was jailed and tortured by his government, and after returning clandestinely to El Salvador, murdered by his former revolutionary associates.

His writings empathize eloquently with humankind, especially the powerless. To help make new perspectives understandable, Dalton advocated a "pedagogy of laughter." *Historias prohibidas del pulgarcito* (1974; Forbidden Stories of Tom Thumb) humorously chronicles life in El Salvador. A somewhat autobiographical novel, *Pobrecito poeta que era yo* (1975; Poor Little Poet That I Was) was published posthumously. Dalton's narratives demonstrate a testimonial nature and collective vision. He composed scintillating, at times anguished, poetry. Themes of his work, including friendship, were diverse, but his sharpest evocations depict the countryside and the common people.

Elizabeth Coonrod Martínez

See also Guerrilla Poetry; Testimonial Writing in Central America.

Work By:

Miguel Mármol. Trans. Kathleen Ross and Richard Schaaf. Willamantic, CT: Curbstone, 1987.

Small Hours of the Night: Selected Poems of Roque Dalton. Trans. Jonathan Cohen et al. Willamantic, CT: Curbstone, 1996.

Work About:

Beverley, John, and Marc Zimmerman. "Salvadoran Revolutionary Poetry." *Literature and Politics in the Central American Revolutions.* Austin: University of Texas Press, 1990, 115–43.

Lindo-Fuentes, Héctor, Erik Ching, and Rafael A. Lara-Martínez. *Remembering a Massacre in El Salvador: The Insurrection of 1932, Roque Dalton, and the Politics of Historical Memory.* Albuquerque: University of New Mexico Press, 2007.

Darío, Rubén (1867–1916)

This Nicaraguan poet and prose author became the most important representative of *Modernismo*, the Hispanic literary response to modernity's forward strides during the final decades of the 19th century and the first two decades of the 20th century. Inheriting from *romanticism the idea of the poet as the antenna of society's sensibility, Darío constantly pursued technical perfection and rescued from oblivion all manner of forgotten verse forms, and he adapted others used in France into Spanish. His first important book, *Azul* (1888; Blue), evolved over several editions. It champions moral aestheticism and identifies the imagination with Spanish America, and is considered *modernismo*'s most authentic manifesto. It is mostly a collection of short stories with some poems. In this complex text, consisting primarily of short stories and poems, the fulfillment of sexual desire and the search for new themes and new poetic forms function as a related pair.

In *Prosas profanas* (1896; *Prosas profanas and other poems*, 1922) Darío declares himself the father of *modernismo*; these poems continue his fascination with sexual bliss and its profane association with Catholic religious elements. His creation in poetry of a world rich in luxury and exquisite elements stands as a rejection of middle-class mediocrity. On the literary level, Darío spurns realism and the tacky remnants of late romanticism. Art nouveau writing, modernist painting, and modernist industrial arts (furniture, china sets, appliances) also figure as influences of his writing, but Darío identifies music as the source of poetry's salvation. In "Sonatina" (sonatine), music is a religion that transforms the poem.

Darío declared with pride that *modernismo* was the first literary movement to originate in Spanish America and to then be adopted later in Spain. He defends equally the aristocracy of his verse and the dignity and value of Hispanic culture against U.S. imperialism. *Cantos de vida y esperanza* (1905; *Songs of Life and Hope*, 2004) initiates a return to idealism, religious abstraction, spiritual search, doubt and anguish. All of these become recurrent topics, as the poet aims for a transcendent nature and art as social morality. The poet's religious confusion continues as he veers from Catholic orthodoxy to agnosticism to heterodoxy to pure aesthetics, in which the purpose of religion is to make art sacred. Confession and pilgrimage are also present in the book. As he moved from aestheticism to political engagement in art, his most important formal legacy is that he successfully reproduced in Spanish the flexibility of French syntax.

Salvador A. Oropesa

See also *Modernismo* in Hispanic Literature.

Work By:

Selected Poems of Rubén Darío. A Bilingual Anthology. Ed. and trans. Will Derusha and Alberto Acereda. Lewisburg, PA: Bucknell University Press, 2001.

Songs of Life and Hope. Ed., trans. Will Derusha and Alberto Acereda. Durham, NC: Duke University Press, 2004.

Work About:

Jrade, Cathy Login. *Rubén Darío and the Romantic Search for Unity: The Modernist Recourse to Esoteric Tradition.* Austin: University of Texas Press, 1983.

Orringer, Nelson. "Modernism and the Initiation of Rubén Darío's Centaurs." *Hispania* 85.4 (2002): 815–25.

Dávila Andrade, César (1918–1967)

This Ecuadorian poet and short story writer belonged to the 1944 Madrugada poetry group. His first collection, *Espacio, me has vencido* (Space, You Have Conquered Me) was published in 1946. His verse, the most recognized part of his literary production, speaks of such diverse themes as childhood, the maternal, moments of unreciprocated love, his indigenous heritage, faith, and the divine, but, as Schwartz observes, most writings are underscored by an obsessive focus on death, and its possible meaning. For Dávila Andrade, life's reality translates to unreciprocated love, loneliness, sadness, and spiritual anguish, emotions that lead him to deny the sensory world.

Raised an orthodox Christian, he gradually turned to Buddhism, and also studied Eastern philosophies, parapsychology, and magic. He also spent an extended period of time in Caracas, Venezuela, working as a journalist for the periodical *Zona Franca*.

Maureen Ihrie

Work By:

Arco de instantes. Quito: Casa de la Cultura Ecuatoriana, 1959.
Cabeza de gallo. Caracas: Arte, 1966.
13 relatos. Quito: Casa de la Cultura Ecuatoriana, 1955.

Work About:

Dávila Vázquez, César. *César Dávila Andrade. Combate poético y suicidio*. Cuenca, Ecuador: Universidad de Cuenca, 1998.
Schwartz, Kessell. "Death and Transfiguration in the Poetry of César Dávila Andrade." *Hispania* 65.4 (December 1982): 562–69.

Décima

Invention of this style of poetry is credited to Spaniard Vicente Espinel (1550–1624). Consisting of 10-line verses with eight-syllable lines and a rhyme scheme of abbaaccddc, it was popular during *Renaissance and baroque Spain, and then traveled to the Canary Islands and the Americas where, particularly in Cuba, Puerto Rico, Mexico, New Mexico, and Argentina, it is popular even today. Topics of the *décima* include love, politics, honor, and satire.

Décimas are composed for publication by poets and folk singers, and they can also be improvised. In present-day Puerto Rico, the *güira*, a musical instrument made from a gourd, often accompanies a singer who extols the virtues of rural life, and praises the pleasure of poetry, music, and improvising *décimas*. Gross observes that in 1988, the Institute of Puerto Rican Culture counted 105 improvisers on the island, and that since then, the genre has been actively encouraged by the Institute via sponsorship of improvisation competitions.

Lestrade, who has studied the *décima*'s presence in Louisiana, notes that it has provided a bond between present-day Canary Island practitioners and those from the New Orleans *isleño* community of St. Bernard's Parish. *Décimas* composed by *isleños* speak of local history, job woes, and even recent concerns like conservation. In 2004, she identified and interviewed the only two remaining *décima* composers among the population.

Maureen Ihrie

Work About:

Lestrade, Patricia Manning. "The Last of the Louisiana *Décimas.*" *Hispania* 87.3 (September 2004): 447–52.

Gross, Joan. "Defendiendo la (Agri) Cultura: Reterritorializing Culture in the Puerto Rican Décima."*Oral Tradition* 23.2 (October 2008): 219–34.

Delibes, Miguel (1920–2010)

Best known for his novels, travel books, short stories, and journal articles, Delibes is one of the most prolific writers of 20th-century Spain. Born in Valladolid, he began to teach himself how to write after having studied business and law. Delibes published more than 40 books; many have been translated into several languages. He received numerous prestigious literary prizes, and 12 of his novels have been adapted to film or theater.

His remarkable early novel *El camino* (1950; *The Path*, 1961) recounts a boy's contradictory feelings on the eve of his departure for boarding school in the city, as he leaves behind friends, family, and rural life. Using a nostalgic, intimate tone, Delibes explores topics including life, death, and destiny, the principal leitmotifs of his narrative. His most experimental work, *Parábola del náufrago* (1969; *The Hedge*, 1983), narrates the story of a man who sees himself shipwrecked, isolated, and doomed.

Using realistic prose and a colloquial, ironic style, this author is known for the denunciation of social injustice, elaborate descriptions of provincial and rural life, and the psychological analysis of middle- and lower-class characters. Delibes interprets with surprising accuracy the desires and sufferings of postwar Spanish society.

Ana Corbalán

See also Novel in Spain: 1900 to Present.

Work By:

The Wars of Our Ancestors. Trans. Agnes Moncy. Athens: University of Georgia Press, 1992.

The Stuff of Heroes. Trans. Frances M. López Morillas. New York: Random House, 1990.

The Heretic. Trans. Alfred MacAdam. Woodstock, NY: Overlook, 2006.

Work About:

Agawu-Kakraba, Yaw B. *Demythification in the Fiction of Miguel Delibes.* New York: Peter Lang, 1996.

Boucher, Teresa C. *Existential Authenticity in Three Novels of Spanish Author Miguel Delibes.* Lewiston, NY: Mellen, 2004.

Denevi, Marco (1922–1998)

One of the most prominent, prolific Latin American writers of contemporary fiction,

Argentine Denevi launched his literary career with the best-selling novel, *Rosaura a las diez* (1955; Rosaura by Ten). In 1960, he published the acclaimed *Ceremonia Secreta* (*Secret Ceremony*, 1961), a psychological novel that incorporates elements of parody with detective fiction. As master of the psychological thriller, Denevi's characters are usually alienated beings who border on madness, either tormented by their past or victims of multiple personalities.

In *Enciclopedia completa de una familia argentina* (1986; Complete Encyclopedia of an Argentina Family) and *La república de Trapalanda* (1989; The Trapalanda Republic), Denevi presents a critical, insightful perspective on the country's history and a humorous vision of Argentine society. In addition to narrative fiction and essay, Denevi wrote several plays.

María Claudia André

See also Detective and Mystery Fiction in Spanish America.

Work By:

The Redemption of the Cannibal Woman and other stories. Trans. Alberto Manguel. Toronto: Coach House, 1993.

Work About:

Lichtblau, Myron. "Narrative Perspective and Reader Responses in Marco Denevi's *Rosaura a las diez*." *Symposium* 40.1 (Spring 1986): 59–70.

Vigliani de La Rosa, María Elena. "La literatura carnavalesca en la ficción de Marco Denevi." *Alba de América: Revista Literaria* 21.39–40 (2002 July): 261–79.

Detective and Mystery Fiction in Spain

The short story *El clavo* (1853; *The Nail*, 1997), by Pedro Antonio de *Alarcón (1833–1891), is generally considered the first detective fiction of Spain; while a few other authors occasionally tried their hand at the genre, only during the last two decades of the 1900s did the genre become popularized. One reason for this is that Spanish detective fiction often includes a pointedly negative portrayal of political institutions and authority figures, views expressly prohibited under the Francisco Franco regime (1939–1975).

While there are many variations of Spanish detective fiction, common characteristics generally include these elements: the crime to be solved is usually a murder, there exist multiple false trails and clues, the detective is the novel's main character, the cause of death is not what it first appears to be, and the setting is usually an urban environment. In addition, crime mysteries are filled with street slang and the detective, the Spanish authorities, and the police are often portrayed as bumbling, incompetent, or corrupt.

Joaquin Belda (1883–1935), one of the most prolific writers of the pre-Franco era, wrote *¿Quién disparó?* (1911; Who Shot?), in which protagonist Gapy Bermúdez spoofs Sherlock Holmes and the narrator/author parallels Dr. Watson. Mario Lacruz (1929–2000) typifies the author whose detective fiction could be published under Franco's censorship; his style—represented by *El inocente* (1953; The

Innocent One)—places the narrative action, and thus any political implications of the corrupt police, in a foreign setting. Francisco *García Pavón (1919–1989), whose novels abound in *costumbrismo* (local color) and take place in rural Spain, circumvented the Franco censorship by making the local police chief—Plinio—a force for positive societal change.

Manuel *Vázquez Montalbán (1939–2003) won multiple Spanish and international prizes with his famous gourmet detective Pepe Carvalho, a former Marxist and CIA agent. A leading member of Catalonia's Communist Party, Vázquez Montalbán included a strong political element in such novels as *Asesinato en el Comité Central* (1981; *Murder in the Central Committee*, 1996). The 22-volume Carvalho series has been translated into over 20 different languages.

Another author with tremendous international readership is Arturo *Pérez-Reverte (1951–). The vast majority of Pérez-Reverte's works—translated into more than 30 languages—are of a historical nature, examining the influence of the Catholic Church. Some, such as the Captain Alatriste series, are more loosely related to the detective/mystery genre; *Limpieza de sangre* (1997; *Purity of Blood*, 1997), for example, contains a murder, an innocently accused victim, intrigue, and an unexpected ending, but centers primarily on Captain Alatriste's efforts to get his charge out of the clutches of the Spanish *Inquisition rather than discovering the murderer's identity. Many other texts fit squarely within the detective fiction genre, although the mystery to be

solved is something other than a murder. Pérez-Reverte's international best seller *Piel del tambor* (1995; *The Seville Communion*, 1998) combines the intrigue of a hacker breaking into the Pope's computer with the erotic temptation of Vatican dispatch Father Lorenzo Quart's attraction to an aristocratic woman also involved in the mystery.

While Eduardo *Mendoza's (1943–) *La verdad sobre el caso Savolta* (1975; *The Truth about the Savolta Case*, 1992) was the first detective novel published after Franco's death, Mendoza is more frequently cited for his humorous fiction featuring a detective whose real name is unknown. "X," as the character is called by critics, is an inpatient at the local mental institution; he is occasionally released to solve a crime because of his contacts and ability to function in society's lower levels. Works like *El misterio de la cripta embrujada* (1979; The Mystery of the Bewitched Crypt) and *La aventura del tocador de señoras* (2001; The Adventure of the Lady's Boudoir) reveal the cultural transformations occurring in Barcelona during the transition to democracy after 1975.

Many other Spanish detective fiction writers have recently emerged. Andreu Martín's (1949–) detective, Javier Lallana, is noteworthy for being the only honest cop in the corrupt force (*Prótesis* [1980; Prosthesis]). Jorge Martínez Reverte's (1944–) detective, Julio Gálvez, is a journalist whose attempts at crime solving portray the complexities of the Basque desire for independence (*Gudari Gálvez* [2005; Gálvez, the Basque Fighter]). Juan

Madrid's (1947–) gangster/mafioso private eye, Toni Romano, first appeared in *Un beso de amigo* (1980; A Friend's Kiss). And Alicia Giménez Bartlett employs a strongly independent female detective, Petra Delicado, in her mysteries; *Día de perros* (1997; *Dog Day*, 2006), for example, offers a moving portrayal of the underground world of fighting dogs. And finally, Lorenzo Silva (1966–) has created the most dynamic duo of sleuths in Spain, seargant Rubén Bevilacqua of the Civil Guard and his partner, Corporal Virginia Chamorro. They represent police work carried out within the frame of the Constitution and a strict compliance with human rights. Silva's *El alquimista impaciente* (2000; The Impatient Alchemist) captured the prestigious Nadal Prize that year.

Clearly, the years since 1975 have been quite fruitful for Spanish detective and mystery fiction, with detectives ranging from the traditional career-minded investigator to the accidental private eye, from the male sexist to the take-charge feminist, and from the inept police bungler to the detective unafraid of using any means necessary to solve the crime. Spanish detective and mystery fiction offers a more critical view of society than other literary genres, as authors use these characters to expose societal, cultural, and/or governmental problems.

Jeffrey Oxford

See also Censorship and Literature in Spain; Detective and Mystery Fiction in Spanish America.

Work About:

Collins, Jacky, and Shelley Godsland, eds. *Mujeres Malas: Women's Detective Fiction from Spain*. Manchester: Manchester University Press, 2005.

Colmeiro, José. *La novela policíaca española: Teoría e historia crítica*. Barcelona and Santafé de Bogotá: Anthropos and Siglo del Hombre, 1994.

Craig-Odders, Renée, Jacky Collins, and Glen S. Close, eds. *Hispanic and Luso-Brazilian Detective Fiction: Essays on the Género Negro Tradition*. Jefferson, NC: McFarland and Co., 2006.

Detective and Mystery Fiction in Spanish America

This genre encompasses all short stories and novels in which crime, and the investigation of crime, are of utmost importance. The detective (represented by a private sleuth, police investigator, or even a literary critic) is often the main character, and progresses from discovering initial clues to solving an enigma or dismantling organized crime.

In 1966, Tzvetan Todorov wrote "The Typology of Detective Fiction" (*The Poetics of Prose*, 1977); in it, he spoke of two main subgenres. The first is the "whodunit," or classical detective fiction where the story opens with a corpse and several clues that may lead to the killer's identity. The second type, the "thriller," shares with suspense novels the follow-up or progression of further criminal actions. Here, the detective or investigator is vulnerable and can be hurt—unlike the original whodunits, whose detectives were completely immune to personal harm. In Spanish American countries (all Spanish-speaking nations in north, central, and South America and the Caribbean), both subgenres have been well represented, although the most recent detective fiction better aligns with the "thriller."

Beginning with the editorial and creative work of Argentine writers Jorge Luis *Borges and Adolfo Bioy Casares (in the 1940s), detective and mystery fiction have a much stronger presence in Spanish America. The first significant work in the genre was published in Argentina in 1942: *Seis problemas para don Isidro Parodi* (*Six Problems for Don Isidro Parodi*, 1981)—a collection of six crime fiction short stories coauthored by Borges and Bioy Casares. The following year, the same authors coedited a two-volume short stories anthology, *Los mejores cuentos policiales* (1943; The Best Short Stories in Detective Fiction), in which a small group of Argentine writers (including Borges, Bioy Casares, Silvina *Ocampo, and Manuel Peyrou), appeared next to such established authors in the genre as Edgar Allan Poe, Arthur Conan Doyle, Ellery Queen, and Agatha Christie. Almost simultaneously, Borges published "El jardín de senderos que se bifurcan" (1941; "The Garden of Forking Paths," 1948) and "La muerte y la brújula" (1942; "Death and the Compass," 1954). These two stories introduced a strong tendency in Argentine, and later Spanish American, crime fiction: a poetic by which death and crime could be both committed and solved through the intellectual activities of reading and writing (a reader could be tricked into death through his reading of a text; at the same time, a detective could find the solution to the mystery in the victim's readings), thereby establishing a strong relationship between the detective figure and the literary critic, as first proposed by Marjorie Nicolson in her 1929 article "The Professor and the Detective."

Although the earliest short stories of detective fiction were published in Argentina, the first important novel came from Mexico, *Ensayo de un crimen* (1944; Rehearsal for a Crime), by playwright Rodolfo *Usigli. This novel inquires into the murderer's psychological profile by presenting its protagonist, Roberto de la Cruz, as a man obsessed with committing a crime for which the police (and society) will find no motive.

If Borges and Bioy Casares were responsible for the translation and anthology of detective fiction classics—the type best represented by Poe and Doyle—Argentine Ricardo *Piglia is credited with promoting the thriller (also known as hardboiled crime fiction, noir fiction, or *novela negra*)—a subgenre of crime fiction best illustrated by the works of American writers Dashiell Hammett and Raymond Chandler. These texts emerged in response to organized crime, Prohibition, and corruption during the first decades of the 20th century in the United States. In Argentina, Piglia directed *La Serie Negra* (The Noir Series), a project in which he translated and published works by authors like Hammett and Chandler, and including James Cain, David Goodis, Charles Williams, and other writers who continued the thriller vein of the genre. Besides his editorial work in the 1960s and 1970s, Piglia penned one of Spanish America's most recognized short stories, "La loca y el relato del crimen" ("The Madwoman and the Story of the Crime," 1995), which earned him first place in the 1975 Latin American Crime Fiction Short Story Competition.

Mexico's production in the genre excelled in the works of Jorge Ibargüengoitia, whose novels *Las muertas* (1977; *The Dead Girls*, 1982) and *Dos crímenes* (1979; *Two Crimes*, 1984) depart markedly from the classical model. Ibargüengoitia's works prove important in that they exhibit a playful relationship with pioneer models of the genre, redefining the tendencies of what would become the Spanish American crime fiction novel at the turn of the century: a text showing strong concern for historical injustices, government corruption, and obsolete cultural norms.

Sharing the same goal of social and government denunciation, several authors wrote serialized novels with an investigator as the sole protagonist: the works of Mexican writer Paco Ignacio Taibo II concentrate on his country's postrevolutionary and post-1968 years as the most relevant crime setting; Cuban writer Leonardo Padura Fuentes's *Las cuatro estaciones* (2001; The Four Seasons) sets the crime in the years following the Cuban revolution (1959); and the works of contemporary Chilean writers Roberto Ampuero and Ramón Díaz Eterovic review the years after Pinochet's 1973 coup d'état.

During the 1980s, recognition is due to the works of Colombian Gabriel *García Márquez (*Crónica de una muerte anunciada* [1981; *Chronicle of a Death Foretold*, 1983]), and Peruvian Mario *Vargas Llosa (*¿Quién mató a Palomino Molero?* [1986; *Who Killed Palomino Molero?*, 1987]), whose use of journalistic and melodramatic discourse resemble that of other canonical works produced in those years in Spanish America outside the genre of detective fiction.

While Spanish America's mystery and detective fiction has been dominated by male writers, the most significant contribution by women writers comes from Chile, with the works of Marcela *Serrano and Alejandra Rojas. Rojas's *Stradivarius penitente* (1999; Penitent Stradivarius) is among the genre's best novels written by a Spanish American woman. Finally, although the majority of her work falls outside the genre (as opposed to Serrano and Rojas), Colombian Laura *Restrepo's mystery novel *Delirio* (2004; Delirium) won the prestigious Alfaguara Prize that year.

Detective and mystery fiction has been a strong force in Spanish American countries for decades. While incorporating some of the original rules of the genre, most of the work in these countries has taken a denunciatory tone, with its most established elements being exposure of government corruption, police inefficiency, and the retelling of history.

Jimena Ugaz Pereda

See also Corpi, Lucha (1946–); Detective and Mystery Fiction in Spain.

Work By:

García Márquez, Gabriel. *Chronicle of a Death Foretold*. Trans. Gregory Rabassa. New York: Knopf, 1983.

Piglia, Ricardo. *Assumed Name*. Trans. Sergio Gabriel Waisman. Pittsburgh: Latin American Literary Review Press, 1995.

Rojas, Alejandra. *Stradivarius penitente*. Madrid: Ollero y Ramos, 1999.

Work About:

Chandler, Raymond. *The Simple Art of Murder*. New York: Norton, 1968.

Mandel, Ernest. *Delightful Murder*. Minneapolis: University of Minnesota Press, 1986.

Piglia, Ricardo. "Lo negro del policial." *El juego de los cautos*. Ed. Daniel Link. Buenos Aires: La marca, 2003, 78–83.

Porter, Dennis. *The Pursuit of Crime*. New Haven, CT: Yale University Press, 1981.

Todorov, Tzvetan. *The Poetics of Prose*. Ithaca, NY: Cornell University Press, 1977.

Díaz, Jesús (1941–2005)

This Havana-born Cuban intellectual, writer, and film director initially became a major representative of Cuba's new revolutionary narrative after winning the 1966 Casa de las Américas Prize that year for his short story collection *Los años duros* (1966; The Hard Years). The text set the tone for the new Cuban narrative by rejecting three tendencies in place: the baroque style of Alejo *Carpentier and José *Lezama Lima, the poetic transcendentalism of the *Orígenes* group, and indigenous populism or *criollismo*. Díaz later moderated his discourse and finally left the island, going first to Germany and later to Spain, where he founded and directed the journal *Encuentro de la Cultura Cubana* until his death in Madrid.

Although he did not criticize Castro's regime in the 1990s as directly and strongly as other exiles, he did show his disagreement with the island's politics in his narrative and used his journal *Encuentro* as a meeting point for artists and creators on and off the island. As novelist, Díaz's works reflect the evolution of Cuba's revolution and the increasing political repercussions faced by authors on the island. Many critics consider *Las iniciales de la tierra* (1987; *The Initials of the Earth*, 2006) to be his finest work and the quintessential novel of the Cuban Revolution.

Miguel Ángel González-Abellás

See also Criollista Novel in Spanish America; Cuban Exile Writing outside the United States; Novel of the Cuban Revolution.

Work By:

The Initials of the Earth. Trans. Kathleen Ross. Durham, NC: Duke University Press, 2006.

Work About:

Collmann, William Oliva. *Jesús Díaz: El ejercicio de los límites de la expresión revolucionaria en Cuba*. New York: Peter Lang, 1999.

De Ferrari, Guillermina. "Embargoed Masculinities: Loyalty, Friendship and the Role of the Intellectual in the Post-Soviet Cuban Novel." *Latin American Literary Review* 35.69 (January–June 2007): 82–103.

Díaz Arrieta, Hernán (pseudonym Alone) (1891–1984)

This self-taught intellectual became one of 20th-century Chile's most polemical and influential literary critics. He worked at the Ministry of Justice for 25 years in a position that allowed him to dedicate much time to literature and writing.

In 1913, Díaz Arrieta adopted his pseudonym as writer and critic, and for the next 60 years used his growing influence to evaluate Chilean writers in magazines and newspapers, thereby codifying the literary canon for those decades. He also funded publications and edited the literary manuscripts of rising authors. Among writers he positioned and advanced were Marta *Brunet, María Luisa *Bombal, and Nobel laureate Gabriela *Mistral.

Alone's weekly "Crónica literaria" column for the influential conservative newspaper *El Mercurio* brought him journalistic and literary prestige and recognition for its fluid, amusing prose. In 1954, he published *Historia personal de la literatura chilena* (Personal History of Chilean Literature), in which he gathered his views of Chilean literary works and authors. It was followed by *Leer y escribir* (1962; To Read and Write). Díez Arrieta's originality resides in his ability to combine stylistic criticism with a queer perspective. In recognition for a life dedicated to writing and discussing literature, Alone received Chile's National Literature Prize in 1959. *Pasado imperfecto* (1976; Past Imperfect) is his memoir. The posthumous collection *El vicio impune* (1997; Unpunished Vice) gathers his *crónicas* of the past 50 years.

Bernardita Llanos

See also Queer Literature in Spanish America.

Work About:

Cortés, Hugo Rolando. *Conversaciones con Alone*. Valparaíso, Chile: no publisher, 1974.

Sutherland, Juan Pablo. *A corazón abierto. Historia literaria de la homosexualidad en Chile*. Santiago, Chile: Sudamericana, 2001, 139–43.

Díaz Castro, Eugenio (1803–1865)

This novelist and essayist is considered one of Colombia's first *costumbrista* writers; his depiction of local customs, language, and color affirmed Colombian nationality and attempted to assess autochthonous Colombian values. Lifelong poor health prevented his participation in Colombia's war of Independence (1810–1819) and civil wars (1821–1841). In 1858, he published his first novella, *Una ronda de don Ventura Ahumada* (A Patrol of Don Ventura Ahumada), in which a monk escapes from his monastery, and Ahumada, Bogotá's police chief, is charged with finding him.

That same year Díaz Castro and José María Vergara y Vergara founded *El Mosaico*, an important literary magazine of the day, and where his best known novel, *Manuela* (1889) was first published as a serial. In 1861, illness forced him to give up journalistic writing, but during this period of seclusion he composed three novels, all published posthumously.

Díaz Castro lived in turbulent times; Colombia's new republic was emerging and yet a feudal system remained prevalent. This reality is reflected in *Manuela*, whose town of Parroquia becomes an allegorical representation of Colombia. Manuela lives and works on the land of wealthy landowner and *caudillo* (town chief) don Tadeo. She is sexually harassed and the other workers are underpaid. Through *Manuela*'s characters and *cuadros de costumbres*, Díaz Castro explores the social conflicts that followed independence from Spain.

Jaime A. Orrego

See also Costumbrismo in Spanish America.

Work By:

Novelas y cuadros de costumbres. Ed. Elisa Mujica. Bogotá: Procultura, 1985.

Work About:

Ortiz, María Mercedes. "De patrias chicas y grandes: La representación de la nación en *María* de Jorge Isaacs y *Manuela* de Eugenio Díaz Castro." *Literatura y otras artes en América Latina*. Ed. D. Balderston, O. Torres Duque, L. Gutierrez, B. Bollnick, E. Willingham. Prol. O. Hahn. Iowa City: University of Iowa Press, 2004, 141–49.

Díaz del Castillo, Bernal (1492–1584)

Born in Medina del Campo, Spain, and probably the most prominent of Hernán Cortés's soldiers, he went on to write what is now considered the most faithful account of the Mexican conquest, *Historia verdadera de la conquista de la Nueva España* (1632; *The Conquest of New Spain*, 1963). Despite the fact that he wrote it years after the events transpired, between 1555 and 1575, his account of what occurred in 1519 aims to correct and clarify Francisco López de Gómara's *Historia general de las Indias* (1554; *The Conquest of Mexico*, 2000). Unlike Gómara, Díaz del Castillo acknowledged the conquest as a collective rather than an individual enterprise. His prologue explicitly states that while he does not question Cortés's achievements during that time, he feels that those who accompanied Cortés and participated in the many ensuing battles deserved equal recognition, recognition that eluded them before publication of his first-person account. The title of Díaz del Castillo's text is particularly revealing, as it functions to underscore the traditional "subjective" nature of history: by stating that his text reflects the "true" account of events, he implies that a "false" account coexists alongside or precedes it. While some scholars may question the work's agenda, his tone, considered as straightforward and candid, does reflect a sincere desire to make history more inclusive. Díaz del Castillo wants to right a wrong in the name of all the nonglorified soldiers who helped Cortés realize his conquest. While he includes himself among these men and women (unlike Cortés, he gives the interpreter Malinche her due credit), his intentions are not regarded as self-serving.

Díaz del Castillo is a man of arms and not letters. His writing style is simple and unornamented, yet intricate. Selective in his words, he describes only what he or other soldiers experienced or beheld, including the bravery and tenacity of the Aztecs (Mexicas). Although his writing lacks the syntactic, grammatical, and literary prowess of Gómara, his deficiencies as an untrained writer ironically make his text all the more guileless and credible. Despite the fact that he was about 80 years old when *Historia Verdadera* was published, most critics do not question his historical accuracy, especially considering that Gómara, his historical opponent, never stepped foot on New World soil. As such, Díaz del Castillo's eyewitness narrative affords him a textual authority Gómara can never claim.

Bonnie L. Gasior

See also Discovery and Conquest Writings: Describing the Americas.

Work By:

The Conquest of New Spain. Trans. John M. Cohen. New York: Penguin Classics, 1963.
Historia Verdadera de la Conquista de la Nueva España. Ed. Joaquín Ramírez Cabañas. México: Porrúa, 2005.

Work About:

Cascardi, Anthony. "Chronicle toward Novel: Bernal Díaz' History of the Conquest of Mexico." *Novel: A Forum on Fiction* 15.3 (1982): 197–212.
Serés, Guillermo. "Vida y escritura de Bernal Díaz del Castillo." *Literatura: Teoría, Historia, Crítica* 6 (2004): 15–62.

Díaz-Mas, Paloma (1954–)

Born in Madrid, Spain, this fiction author published her first collection, *Biografías de genios, traidores, sabios y suicidas según antiguos documentos* (1973; Biographies of Geniuses, Traitors, Wisemen, and Suicides), at age 19 and has since continued to distinguish herself in literature and academia. A professor of Spanish literature specializing in Sephardic studies, she has won many prestigious awards for her essays, fiction, and theater.

Combining a love of history and literature, Díaz-Mas's creative works often masquerade as period pieces, but always contain a contemporary, postmodern twist that questions and undermines the assumptions of privilege, class, and power associated with the depicted eras. Humor, parody, and intertextual references are trademarks of her texts, making them pleasurable for experienced readers and novices.

Jessica A. Folkart

Work By:

Como un libro cerrado. Barcelona: Anagrama, 2005.
El sueño de Venecia. Barcelona: Anagrama, 1992.
Sephardim: The Jews from Spain. Trans. George K. Zucker. Chicago: University of Chicago Press, 1992.

Work About:

Bellver, Catherine G. "Humor and the Resistance to Meaning in *El rapto del Santo Grial.*" *Romanic Review* 87.1 (Jan 1996): 145–55.

Diego, Gerardo (1896–1987)

The avant-garde brought Spain a new kind of poet, the literature professor, one whose erudition imbues his writing. Most certainly, a deep knowledge of literary traditions, especially popular medieval poetry, Spanish baroque, and European romanticism (including its music) all resonate in the writing of Gerardo Diego. Also a skilled musician, his scholarly research of Luis de *Góngora remains a key reading for understanding the revival of baroque in Spanish literature. Diego also compiled the 1927 poetic anthology in honor of Góngora that brought Spain's *Generation of 1927 to fame.

His poetry employed traditional forms (sonnets, ballads, and *décimas*) to speak of love, death, Catholicism, bullfighting, and the Spanish landscape. As an avant-garde poet, he espoused creationism, the cubist "ism" invented by Chilean Vicente *Huidobro, which did not follow regular syntax, used irrational images that broke with traditional metaphor, and, on the printed page, made the visual arrangement of poems evoke their subject; that is to say, if the poem subject was the sea, the outline of the poem's words resembled waves.

Diego links both tradition and avant-garde in his masterpiece, *Fábula de Equis y Zeda* (1932; Fable of X and Z), written between 1926 and 1929; in it, he experiments with traditional stanzas and radically abstract metaphors. He wrote more than 50 collections of poetry; many poems flow from book to book as different versions emerge over the years. From *Sonetos humanos* (1925; Human Sonnets), his poem "El ciprés de Silos" (On the Cypress of Silos), about the majestic cypress in the middle of the cloister of this Romanesque monastery in Burgos, is considered the epitome of Spanish classicism in the 20th century. Diego won the National Literature Award in 1925 and captured the Cervantes Award in 1979.

Salvador A. Oropesa

See also Poetry in Spain: 1900 to Present.

Work By:

Songs and Sonnets of Love Still Innocent: A Representative Anthology of the Poetry of Gerardo Diego. Trans. Carl. W. Cobb. University, MS: Romance Monographs, 1997.

Work About:

Mandlove, Nancy B. "Ultraísmo and Tradition: Two Sonnets of Gerardo Diego." *At Home and Beyond: New Essays on Spanish Poets of the Twenties.* Ed. Salvador Jiménez Fajardo and John C. Wilcox. Lincoln: University of Nebraska, 1983, 69–76.

Rogers, Timothy J. "Reader Cognition and the Dialectical Imagery in the Poetry of Gerardo Diego." *New Essays on Spanish Poets of the Twenties.* Ed. Salvador

Jiménez Fajardo and John C. Wilcox. Lincoln: University of Nebraska, 1983, 77–86.

Diosdado, Ana (1938–)

Born of Spanish parents in Buenos Aires and connected to the theatrical world since childhood (her father was actor and director Enrique Diosdado; her stepmother, actress Amelia de la Torre; and her godmother, actress Margarita Xirgu), Ana Diosdado debuted as an actress in Spain with Federico *García Lorca's *Así que pasen cinco años* but abandoned her studies in humanities at the University of Madrid to pursue a writing career. She published her first novel in 1965, and in 1970 received the *Maite* and *Foro Teatral* Awards for her first play, *Olvida los tambores* (Forget the Drums). In 1973, she obtained the *Real Academia Española's Fastenrath Award for the innovative language of *Usted también podrá disfrutar de ella* (1995; *Yours for the Asking*, 1995).

Married to actor Carlos Larrañaga from 1979 to 1999, the 1980s was her most acclaimed decade due to the originality of texts like *Los ochenta son nuestros*—both novel and play (1988; The Eighties Are Ours) and her success in three TV series adapted from her scripts: *Juan y Manuela* (1972; John and Manuela), *Anillos de oro* (1983; Golden Rings), and *Segunda enseñanza* (1986; Secondary Education). Her plots, ridden with generational conflicts, fresh depictions of an ever-changing Spain, and new roles for women, caught the attention of the Spanish public. Diosdado has adapted plays from other playwrights, prepared scripts for radio, and written for national newspapers. A member of the General Society of Authors and Editors' board of directors since 1983, in 2001 she became its first woman president.

Judith García-Quismondo García

Work By:

Yours for the Asking. Ed. Patricia Walker O'Connor. University Park, PA: Estreno, 1995.

Work About:

Zatlin, Phyllis. "Traditional Sex Roles in the Theatre of Ana Diosdado." *Mid-Hudson Language Studies* 10 (1987): 71–77.

Discépolo, Armando (1887–1971)

This Argentine playwright and director was the creator of the *grotesco criollo* (creole grotesque). For Discépolo, the Creole grotesque was a way to show the reality of thousands of immigrants fighting with themselves and others to adjust to their new homeland. Isolation, pessimism, and the defeat of its characters are the main notes of this genre. His plays offer a commentary on his day's reality: social and economical turmoil, the immigration experience, repressive government legislation, and family life during the first three decades of the 20th century. A fully developed example of *grotesco criollo* is found in *Stefano* (1928), whose protagonist makes futile efforts to communicate and improve his social and family situation; his string of pathetic failures turn him into a caricature and his final death represents a metaphor of the problems affecting Argentina.

Discépolo's first text, the melodramatic love story *Entre el hierro* (1910; Between Iron), enjoyed great success. Thereafter, Discépolo wrote one to two plays per year. Other well-known works are *Mustafá (1921)*, *Mateo* (1923), *Giacomo (1924)*, *Muñeca* (1924; Doll), *El Organito* (1925; Street Organ), and *Cremona* (1932). His last play, *Relojero* (1934; Clock Maker), revolves around the disintegration of the family and generational conflict, showing the impossibility of change. His views of progress are reactionary and offer no hope for the future. For the remainder of his career, Discépolo focused on directing.

María R. Matz

See also Género chico criollo and the Río de la Plata *Saineteros* (*Sainete* Composers).

Work By:

Obra dramática de Armando Discépolo. Intro. Osvaldo Pellettieri. Buenos Aires: Editorial Universitaria de Buenos Aires, 1996.

Work About:

Troiani, Elisa A. "Stéfano: Promises and Other Speech Acts." *Things Done with Words: Speech Acts in Hispanic Drama.* Ed. Elias L. Rivers. Newark, DE: Juan de la Cuesta, 1986, 85–99.

Discovery and Conquest Writings: Describing the Americas

In the late 15th and 16th centuries, Europeans—in this case Spaniards—navigated across the seas following an expansive cultural worldview. From the indigenous American perspective, there was no "discovery" of the Americas, and for this reason many scholars use the term "encounter" to describe the event. Such concepts as "discovery," "conquest," and "conversion"; and names like "the New World," "America," "the Indies," and "Indians" are purely European creations that express a Eurocentric perspective. Nonetheless, the immediate reaction of these men coming from an Old World viewpoint was to evaluate America and its inhabitants according to their Eurocentric worldview.

The "invention of America" was an ongoing process in which acts of conquest were seen to be what Francisco de Gómara called "the greatest event in the world since Creation." These events were narrated down to the smallest detail by explorers, soldiers, and missionaries who participated in the New World conquest, providing eyewitness accounts of the discovery and conquest of existing civilizations and natural wonders of the flora and fauna.

The Indies: First Accounts

With a contract from the Spanish government that promised a hereditary title, the position of admiral and governor, and a fixed share of profits, Christopher

Columbus left Spain in 1492 and after 66 days reached the New World, announcing the "discovery" of a new land. Columbus writes about discovering a new route to the Orient, not a new world. He describes the indigenous people living in these newly found territories as pleasant in aspect and easy to convert and the land as fertile and abundant in water. The first account of this "discovery" was Columbus's letter to Luis de Santángel; its portrayal of the land and ways of life helped create a mythical world resembling a Biblical paradise that was also filled with economic possibilities for the new owners. This paradise was a product of Columbus's imagination, but the image served to bring other expeditions to the newly discovered territory.

Within a few years, it became clear to Europeans that rather than reaching Asia, Columbus had encountered new lands and peoples. The Italian Amerigo Vespucci, who remains a controversial historical figure, was first to acknowledge in writing that these lands were indeed a New World, and in 1507, two German geographers proposed naming the new territory America after him.

In 1499, due to Columbus's limited success, the Spanish Crown began to authorize contracts (*capitulaciones*) with other entrepreneurs and explorers. The first accounts of explorations in Central and South America are a series of letters grouped in the book *Décadas* (1511–1530; *The Decades of the Newe Worlde or West India*, 1966) written by Pedro Mártir de Anghiera, an Italian-born Spanish historian. In 1511, Charles I of Spain (who was also Charles V of the Holy Roman Empire) appointed him chronicler of the newly formed Council of the Indies; his duty was to describe the New World.

Debates about the Nature of Indians

From the outset, Spain harbored serious doubts regarding the ethics of the colonization. The writings of Dominican defender of the Indians Bartolomé de las Casas are essential for understanding the cultural and political history of Spain's colonization in the Americas. Among his works are the *Apologética historia sumaria* (written 1527–1531, published 1566; *Apologetic History*, 1946), which takes classical and medieval environmental theories and applies them to the Antilles; and the *Historia de las Indias* (written 1527–1560, published 1875; *History of the Indies*, 1971), one of the earliest chronicles of the Indies—its account of Spanish colonization from 1527 to 1561 is considered by many to be his most ambitious text. Finally, his *Brevísima Relación de la Destrucción de las Indias* (written 1542, published 1552; *Brief Account of the Destruction of the Indies*, 1992) offers one of the harshest views of colonial violence. It calls for justice and contributes to what has been known as the *Black Legend (leyenda negra), an anti-Hispanic and anti-Catholic sentiment advocated by Spain's political and religious rivals. Las Casas's writings have generated rich discussion that even reaches contemporary considerations of topics like national movements in Latin

America, human rights, and globalization, among others.

Indies Historians

Accounts about the Indies were also produced by what are now called *historiadores de Indias* (Indies historians), although they were not technically historians: in addition to narrating historical events, they gave their impressions and thoughts about the new territories as they organized the new information. In other words, they compiled narratives that organized what they had seen firsthand or had learned secondhand (verbally or in writing), thanks to the accounts of others. All were called "histories," but they differed markedly: Jesuit missionary José de Acosta (1539–1600) targeted natural and ethnographic information, as did Gonzalo Fernández de Oviedo, while such authors as Bernardino de Sahagún and Fray Diego de Landa used a more encyclopedic approach.

In 1523, Gonzalo Fernández de Oviedo was appointed historiographer of the Indies. He wrote *La General y natural historia de las Indias* (written 1514–1549; *The General and Natural History of the Indies*, 1941) was not published as a whole until 1851. Francisco López de Gómara is particularly noted for the *Historia de las Indias y conquista de México* (1552; *The Conquest of the West Indies*, 1966), which describes Hernán Cortés's expedition. Although Gómara himself did not accompany Cortés and never visited the Americas, he used firsthand sources for his account. His contemporaries, among them Bernal *Díaz del Castillo, criticized his work as inaccurate and exaggerated in its portrayal of Cortés's role.

Mexico

The conquest of Mexico is one of the most well-known episodes in Spain's conquest of the Americas, and Hernán Cortés is one of the most recognized conquistadors. Cortés landed on the eastern coast, founding the city of Veracruz in 1519; two years later, the Aztec empire had surrendered. This conquest has been chronicled in several accounts: in letters that Hernán Cortés wrote personally to the Spanish emperor; in the account of Cortés's Lieutenant Bernal *Díaz del Castillo, *La verdadera historia de la Conquista de la Nueva España* (1632; *True History of the Conquest of New Spain*, 1973), and by the Aztecs themselves.

Bernardo de Balbuena's *La grandeza mexicana* (1604; *Mexican Greatness*, 1930) used both Cortes's and Díaz del Castillo's texts as inspiration for his encomium to *Mexico City. This work presents the capital as a Renaissance metropolis that matches or even surpasses its European rivals, marking the end of the conquest process.

Peru

The defeat of the Inca empire constituted another great episode in Spain's conquest of America, but its author, Francisco Pizarro, never achieved the same reputation that surrounded Cortés. Peru's primary chronicler, Pedro Cieza de León, was also a Spanish conquistador. Written in three parts over the span of a decade (1540–1550) *Crónicas del Perú* (*Chronicles of Peru*, 1998) offers a historically oriented narration of the conquest and of civil wars among the Spaniards, but much of its importance lies in the detailed descriptions of geography, ethnography, flora, and fauna. The three parts were respectively published in 1553, 1871, and 1909.

Indians and Mestizos

When the acculturation process began, indigenous and mestizo writers, some of whom belonged to Aztec and Incan royalty, produced conquest accounts. In Mexico, a group of manuscripts written during the early colonial years related the history of the Nahuatl people using their traditional way of writing. These manuscripts are known as the *Códices postcortesianos* (Postcortesian Codices); among the most important are the *Códice Boturini* (Boturini Codex) and the *Códice Mendoza* (Mendoza Codex). Also of note in Mexico is Hernando Alvarado de Tezozomoc, of royal Náhuatl lineage, who composed the *Crónica Mexicayotl* (1598; Mexicayotl Chronicle), a record of the Aztec empire. Written in Spanish and Nahuatl, it provides an account of Aztec history from Acamapichtli (1350–1403), the first Tlatoani (ruler), to the Spanish-appointed rulers in the mid-16th century.

The voice of the defeated culture figures importantly in writings about the conquest of Perú. Felipe Guaman Poma de Ayala's *Nueva Crónica* (1600; *New Chronicle* 2006) records the history of Peru from the beginning of time up to the Spanish conquest (1532–1572), and *Buen Gobierno* (1615–1616; *Good Government*, 2006) offers a mix of history, social criticism, political science, and Christian morals. Also of note are writings by the son of a Spanish conquistador and an Inca princess, the Inca *Garcilaso de la Vega. Educated in Lima and Spain, his most important work is *Los Comentarios reales* (1609; *Royal Commentaries*, 2006), an account of the Inca empire's history up to the Spaniards' arrival. In his narration, Garcilaso shows pride in being part of an educated Inca elite with no reason to envy its Spanish counterpart.

Travelers and New Discoverers

As Spaniards conquered the islands of the Caribbean, they also explored the coastlines of the American mainland. Several expeditions moved northward into Florida and the southwest of the future United States. Among many is the well-documented 1526 exploration led by Pánfilo de Narváez that shipwrecked in West Florida; after numerous subsequent disasters and hardships, by 1536 a handful of survivors led by Álvar Núñez Cabeza de Vaca had worked their way to the west coast of Mexico. Written with a quick, clear, and passionate prose, Cabeza de Vaca's account of their wanderings was published as *Naufragios* (1542; *Shipwrecks*, 2003).

As the conquest progressed, rumors of fabulous richness spread: large cities with streets of silver, people who ate from golden dishes and possessed priceless jewels, and an Indian chief who painted himself with gold dust, among others. These fantastic stories were the result of a mentality still transitioning from the Middle Age to the *Renaissance. Such stories of wonders or even monstrosities in the new lands motivated Spaniards to explore unknown territories in search of *El Dorado* (the golden one), *las siete ciudades de Cíbola* (the seven cities of Cibola) or the fountain of eternal youth.

People of the Cloth

After the initial accounts by soldiers, a second wave of writings by men of faith documented their spiritual conquest, which progressed more slowly than that of the sword. They came in several stages, depending on their specific religious denomination. One of the first arrivals to the new lands were Franciscans friars like Toribio de Motolinia, author of *Historia de los indios de la Nueva España* (written 1536–1541, published 1858; *History of the Indians of New Spain*, 1970), and Bernardino de *Sahagún, who used Nahuatl and Spanish in the *Historia general de las cosas de la Nueva España* (written 1547–1577, published 1829–1830; *General History of the Things of the New Spain*, 1982). Such Dominicans as Diego Durán soon followed the Franciscans, after which came the Augustine Order, with such friars as Juan de Grijalba. Of particular note are Antonio de Remesal (in Guatemala) and Francisco de la Calancha (in Peru). Finally, the Jesuits were the last religious order to spread throughout the new lands.

Guatemala and Yucatán

Bishop Diego de Landa of Yucatán authored the *Relación de las cosas de Yucatán* (1566; *The Relationship of the Things of the Yucatan*, 2002), which catalogs the Maya language, religion, culture, and writing system. Paradoxically, at the same time, Landa took aggressive measures to spread the Christian faith. On July 12, 1562, he conducted an *auto de fé* (act of faith) in which a significant body of Mayan cultural objects were destroyed in a public act of penance.

Chile

Mention must also be made of *La Araucana* (*The Araucana*, 2006), the vivid poetic narration of the conflict between Chile's Araucan people and Spanish soldiers. This epic poem by cultivated nobleman and soldier Alonso de Ercilla y Zúñiga consists of 37 cantos divided into three parts, published in 1569, 1578, and 1589.

Conclusion

The conquerors and settlers of the New World were men of the sword, of faith, or the law. The earliest writings share a curiosity toward the new lands and inhabitants. Exoticism is a major characteristic of 16th-century accounts of the land, its fauna and flora, and more importantly, its native populations, including their beliefs, traditions, and different cultural habits.

As the conquest of territories progressed, a new type of writing emerged, in which the heroic actions of conquistadors dominate, and that included detailed descriptions of epic victories against great empires like those of the Aztecs and Incas.

At this point, moral judgments begin to appear, along with reflection about the rightness of the conquest enterprise and the treatment that natives received.

Each type of writing differs, despite their common elements of description and narration of events that often relate to Old World events or places. Nonetheless, the underlying intents of each group of authors were unique. Documents written by a Columbus or Cortés responded to the need to communicate with the Spanish monarch. The desire for knowledge of the New World inspired accounts like that of Cabeza de Vaca. Authors like Díaz del Castillo offered different versions of events, aiming to correct the mistakes of other texts. Mestizo author Inca Garcilaso strove to praise the indigenous culture, and indigenous writer Guaman Poma de Ayala protested abuses in colonial government. Finally, such friars as Las Casas wrote to defend the Indians from abuses of the conquistadors.

Many modern Latin American writers—Gabriel *García Márquez, Alejo *Carpentier, Carlos *Fuentes, and Abel Posse, to name a few—have rediscovered the works of these men and their writings, presenting the impact of the encounter and reinterpreting their writings.

Maria R. Matz

See also Alva Ixtlilxóchitl, Fernando de (1568–1648); Colonial Religious Chronicles in Spanish America; Mayan Literature.

Work By:

Castillo, Susan P., and Ivy Schweitzer, eds. *The Literatures of Colonial America: An Anthology.* Oxford: Blackwell, 2001.

Work About:

Adorno, Rolena. "Discourses on Colonialism: Bernal Díaz, Las Casas, and the 20th-Century Reader." *Modern Language Notes* 103 (1988): 239–58.

Adorno, Rolena. *Guaman Poma: Writing and Resistance in Colonial Peru.* 1986. 2nd ed. Austin: University of Texas Press, 2000.

Elliot, J. H. *The Old World and the New 1492–1650.* Cambridge: Canto, 1994.

Padgen, Anthony. *European Encounters with the New World: From Renaissance to Romanticism.* New Haven, CT: Yale University Press, 1993.

Padgen, Anthony. *The Fall of Natural Man: The American Indian and the Origins of Comparative Ethnology.* Cambridge: Cambridge University Press, 1987.

Documentary Narrative in Spanish American Literature

Latin American literature has a long history of testing the epistemological and generic boundaries between history and literature. Sixteenth-century *crónicas*, which documented the new world of the Americas for the Spanish crown, employed elements of both objective reportage and fantasy to describe their encounters in a foreign space. Argentine intellectual Domingo *Sarmiento blurred the limits of biography, history, and invention in his 1845 *Facundo: Civilización y barbarie* (*Facundo, or Civilization and Barbarism*, 1998), a biography of federalist *caudillo* Juan Quiroga Facundo and the landmark evaluation of

Argentine cultural mores. But the possibility of grafting storytelling techniques and historical documentation took a decidedly more political tack in the mid-20th century. In response to an increasingly fierce appropriation of the production and dissemination of an official, invariably distorted history by their governments, Latin American authors began to narrate their own versions of historical events using techniques of journalism and fiction writing.

Documentary narrative blurs the boundaries between history and fiction, novelistic subjectivity and real-world events, and documentation and storytelling. This largely postmodern hybrid genre is variously known as literary journalism, new journalism, *el relato real*, and the testimonial novel. It is inherently and overtly concerned with how history is told, who gets to tell it, to what end, and to whom, but uses such literary techniques as point of view, multiple shifts in narrative voice and perspective, reported speech, and scenic development to construct an historical account.

Perhaps the first example of Latin American new journalism, Argentine Rodolfo Walsh's 1957 *Operación masacre* (*Operation Massacre*, 2006) documents the 1956 illegal arrest and attempted murder of a group of Peronist loyalists. Eleven men were detained and shot by police and army officers near a city dump on the outskirts of Buenos Aires, but six of them survived the intended assassination. Walsh, a local journalist, met with one of the survivors who had gone into hiding, and wrote *Operación masacre* in order to counter official government accounts that claimed that a group of violent Peronist rebels had been quelled. Walsh continued to rebut the falsification of historical record with his 1958 *Caso Satanowsky* (Satanowsky Case) and 1969 *¿Quién mató a Rosendo?* (Who Killed Rosendo?), which reported the cover-ups surrounding the political murders of a judge and a union leader in Buenos Aires.

In 1966, Cuban ethnographer Miguel *Barnet published *Biografía de un cimarrón* (*Biography of a Runaway Slave*, 1995), based on a series of tape-recorded interviews he conducted with the 105-year-old Esteban Montejo. The illiterate Montejo recounted to Barnet his life as a slave in captivity, a fugitive slave, and a soldier in the Cuban War of Independence, and Barnet transcribed, edited, and published the account. Insomuch as Barnet served as an intermediary for the production of Montejo's autobiography, this early example of testimonial narrative raises questions of authenticity and authorship.

Mexican author Elena *Poniatowska's 1969 *Hasta no verte Jesús mío* (*Here's To You, Jesusa*, 2002) follows Barnet's lead by relating the life story of the resilient Oaxacan Josefina Bórquez through the invented narrator and character Jesusa Palancares. Basing her text on the transcribed interviews she had conducted with Bórquez over several years, Poniatowska's testimonial novel blurs the identification of author and agent to document the life of Bórquez, a poverty-stricken, rebellious, inventive woman.

Poniatowska again penned a documentary narrative, albeit in a more historical vein, two years later with *La noche de Tlatelolco* (1971; *Massacre in Mexico*, 1992). Here, she compiles an oral history of the events of October 2, 1968 in Mexico City, when the military opened fire on and killed approximately 325 student demonstrators who were peacefully protesting the government's elaborate financial sponsorship of that year's Olympic Games in the face of widespread national poverty. Poniatowska's montage of eyewitness accounts, interviews, letters, newspaper articles, poetry, and photographs documents the massacre through the voices of those who lived it.

Colombian author Gabriel *García Márquez published a watershed work of new journalism with his 1970 *Relato de un náufrago* (*Story of a Shipwrecked Sailor*, 1986). García Márquez uses a first-person narrative voice to reconstruct the story of Luis Alejandro Velasco's 10-day survival at sea in 1955, a discursive methodology of autobiographical legitimization that he adopts in order to mitigate political repercussions from the work's implicit critique of the Colombian government for overloading Velasco's navy ship with contraband, which helped provoke the shipwreck. Certainly a result of his training as a journalist, García Márquez returns to documentary narrative with the novella *Crónica de una muerte anunciada* (1981; *Chronicle of a Death Foretold*, 1983), a prosaic retelling of events surrounding the murder of young Santiago Nasar; and with the journalistic *Noticia de un secuestro* (1996; *News of a Kidnapping*, 1997), which recounts the kidnapping of a group of prominent Colombian journalists by the Medellín drug cartel.

While documentary narrative takes various generic forms and sometimes bumps up against the shores of historical fiction, its aim is always to provide an alternate interpretation of history, historical agents, and the representation of these agents.

Karen Elizabeth Bishop

See also Discovery and Conquest Writings: Describing the Americas; Testimonial Writing in Central America; Torture in Modern Spanish American Literature.

Work About:

Gugelberger, Georg M., ed. *The Real Thing: Testimonial Discourse and Latin America*. Durham, NC: Duke University Press, 1996.

Dominican Republic: Contemporary Literature by Women Writers

Socially isolated and disempowered for years, in the 20th century, literature written by Dominican women has assumed prominence in the public arena. Between 1820 and 1990 only 25 novels were published by Dominican women, but during the last 20 years they have produced over 50 texts, and critical research on their writings has become a particular focus of women critics.

A solid group of women emerged in the 1980s; each possessed a very personal, unique style, but they all strongly questioned women's subordinate role in the patriarchal Dominican society and essentially denounced such oppression. With increased access to broader publishing venues, the 1990s ushered in a true boom of literature written by women that encompasses poetry, short stories, novels, essays, and plays. In the capital city, Santo Domingo's Casa de Teatro Award and La Trinitaria bookstore's assiduous efforts to promote new writers further contributed to this boom of women writers.

Poet and short story author Aurora Arias (1962–) started writing in the 1980s, initially publishing in newspapers and magazines. Her texts take place in noisy, car-infested Santo Domingo, a city that epitomizes social chaos. Her short story collection, *Invi's Paradise y otros relatos* (1998: Invi's Paradise and Other Tales), explores the impact of urbanization and migration in the district of INVI, a poor neighbourhood filled with social problems. Arias gives voice to urban mothers and youth without opportunities who struggle to survive.

After a successful career as judge, law professor, and journalist, Ligia Minaya (1941–) turned to literature, publishing a collection of articles, short stories, and two novels. *El callejón de las flores* (1999: The Backstreet of Flowers), a collection of 12 erotic tales, represents the first erotic narrative by a Dominican woman. Its stories tackle such issues as paedophilia, incest between brother and sister, sexual awakening, female infidelity, adultery, and sexual corruption within the Church.

Novelist Martha Rivera (1960–) penned *He olvidado tu nombre* (1997: *I've Forgotten Your Name*, 2004), which traces different psychological issues faced by young people growing up in the 1970s and 1980s, in the aftermath of the nation's 1965 political crises. Primarily a poet,

Rivera's use of obscure, often ambivalent language enriches the novel's poetic analysis of a generation in crisis.

Ángela Hernández (1954–) developed an interest in human rights as a university student; her essay collection *¿Por qué luchan las mujeres?* (1985: Why Do Women Fight?) and short story volume *Las mariposas no temen a los cactus* (1985: Butterflies Are Not Afraid of Cacti) constitute examples of feminist writing.

Chiqui Vicioso (1948–) evinces particular interest in the situation of women and the concept of myth within a Caribbean context, as in *Un extraño ulular traía el viento* (1985: A Strange Howling Brought by the Wind). Her play *Wish-ky Sour* (1998) deals with women's sexuality and inequalities of gender, where older men can still look attractive but women cannot. The play's very title reflects this situation for women, who tend to drink whisky when socializing in bars, hoping to find male company, and find their desire turns sour when a male partner does not materialize. Similarly, multifaceted author Carmen Imbert Brugal (1955–) communicates strong concern for women's issues in *Prostitución: esclavitud sexual femenina* (1985: Prostitution: Feminine Sexual Slavery) and in *Tráfico de mujeres: visión de una nación explotada* (1991; Trafficking in Women: Vision of an Exploited Nation).

A number of contemporary Dominican women writers currently reside in the United States and, like Julia Álvarez (1950–), publish in English. Her internationally recognized first novels, *How the Garcia Girls Lost their Accent* (1991) and *In the Time of the Butterflies* (1995), explore in different ways the topics of Dominican identity and history. In 1999, Loida Maritza Pérez (1963–) published *Geographies of Home*; this novel maps the problem of diaspora lived by a Dominican family. Angie Cruz (1972–) deals with the same situation with her first novel, *Soledad* (2001), whose protagonist develops a very distinctive psyche as an immigrant living in Manhattan. Finally, Nelly Rosario (1972–) highlights the idiosyncrasies of three different female protagonists in *Song of the Water Saints* (2002); her first novel, it won the 2002 PEN Open Book Award.

Enrique Ávila López

Work By:

Cocco De Filippis, Daisy, ed. *Desde la diáspora: Selección bilingüe de ensayos. A Diaspora Position: Bilingual Selection of Essays*. New York: Alcance, 2003.

Cocco De Filippis, Daisy, ed. *Documents of Dissidence. Selected Writings by Dominican Women*. New York: CUNY Dominican Studies Institute, 2000.

Work About:

Rosell, Sara. *La novela de escritoras dominicanas de 1990 a 2007*. New York: Edwin Mellen, 2007.

Dominican Republic: History, Culture, and Literature

History

The Dominican Republic shares with Haiti the island of Santo Domingo, also known as Hispaniola, the second-largest island in the Greater Antilles. Dominican territory consists of 18,704 squares miles, with a population estimated at 9, 956,648 (July 2011). Its capital is Santo Domingo.

Christopher Columbus colonized Hispaniola, landing on its north coast on December 5, 1492. On his second journey the following year, he founded Isabela, the first European town in the New World. In the city of Santo Domingo de Guzmán, founded August 4, 1496, by Columbus's brother Bartolomé, the Alcázar (Palace) was built for the first viceroy, Diego Colón, and the Real Audiencia (Royal Tribunal) was founded there in 1511. Santo Domingo became the site for the first hospital (begun in 1509), first cathedral (begun in 1514), and first university (1538) in the Americas.

The Dominican Republic gained independence from Haiti in 1844 and from Spain in 1865. Between 1916 and 1924, the country experienced its first invasion by the United States. In 1930, Rafael Leónidas Trujillo came to power, ruling with an iron hand for the next 31 years. His 1961 assassination threw the country into chaos, culminating in the nation's first democratic elections, which brought Juan Bosch to the presidency. He was overthrown by a military coup seven months later. In 1965, the April Revolution, led by Colonel Francisco Alberto Caamaño, erupted; as a consequence, the United States invaded a second time. For the next 12 years, a series of repressive governments headed by Joaquín Balaguer dominated the country's political life. After that, governments under the PRD (Dominican Revolutionary Party) and the PLD (Party of Dominican Liberation) have alternated in democratically elected political power leading up to the elections of 2008.

Literature, Fine Arts, and Culture

The two U.S. invasions, the Trujillo dictatorship, and the April Revolution have provided thematic material for many artists since 1960. Pedro Mir's novel *Cuando amaban las tierras comuneras* (1978; When They Loved the Common Lands), is set in the period between the two invasions. Divided in two parts, the first narrates the lives of Romanita, her husband Bonifacio Lindero and son Bonifacio Junior, and Suzy (Doña Susanita). The second part opens with the chapter "Introducción tardía," in which the character of Professor Enrique Villamán explains how the Common Lands were appropriated by sugar mills and U.S. troops in 1916. Most of the plot occurs during the second U.S. invasion in 1965. The character Silvestre symbolizes the Common Lands and also links the two U.S. invasions (1916, 1965) in a spiral structure. Marcio *Veloz Maggiolo, who wrote several novels about Trujillo (including *Uña y carne* [1999; Fingernail and Flesh]), also penned *De abril en adelante* (1975; From April On), the best-known novel about the second invasion. The 1965 American invasion produced reactions in literature from an important generation of writers, including René del Risco Bermúdez, Tony Raful, Andrés L. Mateo, and Norberto James.

Dominican literature and painting have followed the same course as artistic movements of Europe and Latin America. The early 20th century also saw the formation of several avant-garde movements, including *vedrinismo*, *postumismo*, and *Los Nuevos*. These movements were informed by Latin American avant-garde movements, and as such, tried to break with literary tradition and experiment with language. During the 1940s new writers' movements and groups emerged, among them Poesía Sorprendida, the Independientes del 40, and the *Generación del 48*. In the fine arts, an important group of painters arose that employed abstraction, symbolism, and *tenebrismo* (related to darkness, or obscurity) to avoid dictatorial censorship; Silvano Lora, Guillo Pérez, Eligio Pichardo, Ada Balcácer, and Domingo Liz belong to this generation. Artists emerging in the 1960s took Dominican art in a different direction; Ramón Oviedo, Iván Tovar, Cándido Bidó, José Félix Moya, Alberto Ulloa and Soucy de Pellerano turned to new forms, from figurative expressionism to chromatic drama, embracing surrealism and sometimes developing social and political themes.

In cinema, René Fortunato produced several documentaries about the 1965 American invasion and Trujillo's dictatorship, including *Abril, la trinchera del honor* (1988; April: The Trench of Honor) and *Trujillo: El poder del Jefe* (1991; Trujillo: The Power of the Strongman). Massive Dominican immigration to the United States has been reflected both in literature and film. In his films *Nueba Yol* (1995) and *Nueba Yol III* (1997), Ángel Muñiz depicts the conflicts of Balbuena, a charismatic character in New York.

Dominican music is strongly influenced by Africa. The *merengue*, which Trujillo used for propaganda purposes, has become the national musical genre. Johnny Ventura, Wilfrido Vargas, and Juan Luis Guerra are among the artists and composers who have made this musical form known throughout the world. The Dominican tradition embraces other such rhythms as *bachata*, *mangulina*, *carabiné*, and *atabales*. Traditional groups like *Convite* and singers like Xiomara Fortuna e Irka Mateo have researched and interpreted national folk traditions.

Dominican culture is a melting pot, fusing different aspects of African, Spanish, indigenous, Asian, and Arabic cultures. The official national language is Spanish, with strongly Andalusian features reinforced by linguistic patterns derived from African languages. Catholicism is the majority religion, though others, like evangelical Protestantism, are also practiced; in some parts of the country a form of voodoo is also practiced. One typical dish, the meat and root vegetable soup called *sancocho*, serves as a most appropriate representation of Dominican culture itself.

Fernando Valerio-Holguín

See also Appendix B for other entries related to the Dominican Republic.

Work About:

Ferguson, James. *Dominican Republic: Beyond the Lighthouse*. London: Russell Press, 1992.

Zakrzewski Brown, Isabel. *Culture and Customs of the Dominican Republic*. Westport, CT: Greenwood, 1999.

Don Juan Archetype in the Hispanic World

Early Spanish ballads and folk traditions depicting an arrogant seducer of women considerably predated *El burlador de Sevilla y el convidado de piedra* (*The Trickster of Seville and the Stone Guest*, 1986), a drama published in 1630, yet completed several years earlier. Attributed to Mercedarian friar *Tirso de Molina (Gabriel Téllez), the work immortalized Don Juan, the mythic figure who has for four centuries undergone numerous transformations. Through his social status, superior physical attributes, or sheer cunning, this mortal with a seemingly insatiable sexual appetite usually succeeds in deceiving naïve females, each of whom realizes far too late that, rather than having inspired genuine love, she has merely permitted him to add her name to his catalogue of conquests.

In addition to Don Juan's powers of seduction, the thread common to many treatments of the archetype, especially in the earliest versions, is his confrontation with a supernatural force. Although he has at times been represented as a diabolical figure, he often repents; however, questions often persist as to whether his contrition is sincere and if there remains time for him to escape damnation.

In Tirso's work, the supernatural is represented by a statue of the Comendador (Commander), the father to one of the rogue's victims. When the dead Comendador invites Don Juan to dine with him, the fearless libertine accepts, despite repeated warnings from Catalinón, his servant. To each admonition, Don Juan smugly responds, "Qué largo me lo fiáis," loosely translated as "There is yet abundant time for me to repent." At the dinner, however, Don Juan discovers that the time for contrition has expired, and, with his hand grasped mercilessly by the stone statue, he is drawn into a fiery underworld. Popular Spanish ballads and folk tales prior to Tirso's era provide similar accounts of mortals who insult the deceased, kick a skull, or invite a dead person to a feast, only to meet a similar fate.

The motif has been reworked repeatedly, and studies of the character in literature, music, art, and film number in the thousands. Critics have suggested that it is only logical that an antihero who is a man of action would achieve his greatest success in stage and film versions, where dialogue and gestures are far more dynamic than mere prose. It is thus unsurprising that Spain's other great version of the myth is José *Zorrilla's *Don Juan Tenorio* (1844), a drama written and performed during the apogee of *romanticism. Though faithful to the original in many ways, Zorrilla's play varies in that Don Juan repents and is then redeemed by the intervention of Doña Inés, the heroine. Central to Zorrilla's treatment is a contest of bravado between Don Juan and a rival, each of whom catalogues the number of women he has seduced and the number of men he has killed. This phenomenally successful work has eclipsed Tirso's drama in popularity and remains an integral part of activities surrounding All Saints' Day

and All Souls' Day (November 1 and 2, respectively) in many locales in Spain and Hispanic America. The popularity of Zorrilla's sentimental and somewhat conservative treatment and that of similar versions underscores its didactic potential, as those attending the theater witness firsthand the dangers of profligacy. Given both the power of a Catholic Church that eagerly condemned promiscuity and the presence of a spirited figure anxious to rebel against such restraints, Spain provided the ideal atmosphere for the archetype to flourish.

Another Spanish romantic, José de *Espronceda, provided a more liberal treatment of the type through the dashing, unrepentant Don Félix de Montemar in *El estudiante de Salamanca* (1840; *The Student of Salamanca*, 1991), a lengthy narrative poem considered by some to be his finest work. Similar Don Juan types appear in the form of the Marqués de Bradomín, who is observed by readers during several stages of his life in Ramón del *Valle-Inclán's *Sonatas* (1902–1905), a four-volume series in the modernist vein, and in some of Jacinto Grau's dramas, most notably *El burlador que no se burla* (1930; The Trickster Who Plays No Tricks).

The most popular treatments of the archetype in Western literature beyond Spain are found in Molière's *Dom Juan ou le Festin de Pierre* (1665; Don Juan or the Stone Guest), Lord Byron's mock epic, *Don Juan* (1819–1824), Alexander Pushkin's *The Stone Guest* (1830), and George Bernard Shaw's drama, *Man and Superman* (1903). Contemporary reworkings of Zorrilla's Don Juan have occurred in the

Chicano theater through Octavio Solís's *Man of the Flesh* (1998) and Carlos Morton's *Johnny Tenorio* (2003).

The universal appeal of the Don Juan character has extended beyond literature into the arts, the most successful musical adaptations being those by Wolfgang Mozart in his opera *Don Giovanni* (1787), with its libretto by Lorenzo da Ponte; and Richard Strauss, in the tone poem *Don Juan* (1889). Mozart's opera owes much of its success to the depiction of Leporello, who, like Tirso's Catalinón, represents both the comic figure and the moral compass for the work.

Psychological studies of Don Juan abound, and their conclusions vary substantially because they analyze a figure constantly being reinvented. Because characterizations range from a virile superman to an effeminate fop, those seeking a Freudian explanation for Don Juan's persona have on occasion concluded that he possesses an Oedipus complex or that he is a homosexual, latent homosexual, or bisexual personality. The antihero's obsession with seduction has been variously attributed to the fact that he is more amoral than immoral, that his actions bespeak a sadistic quest for power, and that his conquests spring from an inferiority complex that constantly impels him to prove his manhood through serial seductions.

Charles Maurice Cherry

Work About:

Mandrell, James. *Don Juan and the Point of Honor: Seduction, Patriarchal Society, and Literary Tradition.* University Park, PA: Pennsylvania State University Press, 1992.

Tirso de Molina. *The Trickster of Seville.* Trans. Gwynne Edwards. Warminster, England: Aris and Phillips, 1986.

A Translation of José Zorrilla's Don Juan Tenorio. Trans. Robert G. Trimble. Lewiston, NY: Edwin Mellen, 2003.

Donoso, José (1924–1996)

This Latin American literary *Boom* author was born in Santiago de Chile to a family of lawyers and doctors. He learned English at a prestigious English day school in Chile and later, when studying at the University of Chile, won a two-year scholarship to Princeton University. While there, he published his first two stories in English. After returning to Chile, Donoso continued writing, and in 1962 won the William Faulkner Foundation Prize for his first novel, *Coronación* (1957; *Coronation*, 1965). In this story of degradation within a Chilean aristocratic family, Donoso's signature grotesque style and social satire were already present.

Between 1965 and 1980 Donoso lived in self-imposed exile in the United States and Spain. He taught creative writing at the University of Iowa before moving to Spain in 1967. In 1970 Donoso published perhaps his most ambitious novel, *El obsceno pájaro de la noche* (*The Obscene Bird of Night*, 1973). This novel tells the story of two men, Humberto Peñaloza and Jerónimo de Azcoitia. Humberto is obsessed with the need to find his roots and, consequently, his past. Jerónimo, on the other hand, is a millionaire without an heir. Donoso's text explores each man's search for identity through narrative techniques that, characteristic of *Boom* texts, combine reality with fantasy, filling the novel with surreal imagery and linguistic experimentation.

In 1977, Donoso published *La historia personal del "Boom"* (*The Boom in Spanish American Literature: A Personal History*, 1977) in which he considered the "internationalization" of the Spanish American novel as its most important characteristic. Donoso viewed the innovative power of the *Boom* in its opposition to, in his words, the estranged, static, limited, xenophobic, and chauvinistic characteristic of all earlier Spanish American narrative. *Boom* narratives collectively broke free of Spanish America's national and cultural borders and engaged, as Donoso notes, internationally.

Donoso wrote of the exile experience and the artistic paralysis it imposed in his novel *El Jardín de al lado* (1981, *The Garden Next Door*, 1992). Homesickness and the desire to be part of Chile's social and literary life brought him back to Chile in the 1980s. He was awarded Chile's Premio Nacional in 1990. The author died of cancer at age seventy-two.

Ketevan Kupatadze

See also Novel in Spanish America: *Boom Literature*: 1950–1975.

Work By:

Curfew. Trans. Alfred MacAdam. London: Pan Books, 1988.

Hell Has No Limits. Trans. Suzanne Jill Levine. Los Angeles: Sun and Moon Press, 1995.

A House in the Country. Trans. David Pritchard and Suzanne Jill Levine. New York: Knopf; London: Allen Lane, 1984.

Work About:

Adelstein, Miriam. *Studies on the Works of José Donoso: An Anthology of Critical Essays.* Lewiston, NY: Mellen, 1990.

González Mandri, Flora. *José Donoso's House of Fiction: A Dramatic Construction of Time and Place.* Detroit: Wayne State University Press, 1995.

Swanson, Philip. *José Donoso, the "Boom" and Beyond.* Liverpool: Francis Cairns Publications, 1988.

Donoso Pareja, Miguel (1931–)

One of Ecuador's principal literary icons of the last 50 years, his contributions as novelist, short story author, critic, essayist, journalist, poet, and creative writing teacher summarize the breadth and scope of his work. In 1963, he was exiled to Mexico where he lived for 18 years and served as the national supervisor of writing workshops sponsored by the Fine Arts Institute; during his years in Mexico, he also distinguished himself as a literary journalist and organizer of important international literary and cultural events and publications. In 1981, he returned to Ecuador and introduced his writing workshops to develop and promote young talent there. Many of Ecuador's most accomplished contemporary writers have come from his writing program.

Among his major publications are such experimental and introspective novels as *Henry Black* (1969), *Día tras día* (1976; Day After Day), *Nunca más el mar* (1981; Never Again the Ocean), *Hoy empiezo a acordarme* (1994; Today I Begin to Remember), and *A río revuelto* (2001; Agitated River). In each case, Donoso Pareja mixes traditional and nontraditional forms of narrative expression while blending dense prose with mass culture. He has also published short stories, poetry, and essays about cultural, literary, and historical themes that transcend geographical boundaries. A most significant book-length essay is his *Ecuador: identidad y esquizofrenia* (1998; Ecuador: Identity and Schizophrenia), which interprets the country's complex identity and the regional conflicts that continue to foment fragmentation. In 2007, he received the Eugenio Espejo Prize, which is Ecuador's most prestigious literary award.

Michael Handelsman

Work By:

El otro lado del espejo. Quito: Campaña Nacional Eugenio Espejo por el Libro y la Lectura, 2004.

"Fútbol, pobreza y abundancia, identidad y emigración." *Cuadernos Hispanoamericanos* 675 (September 2006): 53–60.

Don Quijote de la Mancha in Spanish American Literature and Culture

This iconic masterpiece of Spanish literary giant Miguel de *Cervantes (1547–1616) has always been at the heart of Spanish American culture. Despite laws prohibiting the sending of fiction writings to the colonies, within weeks of its publication, copies of the first part of *Don Quijote* (1605; *Don Quixote*, translated to English many times between 1612 and 2009) were shipped to Colombia, Mexico, and Peru. Within a few years, several hundred copies (maybe over 1,000) of early printings of the novel wound up in Spanish colonies in the Indies (none of these copies has ever been located). As early as 1607, figures from Cervantes's novel began to appear in popular festivals and processions, just as they did in Spain. Apparently, there is no record of volumes of the 1615 second part being shipped to the New World, but since the traffic in books was consistently strong, it, too, must have made the voyage. Don Quijote and Sancho, Dulcinea, Rocinante, the windmills, and Mambrino's helmet are almost as well known and easily recognized throughout Spanish America as they are in Spain itself. Themes of quixotism—romantic, chivalric idealism; romantic exaltation; visionary and/or imaginative capabilities; delirium and/or hallucination; impractical but earnest efforts to do well; detachment from reality; a book-inspired understanding of reality; and an attempt to cope with the world according to, or in imitation of, literary (or filmic, television, or other media) models—permeate the literatures of Spanish America. In the paragraphs that follow, the influential presence of *Don Quijote* in the novel and short fiction will be discussed at some length. Much briefer remarks on poetry, theater, and essay, as well as other aspects of culture, will follow.

Novel

Some of the greatest novels written in Spanish America have been conceived and executed specifically under the influence of *Don Quijote*. In Mexico, José Joaquín Fernández de Lizardi is generally credited with authorship of the first Spanish American novel, *El periquillo sarniento* (1816; *The Itching Parrot*, 1942), a didactic and digressive story modeled largely on Spanish *picaresque fiction and *Don Quijote*. Lizardi's later satire *La educación de las mujeres, o la Quijotita y su prima: Historia muy cierta con apariencias de novela* (first part 1818, complete work 1831–1832; Women's Education, or Quijotita and her Cousin: Very True Story with Novelistic Features) makes his debt to Cervantes even more explicit. His *Don Catrín de la Fachenda* (1832; Eng., trans., 1943) is in the same mold.

Guatemalan Antonio José de Irisarri (writing as Hilarión de Altagumea), sometimes called the father of that nation's novel, composed *El cristiano errante* (1847; The Wandering Christian) and *Historia del perínclito Epaminodas del Cauca* (1863; History of the Illustrious Epaminodas of Cauca), works that combine satire, sermon, and political propaganda with quixotic themes and characters. The use of Cervantes's novel and characters for purposes of political satire has a long tradition in Spanish America. Some of the best examples are works by Argentines Juan Bautista *Alberdi, Luis Alberto de Borja-Moncayo, and Leonardo Castellani;

Chilean Daniel Barros Grez; Guatemalan Máximo Soto-Hall; Nicaraguan Gustavo Alemán Bolaños (El Pobrecito Hablador); Peruvian Juan Manuel Polar; and Venezuelan Tulio Febres Cordero. Don Quijote as a political symbol, of both the right and the left, is one of the most interesting and enduring characteristics of Spanish American fiction.

Ecuadorian Alfredo Pareja Díez Canseco is the author of the curious *Hechos y hazañas de don Balón de Baba y de su amigo Inocente Cruz* (1939; Deeds and Feats of Sir Balón de Baba and His Friend Innocent Cross), the story of a truly extravagant quixotic figure. Don Balón is a combination scientist, messiah, inventor, revolutionary, knight-errant, platonic lover, and egomaniac. He dreams, imagines, invents, rationalizes, exaggerates, and lies in his relations with everyone. Maintaining a frantic pace of activity, he defends the needy, rescues damsels in distress, and dismisses and insults anyone who questions his interpretations. His Dulcinea is Cándida, an attractive young woman who lives across the street and strings him along in her answers to his rhetorical love letters. Sancho's reincarnation, the proverb-spouting Don Inocente Cruz de Sepedillo, tries in vain to point out reality as he is drawn into Don Balón's adventures. At the end of the novel, after a political speech fails and he is pursued into the forest by police, Don Balón dies and is eaten by dogs.

Cuba's greatest novelist, Alejo *Carpentier, is author of several novels that echo Cervantes and *Don Quijote*. *Los pasos perdidos* (1953; *The Lost Steps*,

1971) is probably his best and certainly his most quixotic text. The narrator and protagonist is a music composer who specifically refers to himself as a kind of Don Quijote on a quest for an idealized world and a Dulcinea-like ideal woman to love. In this instance, however, Dulcinea is not the traditional ideal, blue-eyed, blonde, noble woman, but an American hybrid of Indian and black heritage. Other books that draw on *Quijote* include *El derecho de asilo* (1972; Right of Asylum), *Concierto barroco* (1974; Eng. trans., 1988), *El recurso del método* (1974; *Reasons of State*, 1976), and *El arpa y la sombra* (1978; *The Harp and the Shadow*, 1990).

The great name in Colombian literature is Gabriel *García Márquez, winner of the 1982 *Nobel Prize for Literature. He is the author of what may be the best and most influential novel ever written by a Spanish American: **Cien años de soledad* (1967; *One Hundred Years of Solitude*, 1970), sometimes even called the "*Don Quijote* of Latin America." The novel relates the story of the Buendía family's quixotic members; the city of Macondo; an endless revolution; cyclical time; an allegory of Colombian history; the invention of ice; and Melquíades, a sage historian (reminiscent of Cervantes's Cide Hamete Benengeli) and his manuscript about the events of the novel. Few novelists have ever captured the spirit of Cervantes as thoroughly and in such an original way as García Márquez.

The leading Mexican figure with respect to Cervantes is undoubtedly Carlos *Fuentes, who rereads *Don Quijote* annually and has written an important and original essay on both *Don Quijote* and the act of reading titled "Cervantes, o la crítica de la lectura" (1976; "*Don Quijote*, or the Critique of Reading," 1976). This influential work came just a year after Fuentes published his most ambitious, most highly acclaimed, and most quixotic novel, *Terra Nostra* (1975; Eng. trans., 1976), in which Cervantes ("the Chronicler"), Don Quijote, and Sancho join with other classic literary and historical figures in a fantastic evocation of the Spanish heritage of the New World. Other novels by Fuentes also bear reminiscences of Cervantes, especially *La cabeza de la hidra* (1978; *The Hydra Head*, 1980) and *Gringo Viejo* (1985; *The Old Gringo*, 1985).

Peruvian Manuel *Scorza's most ambitious novel is *La danza inmóvil* (1983; The Motionless Dance), an explicitly and profoundly quixotic novel. Just as Cervantes is the narrator of *Don Quijote*, Scorza narrates his fiction and makes frequent reference to books he has written, others he has in progress, and the text being read. The novel's interplay of reality and imagination (or fantasy and literature), ideal and fact, theory and praxis; its shifting, alternate realities and its juxtaposition of art and life; and its frequent allusions to and citations of *Don Quijote*, make it constantly reminiscent of Cervantes's work.

Mexican Angelina Muñiz-Huberman's *Dulcinea encantada* (1992; Enchanted Dulcinea) tells the story of an autistic Dulcinea, a refugee in Mexico after the Spanish Civil War (1936–1939). This enchanted Dulcinea does not speak, lives in her own fantasy world, and constantly composes-revises-reviews-remembers novels that she never actually writes. The novel shifts constantly and rapidly between first-person and third-person narrative; it consists of disjointed fragments, phrases, and words. Rarely has the enchanted world of autism been so movingly and authentically evoked, and the intertextual Cervantes connection deeply enriches an extraordinary achievement.

Guatemalan Eduardo Halfon produced a short novel titled *De cabo roto* (2003; From a Broken End [a verse form used in preliminary poems of *Don Quijote*, 1605]), in which a historical scholar, Eugenio Salazar, discovers a document dated 1602 and signed by Miguel de Cervantes. His efforts to verify the historical veracity of the discovery, which places Cervantes in Guatemala for a while at that time, is filled with tantalizing leads, frustrating hints, and profound ambiguity. Mixing real people with fictional characters, and written through multiple narrative levels, the novel calls into question the nature of truth, fiction, reality, and history.

Other writers of quixotic fictions include the following names:

- **Argentina:** Enrique Larreta, Carlos Bosque, Carlos B. Quiroga, Alicio Garciatoral, Ernesto *Sábato, Vidal Ferreyra Videla, Irma Cairoli, Nasim Yampey, Federico Jeanmaire, Francisco José Figuerola, Adolfo Bioy Casares, Rodrigo Fresán, and Marcelo Estefanell
- **Bolivia:** Natanial Aguirre
- **Chile:** Daniel Barros Grez, Juan Barros, Eduardo *Barrios, Eugenio

Orrego Vicuña, Darío Oses, and Roberto *Bolaño
- **Colombia:** José Eustasio Rivera, Julián Motta Salas, Eduardo Camacho Guizado, and Héctor Abad Faciolince
- **Costa Rica:** Alfonso Chacón Rodríguez
- **Cuba:** Luis Otero y Pimentel, Luis Felipe Rodríguez, Reinaldo *Arenas, and José *Lezama Lima
- **Ecuador:** Luis Alberto de Borja-Moncayo and Carlos Bolívar Sevilla
- **Guatemala:** Máximo Soto-Hall, Miguel Ángel *Asturias, David Vela, Rigoberto Juárez-Paz, and Luis Eduardo Rivera
- **Mexico:** Heriberto Frías, Jorge Ferretis, José Rubén Romero, Armando Chávez Camacho, Juan Miguel Mora, and Carmen *Boullosa
- **Nicaragua:** Gustavo Alemán Bolaños (El Pobrecito Hablador)
- **Paraguay:** Augusto *Roa Bastos
- **Peru:** Juan Manuel Polar, José Félix de la Puente, and César Falcón
- **Venezuela:** Carlos Reyles, Mario Briceño-Iragorry, Oswaldo Trejo, and Carlos Sosa

In the Hispanic literatures of the United States, the quixotic presence is also notable. One of the earliest examples is Daniel Venegas's *Las *aventuras de Don Chipote, o, Cuando los pericos mamen* (1928; *The Adventures of Don Chipote, or, When Parrots Breast-Feed*, 2000). Usually considered the first *Chicano novel, it draws upon twin Spanish sources for the novel: the *picaresque and the quixotic. It tells the story of Don Chipote de Jesús María Domínguez as he makes his way from Mexico to the United States and back, never finding the fabulous riches of the North. Perhaps the best Chicano quixotic novel is Genaro González's semiautobiographical *The Quixote Cult* (1998), the story of a Chicano named De la O, who gets idealistically involved in the Mexican American National Organization (MANO) and tries to organize migrant workers. With explicit references to Cervantes and Don Quijote, and characters based on and named after Dulcinea and Rocinante, González brings quixotism to the socially active world of marginalized Chicanos in the late 20th century. Other American quixotic fictions include Chicano Ron Arias's *The Road to Tamazunchale* (1975); Chicana Ana Castillo's *The Mixquiahuala Letters* (1986); Dominican American Julia Álvarez's partly autobiographic *How the García Girls Lost Their Accents* (1991) and its sequel *¡Yo!* (1997; I); and Cuban American Robert Arellano's wild and extravagant *Don Dimaio of La Plata* (2004).

Short Story

If the Cervantine element informs much of the best writing of Spanish American novelists, the same is also true in short fiction. Two Argentine writers stand out in this area: Jorge Luis *Borges and Marco *Denevi. Perhaps the most celebrated piece Borges ever wrote is the fascinating metafiction "Pierre Menard, autor del *Quijote*" (1941; "Pierre Menard, Author of the *Quixote*," 1962); this may be the most frequently read and discussed of all his works. In many ways it is both the prototype of a postmodern metafiction and a tribute to Cervantes, while calling authorship itself into question. In addition, Borges wrote a series of subtle meditations on Cervantes and his novel: "La conducta novelística de Cervantes" (1928; Cervantes's Novelistic Behavior), "Nota sobre el *Quijote*" (1947; Note on the *Quixote*), "Magias parciales del *Quijote*" (1952; "Partial Enchantments of the *Quijote*," 1964), "Análisis del último capítulo del *Quijote*" (1956; Analysis of the Final Chapter of the *Quixote*), "Un problema" (1957; A Problem), "Parábola de Cervantes y de Don Quijote" (1960; "Parable of Cervantes and Don Quixote," 1972), and "El acto del libro" (1981; The Act of the Book).

In a series of short fictions, Marco *Denevi has made clear his own fascination with Cervantes and his novel. The first of these stories is "El precursor de Cervantes" (1966; Cervantes's Precursor), in which Dulcinea invents Don Quijote. In "El nacimiento de Dulcinea" (1970; Dulcinea's Birth), Aldonza Lorenza comes to be revered as Dulcinea by her parents and Teresa Panza. In addition, Denevi has published several other short short-stories (*microcuentos*) about the novel: "Proposición sobre las verdaderas causas de la locura de don Quijote" (1966; Proposal regarding the True Causes of Don Quixote's Lunacy), "Don Quijote cuerdo" (1973; Don Quijote Sane), "Los ardides de la impotencia" (1984; The Strategies of Impotence), "Crueldad de Cervantes" (1984; Cervantes's' Cruelty), "Dulcinea del Toboso" (1999), "Realismo feminino" (1999; Feminine Realism), "La mujer ideal no existe" (1999; The Ideal Woman Doesn't Exist), and "Epidemia de Dulcineas en el Toboso" (1999; Epidemic of Dulcineas in El Toboso). Few Spanish American writers have returned to the theme of Don Quijote as frequently or as brilliantly as Borges and Denevi.

But beyond the work of these two famous writers, there is a long tradition of individual short fictions, often by lesser-known but talented writers, that deserve recognition as outstanding fictions. Most of them are metafictions, rewritings of scenes and characters from *Don Quijote*, or variations on a theme. These works include Rubén *Darío's "D. Q." (1899), about a Spanish soldier, called simply D. Q., in Cuba near the end of the Spanish–American War; Mexican Efrén Rebolledo's "El desencanto de Dulcinea" (1914; The Disenchantment of Dulcinea), in which Dulcinea comes to encourage a dying Don Quijote; Chilean Mariano Latorre's "On Panta" (1935), about the quixotic Don Pantaleón Letelier, who hunts constantly for lions that exist only in his imagination; Mexican René Avilés's *"El Profesor Vidriera," precedido de "El Retablo de Maese Pedro"* (1942; "Professor Vidriera," preceded by "Maese Pedro's Puppet Show"), ingeniously reaccentuates Cervantes's characters; Mexican Juan José *Arreola's "La lengua de Cervantes" (The Language of Cervantes) and "Teoría

de Dulcinea" (Theory of Dulcinea)—both from his *Bestiario* (1958; Beastiary)—especially the latter, which brings reality to Dulcinea in Alonso Quijano's life; Mexican Miguel Aguayo's "Dulcinea en la ventana" (1964; Dulcinea at the Window), in which a servant at an inn reinvents herself as Dulcinea and waits in vain for Don Quijote to return; Colombian Pedro Gómez Valderrama's "En un lugar de las Indias" (1970; In a Village in the Indies), a work that has received considerable recognition, tells how Alonso Quijano writes the story about Miguel de Cervantes's immigration to America and how his long manuscript is lost forever; Peruvian Luis Enrique Tord's ingenious "Cide Hamete Benengeli, coautor del *Quijote*" (1987; Cide Hamete Benengeli, Coauthor of the *Quixote*), in which Cervantes listens in the Seville jail to the tales of a certain Hamete ben Gelie and uses this material to write *Don Quijote;* and Chilean Luis Agoni Molina's "El hombre que asesinó a Don Quijote" (1997; The Man Who Murdered Don Quixote), about a practical joke, a possible murder, and a mysterious disappearance.

Other writers of short fictions inspired by Cervantes include the following:

- **Argentina:** Alberto Gerchunoff, Bartolomé Galíndez, Manuel *Mújica Laínez, Enrique Anderson Imbert, Juan José Delaney, Ricardo *Piglia, Federico Peltzer, Ana María Shua, Ana María Mopty de Kiorcheff, Ramón Fabián Vique, and David Lagmanovich

- **Bolivia:** Juan Francisco Bedregal

- **Chile:** Egidio Poblete, Andrés Gallardo, Mario Olea, Juan Armando Epple, Luis Correa-Díaz, Pía *Barros, Lilian Elphick, Jorge Etcheverry, Lina Meruane, and Diego Muñoz Valenzuela
- **Colombia:** Rocío Vélez de Piedrahita, José Cardona López, and Enrique Hoyos Olier
- **Cuba:** Esteban Borrero Echevarría, and Félix López
- **Ecuador:** José de la Cuatra
- **El Salvador:** Ernesto Rivas Gallont
- **Guatemala:** Augusto *Monterroso
- **Mexico:** Agustín *Yáñez, Teresa Aveleyra A., María Elvira Bermúdez, José Emilio *Pacheco, Alejandro Aura, Raúl Aceves, Carmen *Boullosa, Beatriz Escalante, Dante Medina, Bruce Swansay, Raymundo Ramos, Raúl Renán, Subcomandante Marcos, and Rogelio Guedea
- **Panama:** Gil Blas Tejeira
- **Peru:** Alejandro Sánchez-Aizcorbe C., Jorge Eduardo Eielson, and Enrique Verástegui
- **Puerto Rico:** Diego Deni
- **Uruguay:** Mario Levrero
- **Venezuela:** Pedro Pablo Paredes, José Balza, Gabriel Jiménez Emán, and Armando José Sequera

Poetry

The two best-known poets whose work is in part a tribute to Cervantes and his novel are Rubén Darío and Jorge Luis Borges. Darío, arguably the most important and most influential poet in Latin American history, is the author of two of the most frequently cited poems ever written about Cervantes and Don Quijote, which he published in *Cantos de vida y esperanza* (1905; *Songs of Life and Hope*, 2004). The first is the gentle "Soneto a Cervantes" ("Sonnet to Cervantes"), a pensive poem in which the poet reflects on hours of sadness and solitude, but states that "Cervantes is a good friend." The second is "Letanías de Nuestro Señor don Quijote" ("Litanies of Our Lord Don Quixote"), where the poet invokes the spirit of Don Quijote, a sort of patron saint and liberator of the downtrodden, and asks him to pray for troubled modern mankind. The long poem "Cyrano en España" ("Cyrano in Spain"), from the same book, also has strong Cervantine elements and references. To these we can add the sonnet "La Gitanilla" (1896; The Little Gypsy Girl), based on Cervantes's protagonist in his novella of the same title.

Less well known than Borges's prose writings about Cervantes and his novel are no fewer than a half-dozen poems that evoke Cervantes, Don Quijote, and La Mancha: "Lectores" (1964; Readers), "Un soldado de Urbina" (1964; A Soldier from Urbina), "Miguel de Cervantes" (1972), "Sueña Alonso Quijano" (1972; Alonso Quijano Dreams), "El testigo" (1972; The Witness), and "Ni siquiera soy polvo" (1977; I Am Not Even Dust). The gentle, poetic, melancholic Borges of these poems only faintly resembles the cerebral, ambiguous, scholarly Borges of his prose, and completes the picture of one great writer's appreciation of another.

Other poets who have written on Cervantine themes include the following:

- **Argentina:** Ignacio B. Anzoátegui, Estanislao del *Campo, Evaristo Carriego, Juan Manuel Cotta, Pedro Manuel Eguía, Arturo Giménez Pastor, Enrique Larreta, Ezequiel *Martínez Estrada, Luis Matharán, Rafael Obligado, and Pedro B. Palacios
- **Bolivia:** Ricardo Mujía and Gregorio Reynolds
- **Chile:** Daniel Barros Grez, Luis Barros Méndez, Antonio Bórquez Solar, Francisco A. Concha Castillo, Ángel Cruchaga Santa María, Ángel Custodio González, Carlos Díaz Loyola (Pablo de Rokha), Washington Espejo, Manuel Gandarillas, Ernesto A. Guzmán, Oscar Lanas, Pedro Lastra, Samuel A. Lillo, Desiderio Lizana Droguett (Pedro Recio), Guillermo Matta, Carlos Roberto Mondaca, Nicanor *Parra, Víctor Domingo Silva, Víctor Torres Arce, Juvencio Valle, and Daniel de la Vega
- **Colombia:** Juan de Dios Bravo, Roberto Liévano, Isabel Lleras Restrepo, Ricardo Nieto, Manuel Reina, Francisco Restrepo Gómez, José Asunción *Silva, and Guillermo *Valencia
- **Costa Rica:** J. Albertazzi Avendaño and Asdrúbal Villalobos
- **Cuba:** Eugenio Arriaza, Emilia Bernal, Emilio Bobadilla (Fray Candil), Eliseo Diego, Lourdes Gil, Miguel González, Eraida Iturralde, Enrique Hernández Miyares, and Eugenio Sánchez Torrentó
- **Dominican Republic:** Manuel del Cabral
- **Ecuador:** Rafael Coronel and Patricio Falconí Almeida
- **Honduras:** Valentín Durón and Santos B. Tercero
- **Mexico:** Raúl Bañuelos, Alberto Blanco, Salvador Díaz Mirón, Enrique Fernández Granados, Juan Manuel Gutiérrez Zamora, Manuel José Othón, Juan de Dios Pezoa, Vicente Riva Palacio, Adam Rubalcava, Eduardo Lizalde, and Ángel Zárraga
- **Peru:** Marcos Martos, Ricardo *Palma, José *Santos Chocano, and Esteban de Terralla y Landa
- **Puerto Rico:** Rosario *Ferré and José Luis Vega
- **Uruguay:** Francisco Acuña de Figueroa, Juana de Ibarbourou, Justo Olarán Chans, and Carlos Roxlo
- **Venezuela:** Francisco Antonio González G., Jacinto Gutiérrez Coll, and Amendoro Urdaneta

Theater

Plays involving characters and/or scenes from *Don Quijote* have been written and performed for over a century. Probably the earliest Spanish American theatrical work based on Cervantes's novel is Agustín Pomposo Fernández de San Salvador's *Las fazañas de Hidalgo, Quixote de Nuevo*

Cuño, facedor de tuertos ... (1810; The Deeds of Hidalgo, a New Quixote, Doer of Wrongs ...), an attack on Miguel Hidalgo's uprising in Mexico and probably the earliest Spanish American theatrical work based on Cervantes's novel. Noteworthy also are Chilean Antonio Espiñeira's trilogy *Alboroto en el cotarro* (1878; The Disturbance), *Martirios de amor* (1882; Martyrs for Love), and *Cervantes en Argel* (1886; Cervantes in Algiers), all based on the life and works of Cervantes. A tireless Argentine political reformer, Eduardo Sojo wrote *Don Quijote en Buenos Aires: Revista bufo política de circunstancias, en un acto* (1884; Don Quixote in Buenos Aires: A Comic Political Review of Circumstances, in One Act), a political satire in dramatic form.

Other dramatists who have sought inspiration in Cervantes and his works include the following writers:

- **Argentina:** Leopoldo *Lugones, Carlos Mauricio Pacheco, Antonio F. Marcellino, Roberto *Arlt, Marco *Denevi, Adela Basch, and Carlos María Alsina
- **Bolivia:** Adolfo Mier Rivas
- **Chile:** Leonardo Eliz and Jorge Díaz
- **Colombia:** Santiago García
- **Costa Rica:** Rubén Pagura
- **Cuba:** Albio Paz and Esther Suárez Durán
- **Guatemala:** Miguel Ángel *Asturias
- **Mexico:** Antonio García, Manuel José Othón, Salvador *Novo, Virginia Guillén Barrios Gómez, Federico Schroeder Inclán, Gerardo Mancebo del Castillo, and Gilberto Guerrero
- **Peru:** Juan Ríos
- **Uruguay:** Carlos Manuel Varela

Essay

Brief mention must be made of the very many Spanish American writers, philosophers, historians, sociologists, literary critics, and intellectuals who have written nonfiction essays and books about Cervantes and *Don Quijote*. Brief mention has already been made of essays by Borges and Fuentes. Their two major predecessors are Ecuadorian Juan Montalvo and Uruguayan José Enrique *Rodó. Montalvo's posthumous *Capítulos que se le olvidaron a Cervantes. Ensayo de imitación de un libro inimitable* (1895; Chapters Forgotten by Cervantes. Essay of Imitation of An Un-Imitable Book), while presented as a fiction, is less an imitation or continuation of *Don Quijote* than it is a pretext for social and political criticism. Montalvo's aim is to emulate, not rival or compete with, Cervantes, and he worked especially hard to polish his style and to evoke that of Cervantes throughout his work; some claim that it is the finest imitation or continuation of *Don Quijote*, especially for its stylistic perfection.

Rodó's "El Cristo a la jineta" (Christ on Horseback), included in *El mirador de Próspero* (1913; Prospero's Window), describes similarities between Jesus Christ and Don Quijote. The essay is one of the most fully developed explorations of the similarities between the two figures, a theme that was to become common in 20th-century letters. Rodó's earlier "La filosofía del *Quijote* y el descubrimiento de América" (1911; Philosophy of the *Quixote* and Discovery of America) treats Cervantes's novel as symbolic of the conquest of America.

The following representative sample of names should be added (even if minimal): Miguel Ángel Asturias, Ernesto *Caballero Calderón, Alejo Carpentier, Rubén Darío, Esteban Borrero Echeverría, Alberto Gerchunoff, Roberto *González Echevarría, Pedro *Henríquez Ureña, Jesús Silva Herzog, Francisco A. de Icaza, Mariano *Latorre Court, Leopoldo *Lugones, Jorge *Mañach, Amado *Nervo, Ricardo *Palma, Octavio *Paz, Mariano Picón Salas, Alfonso *Reyes, Carlos Reyles, Ricardo *Rojas, Ángel Rosenblat, Luis Alberto Sánchez, Luis G. Urbina, Enrique José Varona, José *Vasconcelos, and Leopoldo *Zea.

Art

Special mention should be made of Bolivian artist Walter Solón Romero, an avid reader of Cervantes's novel throughout his life, who has produced a half-dozen series of works in which Don Quijote represents freedom. Especially noteworthy is "*El Quijote y los perros: Antología del terror político*" (1979; *Don Quixote* and the Dogs: Anthology of Political Terror), which depicts the snarling dogs of repression in opposition to Don Quijote, who represents freedom. But the major repository of quixotic art, not just in Spanish America but in the entire world, is to be found in Mexico. In 1987, art collector Eulalio Ferrer established the Museo Iconográfico del Quijote in Guanajuato. It is the only museum in the world devoted to a single literary character and contains over 800 original works of art in all media. Prominently featured in the museum are works by Mexican artists Enrique Altamirano, Juan Chamizo, José Chávez Morado, Pedro Coronel, Rafael Coronel, Gabriel Flores, Francisco de Icaza, José Guadalupe Posada, Jesús Reyes, Mario Orozco Rivera, Andrés Salgó, Alfredo Zalce, and many others.

Film

The two most important film versions of *Don Quijote* made in Spanish America are Mexican. The great comedian Mario Moreno ("Cantinflas") starred in *Un Quijote sin Mancha* (1969; A Quixote Without Stain [directed by Miguel M. Delgado]) as an idealistic young lawyer. Cantinflas later teamed up with Spanish actor Fernando *Fernán-Gómez in *Don Quijote cabalga de nuevo* (1973; Don Quixote Rides Again [directed by Roberto Gavaldón]), in an interesting take on the Quijote theme. Both movies are, as much as anything, pretexts for Cantinflas's unique brand of nonstop verbal humor.

Revolutionary Quijotes

Finally, mention should be made of Spanish American revolutionary leaders who saw themselves as modern Don Quijotes. According to Ricardo Palma, Simón *Bolívar said on his deathbed that the three greatest fools of history were Jesus Christ, Don Quijote, and himself. Argentine guerrilla leader Ernesto "Che" *Guevara, follower of Fidel Castro, read from *Don Quijote* to his troops in Bolivia and saw himself as a Don Quijote sallying forth on Rocinante to promote the revolution. Most recently, Mexican Zapatista leader Subcomandante Marcos called *Don Quijote* the best book of political history every written and kept a copy of the novel by his bedside at all times.

Don Quijote has informed Spanish American culture from its earliest years to the present day. Spanish American literature, especially the novel and short story, are heavily indebted to Cervantes and his classic novel. And Cervantes has, in a way, repaid much of this debt. Since the Premio de Literatura en Lengua Castellana Miguel de Cervantes, the most prestigious literary prize in the Hispanic world, was initiated in 1976 (the year following Franco's death), no fewer than 17 Spanish Americans have been granted the award: Alejo Carpentier, Jorge Luis Borges, Juan Carlos Onetti, Octavio Paz, Ernesto Sábato, Carlos Fuentes, Augusto Roa Bastos, Adolfo Bioy Casares, Dulce María *Loynaz, Mario *Vargas Llosa, Guillermo *Cabrera Infante, Jorge *Edwards, Álvaro *Mutis, Gonzalo *Rojas, Sergio *Pitol, Juan *Gelman, and José Emilio Pacheco.

Conclusion

The figures of Don Quijote and Sancho, as well as Cervantes himself, have inspired literally hundreds of poems, plays, stories, and novels. This is hardly surprising, as *Don Quijote* was in 2002 voted by far the single best and most influential work of literature in the history of the world in a poll of 100 of the world's best-known living writers. Such themes as reality and appearance (sometimes called *the* theme of all literature), literature and life, idealism and pragmatism; techniques of comedy and satire, realism, and metafiction; and some of the greatest characters ever created are all found in Cervantes's novel. José *Ortega y Gasset wrote that every novel carries within it, like an inner filigree, some aspect of *Don Quijote*. The cumulative evidence provided by the literature of Spanish America does nothing to contradict that assertion.

Howard Mancing

Work About:

Barchino, Matías, ed. *Territorios de La Mancha. Versiones y subversiones cervantinas en la literatura hispanoamericana*. Cuenca: Universidad de Castilla-La Mancha, 2007.

Correa-Díaz, Luis. *Cervantes y América, Cervantes en las Américas: Mapa de campo y ensayo de bibliografía razonada*. Kassel: Reichenberger, 2006.

García Sánchez, Jesús, ed. *El Quijote visto desde América*. Prol. Teodosio Fernández. Madrid: Visor Libros, 2005.

González Echevarría, Roberto. "Cervantes and the Modern Latin American Narrative." http://www.lehman.cuny.edu/ciberletras/n1/crit_07.htm.

Mancing, Howard. *The Cervantes Encyclopedia*. 2 vols. Westport, CT: Greenwood Press, 2004.

Viña, Frederick, ed. *Don Quijote: Meditaciones Hispanoamericanos*. Vol. I. Lanham, MD: University Press of America, 1988.

Dorfman, Ariel (1942–)

Born in Argentina, this Chilean American writer, journalist, professor, and human rights activist spent his childhood in the United States. His family returned to Chile in 1954, when he was twelve. Dorfman became a professor at the University of Chile, but after Augusto Pinochet's 1973 coup he went into exile in the United States. He currently splits his time between these two countries. His memoir *Heading South, Looking North: A Bilingual Journey* (1998) and Peter Raymont's 2007 documentary film *A Promise to the Dead: the Exile Journey of Ariel Dorfman* shed more light on his biography.

Dorfman cowrote his first famous essay with Armand Mattelart: *Para leer al Pato Donald. Comunicación de masa y nacionalismo* (1972; *How to Read Donald Duck: Imperialist Ideology in the Disney Comic*, 1975) deconstructs Disney cartoons from a Marxist point of view. The authors describe it as a "decolonization essay." His most widely recognized work is the play *La muerte y la doncella* (*Death and the Maiden*, 1991), first staged in Chile in 1991 and subsequently performed worldwide. It tells the story of Paulina Salas, who 20 years after being tortured and raped during a dictatorial regime, gets her revenge by kidnapping her former torturer. Schubert's "Death and the Maiden" was the musical background used to hide the screams during the torture and rape sessions, hence the title of the play. Roman Polanski made a film based on *La muerte y la doncella* in 1994. The address of Ariel Dorfman's Web site is http://www.adorfman.duke.edu/.

Fabiola Fernández Salek

Work By:

Death and the Maiden. New York: Penguin, 1994.

Work About:

McClennen, Sophia A. "The Diasporic Subject in *Ariel Dorfman*'s Heading South, Looking North." *MELUS: The Journal of the Society for the Study of the Multi-Ethnic Literature of the United States* 30. 1 (Spring 2005): 169–88.

McClennen, Sophia A. *Ariel Dorfman: An Aesthetics of Hope*. Durham, NC: Duke University Press, 2010.

Rostan, Kimberly. "Sweet Are the Uses of Tragedy: *Death and the Maiden*'s 'Almost Aristotelian' Testimony." *Atenea* 25.2 (December 2005): 9–24.

Dragún, Osvaldo (1929–1999)

The son of Jewish immigrants, this Argentine dramatist, nicknamed Chacho, portrayed Latin America's socioeconomic problems in his works. He studied and premiered his early plays with Buenos Aires's experimental and independent Teatro Popular Fray Mocho. His first written play that was staged is the historical drama *La peste viene de Melos* (1956; The

Plague Comes from Melos), that recounts the 1954 coup d'état against Guatemalan president Jacobo Árlenz, ousted by a military junta with backing from the U.S. government.

Dragún adopted many styles in his plays—most notably Bertolt Brecht's theater of the absurd. This is evident in one of his most famous collections of one-act plays, *Historias para ser contadas* (1957; Stories to Be Told). One of the most representative plays, *El hombre que se convirtió en perro* (*The Story of the Man Who Turned into a Dog*, 1974), portrays dehumanization in society. In it, an unemployed man takes the only position available, which is that of a guard dog. Ultimately, both he and those around him believe he has become a dog.

In 1961, Dragún was invited to Havana to organize its first post-revolution convention for playwrights. He stayed for three years, establishing and developing theater groups. This became his mission and he continued this endeavor in other countries of the Americas. Along with Carlos Gorostiza and Roberto *Cossa, he was a driving force behind *Teatro abierto* (Open Theater), started in 1980, and produced plays of critique and resistance against the weakened Argentinean military regime. In 1981, *Teatro abierto* premiered works by Cossa, José Rivera López, Luis Brandoni, Pepe Soriano and others, including Dragún's *Mi obelisco y yo* (staged 1981; published 1983; My Obelisk and I), in the Picadero Theater. The theater was bombed a week later.

Fabiola Fernández Salek

See also Theater in Spanish America: 1900 to Present.

Work By:

Historias para ser contadas. Buenos Aires: Corregidor, 2008.

Work About:

Leonard, Candyce Crew. "Dragún's Distancing Techniques in *Historias para ser contadas* and *El amasijo*." *Latin American Theatre Review* 16.2 (1983): 37–42.

Droguett, Carlos (1912–1996)

This novelist and short story writer became a powerful voice of criticism, alongside other members of the Chilean literary movement known as the Generation of 1938, who spoke out against an aristocratic society that categorically intensified the misery of lower- and working-classes citizens. Although he never finished a university degree, Droguett managed to publish his work at an early age in the numerous Chilean journals and newspapers of the 1930s. Droguett's first novel, *Los asesinados del Seguro Obrero* (1940; The Worker's Bank Murders), a testimony of political crimes that took place in Santiago in 1938, sets the tone of denouncement and the search for Chile's true history that characterize the rest of his work.

Of those texts, the most recognized are the novels *Patas de perro* (1965, Dog Paws) and *Eloy* (1967). *In Patas de perro,*

Droguett invents a boy born with paws rather than feet and hands, a deformity he cannot conceal and for which he is tormented. *Eloy* recounts in a stream-of-consciousness fashion the thoughts of a petty thief from a poor neighborhood who is hunted down by a policeman who intends to kill him. After receiving numerous literary prizes for earlier works, Droguett was awarded the National Prize in Literature in 1970. In 1976, Droguett left Chile, like many other literary figures oppressed by the Pinochet regime, and remained in residence in Europe until his death in Bern, Switzerland.

Laura Senio Blair

Work About:

Carlos Droguett. -http://www.memoria chilena.cl/temas/index.asp?id_ut=carlos droguett (1912–1996).

Noriega, Teobaldo A. *La novelística de Carlos Droguett: aventura y compromiso*. Madrid: Pliegos, 1983.

E

Echegaray, José (1832–1916)

The first Spaniard to win the *Nobel Prize for Literature (1904), this popular playwright was also a distinguished scholar and statesman, an engineer, mathematician, and holder of several high positions in government. His dramas, filled with passion and exuberance, represent an unusual mixture of elements, designed as they were with the craftsmanship of an expert in scientific formulas and with a declamatory rhetoric that kept the romantic sensibility alive. Echegaray had his first successes on stage in the last quarter of the 19th century, when theatergoers had become rather indifferent. His plays brought a wide-ranging public back to the box office. *La esposa del vengador* (1874; The Avenger's Wife) typifies the obsessions, intrigue, and leaps of logic that mark his dramaturgy and captured the interest of a newly enthusiastic audience. At one point, Echegaray left public service to dedicate himself exclusively to his creative work.

His best-known play, *El gran Galeoto* (1881; *The Great Galeoto*, 1922), is built on the themes of hearsay, jealousy, pride, and honor. Public gossip creates a love triangle where none exists, but the scandal it evokes becomes a self-fulfilling prophesy. The husband dies, and his wife goes off with the man with whom she supposedly was having an affair. Echegaray wrote plays of various types, but he is remembered most for those works that reach emotional heights, if not psychological depths.

Edward H. Friedman

See also Romanticism in Spain; Theater in Spain: 1700–1900; Theater in Spain: 1900–1975.

Work By:

Clark, B. H., et al., eds. and trans. *Masterpieces of Modern Spanish Drama: The Great Galeoto, The Duchess of San Quentin, Daniela.* Cincinnati: Steward Kidd, 1922. Reprint New York: D. Appleton, 1969.

Work About:

De Armas, Frederick A. "José Echegaray." *Premio Nóbel: Once grandes escritores del mundo hispánico.* Ed. Bárbara Mujica. Washington, DC: Georgetown University Press, 1997, 1–25.

Ríos-Font, Wadda C. *Rewriting Melodrama: The Hidden Paradigm in Modern Spanish Theater.* Lewisburg, PA: Bucknell University Press, 1997.

Echeverría, Esteban (1805–1851)

The main representative of romanticism in the Río de la Plata region and the most important intellectual of the "Generation of 1837," Echeverría wrote several works important to Argentine literature. Born in Buenos Aires, he led a bohemian life until 1823 when his mother passed away, and he felt that his licentious life had contributed to her death. From 1825 to 1830 Echeverría lived in Paris, studying literature, philosophy, economics, and politics. Back in Buenos Aires, he attended the Salón Literario organized by Marcos Sastre in 1836, and in 1838, founded the Joven Generación Argentina, a group of young intellectuals opposed to Rosas's dictatorship. From 1840 until his death he lived exiled in Uruguay.

His crowning works are the romantic poem *La cautiva* (1837; The Captive Woman), a long narrative about a woman kidnapped by Indians; and the short story "El matadero" (written 1841, published 1871; "The Slaughterhouse," 1997), in which the barbaric slaughterhouse serves as metaphor for Argentina under Rosas's dictatorship. Among other works, Echeverría published *Dogma socialista* (1846; The Socialist Dogma), which delineates his political and social program for Argentina.

Ángel Tuninetti

See also Short Fiction in Spanish America.

Work By:

El matadero; La cautiva. Intro. Leonor Fleming. Madrid: Cátedra, 1997.
"The Slaughterhouse." *The Oxford Book of Latin American Short Stories.* Ed. Roberto González Echevarría. New York: Oxford University Press, 1997.

Work About:

Katra, William. *The Argentine Generation of 1837: Echeverría, Alberdi, Sarmiento, Mitre.* Madison, NJ: Fairleigh Dickinson University Press, 1996.
Mercado, Juan Carlos. *Building a Nation: The Case of Echeverría.* Lanham, MD: University Press of America, 1996.

Ecuador: History, Culture, and Literature

Located in northwestern South America, facing the Pacific, and about 106,888 square miles in size, it is the smallest of the Andean countries. Colombia lies to the north and Peru borders on the east and south. The Andes mountain range traverses the country from north to south, and the highest volcano is Chimborazo, at 20,577 feet. The Galápagos Islands, Ecuador's most famous province, and one of UNESCO's World Heritage sites, are found in the Pacific Ocean, about 600 miles west of the continent. With about 15 million inhabitants (July 2011 estimate), the nation has the highest average population density in South America and the highest percentage of native Americans. In 2000, Ecuador's Congress approved a series of structural economic reforms that included adoption of the U.S. dollar as legal tender. Although now a democracy, the country is plagued by political instability. As of 2009, protests in Quito have contributed to the mid-term ouster of Ecuador's last three democratically elected Presidents.

History

What is now Ecuador formed part of the Inca Empire until the Spanish conquest in 1533. Quito, now the nation's capital, was founded in its present location the following year. The area became part of the viceroyalty of New Granada in 1717. The territories of the viceroyalty gained their independence between 1819 and 1822 and formed a federation known as Gran Colombia. When Quito withdrew in 1830, the name was changed to "Republic of the Equator." A disagreement about the exact border with Peru in the Amazonian part of the country became a cause of constant violence throughout the 20th century; the dispute was finally resolved in 1999.

Culture

An extremely diverse country, its inhabitants prefer to identify themselves as *serranos* (from the Andes) in the national capital of Quito, where strong indigenous communities uneasily coexist with Spanish colonial traditions. The *costeños*, inhabitants of tropical lowlands where the port city of Guayaquil is located, consider themselves to be more modern and politically liberal. The northern province of Esmeraldas reveals a clear African influence, and the country's *Amazon region, *el Oriente*, traditionally has been home to indigenous groups; it experienced a population boom after oil exploitation in the 1970s. Ecuador's indigenous communities are integrated into the mainstream culture to varying degrees, but some also practice their own autochthonous cultures. The indigenous people around the Otavalo area in the northern sector of the country are particularly successful in combining mainstream culture with a traditional way of life. Thousands of tourists travel to the area to see their colorful markets; they also export handmade crafts and sweaters.

Seafood is very popular along the coast, where prawns, shrimp, and lobster are key parts of the diet. Plantain and peanut-based dishes are the basis of most meals. In the highlands, people prefer potatoes, pork, and corn dishes. In the rainforest, a dietary staple is the yucca, a root vegetable that can be boiled or fried. Fresh fruits are available everywhere.

Quito was declared a world heritage site by UNESCO; Cuenca is another well-preserved colonial city. Among contemporary artists, painter and sculptor Osvaldo Guayasamín (1919–1999) is particularly important. In 1988, Ecuador's Congress commissioned him to paint a mural depicting the nation's history. The U.S. government objected to the final work because one of the panels contained a Nazi helmet with the lettering CIA, referring to the U.S. intelligence agency. His house, just north of Quito, has been converted to a museum.

Literature

Ecuador's geographical and cultural divisions are clearly represented in the country's literature, which is little-known abroad, apart from *Huasipungo* (1934, *The Villagers*, 1964), by Jorge *Icaza (1906–1978). A work of social protest, it decries the abysmal living conditions of indigenous people. *Cumandá* (1879; *Cumanda: The Novel of the Ecuadorian Jungle*, 2007) by Juan *León Mera (1832–1894) is considered the nation's first novel. A "foundational fiction," it describes the doomed love affair between a white man and an indigenous woman who discover they are half-siblings. Pablo Palacio (1906–1947) combined social realism with vanguard techniques in *Un hombre muerto a puntapiés* (1927; A Man Kicked to Death) and *Débora* (1927), before succumbing to mental illness.

Palacio is often considered a precursor of the "Golden Age" of Ecuadorian letters (1930–1945), when the so-called *Grupo de Guayaquil* writers combined socialist realism with regional cultures and folklore. The group caused a scandal in Ecuadorian letters in 1930, when Demetrio Aguilera Malta (1909–1981), Joaquín Gallegos Lara (1911–1947), and Enrique Gil Gilbert (1912–1973) published *Los que se van* (Those Who Leave), a short story collection that incorporated the speech and manners of typical peasants and fishermen from the coast. Another important writer, José de la Cuadra (1903–1941), penned the beautiful novel *Los Sanguirimas* (1934; The Sanguirimas Family), concerning a 100-year-old patriarch about whom terrible rumors and legends circulate; it can be read as a precursor of Colombian Gabriel *García Márquez's *One Hundred Years of Solitude*. Another novel deserving a much wider audience is *El éxodo de Yangana* (1949; The Exodus of Yangana) by Ángel Felicísimo Rojas (1909–2003). The son of a primary schoolteacher in southern Ecuador, Rojas had firsthand experience with the way of life and speech of indigenous people in isolated rural communities.

Of Lebanese descent, Jorge Enrique *Adoum (1926–) is an internationally respected translator and poet who remains best known for his novel *Entre Marx y una mujer desnuda* (1976; Between Marx and a Naked Woman), which was adapted to film in 1995. Nelson *Estupiñán Bass (1912–2002) published numerous novels, starting with *Cuando los guayacanes florecían* (1954; When the Guayacans Flourished), which narrates the history of Esmeraldas during the infamous Concha revolts. Also from Esmeraldas province, Adalberto *Ortiz (1914–2003) explored the uneasy relationship between Afro and mestizo cultures. A member of an indigenous group in Otavalo, Ariruma Kowii (no dates) publishes poetry in his native Quechua, most notably in *Tsaitsik: poemas para construir el futuro* (1993; Tsaitsik: Poems for Building the Future).

Although undeniably a country dominated by *machismo*, Ecuador's women have created opportunities to make their voice heard. Manuela (Manuelita) Sáenz (1797–1856) was born before independence and died in exile in Peru; best known as one of Simón *Bolívar's many love interests, her letters to Bolívar and others have survived and were published as *Manuela Sáenz: Epistolario* (1986; Manuela Sáenz: Letters). Another woman unafraid to interfere in national politics was the niece of dictator Ignacio de Veintimilla, Marieta de Veintimilla (1858–1907), nicknamed "La Generala" because of her military support for her uncle. After being betrayed and incarcerated, she published *Páginas del Ecuador* (1890; Pages of Ecuador) in exile in Lima.

Equally combative, although definitely less violent, are the women involved in the group *Mujeres del Ático* (Women of the Attic) a feminist collective in Guayaquil, which includes authors like Alicia *Yánez Cossío (1928–) and Cecilia Ansaldo Briones (1949–). In the 1990s, they organized literary meetings and published editorial pieces on feminist issues in newspapers. Luz Argentina Chiriboga (1940–) examines the struggle for independence in her historical novel *Jonatás y Manuela* (1994).

May E. Bletz

See also Appendix B for other entries related to Ecuador.

Work About:

Handelsman, Michael. *Culture and Customs of Ecuador.* Westport CT: Greenwood, 2000.

Torre, Carlos de la and Steve Striffler, eds. *The Ecuador Reader.* Durham, NC: Duke University Press, 2008.

Edwards, Jorge (1931–)

Born in Santiago, Chile, this prominent Generation of 1950 writer received his law degree from the University of Chile in 1958, and studied political science at Princeton University. As a member of Chile's diplomatic service, he undertook significant missions to Peru, Cuba, and Paris. Upon being dismissed from the diplomatic service in 1973 by Augusto Pinochet's administration, Edwards resided in Barcelona but returned to Chile in 1978 to serve as president of the Defense Committee for Freedom of Expression.

As of 2008, Edwards has published seven novels, numerous short stories, chronicles, and essays that focus primarily on Chile's recent history. Alternating between fiction and history, his writing concentrates heavily on the interrelation between power and the desire for freedom, which is mediated by a sense of precariousness and deception. Among publications that have earned him extensive recognition is *Persona non grata* (1973; *Persona Non Grata: A Memoir of Disenchantment with the Cuban Revolution*, 1993), a memoir of his experiences as Chile's ambassador to Cuba in the early 1970s.

Edwards has received prestigious literary awards, including the Miguel de Cervantes Prize (1999). In 2005, the library at the Cervantes Institute in Manchester, England was named Jorge Edwards in his honor.

Guillermo García-Corales

See also Chile's Generation of 1950.

Work By:

El inútil de la familia. Santiago: Alfaguara, 2004.

Persona non grata: A Memoir of Disillusion with the Cuban Revolution. Trans. Andrew Hurley. New York: Paragon, 1993.

Work About:

Ampuero, Roberto. *La historia como conjetura: reflexiones sobre la narrativa de Jorge Edwards.* Santiago: Andrés Bello, 2006.

Schulz Cruz, Bernard. *Las inquisiciones de Jorge Edwards*. Madrid: Pliegos, 1994.

Égüez, Iván (1944–)

Born in Quito, he was one of several young Ecuadorian novelists whose work came to international attention in the 1970s. During that decade, Ecuador became an oil-exporting nation and experienced intense influence from global commercial interests. When petrodollars began to flow, enterprises from the United States and other nations arrived to advertise and proffer their products. The face of Quito and other major cities changed dramatically within a few months, and so did the culture. Economic prosperity notwithstanding, Ecuadorian writers, both young and established, recognized a cultural crisis and responded with a literary renaissance that included some of the nation's best novels. *La linares* (1976; *La Linares*, 2005), Égüez's first novel, won the prestigious Aurelio Espinosa Pólit Prize in 1975. With humor, satire, and rich poetic language, it tells of a celebrated femme fatale. Through her story, the novel satirizes long-standing government corruption and recent cultural disintegration under the intense influence of outside commercial interests.

Égüez published two more novels, *Pájara la memoria* (1984; Fleeting Memory) and *El poder del Gran Señor* (1985; The Power of the Great Lord). The latter satirizes the use of a religious cult to manipulate the masses for political purposes.

Both novels are written in the same satirical spirit as *La Linares* and share a similar style. More recent novels are *Sonata para sordos* (2000; Sonata for the Deaf) and *Letra para salsa con final cortante* (2005; Lyrics for a Salsa with Its Ending Cut Short). The latter is based on the infamous case of a Hispanic woman who relieved her husband of his virility.

Égüez began his literary career as an avant-garde poet, publishing three collections: *Calibre catapulta* (1969; Heavy Catapult), *La arena pública y loquera es lo-que-era* (1972; The Public Arena and Insanity Is What It Was), and *Buscavida rifamuerte* (1975; Search for Life, Leave Death to Chance). Along with other young poets, he established the literary magazine *La Bufanda del Sol* in the 1960s. He has published six short story collections beginning with *El triple salto* (1981; The Triple Somersault). It includes the most anthologized of his stories, "Gabriel Garboso" (Gabriel the Stylish), a tragic tale of two middle-class Ecuadorian youths who mask their poverty to endear themselves to one another.

C. Michael Waag

Work By:

La Linares. Intro., trans. C. Michael Waag. Quito: Fonsal-Trama, 2005.

Work About:

Waag, C. Michael. "Political Satire through Popular Music and a Popular Vision of Reality: *La Linares*, A New Novel From Ecuador." *Perspectives on Contemporary Literature* 13 (1987): 50–57.

Eguren, José María (1874–1942)

Also a painter and photographer, Eguren can be credited as one of Peru's first modern poets of the 20th century. He lived a quiet, secluded life and published three poetry volumes: *Simbólicas* (1911; Symbolics), *La canción de las figuras* (1916; The Song of Figures), and *Poesías* (1929; Poetry). The latter includes poems from the previous two volumes along with two new collections, *Sombras* (Shadows) and *Rondinelas* (Repetitions). Deeply influenced by the aesthetics of romanticism, *modernismo* and French symbolism, Eguren's poetry believes in language as a medium for exploring vague and mysterious realities through colorful, suggestive visual imagery. Recurring images in his writing evoke nature, the sea, childhood, and the world of dreams. His ideas on art were published posthumously as *Motivos estéticos* (1959; Aesthetic Motifs).

César Ferreira

See also Modernismo in Hispanic Literature.

Work By:

Obra poética. Motivos. Ed. Ricardo Silva-Santisteban. Caracas: Ayacucho, 2005.

Work About:

Higgins, James. "The Rupture between Poetry and Society in the Work of José María Eguren." *Kentucky Romance Quarterly* 20 (1973): 59–74.

Rodríguez-Peralta, Phyllis. "The Modernism of José María Eguren." *Hispania* 56 (April 1973): 222–29.

Elizondo, Salvador (1932–2006)

For most of his life, Elizondo lived in Mexico City, teaching literature and creative writing. He wrote two novels, more than 50 short stories, a play, and two essay collections. Labeled an experimental author, his novels *Farabeuf: la crónica de un instante* (1965; *Farabeuf*; 1992) and *El hipogeo secreto* (1968; The Secret Hypogeum) eschew such conventions of literary realism as linear plot development or deeply developed characters. Nonetheless, his texts do contain clues to facilitate interpretation.

Farabeuf includes such a clue in the form of a photograph, showing a partly dismembered Chinese torture victim. The serene expression on the victim's face suggests an experience of the sacred amidst physical violence. The novel's protagonist, famous French surgeon Farabeuf, maintains a detached, clinical approach to physical pain. His inability to understand the meaning of the victim's calm look parallels the inability of modern science to comprehend the sacred.

Elizondo's most accessible text, the autobiographical novella *Elsinore* (1988), requires readers to focus on the unreliable narrator. In this coming-of-age story, the narrator's nostalgic tone clashes with disturbing experiences of friendship, sexuality, and violence. *Elsinore* shows how a narrator falsifies the past while drawing attention to the distortions inherent in the autobiographical genre. Elizondo's essays on modernist writers (James Joyce, Ezra

Pound) and his translations of Edgar Allan Poe, William James, and Paul Valéry also explore the limits of representation.

Richard Sperber

Work By:

Farabeuf. Trans. John Incledon. New York: Garland, 1992.

Obras. 3 vols. Ed. Adolfo Castañón. México, D: El Colegio Nacional, 1994.

Work About:

D'Lugo, Carol Clark. "Elizondo's *Farabeuf*: A Consideration of the Text as Text." *Symposium* 39.3 (1985): 155–66.

El Salvador: History, Culture, and Literature

This Central American country borders on the Pacific Ocean between Guatemala and Honduras, and shares the Gulf of Fonseca with Nicaragua. The Republic of El Salvador's capital is San Salvador. With a population of approximately 6 million people (July 2011 estimate), and an area of 8,124 square miles, the densely populated country is Central America's smallest nation. Its lush landscape of lakes and volcanoes is very industrialized. Beginning in 2001, the nation adopted the U.S. dollar as its currency. The economic stability this change introduced stimulated an influx of immigrants from neighboring countries, seeking work.

History

The pre-Colombian inhabitants were Pipil Indians, a Mayan branch. Currently, most of the population is mixed race, primarily of Indian and Spanish descent. Spaniards arrived in 1524 under the command of Captain Pedro de Alvarado. His cousin, Diego de Alvarado, established the village of San Salvador in 1525. In 1546, Charles I of Spain granted San Salvador the title of city. Spanish forces conquered Central American indigenous populations with military force and evangelization. The Spanish crown governed all of Central America until 1821, when the *criollo* (ethnic Spaniards born in the New World) and mestizo (mixed race [Spanish and Indian]) populations joined forces and finally secured independence for each nation and established free commerce with European countries.

After securing independence, El Salvador became part of the Central American Federation, which was dissolved in 1838. The nation's early history as an independent state was marked by frequent wars against the other Central American countries. From 1872 to 1898, El Salvador was a prime mover in attempts to reestablish an "isthmian" federation. The governments of El Salvador, Honduras, and Nicaragua formed the Greater Republic of Central America in 1895. Guatemala and Costa Rica considered joining, but an 1898 coup in El Salvador ended the Federation.

From 1900 to 1930, the nation achieved relative stability. In 1932, the government of General Maximiliano Hernández Martínez quelled an indigenous uprising led by the rebel Augusto Farabundo Martí. An estimated 30,000 peasants were slain by the Martínez administration. This massacre has been fictionalized in such novels as

Cenizas de Izalco (1966; *Ashes of Izalco*, 1995) by Claribel *Alegría (1924–).

After the massacre, General Martínez ruled as dictator for some 12 years (1932–1944). In an attempt to remove him, the military joined with the people on April 2, 1944 in San Salvador, but did not succeed until May 9, when the entire country went on strike and marched through the streets of the capital. For the next 35 years, the country was governed by a series of military dictators. At the end of 1979, discontent with the system and concern for social justice motivated formation of the revolutionary movement Farabundo Martí para la Liberación Nacional (FMLN), which provoked a civil war that lasted 13 years and caused the death of 75,000 people. During this war, the U.S. presidential administrations of Jimmy Carter and Ronald Reagan helped support the military government with contributions of roughly 1 million dollars per day. On January 16, 1992, government and revolutionary leaders signed a peace accord that officially ended the conflict.

Culture

Painting is a primary artistic expression in El Salvador. Artistic styles vary from primitive to vanguard and are executed on wood or canvas. Representative painters include Noe Canjura, Carlos Cañas, Julita Díaz, Camino Minero, Rosa Mena Valenzuela, and Roberto Huezo. Traditional musical genres include religious songs and those that incorporate motifs of rural life. Popular music uses such Maya, Pipil, and African instruments as scrapers, gourds, flutes, and wood drums. After Spanish colonization, European classical music mixed with native styles. *Soccer is the most popular sport.

El Salvador is rich in agricultural products, especially corn, sugar cane, coffee, tropical fruits and vegetables, and grain. Fishing and cattle raising are other common occupations. With Mayan, Lenca, and Pipil influences, traditional appetizers include *pupusas* (stuffed corn tortillas), *shuco* (a beverage made from purple corn, beans, and pumpkin), and tamales. Salvadoran main dishes include seafood and red and white meats mixed with vegetables.

Literature

After the 1932 massacre, Salvadoran writers produced socially engaged literature inspired by their political ideals. Their focus on social justice has continued in successive literary generations and has been enriched by a colorful backdrop of cultural and mythological traditions as in "Canto a Huistalucxilt" (no date; Song to Huistalucxilt) by Manlio *Argueta (1935–). This poem reflects indigenous traditions as well as the author's solidarity with the defeated people in the fight for human rights.

Since 1956, with writers of the *generación compropetida* (Committed Generation), the national literature has intertwined increasingly with its political scene. These authors proclaimed their intent to engage directly with fellow Salvadorans and the issues they face. As a result, writers have since attempted to meld ethics and aesthetics to serve their countrymen. Most poets are also novelists and playwrights, such as Álvaro Menen Desleal (1931–2000), author of the play *Luz negra* (1965; Black Light). Its plot revolves around two recently beheaded prisoners (a common robber and a revolutionary) in San Salvador's Plaza Libertad, where their two bodies and heads have been left for public viewing. As the play begins, the heads open their eyes and proceed to tell their stories, which are allegories of the political violence in El Salvador and the U.S. involvement there, in Vietnam, and in Third World countries. *Las historias prohibidas del pulgarcito* (1974; The Forbidden Tales of Tom Thumb) by Roque *Dalton García (1935–1975) is an essay and poetry book about the history of El Salvador from a revolutionary perspective.

As seen in other countries afflicted by dictators and war, the civil war experiences (1979–1992) have yielded a proliferation of "testimonial" writings in novels and essays, such as Claribel *Alegría's *No me agarran viva. La mujer salvadoreña en la lucha* (1983; They Won't Take Me Alive: Salvadoran Women in Struggle for National Liberation, 1990). Similar topics are touched upon in *Nunca estuve sola* (1979; I Was Never Alone, 1992) by Nidia Diaz (1952–) and by Mario Bencastro (1949–) in *Disparo en la catedral* (1990; A Shooting in the Cathedral, 1996), a fictionalized account of the war and the assassination of Archbishop Óscar Romero. Besides these texts, new novels, plays, and poems have been written by Jacinta Escudos, Claudia Hernández, Ricardo Lindo, Silvia Regalado, David *Escobar Galindo, Horacio Castellanos Moya, and others.

Rhina Toruño-Haensly

See also Guerrilla Poetry; Testimonial Writing in Central America.

Work About:

Armstrong, Robert and Janet Shenk. *El Salvador the Face of Revolution*. Boston: South End, 1982.

Lindo, Hector. *Weak Foundations. The Economy of El Salvador in the Nineteenth Century*. Berkeley: University of California Press, 1990.

El Salvador's *Generación Comprometida* (1956–1972)

Every era and culture creates a distinct form of expression. In January 1956, Salvadoran poet, novelist, and revolutionary Roque *Dalton García (1935–1975), joined by 25 university law school students, founded the *Círculo Literario Universitario* (University Literary Circle) in San Salvador. This gathering soon evolved into the *Generación comprometida* (Committed Generation). The name was coined by leftist poet Italo López Vallecillos, who had returned to El Salvador after studying journalism in Spain. He published the movement's opening salvo in *Hoja* magazine, accusing previous generations of Salvadoran writers of aesthetic superficiality and rejecting an aesthetic where "poetry is a medium of expression for crying hopelessly over roses, crying over geraniums." Dalton agreed that art and literature should be socially engaged, and capable of producing political reform.

Committed Generation members took inspiration from the Cuban Revolution, leftist Latin American writers like Guatemalan Miguel Ángel *Asturias and Chilean Pablo *Neruda (both *Nobel Prize–winners), Peruvian César *Vallejo, and Spaniards Federico *García Lorca and Miguel *Hernández. They quickly adopted the motto, "No hay estética sin ética" (There is no aesthetic without ethics). Other Committed Generation writers include Roberto Armijo, Otto René Castillo, Pepe Rodríguez Ruiz, Manlio *Argueta, Tirso Canales, Danilo Velado, José Roberto Cea, and later on, Waldo Chávez Velasco, Álvaro Menen Desleal, Rafael Gochez Sosa, and Alfonso Quijada Urias. Female voices include Mercedes Durand and Irma Lanzas.

Dalton, however, remains the group's most compelling poet. His poetry, essays, novels, and journalism depict contemporary Salvadoran society and its history of exile, protests, prison, politics, love, and death. These constant themes are particularly vivid in *Las historias prohibidas del pulgarcito* (1974; The Forbidden Tales of Thumbelina [a reference to El Salvador's status as Latin America's smallest nation]). The *Generación comprometida* movement also attracted visual artists; painter Camilo Minero's work confronts similar themes. Like many Committed Generation poets, Minero suffered exile and incarceration. The risk inherent in combining art and politics became

apparent in 1975, when Dalton was assassinated by members of the Ejército Revolucionario del Pueblo (ERP)—which eventually became part of the Frente Farabundo Martí de Liberación Nacional—after he fell in disgrace when he asked the ERP to open itself to non-belligerant groups.

Rhina Toruño-Haensly

Work About:

Cea, José Roberto. *La Generación Comprometida*. San Salvador: Canoa, 2002.

López Vallecillos, Italo. "El intelectual como conducta moral." *Hoja* 3.3 (November 1956): 1.

Eltit, Diamela (1949–)

Amidst the oppressive Augusto Pinochet dictatorship and its aftermath, Chilean writer and performance artist Diamela Eltit has achieved expression through experimental language and marginalized characters. Her works contemplate aesthetics, the body, and difficult sociopolitical realities.

A leader in the *escena de avanzada* or postcoup artists' movement in the late 1970s in Santiago, Eltit cofounded the controversial group *CADA (Colectivo Acciones de Arte), which expressed dissent through public artistic "happenings." Her first novel, *Lumpérica* (1983; *E. Luminata*, 1997), defied both convention and censorship while exploring violence, gender, physical space, and ways of speaking. This fragmentary and often film-like text deals with a woman performing sexual acts before a crowd in a public square, and includes a famous photograph showing Eltit's self-mutilated arms as she reads *Lumpérica* in a brothel.

Eltit's experimental approach to social engagement develops throughout five subsequent novels, a collection of essays, and two hybrid texts documenting marginal socioeconomic and linguistic positions. Among her honors are a 1985 Guggenheim fellowship and an appointment (1990–1994) as Chilean cultural attaché to Mexico.

Laura Kanost

Work By:

E. Luminata. Trans. Ronald J. Christ. Santa Fe, NM: Lumen, 1997.

Work About:

Neustadt, Robert. *(Con) Fusing Signs and Postmodern Positions*. New York: Routledge, 1999. 25–82.

Encina, Juan del (1468–1529)

Probably born in Encina near Salamanca, this important Spanish musician, playwright, poet, performer, and theoretician of the Spanish *Renaissance studied with illustrious humanist Antonio de Nebrija at the University of Salamanca. Working as a writer and composer in the service of the Duke of Alba, he went to Rome in 1949 and began to serve Pope Alexander VI. His successor, Pope Julius II, sent him to Málaga as archdeacon in 1509. Between 1512 and 1516, del Encina

served as Papal Musician to Leo X. In 1519, he was named primary priest of León cathedral, where he spent his last years.

Encina compiled his works under a single volume titled *Cancionero* (1496; Songbook), which had seven editions during his life. Its final version begins with the theoretical work titled "Arte de la poesía castellana" (Art of Castilian Poetry), followed by lyric and burlesque poetry, "Visiones alegóricas y de amor" (Allegorical and Love Visions), and a number of dramatic texts. Particularly important for the history of Spanish music are 68 compositions that he wrote that Francisco Asenjo Barbieri included in his *Cancionero musical de los siglos XV y XVI* (1890; Music Songbook of the Fifteenth and Sixteenth Centuries). These musical pieces, mostly *villancicos* for three or four voices to be performed and danced by actors, contain a characteristic mixture of cultured and popular musical traditions of the period.

Rafael Lamas

See also *Cancionero* Poetry in Spain; Humanism in Spain.

Work By:

Teatro. Ed., study. Miguel Ángel Pérez Priego. Ed., prol., notes. Alberto del Río. Barcelona: Crítica, 2001.

Work About:

Kidd, Michael. "Myth, Desire, and the Play of Inversion: The Fourteenth Century Eclogue of Juan del Encina." *Hispanic Review* 65.2 (September 1997): 217–36.

Enlightenment in Spain: 1700–1800

The new French Bourbon dynasty (Philip V) that ruled in Spain after the War of Succession (1701–1714) brought with it theories focused on a reform of culture and society and religious tolerance. Reform theories were already present in late-17th-century Spain through the work of *novatores*—intellectuals or innovators—such as Juan de Cabriada, who spread news of European scientific discoveries. These new ideas were propagated during the 18th century as French texts were translated, newspaper publications were born (*Diario de los literatos*, *El pensador*, *El censor*), and cultural institutions promoting progress (Amigos de la Patria) were established. Not least of all, the essay played a critical role in this process, and made prose the century's most important literary mode.

The 18th century presented significant changes for women's position, since intense debates were being held over their nature, their emerging role as avid consumers and readers, their newly expanded social acceptance to cafés and halls, and even their need to work and be active, as the debate regarding their inclusion in the Madrid Economic Society indicates. Additionally, women writers stood out, reflecting on the situation of their gender and demanding the equal rights proposed by intellectuals for all men. Josefa Amar y Borbón (1753–1833), Inés Joyes (1731–?), María Rosa Gálvez (1768–1806), and Margarita Hickey (1753–after 1793) represent just a sample of numerous women who strove to denounce social injustice and to reform inequalities and the situation of eighteenth-century women.

Literature of this period has been frequently judged as rigid, and lacking in quality and emotion. Although enlightened Spanish literature is eminently didactic, its rich variety reveals two stages in which, ironically, opposing periods coexist. Baroque aesthetics (highly rhetorical, ornamental language) and antibaroque stylistics (an interest in pure and simple expression) dominate the first half of the century, while neoclassicism (imitation of the Classics, strict adherence to Aristotelian rules) and romanticism (consolidation of neoclassic ideas but with the predominance of personal feelings over reason) prevail in the second half.

Outstanding Enlightenment prose begins with Friar Benito Jerónimo Feijoo, who grouped all his didactic writings in *El teatro crítico universal* (1726–1739; *Universal Critical Theater*, 1968) and *Cartas eruditas y curiosas* (1742–1760; *Erudite and curious letters*, 1928), which condemned superstition and sought to bring modernity to Spain. Gaspar Melchor de *Jovellanos applied his reformist ideas to the sentimental drama *El delincuente honrado* (1794; *The Honored Delinquent*, 1928), which criticizes an existing law on duels. José *Cadalso consolidated the epistolary genre with *Cartas marruecas* (1789; *Moroccan Letters*, 1952), in which the exchange of letters between a Moroccan visitor, his teacher, and his Spanish friend enable a review of Spanish history with special attention to its customs. *Romanticism is obvious in Cadalso's *Noches lúgubres* (1771; *Lugubrious Nights*, 1950), whose protagonist exhibits a morbid obsession with recovering the corpse of his deceased lover. Differing from the above, Diego Torres de Villarroel gained enormous success with a *picaresque account of his adventurous life, *Vida, ascendencia, nacimiento, crianza y aventuras del Doctor don Diego de Torres Villarroel* (1727–1751; *The Remarkable Life of Don Diego*, 1958).

Neoclassic ideas also regulated poetry, recommending utility and decorum over traditions. Ignacio Luzán's *Poética* (1737; *Poetics*, 1956) confirmed poetry's practical purpose. Poets of the day were grouped in schools in the cities where they wrote, namely Salamanca, Madrid, and Seville. The Salamanca school, best represented by Juan Meléndez Valdés, initially exhibited a rococo style (development of pastoral themes centered on love and pleasure), but later produced poems opposing social inequalities. From the Madrid group, Tomás de *Iriarte and Félix María de Samaniego chastised national character defects by means of fables. The Seville school included such figures as José María Blanco White, well known for his translations from English and his active participation in the English cultural magazine *The New Monthly*, for which he composed his famously critical *Cartas desde España* (1821; Letters from Spain). Alberto Lista, founder of the Ateneo (Madrid's free university), defended neoclassical principles of balance and good taste most evidently in *El imperio de la estupidez* (1789; The Empire of Stupidity).

Theater also reflected a gradual evolution from adherence to classical rules toward a search for popular appeal. Madrid group members Vicente García de la Huerta, Ramón de la *Cruz, and Leandro *Fernández de Moratín were particularly successful dramatists. García de la Huerta's *Raquel* (1778; *Raquel*, 1950) showed that a Spanish historical tragedy could conform to prerequisites of classical theater. Moratín (son of Nicolás Fernández de Moratín) used neoclassical didacticism in three major comedies: *El viejo y la niña* (1790; The Old Man and the Young Girl), *El sí de las niñas* (1806; *A Daughter's Consent*, 1938), and *La comedia nueva o el Café* (1792; The New Comedy); the first two works attack family interference in the marriage of young women and the third ridicules contemporary dramatists who disregard Aristotelian rules. The earlier mentioned Ramón de la Cruz, the most popular author of his day, composed over 400 *sainetes* (short comic sketches concerning the problems of urban working-class characters). Two examples are *La Pradera de San Isidro* (1765; The Prairie of San Isidro) and *Manolo* (1769; Manolo); the latter satirizes bad neoclassical theater of that time, where tragic roles and lofty qualities are linked to an antihero and similar low-life characters of Madrid's picaresque milieu. Overall, in each genre, key writers tried to use their intellect to improve the self-government of mankind by reforming society and its structures. At the close of the 18th century, John Locke's idea of the self as the identity of a human being and his influence on Jean Jacques Rousseau's theory of the natural man paved the way for a romantic era, which would focus on literary displays of feelings and human sensitivity.

Judith García-Quismondo García

See also Novel in Spain: 1700–1900; Romanticism in Spain; Short Fiction in Spain: 1700–1900; Theater in Spain: 1700–1900; Women Writers in Spain: 1700–1900.

Work About:

Godzich, Wlad, and Nicholas Spadaccini, eds. *The Institutionalization of Literature in Spain*. Minneapolis: Prisma Institute, 1987.

Haidt, Rebecca. *Embodying Enlightenment: Knowing the Body in Eighteenth-Century Spanish Literature and Culture*. New York: St. Martin's, 1998.

Smith, Theresa Ann. "Writing out of the Margins: Women, Translation, and the Spanish Enlightenment." *Journal of Women's History* 15.1 (Spring 2003): 116–43.

Enlightenment in Spanish America

This philosophical movement emphasizes objective reason, as opposed to faith, emotions, or past tradition as the key to developing the potential of humankind. Reason is seen to further knowledge, which in turn promotes goodness and equity among all citizens. The movement was introduced to Spanish America with the widely distributed writings of Spanish *ilustrados* like Benito Feijoo (1674–1764), Pedro Campomanes (1723–1802), Gaspar Melchor de *Jovellanos (1744–1811), and

Melchor Rafael de Macanaz (1670–1760). Additionally, the French *Encyclopedia* (1751–72), a compendium of universal knowledge from a scientific and lay viewpoint, and similar writings by international figures ranging from René Descartes (1596–1650) to Voltaire (1694–1778) were read in universities, chambers of commerce, academies, and clubs. In 1785, the Real Academia de Bellas Artes de la Nueva España was founded to channel Enlightenment ideas regarding the arts in the colonies in a more purposeful manner. The spread of journalism to a mass audience constitutes one of the Enlightenment movement's most remarkable developments.

The Spanish crown commissioned and authorized European trips to Hispanic America to produce key texts for understanding the state of the colonies and how these territories perceived themselves. Numerous scientific experiments were undertaken. Jorge Juan y Santacilia (1713–1773) discovered that the Earth was not perfectly round but flattened at both poles, and he measured the height of the Andes. Antonio de Ulloa (1716–1795) identified an infrequent meteorological phenomenon now known as Ulloa's halo and was a codiscoverer of platinum as a new element in the periodical table. These scientists, like Alexander von Humboldt (1769–1859), extended scientific understanding on the continent.

Literary texts followed a similar path of rational inquiry. Spaniard Alonso Carrió de la Vandera (1714?–1783) wrote *El Lazarillo de ciegos caminantes* (1773; *El lazarillo: a guide for inexperienced travelers between Buenos Aires and Lima,*

1965); it defends the colonial system and reflects on its history, geography, and economy. Peruvian born Pablo de Olavide (1725–1803) wrote sentimental novels in the style of Jean Jacques Rousseau (1712–1778). Using women protagonists, the stories emphasized man's inherent goodness and the need to preserve harmony with nature; the various women characters each correspond to different moral virtues. Olavide's *Teresa o el terremoto de Lima* (written c. 1800, published 1829; Theresa or Lima's Earthquake) demonstrates the resilience of true love. José Joaquín *Fernández de Lizardi (1776–1827) penned the "first" Spanish American novel, *Periquillo Sarniento* (written 1816, published 1831; *The Mangy Parrot*, 2004), using techniques vaguely akin to *picaresque literature. It depicts the end of colonial society and voices the need for social reform and independence from Spain.

In 1767, the Jesuit Order was expelled from Spain and its colonies because the Enlightenment crown believed its more conservative Catholicism delayed the adoption of necessary reforms. Father Francisco Javier Clavijero (1731–1787), one of the expelled members, wrote the first history of Mexico with a *criollo* (Spaniard born in the Americas) and new-world sensitivity, using the words *patria* (fatherland) and *nación* (nation) with their modern meanings. Another expelled Jesuit, Juan Ignacio Molina (1740–1829), compiled a history of Chile employing the same presuppositions. Finally, the indigenous Ecuadorian physician, Francisco Eugenio Javier de Espejo y Santa Cruz (1747–1794), founded the journal *Primicias de la Cultura de Quito* (1792; Scoops of Quito's Culture). He was also a satiric writer.

Spanish America's first modern history that used new documents and a critical reading of previous sources is the *Historia del Nuevo Mundo* (1793; History of the New World) by Juan Bautista Muñoz (1745–1799?). Others who helped update modern knowledge of the colonies include Antonio de Alcedo (1736–1812), with *Diccionario geográfico-histórico de las Indias Occidentales o América* (1786–1788; Geographical–Historical Dictionary of Western Indies or America); Juan José de Eguiara y Eguren (1695–1763), who wrote *Bibliotheca Mexicana* (1755; Mexican Library); and José Mariano Beristáin de Sousa (1756–1817), publisher of *Biblioteca hispanoamericana septentrional* (1816–1821; Septentrional Hispanic American Library). These encyclopedic volumes advanced knowledge of the history, geography, and unique aspects of Spanish America. Father Manuel de Lacunza (1731–1801) wrote the posthumously published *La venida del Mesías en Gloria y majestad* (1812; *The Coming of the Messiah*, 1816), presenting a millenarist account of Christ's second coming that became very popular and was widely translated.

A second wave of Enlightenment in Hispanic America relates to the independence process. Expelled Jesuit Juan Pablo Viscardi (1748–1798) wrote *Carta a los americanos* (1792; Letter to Americans) asking for independence in the Americas. Dominican Friar Servando Teresa de Mier (1763–1827) explained his personal experiences as witness of the independence process, particularly his own account as a member of the privileged minority of Latin American exiles in Europe; his principal books are *Historia de la revolución de la Nueva España* (1813; History of the Revolution of the New Spain) and *Memorias* (1917; Memories). Simón *Bolívar (1783–1830) published numerous accounts of his participation in the independence process and theoretical treaties on the topic. The anonymous novel *Xicotencal* (1826) tells the history of Mexico's conquest from the viewpoint of the new independence movement, depicting the Aztecs as good, and the Spaniards, evil.

Andrés *Bello (1781–1865) is the most important figure of the Spanish American Enlightenment. In addition to his highly esteemed poems, his writing ranges from a famous Spanish language grammar book to the Civil Code of Chile. As a poet, his "Silva a la agricultura de la zona tórrida" (1826–1827; Poem to the Agriculture of the Torrid Zone [in *The Odes of Bello*], 1920) describes American products and exalts the telluric values, natural lands, and riches of America. To conclude, the Spanish American Enlightenment exhibits two halves. The first involves the continent's self discovery, the second uses reason to justify the independence process. Spaniards and *criollos* compiled the first part and the citizens of the new republics composed the second.

Salvador A. Oropesa

See also Enlightenment in Spain: 1700–1800.

Work About:

Jaffe, Catherine Marie and Elizabeth Franklin Lewis, eds. *Eve's Enlightenment*: *Women's Experience in Spain and* *Spanish America, 1726–1839*. Baton Rouge: Louisiana State University Press, 2009.

Paquette, Gabriel B. *Enlightened Reform in Southern Europe and Its Atlantic Colonies, c. 1750–1830*. Burlington, VT: Ashgate, 2009.

Epic Poetry in the Hispanic World

These long narratives in verse form recount heroic, historic, and fantastic deeds and, in the process, create a sense of cultural identity. Within Hispanic literature, the *Cantar de Mío Cid* (written c. 1140; *Song of the Cid*, 2009) is the oldest-known Spanish epic. Also known as the *Poema del Cid*, the work demonstrates many of the genre's recurring themes: El Cid is a heroic protagonist who participates in a series of challenges to defend his honor, demonstrating incredible, almost supernatural abilities and providing readers with a heightened sense of communal identity.

Early History

Many scholars argue that early or primary epics developed out of oral and musical performances (*cantares de gesta*) that circulated in the recitations of *juglares* (actor-performers) before being compiled by anonymous authors. Others, however, claim that individual authors composed existing epics; still others think it was some combination of the two. The *Cantar de Mío Cid* offers a helpful analysis of the relationship between history and the epic tradition in Spain. The hero is based on the historical figure Rodrigo Díaz de Vivar, and while the historical Cid was exiled and demonstrated great military prowess (as in the famous epic), historical documents indicate that El Cid actually fought with Muslim caliphs against Christian kingdoms, as well as with Christian kings against a variety of foes, shifting allegiances according to political and economic needs. The *Cantar del Cid*, however, ignores this complex history, and presents El Cid as a warrior uniting Christian kingdoms and foreshadowing domination over Muslim territory. The epic genre thus modifies historical events to support a sense of cultural identity and the aims of nation building.

Many other epic texts circulated in medieval Spain, although very few have survived in poetic form: Along with the *Cantar del Cid*, we have fragments of *El Roncesvalles*, which deals with Frankish hero Roland's exploits, and *Las mocedades de Rodrigo* (The Youthful Deeds of Rodrigo [the Cid's given name]). Other epic poems have been reconstructed based on prose versions found in medieval histories, like *Los siete infantes de Lara* (The Seven Infantes [king's sons] of Lara) and the *Cantar de Sancho II* (Song of Sancho II). Scholars note many parallels between Spanish, German, and French epics, but Islamic influences are now also seen as critical in the development of the genre.

Renaissance and Colonial Epic

While medieval Europe proved particularly conducive to the epic genre, the tradition continued into the Renaissance, when literary epics were composed by known authors. After 1492, when the Catholic Monarchs Ferdinand and Isabella conquered the last Muslim stronghold of Granada, new encounters in the Americas provided epic poets with fresh material about the deeds of Spanish conquistadors. Long narrative poems about Spanish soldiers and native peoples, such as Alonso de Ercilla's *La Araucana* (1569–1589), provided new if familiar subjects for epic poetry. Ercilla's text deals with the Spanish conquest of the Mapuche tribes in Chile, and while it is sympathetic toward the indigenous warriors, portraying their heroism in battle, these representations are ultimately meant to highlight Spanish bravery. Even Ercilla's critique of the harsh governance forced on the Mapuche is always contextualized by an insistence on the sovereignty of the Spanish crown and the need for Christian and Spanish domination in the region. Other Golden Age authors like Lope de *Vega composed similarly revisionist epics, such as *Jerusalén Conquistada* (1609; Jerusalem Conquered), which focused not on the colonies but on Spain's relationship to the rest of Europe, in this case fabricating Spanish involvement in the Crusades, thereby focusing on an Islamic enemy against which the broader forces of Europe (including Spain) could unite.

The influence of epics waned rapidly, but the *romance*, the popular ballad verse form that reprises or elaborates memorable fragments of epic poems, remained widely employed, and snippets of ancient epics can still be found in short *romance* poems. While books of chivalry (*libros* de caballerías) and the *picaresque soon dominated, the development of these genres and even the modern novel can be traced to epic roots. Don Quijote can be seen as a type of antihero, and the scope of *Don Quijote*, despite its narrative form, focuses on the quests and deeds of a central figure who seeks to defend honor.

Romanticism and the Epic

The epic regained popularity in the romantic movements of the 19th century, focusing on heroic, exotic, and nationalist themes. Spanish poets created a new semi-epic form, the *leyenda*, a narrative poem that revived traditional concepts (such as battles against Moors) through fantastical imagery and fake realism. Duque de Rivas wrote *leyendas* about the last Visigothic King and the Seven Infantes of Lara, and José de *Espronceda produced the unfinished epic *El diablo mundo* (1841; The Devil World), a philosophical study of Adam's search for freedom as he moves from innocence to experience. The real champion of romantic epic poetry, however, was José *Zorrilla, whose works, such as *Granada* (1852), skillfully evoke a chivalric medieval past, combining history and legend in colorful, romantic forms.

Spanish American literature was particularly influenced by the epic's revival, being newly drawn into the heroics of nation building. José Joaquín Olmedo celebrated Simón *Bolívar's victories over the Spaniards in the epic poem *La victoria de Junín* (1825; The Victory of Junín). Olmedo voices the action through the Incan emperor Huayna-Cápac, overlooking the fact that

criollo (American-born Spaniard) interests drove independence movements and offered no restitution for indigenous populations. Other Spanish American epics like Juan Zorrilla de San Martín's *Tabaré* (1886) explore native history and tradition, seeking national identity within indigenous roots. In Argentina, José Hernández wrote the most famous gaucho epic, *Martín Fierro* (1872–1879), which explores rural life and the plight of an impoverished cowboy on the pampas. The gaucho offers a heroic foundational figure for Argentine national identity, and the work criticizes the Europeanizing, modernizing strategies of the new nation. In Mexico, the epic tradition can be seen in the development of *corridos*, long narrative ballads about famed heroes or criminals on Mexico's frontier. These songs began circulating during the War of Independence (1810–1821) and gained increasing popularity during the Mexican Revolution (1910–1920).

Modern Decline of the Epic

In modern times, the role of the hero holds less appeal, and perhaps for this reason, along with the general decline of narrative poetry, the epic has not been a popular genre. In the 20th century, long poems with sweeping historical scope like Pablo *Neruda's *Canto General* (1950) employ aspects of epic form but reject nationalist aims. Today, with the negative associations held toward the glorification of war, the traditional epic has little attraction. Its influence can still be seen, however, in the tendency to develop antiheroes and in the success of the novel, a lengthy narrative often focused on a central protagonist and the development of identity. In addition, border tensions between the United States and Mexico have produced epic-inspired texts like the *narcocorridos* (*corridos* focused on drug smuggling) as well as the Chicano (Mexican American) epic "Yo soy Joaquín" (1967 I Am Joaquín) by Rodolfo "Corky" Gonzales and the feminine response by Carmen Tafolla, "La Malinche" (1978). While the epic is a notoriously masculine genre, recent studies have also opened the field to questions of gender and women's roles in the epic tradition.

Debra Faszer-McMahon

See also Chivalry Literature in Spain and the New World; *Don Quijote de la Mancha* in Spanish American Literature and Culture; Gaucho Literature; *Indigenismo* in Spanish American Literature; *Romance* (Ballad) Tradition in the Hispanic World.

Work By:

Bailey, Matthew. *Las mocedades de Rodrigo (The youthful deeds of Rodrigo, the Cid)*. Toronto: University of Toronto Press, 2007.

The Song of the Cid. Trans. Burton Raffel. Intro. María Rosa Menocal. New York: Penguin, 2009.

Work About:

Davis, Elizabeth B. *Myth and Identity in the Epic of Imperial Spain*. Columbia: University of Missouri Press, 2000.

Poor, Sara S., and Jana K. Schulman. *Women and Medieval Epic: Gender, Genre, and the Limits of Epic Masculinity*. New York: Palgrave Macmillan, 2007.

Equatorial Guinea: History, Culture, and Literature

History

The Republic of Equatorial Guinea, the country's official name, is located on the west coast of equatorial Africa, sharing boundaries with Gabon to the south and east and Cameroon to the north; the Gulf of Guinea forms its western border. It occupies an area of about 10,830 square miles with an estimated population of 668,225 inhabitants (July 2011 estimate) spread over a mainland territory called Río Muni and five islands in the Gulf of Guinea. Malabo, the nation's capital and largest city, is located on the island of Bioko.

It is believed that the first settlers of today's mainland of Equatorial Guinea were Pygmies and Ndowe tribe people. In the 12th and 13th centuries, migrations by Bantu tribes brought Fang people to the mainland. At about the same time, Bioko Island was settled by the Bubi. In 1472, Portuguese navigators claimed Bioko, naming it Fernando Po. Spanish domination of the area began in 1778 when Portugal ceded the islands and commercial rights to some coastal areas, including Río Muni. The Spanish withdrew in 1781 because of their low resistance to diseases, such as yellow fever. Between 1827 and 1858, Spain leased bases on Bioko to Britain to set up antislavery patrol stations; some freed slaves eventually settled on Bioko. In 1844, the Spanish returned to Bioko and began to develop plantations. The Río Muni area was awarded to Spain at the 1885 Berlin Conference, and in 1900, precise boundaries were established via a treaty with France. Río Muni and the islands then became the colony of Spanish Guinea. In 1963, the colony was renamed Equatorial Guinea and granted limited autonomy.

On October 12, 1968, Equatorial Guinea became an independent nation under president Macías Nguema, who ruled as a dictator for 11 years. He was deposed in a bloody 1979 military coup and replaced by his nephew, Teodoro Obiang Nguema, who has been reelected several times in contentious, controversial elections. A crackdown on freedom of speech and political dissension in Equatorial Guinea has resulted in the exile of several prominent figures, mainly to Spain.

Culture

Fang and Buti cultural and ethnic traditions dominate the nation. Descendants of *Fernandinos* (slaves freed by the British) remain on the islands as well. Minority tribes include the Balengue, Kombe, Igbo, Bujebas, and a small group of Europeans—mainly Spanish descendants. The family unit remains the most important link among Equatorial Guineans and people often identify first with their ethnic group. Polygamy is still common among the Fang, and normally the bridegroom or his family pays a dowry to the bride's family at marriage. Although about 80 percent of Equatorial Guineans are Catholic, some traditional rites still prevail. Ancestors are believed to exert influence on the living, and such rituals as the *abira* (cleansing the communities of evil) are still performed.

Spanish has been the official language since 1844, but a constitutional statute in 1998 also identified French as an official language. Equatorial Guinea entered the CFA monetary zone (a group of 14 African nations who use the franc) in the late 1980s. Portuguese became Equatorial Guinea's third official language in July 2007. Pidgin English has become a lingua franca, especially in Bioko, and many daily activities among inhabitants are conducted in such indigenous languages as Fang, Bubi, or Igbo.

At 86 percent, Equatorial Guinea enjoys one of the highest literacy rates in the developing world, yet many Equatorial Guineans remain in abject poverty. Prior to independence, the agricultural sector employed about half of the labor force. The discovery of offshore oil and natural gas reserves in the 1990s increased economic growth, but this has not significantly improved the country's standard of living, as the wealth is squandered by a select few. Indeed, *Forbes* magazine credits Obiang with becoming one of the world's wealthiest dictators in record time.

Literature

Like many African communities, Equatorial Guinea's literary tradition is oral, with myths and legends passed on from one generation to the next, mainly in such vernacular languages as Fang, Bubi, and Ndowe. In modern Equatorial Guinean literature—written mainly in Spanish—

themes of national identity, colonialism, and dictatorship prevail among resident and exiled writers. Juan Balboa Boneke, María Nsué Angüe, and Donato Ndongo-Bidyogo are some of the most celebrated contemporary writers. Nsué Angüe's eponymous novel *Ekomo* (1985), the first to be published by an Equatorial Guinean woman, discusses women's rights and postcolonial African society from the perspective of a Fang widow who speaks out about her marriage after her husband's death. Ndongo-Bidyogo's *Las tinieblas de tu memoria negra* (2000; *Shadows of Your Black Memory*, 2007), the first novel of his trilogy *Los hijos de la tribu* (Children of the Tribe), chronicles the story of a generation of Equatorial Guineans from colonialism through independence and dictatorship. The struggle between the past—characterized by superstition, initiation rites, and racism—and the present desire to modernize define this novel.

Other writers of note include Juan Tomás *Ávila Laurel, Carlos Nsue Otong, Jerónimo Rope Bomaba, Ciríaco Bokesa Napo, and Maximiliano Nkogo Esono. *Voces de espuma* (1987; Froth Voices), Bokesa Napo's first poetry collection, expresses the individual and collective drama of a nation anxious to discover itself postindependence. In *Adjá Adjá y otros relatos* (2000; Adjá Adjá and Other Stories), Nkogo Esono recounts the people's daily struggle for survival, set against official corruption symbolized by the police force, torture, mutilation, dreams of emigration, and death.

Andrew Sobiesuo

See also Appendix B for other entries related to Equatorial Guinea.

Work About:

Lewis, Marvin A. *An Introduction to the Literature of Equatorial Guinea*. Columbia: University of Missouri Press, 2007.

Sundiata, Ibrahim K. *Equatorial Guinea: Colonialism, State Terror, and the Search for Stability*. Boulder, CO: Westview, 1990.

Ugarte, Michael. *Africans in Europe. The Culture of Exile and Emigration from Equatorial Guinea to Spain*. Chicago and Urbana: University of Illinois Press, 2010.

Equatorial Guinea: Poets

A Spanish colonial possession between 1778 and 1968, Equatorial Guinea has produced many excellent poets, among them Raquel del Pozo Epita ("Raquel Ilombé," 1939–1992), Juan Balboa Boneke (1938–), Ciriaco Bokesa Napo (1939–), and Juan Tomás *Ávila Laurel (1966–). Each uses Spanish as his or her primary literary language. Most express appreciation of Spanish and Hispanic culture, blending Spanish and African cultural referents and traditions. In general, they write about Equatorial Guinea from an outsider's perspective. Ilombé and Balboa Boneke alternate between geographical spaces and perspectives, while Bokesa Napo and Ávila Laurel write from within Equatorial Guinea. These poets tend to divide their poetry collections thematically, dealing with such subjects as exile, suffering, hunger, nostalgia, and nature. These themes allude to the country's current political and economic situation, dominated by a repressive, discriminatory regime and recent world interest in the country after the discovery of oil in its territory.

Ilombé was one of the earliest Guinean poets to publish a poetry collection. Poems collected in *Ceiba* (1978) are written from the perspective of a speaker in Madrid and accompanied by their place and year of composition. Meta-poetic references to the speaker's attempts to voice and represent the past highlight language's role in the representation of experience. Anaphora, parallel structure, and assonant rhyme are common techniques in her poems, which deal with nature, memory, and nostalgia. Hope for the future also appears as a common theme.

Balboa Boneke's verse expresses nostalgia for the landscape and geography of Equatorial Guinea, and exhibits hope for the future and an eventual return to his homeland. Poems in *Sueños en mi selva (Antología poética)* (1987; Dreams in My Jungle [Poetry Anthology]) include references to specific places and geographical features and often supply footnotes that explain these references to a peninsular Spanish audience. Much of his work also displays a political commitment to the situation of Equatorial Guinea's people and sometimes has epigraphs that situate poems in the context of specific political events. Many poems employ anaphora, onomatopoeia, and other tropes that lend themselves well to the oral performance

of poetry. *Requiebros* (1994; Flirtations) returns to many of the themes presented in earlier writing, including nostalgia for youth and hope for the future. Meta-poetry also figures prominently in this collection.

Bokesa Napo's verse shares many of the characteristics found in Balboa Boneke's work. *Voces de espuma* (1987; Voices of Foam) uses footnotes to explain references to Guinean geography and culture, meta-poetic references, anaphora, and references to Spain's poetic tradition, seen in epigraphs taken from Jorge *Guillén's poetry. Bokesa Napo uses a variety of poetic forms, ranging from short to long verses.

Ávila Laurel's book *Poemas* (1994; Poems) is divided in two sections, combining the previous collections *Versos del alma* (1989; Verses of the Soul) and *Ramblas* (1990; Promenades); it is preceded by a prologue from Bokesa Napo. Poems in the first section deal with nature, social injustice, hunger, Africa's place within 20th century history, and its place vis-à-vis Europe. Some poems in the second section address the economic underpinnings of social inequality and such issues as the African AIDS epidemic.

Historia íntima de la humanidad (1999; Intimate History of Humanity) continues a technique also employed in *Poemas* whereby the poet creates a dialogue within poems between the poetic voice and voices of everyday people. This collection, even more explicitly political than *Poemas*, incorporates direct references to the United Nations and the global economic and political situation. Ávila Laurel frames this representation of the situation within Christian religious discourse and mainstream notions of Spanish history, including a reference to the Visigoths.

While the abovementioned poets are some of Equatorial Guinea's best known, they are by no means the only ones. Other noteworthy poets are Francisco Zamora Loboch (1947–), Anacleto Oló Mibuy (1951–), and Jerónimo Rope Bomabá (1953–).

Paul Cahill

See also Equatorial Guinea: Writers in Exile; Equatorial Guinea: Writers Living in the United States; Equatorial Guinea's *Generación del Silencio* (The Generation of Silence).

Work By:

Ávila Laurel, Juan Tomás. *Historia íntima de la humanidad*. Malabo: Centro Cultural Hispano-Guineano, 1999.

Ávila Laurel, Juan Tomás. *Poemas*. Malabo: Centro Cultural Hispano-Guineano, 1994.

Balboa Boneke, Juan. *Requiebros*. Malabo: Centro Cultural Hispano-Guineano, 1994.

Balboa Boneke, Juan. *Sueños en mi selva (Antología poética)*. Malabo: Centro Cultural Hispano-Guineano, 1987.

Bokesa, Ciriaco. *Voces de espumas*. Malabo: Centro Cultural Hispano-Guineano, 1987.

Ilonbé, Raquel. *Ceiba*. Madrid: Editorial Madrid, 1978.

Ndongo Bidyogo, Donato, and Mbaré Ngom, eds. *Literatura de Guinea Ecuatorial: antología*. Madrid: SIAL, 2000.

Work About:

Lewis, Marvin A. *An Introduction to the Literature of Equatorial Guinea: Between Colonialism and Dictatorship*. Columbia: University of Missouri Press, 2007.

Martin-Márquez, Susan. *Disorientations: Spanish Colonialism in Africa and the Performance of Identity*. New Haven: Yale University Press, 2008.

Ugarte, Michael. *Africans in Europe. The Culture of Exile and Emigration from Equatorial Guinea to Spain*. Urbana and Chicago: University of Illinois Press, 2010.

Equatorial Guinea: Writers in Exile

African literature written in Spanish is a cultural project that has received very little critical and theoretical attention in Africa, Europe, or the United States. In Spain, the former colonial power, this void is evident in university and secondary school curricula. A cursory look at the body of texts (anthologies of African literature, Hispanic literature, or critical studies) published in the 1970s, 1980s, and most of the 1990s in Africa, Europe, and the Americas shows the striking neglect of African literature of Spanish expression.

Located in the Gulf of Guinea, or Biafra, between Gabon, Cameroon, and Nigeria, the Republic of Equatorial Guinea is the only sub-Saharan country with a literature written in Spanish, or, as Equato-Guinean historian and writer Donato Ndongo-Bidyogo puts it, *"es la única expresión española en el África negra"* (it is the only Spanish-language expression of black

Africa). In their attempt to write and/or define national and cultural identity, most scholars draw upon the Hispanic aspect of their historical heritage in order to highlight the central and bridging role that Spanish and Hispanic culture play in voicing this discourse of identity. Hispanic heritage is part of various materials and discourses called upon by Equato-Guineans in the construction of national identity. Unlike other African countries with a native *lingua franca* that enables members of different ethnic groups to communicate, in Equatorial Guinea, Spanish is the primary vehicle of interethnic communication that reaffirms the shared Hispanic connection between such groups.

African Hispanic literature has followed a different path than that of the "other" African literatures. It was late to arrive to the African literary scene. Further, unlike what occurred in former French and British colonies, in colonial Spanish Guinea, literature did not develop alongside the nationalist movement for freedom from colonial rule. Madrid in the first half of the 20th century was not a cosmopolitan city, nor did it not serve as a cultural hub and breeding ground for intellectual and cultural exchange, as did Paris for Caribbean, African, and U.S. African American cultural producers. During that early period, most Equato-Guineans who traveled to Spain to further their studies were seminarians, and once in Spain, they were assigned to remote seminaries across the country. Though most of them later withdrew from seminary studies, they enjoyed no exposure to an open cultural ambiance like what existed in Paris.

On October 12, 1968, Equatorial Guinea gained its freedom from Spain. Like all newly independent African nations, the country sought to articulate a unique and specific discourse of national identity, but, as Cusack has noted, soon found that different individuals and groups understood this new national identity in numerous different ways. In Equatorial Guinea, like most African nations, the population's multiethnic composition warranted that the formation of national identity be closely associated with the country's internationally recognized, fixed borders. The geographic territory, then, became a defining factor and the primary site for the construction(s) of national identity. This territorial space, however, had been arbitrarily delineated by the former European colonial powers, and in most cases did not correspond to social, ethnic, and political realities of that environment, making the articulation of identity even more problematic, given the disparate collage of elements.

The Republic of Equatorial Guinea is inhabited by several ethnic groups, including the Fang, Ndowe (also known as Combe), Benga, Baseke, Balengue, Annobones, Bujeba, and the Fang of Río Muni, which is the largest. As a consequence, nation building and the formation of national identity could not rely on one single ethnic group to the detriment of others. Each element had to be based on the construction of national unity in terms of a common history of experience in the geographic territory. Given the heterogeneity and multiple ethnicities and identities, speaking of a single national identity becomes difficult. This is the context surrounding the reality of Equatorial Guinea during the first republic.

Five months after his election, President Francisco Macías Nguema denounced a coup attempt, declared a state of emergency, suspended the constitution, abolished political and social debate by banning all political parties, instituted a one-party rule, appointed himself commander in chief of the armed forces, and proclaimed himself president for life. Macías Nguema embraced the postindependent African discourse of authenticity of that time, also known as "African authenticity." Swiss historian Max Liniger-Goumaz describes his ideological platform as *Afro-fascism*, and labeled the Equato-Guinean version *Nguemismo* because it was ethnic based. Throughout his presidency (1969–1979), the government dealt brutally with opponents who were not members of Macías Nguema's clan, the Fang-Esangui, seeking legitimacy and national unity through violent practices and the establishment of what Ngugi Wa Thiong'o has called the "culture of silence and fear." Macías Nguema rewrote the country's national history (both traditional and contemporary) in order to achieve national unity, calling himself Great Teacher of education, science, and culture of the Republic of Equatorial Guinea; Supreme Leader and national hero; Father of the revolution and Founder of the Guinean State; Supremely Responsible for the historical destinies of our nation; First Sacred Name and Revolutionary of Equatorial Guinea; and Father of all revolutionary children.

In addition, each day, everywhere in the country, be it at work, school, or church, everybody had to sing "*Dios creó a Guinea Ecuatorial gracias a Macías, y sin Macías no hay Guinea*" (Thanks to Macías, God created Equatorial Guinea, and without Macías there is no Guinea). As several scholars have noted, Macías followed the strategy of other African dictators, using his position to define the nation's character and undermine any individual or group attempts to voice collective memories and personal stories. Additionally, he restricted cultural activities, established censorship, and banned local and foreign media, leading to what has been called "*los años del silencio*" (years of the silence).

While silence settled in Equatorial Guinea, what could be described as a discourse of resistance began to take shape outside the country's boundaries. Most Equatorial Guinean writers in exile lived in Spain at the time of the takeover. The vast majority were students who became de facto exiles when Macias seized power, forming what Edmundo Sepa Bomaba calls "La Guinea de la Diáspora" (the Diaspora Guinea). The cultural production of the diaspora was semiclandestine, disseminated through an underground distribution circuit. Given these precarious circumstances, it failed to reach most individuals of the diaspora and even less of a large Spanish readership. Nonetheless, adversity and marginality were being articulated into a site of resistance. Both of these experiences became stepping stones for constructing a discourse of common national identity in exile, that is, a national project that transcended ethnic division and differences. Produced from the geography of trans-territoriality, in which the nation exists wherever its people are, this diaspora literature was, despite its varied discursive practices and forms of expression, the first attempt to condense and reflect on national unity and identity.

In the early 1970s, the Spanish government declared Equatorial Guinea *materia reservada* (classified information) and imposed a total blackout on all news coming out of the country. Further, all organized opposition to Macías Nguema's regime was prohibited. Thus, Equatorial Guinean exile writing sought to build a sense of national unity by drawing upon the common experience of shared oppression, dislocation, and pain. These literary texts were mainly poetic and characterized by what Balboa Boneke described as *la orfandad de tierra* (orphanhood of land). On the one hand, texts were permeated by nostalgic evocations and descriptions of Equato-Guinean geographies as a lost, distant, forbidden land. The writings also narrated the traumatic experience of exile in a foreign land. This experience of displacement and dislocation can be found in Balboa Boneke's poetry collections *O' Boriba (El exilio)* (1981; O'Boriba [The Exile]) and *Susurros y pensamientos comentados: desde mi vidriera* (1983; Whispers and Thoughts: From My Window); Raquel Ilonbe's *Ceiba* (1978), Francisco Zamora Loboch's poem "Prisionero de la Gran Vía" (1984; Prisoner of the Gran Vía [a main thoroughfare in Madrid]), Pedro Cristino Bueriberi's "Nostalgia de mi tierra" (1984; Nostalgia for My Land)", and Maplal Loboch's

Lamento sobre Annobón, Belleza y soledad (1984; Lament on Annobón, Beauty and Solitude).

Other texts are openly subversive and denounce the violence wrought upon Equatorial Guinea and its citizenry, as in Anacleto Oló Mibuy's *A un joven fusilado en Santa Isabel* (1984; To a Youth Executed in Santa Isabel). In some cases, violence, a call for insurrection, and the elimination of the tyrant mediate the poetry of such authors as Francisco Zamora Loboch, in "Vamos a matar al tirano" (Let's Kill the Tyrant).

Fiction and nonfiction prose were other alternative discursive practices used by writers in exile to describe the traumatic experience in Equatorial Guinea. *Nueva narrativa guineana* (1977; New Guinean Narrative), a collection of short stories by Francisco Abeso, Francisco Zamora Loboch, Donato Ndongo-Bidyogo, and Maplal Loboch and the anthology *Poetas guineanos en el exilio* (198?; Guinean Poets in Exile) were published, according to Donato Ndongo, to raise funds for anti-Macías political resistance. These works represent the first legitimate attempt to represent Equatorial Guinea as a multiethnic, multicultural nation with no loyalty to any specific ethnic group; that is, an entity with an "official" national identity. They also narrate the experience of forced displacement and exile. Eugenio Nkogo Ondo's *La condición humana* (1985; The Human Condition) and Balboa Boneke's *¿Dónde estás Guinea?* (1978; Where Are You Guinea?) re-create the quest for identity as way to overcome the fragmentation, dislocation, and alienation caused by exile.

Nearly 20 years after the *Golpe de libertad* (Freedom Coup), cultural reality in Equatorial Guinea remains mediated by fragmentation. The vast majority of writers still operate from trans-territoriality. Equatorial Guinean cultural creators continue to search for national identity and, as Ndongo-Bidyogo argues, his novel *Las tinieblas de tu memoria negra* (1987; *Shadows of your Black Memory*, 2007) tries to answer a series of questions: Who is the Guinean? Why is the Guinean like this, and not different? (*¿Quién es el guineano? ¿Por qué el guineano es así y no de otra manera?*) In Equatorial Guinea, literature appears to be a leading platform for developing and voicing national identity. Marked by deterritorialization and dislocation on one hand, and cultural ethnic heterogeneity on the other, it is diverse, open to influences, and mediated by tension.

M'Bare N'Gom

See also Equatorial Guinea: Writers Living in the United States; Equatorial Guinea's *Generación del Silencio* (The Generation of Silence).

Work About:

Cusack, Igor. "Hispanic and Bantu Inheritance, Trauma, Dispersal and Return: Some Contributions to a Sense of National Identity in Equatorial Guinea." *Nations and Nationalism* 5.2 (1999): 207–236.

Mbomio Bacheng, Joaquín. *El párroco de Niefang*. Malabo: Centro Cultural Hispano-Guineano, 1996.

Ndongo-Bidyogo, Donato. *Antología de la literatura guineana*. Madrid: Nacional, 1984.

Ndongo-Bidyogo, Donato. Letter to M'Bare N'Gom from Malabo, Equatorial Guinea dated October 22, 1990.

Oló Mibuy, Anacleto. "Gritos de libertad y de esperanza" (poesías). *Africa 2000* 2.4–5 (1987): 14, 34.

Ugarte, Michael. *Africans in Europe. The Culture of Exile and Emigration from Equatorial Guinea to Spain*. Chicago and Urbana: University of Illinois Press, 2010.

Wa Thiong'o, Ngugi. "The Culture of Silence and Fear." *South* (May 1984): 37–38.

Equatorial Guinea: Writers Living in the United States

The intellectual production of Equato-Guinean writers living in the United States in recent decades has grown substantially, while remaining largely beyond the periphery of conventional academic fields (such as Latin American, Spanish, Latino, Afro-Hispanic, African American, and African Studies). As in the case of writers working from Equatorial Guinea itself, this efflorescence has followed the securing of independence from Spain on October 12, 1968, and has been most prominent from the late 1980s. These authors represent a variegated spectrum: despite their common migration (forced or voluntary) to the United States, their differing ethnic origins are often reflected in radically disparate approaches to their history and their individual and collective pasts.

Born in Luba (on the island of Bioko) into a Fernandino and Bubi family, Juan

Manuel Davies Eiso (1948–) was sent in his late teens to attend university in Spain. From there, he witnessed the moment of his country's independence. Faced with the impossibility of a prompt return, he came to form part of the so-called *Generación perdida* (lost generation) comprised of the educated youth—from elite Equato-Guinean families—who were excluded from postindependence projects of the Francisco Macías dictatorship (1968–1979). Moving to the United States in the 1970s, Davies Eiso became a prolific writer committed to the cultures of his native island, and to his country's constant political struggles for democracy and freedom. He has authored two poetry books: *Abiono* (2004) offers homage to a young cousin whose life ended prematurely, and *Héroes* (2008; Heroes) presents an encomium to a range of leaders from Guinea's ethnic groups at the dawn of independence, who were erased from the public imagination by the two regimes in power to date. He is also engaged in a long-term project to publish a series of illustrated traditional oral narratives from Bioko, echoing stories he heard from his grandfather, sitting in a circle with other children from the community. These publications currently include *La guerra de Hormelef* (2005; Hormelef's War), *La huida de Mamá Uro* (2005; Mama Uro's Escape), and *Nsabi* (2009); they contain lessons in moral wisdom and ethnic tradition as well as complex cosmologies. Finally, Davies Eiso is the author of two important novelistic essays that critique the historical and political developments of his country since independence through an autobiographical prism: *Siete días en Bioko* (2007; Seven Days in Bioko), and *El rincón de Polopó* (2009; Polopó's Corner).

Of Bubi ancestry, Gerardo Behori Sipi Botau (1960–) is originally from Rebola (on Bioko island), but moved to the United States in the 1990s, in the face of his country's political intransigence. He has published extensively in collective volumes, and his first book—a work of poetry—is titled *Sueños y realidad* (2009; Dreams and Reality). He has two forthcoming projects: a second poetry collection and a volume of essays on the sociology of the Bubi people in connection with postindependence political developments.

Enenge A'Bodjedi (1963–) belongs to the Bobalo clan of Mapanga (a Ndowé ethnic group) and was born in the city of Bata (Río Muni). He came to the United States as a child following his father's appointment as Equatorial Guinea's ambassador to the United Nations during the Nixon administration. He returned to Equatorial Guinea as a student, to gather oral narratives from Ndowé elders, and to master the language and linguistics. In 1998, in New York, he founded the Ndowé International Press, an editorial enterprise devoted to disseminating scholarly work by Ndowé authors writing in English, Spanish, French, and the various Ndowé languages. One of the press's first publications was A'Bodjedi's *Ndowé Tales* (1999), translated into Spanish as *Cuentos Ndowé* (2003; Ndowé Stories). This collection of 15 tales, in an annotated edition with glossary, introduces nonspecialists to the Ndowé worldview and forms of knowledge.

A'Bodjedi's next publications follow an epistemic practice discussed earlier in association with Davies Eiso—illustrated traditional tales, this time in English, with a strong didactic function. As of 2009, he has published *The Present for a Relative* (2004), on the different species of animals; *Tortoise and Gazelle* (2005), a warning to be attentive to what animals say; and *Tortoise, Chameleon, and Lizard* (2005), on the virtues of hard work and dedication. A'Bodjedi has written several essays on American Presbyterian missions in the Ndowé territories. He has reconstructed the history of the nine Presbyterian churches established between 1843 and 1890, along with associated sociopolitical, economic, and cultural transformations in the Ndowé society. He has also written about the 13 Ndowé Presbyterian ministers ordained in their territories between 1870 and 1961, examining the ways in which these Ndowé ministers used the written word, in combination with oratory, to resist Western imperialism during the 19th and 20th centuries. Finally, his writings and professional lectures on the Ndowé ritual use of the hallucinogenic *iboga* plant, and on Ndowé tales and proverbs of psychiatric content, represent concrete examples of how West African Ndowé medical practices and forms of knowledge dialogue with traditional Western medicine (A'Bodjedi practices as a physician in New York). His two forthcoming books are provisionally titled *Ancestral Voices*, and *Bweti. An African Near-Death Experience.*

Born in Egombegombe (Río Muni), Adolfo Obiang Bikó (1940–) is the direct descendant of Ngwa-Nzé or Ngwaza, who was the supreme chief of all Fang peoples in Equatorial Guinea in about 1840, and cosignatory of several treaties with German, French, and English traders, and with Spain, that eventually led to the Spanish colonial presence in the country. He is also the great-grandson of Obama-Nveiñg, a notorious Fang-Atamakek chieftain and freedom fighter against Spanish colonialism who was executed by the colonial government in Puerto Iradier (now Kogo) in the early 20th century. His life and family history steeped in politics, Obiang Bikó arrived in the United States in the mid-1960s as the political observer to the United Nations of the MONALIGE (National Movement for the Liberation of Equatorial Guinea), a party which he helped found, and as its representative to the United States; he also belonged to the foreign section of MONALIGE's executive committee during the struggle for independence. He participated actively in drafting a constitution and advocating the country's independence both in Spain and the United Nations in 1967–1968. After campaigning unsuccessfully for his party during the elections that led to the first postindependence government, he worked with different lobbies and organizations in Washington, DC, to establish a political group in exile to oppose the dictatorship of Francisco Macías Nguema (1968–1979) and the regime of Teodoro Obiang Nguema (1979–present). A frequent guest speaker at academic and political gatherings, and on TV and radio programs, he has penned numerous essays and three books. *Guinea*

Ecuatorial. Del colonialismo español al descubrimiento del petróleo (2000; Equatorial Guinea. From Spanish Colonialism to the Discovery of Oil) and *Fernando Poo: The Myth of Spanish Colonialism* (1994) are both narrative histories of his country, imprinted with his firsthand political experiences. Most recently, he published in New York, *Naked Like the Others. In Prison in Gabon, Africa* (2006), a denunciatory memoir of his years in the jails of Equatorial Guinea's West African neighbor.

The momentum of Equato-Guinean literary recognition in the United States appears to be increasing. The first English-language translation of a novel by an Equato-Guinean writer—Donato Ndongo Bidyogo's *Las tinieblas de tu memoria negra* (1987; *Shadows of your Black Memory*, 2007)—was recently published, and the translation of María Nsue Angüe's pioneering novel *Ekomo* (1985) is forthcoming. Other Equato-Guinean intellectuals residing in the United States, among them Annobonese lawyer, human rights activist, and executive founder of EGJustice Tutu Alicante (1973–), have played key roles in promoting the visibility of their nation, and its current challenges.

Benita Sampedro Vizcaya

See also Equatorial Guinea: Writers in Exile; Equatorial Guinea's *Generación del Silencio* (The Generation of Silence).

Work By:

A'Bodjedi, Enenge. *Ndowé Tales*. New York: Ndowe International Press, 1999.

Davis Eiso, Juan Manuel. *El rincón de Polopó*. Barcelona: Mey, 2009.

Davis Eiso, Juan Manuel. *La Guerra de Hormelef*. Barcelona: Carena, 2005.

Davis Eiso, Juan Manuel. *Siete días en Bioko*. Barcelona: Carena, 2007.

EG Justice: http://www.egjustice.org/.

Ndongo Bidyogo, Donato. *Shadows of Your Black Memory*. Chicago: Swan Isle, 2007.

Sipi Botau, Gerardo Behori. *Sueños y realidad*. Barcelona: Mey, 2009.

Equatorial Guinea's *Generación del Silencio* (The Generation of Silence)

This is the name Equatorial Guinean writer Donato Ndongo Bidyogo gave to a group of writers, intellectuals, and artists from Equatorial Guinea who lived their early adulthood during the years of the dictatorship of Francisco Macías (1968–1979). In Donato Ndongo Bidyogo's influential *Antología de la literatura guineana* (1984; Anthology of Guinean Literature) he refers to the years of exile and lack of literary production inside Equatorial Guinea as "the years of silence." Another writer, Juan Balboa Boneke, calls this group *la Generación perdida* (the lost generation). Representative writers of this first generation of Equatorial Guinean writers after independence include Donato Ndongo Bidyogo, Francisco Zamora Loboch, Maplal Loboch (father of Francisco Zamora Lobach), Raquel Ilonbé, Ciríaco Bokesa, Juan Balboa Boneke, Julián Bibeng Oyee, Eugenio Nkogo Ondo, Cristino Bueriberi Bokesa, Anacleto Oló Mibuy,

Joaquín Mbomio Bacheng, and María Nsue Angüe.

Writers of the *Generación del Silencio* can be divided in two groups, those who chose or found themselves in exile during the Macías dictatorship, and those who survived the dictatorship inside the country. The experience of *Nguemismo*, as the political regime of Macías Nguema is known, and the end of colonialism mark their work even during the first decade of the 21st century in ways that distinguish them from the younger group of Equatorial Guinean writers who experienced the Macías regime in their childhood or adolescence, or who were born, in some cases, after 1979.

Given the peculiarities of Equatorial Guinea's independence process and the almost total absence of formal education for blacks during the Spanish colonial period, writers of the *Generación del Silencio* did not have a national anticolonial discourse of their own. One of their tasks during the period of exile and after the end of the Macías regime in 1979 was to carry out a critique of the Spanish colonial past, which until then had been presented as benevolent. At the same time, they dismissed the Macías regime's anti-Spanish speeches that justified the suppression of all intellectual activity in the country, as the regime prohibited the use of Spanish in writing and even the possession of books or papers written in Spanish.

With the death of General Francisco Franco in Spain (1975) and an easing of the political climate, for the first time Equatorial Guinean exiles found a chance to denounce the process of decolonization and the Macías dictatorship. Historical essay was the tool employed in two main works: Donato Ndongo's *Historia y tragedia de Guinea Ecuatorial* (1977; History and Tragedy of Equatorial Guinea) and Eugenio Nkogo's collection of shorter essays, *El problema humano* (1985; The Human Problem).

The point of departure for this "generation of silence" is *Nueva narrativa guineana* (1977; New Guinean Narrative), with four short stories: "El sueño" (The Dream) and "La travesía" (The Middle Passage) by Donato Ndongo, "Bea" by Francisco Zamora Loboch, and "La última carta del Padre Fulgencio Abad, C.M.F" (The Last Letter of Father Fulgencio Abad, C.M.F.) by Maplal Loboch, published posthumously. This four-story booklet was compiled specifically to obtain funds for opposition to the Macías regime; it also established the basis of Equatorial Guinean literature as no other publication had before. The stories touch on four different themes of postcolonial literature: "El sueño" and "Bea" tell narratives of the African migration to Europe after independence, "La travesía" offers a fictional slave narrative, and "La última carta . . . " presents an ironic evaluation of the colonial period and its cultural and religious impositions.

The 1970s saw almost all literary and intellectual production come to a standstill in the country, as *Generación del Silencio* writers shared the experience of exile or imprisonment. Most writers in exile lived in Spain, where they had been studying since about 1968. They wrote despite the vacuum of readership, as Equatorial Guinean society was totally isolated and education levels had plummeted. At the same time, General Franco's Spanish government decreed all matters related to Equatorial Guinea to be *materia reservada* (classified information) and no books or newspaper articles could be published about Spain's former colony. Some writers—Bokesa, Matogo, Simplicio Nsue Avoro, Secundino Oyono—who had been active in the years prior to 1968, remained unaccounted for even five years after the end of the Macías dictatorship, according to Ndongo's anthology.

Poetry became the preferred genre for *Generación del Silencio* members. Exile, nostalgia, and the denunciation of Equatorial Guinea's political situation were the common thread of poetic production between 1968 and approximately 1985. Zamora Loboch's "Salvad a Copito" (Save Copito), dedicated to the Barcelona zoo's famous albino gorilla; "El prisionero de la Gran Vía" (The Prisoner of Gran Vía Street), a cry of the loneliness of exile in the center of Madrid, the former capital metropolis of Equatorial Guinea; and "Nuestros eróticos viciosos círculos" (Our Corrupt Erotic Circles)—a longer elegy to the African diaspora over centuries—summarize the best of this poetry. Balboa Boneke, like other writers, responded to the oppression of Equatorial Guinea's ethnic culture during the Macías dictatorship with the bilingual composition, "O Bulahelea/Deseo de libertad" (O Bulahelea/Desire of Freedom), published in *O Boriba (El exiliado)* (1982; O Boriba [The Exile]). Balboa Boneke

made his exile in Spain the central theme of *¿Dónde estás Guinea?* (1978; Where Are You Guinea?); his novel *El reencuentro: el retorno del exiliado* (1985; Meeting Again: The Exile's Return); and his two books of poetry, the abovementioned *O Boriba*, and *Desde mi vidriera (susurros y pensamientos comentados* (1983; From My Window [Whispers and Thoughts Explained]). Ilonbé, one of the group's few women writers, chose a less overtly political, more mystical tone to express nostalgia for the lost land and the sentiment of imprisonment in her collection of poetry titled *Ceiba* (1977).

The decade of the 1980s was the period of maturity for the majority of these writers. In 1985, Nsué published *Ekomo*, the first novel ever published by an Equatorial Guinean woman. The protagonist is a young Fang woman, whose story of love and betrayal by her husband moves her to reject the role traditionally reserved for widows in Fang society; this occurs amidst a mythical past that announces tragic times that African independent countries will experience in the future decade of the 1960s. In 1987, Donato Ndongo published *Las tinieblas de tu memoria negra* (*Shadows of Your Black Memory*, 2007) in the *bildungsroman* (coming-of-age story) tradition. Its protagonist, a young Equatorial Guinean seminarian, reflects on his childhood and adolescence during the last years of Spanish colonial rule, in which Francoist education, Catholic religion, and the traditional Fang worldview coexisted in both subtle and violent confrontation. The nameless male protagonist learns to be a translator of ideas and words for two antagonistic worlds that have put their future hopes in him. The choice of a Catholic seminarian reflects the fact that many writers of the *Generación del Silencio* were or had been Catholic priests, or had attended Bonapá Seminary in Equatorial Guinea. The same nameless protagonist faces the ravages of the Macías dictatorship on his return to the now independent country in Ndongo's second novel, *Los poderes de la tempestad* (1998; The Powers of the Storm).

The work of writers who spent the Macías period inside Equatorial Guinea started to appear only a decade after the dictator's death. Such is the case of Mbomio Bacheng, who was imprisoned by Macías and condemned to forced labor. He has published two novels that give testimony of that time: *El párroco de Niefang* (1996; Niefang Parish Priest) and *Huellas bajo tierra* (1998; Underground Markings). The publication of *El Patio*, the literary magazine sponsored by the Centro Cultural Hispano-Guineano, and *África 2000*, allowed some of these silenced writers to resume publishing or publish for the first time. This was true for Antimo Esono (1954–1996) and Bokesa. These two magazines, the work of Ndongo Bidyogo and *Generación del Silencio* authors, allowed the public of Equatorial Guinea to read literature by exiled writers for the first time.

After the change of regime in 1979, some *Generación del Silencio* writers returned to the country. Most of them, however, ran afoul of the new president, Teodoro Obiang Nguema. Initially invited to participate in the new political situation, authors including Donato Ndongo, Balboa Boneke, and Anacleto Oló Mibuy returned from exile. Of them, only Oló Mibuy continued to reside in the country and participate in politics after 1995. Nsue divides her life between Madrid and Malabo. In their public presentations, most writers of this generation have expressed disillusionment at the lack of political freedom under the Obiang regime.

Baltasar Fra-Molinero

See also Equatorial Guinea: Poets; Equatorial Guinea: Writers in Exile; Equatorial Guinea: Writers Living in the United States.

Work About:

Lewis, Marvin A. *An Introduction to the Literature of Equatorial Guinea: Between Colonialism and Dictatorship.* Columbia: University of Missouri Press, 2007.

Ndongo Bidyogo, Donato. *Antología de la literatura guineana.* Madrid: Nacional, 1984.

Ndongo Bidyogo, Donato, and Mbare Ngom. *Literatura de Guinea Ecuatorial (Antología).* Madrid: Casa de África, 2000.

Ugarte, Michael. *Africans in Europe. The Culture of Exile and Emigration from Equatorial Guinea to Spain.* Chicago and Urbana: University of Illinois Press, 2010.

Erauso, Catalina de (1592–1650)

This Basque writer is recognized for her dramatic autobiographical novel, *La monja alférez* (1626; The Lieutenant Nun, 1997), that details her escape from a San

Sebastián convent and subsequent travels and adventures throughout Peru and Chile. Erauso's text is considered a hyperbolized account of her life story, but it is the only extant memoir from her, and as such, is treated as nonfiction. Two 17th-century dramatists, Luis Belmonte Bermúdez and Juan Pérez de Montalbán, also wrote plays based on Erauso's life.

Erauso recounts how, as a teenager, she escaped the convent, cut her hair, and began cross-dressing to attain mobility in Spain and, later, the New World. Once on American soil, her travels assumed a dynamic, incessant nature: Erauso frequently fought with groups of men, argued over gambling bets, fled crime scenes, and assumed multiple masculine identities. She also comments on her potential romantic relationships with other women, brief stints in local jails, and her opinion of certain ethnic and racial groups, particularly indigenous and black. She consistently refers to herself in the masculine, intentionally estranging herself from her true gender. Whether Erauso did so to maintain the integrity of her travels or out of concern that society see her as a man is debated.

Erauso's transgressions finally catch up with her when she is sentenced to death for murder. To save herself, she confesses her true gender to a local bishop and eventually returns to Europe. Once there, Pope Urban VIII allows her to continue dressing as a man and Phillip IV of Spain awards her a pension. She lived out the rest of her life in Mexico, purportedly working as a mule driver.

Bonnie L. Gasior

See also Gender in Spanish Literature.

Work By:

Erauso, Catalina de. *The Lieutenant Nun.* Trans. Michele Stepto and Gabriel Stepto. Boston: Beacon, 1997.

Work About:

Merrim, Stephanie. "From Anomaly to Icon." *Coded Encounters: Writing, Gender, and Ethnicity in Colonial Latin America.* Ed. Francisco Javier Cevallos-Candau. Amherst: University of Massachusetts Press, 1994, 177–205.

Perry, Mary Elizabeth. "From Convent to Battlefield: Cross-Dressing and Gendering the Self in the New World of Imperial Spain." *Queer Iberia: Sexualities, Cultures, and Crossings from the Middle Ages to the Renaissance.* Ed. Josiah Blackmore and Gregory S. Hutcheson. Durham, NC: Duke University Press, 1999, 394–419.

Velasco, Sherry. *The Lieutenant Nun: Transgenderism, Lesbian Desire, and Catalina de Erauso.* Austin: University of Texas Press, 2000.

Eroticism in Contemporary Spanish Women Writers: 1975 to Present

In her essay "Erotismo y literatura" (1992; Eroticism and Literature), Ana María *Moix explains that after the sexual liberation provoked by Freud's psychoanalytical theories, sex ceased being a taboo subject and opened new options for writers. In Spain, however, Francisco Franco's dictatorship (1939–1975) continued to impose strict morality through *censorship. Following his death, Spain experienced *el destape* (the undressing), as Catholic influence waned and naked women appeared in the media and arts. The whirl of new freedoms acquired during the transition to democracy allowed writers to introduce elements of sexual awakening. Thus, Rosa *Chacel, Esther *Tusquets, Moix, Carme Riera, and Rosa *Montero became pioneers by defying gender roles and exploring sexual alternatives like homosexuality and bisexuality in their writing. Moix, Tusquets, and Riera examine lesbianism and demystify the patriarchal ideology. Additionally, Riera and Moix have highlighted the significance that seduction and sensuality play in erotic texts, allowing ambiguity and innuendo to characterize many of their works.

In the Catalan-language short fiction collection *Epitelis tendríssims* (1981; Very Tender Ephithelia), Riera presents absurd, humorous situations but also serious moments, as in "Joseph Luis Jacotot agonitza," in which a young girl is sexually exploited by her family. Women authors reveal abuses and other deviations as in "Alice" (found in *Relatos eróticos*; [1990; Erotic Short Stories]), in which Lourdes Ortiz portrays a pedophile, echoing Lewis Carroll's *Alice in Wonderland*.

In addition to new freedom and relaxed moral codes, in 1977 new events helped to promote erotic literature in Spain. The Bruguera publishing house facilitated access to erotica by launching the *Clásicos del erotismo* series, and Tusquets initiated the collection "La Sonrisa Vertical" (The

Vertical Smile) collection and awarded an annual prize to new erotic prose in Spanish.

As Spain reached full democracy, erotic literature included detailed sexual encounters described in explicit language. In *Un espacio erótico* (1982; An Erotic Space), Marta Portal reveals different types of abuse and humiliation suffered by Elvira in the course of her marriage in México, and the exploration of her sexuality in a love triangle with a colleague and her female cousin in Spain. The same year, Consuelo García completed *Luis en el país de las maravillas* (1982; Luis in Wonderland), a novel that criticizes male chauvinism and pokes fun at men's insecurities and ignorance regarding female sexuality. María Jaén published the Catalan-language *Amorrada al piló* (1986; The Neckline) and *La sauna* (1987; The Sauna), novels whose protagonists are sexually liberated, financially independent, and eager to experience new pleasures.

Mercedes Abad became the first Spanish woman to earn the La Sonrisa Vertical prize for *Ligeros libertinajes sabáticos* (1986; Frivolous Weekend Libertines). Her short stories introduce a pivotal change by depicting all manner of sexual transgressions—orgies, sadomasochism, necrophilia—performed by eccentric and absurd characters. Her collection opened the door to works interweaving perversions, violence, and sex. Abad claims that all eroticism is pornography and that, at times, descriptive sexual encounters are boring. Certainly, not all critics and writers agree. Another La Sonrisa Vertical–winner featuring sexual deviance is

Almudena *Grandes's best-selling *Las edades de Lulú* (1989; *The Ages of Lulú*, 1994). This novel marked the boom in erotic literature by Spanish women and raised great controversy for the risky sexual practices presented and the depiction of a character driven primarily by lust.

Following readers' interest in erotic literature, Castalia and the Instituto de la Mujer publishers produced *Relatos eróticos* (1990; Erotic Short Stories), tales written by Argentina's Susana Constante and Spanish authors Paloma *Díaz-Mas, Marina *Mayoral, the earlier-mentioned Ortiz, Ana *Rossetti, and Tusquets. Scholar Janet Pérez has noted the compilation's common features: frequent subplots, interruptions and humorous deviations, women's ability to separate love and eroticism for women, depiction of sexual deviance and unconventional sexual practices, varied technique and form, and disinterest in the size of male genitalia.

In other works, size and appearance do take on significance, as in Mayoral's *Recuerda, cuerpo* (1998; Remember, Body). In her tales, the penis is admired for its beauty, exotic features, and sexual prowess but also mocked when it fails to excite or perform satisfactorily. Because gender roles are inverted in women's erotic writing, the male body attains visual importance, as the female gaze undresses and explores what has been covered for centuries. Increasing interest in the male physique motivates *Verte desnudo* (1992; Seeing You Naked), a multiauthored collection focused on different parts of the male anatomy: the mouth, neck, chest, belly button, hands, genitalia, buttocks,

and feet. Two of the nine stories are written by Clara *Janés and Rossetti, acclaimed poets with strong erotic components in their work, especially the latter. Janés plays with erotic discovery, sexual pleasure, and exotic undertones in *Eros* (1983), *Vivir* (1986; To Live), and *Creciente fértil* (1989; Fertile Crescent). Her short story "La boca: El banquete" (The Mouth: The Feast) seduces the reader with a retrospective narration of intimate encounters filled with feasts of fruits, erotic games, and many pleasures awakened by Nuri, the man who has pleased her as no other. In "Dedicado a sus plantas" (Dedicated to His Soles), Rossetti combines fetishisms, homosexuality and religious rituals. She earned the La Sonrisa Vertical prize for *Alevosías* (1991; Treacheries), in which she incorporates her usual themes in highly poetic prose. Prior to this recognition of her prose, Rossetti published many critically acclaimed poetry books with innovative erotic language and exquisite expression. Her texts expose an array of sexual boundaries ranging from varied sexual activities to sexual traumas and pathological cases.

Although the La Sonrisa Vertical prize was canceled in 2004 due to the progressive integration of the genre and the general inattention that critics have given to awarded works, the collection remains active. Tusquets and other publishers have helped promote erotic works by careful marketing and book releases at different seasons: *Cuentos eróticos de Navidad* (1999; Erotic Short Stories for Christmas) and *Cuentos eróticos de verano* (2007; Erotic Short Stories for Summer), and even Valentine's Day, *Cuentos eróticos de San Valentín* (2007; Valentine's Day Short Stories). Even though these three works produced by Tusquets offer a larger selection of stories authored by men, noted women authors also continue to delight readers. Abad and Moix penned two new stories in the Christmas collection. Abad plays with common techniques and themes—mystery, cruelty, masturbation, and a conspiratorial irony in "Ideogramas húmedos" ("Wet Ideograms"). Mysterious undertones take a tragic turn in Moix's "Un árbol en el jardín" ("A Tree in the Garden") whose protagonist hangs himself because he has lost his vital desire and is unable to perform sexually. Having heard that death by hanging obtains an erection, he thus shows his wife that he died aroused. In the summer collection, Rossetti plays with passion and spells in the relationship between Miriam and Joaquín, who end up joined for eternity in "La noche de los enamorados" (The Lovers' Night).

In the late 1990s, a new controversial author began to publish novels in which sexual freedom and the desire to live each day to the fullest became ordinary. Lucía *Etxebarria received notable attention when *Amor, curiosidad, prozac y dudas* (1997; Love, Curiosity, Prozac, and Doubts) and *Beatriz y los cuerpos celestes: una novela rosa* (1998; Beatriz and the Celestial Bodies: A Romantic Novel) were released. Each novel deals with sexual practices and recreational drugs motivated by consumerism, apathy, or a quest for a harmonious identity. Etxebarria's characters embody a generation lacking the sexual repressions and inhibitions that

predominated in previous decades. Nevertheless, the marketing of Etxebarria's works and her persona propitiated heated discussions about the role of the mass market in the boom of literature written by women and questions regarding sales, visibility, and quality. Contemporary authors offer new models of female subjectivity and relationships where sex is neither a taboo nor a surprise. Spanish women writers' works display a wide range of themes, techniques, and subversions in the erotic genre, but now that descriptions of sexual practices with explicit or implicit expression are commonplace, eroticism and sexuality may cease to be seen as literary transgressions.

Mayte de Lama

See also Gender in Spanish Literature; Short Fiction in Spain: 1900 to Present; Women Writers in Spain: 1900 to Present.

Work About:

Bermúdez, Silvia. "Let's Talk About Sex?: From Almudena Grandes to Lucía Etxebarria, the Volatile Values of the Spanish Market." *Women's Narrative and Film in Twentieth-Century Fiction Spain: A World of Difference(s)*. Ed. Ofelia Ferrán and Kathleen Glenn. New York: Routledge, 2002, 223–37.

Drinkwater, Judith. " 'Esta cárcel de amor': Erotic Fiction by Women in Spain in the 1980s and 1990s." *Letras Femeninas* 21.1–2 (1995): 97–111.

Maginn, Alison. "Female Erotica in Post-Franco Spain: The Will-to-Disturb." *Ciberletras: Revista de crítica literaria y de cultura* 8 (2002). http://www

.lehman.cuny.edu/ciberletras/v08/maginn
.html.

Pérez, Janet. "Characteristics of Erotic Brief Fiction by Women in Spain." *Monographic Review/Revista Monográfica* 7 (1991): 173–95.

Escobar Galindo, David (1943–)

Born in El Salvador, this professor, attorney, and poet also founded and, as of fall 2009, is the current president of Dr. José Matías Delgado University in San Salvador. To date, he has published nearly 100 texts, including 62 poetry books, 10 short story collections, two novels, and two collections of fables. He has used his personal experiences during the violent, pre–civil war years (1971–1979) as inspiration for his fiction. The best-selling psychological novel *Una grieta en el agua* (1972; A Crack in the Water) is built around a character's kidnapping by revolutionaries. In reality, Escobar Galindo's father was kidnapped and later released for ransom in the 1970s; the play *Después de medianoche* (1988; After Midnight) also explores this theme. Escobar Galindo's poetry for adults addresses wartime experiences, as well as religion, love, and peace. His verse for children, however, draws from fables and mythology, as in *Fábulas* (1979; Fables).

The most prolific and prizewinning author in Salvadoran history, Escobar Galindo also figures as a key player in national politics: He helped negotiate the 1986 Peace Accord between El Salvador and Honduras, and the accord that ended El Salvador's Civil War, signed January, 16, 1992.

Rhina Toruño-Haensly

Work By:

Casi todos los ángeles tienen alas. San Salvador: Delgado, Universidad Dr. José Matías Delgado, 2007.

Work About:

Montes, Hugo. "Poesía de David Escobar Galindo." *Revista Chilena de Literatura* 59 (Nov 2001): 111–16.

Escoto, Julio (1944–)

This Honduran novelist, essayist, and nonfiction and short story writer focuses on questions of identity from the personal to the national level. At an early age, Escoto began writing short stories based on his experiences of everyday life, and then moved to a consideration of regional and national topics within a historical context.

His first published short story collection was *La balada del herido pájaro* (1969?; Dance of the Wounded Bird). Three years later, *Bajo el almendro . . . junto al volcán* (1988; Under the Almond Tree . . . Next to the Volcano) takes as its starting point the July 1969 four-day "Soccer War" between Honduras and El Salvador, in which rising tensions related to the illegal immigration of Salvadorans (fleeing their nation's civil war violence) to Honduras coincided with a riot during the second qualifying match between the two countries at the 1970 FIFA

(International Federation of Football Association) World Cup.

In 1990, two nonfiction volumes by Escoto were published. *El ojo santo: La ideología en las religiones y la televisión* (The Holy Eye: Ideology in Religion and Television) reflects on spirituality in terms of inner harmony, while *José Cecilio del Valle: Una ética contemporánea* (José Cecilio del Valle: A Contemporary Ethic) profiles the leader of Honduras's and Central America's early 19th-century independence movement. Similarly, *El general Morazán marcha a batallar desde la muerte* (1992; General Morazán Comes Back to Fight from His Death) celebrates a Central American advocate of unification.

Escoto's most acclaimed novel, *Rey del albor: Madrugada* (1993; King of the Dawn: Madrugada), combines fiction and history to explore Honduran history and highlight ongoing U.S. intervention in Central American politics. As Craft explains, Madrugada is the code name for a secret U.S. plot to use information technology to manipulate and ultimately control Central America. As part of this agenda, a U.S. professor, Jones, is sent to Honduras to rewrite its national history and to erase/rewrite all mention of the negative role the United States has played and manipulate the historical record of actions by other nations. Jones soon becomes aware of the Madrugada conspiracy and, as he works backward through the historical records, he also collaborates secretly with the underground and tries to hack into Madrugada. Among other observations, Craft notes that the parallels drawn between Honduras's present-day cultural situation and that of the 16th century imply the need to support a polyethnic national identity. More recently, Escoto published *El génesis, en Santa Cariba* (2006; Genesis in Santa Cariba).

Maureen Ihrie

Work By:

Rey del albor, Madrugada. San Pedro Sula, Honduras: Centro, 1993.

Work About:

Craft, Linda. "Ethnicity, Oral Tradition and the Processed Word: Construction of a National Identity in Honduras." *Kánina* 23.1 (1999): 157–66.

Espronceda, José de (1808–1842)

One of Spain's most prominent romantic poets, his literature diverges into two periods marked by his exile from Spain for his liberal political stance. Espronceda followed neoclassic aesthetics until his stay in London (?–1833), where he embraced the romanticism practiced by British poets like Byron. After returning to Spain, he became active politically and spearheaded the romantic movement there.

He practiced journalism, wrote plays, and penned novels like *Sancho Saldaña* (1835), but is best remembered for his poetry, which touches on such topics as politics in "El verdugo" (1835; The Executioner), freedom and individualism in "La canción del pirata" (1840; Song of the Pirate), and extreme, painful love in

"Canto a Teresa" (1840; Song for Teresa). His best-known collections of poetry are *El estudiante de Salamanca* (1837; *The Student of Salamanca*, 1991) and *El Diablo Mundo* (1840; The Devil World). The first provides a textbook example of romanticism with its hero's individualism and his incarnation as diabolical hero, laughing at God and the Devil, rebelling for rebellion's own sake. The poem's heroine Elvira embodies the recurring romantic theme of a victim, pure and beautiful, riddled by pains of love. The second collection voices a strong preoccupation with existential issues of pessimism and a questioning of God's relationship with the world.

Vicente Gomis-Izquierdo

See also Enlightenment in Spain: 1700–1800; Romanticism in Spain.

Work By:

El Diablo Mundo. El Pelayo. Poesías. Ed. Domingo Ynduráin. Madrid: Cátedra, 2004.

El estudiante de Salamanca. The Student of Salamanca. Trans. C. K. Davies. Ed. Richard A. Cardwell. Warminster, UK: Aris & Phillips, 1991.

Work About:

Schurlknight, Donald. "Of Subversion and Narratology: *El estudiante de Salamanca.*" *Letras Peninsulares* 12.2–3 (1999–2000): 171–83.

Talens, Jenaro. "The Collapse of Literature as Institutionalized Discourse: Espronceda's *El diablo mundo.*" *The Crisis of Institutionalized Literature in Spain.* Ed. Wlad Godzich and Nicholas Spadaccini. Minneapolis: Prisma, 1988, 67–97.

Esquivel, Laura (1950–)

Born in Mexico City, this prose author began her career as a film script writer. Her vocation as novelist commenced in 1989 with publication of the best-seller *Como agua para chocolate* (*Like Water for Chocolate*, 1989), which soon became a film based on her screenplay. It is the largest-grossing foreign film in U.S. history.

Set during the Mexican Revolution (1910–1920), the narration has 12 chapters, one for each month of the year. Each chapter begins with a recipe connected to events of those pages; best known of these is "Quail in Rose Petal Sauce," which transfers the passionate desire with which protagonist Tita crushed the rose petals in the sauce to all those who later eat it. The central characters, all women, deal with changes in Mexican culture as it evolves from a traditional, rural culture to a modern, urban society. Written in the *magical realism style, the work is considered a classic of Latin American letters.

Esquivel's next novels, which have met with less acclaim and commercial success, include *La ley del amor* (1995; *The Law of Love*, 1995), a law which dictates that acts of brutality upset the cosmic order, which must then be realigned; *Tan veloz como el deseo* (2001; *As Swift as Desire*, 2001), inspired by Esquivel's father, and *Malinche* (2006; Eng. trans., 2006), about the mother of the Mexican race.

Jerry Hoeg

Work By:

Like Water for Chocolate: A Novel of Monthly Installments, with Recipes, Romances, and Home Remedies: Trans. Carol Christensen and Thomas Christensen. New York: Doubleday, 1991.

Work About:

Skipper, Eric, ed. *Critical Approaches to Laura Esquivel's* Like Water for Chocolate." Amsterdam: Rodopi, 2009.

Estévez, Abilio (1954–)

One of Cuba's leading contemporary writers, he studied literature and philosophy at the University of Havana and has taught at universities in Italy and Venezuela. In Cuba, Estévez has directed a theater troupe and written for and edited numerous journals, including *El caimán barbudo*. His award-winning novels, short stories, plays, and essays exhibit an ethereal, dreamlike quality that recalls the neobaroque style of Alejo *Carpentier. Estévez's first novel, *Tuyo es el reino* (1998; *Thine Is the Kingdom*, 2001), challenges readers by experimenting freely with narrative voice and making numerous erudite allusions to the world of art. His subject matter includes Havana (*Inventario secreto de La Habana* [2004; Secret Inventory of Havana]), particularly in terms of how change over time has furnished the city with a rich cultural texture. Temporality is the focus of his short story "Tosca," from the 1998 collection *El horizonte y otros regresos* (The Horizon and Other Returns), in which the central character attempts to recapture early 20th-century Havana's glory by making all the clocks in his house run backward. *Los palacios distantes* (2002; *Distant Palaces*, 2004) similarly recounts a search for a Havana from a bygone era.

Rudyard J. Alcocer

See also Havana in Literature.

Work By:

Distant Palaces. Trans. David Frye. New York: Arcade, 2004.
Inventario secreto de La Habana. Barcelona: Tusquets, 2005.
Thine Is the Kingdom. Trans. David Frye. New York: Arcade, 1999.

Work About:

Rodríguez-Mangual, Edna. "Un caos lúcido: Delimitaciones de la ciudad antillana en *Tuyo es el reino* de Abilio Estévez." *Torre: Revista de la Universidad de Puerto Rico* 10. 35 (January–March 2005): 121–33.

Estrada, Santiago (1841–1891)

Born in Buenos Aires into a well-known Catholic family of public personalities, Estrada became an intellectual at a very young age, even though he did not pursue university studies. He began his career as a journalist and writer early on, publishing articles on literature and art criticism in several newspapers, as well as several books with historical or religious topics, like *El santuario de Luján* (1867; The Luján Sanctuary) and *El conventillo de Buenos Aires* (1874; Buenos Aires Boarding Houses). His most important work, *El hogar en la pampa* (1866; The Home in the Pampa), can be considered one of the first novels in gaucho literature.

As a diplomat, Estrada participated in a mission to Chile to discuss a border treaty on Patagonian lands. After this trip, he became a passionate advocate of Argentine sovereignty over Patagonia. Under his direction, the newspaper *La América del Sur* became one of the main voices for this position, and in 1879, he established another newspaper, *La Patagonia*, with the same agenda.

Estrada later moved to Spain, living there until his death. Named a member of the *Real Academia Española, most of his works, including two volumes of *Viajes* (1889; Travels), were published in Barcelona in eight volumes with prologues by eminent Spanish writers. To date, there are no modern editions of his work.

Ángel Tuninetti

See also Gaucho Literature.

Work About:

Tuninetti, Ángel. "Primitivism and Progress in the Representation of Patagonia and the Pampas in the Travel Literature of Estrada, Onelli and Rusiñol." *L'Ailleurs de l'autre: Recits de voyageurs extra-européens*. Ed., intro. Claudine Le Blanc, ed. Jacques Weber. Rennes: Presses Universitaires de Rennes, 2009, 159–67.

Estupiñán Bass, Nelson (1912–2002)

Noted for his strongly activist defense of his racial identity, this Afro-Ecuadorian novelist, poet, and essayist was born and raised in Esmeraldas province, a predominantly black, northern coastal province. As a writer of fiction and poetry, he established himself as a major literary figure within the African diaspora. Several writings emphasize black pride and social change.

His first novel, *Cuando los guayacanes florecían* (1954; *When the Guayacanes Were in Bloom*, 1987) is based on a historical uprising led by a black, Colonel Carlos Concha. Much of the novel focuses on Esmeraldas blacks who are victims of enslavement and understand that their race and social conditions are intricately intertwined.

Like many of his contemporaries from the United States, Estupiñán Bass's novels initially express intense racial hatred, but eventually adopt greater tolerance and recognize that all men are equal, as in the novel *El último río* (1966; *Pastrana's Last River*, 1993). This same message resonates in *Canto negro por la luz: Poemas para negros y blancos* (1954; Black Song Brought to Light: Poems for Blacks and Whites), in which he uses African sounding words and rhythms, as illustrated in the poems "Negra bullanguera" (Fun-Loving Black Woman) and "Lola Matamba" to affirm black pride in the context of peace and brotherhood.

Rebecca G. Howes

See also Afro-Hispanic Literature in Spanish America.

Work About:

Jackson, Richard L. *Black Writers in Latin America*. Albuquerque: University of New Mexico Press, 1979, 153–70.

Lewis, Marvin A. *Afro-Hispanic Poetry 1940–1980: From Slavery to "Negritud" in South American Verse*. Colombia: University of Missouri Press, 1983, 107–20.

Etxebarria, Lucía (1966–)

Born in Bermeo, Valencia, this prolific Spanish novelist studied foreign languages and journalism at the Universidad Complutense in Madrid, where she currently resides. Young, sexy, and outspoken, Etxebarria became a highly controversial figure with her best-selling novel *Amor, curiosidad, prozac y dudas* (1996; Love, Curiosity, Prozac, and Doubts), which made her a cultural icon of Generation X. Loved and hated with similar intensity, she has won two prestigious Spanish literary prizes: the Nadal Award for her second novel *Beatriz y los cuerpos celestes* (1998; Beatriz and the Celestial Bodies) and the Planeta Prize for *Un milagro en equilibrio* (2004; A Miracle in Balancing). Mixing popular culture and innovative literary techniques, she voices the existential uneasiness of a kaleidoscope of female subjects who struggle to achieve comfortable roles in a society devoid of positive models.

Etxebarria's numerous novels, short stories, poems, essays, and film scripts never cease to surprise readers with transgressive themes. These center to a greater or lesser degree on self-destructive love and emotional dependence, concerns she developed in the self-help book *Ya no sufro por amor* (2005; I No Longer Suffer for Love). Overcoming traumatizing sexual initiations as well as emotional and physical abuse, her characters articulate the social fragmentation that constitutes Spain's postmodern condition.

Marina Bettaglio

See also Generation X in Spain.

Work By:

Cosmofobia. Barcelona: Destino, 2007.
La Eva futura/La letra futura, Barcelona: Destino, 2000.

Work About:

Tsuchiya, Akiko. "The New Female Subject and the Commodification of Gender in the Works of Lucía Etxebarria." *Romance Studies* 20.1 (2002): 77–87.

Exile Literature by Spanish Civil War Émigrés

In 1939, thousands of artists, writers, scientists, and philosophers left Spain to escape from political repression or even certain death from General Francisco Franco's coup d'état. Critics agree that this intellectual Republican diaspora caused a cultural impoverishment in Spain and resulted in a severe step backwards in the development of a nation already shattered by a brutal three-year civil war. Summarizing the literature written by Spanish exiles after the postwar period has proven to be a very painstaking process. First of all, due to severe *censorship, the literature of exile has always been on the margins of the peninsular literary canon, and therefore is still unknown to a great majority. Secondly, producing a clear taxonomy of the literary production in exile proves problematic because of the generation gap between exile writers, the variety of aesthetics, and the varying ideological tendencies that agglutinate hundreds of exiled writers. To this diversity one must add also the spatial plurality, that is, the variety of countries (with their own political, social, and environmental circumstances) that took in this Republican exodus and directly influenced its literary production.

Since Spain's political transition in 1975, critics and some publishing houses have concentrated mainly on disseminating the individual works of certain prominent authors as a representation of a great unknown majority of exiled writers. Thanks to these sporadic efforts, novelists like Ramón J. *Sender (1901–1982) and Francisco *Ayala (1906–2009), dramatists like Max *Aub (1903–1972) and Alejandro *Casona (1903–1965), and poets like Pedro *Salinas (1891–1951) and Luis *Cernuda (1902–1963), to name but a few, received the historical and literary recognition that for decades the dictatorial regime had denied them by excluding most of them from the Spanish literary scene. Unfortunately, most exiled authors remain unknown to the general contemporary Spanish population. However, with the new millennium, new research groups like GEXEL (*Grupo de Estudios del Exilio Literario* [Research Group for Literary Exile]), from the Autonomous University of Barcelona have created such projects as the collection *Library of Exile*

(established in 2000), whose purpose is to recover the historical and literary memory of hundreds of exiled Republican authors who left Spain.

The variety of genres, aesthetic tendencies, and styles surrounding the literature of Republican exiles calls for a thematic taxonomy, rather than a long list of writers and works, to establish some criteria for classifying the production of this array of individuals. Apart from their common identity as political exile authors, the majority of critics praise the quality of literature produced outside Spain during the postwar period. It is evident that exiled writers did not encounter the brutal censorship faced by authors who never left the country. However, critics also emphasize the intellectual and artistic excellence of many exiled writers compared to those who remained in Spain. One such example can be found in the writing of the *Generation of 1927; of this illustrious group, only Vicente *Aleixandre (1898–1984), Dámaso *Alonso (1898–1990), and Gerardo *Diego (1896–1987) declined exile. Remaining authors of this generation like Rafael *Alberti (1902–1999), Cernuda, Manuel *Altolaguirre (1905–1959), and Emilio Prados (1899–1962), to name a few, as well as the generation's highly influential member, 1956 *Nobel Prize laureate Juan Ramón *Jiménez (1881–1958), consolidated their literary fame and composed some of the most poignant works of Spanish and European literature while in exile. With the exception of Alberti and Jorge *Guillén (1883–1984), the rest of this brilliant artistic generation never returned to Spain.

Another paradigmatic characteristic that unifies these exiled writers and their texts is the ever present commitment to the Republican political cause of liberty and progress. For years, the expectation of returning soon to a free, democratic Spain prevented them from establishing roots in their new environments. This in turn impaired their adaptation to new surroundings far away from a beloved homeland. Jiménez consciously alluded to this alienating state in the poetic volume *En el otro costado* (1974; On the Other Side), observing that what really characterizes "the exiled" is a strange feeling "of not belonging to any nation and never again being a Spaniard."

These characteristics shared by the majority of exile writers helped generate a thematic configuration that permeates their literature. A great majority express nostalgia for a nation from which they were violently uprooted, which brings about a sense of temporal and spatial displacement. This sentiment encourages exiled writers to idealize their past by revisiting intimate childhood and adolescent memories in order to escape painful, alienating circumstances of the present. Two prominent examples of this tendency are *La forja* (1951; *The Forging*, 1941), the first novel of the trilogy *La forja de un rebelde* (1941–1946; *The Forging of a Rebel*, 1951), by Arturo *Barea (1897–1957), and *Crónica del alba* (1942; *Chronicle of Dawn*, 1944) by Sender. Some exiled writers, however, also looked back on Spain's historical situation with a critical, ironic eye that aimed to explain the reasons that led to the disintegration of a nation and its people. The intellectual Ayala explored this topic in his essay *Razón del mundo: preocupación de España* (1962; World's Reason: Spain's Preoccupation).

Another recurrent motif in the literature of Spanish exile is the civil war and its negative impact on the existential condition of the individual. This focus is found in the lengthy novelistic and short story series *El laberinto mágico* (1943–1968; The Magic Labyrinth) by Aub; stories by Ayala compiled in *La cabeza del cordero* (1949; The Lamb's Head); the autobiographical testimony of María Teresa León (1903–1988) in *Memoria de la melancolía* (1970; Memory of Melancholy); the philosophical poetry of María Zambrano (1904–1991) in *El hombre y lo divino* (1953; Man and the Divine); such political dramas by Alberti as *Noche de guerra en el Museo del Prado* (1956; A Night of War in the Prado Museum); and Salinas in *Los santos* (1946; The Saints), to name a few of many such works.

Following this idea, many exiled writers turned their attention to exploring the causes of the civil war, like Ayala's short story volume *Los usurpadores* (1949; *Usurpers*, 1986) and Manuel Andújar (1913–1994) in his first novel *Cristal herido* (1945; Broken Glass), and the subsequent trilogy *Vísperas* (1947–1959; Vespers). As mentioned before, the chimerical return to a liberated, democratic Spain represents a common theme among some of these authors. The disillusion that generates the return to a nation that for decades had been idealized in exile by writers is brilliantly epitomized in the short stories of Aub's autobiographical *La gallina ciega, diario español* (1971; Blind Chicken, Spanish Diary), and Ayala's *El regreso* (1992; The Return).

As well as turning their attention to an idealized past in Spain, exiled writers concentrated on the immediate spatial and temporal present by representing universal problems affecting the existential conditions of people. Poets like Guillén were no stranger to the brutal Nazi atrocities of World War II, as seen in the poem "La afirmación humana (Anna Frank)" (The Human Affirmation [Anna Frank]), part of the *Clamor* (1957–1963) poem collection, and other such themes current during his exile as the Vietnam War and the segregation of blacks in the United States. Other authors like Ayala used a Latin American setting to denounce the debasement of humanity as in his paradigmatic novel *Muertes de perro* (1958; *Death as a Way of Life*, 1964).

Juan Carlos Martín

See also Censorship and Literature in Spain; Francoism, Fascism, and Literature in Spain; PEN Club in the Hispanic World; Spain and Self-Identity in the Nation; Spanish Civil War and the Dictatorship of General Franco (1936–1975).

Work About:

Faber, Sebastiaan. *Exile and Cultural Hegemony: Spanish Intellectuals in Mexico, 1939–1975*. Nashville: Vanderbilt University Press, 2002.

Kamen, Henry. *The Disinherited: Exile and Making of Spanish Culture, 1492–1975*. New York: HarperCollins, 2007.

Exile Writing in the Hispanic World

Exile represents a foremost reality in the Hispanic world during the 20th century. In the case of Spain, the end of the civil war in 1939 and subsequent consolidation of Francisco Franco's repressive system forced many intellectuals to flee their country. Similarly, countless Spanish American authors were forced to live away from their home countries as a result of political totalitarianisms. The late 1960s and 1970s constituted dark decades in many Latin American nations. Characterized by brutal dictatorships, these years brought waves of human rights violations, killings, tortures, and for those able to escape the violence, the bitter experience of exile.

For the Chilean-born writer Roberto *Bolaño, obliged to escape his country after the 1973 military coup and exiled during most of his life, literature and exile are two sides of one coin. This entwined experience of uprooting and writing is symptomatic for many authors of these years; the enforced silence and awareness of a physical and psychological rift lie at the origin of their creativity, and they often show a propensity for the testimonial and autobiographical genres.

Language shapes and reflects one's knowledge and understanding of the world, of oneself, and of others. If this lived world suffers an abrupt change, one's language itself alters significantly. Thus, exile writing represents not merely the writing of separation from home and the insecurity of space, it also expresses the search for a specific, new language that mediates the shock of linguistic, cultural, and spatial change and the experience of solitude. In many texts written in exile, the narrative voice is precarious, tentative, and even contradictory. Language is presented as an unstable, shattered string of words written in the face of the peril of silence. Instead of following chronological order, many narrations center on selected details, to which they return in a sometimes obsessive manner, portraying the traumatic experience as a series of anxieties beyond chronological order. Space, the vulnerability of the human body, and the possibility or impossibility of sense-making through language become constant themes of writing in exile.

At the end of the Spanish Civil War (1936–1939), defeated International Brigade members returned to their home countries, and many Spanish opponents to Franco's regime joined them. Among them were Rafael *Alberti, author of the collected poems *Retornos de lo vivo lejano* (1952; Returns of What Is Alive from Afar) and Pedro *Salinas, author of *El contemplado (Mar; poema)* (1946; The Contemplated [Sea; Poems]), and prose author Jorge *Semprún, with his autobiographical memoir *Autobiografía de Federico Sánchez* (1977; *The Autobiography of Federico Sanchez*, 1980). Each reflected on the uprooting experience. One of the most radical dissident writers is Juan *Goytisolo, whose opposition to Franco led him into exile in Paris in 1956. His trilogy *Señas de identidad* (1966; *Marks of Identity*, 1969), *Reivindicación del Conde don Julián*

(1970; *Count Julian*, 1974), and *Juan sin tierra* (1975; *Juan the Landless*, 1977) radically demystify his country's conservative, dehumanizing institutions and traditional ideologies. In France, Goytisolo also helped found the Spanish-language magazine *Mundo Nuevo*, which promoted work by Latin American exiles who had fled to Paris to escape repressive regimes.

The largest wave of exiles from Argentina took place during the last, most brutal dictatorship, known as the *Guerra Sucia* (Dirty War) from 1976 to 1983, carried out by Rafael Videla against Argentine citizens. Among others, writers Juan *Gelman, Alicia Partnoy, Tununa Mercado, and Jacobo Timerman described the tortures and killings they witnessed in Argentina, giving voice to the trauma of everyday life experienced by émigrés. Partnoy also edited the anthology of testimonies *You Can't Drown the Fire: Latin American Women Writing in Exile* (1988).

Mario *Benedetti is perhaps the best-known Uruguayan author to discuss the experience of the approximately 10 percent of Uruguay's population who emigrated during the military regime of 1973–1985. Benedetti, who lived in exile in several Spanish American countries and Spain, meditated on this situation of nonbelonging and on his firm belief in the return of democracy in many poems and in the novel *Viento del exilio* (1982; Wind of Exile).

Chile experienced its own dark "9/11": Augusto Pinochet's military coup on September 11, 1973, against president Salvador Allende's government initiated a repressive system that lasted until 1990.

This traumatic event indelibly marked the writings of many authors forced into exile. Among them stands out the novelist and playwright Ariel *Dorfman, who had served as a cultural advisor to Allende. His play *La muerte y la doncella* (1992; *Death and the Maiden*, 1992 [made into a film in 1994]) and memoir *Rumbo al sur: deseando el norte: un romance en dos lenguas* (1998; *Heading South, Looking North: A Bilingual Journey*, 1998) each confront the horrors of state terror and the trials of exile.

Author and human rights activist Victor Montejo is possibly the most-read Guatemalan writer living in the United States. His hybrid testimony and critical analysis *Voices from Exile: Violence and Survival in Modern Maya History* (1999) describes the repressions and massacres of mainly rural indigenous populations during the civil war (1960–1996). He presents the consequences of exile as a cultural, political, and psychic shock for thousands of Mayas who fled their country in the 1980s.

In El Salvador, the civil war between the ultraconservative, U.S.-backed military government and left-wing guerrilla groups (1980–1992) was a time of extreme violence and terror. In his short story collection *Árbol de la vida: Historias de la guerra civil* (1993; *The Tree of Life: Stories of Civil War*, 1997), Mario Bencastro, exiled in the United States since the mid-1980s, fictionalizes the experiences of everyday panic and sheer helplessness felt during the disappearances and assassinations, as well as the aftermath of turmoil in the diaspora. Several of Bencastro's texts have been adapted for the stage.

With its single-head of state for almost half a century—Fidel Castro was its leader from 1959 until 2008—the case of Cuba is unique within Latin America. Yet similar to many other countries of the Southern Hemisphere, the island suffered a decidedly repressive period during the 1970s. Reinaldo *Arenas became one of the most outspoken critics of Castro's repressive system during those years of brutal silencing of dissidents. His biographical novel *Antes que anochezca* (1992; *Before Night Falls*, 2000 [adapted to film in 2000]), and the essay collection *Necesidad de libertad* (1986; Need for Liberty) described the persecutions of Cuban intellectuals and his own desperate attempts to flee the island. In one essay composed in New York, he wrote that Cuba had become an incessant question, an almost nonexistent site for the exile, which might only be recovered as a "moving home" that resides in literature.

Despite responding to very heterogeneous political and sociocultural circumstances, the writings of exile in the Hispanic world possess several key commonalities. They present themselves as examples and emphasize their role as voices for those who have been silenced. Writing becomes a counterforce to trauma and forgetting—a partial and subjective remembrance of the past space, a painful memory of the injustice, and an account of the life at a new place which may, in some but not all cases, become a new home.

Ilka Kressner

See also Cuban American Writers; Cuban Exile Writing outside the United States; Equatorial Guinea: Poets; Equatorial Guinea: Writers in Exile; Equatorial Guinea: Writers Living in the United States; Equatorial Guinea's *Generación del Silencio* (The Generation of Silence); Exile Literature by Spanish Civil War Émigrés; Mariel Writers Generation; PEN Club in the Hispanic World.

Work About:

Aves de paso. Autores latinoamericanos entre exilio y transculturación (1970–2002). Ed. Birgit Mertz-Baumgartner and Edna Pfeiffer. Frankfurt: Iberoamericana, 2005.

Kaminski, Amy. *After Exile: Writing the Latin American Diaspora*. Minneapolis: University of Minnesota Press, 1999.

Ugarte, Michael. *Shifting Ground. Spanish Civil War Exile Literature*. Durham, NC: Duke University Press, 1989.

You Can't Drown the Fire: Latin American Women Writing in Exile. Ed. Alicia Partnoy. San Francisco: Cleis, 1988.

F

Fagundo, Ana María (1938–2010)

Born in Tenerife, Canary Islands, this Spanish poet lived in the United States from 1958—completing undergraduate and graduate studies and teaching Spanish literature at the University of California, Riverside—until 2002, when she returned to Spain. Despite these decades in the United States, the landscape and nature of Tenerife remained the constant setting of her verse. In 1969, she founded *Alaluz*, a highly respected poetry and literary journal. She was its editor until 2001.

Fagundo published over 10 collections of poetry. Nature, personal identity, her autobiography, separation from her homeland, and the mysterious power of words (or metapoetry), are ongoing threads of her verse. Their language, as Gala notes, is aural and tactile, underscoring the material nature of words. Her first poetry collection, *Brotes* (1965; Buds), was followed by *Isla adentro* (1969; Within the Island), an expression of self-affirmation. Three books of poetry published after her father's death (*Configurado tiempo* [1974; Configuration of Time], *Invención de la luz* [1978; Invention of Light], and *Desde Chanatel, el canto* [1982; Chant from Chanatel]) recapture memories of her childhood in Tenerife.

Fagundo has also published a short story collection, *La miríada de los sonámbulos* (1994; The Myriad of Sleepwalkers) a collection of 26 short stories in which the values of traditional society are set against individual "otherness."

Maureen Ihrie

Work By:

Materias en olvido. Santa Cruz de Tenerife, Spain: Idea, 2008.

The Poetry of Ana María Fagundo: A Bilingual Anthology. Ed., intro. Candelas Gala. Multiple translators. Cranbury, NJ: Associated University Presses, 2005.

Work About:

Brooks, Zelda. *Struggle for Being: An Interpretation of the Poetry of Ana María Fagundo*. Miami: Universal, 1994.

Cavallari, Héctor Mario. "Journeys of Desire: The Poetry of Ana María Fagundo." *Pacific Coast Philology* 39 (2004): 1–8.

Falcón, Lidia (1935–)

This activist, thinker, novelist, dramatist, essayist, and journalist can also be considered the mother of Spain's feminist movement. A prolific writer in many genres, she has authored 36 books with women protagonists. Her political activism and outspoken feminism prompted Francisco Franco's regime (1939–1975) to persecute and arrest her.

A highly educated scholar, Falcón holds degrees in theater, journalism, law and a doctorate in philosophy. She founded Spain's first political feminist party and created and directed the journals *Vindicación Feminista* (Feminist Vindication) and *Poder y Libertad* (Power and Freedom). Her participation in the International Court for Crimes against Women in Brussels, and in international feminists forums of New York, Nairobi, and Beijing are intended to encourage open debate on national and international issues from a feminist perspective.

Falcón has published four memoirs. The autobiographical *La vida arrebatada* (2003; The Stolen Life) describes the sufferings of postwar Spain, the difficulties women face, and her clandestine political involvements, thus conflating her private life with a subjective interpretation of issues pertaining to the Francoist dictatorship. She is also an active playwright, producing a dozen plays, including *No moleste, calle y pague, señora* (1994; *Shut Up, Don't Bother Me, and Pay on Your Way Out, Lady*, 1998) and *Tu único amor* (1991; Your Only Love). Her theater shows a dynamic interplay between male and female characters. Falcón's work uses strong social satire to portray and denounce social injustices against women to promote cultural and political consciousness.

Ana Corbalán

See also Feminism in Spain: 1700 to Present; Francoism, Fascism, and Literature in Spain.

Work By:

Mujer y sociedad: Análisis de un fenómeno reaccionario. Barcelona: Fontanella, 1984.

"Shut Up, Don't Bother Me, and Pay on Your Way Out, Lady!" *One-Act Spanish Plays by Women about Women.* Ed. Patricia O'Connor. Madrid: Fundamentos, 1998, 143–69.

Work About:

Gabriele, John P. *Lidia Falcón: Teatro feminista.* Madrid: Fundamentos, 2002.

Gabriele, John P. "Toward a Radical Feminist Stage Rhetoric in the Short Plays of Lidia Falcón." *Symposium: A Quarterly Journal in Modern Literatures* 51.1 (1997): 3–19.

Levine, Linda Gould. "Remapping the Left in *Camino sin Retorno:* Lidia Falcón's Feminist Project." *Women's Narrative and Film in Twentieth-Century Spain: A World of Differences.* Ed. Ofelia Ferrán and Kathleen Glenn. New York: Routledge, 2002, 136–51.

Falcones, Ildefonso (1958–)

This Catalan-born Spanish novelist has enjoyed notable commercial success in historical fiction. His first novel takes inspiration from the Spanish translation of Ken Follett's *The Pillars of the Earth* (1989), which sold hundreds of thousands of copies in Spain. Among numerous adventures, Follett's story of a Gothic cathedral in medieval England narrates the pilgrimage to *Santiago de Compostela and depicts the Spain of the three religions (Christianity, Judaism, Islam) in Toledo and its School of Translators. Falcones managed to repeat Follett's success in his own novel, *La catedral del Mar* (2006; *The Cathedral of the Sea*, 2008), which became an instant best seller. It tells the story of Arnau Estanyol, a stevedore in Barcelona's harbor during the 14th century. Using as background the construction of the Gothic cathedral Our Lady of the Sea, the novel's true protagonist is the city of Barcelona and its main topic is how the concept of a "free man" developed in European cities during the late Middle Ages.

Falcones's second novel, *La mano de Fátima* (2009; *The Hand of Fatima*, 2011), tells the story of *moriscos* (the Spanish-blood minority that practiced Islam) in Spain in the second half of the 16th century, after the last Islamic kingdom of Granada fell to Christian monarchs Ferdinand and Isabella in 1492 and initiated the compulsory Christianization of the country. Set in a little village in the mountainous Alpujarra region of Granada, it features the protagonist Hernando Ruiz de Juviles, the bastard son of a Catholic priest who raped a *morisca*. For more than 50 years, Hernando, a muleteer, tries to practice his Muslim faith and keep his Arabic name, Ibn Hamid. With historical rigor, Hernando takes readers to the *morisco* wars; the expulsion of *moriscos* from all kingdoms of Spain; the traumatic construction of the Córdoba cathedral inside the great mosque of Córdoba; the schizophrenic, traumatic Christianization of Granada; and the forgery of an apocryphal Gospel of Sacromonte. Using the structure of adventure of the Byzantine novel, Falcones meticulously represents the life of *moriscos*. The moral of the novel is that the peaceful coexistence of the three religions that adore the God of Abraham is as necessary today as it was in the distant past.

Salvador A. Oropesa

See also Hispano-Arabic and Hispano-Judaic Literature and Culture in Spain; Islamic Presence in Spain; Novel in Spain: 1900 to Present.

Work By:

Cathedral of the Sea. Trans. Nick Caistor. New York: Dutton, 2008.

Fallas, Carlos Luis (1909–1966)

Considered one of Costa Rica's most important social realist writers, this novelist and politician worked for the United Fruit Company as a young man and became a union organizer and Communist Party member. He helped organize the 1934 banana workers' strike and in 1940 was assigned by the Vanguardia Popular political party to supervise elections in a banana region. His report, which appeared in installments in the *Trabajo* newspaper, became the core of his most important novel, *Mamita Yunai* (1941). Narrated in the first person, the text records the abuses committed by the United Fruit Company as it exported bananas and other tropical fruits from the Caribbean region of Limón to the United States and other parts of the world.

Fallas's novel *Gentes y gentecillas* (1947; People and Little People) continues the social realism of *Mamita Yunai*. Its protagonist, Jerónimo, witnesses unfair treatment of workers on a plantation and feels nostalgia for his homeland, Costa Rica's Central Valley.

Jaime A. Orrego

Work By:

Mamita Yunai. San José, Costa Rica: Costa Rica, 1986.

Work About:

Grinberg Pla, Valeria, and Werner Mackenbach. "Banana novel revis(it)ed: Etnia, género y espacio en la novela bananera centroamericana. El caso de *Mamita Yunai*." *Iberoamericana: América Latina-España-Portugal* 23 (2006): 161–76.

Felipe, León (1884–1968)

Considered one of Spain's most profound poets, Felipe Camino Galicia de la Rosa (pseud. León Felipe) studied pharmacy and worked as an actor in Madrid, a hospital director in Guinea, but mostly as a teacher in the United States and Mexico, where he exiled himself after the Spanish Civil War (1936–1939). He wrote several poetry books and adapted a number of Shakespeare's plays to Spanish; the expressiveness and humanistic commitment of his poetry continue to touch modern readers.

Felipe's verse has biographical content, but this personal experience resembles the existential anguish of all mankind. He defines the poet as a prophet, the "great responsible one" who must denounce injustices caused by egotism and defend the absolute values of life and humankind. Walt Whitman, whose poetry he translated, clearly influenced his thought.

During the war, he volunteered with the Republicans and called for fraternity among Spaniards. In his poetry, which exhibits a clear redeeming intention, he dialogues with man and God, declaiming the perils of existence and the mystery of God's justice. Concerned with the suffering and destiny of the world, he addresses such themes as love, justice, dignity, and self-fulfillment. He turns to literary and biblical figures, including Prometheus, Oedipus, Don Quijote, Jesus, and Job to portray humankind's struggle on earth. Natural symbols like light, wind, and fire figure in his verse, and he finds in Jesus a proof of how humans, in their encounter with God, can transform a suffering existence into one of triumph.

Felipe defined himself as a pilgrim and conceived his poetry as a vital process for exploring, and maybe discovering, the keys of human existence. His ethically charged writing overcomes suffering and exhorts readers to seek justice and to pursue their "divine nature."

María-Cruz Rodríguez

See also Exile Literature by Spanish Civil War Émigrés; Poetry in Spain: 1900 to Present.

Work By:

The Last Troubadour: Selected Shorter Poems. Trans. Robert Houston, Criss Cannady, et al. Tucson, AZ: Blue Moon, 1979.

Lakes and Legacies. Trans. Criss Cannady. Tucson, AZ: Blue Moon, 1978.

Work About:

Costa, Luis F. "The Failed Ideal in León Felipe's poetry of the Spanish Civil War." *The Spanish Civil War in Literature.* Ed. Janet Pérez and Wendell Aycock. Lubbock: Texas Tech University Press, 1990, 139–48.

Jiménez Fajardo, Salvador. "León Felipe: The Voice Without/The Voice Within." *Crítica Hispánica* 12 (1990): 103–14.

Feminism in Spain: Precursors to 1700

Although women writers have rarely had access to a prominent position in the literary canon, Spanish literature exhibits a prefeminist, *avant la lettre* mentality in representing women's roles within society. The female voice and feminine attitudes toward society can be traced back to antiquity. Spain's earliest literature manifestation (probably predating the 11th century) is the *kharja*, a lyric of four short verses expressing a woman's love. The *kharjas* of Muslim Spain, along with the Galician-language *cantigas de amigo* (songs about a boyfriend), represent a lyric tradition descending from women's love songs written in Vulgar Latin. Widely diffused in the Roman Empire but never written down, these songs are often attributed to male authors, but likely originated from popular poems by women.

Despite the fact that the origins of Spanish literature express a feminine sensibility toward love within a patriarchal society, the first works openly attributed to women appear late. Only three women writers have left proof of substantial literary work during the late Middle Ages: Leonor López de Córdoba (c. late 14th–early 15th century), Teresa de Cartagena (c. 1420–after 1460?), and Florencia Pinar (15th century). These authors share a common poetic of imprisonment—a result of the restraints imposed by gender and the reigning social environment.

López de Córdoba's *Memorias* (no date; *Memoirs*, 1984) constitutes Spain's first text attributed to a woman. It details her experiences as a victim of high politics in a violent, treacherous age, and as a witness to the civil wars between Pedro I of Castile and his half-brother Enrique de Trastámara. Cartagena, from a prominent **converso* family, studied in Salamanca, became a nun, and composed two works: *Arboleda de los enfermos* (no date; *The Grove of the Sick*, 1998) and *Admiración operum Dey* (no date; *Wonder at the Works of God*, 1998). *Arboleda* is a work of self-consolation in the tradition of the consolatory treatise, a widespread 15th-century genre, which aims to derive comfort in the face of hardship or tragedy. In *Admiración*, Cartagena reflects on the creative process and answers her critics, who viewed with suspicion the intellectual life of *conversos*. Little is known about Pinar, whose name is attached to a few poems in *cancioneros* (late medieval songbooks). Even though the great majority of **cancionero* poets are male, these songbooks include a half-dozen named and two anonymous women poets. Pinar's poems deal with love and erotic themes and appear in three *cancioneros* from the late-15th and early-16th centuries.

The number of Spanish women writers increased particularly during the 16th and 17th centuries through participation in literary circles (*academias* and *saraos*), where women sometimes achieved acceptance and admiration from contemporary male writers, although few achieved a place in canonical literature. The most famous is Santa *Teresa de Jesús (1515–1582), writer of prayers, autobiography, poetry, and religious reforms. Her works *Libro de la vida* (written 1562–1565; *Book of Her Life*; 1988), *Camino de perfección* (written 1562; *Way of Perfection*, 1964), and *Moradas del castillo interior* (written 1577; *Interior Castle*, 1961) constitute the most extraordinary example of early modern Spanish mystical literature. Although Santa Teresa's representation of women's intellect, religiosity, and spirituality ultimately resulted in her silence, the reforms she inspired within her religious order challenged the roles and mission that church authority imposed on 16th-century women.

The 17th century produced a number of women poets and prose writers. Among those who achieved popularity is María de *Zayas y Sotomayor (1590–after 1647), who contributed to the *novela corta* (short novel) genre with her *Novelas amorosas y ejemplares* (1634; *Enchantments of Love*, 1990) and *Desengaños amorosos* (1647; *The Disenchantments of Love*, 1997). Using the framed-narrative structure of Italian Giovanni Boccaccio's *Decameron*, these short novel collections discuss the complications of married life and mistreatment suffered by women; her female characters denounce their inferior position in a society which subjects them to violence and abuse.

Early modern women dramatist rarely saw their works performed. Nonetheless, several did bring significant and subversive innovations to the stage, including Ana Caro Mallén de Soto (1565?/1600?–1652?), Ángela de Acevedo (early 17th century? –?) and Leonor de la Cueva (early 17th century–?). Worth mention also is Catalina de *Erauso (1578?/1585?/1592?–after 1630), known as *la monja alférez* (the lieutenant nun); her autobiography stunningly embodies the transgression of gender and social boundaries of her time.

Jesús David Jerez-Gómez

See also Convent Writing in Spain and the New World; Gender in Spanish Literature; Mysticism and Asceticism in Spain; Women Writers in Spain: Beginnings to 1700.

Work About:

Kaminsky, Amy Katz. *Water Lilies: An Anthology of Spanish Women Writers from the Fifteenth through the Nineteenth Century*. Minneapolis: University of Minnesota Press, 1996.

Vollendorf, Lisa, ed. *Recovering Spain's Feminist Tradition*. New York: Modern Language Association of America, 2001.

Vollendorf, Lisa. *Reclaiming the Body: María de Zayas's Early Modern Feminism*. Chapel Hill: University of North Carolina Press, 2001.

Feminism in Spain:
1700 to Present

Although women writers like Santa *Teresa de Jesús, Ana Caro Mallén de Soto, María de *Zayas y Sotomayor, Ana de San Bartolomé, or Sor Juana Inés de la *Cruz competed successfully with male counterparts and confronted restrictive norms of their day as long as 400 years ago, critical recognition of this fact is quite recent. Likewise, many contemporary feminist critics consider Spain's history of feminism to date back barely two centuries. One must not discount, however, such illustrious 18th-century forerunners as Josefa Amar y Borbón, Inés Joyes, María Rosa Gálvez, and Margarita Hickey.

Amar y Borbón belonged to the Royal Societies of Friends, a loose association of clubs throughout Spain that strove to reform national vices. An avid reader, translator, and bibliographer, she delivered several speeches (1786–1790) defending women's equal abilities in all arenas. Inés Joyes y Blake, daughter of Irish Catholics settled in Madrid, authored the *Apología de las mujeres* (1798; Apology of Women), which denounces the overwhelming situation of inequality and blames men for women's ostracism. Margarita Hickey centered her poetry (*Poesías varias sagradas* [1789; Selected Sacred Poems]) on women's issues and called for free thought and speech for women.

During the 19th century, Spain moved gradually toward laicism (nonreligious control) and political combativeness.

Concepción Arenal, the founder of Spain's feminist movement, combined revolutionary fervor with Christian doctrine in her work with the poor and marginalized. Novelist Emilia *Pardo Bazán discussed feminism in various essays and directed and published the book series *La biblioteca de la mujer* (1892; The Woman's Library). This collection included modern versions of 17th-century writer Zayas y Sotomayor's novellas, biographies of notable women, and translations of texts on women by popular contemporary theorists like John Stuart Mills and August Bebel. She constantly defended women's rights and access to education and criticized society's double moral standard for men and women. Textile worker Teresa Claramunt, Spain's first feminist revolutionary, protested the exploitation of women at work and suffered repeated arrests. After being exiled to England for allegedly participating in anarchist activities, she returned in 1898, collaborated with socialist newspapers and joined several workers' unions. In 1903, she published *La mujer, consideraciones sobre su estado ante las prerrogativas del hombre* (Women, Considerations on Their Status with Regard to Male Prerogatives).

During the 20th century, women concerned themselves with various broader political issues, including the expansion of education opportunities, promotion of suffrage, and improvement of working conditions. In 1918, ANME (National Association of Spanish Women) was founded, which consisted of middle-class women, teachers, writers, university students, and intellectuals. Most other women's associations of the time were composed of well-off wives with strong Catholic beliefs who pursued a conservative feminism that conceived woman as different from man—an intelligent collaborator but still a domestic consort whose proper role was to raise and educate children. Under the dictatorship of Miguel Primo de Rivera (1923–1930), a paternalist attitude toward women prevailed. Women were allowed to vote if they were unmarried, and could organize in unions dedicated to promoting the active political participation of Catholic women reformers, a tendency observed in members of the rightist *Partido Popular* (Popular Party). This was the case in Esperanza Aguirre and Rita Barberá, whose political corpus is directly linked to Catholic moral beliefs.

Nonetheless, divorcée Carmen de *Burgos as reporter, novelist, translator, and feminist activist defended women's right to live with total freedom. Using the pen-name "Colombine" she composed *La mujer moderna y sus derechos* (1927; Modern Woman and Her Rights). Clara Campoamor, who earned a law degree at the University of Madrid, vociferously advocated women's civil liberties and political rights. Elected to congress in 1931 by the Radical Party, she helped drafting the Constitution for the Spanish Second Republic, particularly Article 36, which granted women unrestricted suffrage. In this, she opposed feminist congresswomen like Victoria Kent and Margarita *Nelken y Mausberger, who approved suffrage for women only after they became more educated politically.

Campoamor also contributed decisively to passage of the divorce law.

Two women activists emerge with particular force in the years preceding the Spanish Civil War (1936–1939). The first, Dolores *Ibarruri, known as *La Pasionaria* (The Passion Flower), was born into a mining family; several tragic life events (poverty, the death of four children, her unionist husband's arrest) led her to fight for social justice. A congresswoman, during the Spanish Civil War (1936–1939) she served as the Republican spokesperson and collaborated with the International Communist Party, organizing European meetings to denounce fascism. After the war, Ibárruri fled to the Soviet Union, where she became general secretary and president of Spain's Communist Party. In 1977 (two years after Francisco Franco's death), she returned to Spain and worked in Parliament as a delegate for the Communist Party. The second was Federica *Montseny Mañé, a Spanish anarchist leader, who served as minister of health and social assistance to Francisco Largo Caballero's socialist government during the war. Her texts in defense of women include *La mujer: problema del hombre* (1932; Woman: A Man's Problem) and *Cien días en la vida de una mujer* (1949; One Hundred Days in A Woman's Life).

From the second half of the 20th century to today, strong feminist women denounced the gender segregation under Francisco Franco's regime (1939–1975). Democracy, however, brought political equality for both men and women—the Constitution of 1978 includes a clause conferring this status—and the Institute for Women was funded in 1983. Since then, numerous Spanish feminists have joined in national and global efforts to promote equality. Lidia *Falcón, founder of the Spanish Feminist Party and fighter for women's rights in four United Nations World Conferences on Women, has also studied in her theater how gender relations still impose the social constructs (behavior roles) of masculine or feminine on individuals. Sociologist Inés Alberdi, named executive director of the United Nations Development Fund for Women in 2008, fights to empower women and reform conditions in less-developed countries.

Feminist theorist and philosopher Celia Amorós, who directed the Institute for Feminist Research until 1993, has proposed a so-called *equality feminism* as a possible solution to the prevailing bipolar division between masculine and feminine and the victimist exaltation of women. Her influential permanent seminar on "Feminism and Enlightenment" has also received contributions from theorists like Cristina Molina Petit and Ángeles Jiménez Perona. A group of Catalan writers, including Montserrat Roig, Maria-Mercè Marçal, and Carme Riera have dealt similarly with feminist concerns in journalism and fiction.

Finally, feminism has also gained strength from recent fiction by illustrious Spanish women writers that reflect on pervasive mind-sets like *machismo*, religion, and tradition in daily actions, attitudes that still haunt relations between the sexes. Carmen *Martín Gaite has vividly depicted the patriarchal society of Franco's regime, Rosa *Montero has reflected on the alienation of the working woman, Esther *Tusquets has dealt with lesbian love, and Maruja Torres has shown generational differences among women while pleading for women's rights.

Judith García-Quismondo García

See also Chacel, Rosa (1898–1994).

Work About:

Charnon-Deutsch, Lou, and Jo Labanyi, eds. *Culture and Gender in Nineteenth-Century Spain*. Oxford: Clarendon, 1995.

Cruz, Anne J. "Feminism, Psychoanalysis, and the Search for the M/Other in Early Modern Spain." *Indiana Journal of Hispanic Literature* 8 (Spring 1996): 31–54.

Enders, Victoria Loree, Pamela Beth Radcliff, and Karen Offen, eds. *Constructing Spanish Womanhood: Female Identity in Modern Spain*. Albany: State University of New York Press, 1999.

Vollendorf, Lisa, ed. *Recovering Spain's Feminist Tradition*. New York: Modern Language Association, 2001.

Feminism in Spanish America

Geographically, Spanish America spans portions of North America (i.e., Mexico and the growing Spanish-speaking population of the United States), the Caribbean, Central America, and South America. To speak of feminism in Spanish America, then, is to negotiate the complexities of an extremely diverse geographical, political, and cultural region. Although the theoretical origins of feminism in its most basic form exceed national boundaries by positing gender oppression as an experience common to all women, there are conditions particular to Spanish America that feminists had to and, in some cases, continue to confront. They include the lasting impact of conquest and colonialism, the genocide and marginalization of indigenous populations, the legacy of slavery, the influence of a rich Catholic tradition, the significant delay in legalizing women's suffrage, the interference of Cold War politics in national leadership, and the struggle to maintain autonomy for their political agendas.

Miller argues that the timeline of feminism in Latin America is often misread, especially by those who analyze it in terms of the first wave and second wave feminism of the United States. Miller claims that critics disregard the fact that, despite the suffrage movement being well under way by the early 20th century, in many countries of the region women did not gain the right to vote until during or after World War II, with Paraguay being the latest in 1961. Women's movements in Spanish America have not always necessarily implied a critical engagement with the concept of gender or a particularly feminist stance; many times such movements articulated their demands in terms of performing their duties as wives and mothers properly, which gave them greater political expediency. Miller uses the term "social motherhood" to refer to this platform, which was often employed in the early stages of the feminist movement to argue for women's right to vote, to get an education, and to have access to social welfare programs. Chilean *Nobel Prize–winner Gabriela *Mistral's campaign for women's education in Mexico, for instance, was based on the assumption that, as mothers, women hand down tradition, culture, and values to the future of the Mexican race, and therefore, their education would contribute to the betterment of the nation itself. The Buenos Aires protests of *Las Madres de la Plaza de Mayo* (1977–present; The Mothers of the Plaza de Mayo) offer a later example of this ideology, since these women placed state practices of torture, violence, and disappearing citizens into question by claiming the need to locate their children's bodies as an expression of their natural role as mothers.

The Cuban Revolution (1953–1959) provided the impetus for other social revolutions throughout the region in which feminists often participated and found a medium through which to express their own sociopolitical concerns. In several cases, the formulation of a feminist ideology emerged from women's participation in leftist movements, which often had socialist leanings and were created in opposition to military dictatorships and the violence of oppressive regimes. In these instances, some women were empowered by political participation at the very same time that others noticed that their concerns about patriarchy were subordinated to the "more important" issue of class oppression, and the accompanying belief that women's freedom would later yield a natural result of economic liberation. However, fears about the spread of socialism during the Cold War following the Cuban Revolution, especially on the part of the United States, led to U.S. support for installing a series of military dictatorships throughout the Americas. These dictatorships posed a particular threat to feminist agendas, given that many of these regimes touted a return to traditional gender roles and expected women to revert to the private sphere, namely the home.

Politically subversive men and women were often the target of torture, rape, and "disappearance." Women's experiences in Spanish America garnered international attention when the Mirabal sisters were assassinated by the Dominican Republic's Trujillo regime in 1960. The United Nations later declared the anniversary of their death as the International Day for the Elimination of Violence against Women (1999).

Ultimately, Spanish American feminists faced a choice—whether to work within or in conjunction with a preestablished political movement, or to preserve their political and economic autonomy. Many women did both. This choice continues to be an issue; certain feminists have been criticized for "selling out" by becoming part of government organizations, especially given their assigned role of speaking on behalf of all interests of women in their country. More recently, many feminist groups receive sponsorship and financial support from international organizations supporting human rights; they often must work to prevent their resources from being co-opted by other groups wishing to collaborate with them,

especially following the UN's declaration of the decade for women (1976–1985) and the funds now available from NGO's and not-for-profit organizations in support of women's issues.

Many Spanish American feminists took up the language of human rights to ground their arguments for bettering the conditions for women's and men's participation in public and private spheres. The United Nation's Fourth World Conference on Women in Beijing (1995) garnered international attention for the concerns of Spanish American women and fostered a transnational approach to feminism that united many feminists, especially in the Americas, in the common goal of achieving human rights for all (including reproductive rights). Indeed, feminists in Spanish America found solidarity through such a variety of venues as the circulation of women-run and feminist publications and the participation in and organization of transnational conferences on the subject of women's rights and feminist issues, well before the Beijing Conference. This evidence suggests that Spanish American feminists recognized and continue to recognize that establishing a transnational network is crucial to achieving their goals.

In addition to political movements and community organizations, feminists in Spanish America also developed their own theories of feminism and aimed to reconstruct a history of women's experience in their own terms. Such literary figures as 17th-century Mexican nun and poetic genius Sor Juana Inés de la *Cruz, who brilliantly defended her right (and the rights of all men and women) to a liberal arts education in opposition to the Spanish *Inquisition, and Doña Marina, the indigenous translator without whom Hernán Cortés could not have conquered the Aztecs, have been sources of feminist musings and reimaginings. Other important figures include the earlier-mentioned Mistral and Mexican Rosario *Castellanos, whose *Mujer que sabe latín* (1973; Woman Who Knows Latin) is a seminal work for any study of Spanish American feminism.

Other important historical feminist figures and writers include María Luisa *Bombal (Chile), Gertrudis *Gómez de Avellaneda (Cuba/Spain), Camila *Henríquez Ureña (Dominican Republic/Cuba), Clorinda *Matto de Turner (Peru), Teresa de la *Parra (Venezuela), Alfonsina *Storni (Argentina/Switzerland), and Flora Tristán (Peru/France). Such contemporary writers, theorists, and activists as Isabel *Allende (Chile), Griselda *Gambaro (Argentina), Angélica Gorodischer (Argentina), Diamela *Eltit (Chile), Rosario *Ferré (Puerto Rico), Julieta Kirkwood (Chile), Marta Lamas (Mexico), Sylvia Molloy (Argentina), Raquel Olea (Chile), Cristina *Peri Rossi (Uruguay/Spain), Nelly Richard (France/Chile), Beatriz *Sarlo (Argentina), and Luisa *Valenzuela (Argentina) have engaged creatively and critically with such themes as exposing violence against women, especially under dictatorship; establishing the relation between the Third and First Worlds; creating theories of identity and difference; assessing the current state of feminism; exploring alternate ways of knowing; and proposing more ethical modes of representation.

Social activists like Domitila Barrios de Chungara (Bolivia), Rigoberta *Menchú (Guatemala), and Elena *Poniatowska (Mexico), employ the genre of *testimonio* to express the urgency of their current situations and to give voice to those who lack the ability or means to share their stories publicly. Puerto Rican Aurora Levins Morales, Chicana Gloria *Anzaldúa, and Chicana Cherríe Moraga have articulated the particular implications of being Latina/Chicana women living in the United States. They have challenged the predominantly white feminist movement there to recognize and incorporate notions of difference in their conceptualizations of feminist theory and policy changes. This can be seen in their coauthored volume *This Bridge Called My Back: Writings by Radical Women of Color* (1981), along with Anzaldúa's *Borderlands/La frontera* (1987)—both are examples of this intellectual movement.

Also of note are contributions of Spanish American exiles like Marjorie *Agosín (Chile/United States), who fled from Chile during the dictatorship and moved to the United States, and Cristina *Peri Rossi, who fled Uruguay and settled in Spain. Both continue to engage in women's issues and women's rights by telling their stories. In the same vein, feminist Latin Americanists living in the United States who may or may not have Latin roots, such as Debra Castillo, Jean Franco, Amy Kaminsky, Mary Louise Pratt, Sara Castro Klarén, Sonia Álvarez, and María Inés Lagos have made important contributions to the field.

Nicole Sparling

See also Brunet, Marta (1897–1967); Spanish American Poetry by Women; Trujillo as Theme in Dominican Republic and Hispanic Writing; Women Writers in Cuba: 1900–1959.

Work About:

Brooksbank Jones, Anny, and Catherine Davies. *Latin American Women's Writing: Feminist Readings in Theory and Crisis.* New York: Oxford University Press, 1996.

Castillo, Debra. *Talking Back: Toward a Latin American Feminist Literary Criticism.* Ithaca, NY: Cornell University Press, 1992.

Femenías, María Luisa, and Amy Oliver, eds. *Feminist Philosophy in Latin America and Spain.* New York: Rodopi, 2007.

Miller, Francesca. *Latin American Women and the Search for Social Justice.* Hanover, NJ: University Press of New England, 1991.

Richard, Nelly. *Masculine/Feminine: Practices of Difference(s).* Durham, NC: Duke University Press, 2004.

Fernández, Macedonio (1874–1952)

Described as one of the most eccentric writers working in Spanish, the oeuvre of this Argentine author is largely unclassifiable. Fernández is noted as a novelist, poet, essayist, and philosopher, but his writing defies traditional generic and disciplinary boundaries. Born in Buenos Aires, he practiced law for 25 years while publishing poetry and essays in local reviews, but in his lifetime refused to publish his most important narrative work, *Novela de la Eterna* (1967; The Novel of Eterna). This unfinished avant-garde "novel" features often philosophical dialogue between the author, in the guise of "El Presidente," and the work's disembodied characters. Foregrounding Fernández's abiding preoccupation with the very possibility of constructing a novel, the work comprises a series of prologues, postprologues, notes to real and imaginary readers and authors, editorial observations, intertextual references, and reflections on writing, time, and the imagination.

Fernández's influence on contemporaneous and subsequent generations of Argentine authors is difficult to overestimate. In 1921, he became friends with the young Jorge Luis *Borges, whose own work would reflect Fernández's mostly unpublished obsessions with metaphysics, alternate dimensions, utopias, originality, and textual relationships.

Karen Elizabeth Bishop

See also Avant-Garde Poetry in Spanish America; Avant-Garde Prose in Spanish America.

Work By:

Engelbert, Jo Anne, ed. *Macedonio: Selected Writings in Translation.* Fort Worth, TX: Latitudes, 1984.

Work About:

Englebert, Jo Anne. *Macedonio Fernández and the Spanish American New Novel.* New York: New York University Press, 1978.

Garth, Todd S. *The Self of the City: Macedonio Fernández, the Argentine Avant-Garde, and Modernity in Buenos Aires.* Lewisburg, PA: Bucknell University Press, 2005.

Macedonio.net. May 15, 2009. http://www.macedonio.net.

Fernández Cubas, Cristina (1945–)

Born in Arenys de Mar and a resident of Barcelona, Cristina Fernández Cubas initiated a renaissance in Spain's short story genre with her first collection, *Mi hermana Elba* (1980; My Sister Elba). She continues to produce remarkable works of short fiction, in addition to publishing novels (*El año de Gracia* and *El columpio* [1985; The Year of Grace] and [1995; The Swing]), a book of memories (2001; *Cosas que ya no existen*; Things That No Longer Exist) and a play (1998; *Hermanas de sangre*; Blood Sisters).

Fernández Cubas's award-winning works provide an intriguing, unsettling, humorous, and provocative view of post-totalitarian Spain. Often playing with concepts of identity, difference, and doubling, they undermine the expected world order, projecting a fictional cosmos where the illogical rules as much as logic. Fernández Cubas's texts are highly entertaining, yet thought provoking. Ultimately, they incite readers to reconsider their perception of reality and identity, and what it is possible to know through language.

Jessica A. Folkart

Work By:

Blood Sisters. Trans. Karen Piano Dinicola. New York: Estreno Plays, 2004.
Cosas que ya no existen. Barcelona: Lumen, 2001.
Parientes pobres del diablo. Barcelona: Tusquets, 2006.

Work About:

Folkart, Jessica A. *Angles on Otherness in Post-Franco Spain: The Fiction of Cristina Fernández Cubas.* Lewisburg, PA: Bucknell University Press, 2002.

Fernández de Lizardi, José Joaquín (1776–1827)

Born in Mexico City, Fernández de Lizardi is considered the father of the Latin American novel and a writer who shaped 19th-century Mexican narrative style and influenced that of future generations as well. In 1812 he founded a very liberal newspaper, *El pensador mexicano* (The Mexican Thinker), in which he narrated events during the anti-imperial viceroyalty period (1521–1810). A prolific writer, journalist, and editor, he also published more than 200 pamphlets (*folletines*) on diverse topics such as the true meaning of "civilization," "Christian salvation," and the ideological framing of Mexican decolonization.

His most famous work, *El periquillo sarniento* (1816; *The Mangy Parrot*, 2005) narrates in colloquial, popular language the story of Pedro or Periquillo (Parrot), a young, mischievous orphan who, as a result of social forces, descends the social and economic ladder. After a variety of jobs, Periquillo finally becomes a criminal and gambler. In satiric fashion, Lizardi portrays the voice of charlatans, developing ideas of picaresque conventions in which Periquillo is both enjoyable and repugnant. The text's topics included fierce criticism of social injustice and a moralist desire to educate the economically less fortunate. This first novel continues to propagate ideas of freedom and political independence from Spain but with greater focus on the social injustice suffered by working classes; his later novel *Noches tristes y días alegres* (1818; Sad Nights and Happy Days) again defends the working class. Lizardi's preoccupation with Mexican social justice took precedence over a concern for form in his prose, making him a hero to many for his progressive, democratic ideals and his vocal opposition to the exploitation of Mexico's poor and oppressed.

María Calatayud

See also Novel in Spanish America: 1800–1900; Picaresque Literature in the Hispanic World.

Work By:

The Mangy Parrot, abridged: The Life and Times of Periquillo Sarniento Written by Himself for His Children. Ed., trans. David Frye. Intro. Nancy Vogeley. New York: Hackett, 2005.

Work About:

Vogeley, Nancy. *Lizardi and the Birth of the Novel in Spanish America.* Tallahassee: University Press of Florida, 2001.

Fernández de Moratín, Leandro (1760–1828)

This illustrious Spanish playwright, critic, and spectator, son of the great writer Nicolás Fernández de Moratín, was born and raised in Madrid. He suffered from smallpox as a child, which left him physically scarred. At age 17, he traveled to France for the first time as secretary to Francisco Cabarrús, who introduced him to Enlightenment ideas.

Moratín began his literary career writing satirical prose against bad poets in *La derrota de los pedantes* (1789; Defeat of Pedants). In 1790, his play *El viejo y la niña* (The Old Man and the Girl) focused on inequality in marriage between an older man and a younger woman. Two years later, he published *La comedia nueva o el Café* (1792; The New Comedy or the Café), an unsuccessful attempt to shed light on ideas about reform. Moratín returned to social critique in subsequent plays, centering on the institution of marriage and unjust arrangements made by parents for their daughters. He reached the pinnacle of his career with his last play, *El sí de las niñas* (1806; *A Maiden's Consent*, 1962). Increasingly discontented with the state of Spanish theater, he never wrote another play. Moratín never married. Political tensions and unrest marked his life, forcing him to leave Spain repeatedly. He left for the last time in 1820, dying in exile in Paris.

Joseph McClanahan

See also Enlightenment in Spain: 1700–1800; Theater in Spain: 1700–1900.

Work About:

Gabriele, John P. "Voice as the Locus of Narrative Struggle in *El sí de las niñas.*" *Torre: Revista de la Universidad de Puerto Rico* 9. 34 (October–December 2004): 537–53.

Fernández Retamar, Roberto (1930–)

A Cuban poet, essayist, and philology professor, his publication of "Calibán" (1971; *Caliban and Other Essays*, 1989) challenged Eurocentric colonial thought and became a kind of manifesto for Latin American intellectuals. In Retamar's hands, Calibán, the brute of Shakespeare's *Tempest*, becomes a powerful metaphor for Latin America's cultural situation both in terms of its marginality and its attitude of resistance.

Retamar has elaborated on another idea related to that of Calibán, the dichotomy between civilization and barbarism, a theme examined earlier in Domingo Faustino *Sarmiento's iconic *Civilización y barbarie* (1845). Using counterdiscourse, *Algunos usos de civilización y barbarie* (1988; Some Uses of Civilization and Barbarism) criticizes Sarmiento's Eurocentric and, according to the author, "racist" approach to Latin America, which Sarmiento described as a vast land peopled by primitive, abject tribes incapable of evolving.

In 1986, Retamar concluded his Calibán project with the essay "Calibán revisitado" (Caliban Revisited) in which, after stating that he will not dwell on Calibán's anagrammatic history, he clarifies some ideas proposed in the essay and responds to critics like Jorge Luis *Borges, Carlos *Fuentes, and Emir Rodríguez Monegal.

Silvia Nagy-Zekmi

See also Colonialism and Anticolonialism in Spanish American Literature.

Work By:

Caliban and Other Essays. Trans. Edward Baker. Minneapolis: University of Minnesota Press, 1989.

Work About:

Gillman, Susan. "Otra vez Caliban/Encore Caliban: Adaptation, Translation, Americas Studies." *American Literary History* 20.1–2 (Spring–Summer 2008): 187–209.

Millán-Zaibert, Elizabeth. "A Great Vanishing Act? The Latin American Philosophical Tradition and How Ariel and Caliban Helped Save It from Oblivion." *The New Centennial Review* 7.3 (Winter 2007): 149–69.

Fernández Santos, Jesús (1926–1988)

This distinguished narrator of the period covering the Spanish Civil War (1936–1939) and its aftermath is credited with introducing the social realist novel to Spain. Social realist narratives offer a mimetic view of postwar realities, including hunger, injustice, and class struggle, thereby providing a critique of the Francisco Franco regime's effects. Like the child protagonist in the poignant, quasi-autobiographical short fiction "Muy lejos de Madrid" (Far From Madrid), he and his family were on vacation when war broke out, and he did not return to his hometown until its end. Fernández Santos penned at least three slightly different versions of this story (in 1958, 1966, and 1986), suggesting the lifelong pull those days exerted on him.

His works consistently garnered literary awards. In addition, he collaborated with film and television production. The same eye for detail and technical skill that allows for multiple viewpoints in the visual arts focuses his prose. His writing style, which expanded beyond social realism, reveals a filmographer's vision, with cuts to and from different angles of perspective, particularly in his short fiction. In *Los bravos* (1954; The Untamed), he explores rural life and location, not events, centers the narrative. *Extramuros* (1978; Eng. trans., 1984)—understood as "Beyond the Walls"—is the story of two 17th-century nuns who are lovers. To save their convent and their lives together, they perpetrate a hoax around the self-inflicted wounds on one of the women's hands. Eventually, both are brought before the *Inquisition and, although their punishment is limited to banishment and acts of atonement, the story ends with their death. Beyond the prurient interest that lesbian nuns might inspire, the novel, which won Spain's National Prize for Literature, raises important questions about love, spirituality, and historiography.

Paula M. Bruno

See also Civil War Literature in Spain.

Work By:

Extramuros. Trans. Helen R. Lane. New York: Columbia University Press, 1984.

Work About:

Blackwell, Frieda. "Subverting Establishment Morality in *Extramuros* by Jesús Fernández Santos." *Monographic Review/Revista Monográfica* 18 (2002): 120–33.

Herzberger, David K. *Jesús Fernández Santos.* Boston: Twayne, 1983.

Fernán-Gómez, Fernando (1921–2007)

Born in Peru while his Spanish mother was on tour with an acting company, he moved to Spain in 1924. Known primarily as an actor and director, he was also a successful writer of plays, novels, essays, scripts, and newspaper articles. He was honored at the Berlin and Venice film festivals, and received highly prestigious awards within Spain, including the Gold Medal of Fine Arts, the Prince of Asturias Award in the Arts, the Academy of Motion Picture Arts and Sciences Gold Medal, the National Theater Award, the National Cinematography Award, the Donostia Prize, the Lope de Vega Prize, and several Goyas (Spain's Oscar). In 2000, Fernán-Gómez was named a member of the *Real Academia Española, occupying the chair for the letter B.

His literary works combine irony, humor, tenderness, and satire to highlight the humanity of his characters as they struggle in their everyday lives to fulfill their aspirations. His most famous play, *Las bicicletas son para el verano* (staged 1982; Bicycles Are for the Summer) focuses on the deprivations and dangers experienced by a middle-class family and their neighbors in Madrid during the Spanish Civil War (1936–1939). His novel *El viaje a ninguna parte* (1985; The Trip to Nowhere) about a traveling theater troupe was cinematically adapted and became his most critically acclaimed film as a director. Upon his death, the city of Madrid renamed a major theater in his honor and the Spanish government posthumously awarded him the Great Cross of the Civil Order of Alfonso X "el Sabio."

Linda M. Willem

Work By:

El viaje a ninguna parte. Madrid: Cátedra, 2002.

Las bicicletas son para el verano. Madrid: Espasa Calpe, 1999.

Work About:

Brasó, Enrique. *Conversaciones con Fernando Fernán-Gómez*. Madrid: Espasa Calpe, 2002.

http://www.cervantesvirtual.com/FichaObra.html?Ref=3367.

Ferré, Rosario (1938–)

This Puerto Rican writer was born in Ponce to a politically influential family. Her father, Luis A. Ferré, was the pro-statehood governor of the island from 1968 to 1972. Unsurprisingly, many of her works discuss social issues and the political situation of Puerto Rico. Her first novel, *Maldito amor* (1987; *Sweet Diamond Dust*, 1988), deals directly with these factors as it examines from a mythical perspective the political and cultural struggles that face the island as a commonwealth of the United States.

While in college, Ferré generated controversy by supporting the Independent Party in direct opposition to her father's political ideology. In recent years, however, her political affiliations have changed and she now supports statehood for the island.

The *House on the Lagoon* (1995), which was originally published in English, generated criticism from Puerto Rican nationalists. Proud of her heritage and loyal to her roots, Ferré discredits negative comments and asserts that her choice of language has no bearing on her national identity. The novel, in turn, does explore the issue of nationalism by establishing a parallel between the struggles of the Mendizábal family and the conflictive relationship between the United States and Puerto Rico.

Ferré is also very concerned with the struggle faced by Puerto Rican women in a *machista* (male exalting) culture. Women in her novels constantly search for identity in a male-dominated society. Her first book, *Papeles de Pandora* (1976; *The Youngest Doll*, 1991), questions the patriarchal myths that permeate Puerto Rican culture. She asserts that language is not gender specific but determined rather by the individual experiences of men and women. Many of her works reflect influences from Virginia Woolf, Julia Kristeva, and Sor Juana Inés de la *Cruz.

Delmarie Martínez

See also Feminism in Spanish America.

Work By:

Eccentric Neighborhoods. New York: Farrar, Strauss and Giroux, 1998.

Work About:

Hintz, Suzanne S. *Rosario Ferré, A Search for Identity*. New York: Peter Lang, 1995.

Rosario Ferré. www.ensayistas.org/filoso fos/puertorico/ferre.

Figuera Aymerich, Ángela (1902–1984)

A poet of the Spanish postwar era, Figuera stands out as a vigorous feminine voice that brings the intimacy of the domestic space to the social order. She proclaims the value of fraternity and demands a social transformation to bring peace and justice to the human family.

Born in Bilbao, she worked as a teacher and in the National Library and wrote several books of poetry, including collections for children. Her poetry started as an intimate lyric and, through existential considerations, evolved into a compelling indictment of human suffering. Defining herself as a "mud woman," made of the same mud as men, Figuera defies the submissive role of women and celebrates all aspects of life, including her sensuality. For this, she was censored. Her feminine perspective gave her an advantage in understanding the suffering of others, and hence, her poetry combines subjective perspective with an attitude of collective consciousness. She aimed to give voice to all oppressed women and men with her verse.

Motherhood is a core theme of her writing. She describes the joy of domestic life, exalting her love of her husband and son, but also relates it to fratricide. Using the images of Eve and Mary, Figuera exhorts all mothers to break the circle of hate that led to the Spanish Civil War (1936–1939) by taking an active role in shaping a harmonious world for their children. Aware of the utopian aspect of her humanistic poetry, she laments human fragility, especially the limitations of women in a patriarchal society.

Figuera played a very important role as the link between Spanish poets in exile and those poets who remained in Spain after the Spanish Civil War. She completes, along with Gabriel *Celaya and Blas de *Otero, Spain's trio of Basque social poets.

María-Cruz Rodríguez

See also Civil War Literature in Spain.

Work By:

The Three Pups. Carmel, CA: Hampton-Brown, 1991.

Work on:

Arkinstale, Christine. "Rhetorics of Maternity and War in Ángela Figuera's Poetic Work." *Revista Canadiense de Estudios Hispánicos* 21.3 (1997): 457–78.

Evans, Jo. *Moving Reflections: Gender, Faith and Aesthetics in the Work of Ángela Figuera Aymerich*. London: Tamesis, 1996.

Wilcox, John C. "A Reconsideration of Two Spanish Women Poets: Ángela Figuera and Francisca Aguirre." *Studies in Twentieth Century Literature* 16.1 (1992): 65–92.

Flores, Marco Antonio (1937–)

A Guatemalan novelist, poet, journalist and essay writer, he was twice forced into exile but returned to his country in the 1990s. A controversial figure, Flores captured the Miguel Ángel Asturias National Prize in Literature in 2006. His novel *Los compañeros* (1976; The Comrades) started a trend in Guatemalan narrative, combining realism, political criticism, avant-garde narrating techniques, and colloquial language. Flores denounced both state repression and the corruption of guerrilla organizations, and consequently received reluctant acceptance by intellectual and political circles. The revolutionary struggle, central in contemporary Guatemalan history, remains the main topic of many of his novels. Flores has strongly influenced creative writing in his country.

Claudia S. García

Work By:

En el filo. Guatemala: F&G, 2002.

Los compañeros. México: Joaquín Mortiz, 1976.

Poesía escogida. Guatemala: La Ermita, Oscar de León Palacios, 1998.

Work About:

Menton, Seymour. "Los Señores Presidentes y los Guerrilleros: the New and the Old Guatemalan Novel (1976–1982)." *Latin American Research Review* 19: 2 (1984): 93–117.

Flor y canto

The Nahuatl phrase *in xochitl in cuicatl* (*flor y canto* in Spanish; flower and song) is a metaphor of artistic endeavor in general, but specifically poetry (oral and pictographic), music, and dance. The heart-purifying practice of *flor y canto* formed the metaphysical base of Nahua (pertaining to indigenous peoples of central Mexico, including Aztecs) philosophy, exemplified in the poems on temporality attributed to the poet-king Nezahualcóyotl.

Bruce Dean Willis

Work By:

León-Portilla, Miguel, ed. *Fifteen Poets of the Aztec World.* Trans. Grace Lobanov. Norman: University of Oklahoma Press, 1992.

Formica, Mercedes (1918–2002)

As a journalist, lawyer, and novelist, Formica revealed the inequality of Spanish laws for women and men concerning adultery, separation, divorce and its repercussions, and even competitive examinations for jobs. Her parents' divorce in 1933 provoked a dramatic aftermath: the women in the family had to move from Andalusia to Madrid, suffering financial troubles and separation from their only brother. Encouraged by her mother, Formica enrolled at the university and became one of Spain's first women attorneys in 1948. The nation's inequitable laws moved her to write "El domicilio conyugal" (1953; The Conjugal Domicile) denouncing the legal abandonment of women abused by their husbands. The article, which was printed in the popular newspaper *ABC*, her lectures, and the novel *A instancia de parte* (1955; On Behalf of the Third Party), stirred heated debate that resulted in the reform of 66 statutes of the Spanish Civil Code in 1958.

The Spanish Civil War (1936–1939) exercises considerable prominence in her work; her first two novels incorporate the tragic conflict and its consequences, and it appears in her memoirs published in three parts (1982, 1984, 1998); these texts also includes sociohistorical details. Formica's campaigns and defense of equal rights seem to pose a certain contradiction between her political views, quite fascist for many critics, and the feminist beliefs of her writing, interviews, and presentations. Her interest in women's lives inspired such novels and historical biographies as *María de Mendoza. Solución a un enigma amoroso* (1979; María de Mendoza. Solution to an Amorous Enigma), awarded the Fastenrath Prize.

Mayte de Lama

See also Civil War Literature in Spain; Feminism in Spain: 1700 to Present; Francoism, Fascism, and Literature in Spain.

Work By:

Collar de ámbar. Madrid: Caro Raggio, 1989.

Espejo roto. Y espejuelos. Madrid: Huerga & Fierro, 1998.

Work About:

Leggott, Sarah J. "Testimony, Gender and Ideology in Mercedes Formica's *Pequeña historia de ayer." Letras Peninsulares* 12.2–3 (1999–2000): 421–35.

Forner, Juan Pablo (1756–1797)

This rabid Spanish nationalist and personification of the Enlightenment poet and essayist wrote the official answer to the *French Encyclopedia*'s aggressively negative portrayal of Spain. The most strikingly innovative aspect of Forner's *Oración apologética por la España y su mérito literario* (1786; Apology of Spain and Its Literature) is his consideration of the nation in modern terms, as a community anchored in the past, but living the present and projecting to a future of wealth, civilization, welfare, and happiness for its citizens. Another relevant work is *Discurso sobre el modo de escribir y mejorar la historia de España* (1785; Discourse on How to Write and Better the History of Spain), a very modern treatise about how to write history. Forner compiles data to understand historical changes and how they have been produced in a logical manner.

For Forner, nations are the only entities possessing history and civilization; nations are formed by a community of people who help each other, doing good for fellow patriots rather than the prince. Love for the fatherland constitutes the essence of the civil man, and the futures of nations depend on this quality. *Exequias de la lengua castellana* (1795; Obsequies of the Spanish Language), written in prose and verse, examines Spanish culture. Forner considers the problems of theater and censorship to be national problems because national culture is precisely what is represented on the stage; thus, the state must protect the health of its culture by formulating proper theater regulations.

He also wrote satiric fables against Tomás de *Iriarte and many other fellow writers and participated in endless literary polemics. Forner's thought is key in understanding the modern conservative Spanish nationalism that developed at the end of the 19th century.

Salvador A. Oropesa

See also Enlightenment in Spain: 1700–1800.

Work About:

Schlig, Michael. "Spain as Orient in Juan Pablo Forner's *Los gramáticos: historia chinesca.*" *Dieciocho* 23.2 (2000): 313–25.

Fortún, Elena (pseudonym of Encarna Aragoneses) (1886–1952)

This Madrid-born daughter of the king's halberdier (armed guard) studied at the School of Philosophy and Arts. She married Eusebio de Gorbea Lemmi, a Republican soldier, writer, and dramatic actor, in 1908. During the Second Spanish Republic (1931–1939), she worked to address illiteracy among women and published articles about social issues and domestic life in such magazines as *Crónica* and *Semana*. One of her two children died in 1920; she finally found solace in 1928, writing for children in the magazine *Blanco y Negro*, using the pseudonym Elena Fortún. Her *Celia* series soon became the most famous children's classic of the day. Through the eyes of imaginative, young, bourgeois Celia, the

world of adults was acutely criticized. Celia's unconventional friendship with a young Arab, her dislike of artificial manners, and her constant rule breaking and similar acts challenged conventional views. Celia's stories were so successful among children that Aguilar Press started publishing the books. Some of Fortún's most famous stories were compiled in the volume *Los cuentos que Celia cuenta a las niñas* (1951; Stories That Celia Tells Girls).

Her husband's involvement in the Spanish Civil War (1936–1939) forced them into exile in Argentina in 1939. There, Fortún would write her most outspoken Celia book, *Celia en la revolución* (written 1943, published 1987; Celia in the Revolution), based on the horrors of the civil war. In 1948, her husband committed suicide in Buenos Aires.

Judith García-Quismondo García

See also Children's Literature in Spain: 1900 to Present; Exile Literature by Spanish Civil War Émigrés.

Work By:

Los libros de Celia. Madrid: Alianza, 2003.

Work About:

Dorao, Marisol. *Los mil sueños de Elena Fortún: Celia.* Cádiz: Universidad de Cádiz, 2000.

Francoism, Fascism, and Literature in Spain

Spanish literature has been profoundly marked by the ideological struggles stemming from Francisco Franco's dictatorship

(1939–1975). Early on, opponents termed Franco's regime "fascist." Nonetheless, it is important to note that Spain's fascism differed from German or Italian models because it developed from a military coup into an absolutist, reactionary authoritarianism that controlled Spain by manipulating constituencies like the army, the Spanish Fascist Party (*Falange*), Carlists (traditional monarchists), and the Catholic church. Francoism can thus be distinguished from other forms of fascism while acknowledging that it employed similar techniques to suppress political dissent through state terror. Many authors who disagreed with Francoist ideology were killed, imprisoned, or fled into exile after the civil war (1936–1939). For those remaining in Spain, censorship became a primary means of enforcing authoritarian control, and thus responses to Francoist ideology greatly impacted Spanish literature.

Works produced in Francoist Spain are typically divided into four periods. The first began during the war and stretched into the 1940s with *triunfalismo* (works celebrating the Nationalist Civil War victory); this was followed by *tremendismo* (texts depicting the bleak, harsh postwar reality). Social literature or critical realism came to prominence in the 1950s and early 1960s, and finally, experimental or "new" literature dominated from the mid-1960s until Franco's death in 1975.

Francoist ideology presented the national conflict as a battle between good and evil, Christian Spain against atheists, anarchists, communists, separatists, masons, Muslims, and Jews. The enforcement of strict ethnic, linguistic, and gender boundaries combined to present Spain as monolithic, homogenous, and divinely ordained. José María Pemán's *Poema de la Bestia y el Ángel* (1938; Poem of the Beast and the Angel) provides a striking example of this ideology. The book-length allegorical poem features Franco (in the person of a youthful Christian soldier) as an angel fighting against beastly Satanic, Jewish, and Republican forces, with the angel slaying the beast in the end. The poem introduces several themes that were later developed within Francoist discourse, particularly Spain's Catholic Christian identity, the equation between Republicans and Jewish or Satanic figures, and historical symbols of the *Reconquista* (the seven-century struggle to end Moorish control of the peninsula, ending in 1492) in which Nationalists strive to recover Spain's imperial glory through a new dawn offered by the Nationalist cause.

Other triunfalista works produced during the war, like Agustín de Foxá's *Madrid de corte a checa* (1938; Madrid from Royal Court to Stalinist Prison), depict events leading to the conflict from a fascist perspective. Narrated by a young Falangist from Madrid, the novel begins in 1931 and describes the Second Republic from the viewpoint of monarchist and fascist groups. It offers interesting intertextualities with canonical authors but maintains a troubling ideological stance. One section narrates the author himself (along with such Fascist leaders as José Antonio Primo de Rivera and Rafael Sánchez Mazas) writing the Falangist hymn. After the war, books like Rafael García Serrano's *La fiel infantería* (1943; The Loyal Infantry) continue to employ

Nationalist propaganda in support of patriotism, discipline, violence, and virility, classic fascist themes. Another typical postwar *triunfalismo* work, José Luis Sáenz de Heredia's film *Raza* (1941; Race [based on a text Franco wrote himself]) narrates events of the civil war through one divided family's struggles and interprets the conflict as a religious battle in which the guilty are punished and national values are redeemed.

One of the earliest novels to depict the war's economic and psychological turmoil was Camilo José *Cela's *La familia de Pascual Duarte* (1942; Eng. trans., 2004); its descriptive style and focus on cruel, even depraved behavior became known as *tremendismo*. Pascual, the narrator, confesses his murderous, violent history before being jailed; eventually he is executed. The recipient of his confession, like a censor, is left to determine whether Pascual's tale should be disseminated. Cela, who had sided with the Nationalists during the war and was himself a censor in the 1940s, knew the system intimately; thus, since Pascual's descriptions of the war's brutality never reveal his specific participation in the conflict, the genius of the work involves this resonant silence. *San Camilo, 1936* (1969) marks the first time Cela addressed events of the war directly. The novel, filled with page-long sentences, focuses on the experience of Madrid's residents in the days surrounding the start of the war. Like other historical novels that deal with the civil war period from a sympathetic Nationalist perspective, it incited polemic for rationalizing Nationalist actions and ideologies.

Controversies continue to surround such contemporary historical fiction sympathetic to Nationalist figures as *Soldados de Salamina*, by Javier Cercas (2001; *Soldiers of Salamis*, 2003), which explores one soldier's decision not to kill a prominent Fascist leader near the end of the civil war.

The first novel to problematize the conflicts of the civil war was José María Gironella's *Los cipreses creen en Dios* (1953; *The Cypresses Believe in God*, 2005). The first book of a trilogy, the novel is set in Girona (Catalonia) and begins prior to the conflict in 1931. It reveals the diverging political, economic, and religious perspectives of the Alvear family, allowing readers to experience the divisions leading to the civil war through personal struggles. The narrator, an atheist from Madrid, is married to a Basque woman, and they live in Catalonia with three children who each experience the political movements in different ways. The author, a Roman Catholic who fought under Franco, managed to publish the trilogy despite the tremendous pressures of Franco-era censorship.

In the 1950s and 1960s, authors aimed to evade censorial limits by presenting objective, realist representations of Spain's economic and social woes. Antonio *Buero Vallejo's play *Historia de una escalera* (1949; *History of a Staircase*, 2003) illustrates social and economic stagnation through a Madrid tenement house whose residents move up and down the stairs during three decades of unchanging prospects. Rafael *Sánchez Ferlosio's *El Jarama* (1956; River Jarama) presents an objectivist snapshot of lower-class youth one Sunday at a swimming hole outside of Madrid. The work gives the young proletariat a voice, showing its emergence from the misery of postwar years, while the setting, and title, recall battle scenes from the civil war and mark the ongoing struggles faced by the war's victims.

Francoist ideology and censorship led other authors to a more personal mode that could resist monolithic interpretations of Spanish identity, particularly in works by women writers like Carmen *Laforet, Ana María *Matute (1926–), and Mercè Rodoreda (1909–1983). Laforet's *Nada* (1945; [Nothing], Eng. trans., 2007), portrays a young woman surrounded by a damaged and dysfunctional family that struggles to adjust to life in postwar Barcelona; the text depicts the dreary, harsh reality that faced even the war's victors. The work interweaves the personal and the national as protagonist Andrea matures and loses adolescent illusions. Readers are left to imagine how the war's vanquished fared, seeing that the winners of the national conflict emerged this badly. Aesthetic experimentation and social commentary were also handled deftly by poets like Gloria *Fuertes, whose playful, ironic attacks on repression produced works like *Aconsejo beber hilo* (1954; I Recommend Drinking Thread), in which the physical hunger facing postwar Spaniards extends as a metaphor for the emotional and intellectual limitations placed on women, the poor, and those left powerless in the new order.

In the 1960s, a group of authors disenchanted with critical realism began to produce works that resisted Francoist ideology through the subversion of language itself, rather than overt social critiques. Novelists and poets like Juan *Goytisolo, Juan *Marsé, Guillermo Carnero (1947–), and Carmen *Martín Gaite (1925–2000) contributed to experimental forms. Marsé's *Si te dicen que caí* (1973; *The Fallen*, 1979) uses shifting narrative voices and unstable temporal perspectives to tell the story of Spain's moral and economic degradation as experienced by Barcelona street kids whose parents were killed, exiled, or imprisoned during the war. Other works like Goytisolo's *Señas de identidad* (1966; *Marks of Identity*, 1969) and *Reivindicación del Conde don Julián* (1970; *Count Julian*, 1974) skillfully parody Francoist language and ideological icons.

While Franco's death in 1975 brought the dictatorship to an end, critics argue that the relatively peaceful transition to democracy allowed many Francoist institutions to survive, and thus vestiges of Francoism continue to echo in Spanish literature and culture.

Debra Faszer-McMahon

See also Censorship and Literature in Spain; Civil War Literature in Spain; Exile and Literature by Spanish Civil War Émigrés; Pen Club in the Hispanic World; Spain and Self-Identity in the Nation; Women's Literature in Spain: 1900 to Present.

Work About:

Gracia García, Jordi. *La resistencia silenciosa: fascismo y cultura en España.* Barcelona: Anagrama, 2004.

Merino, Eloy E., and H. Rosi Song, eds. *Traces of Contamination: Unearthing the Francoist Legacy in Contemporary Spanish Discourse.* Lewisburg, PA: Bucknell University Press, 2005.

Payne, Stanley G. *Fascism in Spain, 1923–1977.* Madison: University of Wisconsin Press, 1999.

Richmond, Kathleen. *Women and Spanish Fascism: The Women's Section of the Falange, 1934–1959.* London: Routledge, 2003.

Fuenmayor, José Félix (1885–1966)

This Colombian journalist, poet, storyteller, and lifelong resident of Barranquilla founded the newspaper *El Liberal* when he was in his twenties. In 1910, he published *Musas del trópico* (Tropical Muses), a book of *modernista* poetry, and between 1917 and 1920 he wrote for *Voces* magazine, founded by Ramón Vinyes of Catalonia. In 1927, he composed his only novel, *Cosme* (1928). Set in an urban milieu, it tells the story of a naïve Barranquilla man, chronicling his life until he is crushed by society. Fuenmayor's short novel "Una triste aventura de catorce sabios" (1928; The Sad Adventure of Fourteen Wise Men) prefigures Colombian literature of the fantastic. It entails a theoretical discussion about truth and verisimilitude in narration while exploring metafictional relations among author, reader and text.

In 1940, a group of intellectuals, writers, and artists congregated around Fuenmayor and Vinyes, forming the influential *Grupo Barranquilla*. Fuenmayor's ideas about humor influenced the first stories by Gabriel *García Márquez and Álvaro *Cepeda Samudio. From 1940 to 1966 he published short fiction in weekly magazines like *Crónica* (1950–1951), directed by his son Alfonso Fuenmayor. These stories were published posthumously in *La muerte en la calle* (1967; Death in the Street).

Yohainna Abdala-Mesa

See also Magical Realism.

Work By:

Cosme. Bogotá: Oveja Negra, 1985.

Work About:

Sims, Robert L. "*Cosme*, precursora de la nueva novela latinoamericana." *Literatura y cultura: Narrativa colombiana del siglo XX.* Ed. María Mercedes Jaramillo, Betty Osorio, and Ángela Robledo. 3 vols. Bogotá: Ministerio de Cultura; 2000. I: 149–75.

Fuentes, Carlos (1928–)

Born in Panama City to a Mexican diplomat, this towering figure of Mexican literature grew up moving from one country to another. During his childhood and youth, he lived in Switzerland, El Salvador, Uruguay, Brazil, Chile, Argentina, and the United States. In his adolescence he returned to his native Mexico, which marked his work decisively. After finishing studies in law with a minor in economics, Fuentes held many diplomatic posts, serving as Mexico's delegate to the United Nations, undersecretary in Mexico's Foreign Relations Ministry, and as Mexican ambassador to France from 1974 to 1977. Fuentes also served as a professor at the universities of Harvard, Princeton, and Cambridge.

In 1955, Fuentes, Emanuel Carballo, and Octavio *Paz cofounded the *Revista Mexicana de Literatura*. The year 1964 marked the beginning of a strong friendship with Colombia's Gabriel *García Márquez. Alongside Peruvian Mario *Vargas Llosa and Argentine Julio *Cortázar, they represent the titans of the Latin American *Boom*.

Fuentes's appeal to popular and academic audiences made him an icon of cosmopolitan intellectuals. He feels that the writer must simultaneously cultivate memory, imagination, and language. His polysemous work includes short stories, plays, cultural and political essays, and a multitude of novels. Among the more meaningful works where he examines Mexico's cultural identity in depth, several titles stand out: *La región más transparente* (1958; *Where the Air Is Clear*, 1960), *La muerte de Artemio Cruz* (1962; *The Death of Artemio Cruz*, 1964), *Aura* (1962; English version, 1965), *Zona sagrada* (1967; *Holy Place*, 1972), *Cambio de piel* (1967; *A Change of Skin*, 1968), *Terra nostra* (1975; English version, 1976), *La cabeza de la hidra* (1979; *The Hydra Head*, 1978), *Agua quemada* (1981; *Burnt Water*, 1980), *Gringo viejo* (1985; *The Old Gringo*, 1985), *Cristóbal Nonato* (1987; Christopher Unborn, 1989), and *Todas las familias felices* (2006; All the Happy Families).

Critical approach to Fuentes's literary production comes from a wide range of perspectives. His own literary criticism may be divided in different periods: a revolutionary stage with *La nueva novela latinoamericana* (1969; The Latin American New Novel) and *Casa con dos puertas* (1970; House with Two Doors); a second stage that corresponds to a process of historical and cultural concepts, which materializes in *Cervantes; o, La crítica de la lectura* (1976; Cervantes, or the Critique of Reading); and a third stage, marked by such texts as *Valiente mundo nuevo* (1990; A Brave New World) and *Geografía de la novela* (1993; Geography of the Novel). More recently, he published *Tres discursos para dos aldeas* (1993; Three Speeches for Two Villages) and *En esto creo* (2002; This I Believe: An A to Z of a Life, 2005). *Contra Bush* (2004; Against Bush) synthesizes his political philosophy regarding international affairs.

Fuentes was awarded several important prizes, including Venezuela's Rómulo Gallegos Prize (1977), Mexico's National Literature Prize (1984), Spain's Cervantes Prize (1987), and Príncipe de Asturias Prize (1994).

Daniel Altamiranda

See also Novel in Spanish America: *Boom* Literature: 1950–1975.

Work By:

The Death of Artemio Cruz. Trans. Alfred MacAdam. New York: Farrar, Straus and Giroux, 1991.

Myself with Others. Selected Essays. New York: Farrar, Straus and Giroux, 1988.

Terra Nostra. Trans. Margaret Sayers Peden. New York: Farrar, Straus and Giroux, 1976.

Work About:

Anderson, Mark. "A Reappraisal of the 'Total' Novel: Totality and Communicative Systems in Carlos Fuentes's *Terra Nostra*." *Symposium* 57.2 (2003): 59–79.

Helmuth, Chalene. *The Postmodern Fuentes*. Lewisburg, PA: Bucknell University Press, 1997.

Westrope, Theron. "The 'Double Flame' of Culture: The Metaphors of Las Meninas and Angelus Novus in Carlos Fuentes' 'Constancia.' " *Interdisciplinary Humanities* 17.2 (2000): 197–205.

Williams, Raymond Leslie. *The Writings of Carlos Fuentes*. Austin: University of Texas Press, 1996.

Fuero Juzgo

Also known as *Forum iudicum* or *Liber iudiciorum*, this is the name that the seventh-century IberianVisigothic law code (*Lex Visigothorum*) acquired after it was translated into the vernacular and modified in the 13th century by order of Castilian King Ferdinand III, who ruled from 1217 to 1252. *Fuero juzgo* is the common body of law that ruled Iberian populations, Visigothic and Hispano-Roman, during the Middle Ages. Organized into 12 books, it includes about 600 laws governing marriage, inheritance, property, business transactions, theft and fraud, acts of violence and injuries, and so on. *Fuero juzgo* was one of the main sources of the most important law code of the Middle Ages, the *Siete Partidas* (1251–1265; The Seven Books of Law), sponsored by King *Alfonso X, "el Sabio," who ruled from 1252 to 1284. Modern historians regard it as the origin of the political principles that govern European nations. In Spain, this *fuero* survived until 1889, when the Civil Code, the *Código Civil Español*, was approved.

Enric Mallorquí-Ruscalleda

Work By:

The Visigothic Code (Forum Judicum). Ed., trans. (from original Latin) Samuel P. Scott. Littleton, CO: Rothman, 1982 [1910]. http://libro.uca.edu/vcode/visigoths.htm.

Fuertes, Gloria (1917–1998)

A self-taught poet and writer of children's literature, she has become one of the most acclaimed figures of 20th-century Spanish poetry, a success due to her inspiring poetic works and charismatic personality. Born to a modest family in Madrid, Fuertes suffered the death of her mother and the horror of the Spanish Civil War (1936–1939) in her youth. She composed verses before she could read and later became a television personality with her own programs for children. From 1960 to 1963 she taught literature in various American universities. Fuertes wrote numerous poetry volumes for children and adults. In her children's poetry, she adopts the perspective of the child to convey a pacifist message that encourages respect for all forms of life.

Her adult work, which is spontaneous, ironic, surrealistic, and above all strikingly direct and sincere, depicts the injustices and day-to-day problems of humankind. The prostitute, the laborer, and the drunk appear as subjects to convey social criticism. Many critics associate her with Spain's group of poets of the 1950s, who were characterized by their denunciation of social oppression under Francisco Franco's regime (1939–1975), yet Fuertes's very personal creative vision and style set her apart. Going against established poetic norms and manipulating words and meanings in a playful manner, Fuertes poeticizes everyday experience.

Though many of her poems are autobiographical, they transcend the individual to recount the experience of ordinary people, developing such themes as solitude, love, social injustice, death, and God. She employs a tone of familiarity to guarantee the communicability of her verses, which she uses as a tool of personal and social liberation. Because of her humane spirit, direct voice, innovative style, and presentation of universal themes, Fuertes reaches all types of readers, and occupies an important place in the panorama of 20th-century Spanish poetry.

María-Cruz Rodríguez

See also Civil War Literature in Spain; Francoism, Fascism, and Literature in Spain; Women Writers in Spain: 1900 to Present.

Work By:

Off the Map: Selected Poems by Gloria Fuertes. Ed., trans. Philip Levine and Ada Long. Middletown, CT: Wesleyan University Press, 1984.

Work About:

Cooks, María L. "The Humanization of Poetry: An Appraisal of Gloria Fuertes." *Hispania* 83.3 (2000): 428–36.

Fundación Gloria Fuertes. December 10, 2006. http://www.gloriafuertes.org/.

Gloria Fuertes in Biblioteca Virtual de Cervantes. www.cervantesvirtual.com/bib_autor/Fuertes/.